The Culture of Protestantism in Early Modern Scotland

The Culture of Protestantism in Early Modern Scotland

Margo Todd

Yale University Press
New Haven and London

For information about this and other Yale University Press publications, please contact:
U.S. Office: sales.press@yale.edu yalebooks.com
Europe Office: sales@yaleup.co.uk www.yaleup.co.uk

Set in Bembo by SNP Best-set Ltd., Hong Kong
Printed in Great Britain by St. Edmundsbury Press

Library of Congress Cataloging-in-Publication Data

Todd, Margo.
The culture of Protestantism in early modern Scotland/Margo Todd.
p. cm.
Includes bibliographical references and index.
ISBN 0–300–09234–2 (cloth: alk. paper)
1. Protestant churches—Scotland—History. 2. Scotland—Church history. I. Title.
BX4840 .T63 2002 280′.4′09411—dc21 2001007254

A catalogue record for this book is available from the British Library.

10 9 8 7 6 5 4 3 2 1

For Peter,
youngest of the brethren

Contents

Plates

Acknowledgments

Research for this book was facilitated by a fellowship from the University of Edinburgh's Institute for Advanced Study in the Humanities in 1997, and the James K. Cameron Faculty Fellowship of the St Andrews University Institute for Reformation Studies in 2000 made it possible to write in the lively atmosphere of the Institute. The warm hospitality of its director, Andrew Pettegree, made the experience a thoroughly pleasant one. For reading an early draft of the manuscript, ridding it of its most egregious errors and offering insights I would have missed, I am indebted to Jane Dawson and Derek Hirst. Jenny Wormald and Joel Harrington also read and commented helpfully on portions of the work. The errors that remain are, of course, my own responsibility. I am grateful for stimulating discussions during the research process with George Dalgleish, Elizabeth Ewan and Louise Yeoman. For the staffs of the National Library of Scotland, the Mitchell Library, the Ayrshire Archives Centre, the Perth Museum and Art Gallery, the A.K. Bell Library of Perth, the Royal Commission on the Ancient and Historical Monuments of Scotland, the Folger Shakespeare Library, the Lambeth Palace Library and most especially the National Archives of Scotland, I have only praise and thanks. That of the Historical Search Room of the General Register House, Edinburgh, was as friendly as it was efficient and went beyond the call of duty to make manuscripts available at the West Register House when their own location was closed for refurbishment in 2000. Vanderbilt University offered not only leave time to pursue research, but also the remarkably able help of two undergraduate research assistants, Justin Memmott and Thomas Smith, and of Lori Cohen, whose skills in on-screen mapmaking were invaluable. And my colleagues as well as my students have endured with patience my compulsion to recount stories from kirk session minutes at every opportunity.

Finally, for the tolerance that my sons have exhibited of early modern intrusions into their lives, and for my husband's steady support (and willingness to proofread), I am ever thankful. This work is dedicated to the youngest of my lads, who accompanied me to Edinburgh and St Andrews and who, with his school stories, his enthusiasm for seaside walks and playing by the burn with his mates, and his unwavering cheerfulness, kept me sane and more fully aware than I might have been of the humanity of the families who lived where we did four hundred years before.

Abbreviations

AAC	Ayrshire Archives Centre, Ayr
APS	*Acts of the Parliaments of Scotland, 1127–1707*, ed. Thomas Thomson and Cosmo Innes, 12 vols (Edinburgh, 1814–75)
BCO	*Book of Common Order*, ed. George Sprott (Edinburgh, 1868)
BUK	*Booke of the Universall Kirk: Acts and Proceedings of the General Assemblies of the Kirk of Scotland, 1560–1618* (Edinburgh, 1839)
Canongate	*The Buik of the Kirk of the Canagait, 1564–1567*, ed. A.B. Calderwood (Edinburgh, 1961)
Dundonald	*The Session Book of Dundonald, 1602–1731*, ed. Henry Paton (n.p., 1936)
Fasti	*Fasti Ecclesiae Scoticanae: The Succession of Ministers in the Church of Scotland from the Reformation*, ed. Hew Scott, 10 vols (Edinburgh, 1915–28)
First Book	*The First Book of Discipline*, ed. James K. Cameron (Edinburgh, 1972)
Folger	Folger Shakespeare Library, Washington, D.C.
IR	*Innes Review*
JBS	*The Journal of British Studies*
LPL	Lambeth Palace Library, London
ML	Mitchell Library, Glasgow
NAS	National Archives of Scotland, Edinburgh
NLS	National Library of Scotland, Edinburgh
PL	A.K. Bell Library, Perth
PMAG	Perth Museum and Art Gallery
P&P	*Past and Present*
RCAHMS	Royal Commission on the Ancient and Historical Monuments of Scotland, Edinburgh
RPC	*Register of the Privy Council of Scotland*, 1st ser. 1545–1626, ed. J.H. Burton and D. Masson (Edinburgh, 1877–96)
RSCHS	*Records of the Scottish Church History Society*
SAU	Saint Andrews University Library

SAKS	*Register of the Minister, Elders and Deacons of the Christian Congregation of St Andrews, Comprising the Proceedings of the Kirk Session . . . 1559–1600*, ed. David Hay Fleming, 2 vols (Edinburgh, 1890)
SHR	*Scottish Historical Review*

All records noted herein with the CH2 prefix are manuscript minute books and are in the NAS unless otherwise indicated.

Spelling, capitalisation and punctuation in early modern sources, excepting only poetry and published titles, are modernised, and the Scots is rendered in English, with apologies to those committed to reviving the Scots language. The intention here is to make the sources easily comprehensible to modern readers. Proper names retain the spelling most consistently used in the sources (where a name might be spelt two or three different ways on the same page), except for surnames of some well-known individuals whose names are generally modernised.

Notes on Scottish Money and Dating

A pound Scots was worth about one-sixth of an English pound sterling in 1565, one-twelfth by 1601. It comprised 20 shillings (s), each shilling in turn consisting of 12 pence (d). In the present work, the £ always denotes Scots pounds.
A merk was valued at about 13s 4d in 1651.
A dollar (a Danish coin) was worth about two Scots pounds.[1]
A labourer in Edinburgh in 1580 could earn about 4d a day, in 1590 5d, and by the beginning of the seventeenth century 6s per day; and would pay about £4 for a boll (= 5.8 imperial bushels) of oatmeal. Wages would have been lower outside the capital, and in many cases varied seasonally.[2]

Readers should keep in mind the relatively depressed value of Scottish money when assessing the impact of, say, a 20s fine for sabbath breach, or the worth of a £100 reader's stipend or a £300 donation to the poor.

Dates are given Old Style, but with the year taken to begin on 1 January rather than 25 March – a change made in Scotland in 1600.

1. For coinage valuation, see J.M. Henderson, *Scottish Reckonings of Time, Money, Weights and Measures*, Historical Association of Scotland pamphlet, ns, no. 4 ([Edinburgh], 1926); John J. McCusker, *Money and Exchange in Europe and America, 1600–1775: A Handbook* (Chapel Hill, 1978); R.W. Cochran-Patrick, *Records of the Coinage of Scotland*, 2 vols (Edinburgh, 1876); J.D. Robertson, *A Handbook to the Coinage of Scotland* (Chicago, 1968); and for mention of the dollar (or daler), David Stevenson, *Scotland's Last Royal Wedding* (Edinburgh, 1997), xiv.
2. A commission established by an act of the Scottish parliament in 1617 approved two different corn measures: a wheat firlot (used also for pease, beans, rye and salt) was slightly less than the imperial bushel (gauged at 2,218 cubic inches, or 80 pounds of water in weight). The barley firlot (used also for oats and malt) was larger by 1,000 cubic inches (Henderson, 7–8, 14). Four firlots constituted a boll, 16 bolls a chalder. For assessments of labourers' wages, see L.M. Cullen, T.C. Smout and A.J.S. Gibson, 'Wages and Comparative Development in Ireland and Scotland, 1565–1780' in *Economy and Society in Scotland and Ireland 1500–1939*, ed. Rosalind Mitchison and Peter Roebuck (Edinburgh, 1988), 105–16; and Gibson and Smout, *Prices, Food and Wages in Scotland 1550–1780* (Cambridge, 1995).

Scottish parishes with extant records, *c.* 1560–1640

Introduction

The Problem of Religion in the Pew

Scottish Christians in the later Middle Ages, like their counterparts elsewhere in Britain and on the continent, had a profoundly sensual experience of religion. The church was a site of image, sound and smell; the central rite of the mass celebrated by taste; the whole defined by movement and ceremony, and designed to elicit an affective response. It is by now a truism that the protestant Reformation replaced this cult of sensual and ceremonial spirituality with a cult of the word – preached, read, repeated, hopefully understood – and that the Calvinist tradition especially was responsible for the destruction of image and ritual in favor of book and sermon.[1] This was a genuinely radical shift, by any measure a cultural revolution. For ordinary folk, the Scots in the pew, it required a profound reorientation of understanding and expression of their most elemental hopes and fears. The rites by which their children entered the Christian community and by which they were married were pared down and stripped of much of their festivity; those by which they entered the next world were virtually abolished. The new kirk banned the processions that had escorted both images of Christ or the saints and the body of the deceased to the graveside, underscoring their elimination of the saints themselves from the process of intercession.[2] It condemned the 'works' –

1. James Kirk, *Patterns of Reform: Continuity and Change in the Reformation Kirk* (Edinburgh, 1989), Introduction (despite the subtitle, change is the dominant theme in these essays to the extent that they deal with matters of religious culture); Ian B. Cowan, *The Scottish Reformation: Church and Society in Sixteenth-Century Scotland* (London, 1982), 1–14, 95–101, 189–92; cf. Denis McKay, 'Parish Life in Scotland 1500–1560' in *Essays on the Scottish Reformation 1513–1625*, ed. David McRoberts (Glasgow, 1962), 85–115; James Galbraith, 'The Middle Ages' in *Studies in the History of Worship in Scotland*, ed. Duncan Forrester and Douglas Murray (Edinburgh, 1984), 20–25.
2. *First Book*, 199–201; Andrew Spicer, '"The Rest of their Bones": Fear of Death and Reformed Burial Practices' in *Fear in Early Modern Society*, ed. William Naphy and Penny Roberts (Manchester, 1977), 167–69; Bruce Gordon and Peter Marshall, eds, *The Place of the Dead: Death and Remembrance in Late Medieval and Early Modern Europe* (Cambridge, 2000); H. Colvin, *Architecture and the After-Life* (New Haven and London, 1991).

pilgrimage, veneration of relics and saints, chantry services – that had assuaged the terrors of purgatory and hell which had been fed so abundantly by ecclesiastical art.[3] Its service was no longer centred on the dramatic, daily re-enactment of Christ's sacrifice in the mass; rather, communion became an annual or biennial affair, the weekly experience of worship instead a logocentric one, with long morning and afternoon sermons separated by catechism. It left anxieties about childbirth or storm or disease unmet by traditional recourse to holy water or appeals to saints. The side altars maintained by guilds for their patron saints, underpinning both group identity and piety, were now abolished, the guild members left to reconstruct their corporate identity without that outward form.[4] How can such a drastic shift have been accomplished, and in Scotland with remarkably little directly religious violence?[5]

The educated elite of the sixteenth century have left us abundant records of why they opted for this shift. Clerics give us the theological underpinning in their diatribes against popish idolatry and superstition; lay authorities reveal the political motivations so evident in the actions of the Lords of the Congregation.[6] Histories of the Scottish Reformation have taken full advantage of these sources, from theological treatises and sermons, to partisan histories penned by participants in the change, to the proclamations of kings and bishops and acts of parliaments, so that we have a very good 'top-down' view of what happened and why.[7]

3. Audrey-Beth Fitch, 'The Search for Salvation: Lay Faith in Scotland, 1480–1560' (Unpublished PhD thesis, Glasgow, 1994); Duncan MacMillan, *Scottish Art 1450–1900* (Edinburgh, 1990); Cowan, *The Medieval Church in Scotland*, ed. James Kirk (Edinburgh, 1995), 170–92; D.E. Easson, 'The Collegiate Churches of Scotland', *RSCHS* 6 (1938), 193–215 and 7 (1939), 30–47; McKay, 105–09.
4. R. Fawcett, *Scottish Architecture from the Accession of the Stewarts to the Reformation, 1371–1560* (Edinburgh, 1994); G. Hay, *The Architecture of Scottish Post-Reformation Churches, 1560–1840* (Oxford, 1957), 21–28; D. Howard, *Scottish Architecture from the Reformation to the Restoration, 1560–1660* (Edinburgh, 1995), 172–77. The *Book of Perth*, ed. John Parker Lawson (Edinburgh, 1847), 59, notes as many as seventy endowed altars in St John's kirk, Perth, forty founded since 1400.
5. Gordon Donaldson makes the telling point that while the Scottish Reformation was much more thoroughgoing than England's, it entailed relatively little explicitly religious violence against persons, on either side: over against Mary Tudor's nearly three hundred protestant martyrs and Elizabeth's more than two hundred catholics, he sets Scotland's twenty or so protestants and a couple of catholics: 'A Backward Nation?' in *Scotland's History: Approaches and Reflections*, ed. James Kirk (Edinburgh, 1995), 46.
6. Most clearly and concisely summarised in Jenny Wormald, *Court, Kirk and Community: Scotland 1470–1625* (London, 1981), ch. 7.
7. For an excellent bibliography of works before 1989, including a survey of key printed primary sources from which much secondary work has been drawn, see James Kirk, 'The Scottish Reformation and the Reign of James VI: A Select Critical Bibliography',

Ecclesiastical polity and administration, theology, the clergy and clerical patronage, and relations with secular authorities have all been well, even brilliantly treated, as have the implications of Reformation for political theory and national policy.[8] In the last twenty years or so, however, this perspective has been found wanting by historians of most national Reformations. Influenced by the social history and historical anthropology that emerged in the 1970s, we no longer accept that the achievements of the Reformation can possibly be identified, let alone measured, by looking only at elite groups, ignoring the masses of people in the pew (or the alehouse) on the receiving end of all those sermons and proclamations.[9] We wonder what they thought about it all; how their own beliefs changed or maintained old assumptions; whether they understood themselves, God and their communities differently after the mandated changes; to what degree they adjusted their behaviour to reflect a new understanding. Historical anthropologists have introduced the possibility that a quite markedly different set of 'popular beliefs' coexisted uncomfortably with elite prescriptions, and that these beliefs might be investigated using some

RSCHS 23 (1989), 113–55. For works published before 1982 for the early seventeenth century, see David Stevenson, 'Scottish Church History 1600–1660: A Select Critical Bibliography', *RSCHS* 21 (1982), 209–20.

8. In addition to works listed in Kirk and Stevenson's bibliographies, see Roger Mason, *Kingship and the Common Weal* (East Linton, 1998) and 'The Scottish Reformation and the Origins of Anglo-British Imperialism' in *Scots and Britons: Scottish Political Thought and the Union of 1603*, ed. R. Mason (Cambridge, 1994); Julian Goodare, *State and Society in Early Modern Scotland* (Oxford, 1999), ch. 6; John Morrill, *The Scottish National Covenant in its British Context* (Edinburgh, 1990). A good recent clerical biography is John Coffey, *Politics, Religion and the British Revolutions: The Mind of Samuel Rutherford* (Cambridge, 1997). David Mullan traces the 'puritan brotherhood' and analyses puritan piety and theology in *Scottish Puritanism 1590–1638* (Oxford, 2000). Efforts to set Scotland's Reformation in a larger British or even European context include Jane Dawson, 'Anglo-Scottish Protestant Culture and Integration in Sixteenth-Century Britain' in *Conquest and Union: Fashioning a British State 1485–1725*, ed. Steven G. Ellis and Sarah Barber (Harrow, Essex, 1995), 87–114; Roger Mason, ed., *Scotland and England* (Edinburgh, 1987); Michael Graham, *The Uses of Reform: 'Godly Discipline' and Popular Behavior in Scotland and Beyond, 1560–1610* (Leiden, 1996), ch. 9 (comparing with Huguenot discipline); Bruce Lenman, 'Limits of Discipline' in *Religion and Society in Early Modern Europe*, ed. Kaspar von Greyerz (London, 1984); T.C. Smout, ed., *Scotland and Europe 1200–1850* (Edinburgh, 1986).

9. There are now a few good, book-length local histories of the Reformation, notably Michael Lynch, *Edinburgh and the Reformation* (Edinburgh, 1981); Margaret H.B. Sanderson, *Ayrshire and the Reformation: People and Change, 1490–1600* (East Linton, 1997); and Frank Bardgett, *Scotland Reformed: The Reformation in Angus and the Mearns* (Edinburgh, 1989). These begin to address questions about larger groups of laity, but there is a relative dearth of such studies for Scotland, as contrasted with England.

of the tools of cultural anthropologists, particularly of the functionalist variety.[10] Literary scholars similarly influenced, especially students of early modern drama, have entered the fray with their own analytical tools, in turn drawing historians to re-examine the Reformation as a cultural revolution in terms of visual, auditory, mimetic and linguistic arts.[11] Historians of the German and French Reformations have been particularly drawn by anthropological studies of ritual, especially rites of violence, to help describe and explain the culture of protestantism in broader terms, examining shifting and often disappearing rites and festivities, rituals of inversion, and highly structured confessional violence as evidence of changing attitudes.[12] Thus far, however, Scottish religious history has resisted these influences, perhaps conservatively (and not unreasonably) sceptical of their claims that history can be a social 'science'.

Recent work looking back on what has been accomplished thus far in sorting out 'belief' in the street, the workshop and the pew has identified both the benefits and the problems of historical anthropology.[13] The problems are certainly myriad, as historians and indeed anthropologists them-

10. Keith Thomas, *Religion and the Decline of Magic* (New York, 1971); Alan Macfarlane, *Witchcraft in Tudor and Stuart England* (London, 1970) and *The Family Life of Ralph Josselin* (Cambridge, 1970); Peter Burke, *Popular Culture in Early Modern Europe* (New York, 1978).
11. Patrick Collinson has produced useful results for English protestantism in *The Birthpangs of Protestant England* (New York, 1988), esp. 94–126, and 'Elizabethan and Jacobean Puritanism as Forms of Popular Religious Culture' in *The Culture of English Puritanism 1560–1700*, ed. Christopher Durston and Jacqueline Eales (London, 1996), 32–57, suggesting some similarities between English puritan and Scottish religious culture. Important influences for literary scholars are Clifford Geertz, *The Interpretation of Cultures* (New York, 1973); Mikhail Bakhtin, *Rabelais and his World*, tr. H. Iswolsky (Cambridge, Mass., 1968) and *Speech Genres and Other Late Essays*, tr. V.W. McGee (Austin, 1986); and Stephen Greenblatt, *Renaissance Self-Fashioning* (Chicago, 1980), *Shakespearean Negotiations* (Oxford, 1988) and *Learning to Curse: Essays in Early Modern Culture* (New York, 1990).
12. Natalie Zemon Davis, *Society and Culture in Early Modern France* (London, 1975) and 'The Sacred and the Body Social in Sixteenth and Seventeenth-Century Lyon', *P&P* 90 (1981), 40–70; David Sabean, *Power in the Blood: Popular Culture and Village Discourse in Early Modern Germany* (Cambridge, 1984); R.W. Scribner, 'Ritual and Popular Belief in Catholic Germany at the Time of the Reformation' in *Popular Culture and Popular Movements in Reformation Germany* (London, 1987), 17–48. Applying ritual studies in anthropology to less religious early modern developments are Edward Muir, *Civic Ritual in Renaissance Venice* (Princeton, 1981), *Mad Blood Stirring: Vendetta and Factions in Friuli during the Renaissance* (Baltimore, 1993) and *Ritual in Early Modern Europe* (Cambridge, 1997); and Michael Bristol, *Carnival and Theatre* (New York, 1985).
13. Robert Scribner, 'Historical Anthropology of Early Modern Europe' in *Problems in the Historical Anthropology of Early Modern Europe*, ed. R. Po-Chia Hsia and R.W. Scribner (Wiesbaden, 1997), 11–34.

selves fully recognise.[14] Anthropology is a discipline much like history, in which scholars tend to impose their own perspectives and concerns on their subjects; in which the sources for understanding a culture, whether aural or written, have their own biases, their own fictions; in which theories are often applied without regard to change over time. Functionalism or structuralism can skew data in a distinctly ahistorical direction, and adherents of an acculturation thesis tend too readily to bifurcate urban and rural, elite and popular.[15] Historical anthropologists have finally begun to realise, moreover, that early modern Europe was not a primitive tribal society. Still, we can employ many of the questions, techniques of observation and explanatory strategies offered by anthropologists, if we keep them within the context of a discipline that must by its very nature set all observations, all data, within a temporal framework in which change features as much as stasis. The symbolic anthropology of Clifford Geertz, van Gennep's rites of passage, Max Gluckman and Victor Turner on ritual and inversion and the former on dispute, Stanley Tambiah's version of performative theories, Marshall Sahlins's historicisation of anthropological structuralism, and Paul Connerton's work on social memory must all find echoes in historical studies of protestantism as cultural revolution.[16]

Ritual studies, and especially the 'performative approach' associated with Turner's later work and with Tambiah, Sally Moore and Barbara

14. Catherine Bell, *Ritual: Perspectives and Dimensions* (Oxford, 1997) and *Ritual Theory, Ritual Practice* (Oxford, 1992); Scribner, 'Historical Anthropology'; Jonathan Barry, 'Keith Thomas and the Problem of Witchcraft' in *Witchcraft in Early Modern Europe*, ed. Barry, M. Hester and Gareth Roberts (Cambridge, 1998); Peter Burke, *History and Social Theory* (Ithaca, NY, 1992); Caroline Walker Bynum, 'Introduction: The Complexity of Symbols' in *Gender and Religion: On the Complexity of Symbols*, ed. C.W. Bynum, S. Harrell and P. Richman (Boston, 1986), 1–20, and *Fragmentation and Redemption* (New York, 1991).
15. Robert Muchembled, *Culture populaire, culture des élites* (Paris, 1978); Burke, *Popular Culture*, cf. *Varieties of Cultural History* (Oxford, 1997), 124–35, somewhat modifying his earlier views.
16. Clifford Geertz, *Available Light: Anthropological Reflections on Philosophical Topics* (Princeton, 2000), *Interpretation of Cultures* (New York, 1973) and 'Religion as a Cultural System' in *Anthropological Approaches to the Study of Religion*, ed. Michael Banton (London, 1960); Arnold van Gennep, *Rites of Passage* (Chicago, 1960, orig. 1909); Max Gluckman, *Custom and Conflict in Africa* (Oxford, 1955), *Essays on the Rituals of Social Relations* (Manchester, 1962) and *Politics, Law and Ritual in a Tribal Society* (Oxford, 1965); Victor Turner, *The Anthropology of Performance* (New York, 1987) and *The Ritual Process: Structure and Anti-Structure* (Chicago, 1969); Stanley Jeyaraja Tambiah, *Culture, Thought and Social Action: An Anthropological Perspective* (Cambridge, Mass., 1985), esp. 1–13, 123–66; Marshall Sahlins, *Historical Metaphors and Mythical Realities* (Ann Arbor, 1981) and *How 'Natives' Think: About Captain Cook, for Example* (Chicago, 1995); Paul Connerton, *How Societies Remember* (Cambridge, 1989).

Myerhoff, have proven particularly suggestive for this study, opening an array of possibilities for analysing the multivalent meanings of recorded outward actions to both participants and observers within a historical setting. A closer examination of early modern ritual (in this study, penitential ceremony, festivity, communion, reconciliation of quarrellers and fasting) helps to balance out the always troubling gaps left by questions of inner, subjective state and private belief, and to deal with evident inconsistencies in doctrine and behaviour. Ritual, as Myerhoff has emphasised, is not religion, but rhetoric. It is a performance that may 'call for belief, but not through the cognitive mechanisms that allow critical thinking to interfere with conviction'. If one may 'become what one performs', then the rituals one finds reflected in sixteenth-century records will tell us a good deal about how the rather difficult intellectual constructs of protestant theology can have permeated and restructured the religious culture of early modern Scottish communities.[17] And since by their very nature rituals, unlike systems of religious ideas, incorporate and even revel in ambiguity and paradox, the protestant performances considered here may reveal more than any number of Calvinist theological treatises and sermons about how Scottish parishioners organised and displayed their multivalent understandings of the new faith in the context of pervasive traditional values, fears and structures.[18] What will emerge is a view of the Reformation as a rearrangement of fundamental beliefs enacted or performed in such a way as to achieve a meaningful new order, relating sacred to secular, individual to God and to community. If ritual itself constitutes a 're-shaping of consciousness or experience', if it establishes 'a view of reality and a corresponding view of self, . . . creating a subjective psychological state that restructures meaning', then exploring early modern protestant ritual will be an essential avenue to discovering the meanings of Reformation in the pew, and how those meanings were achieved and fostered.[19] There is more to the story than ritual, of course; it will not do to play down the cognitive in a religion of the book, where Bible, catechism and sermon were the prescribed (indeed, enforced) ways to an ideal of correct understanding. But considering ritual along with the other evi-

17. Barbara Myerhoff, 'Rites of Passage: Process and Paradox' in *Celebration: Studies in Festivity and Ritual*, ed. Victor Turner (Washington, D.C., 1982), 109–35, quotations at 128–29; Sally Moore and Myerhoff, eds, *Secular Ritual* (Assen, 1977); Moore, *Law as Process* (London, 1987) and *Anthropology and Africa* (Charlottesville, Virginia, 1994).

18. Bell, *Ritual Theory*, 222, reminds us that 'ritual will not work as social control if it is perceived as not amenable to some degree of individual appropriation', making a given ritual's meanings necessarily as diverse as its practitioners.

19. Sherry Ortner, *Sherpas through their Rituals* (Cambridge, 1978), 9; Myerhoff, 129; Geertz, *Available Light*, 118–33.

dence we have of how Reformation worked in the parishes will bring us much closer to the mark than more exclusive traditional approaches.

In its current guise, the performative approach is particularly amenable to historical application. It departs from earlier theory by making room for ambiguity within ceremonial forms, for change over time in the context of ritual, and for word as well as action in its composition. To take the last point first, the reader worried about the ascription of agency to ritual that we find in Myerhoff and others, should keep several points in mind. Not only is ritual performed repeatedly and frequently before a captive audience very often acting as well as observing, not only is it replete with powerful signs and language, it is also in early modern Reformed culture intimately associated with the word preached. One strength of Tambiah's approach is his argument that the ritual communication of cosmologies combines the semantic and the pragmatic, thought and action – a presumption particularly well suited to a study of ceremony contextualised by the theological principles of an intensely logocentric religion. Another strength is his willingness to grant the complicating factors of an individual's situation and of variations, including historial change, in the larger context of ritual action. There were multiple subcultures of protestantism under the Reformed Scottish umbrella – including the especially zealous or puritan, and the more disorderly but still often anxiously religious; the clergy with their distinctive cult of persecution, and the more complacent authorities devoted to a culture of discipline as a means to a more orderly society; and ultimately the Covenanters and their foes, not to mention the more neutral but not irreligious mass caught in the middle of the seventeenth-century wars. Both communal and individual stories, self-concepts and agendas impinged on the universal story enacted in protestant ritual, and sorting out both the 'formalized dimension' and the 'contextual meaning' of each performance is therefore essential to approach the real complexity, the internal tension as well as the external resolution, of protestant culture.[20] Finally, as we shall see in close examination of the rituals retained and modified by the kirk after the Reformation, the capacity for ritual action to embrace and even celebrate ambiguity was an essential element of the triumph of Scotland's extreme form of protestantism.

For all the benefits of cross-disciplinary perspectives and more inclusive theoretical approaches, however, serious problems remain for those who would examine early modern religion in the pew. Reformation historians have had to struggle to access the view from the bottom principally because of the dearth of source material for the illiterate mass of the

20. Tambiah, *Culture*, 2, 4, 13, 123–66.

population. Historians work with texts; how can we know the thoughts of those who did not write? There are ways: English historians have recently made good use of churchwardens' accounts, ecclesiastical court records and the material remains of the Reformation in parish churches.[21] All these sources, however, are limited: the English church courts were not local, certainly not parochial; churchwardens' presentments were formulaic and their accounts concerned mainly with finances and fabric; and extant artifacts are few and far between.

Scotland, however, offers historians a remarkable opportunity to explore the culture of protestantism at the parochial level, because of its Reformed polity. The reader will think immediately of presbyterianism here; but the more significant aspect of the polity for our purposes, the one that has contributed such an abundance of parochial source material and that is in many ways itself the real hallmark of the Reformed church in Scotland, is not presbyterianism or superintendency, about which so much has been written, but rather the most local of the Calvinist church courts, the kirk session. Operating in some parishes from the dawn of the Reformation (indeed, even before, in St Andrews and Dundee) and in most well before the turn of the century, the session was comprised of the minister (in a large parish, ministers) and a sizable group of lay elders (generally a dozen to twenty-five).[22] These were drawn from substantial landholders down to

21. Eamon Duffy, *The Stripping of the Altars* (New Haven, 1992); Ronald Hutton, *The Rise and Fall of Merry England: The Ritual Year 1400–1700* (Oxford, 1994); Laura Gowing, *Domestic Dangers: Women, Word and Sex in Early Modern London* (Oxford, 1996); Martin Ingram, *The Church Courts, Sex and Marriage in England 1520–1640* (Cambridge, 1987); Ralph Houlbrooke, *Church Courts and the People during the English Reformation 1520–1570* (Oxford, 1979); Beat Kümin, *The Shaping of a Community* (Aldershot, 1996) and 'Parish Finance and the Early Tudor Clergy' in *The Reformation of the Parishes*, ed. Andrew Pettegree (Manchester, 1993).

22. Estimates for established kirk sessions by the early seventeenth century are generally three-quarters to 80 per cent of the thousand or so parishes: Lesley M. Smith, 'Sackcloth for the Sinner or Punishment for the Crime? Church and Secular Courts in Cromwellian Scotland' in *New Perspectives on the Politics and Culture of Early Modern Scotland*, ed. John Dwyer, Roger Mason and Alexander Murdoch (Edinburgh, n.d.), 119; Ian D. Whyte, *Scotland's Society and Economy in Transition* (New York, 1997), 50. Such estimates may be too conservative, given the survival rate of session minute books. For Dundee's 1559 session, see Ian Flett, 'The Conflict of the Reformation and Democracy in the Geneva of Scotland, 1443–1610: An Introduction to Edited Texts of Documents Relating to the Burgh of Dundee' (Unpublished MPhil thesis, St Andrews, 1981). For size, see CH2/390/1, f. 1 (an unusual thirty-two in Dysart); CH2/400/1, p. 307 (twenty-nine in Falkirk). CH2/636/34, f. 1; CH2/521/1, f. 84 and CH2/521/2, f. 66v; and AAC CH2/751/1, ff. 1, 133, and CH2/751/2, f. 1 list more typical figures of twenty elders for Kirkcaldy, twelve to fourteen for Perth, twelve to twenty for Ayr. Dron had only nine (CH2/93/1, f. 18); *SAKS* 2:760–61 lists fifty-

working farmers in the countryside, and in towns from a range extending from the mercantile elite to various levels of craftsmen and artisans.[23] English critics claimed that elders, 'popes in the highest degree' in every parish, were of the 'basest sort', an 'unlearned company', but in fact the wealthier and more prominent men tended to outnumber and doubtless dominated their inferiors on the session.[24] Town and village sessions alike included elders from both the population nucleus and its 'landward and links', or surrounding rural areas, often for a radius of several miles, ensuring that those outside the walls were represented.[25]

Sessions met weekly in most parishes, and as often as four times weekly in large urban settings, to deal with matters of ecclesiastical administration

nine St Andrews session members but includes deacons. Highland sessions tended to be dominated by a few prominent kin groups: Inveravon's eighteen elders included seven Grants, five Stewarts, two Innes (CH2/191/1, ff. 59v–60); Mortlach had three Gordons, four Lesleys (CH2/529/1, f. 80).

23. For composition, see W.H. Makey, 'The Elders of Stow, Liberton, Canongate, and St Cuthbert's', *RSCHS* 8, pt 2 (1970), 155–67; Cowan, *Scottish Reformation*, 135. Perth's list included baxters (bakers) and skinners as well as wealthy merchants also sitting on the council (CH2/521/1, f. 11); Dron's included heritors (landed proprietors), knights, bailies, tenants and a miller (CH2/93/1, f. 18). NAS ms RH2/1/35, f. 19v lists Edinburgh elders in 1574 including merchants, cordiners, surgeons, baxters, smiths, skinners, tailors, barbers and cutlers; Trinity College kirk's in 1627 included a skinner, a tailor, an armourer, an advocate, several merchants and a maltman: CH2/141/1, f. 25.

24. LPL ms 3471, ff. 43v, 46 (Patrick Blair, 1589). Lynch, *Edinburgh*, 39–40, finds only one baxter on the Edinburgh session, dominated by wealthy merchants and lawyers. In rural parishes, heritors or lairds were sometimes outnumbered by portioners (small proprietors) or tenants and subtenants (as in Kilconquhar, SAU CH2/210/1, f. 9, or Monifieth, New Register House, Edinburgh, OPR 310/1); however, their presence was required for the most important decisions (CH2/93/1, f. 24; CH2/471/1, f. 4).

25. CH2/636/34, f. 1 (with similar division of deacons). The Dundonald session included elders from the town and one each from eight outlying hamlets: *Dundonald*, 57. Rural sessions and those of towns with very extensive landward areas were often over-large because they included lairds who rarely attended and seem to have been appointed mainly for political reasons: e.g., CH2/400/1, pp. 79, 184 (only four to six of Falkirk's twenty-odd elders present at session meetings; the only elders never fined for absence were the lairds). Brechin initially set lower attendance expectations for its landward elders (twenty-one of their thirty-eight), some of whom lived three miles from the church; later the landward elders began meeting as a separate session after the Sunday sermon to avoid making the trip to town more than once weekly: D.B. Thoms, *The Kirk of Brechin in the Seventeenth Century* (Perth, 1972), 7–10. Many rural districts electing elders to town sessions had themselves constituted parishes at one time but were unable to support resident preachers. Under the discipline of a central session, administered locally by their own elders, they would nonetheless have been forcibly included in the larger parish's round of catechism and sabbath observance which we will examine in the following chapter.

and moral discipline.[26] This must have been an onerous burden on men with farms or businesses to run, and fines levied by nearly every session for absence from meetings suggest that some elders bore it grudgingly. Only very rarely, however, did a man try to decline the office, which clearly carried considerable power and status along with obligation.[27]

A session's jurisdiction could be enormous, geographically in rural areas, numerically in burghs. Although average parish size in late sixteenth-century Scotland was around 150 households, most towns were single-parish, presenting urban sessions a daunting challenge. Even the capital, with ten to twelve thousand at mid-century and perhaps fifteen thousand by 1600, had at the Reformation only one parish church, St Giles. Here, as in Glasgow's cathedral, the congregation was divided into quarters and the church partitioned for separate services; however, a single session oversaw all the quarters for most of our period as the 'General Kirk'. Of the other 'four great burghs', with populations approaching four thousand at the Reformation, only Aberdeen had two parishes; Perth and Dundee made do with one each, St John's kirk of Perth being partitioned like St Giles but governed by a single session.[28] Other burghs were much smaller but still demanding, given the responsibilities that the reformers assigned to elders.

Sessions investigated and rendered judicial decisions in cases of sexual offence, drunkenness, quarrelling, doctrinal error and sabbath breach. They

26. For Perth, CH2/521/3, pp. 2, 25 record two discipline days (Monday and Thursday) by 1597, a third meeting added on Tuesdays in 1598 for hospital business. From 1601 elders were required to attend Friday morning prayers before visiting families in their quarters (p. 177), although this order had to be repeated in 1605 (CH2/521/4, p. 170), when the Tuesday meeting was devoted to poor relief, and hospital business moved to Thursday. They added a regular Friday meeting in 1621, and in fact disciplinary matters were handled on most of the meeting dates. The elders were expected to attend presbytery meetings on Wednesdays (CH2/521/7, p. 276). Elgin's session also met three or four times weekly from at least 1600: CH2/145/2, f. 60 *et passim*.

27. For reluctant and lax elders, see chapter 8 below. Lasswade's session in 1615 complained that some had 'borne the burden very long': CH2/471/1, f. 7.

28. Edinburgh's Southeast and Northwest kirks would continue to share St Giles after the Northeast moved to Trinity College in 1584 and the Southwest to the Upper Tollbooth in 1598 until New Greyfriars' completion in 1620. In the 1640s the Tollbooth and Tron parishes were added to accommodate expanding population: *Fasti* 1:37–86, 122–31; *Early Travellers in Scotland*, ed. P. Hume Brown (New York, 1970), 151. Other nearby parishes – Corstorphine, Duddingston, Liberton, St Cuthbert's, the Canongate and Restalrig/Leith – were all outside the town walls; however, no resident of Edinburgh was more than half a mile from a parish church. Population figures for this period are very rough estimates; these are Gordon Donaldson's, *Scottish Church History* (Edinburgh, 1985), 220, 225.

themselves 'discovered' many of these offences, charged as they were with regularly visiting their 'quarters' of the parish, and with prowling about the town or village during the Sunday service to surprise sabbath-breakers in the act.[29] But they did much more. They also administered poor relief and education; regulated marriage, baptism and burial; administered parochial finances and supervised the physical maintenance, decoration and expansion of the kirk and kirkyard; oversaw catechism and examination; declared fasts and feasts; ordered and administered communion; represented the parish in calling and assessing ministers; and served as liaisons with higher church bodies – presbyteries, synods and, at the national level, the General Assembly. At some point in their lives, most members of the community would have cause to appear before the session, and not necessarily to be censured for an offence. Couples had to seek the session's permission to have their marriage banns pronounced; people came to complain about the misbehaviour of their neighbours or to offer depositions to aid their defence; travellers and the poor came seeking aid, as did schoolboys wanting the means to attend university, or local families fostering abandoned children. The minute books kept by sessions thus offer an extraordinary look at a cross-section of local populations living out their daily lives in the new context of Reformed protestantism, striving to deal with unchanging concerns and anxieties in a drastically changing religious milieu.

Even before a presbyterian system was fully implemented, Reformed parishes formed an interdependent web. They communicated regularly with each other, assisted each other with discipline, offered financial aid in time of disaster and shared ministers when the need arose. Both individually and as part of the larger network, their sessions had real clout. Contumacy – declining to appear when summoned, or to pay penalties or perform repentance when ordered – was not ignored and could result in suspension from communion and ultimately excommunication. No one was permitted to receive the contumacious in their homes.[30] And the co-operation generally forthcoming from secular authorities – town bailies and magistrates, the officers of local heritors – gave the sessions the physical means to enforce their will. These men were often elders themselves; overlapping personnel blurred the line between kirk and burgh authority. Thus the kirk of Glasgow in 1593 was able to call on the laird of Minto's officers to apprehend two men 'disobedient to the admonition and word of the kirk' and ward them until the next presbytery meeting.

29. See chapter 1, below.
30. E.g., CH2/338/1, f. 2v (Stow, 1626).

Burgh sessions often met jointly with councils, co-operating in the administration of schools and hospitals and facilitating corporal punishment of sinners.[31]

The mutual aid that sessions of neighbouring (or even far-distant) parishes lent for discipline was vital: in tracking down fugitives and providing testimonials for the well-behaved, they made it difficult for any offender to escape the system. Upstanding parishioners moving to another community found that, without a signed testimonial from the session of origin affirming their correct doctrine and 'godly and honest behaviour where they were before', no man would 'be received burgess, nor no woman have residence'.[32] Anyone who had just performed repentance or paid a penalty for offence in her parish of origin had to bring a testimonial to that effect.[33] One hoping to escape the session's sentence for an offence not only lacked the requisite document for acceptance in the new place, but was also liable to being picked up by the authorities in the new parish, often at the request of the old, and banished or forcibly returned for punishment.[34] So great was the value of a testimonial that there was an active trade in counterfeits, though if possession of a bogus document were discovered, one could be banished, as Margaret Gray was when she tried to move to South Leith having failed to repent publicly of her adultery in Aberdeen.[35] Suspension by the session meant exclusion from the life of the community, and if the ultimate sentence of excommunication were pronounced (generally upon presbytery order, but at the instigation of the local session), one's neighbours were forbidden to eat or

31. ML CH2/171/1, f. 14v; CH2/521/6, f. 6. On overlap of session membership with magistracy, W.R. Foster, *The Church before the Covenants* (Edinburgh, 1975), 70–71. Perth illustrates the point well: a comparative glance at lists of councillors (PL ms B59/12/9) and elders (CH2/521/1–2) shows that it was not unusual for half to two-thirds of the sixteenth-century elders to be council members as well. By 1631 the overlap was so great that the council simply met with the session as a matter of course: CH2/521/8/1, ff. 2–5. See also *SAKS* 2:650 (eight of fourteen elders on the council, 1589).
32. CH2/521/2, f. 77; CH2/1115/1, f. 8v (Boharm, 1636, a standard order for no outsider to be received 'without testimonial of satisfactoriness of their life and conversation under the hand of the minister of the parish they dwelled last within').
33. CH2/283/1, f. 4 (Newton, 1629); cf. SAU CH2/210/1, f. 5v; CH2/141/1, f. 4; CH2/1026/1, f. 7v (Stirling, Holy Rude, 1597). The network between parishes could function to initiate or forestall discipline, as when Dron send two elders to seek a neighbouring minister's help in persuading an errant Dron husband to return home: CH2/93/1, f. 23.
34. CH2/716/2 (South Leith), ff. 55, 88; CH2/1142/1, f. 98v (a 1619 Fraserburgh elders' 'inquisition concerning a fugitive out of the parish').
35. CH2/716/1, f. 9v (1601); AAC CH2/751/1, f. 136 (Ayr's officer deposed for his by-employment of forgery); CH2/141/1, f. 27v.

drink, shelter or do business with the offender until she had 'made satisfaction'.[36] Once presbyteries and synods came into being, their close oversight of sessions ensured an evenness of local compliance with this policy remarkable for so far-flung and decentralized a realm as Scotland.[37]

Every session had a clerk, and the minute books of more than sixty parishes survive from the three generations or so following the official Reformation of 1559–60. This study is based on the extant volumes from the Reformation through the Bishops' Wars, continuing in some cases into the 1650s, since the wars seem to have unsettled the sessions' operations remarkably little. The terminal date is deliberately vague; the survival rate of minute books steadily increases as the seventeenth century progresses, so that by the 1640s the amount of evidence is simply too great to treat comprehensively. In any case, by mid-century the system was long and well established.

It would obviously be dangerous to draw too many conclusions about the first generation of protestants from second- and third-generation sources. But a comparison of the earliest extant session minute books with those of the early seventeenth century indicates that the first-generation sessions do seem to have become the model for later ones, and where early registers are missing, it seems not too much of a stretch to assume a good deal of continuity in practice, so that later records are surely good indicators of a system put in place in the 1570s or 1580s.[38] Clearly it is wrong to assume, when the first extant record is a seventeenth-century one, that the first session was established that late: for parishes where the earliest surviving records are from the 1610s and 1620s, the first books in the extant series nearly always contain internal evidence of earlier, lost books and already long-standing traditions for their sessions – references to 'the act formerly made' or 'as of old' or 'or fifty years bypast'.[39]

36. AAC CH2/751/1, f. 136 (ordering that 'none set a house to her under pain of £20' when Jonat Bon was excommunicated and banished from Ayr in 1608); see also CH2/448/2, p. 63; CH2/521/2, f. 139; CH2/96/1 (Duffus), f. 7v; *APS* 3:71–72, 421; 4:63 (none to 'haunt, frequent, nor intercommon with them'), 407 (excommunicates to forfeit 'lands, rents and revenues').

37. E.g., CH2/121/1, f. 43v (Edinburgh presbytery, 1588); CH2/294/1 (Paisley presbytery), ff. 2–2v *et passim*; CH2/271/1 (Moray synod), pp. 2–4, 6, 9 *et passim.*

38. Graham, *Uses*, deduces trends on the basis of a handful of kirk session records in the sixteenth century. Sessions did pursue particular clusters of sins at particular times, as one would expect – periodic crackdowns on currently fashionable crimes being a characteristic of modern police forces as well. Overall, though, the surviving records from the eighty years following the Reformation saw more continuities than divergences of concerns and policies.

39. Many minute books begin mid-case: e.g., CH2/472/1 (Kinghorn, 1607), CH2/283/1 (Newton, 1629), CH2/147/1 (Ellon, 1607), CH2/699/1 (Longside, 1620), suggesting

Presbytery and synod records, moreover, note parishes where clearly there are sessions operating but failing to keep written accounts of their proceedings.[40] And we can only guess at how typical was the case of Brechin parish, whose book was 'taken away by the common enemy' in 1644, or Scoonie's, where the account was kept with the minister's books and 'burned with fire which fell out in his chamber chimney' in 1641.[41]

The focus here is in any case on the culture that was established by that system of parochial sessions in the seventy or eighty years following the official Reformation. I am less concerned with the pace of Reformation (which in any case varied considerably by region) than with its mechanisms, how those mechanisms functioned, and what they brought about in reshaping how people found and expressed meaning in external forms, in those repetitive corporate performances we call ritual, in habits and in material tokens. My subject, in other words, is the religious culture of early modern Scotland.

The sources for this study include the parochial records of communities urban and rural, large and small, pastoral and fishing, the Borders to the Highlands and Northern Isles, to the extent that they are available. Most of the surviving minute books are naturally from the more heavily populated south and east, and from towns, which understandably organised sessions earlier than did rural areas and found regular meetings easier to achieve without extensive travel. An important theme of this investigation will be that the session itself was the single greatest factor in establishing a culture of protestantism, so that the 'success' of protestantism demonstrated here is naturally at the earliest stages a rather more urban than rural phenomenon. No claims will be made for rapid or significant cultural change in the Highlands and islands, although recent studies suggest that Calvinism was earlier and more effectively established there than we have previously thought.[42] Clearly the Highlands and other rural

continuation from earlier lost books. Clerks often started a new book when a new minister came, as in Inveravon (CH2/191/1). Only in 1609 did South Leith's session begin to provide for record storage (CH2/716/1, f. 20v), so we are fortunate to have a book beginning in 1597. Dysart's first extant book (CH2/390/1, 1619) is typical in referring to earlier acts of session (f. 10); Innerwick's (CH2/1463/1) has minutes of discipline cases beginning in 1648, but they follow a listing of 1608 acts of session apparently copied from an earlier book that no longer survives. Those 1608 acts on the first folio also complain about persistent absenteeism from session meetings obviously antecedent to 1608. Plate 1 illustrates the appearance of session minutes.

40. CH2/271/1, f. 13. There were also sessions operating in parishes without ministers (*pace* Cowan, *Scottish Reformation*, 134): CH2/146/1 (Ellon presbytery), ff. 15, 19v–20, 27v, 36v–38v, 109–09v, 115–16 (Udny session).

41. Thoms, *Kirk of Brechin*, 11 (a book kept from 1624; earlier ones survived the 1640s but are no longer accessible); CH2/326/1, p. 38.

42. Jane Dawson, 'Calvinism and the Gaidhealtachd in Scotland' in *Calvinism in Europe*

areas had problems that did not confront towns to such a degree: their session meetings were regularly cancelled in winter, for instance, for 'tempestuous weather' or 'great storm and inundation of waters' that made travel over great distances impossible. Highland sessions were also disrupted by the violence of feud, as when 'the great desolations and troubles that were in these parts' prevented the Inveravon session from meeting for much of the winter of 1630–31.[43] But given population distribution in early modern Scotland, and the direct impact of towns on their immediate landward, it is surely the case that the most significant portion of the Scottish population – in the crescent from the northeastern towns of Fraserburgh and Aberdeen, through Fife, the Lothians and Borders, and southwest to Ayrshire – experienced as remarkably successful a Reformation as anywhere in Western Europe, on a vastly larger scale than the Calvinist towns on the continent, and in a more profound, penetrating form than anywhere else in the British Isles. Scotland's Reformation put the English puritan agenda to shame in its thoroughgoing reform.[44] Towns, furthermore, provided the model for the cultural transformation of smaller

1540–1620, ed. Andrew Pettegree, Alastair Duke, Gillian Lewis (Cambridge, 1994), 231–53. Some of Dawson's most convincing evidence is the complaint of Franciscan friars from Antrim that protestant preaching had made the Highlands and Isles by the 1620s impossibly hostile territory (p. 240). Kirk sessions were not a particularly important factor in the Highlands; instead, she argues, Calvinist preachers drawn from the Gaelic learned orders and magnates friendly to the Reformation successfully adapted Calvinism to Gaelic culture. On the other hand, there is counter-evidence of substantial Highlands recusancy pointing to the patchy nature of the reform there. For the fundamental cultural change that underlies Scottish Calvinism, I find that the sessions were the key. Cf. Kirk, *Patterns*, 305–33, 449–87; his 'Jacobean Church in the Highlands, 1567–1625' in *The Seventeenth Century in the Highlands* (Inverness, 1986), 24–51; and James Kirk (ed.), *The Church in the Highlands* (Edinburgh, 1998), 37–88.

43. CH2/191/1, ff. 1–1v (no meetings from Martinmas, 11 November 1630 to 2 January 1631), 2, 8v, 9, 12, 42, 46 etc. (all cancellations because of weather). In Angus, Menmuir's clerk recorded in 1636, 'no session holden in the winter season partly because of the coldness of weather, and partly because of the often absence of our gentlemen heritors', and in February 1640 no meeting 'in respect of the extraordinary storm of snow': CH2/264/1, ff. 13v, 25. Reasonably enough, Upland sessions tended to meet weekly at most, after a Sunday sermon, and to enforce less rigorous sermon attendance on the parishioners for the same reason. Small wonder that protestantism took longer to seize hold of these areas. On the other hand, weather often prevented session meetings even in burghs like Perth and Dalkeith (CH2/521/8/1, f. 160; CH2/424/1, ff. 3v, 4).

44. Lenman, 'Limits of Discipline'; Kirk on 'Scottish Achievements and English Aspirations' in *Patterns*, 334–67. Cf. the struggles and shortfalls of discipline even in English puritan parishes: M.S. Byford, 'The Price of Protestantism: Assessing the Impact of Religious Change in Elizabethan Essex: The Cases of Heydon and Colchester, 1558–1594' (Unpublished DPhil thesis, Oxford, 1988).

and more isolated communities, especially as the presbyteries established in the 1580s and 1590s became more effective at installing Reformed ministers throughout the land and bringing them together at presbytery meetings to compare notes with their more advanced brethren. Towns set the standard for protestant communities, and the records reveal smaller parishes as well as rural districts overseen by landward elders emulating urban ecclesiastical patterns. The self-skewing of our evidence towards towns, then, need not be a problem. It may even be that one effect of Reformed polity in Scotland was precisely to impose urban values of discipline and order on the rest of the realm, formerly less centralised and regimented.

The minute books' quality and comprehensiveness vary, of course, and they must be used with great care. They will not do at all for a statistical study, for many reasons. First, the condition of many books, with large sections of fragmentary, crumbled and torn pages, moisture damage and badly faded ink, makes counting of cases over time impossible.[45] Second, there are significant gaps in even the best records. These may be due to lost pages or lost volumes, or to temporary lapses either in session meetings or in the taking of minutes because of local disasters or the illness of the clerk.[46] In some cases there is evidence of deliberate excision of portions of the record, perhaps to send a particular case on to the presbytery.[47] Burntisland's loss of records may be explained by the peculiar obsession of the clerk, Andro Wilson, who in 1609 refused to turn over his collection of registers to the kirk, 'alleging they were his life' and

45. Mortlach's first book (CH2/529/1) was surely left out in the rain at some point.
46. Perth's voluminous minutes (CH2/521/1–8) are the most complete and detailed, running from 1577 to 1637. But even these have gaps at 1613–14 and 1624–30; the volumes beginning May 1577, January 1615 and January 1631 all indicate continuation from volumes no longer extant. Even the St Andrews session minutes have a gap from August 1585 to June 1586, between the plague death of one minister and the arrival of his replacement: *SAKS* 2:lxvi. More seriously, and typically, Kinghorn is missing 1610–22 and 1632–39, and has only a fragment from the 1580s in its 1605–10 volume (CH2/472/1–2); Elgin has gaps for 1605–13 and 1629–48; St Monans lacks 1617–29 (SAU CH2/1056/1); Newbattle is missing 1628–43 (CH2/276/1–2). Mid-Calder's clerk often skipped over weeks of entries (CH2/266/1), moving directly from January to July on the same page.
47. E.g., CH8/54/1a, a page apparently taken from the Dumfries session book, with evidence from more than the one case in which the presbytery might have been interested (1606). This may explain the sheets of 1590s notes and depositions shuffled at the end of Elgin's 1613–22 book, including records of a child rape case that might have been excerpted for an assize (CH2/145/3, after f. 195); or loose pages at the end of CH2/521/7, depositions against three accused witches, probably cut from the book to be copied and sent to an assize. Most of Perth's books are in the NAS, but odd pages from one seventeenth-century book are in a bundle of hospital documents in the Perth Museum (ms 86/12), labelled 'Miscellaneous Receipts 1583–99'.

'appertained not to the session'.[48] Even worse, some sessions apparently met without keeping records, as we learn from presbytery and synodal complaints.[49] Third, session clerks were individuals with their own particular interests and abilities; they varied in their concern with particular sins and in their diligence and accuracy in taking down evidence. Some recorded every case in painstaking detail, though it is the rare scribe who actually sketches a portrait of the offender in the margin next to her case, as Ellon's clerk did in 1603. Too often, such particularly effusive clerks are succeeded by scribes whose entries are sparse and haphazard.[50] Menmuir's book abruptly changes in 1637 from a record of fifteen years of discipline to one of collections only: should we conclude that the parish was suddenly rid of sin?[51] A historian busily counting cases of fornication or drunkenness needs to be aware that a new clerk less concerned with comprehensive recording than his predecessor may well skew the figures. There is also some unsurprising evidence that a clerk receiving a regular stipend kept better records.[52] Finally, conventions of record-keeping diverge quite

48. CH2/523/1, ff. 36v, 37v, 38, 45 – negotiations from May through December 1609, including 'long reasoning of the pastor' and intervention of presbytery and town council to secure the books. Burntisland's pre-1602 books are not extant; one wonders whether they might have been squirrelled away in Mr Wilson's cache, never to emerge. John Cruikshank of Ellon seems to have had a similar problem, writing in the session-book margin, 'him that seeks this book from me, I will see hang upon a tree': CH2/147/1, f. 47. A deprived minister absconded with the Deer presbytery's early books: CH2/89/1, f. 26 (1604).
49. E.g., CH2/271/1, f. 13 (Moray synod). This seems to have been a problem more in the Highland than Lowland parishes.
50. CH2/147/1, f. 13. CH2/521/8/2 is a striking case of a new clerk dramatically changing the nature (and usefulness) of a minute book: after eight volumes and more than sixty years of detailed and comprehensive narrative recounting of cases, mostly by the notary John Davidson, the Perth minutes abruptly change hand in 1637 (f. 234v) and disintegrate into sporadic listing of almost exclusively sexual cases, marriage contracts, accounts and penitents received. The demise of Mr Davidson ought not lead us to conclude that suddenly Perth was no longer troubled by its previous problems of charming, sabbath drinking or quarrelling. The new clerk simply failed to record the offences of most of the penitents received, or the details of the sexual cases and the prescribed repentances. Perhaps he moved these to a different book. The abrupt change of hand in the Mortlach records is also telling: CH2/529/1, f. 58v marks a sudden change in February of 1637 from recording discipline to listing collections and marriage contracts, with only very scattered cases of the sexual offences, sabbath breaches and slanders that had consistently dominated the book earlier, under a different clerk's hand.
51. CH2/264/1, f. 16. Fornication cases resume f. 19.
52. The Mid-Calder records become much fuller and more regular when the clerk began to get a stipend taken from the penalties of offenders: CH2/266/1, f. 5v. Minutes before that point indicate the session met only about four times a year, but suddenly

considerably from one clerk to another, even within a parish, and they were often modified when a new minister arrived and a new book was begun.[53] Some parishes seem to have kept separate books for particular kinds of business – a volume for financial matters, a separate one for sexual offences, another for marriage banns.[54] Some clerks summarised minutes long after the session meeting had ended, leading to muddled chronology and omitted data.[55] Perhaps most misleading to modern historians, some surviving books are in fact contemporary excerpts or incomplete fair copies of much more comprehensive rough notes taken at meetings. Overlapping rough and fair volumes from the 1590s for South Leith offer fair warning against using session books to render sin quantifiable: if all that had survived were the fair copy, the session would appear to us much less busy, and not at all concerned with the cases of sabbath golfing that are in fact numerous in the rough copy.[56] This study therefore eschews any pretence to statistical investigation.[57]

after 1607 they were meeting almost weekly; how seriously can we take the evidence provided for the earlier period? Ayr's well-kept records doubtless have something to do with quarterly payments of 40s to John Esdaw for 'sure keeping of the book': AAC CH2/751/1, f. 15v.

53. CH2/191/1, f. 1, 'session book since the entry of Mr John Chalmer'.
54. The Dumfries clerk extracted cases of absence from communion in a separate place (CH8/54/1a); many clerks seem to have kept fornicators in a separate book. Bolton, Dunbarney, Edinburgh and Newton kept separate books for accounts, with the occasional intrusion of discipline cases as if, perhaps, the clerk brought the wrong book to a session meeting: CH2/37/1, CH2/100/1, CH2/122/76, CH2/283/1. Kingsbarns's book has a separate accounts section that includes some slander cases not appearing in the discipline section: SAU CH2/819/1.
55. The clerk of Mid-Calder, for instance, records events 'about this time or a little after' and afterthoughts that he had neglected to record earlier and in order: CH2/266/1, ff. 2v, 4.
56. CH2/716/1 (fair copy) and 716/2 (rough). The latter (from 1609) contains many more cases of all sorts than the same years in a volume that initially appears to be a fair copy for cases from 1597. Whoever copied from the original volume opted to summarise favourite cases rather than making a full fair copy. We cannot tell whether the fair volume is actually exhaustive for 1597–1609 (where the rough copy no longer exists), but selective for post-1609; I surmise that most of the cases from 1597–1609 are no longer available to us. How many of what appear complete minute books for particular periods are in fact excerpts of what contemporaries thought the most important cases (though Leith's omitted cases include one of trelapse adultery)? As an indication of how *much* data is omitted from Leith's fair copy, the rough includes for 28 April 1609 six fornication cases not entered in the fair copy for the same date: CH2/716/1, f. 21v, cf. CH2/716/2, f. 9v. While one gets the impression from session books that early modern Scots spent a considerable amount of time fornicating, we may be seeing only the tip of the iceberg.
57. My only exceptions to this rule of not counting cases relate to the question of the double standard. My impression after reading scores of minute books is of equity in the treatment of male and female sexual offenders, which I tested by sampling from

For every topic considered here, I began with as empirical an examination as I could manage of the primary data provided by session minutes, supplemented by presbytery, synod and General Assembly minutes; borough records; diaries, letters and autobiographies; sermons and sermon notebooks; elite concerns expressed in statute; and the more socially inclusive concerns expressed in complaint and deposition.[58] Only then did I turn to theory in order to frame questions and possibilities for interpretation that might not otherwise occur to a data-based historian. I have focused my attention on practices common to all or most of the parishes examined, with exceptions and peculiarities occasionally noted, but *as* exceptions.

That the records of the sessions offer a mediated version of the words of ordinary parishioners goes without saying. Minutes and depositions are taken down by clerks, necessarily literate and so part of a definable elite (though an impressively expanding one by the later sixteenth century). We have been sufficiently warned about how their shorthand, formulae or perhaps even more active editing can shift emphases or distort meaning.[59] This does not render the minute books unusable. For one thing, elders often required deponents to sign their depositions after they had been read back to them; how much distortion would they have tolerated? In Inveravon, the deponents in slander cases were instructed to say 'word by word which they heard'; would they have agreed to an inaccurate version when it was read back to them?[60] For another, the sharp differences one often finds between the language of the minutes and the language of the depositions suggest a significant degree of authenticity for the latter. While one must be aware of formulaic elements and the biases of scribes, then, it is still possible to hear multiple voices in the minute books. Finally, the degree to which people of all sorts resorted to church courts voluntarily suggests that the sessions' proceedings cannot have been so significantly

four arbitrarily chosen parishes (see chapter 3, below). I also sampled flyting (scolding) cases in a few parishes to draw some conclusions about the language of men and women in railing at their neighbours, and about numbers of witchcraft accusations compared to prosecutions (see chapter 5, below). Would-be statisticians ought also to bear in mind that many disputes and sins would have been addressed informally and never come to the session's attention, as Judith Pollman has found for the Netherlands: *Religious Choice in the Dutch Republic* (Manchester, 1999).

58. My methods have been, willy-nilly, empirical: I began this project with a rather different hypothesis that in fact could not be demonstrated from the evidence of the session minutes. Engagement with the sources revealed a whole different set of issues, suggested different themes to be explored, and opened the possibility that some anthropological approaches might prove useful in analysing available data. The evidence itself has thus dictated the structure and content of the study.
59. Most effectively by Natalie Zemon Davis in *Fiction in the Archives* (Cambridge, 1987).
60. CH2/191/1, f. 36.

distorted by some elite agenda that we cannot draw from them conclusions about the concerns and activities of ordinary people. Historians' sources are as problematic as anthropologists' interviews of tribespeople, but they are no less fruitful. If we are not simply to stop asking our questions, we must develop ways to use the data available creatively while fully acknowledging its limitations and hedging our conclusions accordingly. The abundance of kirk session minutes, their remarkable detail, the earthiness of much of the language and the availability of corroborating evidence in depositions, journals, correspondence and other records, makes them a source enviable to historians of the English protestant parish, whose records are so sparse and narrow.

I have attached names to the voices of ordinary parishioners recorded in the minutes rather more often than might be expected.[61] This is not gratuitous, but a deliberate effort to lend some humanity, some individuality, to people too often lumped into statistics because they were not of the literate, 'better' sort. Historians are too often guilty of 'swamping the acting individual in the onrush of surface events'.[62] But while ordinary people in Scottish pews have not been judged by many historians to be worthy of notice except in categories, they were the people who in fact achieved the Reformation in Scotland, if we understand Reformation as cultural change. They may not have done so quite as the Reformers wished, by simply accepting instruction. Instead, they forced protestantism's adjustment to the demands of their own lives, receiving and expanding what they found useful, resisting much, ignoring more, creatively modifying most. It was they who re-formed the Reformation to make it their own, and I depart from more traditional treatments of the Scottish Reformation by taking them together with the ministers and elders as the inventors of the culture of protestantism.

The kirk session minutes do not address all the questions that concern historians of religion in the pew. Above all, protestantism is what puritans called 'heart religion', and the convictions of the heart are an elusive item when dealing with a largely illiterate population unable to leave us much in the way of diaries, letters and spiritual autobiographies.[63] We can read between the lines of session records, and supplement them with other kinds of data, but ultimately the interior spirituality of most people

61. The reader will note that married women retained their patronymics, a function of persistent agnatic kinship in Scotland.

62. Geertz, *Available Light*, 119.

63. For an attempt to get at the interior spiritual lives of literate seventeenth-century Scots, see Louise Yeoman, 'Heart-Work: Emotion, Empowerment and Authority in Covenanting Times', (Unpublished PhD thesis, St Andrews, 1992), and more recently Mullan, *Puritanism*, 85–139.

remains beyond our recounting. But the religion of protestants turns out to be an external affair as well – much more so than traditional accounts suggest. What the kirk session minutes reveal is that the version we have received from an earlier generation of historians – of reformers vigorously discarding all external forms, rituals, garb and symbols in favor of an interior focus on conversion and correct doctrine – is deceptively truncated. Indeed, if our central concern is with *how* Reformation was achieved in a Calvinist setting, we must pay particular attention to the externals, the things that contemporaries saw and experienced as well as the things they heard and read. What we shall find is that, far from being discarded, external forms and ceremonies remained crucial to the protestant conquest of hearts and minds.

How was it possible for the Calvinist version of protestantism, with its rigorous and invasive discipline, its abolition of image and religious festival, its stern doctrinal demands, to succeed at all, anywhere, whether quickly or over time? How was it established in Scotland at a national level by the early seventeenth century, even in many remote areas and small communities?[64] There are obvious structural reasons: the system was highly organised in its arrangement of session, presbytery, synod and General Assembly. It benefited from the keeping of careful records at all levels; from parochial oversight by presbytery visitations and inspections of session books; and from the remarkable amount of communication fostered among sessions, between each session and its presbytery, and among presbyteries in exchanges of testimonials, case referrals and appeals for funds. But this structure would not have come into being without support from a wide range of laity as well as clergy. It required lay elders and deacons to take on remarkably onerous duties at the parish level, and these men were not only lairds and wealthy merchants, but also craftsmen, tradesmen and farmers who worked for a living. More generally, it required popular willingness to resort to the kirk for catechising and sermons, banns and burial; to bring quarrels to kirk arbiters; to report misbehaving neighbours to the elders; and to be taxed for local schools and poor relief, for ransom of pirate captives, for aid in time of fire and natural disaster in neighbouring (and sometimes far-distant) communities, or for persecuted protestants abroad. Whence this acquiescence to a system that was clearly intrusive, rigorous and demanding?

The answer that will be offered here is a combination of elements,

64. The debate over slow or quick Reformation in Scotland could profitably be put in the context of English historiography, where a recent installment of the same debate has 1800 as its terminal date: Nicholas Tyacke, ed., *England's Long Reformation, 1500–1800* (London, 1998).

comprehended under the general principle that the culture of early modern Scotland constituted an ongoing negotiation between elements of change and continuity. First, the new kirk waged an unremitting campaign to provide an educated clergy and to establish a literate and theologically informed laity through catechism, examination, sermons, enforced family 'exercises' and the founding of schools. The logocentric nature of protestantism comprised the fundamental change that drove much of the kirk's new disciplinary effort. But truly radical cultural change depends, ironically enough, on continuity. The two exist in a symbiotic tension, leading to the second of our explanatory elements: far from obliterating all that was time-honoured, the kirk managed to achieve a balance between preservation and innovation in ritual and outward forms. For all the new emphasis on sermon and scripture, ceremony remained – in communion, obviously, but perhaps most significantly in the rites of repentance. Holy space and holy time were retained, if redefined, providing the anxious with comfort, the ordinary person with an affective experience of the sacred. Kirk sessions recognised how traditional rituals operated to meet individual and social needs, and to underpin those essential elements of Christian belief that did not change with protestantism – providential divinity, sin and redemption, the need for repentance. The protestant emphasis on faith over works and the priesthood of all believers hardly required that nothing of catholic Christian practice should survive. The considerable continuities that will be described in this study reflect both a large measure of cultural stability – reassuring in a time of ideological flux – and a common ground of belief between protestants and catholics. At the same time, the evidence shows how the fundamental change required by protestant emphases on word over image and faith over works (including ritual behaviour) were mediated with notable flexibility by authorities, who were willing to compromise on some condemned survivals in order to soften the impact of those transformations that doctrinal shift mandated.[65] Third, parochial sessions correctly perceived that, by providing a range of what we would call 'social services', the kirk could achieve a level of peace and orderliness in the society that would foster popular approval of the system and facilitate the hearing of its message. Among the most drastic cultural adjustments introduced after 1560 was a new programme of rigorous discipline that clearly met a whole range of social needs not satisfactorily addressed by medieval ecclesiastical corporations. Intervention in domestic violence, systematic arbitration of

65. As Bell remarks, 'Any ideology is always in dialogue with, and thus shaped and constrained by, the voices it is suppressing, manipulating, echoing. . . . [People] do not passively follow or obey; they appropriate, negotiate, qualify' (*Ritual Theory*, 191).

quarrels and feud, provision of poor relief and broader educational opportunities, and enforcement of paternal financial responsibilities were all high on the agenda of the Reformed church, which managed to address them effectively enough to build a base of community support for a system that otherwise might have been construed as distastefully invasive and innovative.[66] Finally, the active role of the laity (at least the better and middling sort), with elders assuming a quasi-clerical role, and the rhetoric (and sometimes reality) of full lay participation in the life of the church (even women signing parochial confessions, swearing the Covenant and joining in the vetting of ministers and elders), gave the larger community a vested interest in the success of the enterprise. At the same time, an image of the clergy constructed to instil something of the devotion accorded the holy men and women of medieval catholicism provided reluctant parishioners with models for emulation and even veneration. It was this combination of elements that comprised the culture of Reformed protestantism in early modern Scotland. Emerging from a dynamic era of contested meanings, it bespeaks the way early modern Scottish people understood themselves, their communities, their place in the cosmos – not perfectly, but to a degree that traditional histories of theology, ecclesiology and religious politics at the highest levels have not attained.

66. Regulation of sexual behaviour was a hallmark of this ecclesiastical invasion of what we would regard as private, and cases of sexual offence (almost entirely fornication and adultery) dominate every parish's minute books. Historiographically, this is sufficiently well-covered turf that I have opted to treat it comparatively little in this study. The aspects of it that have been underdone by previous scholars and that are singularly important to my focus I have dealt with under the categories of penitential performance and kirk intervention in family life (chapters 3 and 6, below).

Chapter 1
The Word and the People

Protestantism is above all a religion of the book. The scriptures being the only source of sure knowledge about God's design, bringing people to an understanding of the Bible had to be the reformers' first priority. Particularly in the Calvinist version of the faith, the word – read, preached, sung, remembered and recited back at catechetical exercise or family sermon repetition – became the hallmark of communal worship and individual piety. The sermon came to be the central event of feast and fast, of regular Sunday worship and sacramental seasons. For all the reformers' insistence on pairing word and sacrament as signs of a true church, communion in Reformed guise became an infrequent and intensely logocentric event – preceded by doctrinal vetting and Saturday sermons of preparation, accompanied by two Sunday sermons and followed by a Monday sermon of thanksgiving. Celebration of political events, like the king's deliverance from the Gowrie Conspiracy or the Gunpowder Plot, was marked by sermons. Kirk sessions strictly enforced sermon attendance, on weekdays as well as Sundays, at the expense of morning golf and evening dancing; Sunday afternoon picnics went by the board in favour of catechism between sermons. The new focus on the word preached thus redefined the way people organised their time, spent their leisure and observed special days. At the individual level, ability to read the scriptures, take notes on sermons, sing from the new vernacular psalter and clearly articulate protestant orthodoxy became the new status-markers of the godliest, the 'honest persons of good repute'. The leaders of the new kirk identified ignorance and 'contempt of the word' as 'the mother of error and iniquity', the source of the 'universal coldness and decay of zeal in all estates' that they understood as the cause of plague and tempest in this world, and ultimately the path to eternal destruction.[1] But the man with the word hidden in his heart, the woman who meditated constantly on the scriptures, the community where the word shaped behaviour and

1. CH2/471/1 (Lasswade, 1615), f. 2; *BUK* 3:873 (1596).

belief – there the blessing of the divine would rest. In principle and in practice, the word defined the culture of protestantism.

The problem for the reformers is immediately obvious: how does one convert a largely illiterate population to a religion of the word? Judging by ability to sign, urban literacy as late as the 1630s hovered around 50 per cent, rural closer to 10–20 per cent for men; female literacy was less than 10 per cent. Even in the capital, 32 per cent of men were unable to sign the Covenant in 1638.[2] When the parishioners of Kinghorn signed their confession of faith in 1581, only seventy-seven of the 820 signed with their own hands rather than with 'hand at the pen of the notary', and nearly all of the leading parishioners of Kirkoswald signed the Covenant in 1639 'with our hands at the pen of the notary . . . because we cannot write.'[3] Ability to sign one's name is admittedly a conservative criterion by which to judge literacy in an age when people learned to read before (and sometimes without) learning to write. Still, the parish of Mordington reported as late as 1627 that 'not one of the parish can read nor write except the minister.'[4] The reformers thus faced an uphill battle. Their most evident weapons were sermons, which did not require a literate auditory, and a campaign to expand literacy by establishing schools.[5] Schools, however, depended on funding that was too seldom forthcoming from local ratepayers, and sermons required an educated ministry. Although there was a superabundance of clergy left over from the abolition of cathedral bureaucracies and collegiate chapels devoted to masses for the dead, by no means were most of these men inclined towards the new religion. Even of those who were, or who transferred allegiance for practical reasons, few were equipped to preach. The new kirk, like its counterpart in England, whether in puritan or episcopal guise, agonised for generations after the Reformation over how to supply the thousand or so pulpits of Scotland, knowing that new educational foundations like the Edinburgh seminary would require time to produce sufficient staffing.[6]

2. R.A. Houston, *Scottish Literacy and the Scottish Identity: Illiteracy and Society in Scotland and Northern England 1600–1800* (Cambridge, 1985), 89, 91; Houston, 'The Literacy Myth? Illiteracy in Scotland, 1630–1760', *P&P* 96 (1982), 81–102; John Bannerman, 'Literacy in the Highlands' in *The Renaissance and Reformation in Scotland*, ed. Ian Cowan and Duncan Shaw (Edinburgh, 1983), 214–35.
3. CH2/472/1, ff. 125–35v; AAC CH2/562/1, ff. 28–29.
4. David Cressy, *Literacy and the Social Order: Reading and Writing in Tudor and Stuart England* (Cambridge, 1980), chs 2–3; *Reports on the State of Certain Parishes in Scotland, Made to his Majesties Commissioners for Plantation of Kirks, ... 1627* (Edinburgh, 1835 – henceforth *1627 Reports*), 22.
5. *First Book*, 54–62.
6. T. Craufurd, *History of the University of Edinburgh from 1580 to 1646* (Edinburgh, 1808)

In the Scottish campaign to protestantise the people, however, illiteracy and a dearth of sermons in rural areas were not such impediments as we often suppose. Here sermons and reading were supplemented by several factors that generally get too little attention from historians, but were high on the agendas of the kirk sessions, making regular appearances in their minutes. If we are thoroughly to understand the cultural shift that the Reformation entailed, we must take into account what amounted to preaching supplements – and not 'mere' supplements, but aids with the power to transform the way people understood their faith and lived their lives. The most important of these were the continuing office of reader, the popularity of the metrical psalter, strict enforcement of sabbath observance by sessions, some itinerancy and sharing of ministers in rural areas, and systematic catechism and examination – again, rigorously enforced by sessions. All worked together with sermons and schools to bring to men and women in the pew an experience of the word that would fundamentally shift the way they organised their lives, defined themselves as individuals and families, and understood their relationship with the divine. In addition, when we turn in the following chapter from a close examination of this logocentric programme to that other component of the reformers' 'true church' – the sacraments – we will find that the protestantised version of communion in particular served to tie together new sermon with old ritual, easing the transition from a highly sensual mass to a rather austere Lord's Supper by not discarding ceremony and tradition altogether, but instead placing a re-formed ritual firmly in the context of the supremacy of the word, and constructing the message of the eucharistic word as an active and profoundly affective experience. If our overarching problem is how a radical Reformation managed to garner support in an illiterate and traditional society, then exploring the culture of word and sacrament at the parish level will provide the necessary first step towards a solution.

* * *

To grant a role for the sacrament in establishing Reformation, and to consider the important supplements to preaching that enhanced the reformers' efforts in Scotland, is by no means to diminish the significance

is a contemporary account, from NLS ms Adv. 33.7.23; relevant documents are in Alexander Morgan, ed., *Charters, Statutes and Acts of the Town and Senatus, 1582–1858* (Edinburgh, 1937). Modern treatments include D.B. Horn, *A Short History of the University of Edinburgh* (Edinburgh, 1967); M. Lynch, 'The Origins of Edinburgh's "Toun College": A Revision Article', *IR* 33 (1982), 3–14. For other seminaries, see n. 131, below.

of sermons as vehicles of protestantism in the parishes. It was, after all, sermons that pre-Reformation authorities had identified as the means by which heretical 'new opinions may rise in the common people'.[7] After the Reformation, ordination depended first and foremost on a candidate's ability to expound the scriptures in 'private exercises' and specimen sermons before the presbytery, then preaching in the kirk considering him for its minister.[8] Presbyteries enforced on reluctant ministers at parochial visitations the requirement to 'teach each sabbath twice'.[9] The symbol of his office given at the ordination ceremony was not the pre-Reformation combination of kirk key, font cover, missal, chalice and altar vestments, but 'the book of God called the Bible' and the key to the pulpit. The latter was now the dominant item of furniture in the kirk, with altars demolished and fonts replaced by basins.[10] Sessions allocated very considerable sums to buy Bibles for the church and to build new pulpits – now decorated, significantly, not with the images displayed on medieval pulpits, but with the word itself carved into the wood (see plates 2 and 3).[11] Material culture thus visually reinforced the new ideology. Sermon attendance was a test of faith, especially for suspected catholics. Perth's session in the

7. *Acts of the Lords of Council in Public Affairs, 1501–04*, ed. R.K. Hannay (London, 1934), 422 (Gavin Dunbar's concern about friars' preaching).
8. CH2/299/2, pp. 3, 46; cf. CH2/294/1, ff. 6v, 7v; CH2/121/1, f. 61v; CH2/171/1, f. 141; SAU unnumbered ms/St Andrews presbytery minutes, 1585–1605, *passim*. Assessments of 'specimen doctrines' on assigned texts abound in all presbytery minutes. For presbytery exercises as 'a form of supplementary post-graduate education in theology' for prospective ministers, see Alan MacDonald, 'David Calderwood: The Not So Hidden Years, 1590–1604', *SHR* 74 (1995), 69–74.
9. CH2/198/1, ff. 15v–16 (Jedburgh, 1607).
10. ML CH2/171/1, f. 34v (1594); cf. David Murray, *Legal Practice in Ayr and the West of Scotland* (Glasgow, 1910), 73, 74. For medieval practice, Sanderson, *Ayrshire*, 13. 'Ane Forme of Sindrie Materis to be Usit in the Elderschip 1589–1592' in *Miscellany of the Wodrow Society*, ed. D. Laing (Edinburgh, 1844), 1:529–32, lists psalter and kirk keys as the items transferred at a minister's induction. Entrance to the pulpit was by a wicket, or gate, visible in the sixteenth-century St Andrews pulpit in plate 4.
11. CH2/283/1, f. 10v (£9 'for a Bible to the kirk'); CH2/338/1, f. 15v (Stow's Bible purchased from penalties); NLS ms 2782, f. 31 (a Scots Bible 'for the board in the Blackfriars kirk', 1593, and an English Bible for the High Kirk of Glasgow, 1598). For 'bigging of the pulpit' in Ellon and Mortlach, CH2/147/1, f. 125v; CH2/529/1, f. 46v (£4 for timber). The only additional pulpit decoration was silk to cover the lectern: CH2/521/6, f. 42 (Perth's 1616 purchase of 'a sad [sombre] green cloth fringed with green silk, like the pulpit of Edinburgh' had). St Andrews had a typical two-part pulpit, high for the preacher, low for the reader, both elevated (plate 4); Brechin draped both parts in green silk costing in 1661 £14 3s 6d. In front of the Brechin reader's desk was the session's seat, with its own door and keys: Thoms, *Kirk of Brechin*, 6.

1590s looked for 'resort on the preaching days to the hearing of the word, whereby they may be known to be Christians indeed'.[12] It is fitting, then, to begin with the sermon as the core of the post-Reformation sabbath experience.

The new protestant emphasis on sermons redefined and reorganised the post-Reformation sabbath. Sundays were no longer feast days punctuated by a brief observation of the mass but devoted principally to play, food and drink, and rest from labour. In Scotland they were often proclaimed fast days.[13] Even when they were not, the bells that rang on Sunday mornings in Reformed parishes summoned people not to liturgical festival, but to a round of communal Bible-reading, psalm-singing, sermons and catechism that would last for most of the day. Playing at golf or pennystone, wandering the countryside and dancing were as strictly forbidden as sabbath labour and tippling – not because they were evil in themselves, but because they lured people from sermons.

In parishes supplied with preachers, there were two sermons each Sunday, one in the morning, the other after noon, generally separated by catechetical teaching and exercises.[14] Elderly or infirm ministers who found themselves unable to preach twice in a day appealed to presbytery to supply additional preachers rather than let the afternoon sermon

12. CH2/521/2, f. 80v. Sermon absence by lords, lairds or their ladies brought presbytery intervention on the assumption of recusancy. E.g., repeated absences by Lady Marion Cunningham and the Countess of Glencairne 'to the evil example of others' drove the Paisley commissioners first to 'travail with her ladyship and press her by reason and the authority of God his Word', then to require subscription of a confession of faith: CH2/294/1, ff. 10v, 8.
13. E.g., CH2/266/1, f. 50; SAU CH2/150/1, f. 5v; SAU CH2/210/1, ff. 9v, 16; CH2/1142/1, ff. 21, 104; CH2/198/1, ff. 5–6; CH2/326/1, pp. 53, 58, 60–61, 67; NAS ms RH2/1/35, f. 15v; CH2/84/28, f. 1; CH2/1463/1, f. 7; CH2/521/2, f. 12; CH2/521/8/1, f. 160v; CH2/299/2, pp. 298, 382, 384; CH2/242/1, n.f., 20 January 1591; CH2/145/6, f. 10v.
14. AAC CH2/751/1, f. 133v; ML CH2/171/1, f. 58; CH2/442/74, f. 10; CH2/359/1 (Tyninghame), ff. 5v, 6; CH2/521/8/1, f. 51; CH2/471/1, f. 4 (examples from Ayr, Glasgow, Kirkwall, Tyninghame, Perth and Lasswade); CH2/198/1, ff. 15v–16 (Jedburgh presbytery ordering ministers to 'teach each sabbath twice'). The Fife synod (CH2/154/1, f. 72v; cf. SAU ms 30451, f. 6v) is unusual in requiring only morning sermon and afternoon catechism; however, the Fife parishes whose books survive usually exceeded this requirement (e.g., SAU CH2/624/1, f. 17, Anstruther Wester's morning service ending at 11am, a second sermon ending at 3pm, 'and the rest of the afternoon was spent in catechising'). On the other hand, rural parishes where people had to travel great distances to the kirk on Sunday often made exceptions to the two-sermon rule in winter, when return from an afternoon sermon would be made in the dark: e.g., CH2/383/1, f. 14 (f. 3v shows landward domination of Liberton parish, with only five of twenty-one elders in 1640 representing the town).

lapse.[15] The Edinburgh diarist Robert Birrel recorded that when the 'troubles' of 1596 resulted in 'no preaching in Edinburgh neither before noon nor after noon, the like has not been seen before' – so distant already was his memory of pre-Reformation practice.[16] The same bells that had summoned parishioners to mass before the Reformation were now rung three times at half-hour intervals before each sermon, generally 8.30 for 9.30 and 3 for 4 in the summer, 9 for 10 and as early as 12.30 for 1.30 in winter, when parishioners from outlying areas needed daylight for their trek home from the kirk.[17] An English visitor reported that the second Sunday sermon was 'pretty early in the afternoon because in the interim they eat nothing'.[18] In the capital, the charismatic preacher Robert Rollock actually succeeded in adding a third Sunday sermon in the 1580s. One of his students reported that he was concerned about 'great crowds of people assembling early in the morning' and was 'unwilling that they should sit unemployed' – suggesting that these crowds had arrived at the kirk even before the reading and prayers had begun, so anxious were they to hear the gospel. In view of popular demand,

> on the sabbath mornings at seven o'clock – a thing which had never been done in Edinburgh before – he began to preach, and that with such demonstration of the Spirit and of power, with such mighty force of sentiment, and such grave impressiveness of style, that the minds of the greater part of his hearers were illuminated with a heavenly light, their affections were stirred up, and they were irresistibly impelled to admire the preacher. For he not only excited the ordinary class of hearers, but he affected men of learning.[19]

15. NLS ms 2782, ff. 14–14v records addition of a second Glasgow minister in 1589 to facilitate two sermons, and the 1601 appeal of John Ball, too weak to preach twice on Sunday.
16. NLS ms Wodrow Oct. VII, f. 33v. The king in December charged Edinburgh's ministers with sedition.
17. NLS ms 2782, f. 36; CH2/471/1, f. 2 (defining summer as extending from 11 March to 11 September); CH2/716/1, f. 22; SAU ms 30451, f. 6v; and CH2/154/1, p. 128 give the usual morning hours for Glasgow, Lasswade, South Leith and Fife synod respectively, and Leith's afternoon sermon time, 1.30 or 2pm. Glasgow experimented briefly in 1595 with summer morning sermons at 7, afternoon ones at 5. Afternoon times were more variable, but sessions always allowed for winter's early darkness. CH2/521/2, ff. 111v–12 records that on communion Sundays Perth's first bells actually began at 4am for 5 (cf. CH2/521/3, p. 117; CH2/521/8/1, f. 51 for later schedule revisions).
18. Thomas Morer, *A Short Account of Scotland* (London, 1702), 61. Morer became minister of St Ann's within Aldersgate; he wrote while chaplain to a Scots regiment.
19. Henry Charteris, *Narrative of the Life and Death of Mr Robert Rollock* in Rollock *Select Works*, ed. and tr. William Gunn, 2 vols (Edinburgh, 1849), 1:lxxi–lxxii.

This account is by an admirer of the preacher, but we know more generally that the Edinburgh presbytery found such 'good liking that the congregation of the said town has of him' that they institutionalised his extra sermon in 1587. Mention of the 'ordinary class' being excited, moreover, together with the fact that they showed up in significant numbers at 7 in the morning, indicates a broad-based cult of the sermon in Edinburgh within a generation of the official Reformation.[20]

In addition to multiple Sunday sermons, town parishes offered weekday sermons. In Glasgow from at least the 1580s there were two, in addition to the weekly presbytery preaching, or 'exercise', to which people were summoned by bells at 8.30, to 'continue hearing it till ten'.[21] South Leith had a regular Tuesday sermon, Fraserburgh had preaching on Wednesday, St Andrews had an 8 o'clock sermon on Wednesday and Friday, and Aberdeen and Ayr ministers preached on Tuesday and Thursday.[22] Perth takes the prize, with Monday, Tuesday and Thursday morning sermons in addition to the Wednesday presbytery exercise.[23] The Perth ministers were occasionally so exhausted by their preaching burdens that they had to petition the presbytery to supply substitutes for their pulpits.[24]

Sessions abolished traditional festival days that might compete with

20. CH2/121/1, ff. 28–28v; Charteris, 1:lxxi, n. 2.

21. NLS ms 2782, ff. 35–35v, 36, 58. The weekday sermons shifted from Wednesday and Friday to Tuesday and Thursday in 1600 in commemoration of Tuesday as Gowrie Day. Presbytery exercise 'by interpretation of scripture' was the public portion of the meeting, after which ordinary parishioners would leave so the brethren could handle disciplinary matters.

22. CH2/716/1, f. 22v; CH2/1142/1, ff. 78v, 96v; CH2/448/1, pp. 58–59; *SAKS* 2:828–29 (specifying that the service be over by 9am, 'prayers and all'); CH2/448/2, p. 325; CH2/448/3, 11 August 1611; AAC CH2/751/1, f. 134; CH2/271/1, p. 107 (Elgin's Tuesday sermon 'ever in use since the Reformation', 1639). Weekday sermons may have been unpopular in conservative Aberdeen, though: they seem to have been dropped in the 1630s, and when Dr Gould revived them in 1642, 'his auditories were few', and he gave up: John Spalding, *The History of the Troubles . . . from 1624 to 1645*, ed. James Skene, 2 vols (Edinburgh, 1828–29), 2:43.

23. CH2/521/2, ff. 112 (1587), 114v; CH2/521/3, p. 100; CH2/521/6, ff. 68v, 218v; CH2/521/7, p. 438; CH2/299/2 (Perth presbytery minutes), pp. 43, 50, 54: ministers took it in turn to provide the 'public exercise', one man preaching, another responding at each meeting, and ministerial candidates who had passed their Latin disputations on assigned theological topics also participated to test their preaching ability. John Welch preached daily in Selkirk and Ayr in the 1590s: *The History of the Life and Sufferings of the Reverend John Welch, ... Minister in Ayr* (Falkirk, 1780), 4.

24. CH2/521/7, pp. 250–52, John Malcolm's petition on grounds that he 'through disease and infirmity may not teach upon [all] the said days' of a fasting week. Presbytery responses include CH2/299/1, p. 318, CH2/299/2, p. 112. William Cowper preached five times weekly: *Workes* (London, 1629), 5.

Sunday sermons. Of course, saints' days and the liturgical year had disappeared at the Reformation anyway (at least in theory); subsequent calendar shifts targeted market days, some of them established on particular days of the year centuries earlier and tied closely to the success of the local economy. Nothing was to stand in the way of sermons. Thus, when the Paisley presbytery found in 1602 that the market day called 'the Fair of the Hill held in Lochonn North yearly sixth November this year falls upon the Lord's Day', it moved the market to the Saturday before; likewise, the Perth elders moved the Midsummer Day market from the sabbath in 1593.[25] They found support in national legislation: Parliament in 1592 had moved markets that 'of before were kept on the sabbath' to weekdays, though they left enforcement up to sessions; in the heady atmosphere of reform in 1639, they considered abolishing Saturday and Monday markets as well, lest they undermine sabbath preparation and attendance by those intending Monday journeys. Kingsbarns in Fife was among the parishes that followed through on this initiative in the 1640s.[26]

Sunday sermon attendance was not optional. Sermons would clearly not serve to convert and protestantise unless people could be got into the kirk to hear them. The elders accordingly adopted a strategy of strictly enforced sabbath observance, a device that English puritans would have loved, but that depended on the institution of kirk sessions to work. From the outset, every session placed near the top of its agenda the goal of assembling the whole parish for Sunday preaching. They gave to heads of households the responsibility of getting their children and servants to church, and fined them for failure, on Archbishop Spottiswoode's precept that 'to be punished by the purse is a thing that ever hath been most grievous to Scottishmen, and keepeth them most in awe.'[27] The great were not immune: when the Aberdeen elders found in 1607 that 'sundry landed gentlemen making residence in the town resort not to the preaching', the elders of each quarter set out to take their names, and the minister and a bailie then visited each to admonish him either to come to church for

25. CH2/294/1, f. 3; CH2/521/2, f. 78. For actual survival of traditional festival days, see chapter 4, below.
26. *APS* 3:548, ratified 4:63 (1594); 5:594 (1639); *BUK* 2:769 (1592); SAU CH2/819/1, f. 32 ('as in other provinces').
27. E.g., CH2/448/2, p. 80; CH2/326/1, p. 6; CH2/141/1, f. 12v. Spottiswoode, in *Original Letters Relating to the Ecclesiastical Affairs of Scotland*, ed. D. Laing, 2 vols (Edinburgh, 1851), 2:756. The pre-Reformation church had likewise been concerned about poor attendance at mass, finding 'very few indeed out of the most populous parishes deign to be present'; however, they conducted no comparable attendance campaign: *Statutes of the Scottish Church 1225–1559*, ed. D. Patrick (Edinburgh, 1907), 127–28, 138–39.

the sermon or leave town.[28] The Fife synod set three levels of fines for absence from the kirk, the highest for 'lords or barons', a medium fine for lairds, the lowest for husbandmen.[29] Session minute books are cluttered with the prosecutions of all sorts of people, young and old, great and common, for Sunday 'nineholes' or golf, football, bowls, kyles (ninepins), archery, fishing and dancing.[30] And it is worth noting that when the records indicate who reported offenders, they were not always elders or kirk officers: ordinary parishioners took up the campaign on their own.[31]

The elders were doubtless glad to get the help, but they kept their own searches carefully regulated and recorded. The most predictable weekly entry in nearly every session's minute books apart from collections is the appointment of sabbath 'visitors' or 'searchers' – elders tactically deployed in assigned 'quarters' throughout town to detect absentees and summon them to the next session meeting for censure. Their charge was to 'see that the people were on the word when the exercise of it is offered', and they went about it with alacrity.[32] Generally two elders were appointed for each Sunday service.[33] They were authorised to enter people's homes to see who might be hiding away there, and to collect fines from absen-

28. CH2/448/2, p. 255. See also CH2/523/1, f. 8 (four Burntisland elders to 'deal with' the laird of Orrok for absence); CH2/32/1, f. 2 (Belhelvie in 1623 ordering the laird George Gordon and his family 'of years of discretion' to repent their 'bygone apostasy from hearing of the word' or face the 'penalty of the congregation'. Sessions often sought presbytery assistance to enforce attendance on the nobility: e.g., CH2/521/7, p. 469; CH2/294/1, ff. 8, 10v.
29. SAU ms 30451, f. 7.
30. E.g., CH2/146/1, f. 128v; CH2/89/1, f. 6; CH2/521/2, ff. 58–58v; CH2/716/1, ff. 23v, 24v (forbidding such pastimes 'from morn till even'); CH2/521/3, pp. 335–36; CH2/521/7, pp. 161, 200, 204–05; CH2/521/8/1, ff. 49, 55v; CH2/198/1, ff. 12, 15 (ordering repentance in linen for football players); CH2/448/2, ff. 199–200; CH2/523/1, f. 1; CH2/84/29, ff. 3v, 7v–8, 27v, 31–31v, 57; SAU CH2/819/1, ff. 26, 32; AAC CH2/751/1, ff. 2, 126. In Perth 'walking to landward' or 'vaguing in the countryside' was often targeted: CH2/521/3, pp. 141, 142, 150, 272. In 1585 the minister James Law (later bishop of Orkney and archbishop of Glasgow) was himself prosecuted by his synod for playing football on Sunday: *Fasti* 1:212.
31. E.g., AAC CH2/751/1, ff. 141, 126.
32. SAU CH2/624/2, p. 2 (1603); Dalkeith's periodic crackdowns always showed good results: CH2/84/28, ff. 3v, 7v–8, 11, 12v, 15v, 27v, 31–31v, 41v, 57, 58v, 72.
33. Among many examples, CH2/716/2, ff. 14, 94; CH2/89/1, f. 18v; SAU CH2/150/1, f. 8; SAU CH2/210/1, f. 5v; CH2/472/1, f. 14v; CH2/390/1, f. 2; CH2/338/1, f. 15v; CH2/523/1, ff. 2, 27; CH2/276/1, ff. 1v, 69; CH2/621/1, f. 357; CH2/142/1, f. 23; CH2/1173/1, f. 3 (Kelso targeting especially 'wives that keeps not the kirk'). One elder might suffice in a small parish like Ellon: CH2/147/1, f. 177. Kirkwall, Orkney, is typical of parishes where most members were from the surrounding countryside in appointing one elder to visit the burgh, another for the landward: CH2/442/74, f. 12.

tees on the spot.[34] Sometimes they took along a bailie as a sort of 'strongarm man' to enforce collection, civil and ecclesiastical authority as ever co-operative.[35] In Stow, the burden of Sunday searching was so great that in 1628 the parish elected fourteen new elders for the purpose.[36] The landward elders in Newbattle finally balked at having to 'lose the hearing of the word every other sabbath' to search; the Dalkeith presbytery granted their appeal for release from having to visit the town as well as their own quarters.[37] Contiguous parishes often co-operated in Sunday searches: in 1613, South Leith accepted two extra visitors each Sunday for a month from Edinburgh to help apprehend absentees from the capital trying to hide out in the port town's alehouses. Only in rural parishes too far-flung to allow searching were elders charged simply to 'take notice of the absents' by observing the congregation itself, as in the Angus kirk of Menmuir.[38]

There was, as one would expect, some resistance to the visitors. Isobel Young of Leith admitted 'holding the door closed' against them in 1605, and in 1607 Andro Wylie of Burntisland locked his door when he saw them coming – not that it did either any good.[39] The sessions simply added fines and censures for disobedience to the usual fines for sabbath breach. In Ayr, William Cunningham had to pay double the usual fine for sabbath breach and repent publicly in 1608 for 'giving ill language to the searchers on the sabbath, as also for striking the boy who delated [reported] him'.[40] One wonders how Cunningham had offended this officious lad, now perhaps getting his revenge by aiding the searchers.

The seriousness with which sessions viewed sabbath breach is indicated not only by the amount of time and effort they spent finding it out, but also by the often startling entries in their records effectively equating

34. NLS ms 2782, f. 62v; CH2/521/7, pp. 207, 215; CH2/84/28, f. 72.
35. CH2/521/3, p. 100; CH2/521/7, p. 28. The Tyninghame elders persuaded the laird and lady Bass to lend their officer to aid Sunday searching: CH2/359/1, f. 1v, 1615. In the 1580s, Glasgow used bailies as 'sabbath searchers' (NLS ms 2782, f. 42v), but in most parishes elders and deacons served the purpose.
36. CH2/338/1, f. 15v. Tyninghame was sufficiently worried about Sunday absences in 1615 to order 'every elder to go this day about through the town to see whether any is absent from the kirk in time of preaching', so that presumably none of the elders heard the sermon that day: CH2/359/1, f. 1v.
37. CH2/424/1, n.f., 30 September 1630, ruling the elders 'answerable every one of them for their own'.
38. CH2/716/2, f. 94; CH2/264/1, f. 14v.
39. CH2/621/1, f. 357; CH2/523/1, f. 27.
40. AAC CH2/751/1, ff. 138v, 141. Annabell Chalmer was gaoled by the Elgin elders in 1603 for 'deforcing of the officer' and 'holding fast the door in the time of searching': CH2/145/2, f. 126v.

absence from sermons with real crimes. For instance, the Kirkcaldy session in 1624 summoned John Melville 'for pressing to force Thomas Lamb's servant woman upon the sabbath and not frequenting the kirk'.[41] While giving equal billing to attempted rape and sermon absence may strike modern readers as bizarre, the elders saw a clear relationship between inadequate instruction in godly living and the most egregious, even criminal behaviour. They saw sabbath observance as the solution to a multitude of ills, from plague and famine (divine judgments on sabbath breach), to sexual promiscuity and violence: it was the means to the end of a godly and well-ordered community, and a principal mechanism for establishing the new culture of protestantism.

In urban parishes, sessions even compelled attendance at weekday sermons. Perth elders declared in 1587 that 'it behooves every particular person within a reformed congregation and burgh to resort to the kirk, the place of public preaching, for receiving of instruction and strengthening of the faith . . . at all occasions and especially at appointed times' (that is, for both special occasions and regular services). Being informed, however, that on Thursdays at sermon time the 'masters of sundry vocations are found working . . . or abiding in their booths [shops], absenting themselves . . . when the rest of their godly neighbours are occupied in spiritual exercises', they ordered deacons of crafts and deans of guilds to enforce shop closure for all sermons, and demanded that 'the poorer sort of handlabourers' henceforth pay a 10s fine for failing to show up at weekday preaching.[42] They were not particularly successful, doubtless for good economic reasons: in 1599 they found that still 'the sermons on the weekdays are not reported unto as becomes, to our great dishonour of God, corruption of his word, and great slander of this congregation.' They delegated elders to ask the town council to compel craftsmen to 'report to the hearing of the word in the week days more frequently' – the last phrase perhaps a step back from the original requirement to attend every sermon. The problem arose again in 1617 and 1623, but one does wonder whether some of the town's drastic economic decline in the seventeenth century could be traced to restraints placed on commerce by preaching.[43]

41. CH2/636/34, f. 61, or Burntisland's summons of John Broun for 'not frequenting the word, and his lewd and profane life': CH2/523/1, f. 30 (1607).

42. CH2/521/2, f. 6. The penalty for the better sort was the statutory fine for sabbath breach, 20s, and for the destitute, twenty-four hours in the stocks, although the minutes do not record efforts actually to enforce the penalties – hence renewed complaint in 1595 about poor Thursday attendance (f. 114v).

43. CH2/521/3, p. 100; CH2/521/6, f. 68v (reaffirming the 'ancient act made' for weekday sermon attendance); CH2/521/7, p. 438. The 1630s saw active enforcement even on local aristocracy: CH2/521/8/2, f. 171.

The poor had no option: if those who received regular alms from the session failed to attend sermons 'both on the sabbath and likewise on the weekdays', sitting in their appointed and easily supervised place, they were deprived of their dole.[44]

Other towns followed suit. Aberdeen's elders ordered merchants in 1574 to 'strike their booths' (close their shops) on preaching days from the third bell (the final one summoning people to church) until the end of the sermon; later the elders persuaded the council to send the bailies through the streets during preaching on Tuesdays and Thursdays to detect absentees.[45] The Glasgow elders and deacons themselves took on this duty on Wednesdays and Fridays as well as Sunday in 1594.[46] Ayr's session in 1608 set a two-merk penalty for conducting business during Tuesday and Thursday sermons. Some Fraserburgh elders considered abandoning the sparsely-attended Wednesday sermon in 1616, but their colleagues persuaded them instead to 'take order' to compel 'the whole inhabitants . . . [to] lay aside all their affairs' during Wednesday sermons or be fined 6s 8d. The result was 'great convening of the people thereto'.[47]

In general, of course, the emphasis in the attendance campaign was on the two Sunday sermon times. There were a few exceptions to required Sunday attendance. Legitimate excuses included verifiable illness or childbirth, caring for young children, necessary travel – as for fishermen during their season, or for merchants overseas (though the latter were expected to attend protestant services when in port), unusual distance from the kirk and extraordinarily severe weather. Not surprisingly, the last shows most frequently in the session minutes of Highland parishes in the winter. Mortlach's elders, for instance, typically excused winter absences 'for tempest of storm' or 'storm of water'.[48] Sessions also relaxed attendance requirements in rural areas, where villages could be several miles from the nearest parish church; in Ayrshire, for example, a particularly isolated landward man was allowed to come every fourth Sunday in summer and every

44. CH2/521/3, p. 115 (1599).
45. CH2/448/1, pp. 58–59; CH2/448/3, p. 70.
46. NLS MS 2782, f. 34. They proved remiss, however, themselves being admonished in 1598 'for good example's sake to keep the week days preaching' (f. 35v, recalling Glasgow's 1583 order to 'strike booth doors on Wednesday and Friday at sermon time').
47. AAC CH2/751/1, f. 134; CH2/1142/1, ff. 78v, 96v.
48. CH2/529/1, ff. 57v (December 1634), 58 (January 1635); see also CH2/96/1 (Duffus), f. 24v (January 1643). Weather problems did not excuse the Perth cadger John Gray in 1599, however: claiming his Saturday return from Glasgow was delayed by 'tempest and intemperate weather', he was instructed 'not to away any more of home' so near the sabbath: CH2/521/3, p. 99. Want of clothing was also an insufficient excuse: CH2/521/3, f. 151.

sixth in winter.[49] In Orkney, Barbara Scletir escaped censure for absence when 'keeping her bairn who was sick and heavily diseased'; severe gout served to excuse a Perth woman.[50] Anyone claiming illness, however, could expect a visit from an elder or two to substantiate the claim, and if they had been seen out of doors at either play or labour at any time on the Sunday in question, they would pay the price. When John Forrest tried to excuse his absence by explaining that he 'had sick pains in his hands, and that he was but newly risen forth of his bed', the Perth session countered with reports that he had been spotted travelling to Scone on the sabbath in question and fined him 6s. They did the same when someone reported a supposed invalid selling ale in sermon time.[51] Inclinations by some early sessions to make allowances were short-lived. The 1562 Aberdeen session ordered servants to come to church on Sunday 'if their masters give them leave'. That qualifier disappears after the 1560s, however, and the norm becomes that of sessions like Scoonie's, which ruled that if a master ordered a servant to stay home and work on Sunday, both servant and employer would have to pay 6s 8d and offer public repentance for sabbath breach.[52]

Labour was an admissible excuse only in clear necessity. The Dundonald session in 1629 forgave two shepherds who brought their sheep in from the moors on a fasting sabbath, 'because the moorman came not at the time appointed, whereby they could not come to the forenoon's sermon' without putting their flock at risk. In like manner, when Thomas McGregor was questioned about slaughtering a cow on a Sunday evening in 1634, he got off by explaining that the beast was on the verge of death and 'behoved to be slain and blood let of her before her death or then she would not have been for no man's meat, which certain of the elders

49. John Major, *History of Greater Britain* (Edinburgh, 1892), 30; *Dundonald*, 330.

50. CH2/442/74 (Kirkwall), f. 28v; CH2/521/2, f. 70. Childbirth excused Mortlach and Elgin women (CH2/529/1, f. 40v; CH2/145/2, f. 126), and 'necessary waiting on children' or the ill served routinely (e.g., CH2/521/8/2, f. 219; CH2/523/1, f. 1). Among many examples of illness accepted as an excuse, see CH2/521/8/1, f. 51; CH2/472/1, f. 27; CH2/716/2, f. 79v; SAU CH2/Crail/1, f. 1v.

51. CH2/521/7, pp. 474, 108.

52. CH2/326/1, pp. 5–6; CH2/Crail/1, f. 1v (masters only fined, 20s). In the 1560s the Fife synod recommended that landward ministers read prayers early on Sunday to enable servants to attend before commencing the day's work; the regular Sunday sermon began at 10am. They forbade landlords to require carriage by their tenants, however; and to prevent sabbath fieldwork, they told masters of 'poor cottars' obliged to work the fields six days a week to release them from this 'oppression' during harvest season by giving them 'twelve hours furnished each Saturday to shear and win[now] their own corn': SAU ms 30451, ff. 5, 6v.

knowing, verified.'[53] There were distinct advantages to local enforcement of a system that might have been truly oppressive if common knowledge of people's troubles could not be brought to bear. With an eye to the local economy, the Kirkcaldy elders also construed 'necessity' to include serious alcohol production, noting 'that casting of malt upon the sabbath cannot be eschewed . . . in respect a mask of malt will be twenty days laboured before it can be perfected.'[54]

In much of the Highlands, churches were in such remote and inaccessible areas that sessions not only tolerated necessarily irregular attendance, they also paid for Sunday labour to transport parishioners to the kirk. Inveravon's elders paid the boatman John More two merks to 'ferry the people over the water coming and going from the sermon', and in 1638 they bought him a new currach. The entire congregation of Inishail had to be ferried to the church, which was located on an island in Loch Awe.[55] Leniency about attendance, however reasonable, doubtless contributed to the slower pace of Reformation in such remote areas; but clearly parishes willing to pay for transport to sermons held preaching in high regard and expected the ferries to be full. Protestantism had made measurable headway by the time ferrymen became kirk employees.

One significant portion of the congregation was systematically excluded everywhere from Sunday sermons. While sermons were central, the elders knew that they had to be audible to be effective, and so they barred babies and very young children from attendance lest they disturb the adult hearers – a factor that must be borne in mind when trying to gauge actual church attendance in early modern Scotland. The Glasgow sessions designated eight as the cut-off age; Aberdeen prohibited 'young bairns . . . not at the school and not of such age and disposition as they can take themselves to a seat when they come to the kirk, but vague [wander] through the same here and there in time of sermon and make perturbance and disorder.' These children were to be 'kept at home, for eschewing of clamour and disorder in the kirk'. Kingsbarns's session ordered them not only to be kept away from the kirk, but also to be shut up indoors lest parishioners be troubled by the 'running up and down of little ones and young children on the Lord's day in the time of sermon'. Perth's session in 1582

53. *Dundonald*, 287 (the shepherds did make it to the afternoon sermon); CH2/521/8/1, f. 128v.

54. CH2/636/34, f. 60. Necessity did not, however, include salvage of shipwrecks before the tide took them back – a perennial temptation in coastal towns where such plunder could be vital to the local economy: CH2/96/1, f. 3v (salvage forbidden before 'cockcrowing on Monday' in Duffus); SAU CH2/210/1 (Kilconquhar), f. 6v.

55. CH2/171/1, ff. 8, 46; Dawson, 'Calvinism and the Gaidhealtachd', 243.

actually ordered warding (gaoling) and a 6s 8d fine for 'bairns that perturb the kirk in time of preaching' instead of being kept at home.[56] Such rulings would obviously have reduced church attendance quite considerably, since the adult caretakers would have had to stay at home with their young charges. Sessions routinely excused absenteeism by parents, nurses, and other servants for this reason. On the other hand, the frequency with which they had to repeat the order to keep 'greeting [crying] bairns' and other youngsters at home suggests that some adults, far from resenting required sermon attendance, were willing to risk a fine in order to come to the preaching with children in tow.[57] Services of baptism obviously presented a particular dilemma, since one could hardly exclude the baby. Perth solved this problem with a 1587 order that babies 'be holden in some secret place til the preaching is ended' and only then be fetched for baptism, 'for avoiding of the . . . crying of the infant and bairn which makes din in time of the preaching, so that others incoming thereto are stopped from hearing.'[58] After all, mere presence at preaching was not enough for the religion of the word to take hold: one must be able to hear and understand to be converted.

For those without legitimate excuse, sessions imposed sufficiently stern penalties to turn behaviour around. The usual penalty was warning or censure for a first offence and thereafter a fine, graduated for multiple repeaters, and sometimes augmented by public rebuke or repentance.[59] The statutory fine of 20s was seldom levied on first or even second offenders, although there are exceptions in parishes where lesser penalties had proven ineffective. Anstruther Wester began by simply warning sermon absentees, but started imposing a 12d fine for the first offence (2s and 5s for the next two) in 1594 'because of the great contempt of the word and evil keeping of the sabbath'.[60] Burntisland was in 1602 more typical in setting

56. NLS ms 2782, f. 3v (1607, with violators fined 20s for sabbath breach); CH2/448/3, pp. 227–28 (Aberdeen's more modest 4s fine); SAU CH2/819/1, f. 32; CH2/521/1, f. 83; CH2/521/2, ff. 4, 58. Presumably the incarceration order applied to the parents. See also CH2/326/1, p. 6.

57. CH2/521/6, f. 43 (1616); CH2/521/7, p. 355.

58. CH2/521/2, f. 58 (1587). They also forbade parents to leave the sermon to fetch their children early, 'for the avoiding of the tumult of the incoming of the people with them for outgoing for them'.

59. Perth's repeat absentees were 'rebuked in presence of the whole congregation' with threats of being 'more sharply punished' if the problem persisted: CH2/521/4, p. 58 (the case of a webster's wife 'often apprehended').

60. SAU CH2/624/2, p. 5. Third-time offenders also repented publicly (p. 11). For the statutory fine, *APS* 3:212 (1581). In addition to public repentance, Ayr under the zealous ministry of John Welch in 1603 required 6s 8d for the first offence, 8s 4d for the second, and 20s for the third: AAC CH2/715/1, f. 2. Menmuir was more relaxed:

2s for a first absence from the sermon, doubling it for each of the next two offences, with 12s for the fourth and banishment from the town for the fifth (though in the extant records it never came to that). The hierarchy of sabbath breach comprehended not only the number of offences, but also the offensiveness of whatever activity had been taken up in lieu of sermon attendance. The penalties just listed applied to absence only; if the offender had been found playing games or drinking ale in service time, the range became 6s, 13s, 20s and public confession, and banishment for a fourth offence. The punishment was correspondingly higher for selling ale in service time.[61] Ayr's session set higher fines for ale-selling, milling and cadging, as well as scolding, drinking and fighting, and Perth after the turn of the century imposed the 20s fine for first offenders either selling ale or working on the sabbath. St Cuthbert's, Edinburgh, demanded it of a man found 'running a race in time of sermon'.[62] Other parishes occasionally exceeded it: the Falkirk session by 1617 was so distraught at the failure of its earlier efforts that it introduced a 30s penalty for first offenders; Dysart in the 1620s rose to thrice the statutory penalty, and Stow's session demanded 20s for sabbath breach outside sermon time, but 40s for missing the sermon.[63]

Enforced attendance by the whole community had its drawbacks. Some who came to the kirk either slept through the sermon or behaved so badly that they disrupted the service. The frequency with which such problems appear on sessions' agendas should alert us to the fact that the shift to habits of self-control and attentiveness was not accomplished evenly or without effort. Even the popular preacher William Cowper had to remind his auditors in 1600 that a preacher 'hath impediments enough in himself to hinder from teaching . . . Such therefore among you as are Christians, I bind you with the law of conscience to refrain from

William Tam of Balfour had missed six Sundays before the statutory fine was imposed; at that point he was threatened with a doubled fine and public repentance and promised amendment: CH2/264/1, f. 6v.

61. CH2/523/1, f. 1.

62. AAC CH2/751/1, f. 2; CH2/521/6, f. 99 (for bleaching cloth in sermon time); CH2/718/4, f. 2v (1618). Most earlier Perth offenders were just warned – e.g., CH2/521/2, ff. 30–31 (archery or kyles during the sermon, 1589); CH2/521/3, pp. 142–43 (spreading muck or wandering in the fields, 1600); or charged 10s – e.g., CH2/521/2, f. 22v (weaving, 1588), despite the elders being 'daily troubled with breakers of the sabbath' in 1591 and even threatening warding (CH2/521/2, f. 47v). The fine rose to 13s 4d in 1591, but only for repeat offenders who gave the searchers 'light speeches' (CH2/521/2, f. 55); most absentees were still just admonished even after the turn of the century (e.g., CH2/521/3, pp. 264–65, 267). Only sabbath ale-sellers seem to have paid the statutory fine in the 1580s (CH2/521/1, f. 115, 1585).

63. CH2/400/1, f. 7; CH2/390/1, f. 10, Dysart's £3 fine; CH2/338/1, ff. 6v, 10.

sleeping. And such amongst you as are civilians, let common courtesy be an aweband [obligation] to you, remembering that it is no point of civility to sleep in the house of God' – a charge all the more intriguing for its division of the congregation into godly and merely 'civil'.[64] Visitors of the Kincardine kirk of Durris in 1608 observed that the 'commons . . . occupy the time of teaching in sleeping to the great offence of God and grief of their pastors'; Perth's kirk officer wielded 'his red staff in the kirk on the sabbath day to waken sleepers'; and the Glasgow elders found so many people 'sitting with their heads covered in time of sermon sleeping' that they prohibited anyone to enter the kirk 'with their plaids about their heads, neither [were they allowed to] *lie down in the kirk on their face in time of preaching*' – a remarkable indication of how extreme the problem was, even in the 1630s.[65] Adolescents sitting in the loft in Ayr's kirk in 1605 entertained themselves by 'casting down stones to waken the women that were sleeping in time of sermon' – a dangerous mimicking of the elders' discipline of sleepers, verging perhaps on the ritual inversion of youthful 'misrule'.[66]

Others disturbed the service by coming late or leaving early, leading some sessions to have the kirk doors locked at the last bell, others to have latecomers 'immediately admonished from the pulpit'.[67] But sleepers and early leavers were the least of the elders' worries. More troublesome were people like James Young of Burntisland, who apparently thought his pastor's sermon would be easier to bear if he 'drank a quart of ale before the sermon', or John Ambrose of Leith, summoned 'for drinking himself beastly foul' before the sermon, or Monkton's more generalised 'drinking extraordinarily before sermons' and 'abusing God's house . . . in vomiting and casting out the said drunkenness in the kirk'.[68] There is also a good deal of unspecified 'troubling the kirk in time of sermon' in every session minute book, and an abundance of quarrelling.[69] Schoolboys and appren-

64. NLS ms Adv. 31.1.1, f. 231
65. CH2/1/1, n.f., June 1608; CH2/521/6, f. 43 (1616); NLS ms 2782, f. 33v (emphasis mine).
66. AAC CH2/751/1, ff. 17v–18; cf. stone-casters in Elgin, CH2/145/2, f. 172v.
67. CH2/471/1, f. 1; CH2/141/1, f. 3 (identifying latecomers as 'the meanest sort of people'); SAU CH2/624/2, p. 158 (locking the doors in Anstruther Wester); CH2/521/7, p. 108; CH2/326/1, f. 1; CH2/472/1, ff. 13–14; AAC CH2/751/1, f. 134v.
68. CH2/523/1, ff. 10v–11 (1604); CH2/716/2, f. 106v (1613); AAC CH2/809/1, ff. 69v, 79v. Monkton's drunkards paid 13s and 'repented low' – on the lower of the penitential stools; those who vomited paid double and wore sackcloth.
69. CH2/523/1, f. 1v; CH2/472/1, f. 38; CH2/521/6, f. 87v; CH2/521/7, p. 353; CH2/521/8/1, f. 52v; CH2/390/1, f. 5; CH2/636/34, f. 46v; *Dundonald*, 232, or 63 (a 1604 quarrel in Crosbie chapel, one man 'cutting off the bells of Hew Petticruw's shoes').

tices, 'insolent and wanton youths and young boys', were irrepressibly noisy and given to 'misorder, gaming, playing or speaking' during the sermon, despite most parishes stationing elders or officers where they could observe and control misbehaviour.[70] Many kirks were troubled because 'impudent and shameless persons . . . especially of the baser sort take pleasure and delight to bring their dogs to the kirk with them upon the sabbath day, which troubles both the minister and also the hearers of the word'; in Perth and in Ayr these were simply 'dinged away' or removed by the beadle, but the Scoonie elders ordered every offending dog 'taken and killed if it can be apprehended'.[71] Circumspect behaviour came slowly to a traditional religious culture that had lacked vernacular sermons to command attention, and in which clerical performance of the mass had made the laity's role largely irrelevant.

Not all 'troubling of the kirk' indicated popular disgruntlement with required sermon attendance. In 1622 the Falkirk elders confronted Robert Gib for his 'misbehaviour and troubling of the kirk upon Pasch day by leaning in at the window after the door was closed and the sermon begun.' The godly Mr Gib explained, however, that, being a great fan of preaching, he had disturbed the congregation 'out of no evil intention', but rather 'for the earnest [desire] he had to hear the word preached'.[72] Gib's problem was with punctuality (also a concern of sessions), but not with sermons.

Even after the last sermon, the sabbath remained a sacrosanct day. When John Morton of Perth found himself in trouble for fishing on a Sunday evening in 1632 and protested that he only began after sundown, the elders explained that the Lord's Day continued from midnight on Saturday until midnight on Sunday and fined him 40s. A Dundonald woman repented publicly and paid 13s 4d for cutting hay on Sunday to feed her calf, even though she had attended both services. Everywhere, the poor lost their place on the list of alms recipients for sabbath breach, even if they had come to church.[73] This was not sabbatarianism for its own sake, however; the word was the issue. The expectation was that parishioners would devote sabbath hours at home to sermon repetition, Bible-reading,

70. CH2/326/1, p. 8; CH2/521/6, f. 77; CH2/521/7, ff. 109, 141; CH2/448/2, p. 16. Kirkcaldy stationed elders in lofts 'to keep the people in order' (CH2/636/34, f. 46v); in Perth 'for better and more decent order keeping the elders should sit on the south side of the choir' (CH2/521/7, p. 353).

71. CH2/521/1, f. 115v (1585 order to 'ding away the dogs out of the kirk and to smite the bairns that break the glass windows' while playing in the kirkyard); CH2/521/2, f. 84; CH2/326/1, p. 7; AAC CH2/751/1, f. 124.

72. CH2/400/1, f. 94. He apologised for his 'evil example'.

73. CH2/521/8/1, f. 49; *Dundonald*, 59; ML CH2/171/1, f. 10v (though public confession restored alms); CH2/338/1, f. 31v.

psalm-singing and prayer, either individually or in 'family exercises' – activities that visiting elders were to verify. The Kingsbarns elders explained that Sunday evening was the head of household's opportunity to quiz his children and servants, to 'take account of them and see whether they have been in the kirk or not' and how much they absorbed of the sermon.[74] For an illiterate population, the requirement of repeating the main points of the sermon later to one's master or parent provided an incentive for learning the doctrine by listening very carefully in church.

What the sessions were doing here was very systematically instilling new habits of self-discipline in the population on a very large scale, parish by parish. The habit of listening to reading and extended oral exposition of a text was a new and doubtless difficult one for most sixteenth-century people, accustomed to the brevity of the mass and its stimulating sensory paraphernalia. What the elders' activities reveal is the range of mechanisms they devised to instil this new habit across the social spectrum. They compelled assembly of the whole community in a single space, at regular intervals, and on time. They enforced attentiveness, sobriety and quiet for two-hour periods. They expected results in subsequent required performance before each parishioner's immediate social superior. This was a powerful combination which could certainly effect new habits of behaviour. By contrast, when English puritans urged their sabbatarian programme on the same sorts of people as the only efficient way to protestantise, they must have known that without consistorial discipline, they were just whistling in the wind.[75]

All this is not to say that the Scots elders were inflexible in their enforcement of the policy. In addition to the legitimate excuses that they all acknowledged, we do find them making allowances in light of the general behaviour and reputation of the offender. A group of Perth schoolboys found playing in the Inch during the afternoon sermon in 1599 was let off with an admonition on the grounds that they had been to the morning sermon in Scone, and 'because they are youths of good expectation'. One does not want to discourage adolescents who are making an effort. And when Archibald Redheuch reported that he had missed the afternoon sermon on a June Sunday when he 'went a bonny space from his own house for a walk to take the air' and while resting fell asleep and 'wakened not till the last bell', when he found the town gate locked, he too was let off since 'he uses not to be absent from God's service on the

74. CH2/448/2, p. 16 (children to 'give an account of their edification'); CH2/266/1, ff. 110–10v; SAU CH2/150/1, f. 8 (Ferryport-on-Craig searchers seeking pious exercise in homes after the last sermon); SAU CH2/819/1, f. 26.

75. Kenneth Parker, *The English Sabbath* (Cambridge, 1988).

sabbath day'. There was clearly no need to harass people of this kind. But at the same Perth session meeting, James Clink, who showed only 'formal and feigned excuses' for his absence, and who was known to have had people drinking in his house during sermon time, was fined 12s and ordered to repent on his knees.[76] The elders were not indiscriminate, and this must have garnered them support from many in the community who might otherwise have resented their rigour.

The sessions' efforts appear to have achieved a considerable measure of success. While there were certainly recidivists, recorded as multiple offenders and punished with increasing severity, their numbers – and indeed, the numbers of even first offenders – are remarkably small relative to populations, at least in Lowland parishes. It is imprudent to argue too much from silence, but it is surely suggestive that when the Kinghorn session ordered '*all* absents to appear', the list seldom exceeded two or three, generally from landward districts. The largest number reported in a single week in Ayr in the first decade of its earliest book is nine – again, many from the landward.[77] Whatever their complaints about sabbath breach increasing – a regular jeremiad in all the minute books – the elders' hoped-for results actually do seem to have been forthcoming. Over time, the visitors' reports in the minutes increasingly record 'nothing but good order' both morning and afternoon, and those counting people in the kirk often report 'no contemners' or perfect attendance.[78] This did not mean that they let down their guard, however. After several Sundays in 1637 of 'no misorder' but several empty seats in afternoon sermon time, the Kilconquhar elders decided that some offenders 'had their privy spies and watchers to advertise them of the coming of the visitors, during which time they kept themselves quiet in [their] houses until they were departed, and then they went to their drinking.' Alerted to this ploy, the searchers took a sneakier approach, and for the next several weeks

76. CH2/521/3, p. 121; CH2/521/8/1, ff. 57–58.

77. CH2/472/1, ff. 18 (the largest number ever, ten), 19, 27 *et passim*; AAC CH2/751/1 (from 1603), ff. 5v (nine in 1604, three from one family), 13 (seven in 1605), 16v (nine), 140v–42 (nine in 1608). Cf. CH2/636/34, f. 40v; CH2/1142/1, f. 92v.

78. CH2/84/28, f. 15v; CH2/521/3, pp. 22, 100, 101 (indeed, from the 1590s on, Perth's 'visitors report that good order was kept the sabbath preceding' and 'nothing but good order' occur as regular entries in the minutes); CH2/276/1, ff. 1v, 69 ('good order' recurring in searchers' reports throughout the first extant Newbattle minute book); CH2/264/1, f. 22 (perfect attendance in Menmuir). Elgin searchers in 1602 reported 'no misrule this day but a great convention' with 'all the lofts' full: CH2/145/2, f. 90. There were rare remarkable lapses, like the case of David Anderson, absent from Kirkcaldy's sermons for three years, but the elders were clearly astonished that they had managed to overlook him; he was probably living in isolated circumstances outside the town (CH2/636/34, f. 101, 1628).

apprehended a few ale-sellers, drinkers and collectors of fishing bait each Sunday. Thereafter, 'good order' resumed.[79]

The record is unsurprisingly less impressive in the Highlands, but even there the Inveravon session found absenteeism rates of 20–25 per cent in the 1630s unacceptably high. There were, moreover, good reasons for a fourth of the congregation to have been absent on a given Sunday here. For one thing, it was a multilingual parish, where a certain percentage of the congregation would simply not have understood a sermon preached in English or Scots. Then there was the distance that many of these rural parishioners had to travel to the kirk. This factor explicitly drove session to adjust its expectations, ruling 'in respect the parish is far dispersed' that some absences would be tolerable, particularly in winter. They levied a fine only if an absentee failed to respond to a third summons from the kirk officer, the offence then being contumacy rather than sabbath breach. Finally, this session had taken its time implementing the sabbatarian programme established elsewhere generations earlier: they seem not to have begun regularly appointing sabbath visitors until 1635.[80] After all, distance and weather presented the same obstacles for elder/searchers as for ordinary parishioners. Still, even in the Highlands and Isles, the new requirement for the whole parish to come to the kirk weekly was in some parishes remarkably successful. Thanks in part to synods like that of Argyll replacing Anglophone preachers with Gaelic-speakers, Franciscan missionaries reported protestant preaching as their main problem in attempting to reconvert the Highlands and Isles. And on the Isle of Skye, sermon attendance was so good that it introduced a new tactic in feuding: the MacDonalds of Uist succeeded in wiping out the MacLeods of the Waternish peninsula by locking the kirk door during sermon time and setting fire to the building.[81] By the turn of the century, the Privy Council was forced to confront the problem that sermon attendance was now reliable enough to make the kirk door the logical place to lie in wait to ambush one's enemies 'for the time at the preaching'.[82] Discipline had clearly succeeded in underpinning the sermon.

79. SAU CH2/210/1, ff. 1–6v (quotation at 4v), 10, 17v–18.
80. The Inveravon session began systematically listing its absentees in 1635, twenty-three to twenty-five names appearing most weeks, out of 105 communicants: CH2/191/1, ff. 25v, 29; f. 17 notes the language problem for Gaelic-speakers, f. 60v reports laxer attendance requirements. Only once was the JP recruited to execute a £26 fine for a six-month absence (f. 29).
81. Dawson, 'Calvinism and the gaidheal tachd', 240, citing *The Irish Franciscan Mission to Scotland 1619–46*, ed. C. Giblin (Dublin, 1964), and 250, on the Skye feud and a similar incident in Kilchrist, Easter Ross.
82. *RPC* 11:601 (1619).

Another indication of the ultimate success of the visitors' efforts at detection and the sessions' at penalising sabbath breach is the considerable evidence of severe crowding in Scottish churches on Sundays, particularly in kirk repair and expansion budgets and in new kirk 'planting' in the decades following Reformation. The Aberdeen complaint that the minister 'teaches powerfully and plainly the Word [to] . . . such a fair auditory that the seats of the kirk was not able to hold them' is not an isolated one. Both Kinghorn's and Perth's sessions found in 1608 that there was 'little room and evil ease in hearing the word in respect that sundry sat out of the sight of the preaching, . . . blocking them in hearing the word', though they 'press thereto'; and Kilspindy's elders brought the crowding of 'women who sit in the midst of the kirk' to the attention of the presbytery, which advised using vertical space by building galleries.[83] Clingilkirk in Berwickshire reported in 1627 that its building could not hold half of its four hundred parishioners, and two Clackmannanshire congregations sharing a minister complained that 'none of the fabrics of any of the two churches can accommodate the whole number of both parishes without enlargement.' St Magnus, Kirkwall, was so crowded on sermon days that there was no room to move, and the Brechin session fought a losing battle against seats in the body of the kirk encroaching on the space required for communion tables: in the end they had to resort to portable tables that could be hung on the walls on Sundays when there was no sacrament.[84]

In burghs like Aberdeen with substantial schools, the elders were particularly concerned about lack of suitable space for pupils 'who should have been edified in godliness by the hearing of the word' but instead were 'against conscience neglected in that part by reason they sit in such a place [behind the pulpit] where they cannot hear the voice of the minister.' Even when new seats were built for them, 'on the degrees under the new loft, where they will both hear and see the ministry of the word', their master complained that only half of the students could be accommodated there. The session eventually moved those who had 'come to discretion of years and are able to give an account of their edification' to a loft to 'take their notes of the preaching', and seated the younger

83. Spalding, 2:57 (lofts constructed from timberwork saved from the old altar); CH2/472/1, f. 27v. CH2/521/4, p. 155; CH2/521/7, p. 400; CH2/299/1, p. 276.

84. *1627 Reports*, 7–9, 30–31; CH2/442/74, f. 5; Thoms, *Kirk of Brechin*, 72. There is no mention in session minutes for our period of the expedient we find especially in the eighteenth century during communion seasons, where preaching was offered out of doors: Leigh Eric Schmidt, *Holy Fairs: Scottish Communions and American Revivals in the Early Modern Period* (Princeton, 1989); Hugh Cheape, 'The Communion Season', *RSCHS* 27 (1997), 305–16.

children on the new benches under the loft with a master, who was ordered to see 'no disorder nor perturbation be made by them in time of preaching'. Aberdeen's, however, was not an isolated case.[85]

The frequency of quarrels and even violence in the kirk during service time may well provide additional evidence of crowding. With room at a premium, encroachment on one's neighbour's space was the usual reason for such recorded arguments. Thus, James Mitchell caused a furore in Mortlach by 'misbehaving in the time of the preaching in pulling of a woman violently out of her seat and throwing her in the kirk floor' because she had set her stool in his standing room. Such stool wars were extremely frequent in parishes all over Scotland, and while they had to do in part with violation of status, which was read into movement of one's stool from its accustomed place, they presumably would not have come about had there been adequate room in the kirk for everyone's stool.[86] In practical, physical terms, sabbath enforcement may actually have been too successful.

The problem had multiple roots. First, and most obviously, the church had never before required attendance by all except at Easter, so that many parish churches had probably never been big enough to include everyone. Sixteenth-century population growth exacerbated the problem. So did protestant destruction of some parish churches, like Restalrig, that were in the reformers' judgment 'monuments of idolatry'. Finally, many churches had fallen into serious disrepair long before the Reformation: Patrick Blair reported in 1589 many Scots churches 'ruinous and decayed, and few or none of them well repaired or kept except in cities'.[87]

The solution to overcrowding was in many cases, as we have seen in Aberdeen, to maximise existing space by constructing either lofts or 'degrees' – benches banked in ascending height. Both families and guilds petitioned sessions for the right to construct galleries for 'ease in hearing the word'; even in new, purpose-built kirks like Burntisland's, lofts were under construction within a few years of the building's completion.[88] In

85. CH2/448/2, p. 16 (1603); cf. Thoms, *Kirk of Brechin*, 71 (the schoolmaster complaining in 1628 that 'the seats whereon his scholars did sit were far distant from the pulpit', depriving the boys of 'hearing of the sermons').

86. CH2/529/1, f. 29v (1628). See also CH2/521/7, pp. 225, 378; CH/521/8/1, ff. 145, 256v; CH2/521/8/2, f. 166; SAU CH2/819/1, pp. 14, 31; SAU CH2/624/2, p. 143; AAC CH2/809/1, f. 28; CH2/636/34/1, f. 13; CH2/299/1, p. 317. Chapter 7, below, discusses seats as status symbols.

87. LPL ms 3471; *Fasti* 1:160; F.D. Bardgett, 'Dilapidation of Church Property in Angus after 1560', *IR* 40 (1989), 2–23.

88. CH2/472/1, f. 27v (1608); some of Burntisland's lofts, built on all four sides of this square church, are dated, indicating construction in 1598 and especially from 1602 to 1630. See also AAC CH2/751/1, ff. 11, 12v; and chapter 7, below, for petitions to

other cases, new 'aisles', or projecting transeptal wings, were built onto the kirk, with other buildings used for services while repairs and expansion went on.[89] The obvious long-term solution required either drastic repair of formerly unusable buildings – the cheaper and so more frequent solution; transformation of secular buildings into churches; or construction of new buildings.[90] Examples of new buildings are few in the financially strapped sixteenth century – Kembach in 1582, Burntisland in 1592 and Prestonpans in the later 1590s are among the few. The latter was financed largely by the minister himself, John Davidson finding no building at all when he arrived to take up his office in 1595, and by the Laird and Lady Preston. The Preston contribution paid for an aisle projecting from the south side, giving the kirk its characteristically post-Reformation T-plan – a device that considerably augmented auditory space, accommodating not only the laird and his family, but also his tenants (see plate 6). Early seventeenth-century examples are more numerous. They include most notably Greyfriars, Edinburgh (1612–20), Dirlton (begun 1612), Dairsie (1621), Anworth (1627), Portpatrick (1629), Auchterhouse and Kingsbarns (both 1630), South Queensferry (1633), Anstruther Easter (1634) and Elie (1639), but there is evidence of at least a dozen more .[91] The Perth council

build galleries. John Gifford, *The Buildings of Scotland: Fife* (London, 1988), 146, 170, describes post-Reformation adaptation of Culross abbey choir and the twelfth-century church of Dalgety Bay with lofts.

89. The 'littleness of the Low Kirk not holding the inhabitants' forced such shifting about of Glasgow's congregation during repair and reconstruction beginning in 1588: NLS ms 2782, ff. 14, 26, 33. See also CH2/472/1, f. 27v; CH2/299/1, p. 276; CH2/521/4, p. 155; and on addition of aisles (for burial as well as space for sermon auditors) chapter 7, below; James Grant, ed., *Old and New Edinburgh* (Edinburgh, 1880), 2:312 (the aisle added to Duddingston's Saxon building for the laird of Prestonfield and his tenants); Howard, *Scottish Architecture*, 176–77, 199–203; and Andrew Spicer, '"Defyle Not Christ's Kirk with your Carrion": Burial and the Development of Burial Aisles in Post-Reformation Scotland' in *The Place of the Dead: Death and Remembrance in Late Medieval and Early Modern Europe*, ed. Bruce Gordon and Peter Marshall (Cambridge, 2000), 149–69.

90. Edinburgh turned part of its tollbooth into a church in 1574: NAS ms RH2/1/35, f. 20.

91. Charles Rogers, ed., *Three Scottish Reformers* (London, 1876), 47 (Davidson also collecting contributions from friends in Edinburgh for Prestonpans); Gifford, *Fife*, 34–41, 257, 274; Gordon Donaldson, 'The Post-Reformation Church at Whithorn: Historical Notes', *Proceedings of the Society of Antiquaries of Scotland*, 85 (1950–51), 126–28; W.G.S. Snow, *The Times, Life and Thought of Patrick Forbes* (London, 1952), 112–13; SAU CH2/210/1, f. 16v. New churches were either simple rectangles with west-end belfries, or the T-plan as at Elie, Prestonpans and Kembach (most common after 1640). Burntisland departs from the norm: hoping to create a space for clear audition and room at the centre for communion tables, its builders constructed a square around a central tower supported by heavy piers joined by round arches; it proved a poor

donated substantially to building a church in Ferryport-on-Craig in 1603. Elsewhere heritors built new churches for their tenants.[92] Presbyteries regularly found themselves petitioned by over-large parishes to be divided, with new buildings to be provided or decrepit ones repaired for the new congregation. Dividing a parish rather than simply building a larger church had the added advantage of allowing better pastoral care by reducing each minister's quota of parishioners – something the town ministers clamoured for, quite apart from the crowding problem. But, of course, it involved the expense of placing a new minister as well as providing a new building. Both involved 'stenting' (taxing) the heritors and other substantial members of the parish and so generally required presbytery or synodal intervention. Even with pressure from above, however, session records often show that collections did not go well, 'to the great desolations of the kirks', as the Moray synod lamented.[93] The Jedburgh presbytery despaired in 1606 of being able to provide a second church for Jedburgh town and sent a commission to the General Assembly to ask for financial aid.[94] Such problems arose, however, from the success of the sabbatarian campaign to implement the religion of the book.

* * *

What did the parishioners compelled to the kirk actually hear when they finally settled in for the preaching? What do we know about the sermons they would have repeated on the sabbath evening? Sermons were long as well as frequent, pulpits always equipped with 'sandglasses' or hourglasses (see plate 4) that could be turned over once, though twice would certainly be frowned on. Both presbyteries and sessions fined excessively long-winded preachers.[95] While an hour was probably usual, auditors made exceptions for particularly charismatic preachers like Robert Blair, who,

model since its acoustics were not all its planners had hoped. Other new construction used medieval foundations, as at Whithorn, where parts of the priory church were incorporated.

92. PL ms B59/28/11; Thoms, *Kirk of Brechin*, 7; SAU CH2/210/1, f. 16v – the laird of Ardrose's 'purpose to erect the kirk of Elie into a particular park by itself, and to disunite it from the parish of Kilconquhar'; he paid for substantial rebuilding of an ancient church at Elie (Gifford, 207).
93. CH2/271/1, ff. 1, 7, 13, 15 (the quotation, concerning Inveravon and Kirkmichael), 16–18, 21, 23, 27, 29–30, 33–34, 39, 75; CH2/146/1 (Ellon presbytery), ff. 58–59v, 94, 102v, 128v–29 (problems funding construction of the kirk of Udny); CH2/89/1, ff. 7–8 (Deer presbytery, 1603, considering construction of a new kirk at Longmay when the old one was 'overblown with sand' after a storm shifted the dunes).
94. CH2/198/1, f. 7v. They needed a stipend for another minister as well.
95. Where, as in Leith, afternoon sermons began in winter at 1.30 after a 9.30 morning sermon, the first sermon could not easily go on for two hours if catechism and

still inspired 'when the hourglass was ended', preached for another sixty minutes in his Antrim parish. Robert Rollock referred to his Edinburgh parishioners 'sitting an hour or two hearing'. He reminded them that sermon attendance without the corresponding action of the Holy Spirit would not suffice to save them – perhaps combating an assumption about intrinsic merit in sermon attendance that he found all too common already by the 1580s.[96] English visitors complained that Scottish sermons tended to be 'delivered always by heart and therefore sometimes spoiled by battologies, little impertinences, and incoherence in their discourses' – a result of the emphasis on preaching *ex tempore* to allow for the operation of divine inspiration.[97] A preacher often dwelt for weeks on the same book of the Bible, the reformers having rejected the traditional skipping about of the lectionary.[98] When he finally finished it, he consulted with the session as to what book to begin next.[99] Sermons were didactic as well as hortatory, organised generally in three parts – a point-by-point recounting of the biblical text, an exegetical middle, and a final application or 'use'. This last part was particularly important. For ordinary people to engage fully in the biblical text, they had to see the point of it for their daily lives. Accordingly, the Paisley presbytery, assessing a 'specimen doctrine' offered by the ministerial candidate Thomas Hamilton in 1603, declined to ordain him because they found the 'use [is] not so popular as is required'.[100]

dinner were to precede the afternoon service (CH2/716/1, f. 22). The Edinburgh presbytery (CH2/121/1, n.f., 24 October 1587) fined preachers 'who pass the hourglass in making the exercise' 18d; Ellon's (CH2/146/1, f. 110v, 1604), fined those exceeding three-quarters of an hour or an 'addition' (another minister's response to the exercise) longer than half an hour 10s. The St Andrews session ordered that the 8 o'clock morning sermon to be over by 9, 'prayers and all' (*SAKS* 2:828–29); Elgin threatened a 6s 8d fine unless 'the prayers, psalms and preaching be all ended within the hour', and in 1622 ordered David Philp 'when he teaches that he turn the glass when he goes to the pulpit that the prayers, psalms and preaching be all ended within the hour' (CH2/145/1, f. 71v; CH2/145/3, f. 178).

96. Robert Blair, *The Life of Mr Robert Blair, Minister of St Andrews, Containing his Autobiography from 1593 to 1636*, ed. Thomas M'Crie (Edinburgh, 1848), 85; Rollock, *Select Works* (1849), 381.
97. Morer, 60.
98. CH2/448/3, p. 351 (a discernible note of relief in the report that Dr Forbes had finally finished Hebrews and was 'appointed to teach next, God willing, on Romans'); *First Book*, 185. Rollock's *Certaine Sermons upon Severall Places of the Epistles of Paul* (Edinburgh, 1599) includes five on 2 Corinthians 5.
99. *Canongate*, 35–36.
100. CH2/294/1, f. 7; John Davidson, *Some Helpes for Young Schollers in Christianity* in *Three Scottish Reformers*, ed. Charles Rogers, 133, outlines the three parts for his congregation.

Of course, it is difficult to know precisely what was preached, and even more difficult to discern how it was heard. Most ministers who did engage in *ex tempore* preaching left no record of what they said; others 'penned . . . whatsoever I preached', either before or after delivery, but had few of their sermons published.[101] In some cases, printed sermons may tell us more about the preacher's intentions and afterthoughts in revision than about what he actually said. Fortunately, many were printed not from the minister's text, but from auditors' notes, so that we have some indication of what they heard, rather than what the preacher recalled having said. The preface to a contemporary edition of Andrew Gray's sermons describes the volume's contents as 'no more than notes taken from his mouth in the pulpit', and apologises for omitting many of the author's 'critical explanations' in favour of 'other things which they [note-taking auditors] might judge more edifying'.[102] Some manuscript sermon notebooks have also survived, giving us even more direct access to what at least a few literate auditors received. What strikes modern readers about these notebooks are the repetition of themes, so useful for oral transmission of complex ideas; the frequency of numbered lists of ideas, again a practical device to aid memory; the simplicity and vividness of the language; and the combination of rather dry exposition of text – purely a transmission of data and doctrine – with intensely emotional and evocative language in exhortation.[103] The balance between the two elements of this latter trait is particularly significant.

The first addresses the problem of an auditory unable for the most part to read the scriptures themselves. They became, under the oral tutelage of their ministers, 'Christian professors brought up in the fear and *information* of the Lord' – an interesting departure from the biblical 'fear and admonition' in an Auchterderran sermon notebook. The minister of this parish, John Chalmers, attributed his auditors' 'evil disposition and doing'

101. Cowper, *Workes*, 5, prefacing a collection of comparatively few of his sermons.
102. Andrew Gray, *Select Sermons* (2nd edn, Falkirk, 1792; orig. 1649), vii, ix. The preface claims, 'there was scarce ever a sermon that this youth preached at home or abroad but was thus written and preserved as a precious relic of him' (p. v).
103. SAU Hay Fleming Box 53, it. ii and Folger ms V.a.415 are good examples of sermons as numbered lists, and of the simplicity and power of the language. The latter notebook is written by a single hand, from both ends, generally in full sentences but sometimes in fragments, from edge to edge of the paper and with absolutely no punctuation. The preachers are Andrew Gray, James Blair, Robert Watson, David Bisset, James Wallace, William Erskine and James Ruatt (probably Rowat of Kilmarnock). There is notable variety in the language of the preachers, suggesting that the note-taker was not trying to edit. The sermons were preached at fasts and communions (including preparation Saturdays and thanksgiving Mondays), mostly at the barony kirk of Glasgow or in the parish of Bothwell.

to their 'lack of learning, . . . being ignorant both of the knowledge of God and of nature'; accordingly, his sermons, as heard by our note-taker, are first and foremost informative. This parishioner took down both the main points of biblical texts under discussion and tenets of Calvinist (indeed, Bezan) theology often thought by modern historians to have been too esoteric for popular preaching. 'The sum of history', he records, having learned from a 1624 sermon, 'is the salvation of one . . . and leaving another . . . under damnation in the just judgment of God.'[104] A Glaswegian sermon notebook likewise indicates that the eight preachers its author heard dwelt heavily on the distinction between elect and reprobate.[105] Popular preachers like John Welch did not hesitate to explain their key texts by teaching their hearers a little Greek or Latin along the way.[106] The principle was that 'We must know him in our heads before we know him in our hearts.'[107]

Information, however, was not enough. The General Assembly in 1596 worried that even where there was knowledge, too often there was 'no sense nor feeling' to indicate that knowledge had taken effect. This fear is echoed in sermon notes of 'fleeting knowledge in the brain that has no effect on the heart'.[108] The wilful ignorance of those who have had 'the Lord's covenant both offered and explained to them' makes 'their sin greater and themselves more inexcusable', and produces a mere 'pretence of religion', leading to divine 'chastening' of the whole lukewarm community'.[109] Accordingly, sermons as written by auditors move quickly from imparting knowledge to vigorous denunciations of sin, dire warnings of

104. CH2/21/5, ff. 17, 6, 71. These notes are taken in full sentences with no abbreviations, suggesting that shorthand taken down during the sermon may have been recopied upon return home; however, there are abrupt breaks and numerous corrections.

105. Folger MS V.a.415, f. 137v (my foliation), on how to identify those whom 'God had no mind of . . . from eternity, and that they were never given by the father to Christ', or f. 52, evidences of election. Other examples abound in the sermons of Gray or of Zachary Boyd, e.g., *The Last Battell of the Soule in Death* (Edinburgh, 1629), 21 *et passim*. See also William Livingstone, *The Conflict in Conscience of a Dear Christian, Named Bessie Clarksone, in the Parish of Lanark* (Edinburgh, 1632), 15; SAU Hay Fleming Box 53, it. ii, p. 5 from the back (my pagination); or Welch threatening his hearers with the awful possibility of reprobation, *Forty-Eight Select Sermons* (Glasgow, 1771), 79–80, 92.

106. Welch, 93 (declaiming upon *poenitentia*), 97 (explaining μετάνοια to illumine the nature of repentance).

107. Folger ms V.a.415, f. 47. The first few folios of the notebook are lost, so we do not know the preacher of this sermon.

108. *BUK* 3:873; SAU ms Hay Fleming Box 53, it. ii, p. 6 from the back.

109. CH2/21/5, ff. 5–6.

the wrath to come, wrenching descriptions of the sufferings of Christ and God's disappointment in his unresponsive creation, horrific depictions of the pains of hell – in short, to the sort of oration designed to elicit affect, not just understanding. A Falkirk parishioner noted down next to his numbered list of doctrines and uses which ones offered 'comfort in all our afflictions' and which worked 'to terrorise the wicked'.[110] A less sympathetic English auditor in 1617 wrote off all Scottish sermons as 'nothing but railing'.[111]

Clearly the preachers were often highly successful at eliciting an emotional response. Andrew Gray did it by mastering the Falkirk combination of comfort and terror. Auditors described his preaching as 'very warm, rapturous and heavenly, and well adapted to affect the hearts of his hearers', but at the same time so terrifying that he 'often caused the very hairs of their heads to stand up'. In Carrickfergus, an observer of the monthly summer sermon festivals in the 1620s was similarly struck by Scottish preachers' emotional fervour. Here a group of ministers including the dynamic Robert Blair offered four sermons daily, and often saw their auditors 'stricken into a swoon with the word, yea a dozen in one day carried out of doors as dead, so marvellous was the power of God smiting their hearts for sin'.[112] A fast sermon of John Malcolm's 'moved the people [of Perth] to cry to God with tears, clamours and cries, and to hold up their hands to God [and promise to] amend their lives, . . . both men and women.'[113] The preachers alternately railed and thundered, pleaded and cajoled; they wept themselves and elicited tears from their hearers.[114] A congregation that will 'give Christ one look . . . shall be called a place of weeping for Jesus Christ', noted one parishioner, and where the minister described the true believer as the one 'watering his couch with tears', which of his auditors would not try to come up with an appropriate

110. CH2/400/1, f. 2 (the first few folios of the session book seem to have been used as a sermon notebook). Cf. CH2/21/5, f. 5; Livingstone, *Conflict in Conscience*, sig. A3.

111. Sir Anthony Weldon, in *Early Travellers*, 100. Weldon hoped not to 'make this discourse too tedious unto you, as the sermon was to those that were constrained to endure it.'

112. Gray, *Select Sermons* v–vi; Blair, 71.

113. CH2/521/7, pp. 277–78, recording that 'the whole people came to the kirk' at the 7am bell for this sermon. The emotional response, though, owed something to the cause of the fast, the 'tempestuous wind and rain' that had flooded the river Tay, destroying the bridge on which the town depended. Preaching continued 'all that week'.

114. Welch, 74–80, includes examples of threat and pleading in a sermon on Revelation 2.5 – a text to which Welch devoted eight sermons.

response?[115] One sign of an effective preacher was his ability to transfer his own emotional intensity to the auditory: an admirer of Robert Rollock observed that, 'being a man transported and ravished himself, he ever drew his auditors in the same sense with him.'[116] On the principle that 'the child of God may be brought to degrees of anxiety', Welch demanded, 'O, be afraid, for the harvest of the wrath of God is ripe . . . O be afraid and search yourselves, [for] . . . the wrath of God lies at your door' and he shall 'squeeze you betwixt the two millstones of his wrath'.[117] Sermons were not cold or passive affairs; had they been so, Robert Gib would presumably not have troubled to climb through the kirk window.

Nor were sermons necessarily monologues. Rhetorical questions abound and may have sought silent responses, but sometimes preachers set up what in another setting would be called a litany. The auditor's notes on a communion sermon by Gray, for instance, ended with a rousing call for congregational response:

> Let all the congregation say amen
> Let all the saints in heaven and earth praise him,
> And let all the congregation say amen.
> Let sun and moon praise him. Let fire, hailstorms, winds and vapours praise him,
> And let all the congregation say amen . . .
> Let men and women praise him,
> And let all the congregation say amen.[118]

It is impossible to read these notes without hearing the parishioners calling out their amens. And there is other evidence that questions we would read as rhetorical ('Will ye yet refuse Christ a look?' 'Will ye not answer?') actually did seek an audible answer. One defence offered by people summoned before the church courts for questioning or maligning the

115. Folger ms V.a.415, ff. 41, 45, 52, listing 'evidences' and 'assurances' of election. Robert Rollock warned that 'flesh and blood will never shed a tear for heaven': *Certaine Sermons*, 19.

116. *Certaine Sermons*, sig. A6.

117. Welch, 96; Folger ms V.a.415, ff. 45v–46v; Livingstone, *Conflict in Conscience*, sig. A3v ('hearts being racked with terrors' was thought a good thing by Clarkson's Lanark minister). As Zachary Boyd preached, 'When Christ had a will to ding his enemies upon their back, he sent his word to do it': *The Balme of Gilead* (Edinburgh, 1633), 154; cf. Rollock, *Select Works*, 1:393 (ministers' duty to 'ding down' sin).

118. Folger ms V.a.415, f. 63v.

minister during sermon time was that they had simply been misunderstood in their audible responses to his preaching.[119] Open response itself seems to have been acceptable, even encouraged.[120]

Sermons occasionally turned into heated exchanges between minister and parishioners, as in 1596 when William Seton was censured by the Haddington presbytery for interrupting the sermon in 'reproving and staying so far as he could' the minister's teaching, 'taking upon him[self] to judge of the pastor's doctrine to condemn the same'. People listened closely to sermons, leading in a parish of the Selkirk presbytery to the evolution of a sermon into an angry dialogue: when Andro Jameson decided he had taken quite enough 'thundering judgment' from his pastor, 'he stood up in the midst of the preaching and upbraided the minister' with 'many opprobrious words', announcing that 'he had enough of that and would not hold his tongue'. John Lockie interrupted a 1611 Mertoun sermon to defend his daughter when his minister's denunciation of whoredom hit too close to home.[121] This was not the sort of interactive sermon the preachers would have wished, of course, but it does suggest a significant level of audience engagement with the preaching. And it should serve as a reminder that a religion of the word need not depend on literacy. The sermon was an interactive oral medium that could work to great effect.

As for other elements of style, the ideal was 'lively', 'experimental preaching', 'plain, familiar and engaging'.[122] In the absence of icons in the kirk, the preachers used language to draw pictures in the imagination. One of David Bisset's auditors wrote that the congregation had 'seen [Christ] with their eyes crucified before them . . . and with their hands handled him' after a communion sermon. Gray's saw 'the portraiture of Christ . . . drawn upon the cross' in his description of Christ's face, mouth, 'blessed feet', eyes and hands, in a sermon that dwelt at excruciating length

119. The question before the Selkirk presbytery in 1611 was whether Andro Jameson had replied to the sermon 'Away with him' or 'God save us', as he claimed: CH2/327/1, f. 72v. See also Folger ms V.a.415, a series of sermons where questions are steadily fired at the auditors (e.g., ff. 53–53v); and SAU Hay Fleming Box 53, it. ii, pp. 59–64 from the back.

120. NLS ms Wod. LXIV, f. 268v, ministers 'call[ing] upon the people publicly . . . to propound questions, move doubts, . . . for their better satisfaction'; *The Forme of Prayers and Ministration of the Sacraments, Used in the English Church at Geneva, Approved and Received by the Churche of Scotland* (Edinburgh, 1565) (later referred to as the *Book of Common Order*), 20.

121. CH2/185/2, f. 2v; CH2/327/1, f. 73; cf. CH2/1142/1, ff. 96v, 97v, 99 (James Burnet in Fraserburgh likewise 'railing against the minister . . . in time of divine service', 1619).

122. Gray, v; Rollock, *Certaine Sermons*, sig. A6v.

on the five wounds.[123] The language was often homely, James Ruatt describing Jesus looking down on his people only to 'draw the curtain and say, "Poor things, do ye see that there is a bonny thing, and a worse life? Poor things, . . . I will tell thee a secret, I love ye out of wit."' One wonders whether John Davidson, preaching at Prestonpans, was drawing on his own boyhood cruelty when he told his catechumens that sin makes us 'more miserable than the brute beast, yea than the very toad, for when the brains or harns of it are dashed out, there is no more of it.'[124] The preachers used colloquialisms, Gray describing a believer in a state of speechless awe as having come 'to a what-shall-I-say'. They drew images from agriculture and crafts, from sailors' experiences and from the erotic: 'the naked embracement of a glorified Christ', one notebook records, 'will put us to acts of adoration.'[125] They compared sin to disease and – for all their condemnation of superstition – drew on folklore, Rollock's version of the Pauline 'seeing through a glass darkly' being 'in this life we have a fairy glimmering without any sun'.[126]

The vividness of the imagery helps to atone for the stultifying effect (on the modern reader, at least) of the lists. Some sermons consisted simply of collections of lists, with each element dutifully numbered. Five reasons for 'miskenning Christ', or five burdens the Christian can surrender (1. desires, 2. fears, 3. sorrows, 4. doubts, 5. perplexing hopes) make for a dull read; however, enumeration can also be a very effective mnemonic device.[127] So can conjugation: the auditor of a 1607 sermon on Genesis 42 noted down 'We have sinned, they have sinned, thou hast sinned, he has sinned' as a recurring phrase in a sermon that, however narcotic to the modern ear, would have made it hard to forget the theme of sin as both individual and communal, one's own and one's neighbour's. Repeating the conjugation also reinforced 'sin' sufficiently to get across even to the dimmest auditor the preacher's point about its pervasiveness.[128]

123. Folger ms V.a.415, f. 137v; Gray, 603–04. One thinks of the graphic imagery of the suffering body of Christ in contemporary Jesuit devotional books: Augustine Kelly, 'The Vernacular Devotional Literature of the English Roman Catholic Community 1560–1640' (Unpublished PhD thesis, St Andrews, 2001), 44–47.

124. Folger ms V.a.415, f. 81; cf. Rollock, *Select Works* 1:306; Davidson, *Some Helpes*, 142.

125. Gray, 605; Folger ms V.a.415, ff. 45–47v.

126. Rollock, *Certaine Sermons*, sig. A4v ('The body that is hot is distempered, but the body which is altogether cold is dead), and 13, 15, 51 (earthly life a 'fairy home', glitter without substance).

127. Folger ms V.a.415, ff. 39v–40, 55v–58; SAU ms Hay Fleming Box 53, it. ii, pp. 55–64, 21–34 from the back.

128. NLS ms Wod. Qu. LXXXIV, f. 3, with bits of the conjugation repeated again four times, concluding, 'we have sinned, we have sinned, we have sinned. But who has sinned? We have.'

Together with lively language – the glue holding the lists together – such ploys made for a lesson that could be repeated to the master of the household on Sunday evening and be used to jog the memory at catechetical examinations.

* * *

The problem with placing so much emphasis on the sermon was finding enough preachers to offer them. A 1574 account records 289 ministers placed in 988 parishes, although all but 10 per cent of Lowland parishes had either a minister or a reader by then; even so, in 1596 over four hundred churches were 'destitute of a minister of the word', according to contemporary estimates.[129] The 1569 General Assembly heard that Falkirk, with six hundred souls, 'never heard the word twice preached . . . since the Reformation'. Davidson waxed poetic over the problem of 'four parische kirkis to àne preicheir/ Quhairas, ane only kirk wald craif/ Four preichours rather for to haif.'[130] The new seminaries would eventually produce a supply of properly trained preachers, with all Lowland parishes supplied by 1620, mostly with university-trained preachers.[131] In the meantime, though, even those friars or priests-turned-protestants willing to

129. NLS ms Wod. Oct VII, f. 31; 'Register of Ministers . . . from the Book of the Assignation of Stipends, 1574' in *Wodrow Miscellany*, 1:326; John Knox, *Works*, ed. D. Laing (Edinburgh, 1846–64), 2:207. Typical of numerous petitions from parishes lacking ministers is CH2/171/1, f. 58 (Raglen, 1595); even relatively well-served Fife had shortages: CH2/472/1, f. 138 (1593 complaint from Kinghorn). For the general problem of supplying parishes with preachers, see Kirk, *Patterns*, 96–153, reporting the 'remarkable accomplishment' of 240 ministers planted by the end of 1561 (p. 130); and Michael Lynch, 'Preaching to the Converted?' in *The Renaissance in Scotland*, ed. A. MacDonald, Lynch and Ian Cowan (Leiden, 1994), 307–14.

130. *BUK* 1:163; 'Ane Dialog or Mutuall Talking Betuix a Clerk and ane Courteour' in Rogers, *Three Scottish Reformers*, 53–80, quotation at 53.

131. Foster, 132; for Highland achievements, Kirk, *Patterns*, 449–87, esp. 462, 487. By the latter part of the seventeenth century, Morer reported that every Scottish parish had a preacher, and 'in their larger towns every church hath two preachers, for the ease of each other' (p. 50). On the new seminaries, see D. Stevenson, *King's College, Aberdeen, 1560–1641: From Protestant Reformation to Covenanting Revolution* (Aberdeen, 1990), 61–93; G.D. Henderson, *The Founding of Marischal College, Aberdeen* (Aberdeen, 1947); J. Durkan and J. Kirk, *The University of Glasgow 1451–1577* (Glasgow, 1977); R.G. Cant, 'The New Foundation of 1579 in Historical Perspective', *St John's House Papers* 2, St Andrews, 1979; J.K. Cameron, 'The Refoundation of the University in 1579', *The Alumnus Chronicle of the University of St Andrews* 71 (1980), 3–10; James Kirk, '"Melvillian" Reform in the Scottish Universities' in *The Renaissance in Scotland*, ed. A.A. MacDonald, M. Lynch and I. Cowan (Leiden, 1994), 276–300'; and on Edinburgh, Lynch, 'Origins'. Two more new universities were planned, at Orkney and Fraserburgh, but proved abortive.

supply the new church were often ill-equipped to meet the Reformation's demand for preaching; nor was it entirely clear to what extent some had actually renounced their popery.[132] Progress during the intervening period, moreover, appears to have been uneven.[133] Lay patrons often interfered with appointments.[134] Ministers who had effectively retired declined to demit (resign) their charges in favour of younger men, though presbyters made truly heroic efforts to persuade them.[135] Stipends were often too small to support ministers with families, and ministers were expected to go cap in hand to their wealthy parishioners to finance the building of a manse or a cost-of-living rise.[136] Even where promised salaries were adequate, ministers' pay was often in arrears. Patrick Blair found ministers

132. *SAKS* 1:11–16. Before the Reformation there had been about three thousand clerics, but this number included monks, nuns, friars, various cathedral officials, canon lawyers, vicars choral and of course colleges of priests who occupied themselves saying masses for the dead. In other words, many, perhaps most, were not involved in parish ministry: Kirk, *Patterns*, xvii–xviii; Donaldson, *Scottish Church History*, 71–85. McKay, 85, finds that nine hundred parish benefices had been appropriated before the Reformation, often by cathedrals or monasteries.

133. Lynch, 'Preaching', 307–14, questioning Kirk's rather more optimistic view. See also Cowan, *Scottish Reformation*, 159–81.

134. CH2/299/2, f. 54 (frustrating meetings of Perth presbyters with the lady of Pitcur over her opposition to Andro Forrester for the kirk of Collace); CH2/198/1, f. 17v (Jedburgh presbytery dealing with lairds demanding more say in the process); CH2/185/2, ff. 17–17v (Haddington's similar problems).

135. CH2/327/1 (Lastudden kirk, Selkirk presbytery); ML CH2/171/1, f. 65; CH2/271/1, f. 3 (Moray synod's efforts to persuade pluralists and absentees to demit, e.g., in Kincharden, where Patrick Grant finally agreed to demit with 100 marks); CH2/185/2, ff. 14–17v (Haddington presbytery).

136. SAU CH2/819/1, f. 22, records efforts to secure more income for the Kingsbarns minister, for instance. The Glasgow presbytery in 1596 found two ministers who 'through poverty keeps not the days of presbytery', though they admitted that of their fifteen kirks most were 'well provided in stipend': ML CH2/171/1, f. 65. In St Andrews John Authinleck left for lack of sustenance, and only from 1593 were there two ministers for the parish (*SAKS* lxv). On ministerial stipends, Gordon Donaldson's *Accounts of the Collectors of Thirds of Benefices 1567–1572*, Edinburgh, 1949; *The Scottish Reformation* (Cambridge, 1960), 63–64, 93–95; and *Scottish Church History*, 11–89; also W.R. Foster, 'A Constant Platt Achieved: Provision for the Ministry 1600–1638' in *Reformation and Revolution*, ed. Duncan Shaw (Edinburgh, 1967), 124–40; *RPC* (2nd ser.) 1:cvii–clxxvi (for pre-1600 stipends); Foster, *The Church before the Covenants*, 156–72 (for post-1600 figures). The *Register of Ministers, Exhorters and Readers, and of their Stipends* (Edinburgh, 1830), suggests a general range for ministers of £40–£120 in the 1560s and 1570s, plus payments in kind, mostly of grains. Foster finds the post-1600 range within St Andrews presbytery from 91–1,822 merks per year, with most at or over the 500-merk minimum defined as satisfactory. Paisley's range was 210–1,990 merks, all but two (of thirteen) below 500. All eleven Deer ministers were below 500 merks. By 1627, the *Reports on the State of*

with six to twelve months' salary due 'compelled for very want a great many of them to lay to pledge the best goods they have for relieving of their families'. Even in the vigorously Reformed burgh of Perth, where the town council paid two ministers' stipends, the council's records are full of petitions by John Malcolm and William Cowper for overdue payments for victual, housemail (rent money) and coals, or for augmentation to meet expenses in a time of inflation.[137]

Other problems were peculiar to Highland parishes. Language presented a barrier, the Synod of Moray finding, for instance, that Patrick Dunbar was 'unfruitful' as minister of Dorr 'through want of the [Gaelic] language'. The intolerance of Inverness presbyters from the south cannot have helped; they surely alienated the Gaelic preachers among them when they formally complained about 'brethren [who] haunts to the presbytery with uncomely habits such as bonnets and plaids'.[138] It was difficult to get the linguistic feature of Highland culture without its costume. Efforts to fill the numerous vacant parishes by appointing a single man to two only brought the quite legitimate protests that the Highland kirks were too far apart for pluralism to serve. In the Isles, a single minister served churches on clusters of neighbouring islands that might be separated, as in Nesting parish in Zetland, by 'four miles of dangerous sea', constantly threatened by 'storm of weather'. And here, as everywhere, presbyteries and synods heard complaints about inadequate stipends and lack of glebe or manse.[139]

Certain Parishes suggests that 500 merks was still roughly the norm. Morer thought in the 1680s that 'few exceed £100 sterling [English], as few below £20', so that there was greater parity of ministers than in his native England (p. 50). See also Kirk's edition of *The Books of Assumption of the Thirds of Benefices: Scottish Ecclesiastical Rentals at the Reformation* (Oxford, 1995).

137. LPL ms 3471, f. 45v (1589); PL ms B59/16/1, ff. 8v, 18v, 22, 21v, 37v–38, 96; ms B59/28/7 (Row's stipend). After a 1604 visit from Cowper, the king granted the burgh the teinds (tithes), parsonage and vicarage of Perth to pay him with (B59/16/1, ff. 95v–96); by 1615 the town had acquired the rents of the Charterhouse, Blackfriars and Whitefriars and so added a third minister the next year: B59/28/15 and 17. See also Zachary Boyd's complaints to the archbishop of Glasgow about his stipend, 'the meanest of all the presbytery considering in what a dear place I dwell' and the fact that he served more than a thousand communicants (CH8/87/56, 1637); and Alexander Inglis's 1623 complaint to the bishop of Ross about his seriously overdue stipend (CH8/69).

138. CH2/271/1, f. 7. See also CH2/271/1, f. 19 (the minister of Alvie, Inverness, also without 'Irish language'); *Fasti* 7:82 (1623 translation of a Scots-speaking minister from Creich to Kilmalie for 'want of the Irish tongue'. The 1624 Moray synod visitors (f. 7) found that the Inverness presbytery had only one sermon in thirteen assemblies.

139. *1627 Reports*, 224–26 (the Nesting minister's stipend reported as being 'in some years more, and in some less'); CH2/271/1, ff. 11, 13, 15, 19.

As a result, even in the 'great burgh' of Perth there was only one minister until 1595, when William Cowper came to assist John Malcolm; Glasgow only had one minister until 1587, and the 'parish of Glasgow without the town' lacked its own minister until 1597; and Kirkcaldy only came up with a stipend for a second minister (contributed half by the town, half by local lairds and lords) in 1614.[140] Robert Wilkie told his presbytery that St Andrews 'for bounds and people . . . might well be four parishes', but there simply were not four stipends available.[141] In 1600 John Couper, one of the ministers of Glasgow, asked to no avail that the town be divided into parishes for better pastoral care, discipline and audible preaching. The next year the brethren finally had to act when his colleague John Ball told them that he no longer had the strength to preach twice on Sunday. Even so, finances remained problematic.[142]

★ ★ ★

The same problem arose with the Reformers' second proposed means to achieve a culture of the word in Scotland – the provision of a school in every parish, as 'necessary instruments to come to the true meaning and sense of the will of God revealed in his Word'.[143] They called for 'every several kirk' to 'have one schoolmaster . . . able to teach grammar and the Latin tongue if the town be of any reputation'. The *First Book of Discipline* insisted that parents 'bring up their children in learning', and that notable towns build on the foundation of schools by establishing colleges of arts, with provision for poor boys, 'in special those that come from landward'. The benefits for kirk and commonwealth would be a population educated

140. *Book of Perth*, 59; NLS ms 2782, ff. 14–14v (Glasgow had four ministers by 1595); CH2/636/34, ff. 3 (the stipend in Kirkcaldy 800 merks), 100 (the minister's 1628 request for a 'fellow helper'). All were at these dates single-parish burghs. Kirkcaldy's population was perhaps a thousand, but Perth by the turn of the century may have had five thousand people. Glasgow was smaller in the sixteenth century, but grew rapidly thereafter; a contemporary estimate in 1636 was ten thousand (Brereton, in *Early Travellers*, 150).

141. SAU unnumbered ms St Andrews Presbytery minutes, n.p., 8 January 1590, Wilkie complaining that his burden, 'insupportable to any one man', the parish being three or four miles in breadth, had brought him to 'such infirmities as he may no longer bear it out without the loss of himself'. In 1592 the Edinburgh ministers began a long struggle to divide their town into eight parishes, given the 'ignorance for lack of teaching' that they found rife, 'our pastors, being so few in number', unable to 'discharge a pastoral duty in such a populous city, where vice so much aboundeth': Robert Bruce, *Sermons*, ed. William Cunningham (Edinburgh, 1843), 32.

142. NLS ms 2782, f. 14v.

143. *BUK* 2:723. The Privy Council ordered every parish to have an English school to avoid the 'barbarity' of Gaelic: NLS ms Adv. 29.2.8, ff. 195–97.

in virtue and a pool of future ministers to be trained in the universities. In Davidson's poetic version, schools will 'mak our Preichouris multiplie', but 'quhen the scullis ar not provydit/ How can the kirk be bot misgydit?' Properly schooled children, moreover, could provide 'great instruction to the aged' as they publicly performed their catechism.[144] The Innerwick elders extended the last benefit by ordering every family 'where none can read . . . to train up their children in reading' so that the young could open the scriptures to their elders. They risked reversing the age hierarchy in the family for the sake of the word.[145]

A remarkable number of parishes give evidence in their session books of having met the requirements for schools, or at least of making impressive efforts to do so. Indeed, historians may well have taken too seriously clerical jeremiads about dearth of schools. We need to remember that complaint was a usual route to improvement, and one much loved by early modern reformers of all sorts. It does not necessarily reflect reality. In fact, Scottish parishes did establish schools, paying masters with a combination of kirk funds, contributions from local heritors or town councils, and fees from children whose families were able to pay.[146] A recent count of Lowland schools established before the 1633 parliamentary act made parish schools compulsory reaches 405. These were distributed densely in the Lowlands and along the east coast, but there was a not insignificant number scattered in the Highlands, and five have been identified in Orkney and the Shetlands, five more in the western isles.[147] Some of these were reformed medieval establishments, but such schools, influenced by

144. 'Ane Dialog', in Rogers, *Three Scottish Reformers*, 63–64; *First Book*, 131–33, recommending a curriculum that included the catechism, Latin grammar, 'the arts of philosophy and the tongues, and . . . that study in which they intend chiefly to travail for the profit of the commonwealth'.

145. CH2/1463/1, f. 10v (1649). In this parish the elders visited every family monthly to see that this order was obeyed. The Moray synod in 1639 likewise urged parents to 'put their children to school, even those of the meanest sort, til the rest of the children learn the catechism and be able to practise the family exercise': CH2/271/1, f. 128.

146. CH2/266/1, f. 12v; CH2/185/2, f. 23; CH2/390/1, f. 1; NLS ms 2782, f. 66; CH2/359/1, f. 3v; CH2/636/34, ff. 24, 25; CH2/191/1, ff. 15, 22, 23v, 46v; CH2/141/1, ff. 10, 23v (indicating Trinity College kirk's support for the French School as well); CH2/448/2, p. 40; CH2/716/2, f. 49; CH2/276/1, f. 10; SAU CH2/624/2, pp. 145, 177, 191; SAU CH2/624/3, pp. 12, 21; CH2/471/1, f. 5 (1615, Lasswade listing each of the heritors who 'promised faithfully yearly' contributions for the schoolmaster).

147. *Atlas of Scottish History to 1707*, ed. Peter G.B. McNeill and Hector L. MacQueen (Edinburgh, 1996), 437–49; 'Acts of Parliament and of the Privy Council of Scotland, Relative to the Establishing and Maintaining of Schools' in *Miscellany of the Maitland Club* (Edinburgh, 1840), 10–26.

humanism and the new interest in pedagogy, were already expanding before the Reformation, creating a momentum that protestants could and apparently did exploit to their own ends.[148] The *First Book of Discipline* even proved unduly short-sighted in setting lower standards for the Highlands, 'where the people convene to doctrine but once in the week'. Its authors thought that it would have to suffice there for reader or minister to instruct children 'in the first rudiments and especially in the catechism', but in fact by the early seventeenth century Highland presbyteries were demanding that every parish establish a proper school. Presbytery visitors reprimanded Mortlach's minister for his parish's lack of a schoolmaster – an office they called 'not only expedient, but also most necessary'. They ordered him to secure one straightaway.[149] Elders and ministers visited schools, and examined teachers and pupils to ensure correct doctrine and effective teaching.[150] They contributed substantially to the cost of educating poor children, both at the local level and, in cases where children showed academic ability, at the level of college and university.[151]

Lest we underestimate educational expansion and concomitant literacy rates, moreover, it is vital to remember that the number of schools we find approved in session books was by no means the actual total. The

148. John Durkan, 'Education in the Century of the Reformation' in *Essays on the Scottish Reformation 1513–1625*, ed. David McRoberts (Glasgow, 1962) and 'Education: The Laying of Fresh Foundations' in *Humanism in Renaissance Scotland*, ed. J. MacQueen (Edinburgh, 1990), 123–60; Cowan, *Scottish Reformation*, 13–14; McRoberts, ed., *The Medieval Church of St Andrews* (Glasgow, 1976), 63–120.

149. *First Book*, 129–30; cf. CH2/529/1, f. 82v.

150. Session visitations of the Perth grammar school could be quite rigorous: in 1631 the doctor conducted 'examination of the bairns in the highest class upon their lessons and authors' for the visitors, working his way down through the three classes beneath them, who were 'found to answer distinctly and were approved of the ministers and so many of council and elders who were grammarians and scholars'. The minister, John Malcolm, then gave the highest two classes a 'theme in English' to translate into Latin, judging their performance impressive for 'their young years': CH2/521/8/1, f. 109v, and among earlier visitation reports, CH2/521/3, p. 116 (1599). This long-established grammar school had a pre-Reformation tradition of visitation by council and clergy; it was also a school where the boys seem to have learned of the Reformation before the fact, since in 1559 they reportedly hissed and threw their stools at a visiting friar recounting stories of saints and miracles (*Book of Perth*, 101). See also NLS ms 2782, f. 66.

151. *SAKS* 2:845; CH2/716/1, f. 2v (payment of 30s each six months to Agnes Peirs for lodging a landward orphan whom the session 'hold at the school', 1598); Thoms, *Kirk of Brechin*, 39 (£1 6s 8d quarterly to a widow 'to put a bairn to the school'); SAU CH2/624/2, p. 192. For bursaries (maintenance of students) by sessions at the 'New College of St Andrews' pursuant to a Fife provincial assembly order, ranging from 2 merks to £6, see SAU CH2/Crail/1, f. 4; SAU CH2/210/1, f. 7v; CH2/523/1, ff. 8v, 12v.

minutes very often include complaint by schoolmasters that rival teachers, women as well as men, ran unlicensed schools in the area, drawing their students away.[152] Sometimes the competition from 'adventure schools' was fed by dissatisfaction with the official school, as when Perth's master Patrick Johnston found his pupils flocking to William Lamb's rival establishment because they were apparently less likely to be beaten there. Johnston protested that he had 'used but gentle correction against those for their faults which have departed from his school' to 'the said William, where they may be free of correction and necessary instruction'. Unfortunately for the children, the session agreed.[153] Sessions generally demanded such schools to be disbanded, but in many towns their instructions had to be repeated often enough to suggest that multiple schools remained the order of the day, and that a large portion of the population may well have been educated by teachers not approved by kirk or town, but who were nonetheless probably quite able to teach reading.[154] Finally, sessions did discipline parents who neglected to send their children to school. Tyninghame's elders, responding to a 1615 complaint from the schoolmaster, ordered parents who had 'abstracted their bairnes' from school for farm labour to send them back, 'seeing the harvest was past and the corns all in'. And in Highland as well as Lowland towns, they included parents 'even . . . of the meanest sort' in their orders.[155]

152. To be fair, we should remember that a parish could only afford to hire a schoolmaster by ensuring that he would have enough students to pay the fees that comprised a portion of his stipend. Thus, when Anstruther Wester hired a new schoolmaster in 1627, they disbanded pre-existing 'private schools' in the town and ordered 'the whole bairns within this burgh who are able to learn [to] pass to the school with all diligence and that no person nor woman keep any private school within this burgh in time hereafter': SAU CH2/624/3, p. 12. The new master was to ensure 'the upbringing of the youth in literature and manners', which 'cannot be done without a school'.

153. CH2/521/7, p. 282. Lamb's school had actually been licensed, but on condition that he would not 'prejudice the grammar school' and only recruit children for whom there was no room in Johnston's school.

154. CH2/521/7, p. 282 (the council underpinned the kirk's campaign: PL ms B59/16/1, f. 7); CH2/198/1, ff. 7–7v, 9v (rival schools to those of Jedburgh, Godmary and Hawick). The Longside session also treated tutors hired by well-off parents as rivals to the official schoolmaster, since the latter suffered loss of income with each child who left his school: CH2/699/1, f. 14, complaint about the departure of a laird's children, leaving only 'two or three in the school, not enough to entertain' the master, Robert Martin. When the school had been established, the session announced that 'all [are] desired to send their bairns thereto' (f. 10).

155. CH2/359/1, f. 3v; CH2/271/1, f. 128. A 1496 statute ordered all barons and substantial proprietors to send their eldest sons to grammar schools from age eight or nine until they had 'perfect Latin', then on to an arts course (*APS* 2:238) so that

Schools were provided for girls as well as boys, and though presumably they stopped short of teaching Latin grammar, literacy and the catechism do seem to have been on offer – necessarily so, since young boys often attended predominantly girls' schools as well and had to be prepared for their more advanced study later. Many of these were what would be called in England 'dame schools', taught by women.[156] We hear about them only in passing in the session minutes of many parishes, generally when male schoolmasters complained about competition from them. Historians must be grateful for such document-producing rivalry. We would know nothing about Elspeth Cuthbert's school in Markinch if the town's schoolmaster had not reported to the session that she 'instructs boys among her lasses to his prejudice'; the session made her send the boys to his school, but her own establishment continued to serve girls. In Aberdeen, James Tod, teacher of an English school, found himself threatened by 'a multitude of schools taken up by sundry women in this town having doctors [assistant teachers] to teach the bairns both lads and lasses', as well as by several men with unlicensed schools. In addition to Tod's school, 'for learning bairns to read and write', there was also a licensed 'writing school held by John Nicalson'; Tod was convinced that these two should suffice, since lasses had no need for writing as well as reading. The session agreed and disbanded the schools of Margaret Bairnes, Marion Cheyne, Ammas Bechame, Margaret Lyndsay 'and all others' – suggesting that quite a large number of dame schools had operated in the town.[157] A Newbattle schoolmistress apparently teaching children to write as well as read likewise had her school disbanded in 1618 upon complaint from the schoolmaster that he was losing pupils. The Leith session in April of 1598 allowed Elspeth Morton's unlicensed school to finish the school year at Whitsun, but afterwards the session disbanded 'all schools except James Hayes' and Daniel Blacklaw's' – hinting that Morton's was not the only rival school in town. The elders' concern was both with there being insufficient students to sustain the official masters, and with the qualifications of teachers, who were licensed only upon examination. In any case, one of the two official schools, James Hay's, was designated 'for lasses'. Their 1598 efforts, moreover, proved ineffective: three years later they had to

they would learn to administer justice in their jurisdictions upon adulthood. The protestant orders are obviously much more inclusive, aiming to encompass the whole society in a culture of the word.

156. A few of these may have been heirs of pre-Reformation nuns' schools: Durkan, 'Education', 155–56.

157. CH2/258/1, n.f., 3 February 1644; CH2/448/2, p. 40. Elgin likewise prohibited the schools of Christian Gordon and Jonet Abernethie and her daughter in 1628: CH2/145/4, f. 148v.

order 'by open proclamation and strike of drum that no inhabitant within this town send their bairns to any other school, but all the lads to Mr Thomas Provan and all the lasses to James Hay from this time forth, and all other schools . . . be discharged.' A few years after that, we find them ordering 'Isobel Barclay and Isobel Kennedy to discharge their schools altogether if they teach a manchild past six years of age', though the women were permitted to teach girls and young boys.[158]

What such fortuitous references tell us is that our count of schools for girls is doubtless much too low. This in turn suggests that female literacy may have been much higher than we thought. Even though few women managed to sign their parishes' confessions of faith with their own hand, rather than by mark or 'with her hand on the pen' of a notary, we know that judgment of literacy by ability to write is fraught, since girls were, like boys, taught to read first, and only later to write, if at all. (William Cowper, for instance, reports that at age eight he could read but not write.)[159] The 355 (of 358) women who relied on a notary to sign for them Kinghorn's confession in 1581 may well have been able to read their Bibles; so might the 275 (of 338) men who relied on the notary or made a mark, or the 180 (of 222) men who signed the Covenant in Dundonald by proxy.[160] And even granting high illiteracy rates for women, the fact that they regularly swore or signed confessions or the Covenant, and that they were examined as men were on their knowledge of the faith, indicates that they were expected to have absorbed substantial amounts of information from sermons, catechism in school or kirk, or (another underestimated means) being read to by family members.[161] Literacy was simply not necessary to achieve a culture of the word. It was a boon, and it remained a goal of the reformers; but expanded literacy by the seventeenth century was a result, not a prerequisite, of protestantism.[162]

Schools certainly accomplished something for the protestant cause; however, it will not do to overstress their impact. Just as many parishes

158. CH2/276/1, f. 20 (1618); CH2/716/1, ff. 2 (1598), 10 (1601); CH2/716/2, f. 52 (1610).
159. Cowper, 3; Cressy, *Literacy*, chs 2–3.
160. CH2/472/1, ff. 125–35v; *Dundonald*, xiii. In Kinghorn, sixty-three men and three women signed; an additional eleven signatures are not sufficiently legible to determine gender. There are 820 names in all, 338 men, 358 women, the rest not clear as to forename for gender. Houston, *Scottish Literacy*, 84, counts 414 women in the Kinghorn document and claims that all were illiterate, but there are women's signatures on ff. 124, 127v and 132.
161. CH2/299/1, p. 143.
162. This is not to say protestantism was the sole or even most important cause, availability of printed material and economic advantages being key factors (Cressy, *Literacy*, *passim*).

had trouble attracting and supporting ministers, so also schoolmasters were for many a luxury too dear to maintain. Of the forty-nine extant parish reports responding to a royal commission on the state of the parishes in 1627, only nine could boast of having schools; most simply reported 'great necessity' but 'no maintenance'. Saltoun's and Pencaitland's schools in Haddington presbytery were barely 'sustained by labourers of the ground'; Kirknewton's was 'likely to dissolve the next term for want of maintenance'; and Killin and Strafillan in Perthshire and Cockpen in Edinburgh presbytery reported that they had established schools, but 'for fault of maintenance' they had had to be abandoned.[163]

Sessions' trouble with raising the money to pay teachers' stipends should not be taken to mean that schoolmasters were well remunerated. Except in significant burgh parishes with long-established schools, they generally had to combine other jobs (kirk officer, clerk, reader, precentor) with teaching in order to make ends meet. Payment for teaching alone ranged widely. At the upper end of the scale, in the 1570s Aberdeen, Perth, Stirling and Inverness paid schoolmasters in the range of £26–£33 annually; Cupar managed £40, plus £13 for a doctor. Some parishes added room and board, though this might entail teachers moving regularly from one household to another. Well-off parishes even managed significant cost-of-living increases: Aberdeen's 1574 £33 6s 4d had risen to £133 6s 8d by 1633; Inverness's 1576 £26 13s 4d was £80 by 1628. By 1626 St Andrews' schoolmaster was getting more than £166 yearly.[164] In the middle range, Dysart's master did well in the 1610s with 40 merks annually, as did Mid-Calder's with £20 plus 13s 4d from each child. Here, each parishioner paid an allotted portion of the £20 as he collected his communion token – a graphic demonstration of the connection between the religious knowledge required for the sacrament and the kirk's responsibility for schools, as well as an effective means of putting pressure on proprietors to pay the school tax.[165] These parishes, too, managed rises over time: Kinghorn, which began with a modest £13 6s 8d for a schoolmaster/reader

163. *1627 Reports*, 46, 84, 127, 132, 180. Logie kept an English school, but its grammar [Latin] school was 'decayed' for want of funds (p. 202). Ferryport-on-Craig managed to re-establish a school in 1644, 'very necessary for . . . the good of the kirk . . . that it dissolve not again': SAU CH2/150/1, f. 6.

164. 'Extracts from the Accounts of the Common Good of Various Burghs in Scotland, Relative to Payments for Schools and Schoolmasters . . . 1557–1634' in *Maitland Club Miscellany*, 2:39–50; CH2/521/4, p. 63 (£80 and room and board in Perth by 1605).

165. CH2/390/1, f. 1; CH2/266/1, f. 12v. Newbattle's doctor received the handsome quarterly stipend of £4 from the kirk and 4s from each pupil in 1617 (CH2/276/1, f. 10).

combination in 1575, had brought the stipend to £49 by 1633.[166] At the lower and perhaps more widely representative end of the scale, though, Kirkcaldy's schoolmaster made do with just 'the doctor's meat' and 16s from the parish each quarter, 4s of which went to his assistant, plus modest fees from those students who were able to pay. Ellon's received only board from the parish and a 13s 4d quarterly fee from each pupil, and he had to ask the session to put pressure on 'sundry who subscribed for his victual' but failed to come through.[167] Alexander Gordon in Inveravon received 20 merks annually from the parish and the remainder of his pay 'in victual'; he depended heavily on his fees as kirk officer because of 'not thankful payment' by the heritors. He eventually left for lack of sustenance, and was succeeded by George Chalmer, who taught the children in his own chamber for lack of a school building and went from door to door for his 'school victual, yet none would answer him'.[168] No wonder such parishes had difficulty retaining schoolmasters. Problems with low stipends and unreliable payment also help to explain why the quality of teaching was not all that one might have hoped. Anstruther Wester's session echoed many others in having repeatedly to exhort the schoolmaster to 'attend upon the school more diligently [and] upon the instructing of the youth . . . more carefully and painfully than he has done the year bygone.' They sacked Simon Smyth in 1615, and although his successor, John Mores, passed his six-month probation, by 1619 he, too, was found 'giving evil attendance on the school so that the bairns are thought to profit very little'.[169] The best of the schoolmasters, like the most able readers and exhorters, used the job as a stepping stone to ordained ministry.[170]

166. 'Common Good', 46. Forfar's 1577 £8 had likewise grown to £40 plus lodging by 1622 (p. 44).
167. CH2/636/34, f. 24 (George Buchanan's stipend in 1619, plus victual); George Matheson of Ellon's problems are recounted in CH2/147/1, ff. 3–3v; cf. CH2/146/1 (Ellon presbytery), n.f., 18 September 1605, 19 June 1616, 26 March 1617, 27 December 1620. Ellon had a school by 1605, but in 1616 it dissolved when 'parishioners and heritors were unwilling to contribute'. They placed a new master by 1620.
168. CH2/191/1, ff. 15, 22, 23v, 46v (1634–38). A condition of Gordon's coming as first schoolmaster was that the parish would 'big [build] a school and house to him', but they reneged. The landed subscribers to Innerwick's school also proved unreliable (CH2/1463/1, ff. 8, 11). The schoolmaster at Rhynie, John Duncan, tried moonlighting as an unlicensed preacher in Keith, but was dismissed by the presbytery: CH2/271/1, f. 18 (1626). Only in 1633 did parliament give bishops the authority to levy taxes for schools even without consent of the heritors, though they were to request voluntary contribution first: *APS* 5:21–22; *RPC* 10:671–73.
169. SAU CH2/624/2, pp. 145, 17, 191. Mores was gone by 1626, succeeded by David Mitchell, who agreed to a four-year contract: SAU CH2/624/3, pp. 21–22.
170. As in the case of the schoolmaster of Montrose in 1571: James Melville, *Diary, 1556–1601*, ed. G. Kinloch (Edinburgh, 1829), 23.

* * *

Difficulties with the supply of ministers and schools did not leave the kirk bereft of the word, however, even in the early generations of protestantism and in parishes far from the populous and better-supplied Lowlands. If the Reformation 'worked' in great measure because of the preaching of the word at its centre, then undeniably it achieved its ends at a slower pace where there was less preaching – or where, as in Highland parishes, the preaching was in a language not understood by a large portion of the population. But the difference is in speed of cultural change, not in its substance or means. A combination of creative use of resources, an eye to recruitment and exploitation of auxiliary personnel in the form of readers in time addressed the problem. The first two points can be quickly made. First, parishes in undersupplied presbyteries shared ministers. Rural session books are replete with explanations that there was 'no sermon, reading only the last sabbath' because the minister was supplying a sermon in a neighbouring parish. This was the case in rural Lowland as well as Highland parishes. Tyninghame, for instance, had to forgo afternoon sermons on 12 and 19 May 1616 because their minister was preaching communion sermons in Dunbar and Preston on those days; Monkton in Ayrshire frequently cancelled Sunday afternoon session meetings so that the minister could preach in neighbouring parishes; and Inveravon regularly shared its minister with the little kirk of Skierdustane.[171] The parish of Udny, with a session but no minister in the 1590s, borrowed a neighbouring minister for the occasional sermon and to help with discipline.[172]

Second, one job of rural elders was to observe the local boys to determine which of them might supply a future ministry for the locality. Boys who showed a religious bent and some intellectual capacity were often sent at session expense to the nearest town school, in hopes that they would eventually go on to university and to ministry.[173] Whether they would actually return to their parish of origin was of course uncertain, but sessions did keep their eyes on the pool of potential ministers for underserved areas.

Finally, and perhaps most importantly, we must take seriously the possibility that, if the reformers were right, even if there were no sermon,

171. CH2/359/1, ff. 5v, 6; AAC CH2/809/1, ff. 26, 30v, 31 (1610s–early 1620s); CH2/191/1, f. 49 ('no preaching but prayers and reading' when the Inveravon minister was on loan). See also SAU CH2/210/1, f. 15v; New Register House ms OPR 310/1 (Monifieth, Murroes and Barry sharing a minister in the 1560s).

172. *APS* 4:157; CH2/146/1 (Ellon presbytery), ff. 15, 19v–20, 27v, 36v–38v (1598–99). The parish had no minister until 1604 (ff. 109–09v, 115–16).

173. E.g., CH2/716/1, f. 2v; *SAKS* 2:845; CH2/523/1, f. 12v; SAU CH2/624/2, p. 192.

the Bible read aloud in the vernacular could serve to convince and convert. And whether clergy were present or not, the Bible was certainly read publicly and at length in post-Reformation Scottish parishes, twice every sabbath and in towns on weekdays as well. Literate and illiterate alike would have had enough exposure to the scriptures from being read to in the kirk to make the dearth of schools a much less pressing problem.

The office of reader was a signally important one for the religion of the word.[174] Often doubling as schoolmaster, precentor and clerk of session as well, the reader was essential 'for comforting of the people by the reading of holy scripture every sabbath before sermon'.[175] He was licensed by the presbytery, and even schoolmasters who presumed to read without licence found themselves rebuked for having no 'lawful calling' to this important task.[176] At a reader's installation, the session or town council presented him with the emblems of his office – in fact, the tools of his trade, a Bible and a psalter – and he entered the reader's 'desk'.[177] This was situated immediately before the pulpit (see plate 4), beneath it but still elevated – a figuration of the relative importance of reading and preaching. Elevation served the practical function of aiding audition, but it also displayed significance, as did the locked wicket by which the reader entered his desk as the preacher entered the pulpit. This was space set apart for authority.

In urban parishes the reader might provide prayers and scripture once or even twice a day on weekdays as well as twice on Sundays. The *First Book of Discipline* required 'great towns' to offer daily reading and 'notable towns' to offer it one day besides Sunday; session minutes show that the order was taken seriously. Glasgow ordered in 1596 'that all servants be at morning prayers'; Perth from 1591 had bells rung 'collecting the people' to Saturday morning reading; and Dalkeith required the poor to attend daily or lose their alms. In modest-sized parishes from the Lothian port town of Leith to the Orkney cathedral town of Kirkwall – not just in the

174. Lynch, 'Preaching', 310, calls readers the 'unsung footsoldiers of the kirk' and notes that they comprised 70 per cent of the parish ministry in 1574 outside of Argyll.
175. CH2/264/1, f. 14; cf. *First Book*, 180, judging readers 'profitable but not merely necessary'. For other examples of combined offices, CH2/32/1, f. 33 (clerk, reader and schoolmaster in Belhelvie); CH2/359/1, f. 2 (schoolmaster and reader in Tyninghame); CH2/521/6, f. 87 and CH2/521/7, p. 281 (reader, songschoolmaster and precentor in Perth); CH2/266/1, f. 5v (Mid-Calder clerk and reader); CH2/716/2, f. 49 (songschoolmaster and reader in Leith). Reading of the scriptures, confession, and singing of psalms always preceded Sunday sermons: Cowper, 680, 682.
176. As was the schoolmaster in Restalrig in 1607, CH2/716/1, f. 18.
177. *Chronicle of Perth: A Register of Remarkable Occurrences*, ed. James Maidment (Edinburgh, 1831), 35.

'great burghs' – readers provided morning and evening prayer and reading of scriptures daily.[178] They were clearly understood to be required during a minister's absence, Mid-Calder appointing one in 1607 specifically 'for reading the holy scripture openly in the kirk before preaching and other necessary times in absence of the minister'.[179] He generally read for at least a half-hour before each Sunday sermon, from the second to the third bell summoning people to the kirk, though sometimes reading began at the first bell.[180] While the whole parish would not have been present for the full hour, penalties for coming late to the sermon were such that most would have heard at least some portion of the final half-hour of reading. Scottish reformers having firmly rejected the lectionary, whole books of the Bible were read from beginning to end, 'for this skipping . . . from place to place of scripture, be it in reading or be it in preaching, we judge not so profitable to edify the kirk as the continual following of one text.'[181] In addition, readers generally said the creed and the ten commandments in the course of their pre-sermon reading, and the Lord's Prayer afterwards, aiding the catechetical efforts offered on other occasions.[182] And just as inattentiveness during or disruption of the sermon was vigorously punished by the elders, so misbehaviour in time of reading brought fines, public admonition and even warding.[183]

Readers' stipends varied considerably, those in urban parishes and those doubling as schoolmasters, precentors and kirk officers obviously being best off. Glasgow allotted 20 merks per quarter and a shirt and bonnet for 'him that carries up the line in the High Kirk' in the first decade of the

178. *First Book*, 180–81; NLS ms 2782, f. 33 (1619, 1622, 1630); CH2/521/2, f. 55; CH2/84/28, f. 14; CH2/716/1, f. 17; CH2/442/74, f. 10. Elgin had daily evening prayer and reading at 4pm (CH2/145/1, f. 145; CH2/145/2, ff. 7v–8, 90, 172v; CH2/145/3, f. 178. Culross, its kirk a mile from the centre of town, in 1630 set up seats in its tollbooth for Wednesday and Friday morning prayers at 8 'for the ease of the people'; and St Andrews in 1598 set up twice-daily readings: CH2/77/1, f. 1v; *SAKS* 2:829–30.
179. CH2/266/1, f 5v (1607).
180. In Glasgow's High Kirk in the 1580s, reading 'from the ringing of the bell to the minister's coming in' was interspersed with singing of psalms by William Struthers, the songschoolmaster: NLS ms 2782, f. 36v. The Lasswade reader began at the second bell (CH2/471/1, f. 3v). The reader presented 'what part of scripture he pleases or as the minister directs' (Morer, 60).
181. *First Book*, 185.
182. CH2/471/1, f. 3v; Morer, 60 (ministers also offering prayers of confession, thanksgiving, petition and benediction). For the prescribed order, see *Forme of Prayers*.
183. CH2/278/1, p. 34 (Newburn collecting 40s fines from people who during the reading 'stand without in the kirkyard talking and discanting of their worldly matters and of their profane business'); CH2/521/1, f. 83 (Perth warding disrupters of the reading, 1583).

seventeenth century. Menmuir added £24 per annum in the 1630s to the Brechin grammar schoolmaster's stipend for him to come every Sunday and 'openly read the scriptures between the second and third bell'; the heritors agreed to pay, but were often slow about it.[184] In the 1620s, Forres paid its reader £20, Burntisland £33 6s 9d, Kinghorn £53 6s 8d, and St Andrews a remarkable £100. Markinch, however, paid its reader in grain.[185] But readers, like schoolmasters, were in many cases men on their way to clerical status. With a minister's recommendation, they were examined and licensed by presbyteries to expand their reading into 'instruction and edification of the people' – William Strang's path from reader to exhorter to ordained ministry in Leith provides an example of this.[186] They ought to be regarded as apprentice preachers in many cases, and certainly, whether reading or exhorting, they conveyed at least the *sola scriptura* bit of the protestant message, together with the Calvinist providentialism embedded in the prescribed prayers.[187] At the parish level, with enforced attendance, Reformed doctrine would have been hard to avoid for ordinary people, whether or not a preaching cleric had been 'planted'.

A second important supplement to preaching for the Reformed kirk was the psalter, which by all testimony won widespread approval from congregations unused to singing in church before the Reformation. The Scots' metrical psalter, however narrow its range of metres and tunes by comparison to its continental counterparts, however bereft of 'youthful or heathenish liberty or . . . elegancies and pleasant[ness] of profane poetic authors' (as one defender put it), had the advantage of being quickly learned.[188] The simplicity of the tunes is evident from a glance at the

184. NLS ms 2782, ff. 14, 37v (1594–1608); CH2/264/1, f. 14 (the reader's complaint in 1628 that only half of his stipend was forthcoming from the heritors).
185. *Extracts from the Accounts of the Common Good of Various Burghs in Scotland*, 41–49; CH2/258/1, f. 26. Perth's council paid the reader 170 merks in 1616 (PL ms B59/28/20) plus coals (often in arrears: B59/16/1, ff. 22v, 30, 37v–38, 52, 70v, 89).
186. CH2/716/1, f. 18 (1607). The Fife synod required readers to 'gain knowledge' to continue in office, hoping that eventually they could enter ordained ministry: SAU ms 30451, f. 4v; cf. *First Book*, 14.
187. *Forme of Prayers*, 30–62.
188. NLS ms Wod. Qu. LXXXIV, f. 16, or 'Reasons against the Reception of King James' Metaphrase of the Psalms, 1631' in *Bannatyne Miscellany* (Edinburgh, 1827), 1:225–50. On the music of the psalter generally, John Purser, 'Music' in *Scotland: A Concise Cultural History*, ed. Paul Scott (Edinburgh, 1993), 159–94; and *Scotland's Music* (Edinburgh, 1992), 144–47; Michael Chibbett, 'Sung Psalms in Scottish Worship' in *The Bible in Scottish Life and Literature*, ed. David Wright (Edinburgh, 1988), 143–44; and Millar Patrick, *Four Centuries of Scottish Psalmody* (London, 1949). Seven Scottish psalters were published between 1564 and 1666, with common metre tunes, most the work of Scottish composers.

printed music (see plate 7): one did not need to have the music before one to learn them. From the first generation of Reformation, with cantors lining out the psalms (singing one line at a time) for repetition by the congregation, this particular section of the scriptures could easily be learned by heart without the need for literacy.

Congregations sang psalms both before and after each sermon.[189] The singing was unaccompanied, Genevan style, on the grounds that 'dead instruments give not articulate sign of a sound *to edify the understanding* of the hearer which the lively voice of man can very well do.' The purpose of singing was to embed the word in memory. The reformers 'counted [as] ceremonial' the distraction of musical instruments, a means 'to draw that image of the Jews out of the grave again', and 'to hinder the preaching of the word'.[190] The preacher Zachary Boyd, a great proponent of psalm-singing, charged those who declined to join in with 'secret atheism': 'We often forget our book [of psalms] because we forget that God is in his church.' He nonetheless warned that 'those who in singing psalms are led away more by sound than sense [and] respect the music more than the matter, such sing to man but not to God.' The word was the point; music must serve understanding. Accordingly, when John Swentoun of Perth experimented in 1583 with harmony, also thought to distract from the sense of the words, the session ordered him to 'keep only the tenor in the psalms'.[191]

Where possible, the reader doubled as precentor, though in large towns singing in multiple churches on Sundays and weekdays was closer to a full-time job and required more than one precentor. In 1575, the frugal Edinburgh session succeeded in appointing a father and son jointly to the office. In Montrose, a laird managed in 1570 to combine charity to a poor blind man 'having a singular good voice' with service to church music by paying the school's doctor to 'teach [him] the whole psalms in metre, with the tunes thereof' so that he could line them in the kirk.[192] Sessions were always anxious to hire readers and schoolmasters with musical ability so that they could both line the psalms in church and teach schoolchildren

189. NLS ms 2782, f. 33; CH2/471/1, f. 8 (though the Lasswade clerk had some difficulty persuading the session to add a psalm after the preaching).

190. NLS ms Wod. Qu. LXXXIV, ff. 17v–18, 'A Discourse upon the Organs' (emphasis mine). The author concluded that if organs were reintroduced, next would be 'bagpipes for every congregation' – an eventuality to be avoided at all costs (f. 18). Cowper, 1090 also condemned 'dead instruments'.

191. Boyd, *Balme*, 246–47; CH2/521/1, f. 94. In the sixteenth century, the melody was carried in the tenor line.

192. NAS ms RH2/1/35, f. 34v; Melville, *Diary*, 22.

to sing them.[193] In St Andrews, a child from the songschool sat beside the master before the pulpit 'to help sing the psalms'.[194]

The precentor's job was always made easier by well-schooled children and other literate parishioners bringing their psalters along. The Aberdeen elders ordered that 'whoever can read shall learn to sing' and required 'all men and women in this burgh who can read and are of famous report' to have 'Bibles and psalm books of their own, and bring the same with them to their parish kirks, thereon to read'. They had the backing of a 1579 parliamentary act requiring substantial householders to acquire psalters and Bibles or pay a £10 fine (a third of which rewarded the bailies who discovered the defaulters – no mean incentive). Burgh sessions extended the act to include all the literate, the Elgin elders in 1591 having 'all the young men . . . ordered to have psalm books in times coming that can read'.[195] Personal Bibles and psalters effectively became a new protestant status symbol – visible testimony of one's literacy and 'famous report'.

Reports of lay enthusiasm for psalms suggest that parishioners happily complied with the policy of congregational psalm-singing. As a child James Melville found that the singing of that blind precentor in his kirk of Montrose 'so delighted' him that he 'learned many of the psalms and tunes thereof in metre, which I have thought ever since a great blessing and comfort.' Approval on a wider scale became evident when new metrical versions (including the king's own, published in 1631) were roundly rejected by the parishes both in 1601 after the Burntisland General Assembly and again in 1637, because 'the people has been so long acquainted with the old metre that some can sing all or at least many of the psalms without the book.' The poetry of Sternhold and Hopkins may have had little to commend it beyond simplicity of language; however, that counted for a great deal to defenders of the 1564 version. Having 'none [words] but such as may be understood' was clearly better for a religion of the word than 'to bring in a number of words which have need of a dictionary in the end of the metaphrase', as the new version would require.[196]

193. CH2/521/6, ff. 81, 87; CH2/521/7, p. 281 – Perth's precentor Thomas Garvie, not 'apt nor able to discharge his office in taking up of the psalm in the kirk'. Their reader, Henry Adamson, did a better job of it, but lost part of his salary in 1621 because 'he holds not a music school', a requirement of the burgh's precentor.

194. *SAKS* 2:908.

195. CH2/448/2, pp. 83, 94 (1604); *APS* 3:139 (allowing a year and a day to purchase the books, and ordering bailies to search); CH2/145/1, f. 26v.

196. NLS ms Wod. Qu. LXXXIV, ff. 14–16, manuscripts compiled by David Calderwood arguing that the psalter 'should be sung in the kirks of Scotland as they have been since 1564'; *Bannatyne Miscellany* 1:238, 251. The clinching argument against a new

The boon of simplicity had enabled the people to memorise both tunes and words, so that they knew the psalms 'more than any book in scripture'. Even those who could not read could sing psalms 'by heart as may best serve for their different dispositions and cases of conscience and for the changes of their external conditions' – in other words, ordinary people had the psalms available in memory whenever the circumstances of daily life required direction by the word of God.[197]

Protestants also commended the psalter for use in family religious exercises, and with active enforcement by elders visiting their quarters, psalm-singing became a staple of family religion. Sessions embraced the 1560 charge for 'men, women, [and] children . . . to exercise themselves in psalms, that when the kirk doth convene and sing, they may be the more able together with common hearts and voices to praise God.' Innerwick's ordered 'every family that hath any that can read to have a Bible and a psalm book and make use of them', and Aberdeen's specified that 'families shall daily twice humble themselves privately or openly therein before God.' The Perth elders recorded in 1592 that, when visiting the families in their charge, they systematically encouraged psalm-singing with morning and evening prayers and graces at meals.[198] Having learned the tunes in church, people would easily memorise the words with daily repetition in the family. The psalter thus provided a sensible route to biblical knowledge for the illiterate, and helped to establish a society saturated with and defined by the word.

A final and essential factor in the transformation of Scotland's religious culture into one centred on the word, one again heavily dependent on the sessions' operations, was the kirk's firm commitment both to catechising and to the follow-up procedures of private and public doctrinal examination. The campaign to catechise more regularly had begun before the Reformation, with the 1552 order that Archbishop John Hamilton's catechism be read every Sunday and holy day for a half-hour before high mass; however, this was a case of too little, too late.[199] After the Reformation, everyone was subject to both regular catechism and frequent examination. The latter served not only as a sort of puberty rite for young people coming to their first communion, but also as a mandatory gateway

version was that change would 'make other kirks call us light-headed Scots, inconstant and unsettled in our orders' (p. 241). The Sternhold and Hopkins version had been in use since 1564 and was printed together with the catechism.

197. NLS ms Wod. Qu. LXXXIV, f. 16; Melville, 22.

198. *First Book*, 186–87; NLS ms Wod. Qu. LXXXIV, f. 14; CH2/1463/1, f. 10v (1649); CH2/448/2, pp. 83–84 (1604); CH2/521/2, f. 58v.

199. Patrick Hamilton, *Catechisme*, ed. Alexander F. Mitchell (Edinburgh, 1882); Cowan, *Scottish Reformation*, 184.

to marriage and to baptism of one's children, and more routinely as a prerequisite for communicating. The sessions enforced the requirement as rigorously as they did sabbath observance. But they did more: at failed examinations, they commissioned elders to 'deal with' those whose doctrine was inadequate or in error – an educational supplement impossible for a lone parish minister, as in an English congregation, but quite practicable where a dozen or so elders took on the responsibility.

Catechism classes and performances 'in the audience of the people', generally by children, were regularly on offer on Sunday afternoon, usually between the two sermons, though sometimes after both were concluded. Presbyteries diligently investigated whether all their kirks 'continue sabbathly in catechising'.[200] From age six, children were to be able to say the Lord's Prayer, the creed and the ten commandments, already learned at home from their parents, as the basis for more advanced teaching on Sundays.[201] The Aberdeen elders described these performances as opportunities not only for children to exercise their doctrinal knowledge, but also 'for giving knowledge and edification to the common ignorant people'. They ordered that each Sunday two of the pupils of the English school 'shall stand up before the pulpit, the one demanding, the other answering, and repeat publicly with a loud voice in audition of the people, the short catechism and the form of examination of children' in both kirks of the burgh, 'that by the oft repetition and hearing of the said catechism, the people may learn the same'.[202] Towns held classes on weekdays as well – in Leith, for instance, every Wednesday and Thursday evening in addition to Sunday.[203] In these sessions, ministers were supposed to 'take great

200. SAU CH2/624/1, f. 17; CH2/271/1, ff. 7, 8.

201. *BUK* 3:1052 (1608). The 1570 General Assembly required trial of children's grasp on these to see 'how they are brought up by their parents in the true religion' at ages nine, twelve and fourteen (*BUK* 1:176), but this minimal standard was in practice exceeded everywhere. Parliament ordered catechism to begin by age eight: *APS* 4:596.

202. CH2/448/2, p. 86 (1604). The reader also repeated bits of the catechism after prayers on Sunday mornings and weekdays, along with the ten commandments and creed. This order was part of a catechetical campaign during which the Thursday morning sermons were temporarily replaced by catechism and examination 'aye and until our people be better acquainted with the knowledge of the grounds of their salvation' (p. 84), visiting elders having lately reported intolerable ignorance.

203. CH2/716/1, ff. 22v, 23v. 'The masters or mistresses of families shall present their households' at these sessions on a rotation to allow each parishioner 'to have two several weeks of catechising, sabbath, Wednesday and Thursday at night' before each communion. Derelict masters were fined 3s 4d, servants 2s. Kinghorn's sabbath catechising was supplemented 'every Friday in the week between ten and twelve hours'; Aberlady's every Thursday: CH2/472/1, f. 37; CH2/4/1, f. 50v.

diligence . . . to cause the people [to] understand the questions' and the 'doctrine that may be collected thereof'.[204] It would not suffice merely to repeat by rote Calvin's text. Kinghorn's elders limited the number of individuals questioned in each two-hour Friday catechism class to ten or twelve in order to allow enough time to ensure understanding; of course, they placed no limit on the numbers 'that will come to hear'. In addition, most parishes offered special catechetical sessions just before the pre-communion examinations.[205] Here, adults could presumably get a quick refresher course to ensure their admission to the sacrament. Some parishes required attendance at these special classes, Belhelvie typically dividing its congregation and appointing to each group a specific time for catechism.[206] Catechists took attendance, 'none of any estate, sex or degree excepted', and absentees were fined or admonished.[207]

Finally, elders and ministers also catechised during their regular visits to families assigned to them 'for their reformation and information in godliness'. In some parishes these visits were scheduled at regular intervals throughout the year, with reports then being sent back to the session; in others they were concentrated just before communion, 'to assist . . . the pastors in visitation and in catechising and examination to prepare the people to the Lord's supper'.[208] They were clearly useful for informing and correcting the doctrine held by ordinary parishioners: it was during such a visit, for instance, that an Edinburgh elder found Walter Thomson still praying for the dead in the 1570s; a private meeting for individualised catechism eliminated the error. Robert Blair, bereft of an effective session in his Irish ministry in the 1620s, despaired of his responsibility for '1200 adults besides children to be instructed'. Recognising, though, that preaching alone would not do the job ('though I was in public [in the pulpit] four times every week . . . I saw the necessity of more plain and

204. *First Book*, 182; CH2/145/1, f. 50v (1593); NLS ms 2782, ff. 14v, 15 (Glasgow's ministers in 1595 casting lots to decide which of them would catechise on Sunday afternoon, a strain given their preaching duties). The minister in Belhelvie also preached sermons 'on the belief': CH2/32/1, n.f., 8 May 1631.

205. CH2/472/1, f. 37; see chapter 2, below.

206. CH2/32/1, f. 26v (1627). Highlands sessions like Mortlach's recognised the impracticality of mid-week sessions like this, given 'far distance and remove of the bounds'. They also had only one Sunday sermon and found that people left it so quickly for the long journey home that early afternoon catechisms were ill-attended, so they moved catechism to 'immediately after the sermon before the people dissolve': CH2/529/1, f. 82v (1641).

207. CH2/448/2, p. 297; CH2/400/1, f. 178; CH2/32/1, f. 26v. Davidson, *Some Helpes*, 135, had instructors 'take up the names in writ of so many as . . . were warned to that diet [day]'.

208. CH2/521/2, f. 58v; SAU CH2/624/2, p. 2; CH2/448/2, p. 84.

familiar instruction'), he resolved to 'go out among them and spend one day every week and sometimes two . . . as my bodily strength could hold out' offering family catechism.[209]

Until the Westminster Assembly convened in 1643, the catechism used was an English translation of Calvin's, first published with the *Forme of Prayers* in 1556 and thereafter with each edition of the *Book of Common Order*. Instructors were to be sure that parishioners did not merely memorise and parrot the responses, but that they understood the creed and ten commandments with 'the use and office of the same'; the 'right form to pray unto God; the number, use and effect of the sacraments; the true knowledge of Christ Jesus, of his office and natures and such others – without the knowledge whereof neither any man deserves to be called a Christian, neither ought any to be admitted to the participation of the Lord's Table.'[210] These were high standards. How close did ordinary parishioners come to meeting them? We can approach an answer by resorting to the remarkable body of information provided by examination reports to the sessions.

The kirk would not be satisfied either by mere repetition or by a one-time exposition of correct doctrine. Fully aware that information memorised is quickly forgotten, that interpretation may be skewed over time, and that other influences can corrupt once pure doctrine, ministers and elders required regular and rigorous re-examination of all parishioners, conducted either privately at family visitations or publicly before each communion, and in many parishes even more often. In South Leith, the session ordered that 'every eight weeks the *whole town* shall present themselves to the examinations' – a massive burden for the elders and ministers, not to mention householders closing shops and presenting their families six times a year.[211] Glasgow had weekly examinations by the ministers on Sundays between 4 and 5 o'clock, following the afternoon sermon – making a very long day for ministers and parishioners alike. Perth's examinations in the 1580s had to be scheduled daily to handle the whole population; the elders travelled to landward parts of the parish rather than summoning families to town for examination. In the midst of

209. NAS ms RH2/1/35, f. 34v; Blair, 59.

210. *Forme*, 1–11; *First Book*, 133–34. Supplementary catechisms like Davidson's *Forme of Familiar Instruction and Examination of Rude People . . . Practised in the New-Erected Kirk of Salt-Prestoun* (Rogers, *Three Scottish Reformers*, 135–65, approved in 1599 by the synod of Lothian and Tweeddale) were also popular and offer some idea of how much theological detail even 'rude beginners' were expected to master.

211. CH2/716/1, f. 23v (emphasis mine). Regular examination may have been all the more necessary in a port town where corrupting influences on mariners and travellers to catholic lands were rife: e.g., CH2/716/1, f. 8, or CH2/521/7, pp. 327–30.

a catholic scare in 1596, they divided 'the whole congregation as well burgh as landward' for 'weekly visitation and examination of families, that they may know what profit and progress their people make in Christianity, and especially in the grounds of Christian religion presently professed' and to 'avoid the false doctrines of the instruments of Satan in this country'.[212]

Pre-communion examinations once or twice a year were more usual, and still represented an impressive burden for the examiners. Sessions divided their parishes into 'quarters' (generally more than four), with elders assigned to each for 'uptaking of names' in a roll to be 'affixed to the pulpit' of 'those of age and meet . . . to proceed to examination' so that they could be apportioned among the multiple days of testing.[213] Indeed, good record-keeping is a hallmark of Scottish communion seasons, with lists of those eligible and those who actually appeared at the table routinely compared to ensure that no one had communicated unworthily.[214] On the Sunday before examinations commenced, the minister announced from the pulpit which quarters were to appear on which day, and in large parishes the elders conducted examinations at various locations to prevent gatherings of unmanageable size.[215] In addition to the pulpit

212. NLS ms 2782, ff. 14–14v, 39; CH2/521/1, f. 74 (these formal examinations in addition to visitations of quarters 'for discipline and doctrine', on which elders were to report to the preachers every Friday morning: CH2/521/3, p. 178, 1601); CH2/521/2, quotation at f. 158 (1596); CH2/521/3, p. 99 (minister and four elders examining set parts of the landward in 1599).

213. SAU CH2/624/2, p. 108; CH2/145/1, f. 21v; CH2/521/1, f. 72 (Perth's elders to 'pass through the town . . . to take the names of the inhabitants of the city, thereafter to pass to the examinations'), cf. CH2/521/2, ff. 73v, 91v, 119, 126v, 158; CH2/636/34, f. 60 (3s spent by the Kirkcaldy session for paper 'to make books for uptaking of the people's names before their examinations' in 1624); CH2/523/1, f. 37v (Burntisland elders in 1609 to 'take up the names . . . for examination'); CH2/1463/1, f. 1v (Innerwick elders listing those 'apt for communicating . . . that they may be examined'); CH2/32/1, f. 2; CH2/521/1, f. 42; CH2/141/1, f. 3; NLS ms 2782, f. 39. St Andrews was divided for examination into two halves, each with seven 'districts' in 1593: *SAKS* 2:lxviii.

214. CH2/521/2, ff. 4, 58, 73v: Perth's reader in the 1580s to 'write the names of those that after trial' were 'admitted to be partakers', the lists to be proofread by elders of every quarter and checked against those coming to the table.

215. CH2/359/1, f. 5 (Tyninghame's problems with rural quarters reporting on the wrong day); CH2/77/1, f. 18 (appointing 'special diets of examination'). In a small parish like Markinch, the whole congregation came to the parish kirk for examination (CH2/258/1, f. 30), but Edinburgh designated lists of parishioners for the kirks, 'at the nether tollbooth', and 'over the tollbooth' in 1574–75 (NAS ms RH2/1/35, ff. 23–23v, 28v, 49v, 50), with a minister, two or three elders, and two deacons to examine in each location on a weekday afternoon. Perth elders were to be in their quarters with the ministers for communion examinations: CH2/521/1, f. 42 (1580).

announcement, Perth's bellman rang the handbell through the streets to summon people on examination days.[216] The examination period often extended over several weeks before a communion – in Dysart, it lasted six to ten weeks in the 1620s, suggesting that examinations were more than cursory.[217] Innerwick's elders did not even set a communion date until all the people had been examined.[218] Examinations took longer in Highland and other rural parishes where it was unreasonable to ask parishioners to travel to the kirk on workdays; the Inveravon elders in 1631, noting that 'the greatest part of the parish were far distant from the church so that they in respect of their barbarity and unwillingness could not be income on the workday', asked the minister to commence examination immediately after the Sunday sermon. They examined in 'Irish' as well as English.[219] Visitors generally examined households together, but they sometimes separated out the servants for Sunday examination – perhaps on practical grounds, so that their labour would not be lost on workdays.[220] Heads of households were responsible for getting their families and servants to the examination; in Dumfries, the kirk officer came to each house twice to announce the examination 'so that ignorance could not be pretended'.[221] Sessions vigorously punished absentees, Kirkcaldy depriving the poor of 'silver to pay their housemail [rent]' for failure to appear.[222] In Aberdeen, the absentees' fines, appropriately enough, went to

216. CH2/521/8/2, f. 204. The Perth session succeeded in 1597 in getting the aid of the magistrates to force any who refused to come: CH2/521/2, ff. 169–69v.
217. CH2/390/1, f. 17 (a 25 May announcement for examinations to a 20 July communion), 24 (12 July for 21 August 1625), 34 (25 July for 5 September 1626), 45 (10 June for 29 August 1628); cf. *Dundonald*, 223; CH/2/400/1, p. 343; CH2/636/34, ff. 10, 60; CH2/699/1, f. 17v (Longside, 1623); CH2/84/28, ff. 10v, 29.
218. CH2/1463/1, f. 1v.
219. CH2/191/1, ff. 2v (1631, implying that if the Highlanders were less 'barbaric' they would be willing to take time off work?), 17 (a 1633 complaint that many 'ignorants' present their children for baptism 'who never can say the Lord's Prayer nor the belief. . . either in English or at least in Irish'. John Carswell had produced a Gaelic translation of the *Book of Common Order* in 1567.
220. Leith 'workmen' were examined each Sunday at 4pm in winter, 5pm in summer, as were servants on Sunday afternoons in Elgin: CH2/716/1, f. 22 (1609); CH2/145/1, f. 21v (1590).
221. NAS ms CH8/54/1a (1606).
222. CH2/636/34, ff. 39, 31, 46v (those 'who get their clothes from the parish' examined together in Kirkcaldy). Fines ranged from 40d in Innerwick to 40s in Ellon in 1606, some (like Markinch, Tyninghame and Scoonie) adding public repentance: CH2/1463/1, f. 1v; CH2/147/1, f. 53v; CH2/258/1, n.f., 14 August 1631; CH2/359/1, f. 1; CH2/326/1, f. 4; CH2/819/1, p. 8; CH2/400/1, p. 187; CH2/266/1, ff. 18, 111v; *Dundonald*, 23–25, 77; AAC CH2/562/1, f. 2v; NLS ms 2782, f. 39; CH2/716/1, f. 22, CH2/716/2, ff. 82, 87; CH2/383/1, ff. 17, 18; CH2/276/1, ff. 2v–3, 6v, 13v, 16v, 52.

support an orphaned scholar in the college.[223] During the questioning, there was to be no 'whispering and rounding in the ear by others next you'; better 'one sentence, yea never so small, spoken of your own understanding, than a thousand spoken by suggestion and tickling of others.'[224]

The minimum examination standard everywhere was the ability to repeat the creed, the Lord's Prayer and the ten commandments. How far one was expected to be able to explain each point is harder to sort out, though most minute books express the requirement in terms of being able to 'give an account of' the documents rather than merely to 'repeat' their contents.[225] The standard is clearest in the cases of parishioners suspected of catholicism or of holding specific erroneous doctrines. The Haddington presbytery required a suspected catholic to discuss justification in some detail: she 'answered that she was made righteous before God by faith in Christ only without works'. As to invoking the saints, she explained that she prayed 'to God only, as to him that knew only the secret of her heart'. She denied purgatory with the addition that 'she believed only to be purged from sin and get salvation by the blood of Christ', and as to communion she admitted 'only the spiritual presence of the body and blood of Christ'. This was a reasonably sophisticated declamation, but it came from a laird's wife, who might well have been held to a higher than usual standard of performance. On the other hand, we have evidence of quite ordinary parishioners also engaging in detailed and rather advanced discussions of doctrine, on the streets and in examinations. The Edinburgh elders in 1575 summoned a messenger named Walter Thomson who had been overheard debating in the streets with a litster (dyer), John Leyton, about prayer for the dead, citing texts from Maccabees. It was Leyton who informed him that his source was apocryphal and 'not the dictment of the spirit of God and so no credit ought to be given thereunto'. Thomson at his examination assured the elders that he merely posed the question to his friend and 'did not believe prayer for the dead is necessary, neither would he esteem any purgatory to be'.[226] Perth citizens had to 'give the grounds and heads of Christian religion' in their own words to have their names written on the communion list, identifying themselves as 'true Christians who also professes [*sic*] the religion presently professed in this land, renouncing all papistry, superstition and idolatry'. Even people of the

223. CH2/448/2, pp. 16, 22.
224. Davidson, *Some Helpes*, 137.
225. CH2/326/1 (Scoonie) uses this term (p. 51) to record the failure of sixteen men and fourteen women to do so in 1642; Davidson made allowances for 'capacity . . . to understand': *Some Helpes*, 158. See also CH2/1463/1, ff. 1v–2.
226. CH2/185/2, ff. 20v–21, the examination of Lady Seton; NAS ms RH2/1/35, f. 31v, the minister John Dury reporting the initial street debate to the session.

lowest social orders who had voiced any questionable doctrine underwent close scrutiny so that they might sign or swear the confession in all its details. A servant in North Berwick had the confession of faith read out to him not once but three times, and responded each time by affirming that he understood and approved it and would swear and subscribe it 'in all points', assuring the session that 'he did it not of hypocrisy'; only then was his profession finally accepted.[227]

We also get a hint about the rigour of the examination when, in the 1630s, people complained about ministers intruding Arminianism and Laudian ceremonialism into catechism and examination. John Crighton's prosecution by the presbytery of Paisley included his parishioners' charges that, while examining a young lad, he had asked whether the bread and wine at communion were not 'in effect the real body and blood of Christ' and had accepted an affirmative answer, and that he had repudiated the boy's negative answer to whether one should receive communion kneeling.[228] What is significant about these complaints for the present point is that it did not suffice for the boy simply to repeat the catechism's prescribed answer to the questions about the sacraments; he had to be able to discuss the meaning of the responses and articulate additional positions about posture for receiving. Simple repetition of responses would not do. When the entirety of a parish signed or swore 'with uplifted hands' a confession of faith in the sixteenth century, or in the 1630s the Covenant, all indications are that they had a real understanding of what they were affirming.[229]

Where there was hesitation by the examinee on any point of doctrine, and especially if popery were suspected, the elders charged some of their number to go to the homes of the parishioners in question and 'deal with' them about their beliefs, to make sure that 'their minds be in accord with their written' statements, and to report their results back to the session.[230] The Perth elders in 1622 engaged in 'long dealing' with John Robertson, a ship's captain who had spent rather too much time in catholic waters, finding that his beliefs were 'not agreeable to God's word in special points concerning man's salvation'. He declined to subscribe the confession of faith they presented to him 'til he were better informed', insisting 'that he

227. CH2/521/2, ff. 79, 91v (1593), 126v (1595); CH2/285/1, pp. 5–6 (case of Richard Ferguson, 1608). See also CH2/716/1, f. 8.

228. NLS ms Wodrow Oct. IX, f. 14.

229. CH2/472/1, ff. 125–35v; CH2/400/1, p. 302; CH2/299/1, p. 362; CH2/271/1, f. 106 (requiring that before the Covenant was sworn, ministers 'acquaint the people with the necessary verities and sincerity of the same'); AAC CH2/562/1, ff. 24v–28; *Chronicle of Perth*, 36, 38.

230. NAS ms RH2/1/35, ff. 10–10v, 11v (1575).

is not a scholar to dispute in matters of religion' – a hint about the level of the discussion conducted at his examination.[231] They prescribed remedial catechism in 1582 after thus examining Bessie Glass, sure that her 'ignorance in the principles of religion' would be corrected if 'she be every day an hour before noon hearing the examination public in the kirk in the rudiments of religion, and so to learn' – in addition, of course, to going 'every sabbath twice in the day to hear the preaching'. The Glasgow session sent 'six honest elders' to Archibald Hegat to 'try of him . . . for his apostasy', and in a general anti-catholic sweep in 1592 it required all suspected of being 'favourers of the untrue and popistical kirk in exercise of religion, in reasoning against the truth' to demonstrate that 'now from our hearts we embrace' the true gospel, specifically renouncing 'observing any suspicious rites or . . . abstaining from certain meats upon certain days': both inward and outward conversion were sought.[232] While their English neighbours were busily executing Jesuits in the 1580s, the Edinburgh elders were worried about Jesuits 'flocking home . . . to draw the hearts of the people from the obedience of the gospel . . . to embrace again idolatry and superstition' and so asked every minister to visit susceptible families in his charge to 'confirm them within his flock', then to report back his results. Presbyteries and synods took over the duty of 'conference and reasoning with' particularly well-born parishioners who might not respond to elders who were their social inferiors, as well as with the recalcitrant.[233] Their aim with a catholic was not 'to lose him, but rather if possible to win him back' by means of 'resolv[ing] him of the heads whereof he was in doubt'. Thus, the Paisley presbytery ordered Grissel Stewart's minister in 1602 to 'continue in dealing . . . and not to pronounce her excommunication, but await her conversion'. Small wonder, with this labour-intensive programme of doctrinal vetting, that in the final two decades of the sixteenth century the very active kirk session in St Andrews recorded only one papist left in the parish.[234]

231. CH2/521/7, pp. 327, 330. The 'dealing' was in the end unsuccessful: Robertson was referred to presbytery (CH2/299/1, p. 74) and finally on 'some other business' left town. It was also unsuccessful 'after long dealings' with three Falkirk parishioners in 1629; the point here is that excommunication did not come into the picture until the dealing had gone on for months, with individual meetings in parishioners' homes: CH2/400/1, pp. 210–11.

232. CH2/521/1, f. 74; ML CH2/171/1, ff. 6, 4v.

233. CH2/121/1, ff. 32v, 33 (1587); also *SAKS* 2:lxiii. CH2/271/1, ff. 2, 6–7; CH2/294/1, ff. 1, 4v (Forres and Paisley presbyteries).

234. CH2/121/1, ff. 2, 14, 17; *SAKS* 2:601–07. Even in Morayshire, the early decades of the next century saw numerous reports after examination and 'dealing', of catholics agreeing to 'conform themselves' and subscribing detailed confessions of faith: e.g., CH2/271/1, f. 2.

Lest we paint too glowing a portrait of how far the Reformation had come by the turn of the century, though, it is important to note the frequent expressions of frustration by sessions over poor attendance of examinations, misbehaviour there and failure of the test. The standards were high enough that the elders were bound to be disappointed sometimes; they were also high enough to terrify some parishioners into staying at home in hopes that their ignorance might be overlooked. John Foster told the Tyninghame session in 1615 that he 'was ignorant and durst not come to the examinations'.[235] Others seem to have simply despised the whole process and demonstrated their disdain by language and behaviour. One Canongate woman came so drunk to her examination in 1565 that she 'could not be stenchit [silenced]', and an uppity widow in Levin declined to leave her home, insisting that the examiner could very well 'sit down . . . at her bedhead' if he wished to know what she understood.[236] But anecdotes such as this are rare; most people seem to have shown up and behaved themselves.

By no means, however, did they always pass the test. Perth's elders found in 1595 that 'sundry within this congregation are found ignorant of the principles and grounds of religion notwithstanding that there is a yearly trial and examination', and so added several weekdays more catechism and examination 'that all may be instructed'. In Edinburgh, the Trinity College session was so disappointed by the results of examination in 1631 that they advised examination and sermons on the catechism 'be oftener used' and sent two elders to 'pass to the rest of the parishioners to crave their opinions' about the change, and presumably to drum up support for sticking to high standards of knowledge.[237] The Innerwick session in 1608 created its schedule of fines specifically because they had found 'the most part of the people wanted the commands, belief and Lord's Prayer', and required elders to visit their quarters at least monthly to observe how people spent their time 'between and after the time of public worship', since they apparently were not using the time to repeat the sermon or read the Bible and catechism.[238] Sessions generally set deadlines by which

235. CH2/359/1, f. 6. He promised amendment after the minister 'most heavily rebuked' him, pointing out that 'a special cause of his ignorance was his seldom resorting to the kirk'.

236. *Canongate*, 24; CH2/326/1, p. 37. John Oswald found himself before the Selkirk presbytery for his 'obloquy against the minister at the examination': CH2/327/1, f. 46v.

237. CH2/521/2, f. 126v; CH2/326/1, f. 5 (Scoonie elders in 1630 shocked at 'rudeness and ignorance among the common people . . . [of] the principal heads and common questions of religion'); CH2/141/1, f. 58 (the opinion poll's results not reported). See also CH2/32/1, f. 5.

238. CH2/1463/1, ff. 1v–2, 10v.

those who failed some portion of the examination had to have learned enough to redeem themselves; afterwards they enforced both fines and barring from communion in cases of doctrinal ignorance.[239] Offenders thus found themselves in a quandary: after Jonet Semple's examination, 'for ignorance her ticket [to Burntisland's communion] was denied'; she then had to pay the penalty for absence from communion.[240] Acquiring doctrinal understanding was clearly no more optional for post-Reformation Scots than sermon attendance. And it is worth repeating that this programme of indoctrination by sermon, Bible-reading, psalm-singing, public catechetical performance, home visitation and rigorous examination was aimed at mostly illiterate people, the preponderance of whom did pass the examinations and receive admission to communion, sing the psalms from memory, make their marks on the confession of faith and swear the Covenant.

★ ★ ★

The received version has it that Calvinism 'proved in the long run to be an abstract, intellectual religion of the elite.'[241] Not so. Where the life of the community could be organised around sermons and Bible-reading, and where the most ordinary could be regularly held to a public recitation of their faith, Calvinism became genuinely a religion of the people. Where the institution of the kirk session was available, its combination of close oversight, rigorous enforcement, commitment to teaching and persuasion, and co-operation with neighbouring parishes did, indeed, serve to achieve the Reformers' goal of a religion of the word. What would further ease the process of change in a culture whose religion had formerly been fundamentally sensual and ceremonial was the way the sessions dealt with the sacraments. Here they would evince other characteristics that led to protestantism's victory in Scotland – retention of discreet elements of tradition and careful protestantisation of rite and ceremony, especially the firm embedding of ritual within word.

239. The Stow smith John Purvies in 1630 'obliged him God willing to learn the commands, belief & Lord's Prayer in time' (CH2/338/1, f. 25); an Inveravon man in 1640 'shall have the belief against Whitsun next or pay a £5 penalty' (CH2/191/1, f. 50v); cf. 327/1, f. 1; CH2/326/1, p. 5. For barring from communion, CH2/521/2, f. 79; CH2/521/6, f. 41.

240. CH2/523/1, f. 19v, and the similar case of John Tennent, f. 30.

241. R. Po-chia Hsia, *Social Discipline in the Reformation* (London, 1989), 154.

Chapter 2

Word and Form in the Sacraments

When we turn from sermon to sacraments, two striking themes emerge immediately from parochial records. One affirms the fundamental change that protestantism forced from sensual to logocentric religion; the other points to a continuity that must have smoothed the path to change. Communion in particular was on the one hand redefined by being set into a heavily sermonic and dogmatic context. On the other, it remained a seasonal event with characteristic material symbols and experiences, antecedent fasting, ritual use of physical movement and space, and a perceived spiritual significance that was deeply emotive. Form, in other words, remained important in the religion of the word, satisfying a fundamental human need to express meaning in ceremonial action, not just verbalisation.

Contemporary divines would be quick to remind us that protestant Christianity is a religion of sacrament as well as word, and that sacrament may well accomplish what the word alone cannot. John Livingstone chided his parishioners at a communion service, 'I trow, many of you wot not that the substance of the whole Bible is in these sacramental elements – the whole covenant, a whole Christ in a state of humiliation and exaltation.' Indeed, he thought 'there are more . . . at communions than at any other time or place' who experience 'strokes of conscience' and divine intervention for conversion.[1] He was more aware than are many historians that the individuals sitting in early modern congregations were various, that while some may have been best swayed by preaching, others would more quickly respond to the 'rhetoric of re-enactment' in the Lord's Supper, with its dramatic visual and tactile elements and its communal,

1. *Sacramental Discourses* in *Sermons Delivered in Times of Persecution* (Edinburgh, 1880), 628, 625. It was after ten years of regular 'manifestations' at communions that John Broun, 'an exercised Christian in Glasgow', heard the audible voice of the devil in a preparation service, then experienced Christ during the next day's communion 'with such a power as gave him an entire outgate [release from temptation] and . . . a degree of fervency he scarce ever felt': Robert Wodrow, *Analecta* I (Edinburgh, 1842), 70–71.

participatory nature.[2] We focus on sermon apart from sacrament at our peril; if we are to understand religion in the Reformed pew, we must take seriously the contemporary pairing of 'word and sacrament' as the essential elements of Reformed religion.[3] We have seen that the preachers were quick to grant that knowing the word was not enough; they aimed for an experiential and affective understanding. This was accomplished particularly by communion celebrations, where the sensuality of the sacrament underpinned the emotional intensity of sermons. Word alone, apart from sacrament, would not suffice.

* * *

Every communion in post-Reformation Scotland was celebrated over a period of at least two weeks, so that communion effectively comprised a season in itself. The sacrament was offered twice on each of two successive Sundays, even in quite small parishes, in order to allow time for all the designated segments of the congregation to take it in turn to sit at the communion table on the 'forms' or benches that surrounded it.[4] In large parishes like Elgin and Aberdeen, three Sundays barely sufficed; St Cuthbert's, Edinburgh required four by 1619.[5] Perth and the other Edinburgh parishes kept the days to two, but decided in the 1570s that the bell would have to be rung at 4 in the morning for the first

2. Connerton, *How Societies Remember*, 61–104, deals with the repetitive gestures ('bodily practices') and language that characterise commemorative rituals of re-enactment. 'Performative memory is bodily', never more so than in communion – a corporate commemoration of the *corpus* of Christ.
3. The pairing is Calvin's (*Institutes of the Christian Religion*, ed. John T. McNeill, tr. Ford Lewis Battles, Philadelphia, 1960, 4:1, 9); Scottish reformers added discipline to make a triad (see the *Confession* in Knox, *Works*, 2:110), evident in the sessions' enforcement of the first two, as this and the foregoing chapter show.
4. E.g., CH2/390/1, f. 18v; SAU CH2/210/1, f. 3; CH2/266/1, ff. 5v, 32v; CH2/529/1, f. 93; NAS ms CH8/54/1a, f. 1v; NAS ms RH2/1/35, ff. 55–55v; CH2/122/1, ff. 1v, 3v; SAU CH2/624/2, pp. 131, 135; CH2/264/1, ff. 17v–18, 21v–22, 25v; CH2/141/1, f. 5v (Trinity College kirk, Edinburgh, dividing parishioners into two groups for each Sunday 'however it might be most convenient'), 41v, 46v; CH2/400/1, pp. 165, 291; CH2/521/1, f. 42; CH2/521/3, pp. 144–45, 228–39; CH2/521/8/1, f. 49. Landward Ayrshire parishes were unusual in having only single-Sunday communions in the early seventeenth century: AAC CH2/809/1, f. 7v. On sitting around the table, *The Book of Common Order [BCO] of the Church of Scotland, Commonly Known as John Knox's Liturgy*, ed. George Sprott (Edinburgh, 1868), 125–26; Brereton (1636), *Early Travellers*, 147.
5. CH2/718/4, f. 12; CH2/145/5, f. 102; CH2/448/2, pp. 59, 73 (three Sundays in Aberdeen, February 1604, plus a supplementary service in May for 'merchants, skippers and mariners of this burgh that were at the sail the time of the late ministration'). In Inveravon, the second Sunday was designated for those 'that were sick and might not go to the kirk' on the first: CH2/191/1, f. 9v.

administration, 8 for the second, to allow time for afternoon catechism and the third sermon on communion Sundays.[6] Quite apart from the multiple Sundays of sermon and celebration, there was a Saturday preparation sermon before each communion, and a Monday thanksgiving sermon after the final celebration. Compulsory attendance on Saturday and Monday meant that shops were closed and fields left unattended for the duration of the sermons and the time required to get to and from them – an enforced holiday of sorts.[7]

In most parishes communion was only annual, and therefore a great event. Urban parishes added one or two more celebrations each year over time, Aberdeen after 1606 attempting the ideal of four times a year, 'according to the laudable custom of well-reformed congregations'. In practice this was certainly not the custom of most Scottish churches, despite the 1562 General Assembly's order for quarterly communion in burghs, twice a year in the landward.[8] The Canongate elders resolved to institute thrice-annual communions in 1565, but expressed uncertainty 'how to sustain it' given that many parishioners simply opted out of all but the spring celebration.[9] Glasgow attempted two communions in 1595,

6. CH2/521/1, ff. 42, 72v, 116v; CH2/521/2, ff. 4, 101–01v, 111v–12, 117v, 126v; CH2/521/3, pp. 144, 273, 316; NAS ms RH2/1/35, ff. 4, 55–55v (the north side of Edinburgh on the first Sunday, the south on the second). Elgin's first bell also rang at 4 o'clock from at least 1621: CH2/145/3, f. 180v.
7. CH2/145/4, f. 138, CH2/145/6, f. 10v; CH2/93/1, ff. 11, 19v, 28; CH2/21/5, f. 80v. For continuation of these 'communion seasons' into the eighteenth century and into American revivalism, see Schmidt, *Holy Fairs*.
8. *BUK* 1:30, 58. The *First Book* also recommended quarterly communion (p. 183); cf. Calvin's stern argument against annual communion, *Institutes* 4:17.44–46. For Aberdeen see CH2/448/2, pp. 198–99. Parishes with twice-annual communions include Perth (CH2/521/1, ff. 42, 100v; CH2/521/2, ff. 101–01v, 119, March/September, adding a summer communion after 1580); Newbattle (CH2/276/1, ff. 2v–3, 11, 13v, spring and July); Yester (CH2/377/1, ff. 88v, 96v, 98, May and September); Anstruther Wester (SAU CH2/624/2, pp. 131, 135, 144, 152, 168, spring and October) and South Leith (CH2/716/1, f. 22 (March/August). Even in the 1680s, the Englishman Thomas Morer observed that Scottish communions were once or at most twice a year: *Short Account*, 63.
9. *Canongate*, 16, 18, 25. They added July and December celebrations that year and recorded nine hundred tokens in July as opposed to a thousand from the late February celebration, so their worries seem only to have been about 10 per cent of the parishioners. With only seven hundred communicating in early May 1566, though, things were moving in the wrong direction – perhaps reflecting confusion about which communion mattered. The lapse, however, proved only temporary. By summer, people seem to have adjusted to the new, fluctuating seasonal definitions: 1,200 communicated in August, the same number in January of 1567, and with the omission of a spring communion that year, perhaps because of an unusual amount of discord to be settled by kirk arbitration, 1,250 participated in the July communion (43, 51, 63, 71).

but the elders must have been disappointed by the October turnout: the next such experiment was not until 1632, after which March/April and October/November became the regular practice. Edinburgh seems to have been more successful, with two celebrations a year from at least 1574.[10] It is worth remembering that before the Reformation, for all the popular eucharistic devotion suggested by Corpus Christi celebrations, lay participation (receiving the communion bread as opposed to just observing the mass) was usual only at Easter, so that infrequency of the sacrament would have been the norm in post-Reformation lay perception.[11]

Where the protestant sacrament was an annual affair, it was in most parishes scheduled in the spring, at or around the old Easter (Pasch) – the most important element of communion's continuity.[12] The *First Book of Discipline* complained about 'how superstitiously the people run to that action at Pasch, even as if the time gave virtue to the sacrament' and advised avoiding 'the superstition of times'. An anonymous 'Letter on Celebration of the Lord's Supper . . . on Pasch Day' likewise found that 'it brings the Lord's people under temptation of insolent feasting, frivolous ceremony, and vain superstition', to which, the author regretted, people were 'overmuch inclined'.[13] But in scheduling communions, sessions seem to have bowed to popular demand, an inclination communicated to the General Assembly in 1570 by their question 'Whether the communion

10. NLS ms 2782, f. 38v; NAS ms RH2/1/35, ff. 1v, 4 (April 1574), 28v–30 (November 1574), 50–55v (June 1575, postponed from April because examinations took so long).
11. *Statutes of the Scottish Church*, 190; A.A. MacDonald, 'Passion Devotion in Late-Medieval Scotland' in *The Body Broken*, ed. MacDonald, H.N.B. Ridderbos and R.M. Schlusemann (Groningen, 1998), 109–32; Denis McKay, 'Parish Life in Scotland 1500–1560', and David McRoberts, 'Material Destruction Caused by the Scottish Reformation' in *Essays on the Scottish Reformation, 1513–1625*, ed. D. McRoberts (Glasgow, 1962), 98, 106, 415–62; Fitch, 'Search for Salvation' (chs 9–10 – a very comprehensive look at pre-Reformation Scottish eucharistic devotion), and pp. 1–14, 498, 656–804, with references to annual communion 670, 760.
12. There are few exceptions. Highlands parishes sometimes substituted early summer because of unpredictable spring weather: CH2/93/1 (Dron), f. 11; CH2/191/15v (Inveravon departing from Pasch in 1633 when 'all those that were found worthy to communicate could not leave their houses' because of storms). So did other rural parishes where adverse spring weather prevented travel to the kirk: CH2/1463/1, f. 1v; CH2/147/1, f. 17; CH2/283/1, f. 4v; SAU CH2/1056/1, f. 19v; and SAU CH2/21/5, ff. 20–99 (Innerwick, Ellon, Newton, St Monans and Auchterderran). Other parishes chose harvest time, perhaps unconsciously supposing a propitiatory function for the sacrament, since they often combined it with a fast that God might bless the harvest (see chapter 7, below): CH2/77/1, ff. 18, 67 (Culross, September or October); CH2/326/1, n.p., 2–22 October 1642 (Scoonie); CH2/523/1, ff. 38–38v (Burntisland, September); CH2/716/1, f. 19v (Leith, September).
13. *First Book*, 183; NLS ms Wod. Fol. XXVII, ff. 26–26v.

may be administered on Pasch or not?' The assembly replied even at that early date, 'Why not, where superstition is removed?', its members surely aware of how in their own parishes continuing a well-established pattern of Easter participation had served to assuage anxiety about other changes. Sessions thereafter ordered communions explicitly for the day, 'the last of March called Pasch' in Lasswade's 1616 order, for instance. In Elgin, 'Good Friday before Pasch' was also observed as 'a day of preaching, likewise Saturday thereafter the preparation sermon to communion' in 1628.[14] Getting people to church to hear sermons would, after all, do more than anything to combat superstition, and full participation in an annual communion would cement communal identity with the new kirk in that most fundamental Christian rite of inclusion. It was enough of a shift that, with two-Sunday communions, only half of a parish could receive the sacrament on Easter Day itself; more change would only have exacerbated anxiety over not marking the day.[15] With the season retained, loss of the day itself seems not to have been troublesome – at least, we have no indications in any kirk session minutes of protest. What we are seeing here, in other words, is an example of the sort of *de facto* negotiation between pew and authority that in a multitude of areas would smooth the path to Reformation.

Spring celebration was the norm long before the Perth Articles of 1618 restored communion at Easter, and surely explains why that particular order did not arouse more protest than it did. Glasgow's sixteenth-century communions from the 1560s were in April or early May; Aberdeen's and

14. *BUK* 1:80; cf. 1:346; CH2/471/1, f. 10; CH2/145/3, f. 111; CH2/145/4, quotation at f. 138. For other communions explicitly 'on Pasch day', CH2/100/1 (Dunbarney), f. 15v; CH2/141/1 (Trinity College, Edinburgh), f. 46v; CH2/146/2, n.f., 6 September 1617 (referring to the previous spring's paschal communion in Ellon); *Chronicle of Perth*, 20 (1574); CH2/191/1 (Inveravon), ff. 3, 9v, 15v. Glasgow anticipated the order in 1566: *RPC* 1:492.

15. Also, in those rural parishes sharing ministers (described in chapter 1, above) only one of a group could actually have communicated on Easter Day: Tyninghame, for instance, scheduled its communions in April and lent its minister to neighbouring parishes in May for their communion sermons: CH2/359/1, ff. 5–6 (1615). Among many examples of post-1618 continuity of spring communions, all with two-Sunday celebrations so that only one could be on Easter Day, see CH2/1115/1, f. 11 (Boharm, April); CH2/264/1, ff. 13v, 17v, 21v, 25v (Menmuir, April); CH2/529/1, f. 93 (Mortlach, April); CH2/258/1, ff. 15v, 23v–24, 30 (Markinch, May); CH2/4/1, f. 26v (Aberlady, May); CH2/390/1, f. 6 (Dysart, April); CH2/77/1, f. 50v (Culross, April); CH2/141/1, ff. 5v, 46v (Trinity College, March/April); CH2/266/1, ff. 29v, 32v, 34v, 37 (Mid-Calder, April); CH2/636/34, ff. 31, 49v, 60 (Kirkcaldy, April); CH2/191/1, ff. 2, 3, 9v, 19v, 31 (Inveravon, April); CH2/400/1, pp. 164, 167, 171, 263, 283, 291 (Falkirk, March–April); CH2/718/4, ff. 12v–15 (St Cuthbert's, Edinburgh); CH2/1142/1, f. 104 (Fraserburgh).

Kirkcaldy's pre-1618 celebrations were consistently in March or April; and other parishes from Edinburgh to Dron in the Highlands followed the pattern.[16] The simple fact of the matter is that this particular Jacobean article was not an innovation. Whether the king realised it or not, he had simply asked the Perth Assembly in 1618 to affirm what was going on anyway. Other Articles, like kneeling to receive the sacrament, were by contrast genuinely controversial, particularly once enforcement efforts began in the 1630s.[17] When the Perth schoolmaster John Row objected to innovations in communion, he did it only in 1633 when kneeling was finally required for the king's visit; he had no problem with the scheduling of the sacrament at Pasch from 1618, remarking in his 1633 protest that in communions for the last twenty years he had not found 'the institution by Christ altered in any jot'; only now was there 'straight urging of ceremony on the kirk'.[18] He was quite right: Perth had celebrated spring communions since at least 1593.[19] One almost hears a note of relief in the anonymous observations made on a seventeenth-century fast sermon before communion: 'There is some special times and seasons when a Christian ought to look to Christ. This is holden forth from the scrip[tures].'[20]

Every adult in the community was expected to participate in the

16. NLS ms 2782, f. 38v (the only exceptions in 1589, 1593 and 1595); CH2/448/2, pp. 15, 27; CH2/448/3, p. 181; CH2/636/34, ff. 10, 15; NAS ms RH2/1/35, ff. 1v, 4 (1574); CH2/93/1, ff. 11, 19v, 28. Other pre-1618 examples include CH2/377/1, f. 10v; SAU CH2/624/2, pp. 131, 135, 144, 148, 152, 168; CH2/84/28, f. 60; CH2/359/1, f. 5; CH2/266/1, ff. 2, 4, 5v, 11v, 13v; CH2/699/1, f. 17v (Yester, Anstruther Wester, Dalkeith, Tyninghame, Mid-Calder, Longside).
17. Ian B. Cowan, 'The Five Articles of Perth' in *Reformation and Revolution*, ed. Duncan Shaw (Edinburgh, 1967), 160–75 (the only objection to days he notes was to Yule, p. 175); *Scotland's Supplication and Complaint against the Book of Common Prayer (Otherwise Laud's Liturgy)*, ed. David Hay Fleming (Edinburgh, 1927), 43–44. William Cowper, bishop of Galloway (and former minister of Perth), alone among his episcopal peers, refused to kneel after passage of the Perth Articles and was rebuked by the king, but he was indifferent in the matter of the keeping of holy days: *Workes*, 163. The king and Privy Council launched the campaign for Easter communion in 1614–15; the General Assembly finally consented at Perth in 1618: *RPC* 10:215–17, 316–17.
18. CH2/521/8/1, ff. 90–96; CH2/299/1 (Perth presbytery), pp. 309–10, 313. Row not only objected himself, but 'in open view of the whole congregation did take out his scholars at his back so soon as the minister after doctrine and prayer began his exhortation' and also 'charged his scholars not to communicate and thereafter did threaten some one or two [brave souls!] who did communicate.' In the end he apologised for his 'causeless scruple' (109v).
19. CH2/521/1, f. 100v (March 1593), although Perth also had a second, autumn communion as well from at least that date; CH2/521/2, ff. 117v, 119 (March 1595); CH2/521/3, p. 82 (May 1599).
20. Folger ms V.a.415, f. 28.

communion season. Age at first communion varied. The usual was probably fifteen or sixteen, the cutoff used by parishes reporting their communicant membership to the royal commissioners in 1627: Ednam parish in Roxburghshire, for instance, divided its roll into three groups – an unspecified number of 'bairns capable of learning', 120 'catechists' over eleven, and 550 communicants over fifteen – confirming the impression that first communion would have followed a performance of what had been learned in the four years of catechetical preparation, marking the end of childhood.[21] On the other hand, the Edinburgh session recorded admitting a ten-year-old girl in 1575, despite her having remained in town during the 'troubles' (when the queen's forces held the castle); 'in respect of her tender age' they 'admit[ted] her to the Table' without performing repentance – her age was clearly not regarded as an impediment.[22] Robert Blair and James Melville recorded their first communions at ages twelve and thirteen respectively, Melville recalling of his in 1570 'a greater reverence and sense in my soul than oft thereafter I could find . . . where, coming from the table, a good honest man, an elder of the kirk, gave me an admonition concerning lightness, wantonness, and not taking tent [attending] to the preaching.' One wonders whether first communions were generally accompanied by such impromptu teaching of children on their way back to their places in the kirk. It is a striking illustration of Myerhoff's definition of rites of passage as 'moments of teaching when the society seeks to make the individual most fully its own, weaving group values and understandings into the private psyche'.[23]

A first communion clearly served as a sort of puberty rite in early modern Scotland, ushering the child into the adult community as he or she took a seat at the boards alongside grown-up neighbours for the first time.[24] It was the occasion of a particularly celebrated public performance of the catechism, as in the case of young Blair, chosen to 'repeat all the answers' to John Welch's *Catechism* before the sermon. The boy was effec-

21. *Reports on the State of Certain Parishes*, 195–97; Coldstream and Dirlton reported communicants as those 'past sixteen years of age' (pp. 10, 109). The Fife synod set fifteen as the age of first communion: SAU ms 30451, f. 4v.
22. NAS ms RH2/1/35, f. 51. The orphaned child reported that she had entered the town with one Margaret Betoun, perhaps a guardian, and 'could not get forth again'; surely the remarkable thing is that she was questioned at all. The session took children's sins as seriously as adults'.
23. James Melville, *Autobiography and Diary*, ed. Robert Pitcairn (Edinburgh, 1842), 23; Blair, 6–7; Myerhoff, 'Rites of Passage', 109–35, quotation at 112 (also 118 – 'a moment of conspicuous teaching').
24. Physical approach to the table was a clear initiatory crossing of borders and assumption of new (adult) identity: Myerhoff, 113.

tively 'confirmed' by congregational approbation rather than a bishop after he 'timeously pronounce[d] the words whereby thy people were edified'.[25] Years of catechetical rehearsal had preceded this event. The boy then received the token admitting him to communion, a totemic representation of his accomplishment of the essential, doctrinal feature of adulthood. Processing forward to the table and taking bread from the plate with his elders sealed the transition from one life stage to another. Scottish advocates of a restored episcopal rite of confirmation before first communion found their most palatable argument in identifying confirmation with this catechetical performance, so that all they were really proposing was 'the alteration of the name, that it should be called confirmation, or rather the examination of the said children'.[26]

Ministers announced upcoming communions from the pulpit at least a week or two in advance in urban settings, and from three weeks to three months in advance in rural areas, to allow sufficient time for preparation. To be sure that everyone got the message, the Ellon session dispatched designated elders and the kirk officer to travel to the heads of every barony in the parish to advertise upcoming communions. Dumfries's session did likewise, specifying that the officer go twice to every family. They were clearly intent on getting the whole congregation prepared in good time. The Moray synod in 1623 ordered that the announcement be made to families suspected of popery in the presence of two 'famous witnesses . . . for taking away all pretence of ignorance from them'.[27] There were few admissible excuses for absence from either preparatory activities or the sacrament.

Preparation was by no means limited to attending the Saturday sermon, which was rather the culmination of quite lengthy preparatory activity. The first stage in the process was examination of every prospective communicant for correct doctrine and upright behaviour – a review of that transitional performance of early adolescence, combined with close questioning about behaviour in cases where any reports of aberrant activity or 'suspicious haunting' had come to the elders' ears. Like other examinations, these could be conducted privately, elders visiting each household in their quarters, or publicly, families reporting to designated central locations to meet with the minister and elders. In parishes with large landward districts either could be very time-consuming, taking as long as two or three months in Brechin, though even in the densely populated

25. Blair, 7.
26. NLS ms Wod. Oct. IX, f. 3 (1634).
27. CH2/271/1, f. 2 (the Moray synod ordering twenty days' advance warning); CH2/147/1, f. 17 (1607); NAS ms CH8/54/1a (1606).

urban Canongate, the 1567 examination begun at the end of May was for a 3 July communion, 'an elder and deacon assisting every day with the minister'.[28] Lasswade, typical of rather less far-flung parishes than Brechin, set its landward examinations for particular weekdays in the three weeks before communion, 'to begin at Pendrig upon Tuesday, it being the first day, and the barony of Preston upon Wednesday, it being the fast day, and the barony of Roslin upon Tuesday thereafter, it being the tenth day, and Loanhead upon Friday thereafter, and North Loanhead . . . upon Tuesday thereafter the seventeenth day.' Friday before the communion 'the whole parishioners [were] to be present at the preparation at eleven hours and to convene to five hours' – a six-hour marathon of sermons and prayers. One had to pass the examination in order to receive a token for admission to the sacrament, the Lasswade orders continuing, again typically, by charging that 'no persons should be admitted to the table but such as have tickets, and none get tickets but those that have bidden trial and are found well-instructed in the belief, the Lord's Prayer and ten commandments, with the two sacraments' – 'well-instructed' suggesting standards beyond mere repetition of catechism answers.[29]

The other preparatory activity required for a token was reconciliation, in case one were notoriously at odds with one's neighbour. The 'day of reconciliation' regularly appears in the schedules set up for communion seasons, along with 'exhorting of the whole neighbourhood to mutual peace and love'.[30] Burntisland incorporated reconciliation into examination visits, the elders after doctrinal vetting to 'take away all discords to the end the people may be the better prepared for the communion'. In

28. Brechin's own quarters could be examined in three or four weeks in 1654; only the landward required months (Thoms, *Kirk of Brechin*, 75); *Canongate*, 68. Aberdeen held weekly Thursday afternoon private catechisms and public examinations throughout the year: CH2/448/2, pp. 84ff. Edinburgh examinations were on Fridays before each communion: NAS ms RH 2/1/35, ff. 28v, 55–55v. For pre-communion examinations in Perth, CH2/521/1, f. 72; CH2/521/2, ff. 4, 79, 91v; CH2/521/6, f. 135; CH2/521/7, pp. 22, 136; CH2/521/8/1, ff. 90, 204.
29. CH2/471/1, ff. 5v, 6v (1615). The *Forme of Prayers* includes after the catechism (n.p.) 'A Brief Examination of Doctrine Before They Be Admitted to the Table'. The theological sophistication of the *Forme and Maner of Examination Befoir the Admission to the tabill of the Lord* (Edinburgh, 1581) suggests that the doctrinal bar was set high, as does William Cowper's *A Preparative for the New Passover* [London, 1607]. People who tried to communicate without having passed the examination were severely disciplined: NLS ms Wod. Oct. IX, f. 5v.
30. CH2/718/4, f. 12 (St Cuthbert's 'day of reconciliation' Thursday before the first communion sitting); *Canongate*, 13 ('Thursday for the agreeance of brethren, 1566), 48, 60–61. See also CH2/93/1, f. 19v; CH2/122/1, f. 1v; CH2/77/1, f. 50v; CH2/400/1, f. 116; Thoms, *Kirk of Brechin*, 76–77. Pre-communion reconciliation was not in principle a protestant innovation: Fitch, 693–95. But see chapter 5, below.

Menmuir, it was after the Saturday preparation sermon that 'the elders [were] to take trial if there were any persons at variance that they might be drawn to reconcile before the communion.'[31] The Canongate session actually postponed communion in 1567 because of 'dissension and public discord between the crafts and maltmen' which the minister despaired of settling by private or public admonition. To get at the heart of the quarrel and settle it once and for all, the session appointed arbiters and the quarrelling parties swore to 'stand at the[ir] deliverance'. Requiring 'the table to be deferred [for the whole congregation] in hope of reconciliation' signals the vital importance of communal concord for the sacrament.[32] This was a graphic enactment of an ecclesiology that took seriously the biblical command for believers to love one another. Of course, Reformed reconciliation of enemies before communions corresponds precisely to the traditional peacemaking function of the pre-Reformation clergy, particularly during Lent. The difference was that with involvement of lay elders in the process, more of it could go on, more regularly and more intensely than would have been possible with only clerical mediation – even supposing that medieval clergy did in fact act as their theory prescribed.[33] In communion seasons, continuity with medieval theory was leavened by protestant zeal in practice, meeting an often pressing need in a quarrelsome society.

Parishioners often came to the Saturday sermon fasting, or at least having fasted on designated days of the week before. Indeed, it was not at all unusual for annual spring communions to be preceded by several weeks of fasting – clearly reminiscent of pre-Reformation Lent. Fasting, before a communion and at other, specially proclaimed times, obviously involved abstinence, generally from food other than bread and ale, and also from unspecified other pleasures, including sexual ones.[34] But in the

31. CH2/523/1, ff. 38–38v; CH2/264/1, ff. 21v, 17v–18, 22, 25v.
32. *Canongate*, 62.
33. Given a dearth of evidence surviving from medieval parochial practice, it is impossible to gauge this. On the theory, see John Bossy, *Peace in the Post-Reformation* (Cambridge, 1998). Non-communicants often tried to use failure to reconcile as an excuse, but it never worked, since the 'means of reconciliation' were readily available in the session: e.g., NAS ms CH8/54/1, f. 1v; CH2/718/4, f. 12; SAU CH2/819/1, pp. 6–7 (Kingsbarns elders compelling reconciliation before communion, 1630). See chapter 5, below, for fuller treatment of protestant peacemaking.
34. CH2/145/1, f. 36; NAS ms RH2/1/35, ff. 3v–4, 30, prescribing bread and drink only and 'all kind of sobriety' to be enforced by visiting elders during fast weeks before the 1574 communions; *Dundonald*, 73 – summons of people who ate 'beef and other meat' or were 'at bread and cheese' on fast days. The *BCO* prescribed a 'temperate diet' of bread and drink, rather than complete abstinence from food (pp. 152, 169, 178); the Westminster Directory defined fasting as abstinence from food, labour,

post-Reformation era, it also meant attendance at a fast sermon on each of the announced fasting days. Joined with the continuity of Lenten self-denial, then, we have the innovation of preaching on fast days. And while some would regard this as yet another form of self-denial, there was apparently widespread lay support for the practice. A rare instance of early modern pollsters in the Elgin records demonstrates that this lay approval went beyond the session itself. In 1593, the elders summoned to a special Friday meeting all the 'honest men within the town' to 'give their opinion in respect of the busy time of year touching the communion'. They came away from their survey with the decision that shops must close for fast sermons on Wednesday and Friday before the first communion Sunday, 'fast and preaching to be precisely kept the said days throughout the whole burgh and landward' in order 'to prepare the people' for communion.[35] For the local landholders and businessmen to make such a recommendation, to the loss of labour and income, suggests the perceived importance of the full communion season to the early modern community, and of sermons to a proper fast. In fact, the central event of every fast, as well as every feast, was the sermon.

The Saturday preparation sermon gathered the whole parish together in a sort of orgy of self-examination, recrimination and repentance.[36] Preparation sermons naturally dwelt on themes of sin, the sufferings of Christ and the need for repentance. They were composed to elicit both internal soul-searching and external displays of sorrow. As with other sermons, their language was full of evocative imagery, especially of the crucifixion, and powerful condemnation of sinners as well as sins: 'You are a traitor to the son of God and an enemy to the cross of precious Christ,'

'worldly discourses and thoughts, and from all bodily delights': *A Directory for the Publique Worship of God* (London, 1644), 75. William Cowper defined fasting as abstinence from meat (*Workes*, 612). See also William Struther, *Scotland's Warning; or, A Treatise of Fasting* (Edinburgh, 1628), 49, 60; William McMillan, *The Worship of the Scottish Reformed Church 1550–1638* (London, 1931); and chapter 7, below, for more on fasting.

35. CH2/145/1, f. 49; cf. f. 36.

36. The sermon could be in either morning or afternoon. Morning was preferred so that the session could meet afterwards to allocate the next day's duties among its members, as at Kirkwall (CH2/442/74, f. 33); Edinburgh preferred 3 pm in the 1570s (NAS ms RH2/1/35, f. 30). St Cuthbert's 2 pm Friday sermon was a rare exception (CH2/718/4, f. 12, 1619). Saturday saw preparation sermons throughout the realm: CH2/529/1, f. 93; NS ms 2782, f. 37v; *Dundonald*, 259; SAU CH2/624/2, pp. 131, 135, 168. For an example of Scots preparation sermons in Ireland, see Blair, 84. Blair reported that people who travelled far to the preparation sermons in Antrim then spent the whole night 'in conference and prayer . . . the sabbath night likewise', abstaining from sleep as well as food, but somehow still able to stay awake for the Sunday and Monday sermons (p. 139).

one auditor dutifully copied into his sermon notebook. Preachers deliberately elicited anxiety about the states of their auditors' souls, putting words into their mouths where necessary: 'But oh, says some, I have none of these sweet effects that folk uses to have after that they have looked unto Christ, such as light and joy and comfort and consolation; therefore, I think I am not right [with God].' Some must have been terrified of coming to communion the next day after hearing their preachers warn, 'Yea, there is some that will be here the morn that Christ will propose these three questions unto when they come here: . . . How durst thou come hither without a wedding garment? . . . Does thou betray the son of God with a kiss? . . . How durst thou come here that has lifted up thy hand against me? O search yourself with candles and try if it be not so with you.'[37] Thus ends a sermon designed to prepare hearers for the table apparently by undermining whatever confidence they may previously have had of their election. James Wallace told his auditors, 'put yourselves to the trial, for many are come here who may get unjust testaments and tickets and yet be slight in examination to ken what they are.' They mistake 'formality for grace and so eat and drink damnation'. 'Stand trembling,' he warned, 'thou hast a deceitful heart within thee, and the devil may soon have thee.'[38] The anxiety fostered here was of a sort that only the performance of religious duties could assuage. However worried one might be about participating unworthily, to stay home the next day would be infinitely worse, an admission that one lacked the wedding garment; moreover, the worry and self-doubt that must have been forthcoming from such sermons may well have been calculated as the attitude most conducive to producing an emotional high the next day. Preparation sermons, like fast sermons, were designed as cathartic experiences, eliciting moaning and weeping from the whole congregation at a crucial juncture in the preparation process, just antecedent to the verbal confessions and 'signs of repentance' of the penitents who had been seated beneath the pulpit for the length of the sermon.

The Saturday pre-communion sermon served as a verbal introduction to the highly charged ritual of 'receiving' penitents from the place of their public humiliation back into the bosom of the congregation. The Inveravon session was typical in ordering any penitents who had delayed performance of public repentance to complete it in time for Easter communion 'that so they might be admitted'; they shortened some penitential terms to time reception just before the sacrament, and they cancelled session meetings in order to conduct the last of the penitents'

37. Folger ms V.a.415, ff. 28, 38v–39, 41.
38. Folger ms V.a.415, f. 146.

examinations in time.[39] We shall explore this phenomenon at greater length later; for now, three points should be made relative to the sacramental season. First, this preparation Saturday event should bring to mind catholic absolution of penitents before the Reformation, also timed for the end of Lent; for new elders as for old priests, Easter communion marked a reconstitution or restoration of the Christian community.[40] Second, the performance required of the penitents, including public confession of their sins and visible display of their sorrow, provided in effect a sort of scapegoat for the whole community.[41] The antecedent sermon had made painfully clear that all were guilty of offending the Almighty; in the public humiliation of a segment of the congregation, the weight of the sins acknowledged of all were demonstrably borne, confessed and bemoaned by an all-too-representative group. Finally, however, ritual reincorporation of penitents at this juncture also served to underline visibly for the whole community the theological message of not only the Saturday sermons on sin and repentance, but also of the peculiarly Christian outcome of it all in ultimate forgiveness of the faithful. In ritual 'reception', those who had most notoriously offended God and the kirk were joined back to the community that on the morrow would share the sacramental meal. It served as the final element of communion preparation by reifying a complex theological principle in a way that no amount of preaching could achieve. This was protestant ecclesiology made flesh.

By the time people had gathered on preparation Saturday, they had in most cases already collected the tokens or tickets they needed to be admitted to communion. A prospective communicant could sometimes receive this at the examination – an immediate reward for an acceptable performance, and when this was public, a tangible sign to all of one's neighbours of inclusion among the godly of the community as well as some comfort to spiritually anxious individuals. One imagines auditors of those terrifying preparation sermons holding tightly to their tokens for reassurance that they did, after all, stand some chance of being among the godly. In Edinburgh, it was after all the examinations had been completed that people reported back to their particular places of examination at 2

39. E.g., CH2/191/1, f. 2v; CH2/264/1, f. 25v – reception of a Menmuir penitent at the second preparation sermon; for other examples see chapter 3, below.

40. CH2/400/1, f. 116. See chapter 3, below, for penitential performance and reception. For pre-Reformation penitential practice, see Thomas Tentler, *Sin and Confession on the Eve of the Reformation* (Princeton, 1977); John Bossy, 'The Social History of Confession in the Age of the Reformation', *Transactions of the Royal Historical Society* 5th ser., 25 (1975), 21–38; Bossy, *Christianity in the West 1400–1700* (Oxford, 1985), chs 3–4; and Bossy, 'The Mass as a Social Institution 1200–1700', *P&P* 100 (1983), 29–61.

41. This may be construed as the 'redressive phase' of the social drama: see Turner, *Performance*, 34–35, 38, 67–69, 90–93, 100–07, which informs this paragraph.

on Friday afternoon to receive their tokens in a modest ceremony of inclusion and approbation.[42] In St Cuthbert's, the distribution of tickets was a great event; also on Friday, it was scheduled to take three hours (from 9am to noon).[43] Lasswade departs from the norm in incorporating the distribution into its six-hour Saturday gathering for the preparation sermon. Again, however, the public nature of the event and its inherent communality are apparent. Everyone who had passed the examination could take a break from work and gather with neighbours in a very visible display of righteousness and social acceptability, regardless of economic or social status. The Lasswade elders in fact worried in 1615 that it had become a rather too festive, indeed raucous, social event, and resolved 'to eschew confusion of the ticket-giving, to cause one of every house to stay and to receive the tickets' for the whole family after the preparation sermon; in most parishes, however, individuals received and held onto their own tickets.[44] In the distribution of tokens, the kirk had hit upon a very powerful way indeed to demonstrate godly identity and the coherence of the faithful community. One could carry one's token about for a day or more before giving it up at the communion, displaying it at will as evidence of spiritual status and the approbation of the kirk. On the other hand, to be excluded from this gathering, to be unable during the hours remaining until the next day's service to display one's token, was a form of banning that would surely have encouraged better behaviour or learning next time around.

The tokens themselves were small lead discs, stamped generally with the name of the parish, the date and/or the minister's initials. In the first decades after Reformation they were in at least some parishes stamped on heavy paper stock; the change in material to something more permanent and valuable may well attest to the importance this material object acquired early on, in the absence of so many of the traditional physical aspects of the sacrament banished by the Reformers.[45] Without icons,

42. NAS ms RH2/1/35, f. 30 (1574); CH2/521/1, f. 74 (receiving tokens in Perth from minister, elders or reader).
43. CH2/718/4, f. 12 (1619); cf. CH2/191/1, f. 2v (collection of tokens on the Sunday antecedent to communion in Inveravon, where travel to the kirk was so time-consuming it was sensibly avoided on weekdays).
44. CH2/471/1, f. 5v.
45. Glasgow's session recorded purchasing 'cards for the tokens' in the 1580s; in 1589, 'tickets marked with a sign'. In 1593, however, they spent 50s 'for stamping of the tickets of lead', and in 1604 they melted down old tokens to make new ones: NLS ms 2782, f. 37v. Edinburgh's tokens in 1578 were 'cards to be tickets', though a goldsmith was hired 'for stamping of them', and the St Andrews tokens were not metal, since they were 'written by the clerk' (*SAKS* 1:34–35, n. 2). Anstruther Wester in 1593 paid 5s for molds to form tokens: SAU CH2/624/1, p. 29.

incense, holy water – the whole panoply of holy objects associated with sacramental activity in a catholic setting – there must have been some impetus to seize onto an object that signified the individual's inclusion in the holy. Like the badge of a medieval pilgrim, the token bespoke sanctity. There was actually a livelihood for purveyors of counterfeit tokens, such was the demand both for the material item itself and the sacramental inclusion it made possible.[46]

★ ★ ★

After all this intense preparation, the communion day itself began as early as 4 in the morning and lasted many hours. The early start did not necessarily have the effect of ending a pre-communion fast. On the contrary, Sundays in post-Reformation Scotland were often fast days, and communion Sundays were no exception.[47] Robert Blair recorded his hesitation to receive his first communion in 1605 because he had not fasted first; he was only persuaded by the biblical reference to the disciples receiving the wine 'after supper' that his own participation after breakfast would be permissible.[48] Such recognition that fasting was not a biblical requirement, however, did not stop the practice from becoming quite general in the first generations after the Reformation. Perhaps a fast was construed as a way to make a holy day even holier, if rather less festive. The Edinburgh elders from the 1570s routinely ordered 'public fasting and humiliation before' each communion, timing it from 8 on Saturday evening until Sunday evening at 6.[49]

Other than being earlier than usual, the communion service began like any other, with readings, prayers, psalm-singing and the always-central sermon. Sermon note-takers clearly regarded communion sermons, like preparation sermons, as special; they often set aside a notebook just for the sermons of the communion season, and we certainly have an extraordinary number of surviving manuscript as well as printed communion sermons – the numbers obviously swelled also by there being at least two Sundays of both morning and afternoon sermons for each communion

46. E.g., CH2/32/1, f. 36.
47. Examples of fasts on communion Sundays include CH2/521/1, f. 116v; CH2/521/2, ff. 101–101v; CH2/1142/1, f. 104 (including the Sunday before the 3 April 1620 communion); NAS ms RH2/1/35, f. 30. For fasts on other Sundays, see chapter 1, above, n. 13.
48. Blair, 7, the biblical reference being the text from 1 Corinthians 11 used for the communion service, though the 'supper' reference is, of course, to reception of the bread (Luke 22.20).
49. NAS ms RH2/1/35, f. 30.

season.[50] One such sermon notebook, containing preparation, communion and Monday sermons by eight different preachers, given mostly in Bothwell parish in the presbytery of Glasgow, gives us some notion of what a fairly perceptive parishioner would have heard during the communion season.

The preachers acknowledged the 'hot exercises' and 'scorching heat in the conscience' that the preparation experience had elicited. Now, at last, that self-scrutiny and repentance would be repaid, they promised, for 'after great pains taken in duties wrestling for sweet Christ's face', it is 'at a communion like this that . . . the soul will win in to Christ's bosom', the sacrament being that 'correspondence that God keeps with his own'. The notes hint at the heightened emotionality of communion services, when believers were 'admitted and taken into the chamber of presence and made to rejoice with him with joy unspeakable'. The preachers built up expectations of ecstatic experiences, even visions, at communion time, when 'thou shalt have [more] high and majestic thoughts of him than ever thou had before at any time', and promised that, after a 'sight of Christ' in the sacrament, 'all the duties of religion will be most pleasant unto you, the [next] communion will be sweet and delectable, and meditation will be pleasant unto you, and prayer will be sweet, and reading the scriptures, that will also be pleasant unto you.'[51]

Such promises, of course, raised the spiritual bar considerably and gave place to the other, more sinister themes of communion and thanksgiving Monday sermons – those of pervasive sin, hypocrisy and the need for constant vigilance lest Satan win out. Communion sermons were an emotional roller coaster, the troughs as deep as the peaks were high. 'The hypocrite can give Christ the outside of outward duties: he can fast, pray and communicate, read and meditate, and yet never give his heart to precious Christ,' thundered Andrew Gray, speculating that his audience might be entirely composed of hypocrites, so that 'Christ will return alone from the kirk of Bothwell', no hearts having been given to him. Lest his congregation decline into smugness after the sacrament, he roundly insulted

50. E.g., Folger ms V.a.415; NLS ms Wod. XLVII (notes on Samuel Rutherford's 'exhortations at communion'); Gray, *Sermons* – a printed collection of 'no more than notes taken from his mouth in the pulpit' (p. ix).

51. Folger ms V.a.415, ff. 81v (James Ruatt), 85 (Andrew Gray), 42, 52 (unnamed afternoon preachers). An Auchterderran communion sermon notebook records the purpose of the communion sermon as being 'to instruct and refresh a weak and weary soul in these apostate and corrupt no less nor dangerous days': CH2/21/5, f. 92. This parishioner must have been pleased to note down, 'it is your father's good pleasure to give [crossed out and changed to] elect you to the kingdom' (f. 45, 1625). Most of these communions were in Kirkcaldy or Kinglassie, 1618–25.

them: 'I think if there were none to hear this preaching today but those to whom Christ should speak . . . we would have a thin congregation.' And surely whatever spiritual comfort communion may have offered would have been erased by the conclusion: 'O woe be unto you eternally if so be ye have feasted with an angry Christ.'[52] While the systematic condemnation of the auditory we have observed in preparation sermons is perhaps not surprising, continuation of the same message in the two Sunday sermons is a bit jarring. Here, after the emotional devastation of the fast sermon and in view of the communion table set for reception, one would anticipate at last a message of comfort and forgiveness. It is there, but severely tempered by the reminder that 'there are many painted Christians amongst us'. Even so, communion sermons undeniably contributed to the emotional intensity of the experience and, for the faithful, to continued anxious self-scrutiny on the one hand, and an expectation of spiritual ecstasy through prayer, Bible-reading and sermons on the other. Perhaps most importantly, at their most negative they put all members of the congregation in the same boat: it was the whole parish that bore the brunt of the preacher's question: 'Shall this be the report today, we came there to Bothwell and there was not one that gave Christ a look? . . . Shall it be written upon the doorheads of this place, Christ was not seen by this congregation[?]'[53] In the end, for good and ill, the sacrament was a communal event, joining all the parishioners in a single endeavour to repent truly, to combat sin actively, to achieve sanctity, to experience the holy.

Even after the sermon had ended, the word did not: as each successive table was served, the minister launched into an 'exhortation', a short homily that also found its way into sermon notebooks.[54] These exhortations were at least short; at this point in the service, the focus significantly shifted from spoken word to material form, food and drink, and highly formalised, even choreographed movement. The verbal imagery of the sermon gave way to (though it still emphasised) the sensual participation that obviously remained the most continuous thread from pre-

52. Folger ms V.a.415, ff. 58, 60, 63v–64, 71v; cf. Gray, *Sermons*, 604: 'I think this communion had been better if some of us had not been here', placing the reluctant communicant in a catch-22, since absentees would have been fined.

53. Folger ms V.a.415, ff. 50, 45v, 46–46v.

54. CH2/145/6, f. 17; Blair, 7. It was the words of the second and third exhortations that persuaded Blair to communicate for the first time. Communion exhortations appear in Folger ms V.a.415. Gray's collected sermons include comparatively brief exhortations at the first, second, third and fourth tables of a communion at Kirkliston (pp. 603–10). Parishes often sat eight or ten tables to accommodate the whole congregation (e.g., CH2/145/6, f. 11v).

Reformation eucharists.[55] 'The communion will satisfy all your senses,' Andrew Gray promised his Glasgow auditors – sight in the 'shining cup of red wine', taste in 'spiced wine', touch and smell in handling of bread and sipping of wine, leading to experiences as ecstatic as those of the most visionary of catholic saints: 'Are your hearts in heaven, O Christian[s]? . . . Is it he? Is it he? Is it exalted he? Is it he whom I saw in prayers and sacraments?'[56]

The shining physical implements that contained that 'spiced wine' and the inspirational bread were designed as much as the sermons were to embody protestant messages. Three points should be made about the plate. First, in the sixteenth century, cups – not chalices – seem often to have been borrowed or donated tableware. Those that have survived are for the most part quite plain, frequently marked with a family name, and in an emphatically un-ecclesiastical style (see plate 8).[57] The mass had given way to a common meal, its paraphernalia that of the family table. This may have been as much for practical as for ideological reasons, given the cost of silver, but the message must have been quite clear to those accustomed to watching the mass from afar, only coming near the plate annually, and then only seeing the chalice held by the priest. The mystical transformation of wine to blood at the hands of a sacerdotal clergy was repudiated in the very commonness of the tableware. Of course, there was a danger inherent in eliminating the sacerdotal aspect of communion and in preaching against transubstantiation, at least insofar as the ignorant had not quite managed to grasp the bit in the *Catechism* on communion: the Ayr session had to discipline the chapman John Dalrymple after the spring 1604 communion for 'taking a piece of flesh and casting it from him, saying, "That was the flesh of Christ"'. But this 'odious blasphemy' was unusual.[58] The second point about the plate is that, when more highly decorated and formal cups were introduced from the 1590s, with a particular upsurge of output in the 1630s, they took the style of the traditional Scottish mazer, a cup designed for communal use, rather than the chalice associated with an exclusive priesthood (see plate 9). The priesthood of all believers, the peacemaking function of the kirk and the communal identity of the

55. Tambiah, *Culture*, 2–3 on the relationship between language and action in ritual.

56. Gray, *Sermons*, 606–07.

57. George Dalgleish and Stuart Maxwell, *The Lovable Craft* (Edinburgh, [1987]), 18. The 1617 parliament (*APS* 4:534) ordered parishes to purchase communion vessels, suggesting that many lacked their own previously and would have to have borrowed silver for their celebrations. On post-Reformation communion plate generally, Thomas Burns, *Old Scottish Communion Plate* (Edinburgh, 1892), and his ms notes for that work, NAS ms CH1/5/115, v. 1 and v. 7, p. 14ff on the mazer.

58. AAC CH2/751/1, f. 10v.

faithful were all affirmed by a vessel from which traditionally members of feuding families drank to their reconciliation.[59] Finally, it was only when, for King Charles's contentious visit in 1633, a newly favoured ceremonialist clergy began the use of much more elaborate plate, that we find patens decorated with the sort of iconography that protestants had made such an effort to destroy. Some members of Thomas Sydserf's kirk, Trinity College in Edinburgh, clearly approved this effort by contributing handsomely to communion silver that included a bread plate decorated with the figure of Christ kneeling at the table (see plate 10), but the furore that erupted five years later was surely much more representative of popular reaction to the introduction of what protestants had condemned as idolatry.[60] For generations, communicants had been served from the sort of tableware they used at home; to see images on the silver would to the simplest have communicated a real and alarming innovation, grounds ultimately for taking the Covenant.

The furniture of communion, ritual posture and the way the elements were distributed sent the same message as common tableware, of inclusive communality of the faithful. The elders in charge of the tables saw to the placement of boards, or trestle tables, to extend the length of the nave, with a shorter cross-table at the top from which the minister celebrated the sacrament (though English visitors reported great variety in placement of tables, 'lest the uniform situation of them might end in superstition'). The minister after his exhortation 'cometh down from the pulpit and sitteth at the table, every man and woman in like wise taking their place as occasion best serveth.' He then gave the elements to the people, 'who distribute[d] and divide[d] the same among themselves', while scriptures were read, so that 'hearts and minds' were exercised along with 'eyes and senses'. No man acted as priest; rather, 'each man took his communion bread with his own hand out of the basin', and 'gave the cup to others sitting at the table'.[61] Sitting as a family on forms, or benches, on both sides of the table, rather than kneeling at a rail to receive from the minister's hand, militated against any notion of clerical mediation or sacerdotal hierarchy. And each taking bread and wine with his own hand clearly

59. I owe this point to helpful discussion with George Dalgleish. See also NAS ms CH1/5/115, f. 7; Dalgleish and Maxwell, 21, 23–24; Ian Finlay, *Scottish Gold and Silver Work* (n.p., 1956), 79–80, 86–87.

60. CH2/141/1, f. 68v, 74; 1633 collections produced £1,400 for communion silver from this wealthy parish. Fitch, 683–84, 706, points out that medieval chalices had often been decorated with scenes from the crucifixion, and that Jesus is pictured next to the altar in the Arbuthnott Prayer Book.

61. *BCO* 125–27; Spalding, 2:79; *Chronicle of Perth*, 36; Thoms, *Kirk of Brechin*, 78. For table placement, Morer, 53–54; CH2/271/1, f. 132.

eliminated any notion of inherent holiness in the substance of the bread and wine. The Arminian cleric John Creighton in the 1630s would criticise this deliberately casual form as going 'to the Lord's Table, as [if] we were going to a landward bridal [a country wedding] and sit with God cheek for jowl'; in a sense, he was right.[62] Placing the sacrament in an everyday setting was a conscious endeavour to reduce the distance between believer and divinity by removing the sacerdotal layer of the medieval priesthood and its accompanying and separating ceremony and space – exclusive vestments, denial to the laity of entrance into the chancel and partaking in both kinds, the physical railing of the altar, even the privileged language of the Latin mass had all emphasised the gap between laity and clergy and thus increased the gap between laity and God. The message was even more complicated, since sitting also followed 'the example of the apostles eating the old passover, who did it in a gesture like our sitting at table', implicitly elevating humble lay communicants to sainthood.[63] What is important here is that the means to accomplish in the parish this fundamental protestantising of lay–clerical relationships were just as formal, material and ceremonial as the traditional ones had been. With the verbally preached doctrines of priesthood of all believers and spiritual presence rather than transubstantiation thus closely juxtaposed to symbolic performance, Reformed communions serve as well as any example of that combination of semantic and pragmatic that in Tambiah's scheme allows us to begin to understand the efficacy of ritual as an embodiment of cosmology.[64]

As we have seen, sitting had sufficiently strong support among some laity in Perth to cause a furore when the king wanted to change it.[65] When the 1618 articles attempted to abolish 'Christ's gesture of sitting' as 'common and profane' and insert 'the Antichrist's gesture of kneeling', one protestor predicted, 'Look forward and ye shall see the wide door of tradition cast open, whereby the whole multitude of theatrical pan[oply], not only of England but popish vices . . . will enter', with 'the table of the Lord either taken away or turned into a cupboard, our eating and drinking into a minced and pinched tasting . . . and kindly and Christian

62. NLS ms Wod. Oct. IX, f. 14.

63. Morer's observation, 63; Cowper, 263; NLS ms Wod. Qu. C.

64. Tambiah, *Culture*, 3–4.

65. For efforts to enforce kneeling at communion, see *RPC* 11:68–74, 12:60–68; *BUK* 3:1127–28; Blair, 36; *Bannatyne Miscellany*, 1:211. For further evidence of popular resistance, David Calderwood, *History of the Kirk of Scotland*, ed. Thomas Thomson and D. Laing (Edinburgh, 1845), 457, reporting that at Easter 1621 in Edinburgh's Old Kirk, the tables were 'filled but four times' with those who knelt. Representative of published opposition is Calderwood, *Resolutions for Kneeling* (Edinburgh, 1619).

distribution into a stewardly dispensation.' Only 'such kirks as never saw better may have some comfort in this'. Scots congregations had experienced the 'liberty, affection, [and] large consolation' of a better, communal and familiar practice.[66] The earnest reformer John Row was therefore able to report with obvious glee that, in Edinburgh's High Kirk at the 1627 Easter communion, there were 'not above six or seven persons in all the town that kneeled'.[67] Who can deny the power of external form, material symbol and ritual posture for Scots communicants? When we understand sitting to be as loaded a posture as kneeling, it becomes clear that this is not a church that rejected ceremony, but one for which emblem and ritual action continued to embody meaning, including radical objection to what most people now perceived as 'popish' forms.

Opposition to kneeling clearly does not mean that communion was anything less than a highly formalised event, or that there was not great reverence for the celebration and its material accoutrements. The Trinity College bread plate may have been disturbingly iconic in its medallion image of Christ, but the rest of the picture – the silver arranged on the table, the covering with its fringed edge – is probably a very accurate depiction of what the small or cross table would have looked like (see plate 10). Sessions took scrupulous care at Saturday pre-communion meetings to designate particular elders to be in charge of each item of plate – flagons and cups, basins and platters – of each board cloth, and of the elements themselves, to ensure that everything would be properly arranged the next day. They devoted meeting time to sorting out where the plate and cloths would come from when they were borrowed, how to pay for them if they had to be purchased, and who would wash and mend the linen – the sole contribution of women to the material preparations.[68]

66. NLS ms Wod. Fol. XXVII, ff. 21v, 23. The 'congruity' that Archbishop Laud sought was in Scottish eyes a settling for second best. They pitied the English, and scorned those of their own clergy lured into Laud's deception: cf. John Morrill, 'A British Patriarchy? Ecclesiastical Imperialism Under the Early Stuarts' in *Religion, Culture and Society in Early Modern Britain*, ed. Anthony Fletcher and Peter Roberts (Cambridge, 1994), 209–37; Mullan, *Puritanism*, chapter 7. Lay reaction to the kneeling orders of 1618 was admittedly mixed, however. In conservative Aberdeen, when sitting was restored after 1638, 'sundry people murmured and grudged' it, having had twenty years of kneeling, 'but could not mend it' (Spalding, 2:79). The records convey a sense, though, that these people were the minority.

67. John Row, *The History of the Kirk of Scotland*, ed. D. Laing (Edinburgh, 1842), 343, 45–46. In 1628 Edinburgh's ministers reported that of twelve thousand communicants, five thousand for 'scruple of conscience' declined to participate, and fewer than a hundred knelt: NLS ms Wod. Fol. XLII, f. 228.

68. For expenditures on tables, CH2/266/1, ff. 8 (£8 in Mid-Calder for boards and 6s 8d for a half-hundred nails for them in 1608), 33v, and 50v (£5 6s 8d for more

They also spent considerable sums on communion silver, and those who contributed plate to the kirk clearly saw it as a singularly pious act.[69] The cloths, like pulpit coverings, were not plain, but fringed, often at great cost. And the sessions' horror when the cloths were stolen reflects more than frugality. The Perth elders were outraged at the sacrilege as well as the expense of the 1621 theft that cost £6 from the kirk box to replace the tablecloth borrowed from Patrick Pitcairn's wife.[70] The cost of this cloth suggests that, while it was used in the home as well as the church, it would have been reserved for only the most festive occasions in both; the fact that, like sixteenth-century communion cups, it was a household item communicates not ordinariness, but the deliberate protestant blurring of the line between clerical and lay, kirk and family in view of the priesthood of all believers. The material object carried doctrinal as well as spiritual significance.

The Scottish communion was thus emphatically not a 'mere remembrance' of Christ's death, its elements 'nothing else but naked and bare signs'. Our temptation to charge the reformers with eliminating ritual, ceremony and the sanctity of consecrated objects must be tempered by recalling the Calvinist rather than Zwinglian doctrine involved. As the 1560 *Scots Confession* proclaimed, 'In the Supper rightly used, Christ Jesus is so joined with us that he becomes the very nourishment and food of our souls.' It is more than just remembrance when the faithful in communion 'has such conjunction with Christ Jesus as the natural man cannot comprehend', so that while the reformers denounced those who 'worship

communion tables, 1639); CH2/4/1 (Aberlady), f. 11v; CH2/93/1, f. 34 (£5 6s 8d for 'timber to the table boards' in Dron, 1642). Even portable tables were costly to construct and set up each time: AAC CH2/809/1, f. 77, records Monkton's allocation of 13s 3d 'for setting of the tables and drink to the workmen' for a 1630 communion; CH2/145/6, f. 11v allocates 54s to a wright for nails and setting up the table in Elgin, and the same to officers who kept the doors and helped set up the tables; cf. f. 17v for purchase of 'forms [benches] to the table'.

69. CH2/636/34, f. 25 (£9 for two basins and a laver); Burns, *Communion Plate*; Thoms, *Kirk of Brechin*, 79; CH2/141/1, ff. 68v, 74; and George Dalgleish's unpublished 'Trinity College Church, Edinburgh: Communion and Baptismal Plate, 1632–1698'. Stent (tax) of the parishioners generally paid for silver after the 1617 parliamentary act, and session minutes indicate compliance despite significant cost.

70. CH2/521/7, p. 256. See also CH2/266/1, f. 34v (£3 for 'linen to be the board clothes to the communion tables' in Mid-Calder, 1627); CH2/276/1, f. 12 (16 merks 5s for 15 ells of linen, and 17s 6d for cloth to cover the basins and cups in Newbattle, 1617). These costs pale in comparison to Trinity College kirk's £150 linen expenditure in 1636 for four communion cloths each 37 feet long and two shorter (15-foot) cloths, the minister Thomas Sydserf being of a Laudian bent: CH2/141/1, f. 92v. Dalkeith put an elder in charge of borrowing cups and cloth: CH2/84/28, f. 60.

the signs . . . neither yet do we despise and interpret them as unprofitable and vain, but do use them with all reverence.'[71] The *Confession* goes on to insist that not only the clergy, but all receivers of the sacrament must *understand* this complex theology – an objective the more easily accomplished by retaining a strictly ordered ceremony to reify the meaning of the protestant communion.

The elders' physical placement and movement during the celebration was accordingly as strictly ordered as ever the places of priest and acolytes at the mass had been, with the number of personnel much increased. At those Saturday planning meetings, each elder and deacon was assigned not only his duties, but also the space he must occupy to carry them out. The Perth session in 1580 named two elders 'for keeping of the south kirk door', one 'for the north kirk door of the choir', another for the south choir door, two 'for receiving the alms and tokens', two 'to keep the wicket behind the pulpit', two 'to convey the bread through the tables', four 'to convey the wine', three 'to convey the wine from the vestry to the tables', one 'to prepare the bread', one 'to prepare the kirk tables and napery', and the 'rest of the elders and deacons to wait upon them in the choir'.[72] The bread and wine were to be conveyed with gravity, and the elders designated 'to watch at table' and at the doors were to ensure 'a solemn manner' in communicants.[73] Those collecting the tickets served the practical and thoroughly Reformed function of 'fencing the table', that is, preventing those without tokens from entering that part of the church where the communicants sat, or from approaching too near the table – the table and its elements thus acquiring a visible sanctity.[74] Note, though, that unlike the physical separation of all the laity by a rail before the altar, the only

71. *The Confessioun of Faith Professit and Belevit Be the Protestantis within the Realme of Scotland* in John Knox, *The History of the Reformation* in *Works*, ed. David Laing (Edinburgh, 1848), 2:115.

72. CH2/521/1, f. 42; also for Perth, CH2/521/1, f. 144; CH2/521/2, ff. 4, 42, 117v; CH2/521/3, pp. 144–45, 228–30, 271–72; CH2/521/6, p. 23; CH2/521/7, p. 23; CH2/521/8/1, f. 49; the detail of the assignments is consistent from the 1580s through the 1630s at least. Among many other examples, from Edinburgh to Orkney, see CH2/400/1, pp. 164, 165, 263, 283, 291, 302; CH2/266/1, f. 111; CH2/4/1, ff. 32, 36v, 43v; *Canongate*, 6, 33; CH2/442/74, f. 33; CH2/276/1, f. 11; CH2/718/4, ff. 12v, 15; CH2/450/1, f. 4; NAS RH2/1/35, ff. 55–55v; CH2/122/1, f. 3v; SAU CH2 624/2, pp. 144, 189; CH2/716/2, ff. 89v–90.

73. CH2/716/2, ff. 89v–90; CH2/718/4, f. 12v; CH2/299/1, p. 288.

74. CH2/448/2, p. 59 ('none let enter in the kirk but such as has their tickets' in Aberdeen's instructions to the bailies who attended the doors). The authors of the *Forme of Prayers* were concerned that over-zealous 'fencing' might keep some from hearing the sermon and so specified that those barred from the sacrament must be admitted to the building to hear the preaching (p. 117).

barrier now to entering the holy space, for a most holy action, was the doctrinal and behavioural standard imposed by Reformed discipline. No inherent sanctity of clerical status gave entry to the table; only knowledge of the word and proper adherence to it allowed ingress. The elders' physical presence at the threshold of the kirk served to display the new principles of inclusion and exclusion at work in a community that now defined acceptability in terms of piety and knowledge. A person able to cross the threshold, turning in a token in sight of the neighbourhood, displayed her or his status in the protestant hierarchy. A person turned away at the door was effectively excluded from communion in this world and the next, with the neighbours as with God. A new cultural norm was visibly, tangibly established by the elder at the wicket, the elder with the token basket.

Orchestration of the congregation's movements in the sacramental ceremony sent the same messages, and confirmed the same and indeed a higher reality. In Perth, where those not qualified for admission were to come to the kirk for the communion sermon (and to give their alms), they were to enter by the north door, while those with tickets came in at the south door, turned in their alms and tokens, and proceeded to their assigned places near the tables in the choir.[75] There could be no clearer or more dramatic illustration in any sermon of the line between the godly and the worldly, and potentially of the separation of sheep and goats in the final judgment. With saints and ungodly thus defined for all to see, the minority at the north door would have some motivation to prepare for the south door next time around. Meanwhile, the south-door crowd, having sat through the psalms and sermon in their accustomed places, at the administration of communion processed forward in pre-designated groups to take their turns sitting on the forms around the table and partaking of the sacrament, each wave succeeded by the next in a visible, formal and hopefully grave display of godly order. Lending greater solemnity to the processional interludes were the brief exhortations between each seating.[76] Sitting down at the table itself inaugurated what anthropologists would recognise as the liminal phase ('communitas', to use Victor Turner's now well-known phrase) in a rite of passage. Having been separated out from their ordinary categories – the first stage in such a rite – those seated at the table were in a 'betwixt and between' place where

75. NLS ms Adv. 31.1.1, f. 14. None of the records makes it clear whether children of parents with tokens entered the south door with their families or the north door with the impenitent or ignorant; given the kirk's concern with households as units of catechism and discipline, the former was probably the case, with parents responsible for keeping their children away from the table until the proper age.

76. Gray, *Sermons*, 577–612, esp. 603–12.

social rank no longer matters, where all were in a uniform condition, humbled and passive, and involved in a process of refashioning at the hands of the sacred being.[77] When communicants left their seats or galleries or desks, they were abandoning one of the most visible early modern signs of rank in the world in favour of the equality of a common bench and a common table.[78] With that movement, ordinary hierarchy was erased for the duration of the communicants' passive reception of bread and wine – material representations of a transformative grace that would equip them for a godlier way of living upon return, or reaggregation, to the world. Among its many messages, then, protestant communion ritual affirmed in its central phase the common culture that bound together the community of the kirk, even as it acknowledged in its separative and reincorporative phases the tension between the equality of elect status and the hierarchy of parochial society. More was going on in communion than met the eye; what it accomplished culturally in the end was a credible testimony both of the way things were and the way they might be in the divine order. The protestant rite embedded theological principle in recognisable reality, reifying a spiritual potential with a communal performance readily grasped at some level by even the least articulate.

The Lasswade elders ordered an unusual but even more symbolically loaded orchestration of congregational movement to the table. The kirk being very crowded and movement to the tables having given rise to 'a commotion the last year bypast', they decreed in 1615 that after the sermon 'all the people remove themselves forth in the kirkyard to the intent that we may eschew confusion in the going to the table.' Two elders were

77. This discussion reflects Turner's redaction of Arnold van Gennep's tripartite division of rituals of passage into separation, liminality and aggregation; Turner's treatment of the temporary equalising of those in the liminal state is in *Ritual Process*, 94–130.

78. I have found few qualifiers for this point. Calderwood's *History*, 457, refers in passing to a 1621 Edinburgh communion in which 'lords and their dependers, communicated at the first table', with the lower orders at subsequent sittings. Elgin's elders in the same year designated an early morning service for servants so that so they could return home for necessary work (CH2/145/3, f. 180v – 4 am, 'masters of families at 10'). The *BCO*'s 'as occasion best serveth', and session guidelines like Trinity College's 'as it seems most convenient' (CH2/141/1, f. 5v) left room for a social hierarchy of distribution – lairds, then tenants, then servants – the model of continental Reformed churches. Scottish session minutes, however, give no indication that such an order was observed, while they do provide great detail about other aspects of administration. And when James Hamilton sat the gentlemen of his Cambusnethan parish separately and allowed them to give the elements to each other when commoners had to kneel and take from the minister's hand, his parishioners complained to the General Assembly, and got him deposed: NLS ms Wod. Fol. LXIII, ff. 129–35, 1639.

stationed at the kirk door to prevent more entering than 'shall suffice the table at once'.[79] Now, while the session's intention may have been purely practical, to separate those with and without tokens and keep the processions orderly, what they produced was a ceremony that willy-nilly carried with it a complex web of meanings embodied in the congregation's movement into and out of three different, highly charged spaces. From 'the world' they had come into the holy space of the kirk to hear the word preached. From that they passed *en masse* to another holy space, where their ancestors were buried and symbols of death and resurrection decorated the grave markers that multiplied so dramatically in the seventeenth century. Thence they passed in smaller groups back into the kirk, this time to the table itself, where they would consume food and drink now set apart for ceremonial use. Finally, they returned through the kirk door to the everyday world. Their sojourn in the kirkyard must have brought to mind both memories of the departed and the doctrine they had heard so often of their own union with them in the invisible and eternal church.[80] The sacrament in which they were to participate was a communion of all saints, in and out of time, and the signifiers of that cosmic construction of Christian community in the burial ground can only have heightened the meaning of the communion experience to follow, around a table that might have looked like a family board, but that, in the context of the larger experience, movement and milieu, was the Lord's – a sanctified space for holy rather than everyday actions. The power inherent in such movement in and out of holy spaces served to fix in human experience a now distinctly protestant version of the sacrament, antisacerdotal and logocentric in contextualisation, precisely by confirming fundamental continuity with the traditions of holy space that had always surrounded death and burial, communion and the affirmation of afterlife. The radical cultural shift required by the Reformation was thus accomplished in great

79. CH2/471/1, f. 6v. Blair, in Ireland, dealt similarly with the problem that with the communion tables set up, there was insufficient room in the kirk for all the people. He sent the congregation outside to a nearby castle courtyard for his sermon, then back in for communion in a series of smaller groups: Blair, 84. While outdoor preaching would seem a reasonable solution to the problem of crowding, at least in summer, there is no evidence in session minutes that it was an ordinary feature of Scottish communions until much later, especially in the later seventeenth and eighteenth centuries, as Schmidt has shown in *Holy Fairs*, and Hugh Cheape for the Highlands in 'Communion Season', 305–16.

80. Kirkyards were also traditional sites of parish games and festivities, but this was coming increasingly under attack by protestant authorities (see chapter 4, below), even as the new popularity of markers for kirkyard burials was crowding out revelry: Betty Willsher, 'Scottish Graveyards', *Proceedings of the Society of Antiquaries of Scotland* 118 (1988), 322–23; and chapter 7, below.

measure by means of cultural continuity, drawing on inchoate memory to legitimate and render acceptable fundamentally new meaning.

Another catholic tradition, the paschal offering, also proved enduring and effective – both for practical, fiscal reasons and as a reinforcement of ritual continuity in the midst of change. The spring communion offering, retained by elders ever anxious to replenish the poor box, also served to reinforce the seasonality of the sacrament, to mark it by ceremony when much larger than usual offerings were delivered into almsbasins held by specially designated elders standing at the communion boards or the kirk doors.[81] The offerings were quite substantial by comparison with those of ordinary Sundays: Yester kirk at its 1613 April communion collected £8 3s 9d, compared to usual sabbath offerings of around 18d; Newton's communion offerings in the 1620s ranged between £5 and £6 as opposed to their usual 6–18s; Monkton's 10s became 10 merks; and Menmuir gathered £13 6s 8d at its 1638 spring communion, compared to 14–19s on an ordinary Sunday.[82] Individual motives for giving are impossible to discern; we have no idea how many parishioners were simply continuing habits acquired before the Reformation.[83] Certainly many offerings were less

81. On paschal offering before the Reformation, Fitch, ch. 8; McKay, 101; *Statutes of the Scottish Church*, 178–79, 181–82; Cowan, *Scottish Reformation*, 78; Duffy, 93. Bardgett, 'Dilapidation of Church Property', 19, claims that the kirk rejected the pasch offering. They did judge it 'overburdensome on the poor', but rather than rejecting it altogether they made it voluntary, and generally designated it *for* the poor. Among many examples of paschal offerings after the Reformation, see CH2/258/1, f. 24 (Markinch, where the 'collection at the door and tables' of £11 10s paid for bread and wine as well as poor relief); CH2/266/1, ff. 5v, 29v, 34v, 50v; CH2/191/1, ff. 1, 3, 8–8v, 31; CH2/521/6, f. 88; CH2/100/1 (Dunbarney), f. 15v. Anstruther Wester's paschal offerings were made in 1613 at the Saturday preparation sermon: SAU CH2/624/2, 168. Menmuir also had a special offering on preparation day, but it brought in only 13s 4d in 1638 as opposed to £13 6s 8d the next day: CH2/264/1, ff. 17v, 13v.

82. CH2/377/1, f. 10v, 14; CH2/283/1, f. 4v *et passim*; AAC CH2/809/1, f. 77; SAU CH2/819/1 (Kingsbarns' usual weekly collections of £3 5–6s, spring communion collections of £65 9s 8d in 1637, f. 14, cf. f. 20); SAU CH2/210/1, ff. 3–3v (Kilconquhar sextupling its usual £3). New Register House, Edinburgh, ms OPR 310/1, ff. 45–57v, shows Monifieth collections ordinarily around 30d weekly rising to 300d or 400d at communions. In the Highlands, Dron's usual 26s became £46 16s at a 1638 communion (CH2/93/1, 19v), and Inveravon's 16d to 3s rose to 25s in the 1630s, Pasch and Yule offerings together providing twice-annual contributions to the poor of £3 12s (CH2/191/1, ff. 1, 3, 8v, 31).

83. Post-Reformation paschal offerings generally went to poor relief, but in parishes where lords or heritors could not be persuaded to pay for communion elements – expensive now that the whole congregation partook of the wine – the offering often supplied them. The expense was considerable: £8 in Burntisland in 1610 for the landward portion alone, to be paid by a laird (CH2/523/1, f. 33); £2 for four pints of

than voluntary. In Aberdeen, two magistrates supplemented the elders standing at the end of each table in both kirks during the administration of the sacrament to 'demand of every communicant at their rising from the table some alms to the poor according to the form observed in Reformed congregations in the southern parts of this realm'.[84] Such strong-arm tactics were resented in Menmuir, where in 1638 John Glen and John Finlay committed 'rude and unseemly behaviour upon the communion sabbath towards' the two elders/collectors at the kirk door, 'in that they did cast the silver into the boards upon the ground and used all violence and thrusting without giving anything to the poor'. Perhaps had they at least made a contribution, they would not have had to perform public repentance and pay a fine equal in value to an average week's collection from the whole parish.[85] In any case, giving to the poor at Easter would have been as pious a work after as before the Reformation from the perspective of the pew. And the remarkable and steady increase in size of paschal offerings from at least the turn of the century through the 1630s suggests considerable popular support for seasonal acts of charity that would earlier have been construed as meritorious, still associated with the sacrament of communion.[86]

If sitting at the table was the culmination of the communion season, it was not the final instalment. The dénouement came on the next day, when the congregation returned to the kirk for the Monday sermon of thanksgiving. With the Saturday preparation sermon, this provided a sort of logocentric bookend for the ritual of the sacrament. Where the preacher was particularly charismatic, it proved quite popular. Robert Blair reported

wine and 12s for bread in smaller Anstruther Wester in 1613 (SAU CH2/624/2, p. 135); £3 5s in Dron (CH2/93/1, f. 14v, 1635). The Kirkcaldy elders in 1623 sent delegates to a local lord 'to deal with him for the full entertainment and furnishing of the elements for the communion (CH2/636/34, f. 49v); the same tack was taken in Glasgow and Dalkeith: NLS ms 2782, f. 37; CH2/84/28, f. 60 (also 'to buy the tickets', 1616). In 1632 Kirkoswald's minister, who had been paying for communion out of his own pocket, finally had enough and persuaded the elders to take 10 merks from the poor box to cover the cost: AAC CH2/562/1, f. 9.

84. CH2/448/2, p. 77.

85. CH2/264/1, ff. 18–18v. The session found Glen to have been caught up in the disorder accidentally and so let him off.

86. Mid-Calder's communion offerings were more than tenfold the usual, and they rose substantially from the turn of the century, from £10 9s in 1605 to £13 2s in 1624 to £42 in 1627: CH2/266/1, ff. 5v, 29v, 34v, in each case collected over the two Sundays of the spring communion. Perth's likewise more than kept up with inflation, rising over the course of 1632–36 from 137 merks to 205 merks: CH2/521/8/1, f. 133v; CH2/521/8/2, n.f., 9 April 1635, 2 May 1636. So did Belhelvie's, rising from £31 in 1624 to £80 in 1637 (CH2/32/1), and Trinity College kirk's, going from £1,034 in 1626 to £1,926 in 1631 and £2,423 in 1636 (CH2/141/1).

that his Irish parishioners 'came very early Monday, hours before preaching time'. Where Monday sermons were genuinely giving thanks for the atonement and forgiveness represented in the sacrament, they were surely a relief after the threats of the preparation and communion sermons. Even Blair 'promised a blessing from God' at this point 'unto them that would seek it'.[87] The last phrase, though, may be the most important: Monday sermons were replete with exhortations to upright living in light of forgiveness received, and with continued harping on hypocrisy. David Bisset's Monday auditors must have gone away terribly worried that they were among those who 'have been long near Christ as to ordinances', having seen Christ 'with their eyes yesterday and with their hands handled him, and yet Christ may say of them . . . ye have not believed on me', since 'it is very like that God had no mind of them from eternity'. James Blair devoted Monday sermons to warning his Glasgow congregation about the 'iniquities ye are most in hazard of especially after the communion', for 'the devil he will lay baits to tempt you'. He addressed what must have been for some an affective depression after the emotional intensity of communion, urging those who feared that they had 'gotten no mercy' to 'be about your duty and . . . remember that it was a great mercy and favour that ye got leave to sit down at his table.' He exhorted those who may have taken too much comfort from the experience to 'beware of laziness and security . . . of the sin of worldly-mindedness which will readily creep in after the communion', for 'Satan he will seek to winnow you as wheat'. If to us there appears little encouragement of faith in these dire warnings, however, we must grant with the parishioner who took notes on these Monday sermons that 'it cannot be known what becomes of communions, or what strength and vigour and activity of soul is attained by them even in those who for a long time hath been in Christ.'[88]

Participation in communion was very nearly universal in the protestant kirk. While precise numbers are impossible to judge given our ignorance of seventeenth-century population figures and age distributions, the non-communicants at the north door of St John's kirk in Perth really do seem to have been a small minority. Judging from numbers of communion tokens handed out in Perth – 2,200 in 1621 – and allowing for exclusion of the substantial portion of the population under age sixteen, those caring

87. Blair, 84–85.

88. James Blair preached on John 5.11, Jesus instructing the healed man to 'sin no more lest a worse thing come unto thee'. Quotations are from notes written from the back of the sermon notebook, Folger ms V.a.415, ff. 137v–137 for Bisset, ff. 121v–118v for Blair. The former preached on John 6.35 in Govan, Blair in the barony kirk of Glasgow.

for young children, the ill and infirm, and those away on mercantile or fishing voyages, those without tokens would certainly have been a small minority in a town of perhaps five thousand at this date. Glasgow's production of four thousand tickets in 1604, 6,200 in 1653 for its rising population, suggests first, that the usual 1600 population estimate of two thousand is far too low and the rise to about thirteen thousand by 1700 was well under way by mid-century; and second, that a significant landward population was included: the tokens were divided among the four town preachers and one landward.[89] The Burntisland elders recorded in 1609 seven tables served in the morning, twelve in the afternoon, each with fifty persons, totalling 950 communicants – a sizable crowd for a small parish.[90]

Of course, there were some in every community who either misbehaved at communion or failed altogether to appear for preparative examination and the sacrament. They were prosecuted even more vigorously than ordinary sabbath-breakers. Most session books report isolated cases of people who, though eligible to communicate, regarded the sacrament too lightly and had not yet quite acquired the proper habits of reverence. It is important to recognise, however, that this was not a change from pre-Reformation times – disorderly procession to Easter communions had aroused the priests' ire long before 1560. But it did trouble the elders sorely.[91] Assignments for elders in the Canongate kirk therefore included some 'to stench the rumor' (still the noise) in the body of the kirk, that is to keep quiet those waiting their turn to sit at the table.[92] An unduly officious kirk officer could find his efforts backfiring, as did James Dennis in Perth, who moved from his assigned position at the kirk door and came 'within the body of the kirk six or eight feet . . . the people being convent[ed] in great number', to warn those without tokens who 'interrupted the divine service' with noisy conversation. The communicants tried to stop him from disrupting the solemnity of the service even more than the rabble without tokens were doing; in the end the session referred him to the presbytery

89. CH2/521/7, p. 237; NLS ms 2782, f. 37v; Jan de Vries, *European Urbanization 1500–1800* (London, 1984), 271. The Glasgow session had spent 50s 'for stamping of the tickets of lead' in 1593; ten years later the tokens were melted down and four thousand new ones produced. William Brereton generously estimated Glasgow's population in 1636 to be ten thousand, with six to seven thousand communicants (*Early Travellers*, 150).

90. CH2/523/1, ff. 38v, 44v, recording about twenty-five more in September 1610. Monifieth recorded in the 1570s six to seven hundred at every communion; with slight population growth in the 1580s, the figure reached 780 – probably close to the whole adult population of the town: New Register House, Edinburgh, ms OPR 310/1, ff. 31v, 37v, 41v, 45, 51v, 54v, 57v.

91. McKay, 106–07.

92. *Canongate*, 6.

for violating the choreography of a rite whose message lay partly in its formality.[93] Clearly, despite the misbehaviour of a minority, most of the congregation were committed to maintaining decorum.

As for those who failed to show up for examination or communion, some were doubtless closet catholics, though by the turn of the century it became harder and harder for them to survive in communities enforcing the sort of doctrinal standards we have seen in the kirk. Participation in communion was the litmus test of orthodoxy, so missing it was often construed as tantamount to admitting catholicism. The Aberdeen elders in 1615 actually ordered a communion specifically 'for the discovery of the recusants'.[94] Some absentees brought the acceptable excuse of illness or being at feud and so afraid to come – though the latter reason only served if there had been demonstrable efforts to reconcile.[95] Others claimed to have communicated in neighbouring parishes; the elders demanded testimonials to that effect.[96] Still others did, perhaps, constitute an audaciously irreligious minority. These were often 'landward folks', for whom distance made attendance more difficult and who doubtless took longer to be brought into the rigorously protestant fold.[97] But they were a tiny minority indeed, judging from numbers of prosecutions for recusancy, and it was hard for them to survive, too. The fact is that the elders had clout when it came to enforcing attendance. When, in 1599, Perth's communion was

93. CH2/299/1, p. 288.
94. CH2/448/3, p. 181; cf. CH2/448/2, p. 27, the rejected 1607 claim of a suspected catholic of the powerful Menzies family that he had missed eight communions in two years for illness or travel.
95. CH2/191/1, f. 3v (Grissel Grant afraid to come because of threats by her father's enemies, 'the session admitting her excuse'). Isobel Cuik in Burntisland offered the reasonable excuse that she was denied a token for 'variance between her and her neighbour', but the session apparently expected her to settle the quarrel in time; they disciplined her and appointed two elders to arbiter the dispute: CH2/523/1, f. 12v (1604).
96. CH2/400/1, f. 49.
97. CH2/521/6, f. 138; AAC CH2/809/1, ff. 25–25v; CH2/448/2, p. 27 (the always troublesome 'absents from Futtie', Aberdeen's fishing suburb. Living far away in the countryside in isolated circumstances could explain why twenty-four-year-old James Rannald of Falkirk parish had never been examined or received the sacrament; the presbytery required him to make public repentance, 'answer[ing] to the minister when he shall be called upon', and to prepare for the next communion: CH2/400/1, f. 36. Often the same names recorded among communion absentees show up in prosecutions for quarrelling, drunkenness and other forms of disorder: see, for example, CH2/276/1, f. 67v, Henry Wardlaw, absent in Newbattle and claiming illness in 1624, but earlier summoned for flyting (f. 7v) and attempted sexual assault (f. 21v). He represents the truly disorderly sort. Absentees also included people refused tickets because of poor examination performance (*Dundonald*, 308).

only annual and the miller William Young failed to appear, he found himself warded for his 'scandalous offence'.[98]

Numbers of communion absentees relative to population estimates were small in nearly every parish. Even in conservative Aberdeen, where catholics were occasionally excommunicated as late as the 1610s, named absentees from that April 1615 communion, for instance, numbered only five, out of a burgh population of perhaps seven thousand.[99] Fraserburgh's 1615 campaign against 'backlying' from communion was waged against only two, both merchants' sons who managed to give acceptable accounts of their voyages as excuse for absence. Perth's minister complained of 'many' not attending in 1599 and again in 1603, but each time the session, having summoned '*every one of them* to be called before them and censured', only came up with a handful of cases for prosecution – and Perth's elders were nothing if not sticklers for taking attendance and searching the town on Sundays.[100] Five or six absentees set over against 2,200 communicants suggests extraordinary success at establishing a pattern of communion participation. Cases like that of David Fuird of Kirkcaldy, absent from examination and communion for nine years, stand out in their isolation and often have explanations unrelated to doctrine or discipline – absence abroad, or communicating in a neighbouring parish, for instance. As in the matter of ordinary sermon attendance, sessions did accept excuses like illness, but only after investigation: the reported sickness of a 1606 Dumfries absentee was refuted upon observation that the man had managed to do 'all his other affairs ordinarily notwithstanding . . . being tied to the bed', and on Monday after communion his neighbours had found him up and about.[101] In assessing the culture of protestantism, our focus should doubtless be more on the neighbours who informed the session than on the absentee. The majority not only conformed to the

98. CH2/521/3, p. 108.
99. CH2/448/3, p. 183. Four were excommunicated in 1616 for not subscribing the articles of religion, the other sure test of popery. For seventeenth-century population estimates, de Vries, *Urbanization*, 271. Of course, some absentees may have escaped prosecution; however, session books declare such comprehensive campaigns and record sufficiently active searching to confirm that crediting these numbers is not arguing from complete silence.
100. CH2/1142/1, f. 78; CH2/521/3, pp. 82, 275, emphasis mine.
101. CH2/636/34, f. 43; NAS ms CH8/54/1, f. 1. The elders also noted that his wife and servants had been absent as well. The Dumfries session also rejected the excuse of a traveller who had actually made it home on the last day of communion but claimed that he 'could not upon suddenty be prepared' for the sacrament; the elders noted that announcement of examination had been made at his house twice before he had set off on his journey.

sacramental requirements, they enforced the rigorous standards of the kirk on their neighbours – and sometimes even on their ministers. Much more representative of popular attitudes towards communion than absenteeism is complaint from parishioners whose ministers were dilatory about celebration.[102] Temple's congregation petitioned the Dalkeith presbytery for help when their minister, Thomas Copland, omitted the sacrament three years running, offering the feeble excuse that the 'roof of the kirk being faulty was repairing and he could not get it commodiously'.[103]

It is difficult to know precisely how and to what degree we can construe such complaint, along with attendance figures for communion, to indicate popularity of the sacrament. Certainly people went to a good deal of trouble to learn their catechism and behave themselves lest they be barred from the table. Those who had offended the mores of the Reformed community underwent rigorous discipline in order to be admitted, with flurries of disciplinary meetings just before the communions. These produced demanding penalties, which offenders performed with apparent alacrity against the threat of exclusion.[104] On the other hand, failure to communicate was itself a punishable offence, particularly if it were habitual.[105] If participation in the sacrament demonstrated protestant orthodoxy, people may well have avoided absence lest it be taken as a tacit admission of popery, which brought its own dire penalties.[106] Of course, the most severe of these would be excommunication. Did people fear this ultimate penalty because it also entailed exclusion from the secular life of the community, or principally because it barred one from the sacrament? Fortunately, other kinds of evidence allow us a glimpse of popular devotion to communion.

In attempting to assess lay attitudes towards the sacrament in its protestant guise, it is surely significant that all sessions before every communion in the post-Reformation period found it necessary to appoint men to

102. CH2/198/1, ff. 15v, 16, 19.

103. CH2/424/1, f. 15 (1631). This was not the least of Mr Copland's offences: see chapter 3, below, for more on the troubles of Temple parish.

104. E.g., NAS ms RH2/1/35, ff. 52v–53v.

105. The Dundonald session required repentance barefoot and in linen for 'continual biding from examination and communion'; Mortlach likewise required public confession; and in Tyninghame a single absence was 'heavily rebuked' and required 'public satisfaction on their knees before the people' on Sunday and payment of the fornicators' fine: *Dundonald*, 61, 221; CH2/529/1, f. 18; CH2/359/1, ff. 5v–6.

106. Glasgow's session in 1587 ordered two elders to visit 'all that are suspect of papistry' and order them to communicate at the next celebration. When the visitors reported 'some who under pretence of discord may be papists and will not communicate', their colleagues ordered all such either to 'be resolved in their consciences' or excommunicated: NLS ms 2782, f. 37.

guard the kirk doors against interlopers. One does not trouble to provide a defence against a threat that is not real. The fact is that people without tokens – those we too often dismiss as the 'rude multitude' or the irreligious – were anxious to communicate, so much so that they would risk the public humiliation of discovery at the door, or later at the table, in order to join their neighbours. Far from being unconverted to protestant practice, irreverent or impious, or resentful of the kirk's intrusion into their lives, they sought out the religious experience of their neighbours, tried to sneak into those sermons denouncing their ignorance or misbehaviour, and risked not only discovery but punishment for their efforts. William Wilson of Kilspindy almost succeeded when he made it into the kirk and sat on 'a seat of his own hard by the table, but such a seat wherein divers others used to sit and communicate, neither could he deny but that under pretext of sitting upon his own seat he intended to communicate' despite being under censure. A sharp-eyed elder intervened in time, and Wilson had to repent in sackcloth for his audacity. After seeing two Dundonald women found out in 1610 for 'coming to the Lord's Table being under the censures of the kirk', James Fullarton, likewise debarred, decided to try leaving the parish to communicate at neighbouring Riccarton instead. Much good it did him: he was turned over by the elders there to his own session and required to repent publicly and pay 40s.[107] Belhelvie parish encountered so many 'sundry strangers [who] . . . present themselves to the table of the Lord without testimonials from their own ministers which were debarred in their own parishes' that they admonished the elders attending the 'sacred table' to keep their eyes open and remove such scandalous folk.[108]

Among Anstruther Wester's interlopers were a number of fishermen anxious to communicate just before going off for the summer season, suggesting that some saw communion as a sort of spiritual prophylactic, a source of protection against divine wrath expressed in the tempests that took so many fishermen's lives in the seventeenth century. It was worth risking the elders' wrath to avert the danger faced at sea. While sessions hardly approved such confusion of sacrament with magic, in this parish they may inadvertently have contributed to it, in two ways. First, while

107. CH2/299/1, p. 290; *Dundonald*, 214, 308.
108. CH2/32/1, f. 3. In St John's kirk, Calder, the minister gave each watching elder a list of those from his own quarter who were debarred to check against those coming to the table: CH2/266/1, f. 111. Aberdeen profited from the fines of the audacious, 10s from masters of households 'wanting tickets', 5s from their wives, 3s 4d from servants: CH2/448/2, p. 16. See also CH2/326/1, f. 4; SAU CH2/624/2, p. 124; CH2/521/3, p. 82 (discipline of communicants without tokens in Scoonie, Anstruther Wester and Perth).

their careful orchestration of the distribution was intended to ensure 'that all things may be done in decency', the people in the pew may well have seen more in the formality of the ceremony. 'Decency' can fade easily into sanctity where the latter is sought for security in a dangerous world. A sombre and carefully choreographed communion may well have served the same psychological functions as the mass had earlier, assuaging anxiety in the face of natural forces by offering a sense of the protection inherent in proximity to the holy. Second, Anstruther Wester's elders fed popular belief in the magical utility of the sacrament by appointing a Sunday each March specifically for 'celebration of the communion to the seamen that are in readiness to go to their good voyages'.[109] They allowed the communion to serve much the same function as the elaborate physical decoration of the sailors' gallery in the post-Reformation kirk of Burntisland: here with the date 1602 are depicted ships, angels and most notably the inscription: 'Though God's power be sufficient to govern us, yet for man's infirmity he appointeth his angels to watch over us' (see plates 22–23). Is the post-Reformation really a post-totemic era? It is clear that people in the pew applied communion's protective functions not only to storms at sea, but to other natural disasters as well. An Auchterderran parishioner who recorded in his sermon notebook 'being delivered from a desperate disease wherein almost from Lammas to Michaelmas I lay, restored [beyond] all expectation after communion anno 1619 by God's special favour' indicates that such a popular construction of communion may not have been unusual.[110] We are reminded again of the multivalency of the meanings embedded in ritual and emblem – a frustration to those who wished to achieve doctrinal purity, but *de facto* a boon to a movement that, if it were to succeed among ordinary folk, would need to offer concrete comfort to the anxious in the absence of so many of the tangible comforting devices of catholic tradition.

The horror expressed by congregations when the formality of communion was violated also suggests popular devotion to the sacrament. People seem to have absorbed a notion of communion as a singularly sacred event, however ordinary its table, benches and utensils, and one to be guarded carefully from the profane. Allowing the laity to sit in sacred space, 'cheek by jowl with God', did not reduce the sanctity of that space; rather it elevated the possibilities for the laity to approach the divine. Thus, when John Stirling entered the Cadder kirk on communion Sunday 1595 'with drawn whinger held above his head' demanding to be served, and

109. SAU CH2/624/2, pp. 124, 148; CH2/266/1, f. 111.
110. SAU CH2/21/5, f. 21 (in the midst of his notes on a communion sermon on spiritual disease). On Burntisland's galleries, Gifford, *Fife*, 110–12.

in the mêlée the table was overturned, no fewer than seventeen deponents travelled to the Glasgow presbytery to express the congregation's outrage. 'The whole people was sore troubled,' they reported, when 'the bread and wine of the sacraments of the body and blood of Jesus Christ was cast to the ground.' Stirling 'did terrify the people in the kirk' with his knife, but they were even more appalled, 'sore troubled' and 'staggered' at the sacrilege. The presbytery ordered Stirling imprisoned in the castle, and eventually excommunicated him for this particularly 'heinous sin'.[111]

Finally, communion, so densely patterned with interwoven meanings, could also be a highly charged political statement. This is nowhere more evident than when it sealed the swearing of the Covenant. At Perth in March of 1638, the whole congregation, men and women, gathered and swore the Covenant 'by upholding of their hands' at a communion 'in the old manner', sitting around the table rather than kneeling, as a ritual gesture of solidarity in the face of the English enemy.[112] If the Covenant's text had somehow left doubt in anyone's mind regarding the issues over which the coming wars were to be fought, the ritual action of the communion clarified them. The community joined together with God and each other at the table would gladly take up arms for what by now was a fundamental part of Scottish protestant identity.

* * *

Session minutes have much less to say about the other sacrament. What they do reveal, however, is that our central theme – the coupling of elements of continuity with placement of the sacrament into a clearly logocentric setting – works as well for baptism as for the Lord's Supper. The reformers placed baptism firmly into the context of preaching and doctrinal examination of parents. The people, however, negotiated successfully for elimination of both of these protestant requirements when their own fears for their children's souls drove them to demand a sacrament that they clearly regarded as necessary for salvation, whatever the theologians might say. The reformers did what they could to divorce the sacrament from the raucous festivity that had accompanied it time out of mind. Again, however, the demand from the pew for traditional celebration won the day. What we find in the session books is an ongoing process of negotiation between pew and session house that in the end

111. ML CH2/171/1, ff. 50–56v (process from 14 May to 2 July).
112. *Chronicle of Perth*, 36; cf. 38. The 'auld manner' included 'the minister at the little table, and the elders at the two boards, being people at both sides thereof, [and] every one took the bread first off the plate with their own hand, and *fine* the cup.'

produced a cultural shift, successful precisely because the authorities were willing to compromise.

The protestantisation of baptism lay in is association with the word preached and with the systematic doctrinal vetting of parents. The reformers mandated that baptism be public, performed by a minister (never a midwife), in the kirk, on a preaching day – in fact, the next preaching day following the birth. Its principal feature was lengthy instruction on the meaning, necessity and benefits of the sacrament as a means of grace, and on the nature of Christ and his sacrifice as the grounds of salvation – lest the rite be construed as meritorious in itself.[113] In most parishes baptisms were scheduled just after a Sunday sermon, so that the instruction embedded in the ceremony served to reinforce an hour or so of teaching and exhortation – the word ever dominant in the ritual.[114] Alexander Forrester was typical of ministers in his report to the Haddington presbytery that he 'never did so much as baptise a bairn if it were without preaching', even though he complained that most of his parishioners 'desired but a show of the ministry, *viz.*, to marry and baptise their bairns' without requiring an accompanying grasp of the word.[115]

Such parents would not have got far in the new system: sessions routinely required parents coming to 'book' their infants for baptism first to pass the usual examination on the creed, the ten commandments and the Lord's Prayer.[116] Lasswade's session

> ordained that no children of ignorant parents be baptised except the father first lay a pund [a bond] worth 10s in the hands of some person by the session appointed for the receipt thereof, and a month shall be granted the father to learn the Lord's Prayer, belief and ten commandments, together with some competent understanding of the sacraments and catechism, which he performing, his pund to be surrendered, otherwise to be forfeit.[117]

113. *First Book*, 90–91; *Forme of Prayers*, 62–82 in the 1565 edn; CH2/521/7, p. 198. Examples of sessions acting against midwife baptism include CH2/523/1, f. 2; SAU ms 30451, f. 4v. John Welch's representative argument against female baptism is *A Reply against M. Gilbert Browne Priest* (Edinburgh, 1602), finding midwife baptism of weak infants rooted in the erroneous doctrine that baptism is necessary for salvation (p. 220).
114. CH2/471/1, f. 3v; Morer, 62 (observing Sunday celebration, but noting that weekday preaching services were also admissible times).
115. CH2/185/2, f. 14.
116. NLS ms 2782, f. 39v; CH2/636/34, f. 30v; New Register House ms OPR 310/1, f. 8.
117. CH2/471/1, f. 2v (1615 acts); Inveravon also required a 2-merk deposit of the 'ignorants who presents their bairns to be baptised who never can say the Lord's prayer nor belief . . . either in English or at least in Irish': CH2/191/1, f. 16.

Scoonie levied a 40d fine on parents who failed the examination, in addition to refusing baptism to their children. Some of Robert Blair's parishioners in Ireland were not altogether happy with his strict requirement of ministerial conference with parents, 'for I baptise none till first I had conferred with the father and exhorted and instructed him, as need required'; however, he quickly dismissed those who objected as being under the joint influence of the devil and drink.[118] If ignorant parents took too long to learn their lessons, or if they had sinned and were required to perform a lengthy repentance, the elders did sometimes agree to the child's baptism in the interim, but only if a 'faithful Christian would promise to see the child if she live trained up in the fear of God'.[119] Their overriding interest was instruction of the child in the word; correct doctrine and knowledge of the scriptures overrode blood relationship in the protestant scheme. They took seriously the *Book of Common Order*'s lengthy baptismal section, which sternly exhorted parents to instruct their children in the precepts of the protestant faith. Whoever presented the child, having already passed the session's or minister's private examination, still had to perform before the congregation yet another set of responses to the minister's questions about the creed, and then affirm publicly and audibly in response to his charge that he would take care 'for the education of the infant, to make his behaviour suitable to it'.[120] There is no better material symbol of the definition of baptism in terms of word than the placement of the water basin. In lieu of the medieval font at the kirk door, Scottish protestants put water into a 'basin conveniently fastened to the pulpit side', held by an iron bracket (see plate 5).[121] The sacrament was thus physically as well as theoretically tied to the word preached.

For all the care the sessions took to associate baptism with the word preached and doctrine learned, however, celebration of the sacrament was in practice not limited to preaching days, or even to public gatherings. Even in the thoroughly Reformed town of Perth, William Cowper lamented that by the 1610s baptism only on preaching days was a discarded tradition. What immediately strikes a reader of kirk session minutes

118. CH2/326/1, p. 1 (1626 'acts of session'); Blair, 65–66.
119. CH2/521/7, p. 346; NAS ms RH2/1/35, f. 24v (1574) records Edinburgh allowing a base-born child to be baptised before the parents had performed their prescribed repentance for fornication because the father was soon to depart the realm and the mother was still in childbed; however, the parents had to repent publicly as soon as possible, with a cautioner (see n. 129, below) to ensure their performance and present the child. Cf. f. 20, the bastard of another couple 'received to baptism out of the hands of some faithful'.
120. *BCO* 139; Morer, 62–63.
121. Morer, 63; Brereton, in *Early Travellers*, 146–47. Surviving brackets can be seen in Pencaitland and in the Museum of Scotland, which dispays a bracket from Aboyne, Aberdeenshire.

is how regularly sessions either permitted baptism on irregular occasions or complained that people came 'at extraordinary times . . . to crave it', particularly 'upon occasion of the weakness of their children'.[122] Why would parents not wait for a preaching day, as frequent as these were? Quite simply, they feared for the souls of sickly infants likely to die before baptism. Protestant preachers might 'abhor that blind and merciless sentence of the papists that infants dying without baptism go to any house of Hell', but they had to grant the psychological comfort provided by the sacraments to the parents of a weak child. As Cowper put it, 'albeit it be not necessary to the child's salvation, who will deny but it is a necessary, at the least a profitable help of the parents' faith'?[123] Accordingly, sessions routinely qualified the prescription for baptism only on preaching days, with phrases like, 'unless the midwife deponed on her conscience the bairn was weak'.[124] What we have here is obviously the survival of an older tradition, and one quite at odds with Reformed theology. The sessions' willingness to tolerate it, however, surely helped to make possible the gradual adoption of more thoroughgoing protestant doctrine by offering the solace of 'emergency' baptism in the interim without explicitly granting its theological underpinning. Recognising that this was a religious culture in transition, that such a process takes time, and that the elders could not have been ignorant of this reality, helps to account for what look to us otherwise like an untenable contradiction in early modern protestantism. It is time for historians to acknowledge that a culture in the process of drastic change will necessarily be one in which there is internal tension, but that the tension is not necessarily a liability.

The other pre-Reformation survival associated with baptism was celebration of the event with feasting by family and 'gossips'. Here conflict brewed with the sessions' commitment to sobriety and order, more than with a theological position. The role of godparents in speaking for the child in the catholic form of baptism seems to have gone by the board with no particular complaint. But godparentage itself remained firmly

122. Cowper, 9; CH2/521/7, p. 198; CH2/716/1, f. 22v.

123. Cowper, 9, 699 (insisting that unbaptised infants may still enter heaven); *BCO* 136. Cowper worried that the Perth articles' approbation of private baptism would 'confirm the opinion of absolute necessity of baptism, which is dangerous': *Original Letters*, 2:512–13.

124. CH2/521/1, f. 105 (1584); SAU CH2/624/2, p. 3. They also played into the hands of traditionalists by punishing parents who postponed baptism. The St Andrews elders required public repentance of the ploughwright Robert Wilsoun in 1594 for keeping 'his bairn fourteen weeks unbaptised, till the same deceased without baptism': *SAKS* 2:792; cf. CH2/636/34, f. 45v. Of old, this would have doomed the child's soul, but it ought not to have been a such a problem for protestants.

embedded in the culture, Knox's liturgy specifying that the child be brought to the font by father and godfather.[125] What troubled the sessions was the festivity that the protestant laity were clearly unwilling to forfeit at the Reformation.

Protestant baptisms continued the long-standing tradition of attendance by large numbers of hard-drinking gossips who in the elders' view mocked the sabbath, the seriousness of the sacrament, and the good order of the community with their unrestrained revelry, not just at parties before and after the sacrament, but frequently in the church itself. Often festive traditions were maintained by the crafts guilds. In 1611, for instance, 'it was reported to the [Perth] session that James Blyth younger went to Methven on Sunday . . . to baptise his bairn, accompanied with a number of young men of his own craft and others also, who both in going to Methven and returning home, behaved themselves in a lascivious manner, having a pipe playing, and fighting in the tafthouse when they were rebuked by the constable.'[126] Clearly, the revelry surrounding this baptism had got out of hand. The Perth session was likewise disturbed by the crowds of women who often accompanied the midwife and child to the kirk for baptism. In 1620 they reprimanded the 'great abuse grown within this burgh, in that a great number of women' came to church not to hear the sermon, but to celebrate noisily. Some of the women were reportedly 'altogether careless of the hearing of God's word' and remained at the parents' house during the first part of the service; others came to the church but then noisily 'at eleven hours go forth of the kirk to convoy the midwife and the child thereto, who by their going forth disquiet others to give them passage.' The session ordered that henceforth only two or three women should accompany the bairn to the kirk, although after the baptism 'as many may go home with the child as pleases'. They thus allowed for a party following the sacrament, but insisted on a more limited and restrained celebration before, in order to emphasise the importance of attending and not disrupting the sermon. Their repetition of this order in a 1621 charge to midwives, however, suggests non-compliance even with the compromise.[127]

The women of this 'convoy' were the gossips, chosen by the parents to

125. A. Ian Dunlop, 'Baptism in Scotland After the Reformation' in *Reformation and Revolution*, ed. Duncan Shaw (Edinburgh, 1967), 82–99.

126. CH2/521/5, f. 14 (1611). It is not clear why the child was being baptised in Methven. The revellers were punished by the civil magistrate for their disorder, and by the session as sabbath-breakers. Out-of-town baptisms that drew witnesses away from their own parish churches on the sabbath were a frequent annoyance to the session (e.g., CH2/521/7, p. 105).

127. CH2/521/7, pp. 198, 222.

witness the baptism and to celebrate the birth further with feasting and drinking in the family's house. 'Gossipries' had been a traditional feature of baptismal celebration, and their persistence well into the seventeenth century can only be explained by the complicity of elders who recognised the social utility of festivity at rites of passage and kept their disciplinary efforts against it at best half-hearted. There were limits, though. Perth's elders finally decided to clamp down in 1632 when a party of gossips 'through excessive drunkenness were not able to carry themselves on their own feet, but were borne in barrows' home from the celebration, an 'offence of God and profanation of the Lord's day'. The session banned any further 'meetings for drinking of gossips on the sabbath days', and requested a policy statement from the presbytery. The brethren, 'having considered the great abuse in the conscience of many people, men and women, at the baptising of children . . . and the great excessiveness of drinking and gossipers that follows thereupon', passed an 'Act against the great multitude of gossips'. Not quite meeting the Perth session's stringent limitation, they set the maximum number of witnesses at seven.[128]

The year 1634 saw the elders carrying out the presbytery ruling with alacrity. On 16 June they chastised James Clark 'for holding a gossipry in his house the time of the afternoon's sermon'; the following week their concerns about disorder proved justified when violence broke out among a group of drunken gossips during the afternoon sermon. They prosecuted the maltmen Thomas Smyth and David Thomson for fighting, the wife of James Clark for selling ale to them, and Hew Smyth for hosting them (although he claimed to have 'passed away forth of the company of his gossips before the skyth [fighting] fell out'). A few days later they decided that preventive action was in order. 'Understanding by sure report that notwithstanding the former act ordaining that no convening of gossips be in taverns nor alehouses on the sabbath days, yet it is transgressed, and now lately on the sabbath day at gossiping there fell out through getting drunk great mischief and strife and blood drawn', they summoned two fathers of newborns to make sure they understood the rules. The shoemaker Harie Bell was required to secure a cautioner and 'act himself' (take an oath) not to 'convene his gossips and witnesses to the baptism of his child to drink, neither in tavern nor in any other place under the pain of £10 . . . and in like manner Alexander Richartson who has a child to baptise [in] the morn.' Finally, the session widened the net and passed an act that every father of a child to be baptised so act himself or face

128. CH2/521/8/1, f. 75v; CH 2/299/1, p. 308. Twelve to twenty gossips were usual at baptisms in Trinity College, Edinburgh, in the 1630s (Brereton, in *Early Travellers*, 146–47).

the £10 penalty.[129] No further offences are recorded in the decade, so baptismal celebrations must thenceforth have been more restrained, protestant affairs. What is surely significant, though, is that this campaign was not waged until seventy years after the Reformation.

Perth was not alone in its concern about baptismal festivity. In the Fife village of Newburn, the elders were in 1628 so troubled by 'piping and dancing . . . at the feastings at the baptism of children' that they demanded a bond of 40s deposited beforehand with the elders by the parents, to be forfeited if such profane behaviour were reported.[130] Kirkcaldy in 1615 limited the number of gossips to four, and if more were found, 'he that calls them shall pay 6s for every one'. But the well-off were apparently happy to pay for a greater crowd at their baptismal celebrations. The session in 1621 amended the figure to six female gossips in addition to the midwife and no more than four male witnesses, but (with an eye to its treasury) raised the penalty to 20s for each additional reveller.[131] The elders, no fools, set a low priority on abolition of this festivity, and for their tolerance doubtless won approbation from their neighbours and an accompanying willingness to submit to more fundamental religious demands. As with communion, the way to a culture of the word was smoothed by retention of customary ritual and celebratory tradition.

★ ★ ★

Many of the difficulties encountered by a religion of the book in a non-reading society were thus effectively counterbalanced by the kirk's flexible treatment of pre-Reformation traditions. Keeping the sacrament of baptism readily available to meet perceived need in times of stress made good sense for authorities struggling to achieve much more fundamental changes in religious culture – specifically sufficient indoctrination of parents in protestant theology to make the next generation well-grounded in Reformed principles. Turning a blind eye to some measure of celebration may well have staved off lay rebellion until an alternative system was

129. CH2/521/8/1, ff. 139v, 140v. The fighting maltmen and the alewife had to repent on their knees and pay 20s each; Smyth was warned. A 'cautioner', like a 'surety' in England, was a sort of bondsman who promised to pay the penalty if his client failed to perform an assigned act, behave in a prescribed manner or pay a lesser fine. If one who 'acted himself' failed to do as he had promised, he would be liable for the set penalty. Cautioners were generally drawn from the better sort of townsmen or leaders of the offender's kin.

130. SAU ms CH2/278/1, p. 2.

131. CH2/636/34, ff. 9 (1615), 47 (1622). Dalkeith faced the problem of baptisms on fasting Sundays by making parents promise to delay the inevitable banquet until the Monday: CH2/424/1, n.f. 20 January 1591.

in place. Maintaining ceremonial, affective and seasonally customary observance of communion, preceded by preparatory periods of fasting and followed by communal thanksgiving, served ritually to redefine the community within the context of the sermons that would, over time, inculcate the new doctrine. In their Reformed guise, communion seasons and baptisms were organised around sermons, catechism and examination – the word, preached and learned, an ever-present vehicle of meaning. For the parishioner accustomed to annual Easter participation in the sacrament, however, the (generally) spring communions of Calvinist Scotland would have had a comforting familiarity. The process of gaining the all-important token would have provided a communal experience of doctrinal performance, physical self-denial, enforced freedom from labour and emotional catharsis in 'exercises' of preparation – a protestant Lent with its own potency, both spiritual and social. And however innovative rigorous parental examination before baptism was, ready availability of the sacrament and its continued festal celebration rooted the experience in tradition. In the end, it was word and sacrament together that defined for men and women in the pew their new protestant identity.

Chapter 3

Performing Repentance

In August 1621, the minister and elders of Perth summoned the town's penitents for what would become a regular Saturday evening meeting in the kirk. It seems that the elders were concerned that Sunday penitential appearances on the kirk stool, or seat of repentance, were not having their desired effect because of the inappropriate behaviour of those seated there. The immediate problem was that the fornicators – the majority of the penitents – were not learning their lines: they 'cannot make confession of their sin and declare their repentance therefore as becomes', and required 'instruction of the minister what to confess and say', or as the Glasgow session had put it in 1588, 'that he may the wiselier direct them in their repentance'.[1] The minister, in other words, was now to add drama coach and director to his job description. The script was not the only problem he had to address. The Perth session books from their first meetings in the 1570s are full of concern that some were using their plaids to hide their faces from the disapproving scrutiny of the congregation, or that far from weeping or appearing sorry for their offences, some were laughing during the sermon or even during their own confessions.[2] Others squirmed on the stool, or mumbled their confessions, and some actually turned their prescribed confessions on their heads and used the stool as a forum to rail against their neighbours or the minister.[3] The session had tried to address these problems by further punishing those misbehaving with fines or additional days of repentance, but apparently to no avail. They seem finally to have decided that ignorance and inexperience were

1. CH2/521/7, p. 260; NLS ms 2782, ff. 60–61, the session's order (renewed in 1605 and 1643) for penitents to 'pass to the minister who is to preach, on the Saturday before'.
2. CH2/521/1, ff. 9v (1578), 53 (1581); CH2/521/3, p. 97; CH2/521/8/1, f. 8; CH2/271/1, p. 7. Plaids, long woven mantles, were ordinary dress in the Lowlands as well as the Highlands.
3. CH2/1/1, n.f., 29 December 1608; CH2/338/1, f. 17v; CH2/271/1, p. 7; *Dundonald*, 231; CH2/1142/1, ff. 4v, 78v, 94v; CH2/521/6, ff. 115–15v; CH2/400/1, p. 85; ML CH2/171/1, f. 51v; *SAKS* 2:910.

to blame. The Saturday meeting, like Glasgow's longer-established one, was to be a rehearsal of proper penitential performance for the following day. What the session tacitly acknowledged by this mandate was that 'making one's repentance' (the protestant term for penance), while no longer the sacrament of catholic theology, remained a dramatic performance that must be done properly to convey the message of the rite, both to the performers themselves and to their audience.[4] Costume, set, props, choreography and script all needed careful design and rehearsal for the play to be understood.

What did penitential performance mean in a Reformed setting? Recent work on ritual by both cultural anthropologists and early modern historians has drawn the very sensible conclusion that rituals have multiple meanings.[5] A penitential performance that meant one thing to the authorities who ordered it may have meant something quite different to its actors and to its audience. It may have conveyed different meanings at different times, and for that matter multiple meanings at the same time to the same observer or participant. Certainly, in the era of Reformation its meanings were historically conditioned and shifting. The change in name, from 'penance' to 'making repentance', was meant to signify the most drastic of those shifts, in a theology that now denied any efficacy in penitential 'works' for the individual's salvation, and any power to absolve inherent in the priesthood.[6] What is remarkable, however, is the extent to which many externals maintained medieval practices. Traditional histories of the Scottish Reformation have too quickly claimed that the Reformers

4. The term 'performance' for public repentance is a contemporary one: e.g., CH2/400/1, p. 198. On the performative nature of rituals of disharmony, redress and reintegration, see Victor Turner, *Performance*, 72–98, drawing on social drama analysis; his *Dramas, Fields and Metaphors: Symbolic Action in Human Society* (Ithaca, 1974), 37–41; and Tambiah, *Culture*, 123–66.
5. The work of Catherine Bell is particularly instructive on this point: *Ritual Theory* and *Perspectives*. Tambiah, *Culture*, stresses that in public ritual individual stories necessarily impinge on the universal story (p. 125); Turner, *Performance*, 80–85, introduces the notion of 'idioverse', the 'distributive existence' of a culture as a group of individual personalities, each understanding performances in a reflexive, self-referential way. Both help to explain that ritual performances are therefore necessarily as diverse in meanings as the population itself. See also Turner, *From Ritual to Theatre. The Human Seriousness of Play* (New York, 1982); Mervyn James, 'Ritual, Drama and Social Body in the Late-Medieval English Town', *P&P* 98 (1983), 3–29; and D. Kertzer, *Ritual, Politics and Power* (New Haven, 1988).
6. Although a thoroughly protestant sixteenth-century Scots commonplace book grants, 'I may call repentance a work' since it is less a 'quality or habit' than 'an *action* of a repentant sinner', though rising from true faith: Bodleian Library, Oxford, ms Rawl. C 584, f. 5.

altogether discarded penance and the rites associated with it; in fact, the public confession of sin and demonstration of repentance not only remained in practice a rite of the kirk, it actually expanded to become arguably the central ritual act of protestant worship in Scotland.[7] Of course, in this as in other rituals retained from the old religion, there was an ongoing negotiation between old and new forms, to reflect the differences between old and new doctrines of justification. The forms finally adopted would have generated another, perhaps more difficult negotiation of meanings, with ministerial interpretation struggling against lay associations of traditional actions with now prohibited meanings. A close analysis of penitential rites in post-Reformation Scotland will provide a useful step towards sorting out some of the complexities of interpreting a ritual that, performed at least weekly, in one way or another affected every member of the early modern Scottish parish – rich or poor, godly or profane, lay or clerical, male or female.

Recognising that, as the Perth rehearsal day suggests, making one's repentance was fundamentally a dramatic performance, let us begin with as detailed a description of what actually happened as the sources will allow. The session minutes, together with a few surviving artifacts, permit us a closer and more comprehensive view than any other source and will produce a more detailed account than any previous one. To precisely what external forms did the penitent have to submit? In its Scottish version, protestant penance required not only particular modes of dress adopted from an earlier era, and a traditional use of material accessories to demonstrate the offence that had brought on the penance, but also the construction of special furniture – props, we might say – which, in the decades following the Reformation, became increasingly specialised and prominent in the arrangement of church furnishings. Penance was staged and choreographed, with penitents assuming carefully prescribed positions and moving from one place to another in procession within the church, and through particular doors when entering and exiting the building. It was scripted, with allowances for both prescribed, formulaic utterance and *ex tempore* speech, the whole inserted into the larger script of sermon-centred worship. Once we have defined what the penitent was to do, we shall examine the role of the audience, itself controlled by strict rules of acceptable action and expected to perform the proper response to the penitent's dramatic display. The congregation came to see and hear, but also to act in relation to their neighbours' humiliation and confessions. Finally, having

7. Cf. the more traditional view of Kirk, *Patterns*, xvi, asserting that in discipline 'the penitential system of the medieval church was jettisoned'; or for Calvinism more generally, Bossy, *Peace*, 73–100.

described the actual process of repentance, we will address the problem of meanings – religious, first and foremost, but social and psychological as well. Here anthropological categories of analysis will prove useful in some cases, although the complex soteriology underlying the whole notion of penitential acts, the radical protestant reinterpretation of an older doctrine of salvation incorporating works of penance, and the relative complexity of sixteenth and seventeenth-century Scottish society all make the problem of analysing this aspect of early modern Scotland a quite different order of business from interpreting the rituals of simpler tribal cultures. In many ways, the penitential performance defined the relationship between individual and community as much as that between godly and profane. It reflected economic and gender hierarchies, but both underpinned and undermined them. It divided the community into godly and sinners, only to reunite it in reconciliation or 'reception again' of the second group.[8] Finally, it enacted an understanding of the relationship between the whole human community and the divine that was at its core anxious, even terrified, and ultimately – perhaps desperately – propitiatory. Can the words of the sermon possibly have embodied more meaning that the mimesis of 'making repentance'? However insistent historians have been on protestantism as a shift from image and drama to word read and preached, from passion to rationality, the performance of repentance in the kirk demonstrates the continued and, indeed, affective vitality of ritual in the Reformed community.[9]

★ ★ ★

When asked which item of church furniture best represents the Calvinist reform of the sixteenth century, students of the protestant Reformation will generally respond that it is the pulpit. Certainly, as we have seen, the word preached acquired a predominance over the mass celebrated, and reduction of the altar to a common table and concomitant movement of the pulpit to front and centre tends to support this immediate answer. It works for most Reformed settings, but perhaps not quite so well for Scotland. There, a rival item of furniture confuses the issue. Yes, the sermon was central to the Calvinist service in Scotland, and pulpit would still be the correct answer. But near the pulpit, in general imme-

8. Myerhoff, 'Rites of Passage', emphasises the process of separation and reintegration in ritual performance. See also Turner, *Performance*, 74–79.
9. Cf. Peter Burke, 'The Repudiation of Ritual in Early Modern Europe' in *The Historical Anthropology of Early Modern Italy* (Cambridge, 1987), 223–38; Muir, *Ritual in Early Modern Europe*, 76, 140, 151 (describing 'that breakneck destructuring rush called the protestant Reformation').

diately in front of it, was another item of furniture that excited so much more attention both in the kirk session minutes and in the recorded observations of visitors that one wonders whether we have not perhaps overstressed preaching at the expense of penitential display for this northern realm.[10] This item was the stool of repentance, on which penitents were to sit for the duration of the service for which their 'humiliation' had been prescribed. Variously called stool, pillar, place or seat, it also took more than one form. Two varieties survive from the early seventeenth century in the parish of Holy Trinity, St Andrews. One is what we would recognise as a stool – low, sturdy, four-legged and without back or arms. The other we would call a bench – narrow-seated, long enough for more than one person, with a high back on which is painted in easily legible letters 'Repentance' (see plates 11 and 12). Two other versions survive in the Museum of Scotland: one, from Greyfriars, Edinburgh, is a tall (about a metre high), square-seated, four-legged stool with a footrest, necessary since its height would preclude placement of the feet on the floor (see plate 13); perhaps such a high stool was what contemporaries called a 'pillar'. The other is a low, narrow and backless bench, of the sort contemporaries called a 'form', from Monzie, in Perthshire (see plate 14). Glasgow's High Kirk had both a 'pillar' and a 'form before the pulpit'.[11]

10. Placement of the stool immediately 'before the pulpit' (CH2/141/1, f. 51) was usual: examples in Edinburgh include CH2/141/1, f. 51 and NAS ms RH2/1/35, f. 48 (my fol.). In Aberdeen, the precentor's 'desk' (seat) was beneath the pulpit, the penitents' stool immediately beneath that: Morer, 53. An exception was Temple, where it was moved to the north side of the kirk door because the Dalkeith presbytery at its 1631 visitation thought that location 'most commodious' (CH2/424/1, ff. 15–15v). This move, however, incited a small riot by a group of parishioners who 'with their swords about them and an axe with them and put forth the bairns who were learning in the kirk and so took down and transported the same' (ff. 16–16v).

11. I am grateful to the Reverend Charles Armour for allowing me to photograph the two 'stool-type' and one 'bench-type' penitents' seats in the vestry of Holy Trinity. The bench is only long enough to hold two people; however, session minutes indicate that often many more penitents sat on the stool on any given sabbath, so that either the small stools would have to be multiplied or the bench-type would need to be lengthened. Aberdeen's stool was a 'bench for five or six to sit on' (Morer, 53). 'Pillar' probably indicates the higher form of stool, like Greyfriars' in Edinburgh. The Trinity College, Edinburgh, and Glasgow kirk sessions prescribed 'public satisfaction on a *form* [bench]': CH2/141/1, f. 41; NLS ms 2782, f. 60. Most session books use the terms stool, pillar, place, form and seat interchangeably, with no indication that more than one item of furniture is meant. I have adapted the most usual term, 'stool', as an inclusive term. 'Place' may mean a wooden seat, or simply a location beneath the pulpit where penitents usually stood – like the place before the altar taken by their medieval counterparts. Generally, however, session minutes suggest that there was a piece of furniture in the 'place'.

Whatever its structure, the stool was situated to face the congregation and often seems to have been elevated on some sort of platform. Elgin's pillar was so high, in fact, that Cristane Innes in 1594 failed to make her assigned appearance 'because the ladder that stood at the pillar of repentance was taken away'.[12] One seated on the high stool or standing on the low (as was often ordered) was visible to all of his or her neighbours, on display before the whole community.[13]

A place of repentance was not unusual in either catholic or protestant churches in Western Europe: for centuries before the Reformation, penitents stood just beneath the high altar for the duration of the mass. Afterwards, protestant churches assigned them a place beneath the pulpit for the duration of the sermon, after which they would declare their repentance and be absolved or received.[14] But the Reformed Scots seem to be unique in seating their penitents in that place on a structure that in effect set them off even more definitively from the congregation – in

12. CH2/145/1, f. 64. Penitents were generally said to 'come down' from the stool after repentance (e.g., CH2/521/2, ff. 1v, 12), suggesting that even a low seat may have been placed on a platform. Elevation or use of a high stool is also suggested by the fact that it was possible for lesser offenders to repent 'at the foot of the stool' (f. 43v). In some parishes the stool was consistently called the 'pillar of repentance', e.g., CH2/4/1, ff. 2–2v (Aberlady). Fynes Moryson, a Cambridge student who travelled to Scotland in 1598, noted in St Giles, Edinburgh, a 'seat built a few stairs high of wood leaning on a pillar next to the pulpit' and opposite, 'another seat very like it, in which the incontinent use to stand and do penance'. Another English visitor observed in 1636, 'the stool of repentance . . . is a public and eminent seat, erected . . . about two yards from the ground, either about some pillar, or in some such conspicuous place where the whole congregation may take notice of them'. *Early Travellers*, 83, 144.
13. In many parishes, penitents 'stood' on the pillar, indicating that low stools, where seated penitents might be difficult to see, were actually intended to be stood on rather than sat on. Mid-Calder's elders told penitents to 'stand upon the seat upright': CH2/266/1, ff. 2v, 22v (1604); also NAS ms RH2/1/35, f. 28; CH2/96/1 (Dron), f. 15. In other parishes one is said to 'enter into the pillar' or stool (e.g., CH2/472/1, ff. 14, 21) and to 'sit on the pillar' (f. 19v). Most often, the verb is 'sit', and the fact that penitents are said to 'rise' or 'stand' to make their confessions after the sermon suggests that sitting during the earlier part of the service was usual: NAS ms RH2/1/35, f. 19; NAS ms CH8/42 (1597).
14. For an example of how this was acted out in an English setting, see my 'A Captive's Story: Puritans, Pirates, and the Drama of Reconciliation', *The Seventeenth Century*, 13 (1997), 37–56. Other examples can be found in Laura Gowing, *Domestic Dangers*, 40–41; Susan Karant-Nunn, *The Reformation of Ritual: An Interpretation of Early Modern Germany* (London, 1997), ch. 4; and *Penitence in the Age of Reformations*, ed. Katharine Jackson Lualdi and Anne T. Thayer (Aldershot, 2000). On penance in the pre-Reformation church in Scotland, see McKay, 106, 113–15.

some cases, as in St Andrews, complete with a written label.[15] The fact that the stool remained in that spot when the service ended would have served as a reminder throughout the week of the separate identities of penitent sinner and incorporated saint. Underlining the separation in some instances was empty space before the penitents' seat: in 1597, when the earls of Huntly and Errol made their repentance in Aberdeen seated before the pulpit, an observer noted that 'the greatest part of the body of the kirk [was] empty before the pulpit', despite an unusually large number of people in attendance.[16] Visibility would have been enhanced by the open space. Certainly a premium was put on easy visibility by the whole congregation. An English visitor to Aberdeen described the stool there explicitly as a place for sinners 'to be seen by the congregation and bear the shame of their crimes', and in Perth, when Margaret Mar 'sat in the back side of the stool', the kirk officer ordered her 'to sit on the foreside – that she might be seen'.[17] Mar effectively functioned as the living illustration of a theological point and had to act her part in clear view of all for the point to be made.[18] The elders also took seriously the precept in the *First Book of Discipline* that public sins require public censure. It was because a violator of the sabbath in South Leith had given 'evil example to the whole congregation' that he had to 'sit in a public place where all the whole kirk may see him'; and in Falkirk a drunkard made 'public repentance . . . in respect his offence was publicly known'.[19] In ordering public repentance sessions often underlined the importance of visibility with their formulaic language – 'in the face of the congregation, or 'made a spectacle to the congregation'.[20] Penitents were not a spectacle to be mocked, however. During the English occupation of Glasgow in the 1650s, the session ordered that 'so long as the English continue in town' the kirk

15. The sole English reference I have found to a seat of repentance is in Richard Sheridan's play *A School for Scandal* (II:iii) when Sir Oliver, learning that an old friend had been married for seven months, replies, 'Then he has been just half a year on the stool of repentance.' David Postles, of the University of Leicester, has found a Nottingham archdeaconry court case of 1577 where a woman did penance 'standing on a seat in the midst of the church', but the seat seems not to have been a permanent structure, and this is an isolated case: 'The Performance of Imposed Penance in England: A Long View (c. 1250–1600)', unpublished paper, cited with permission.
16. *Miscellany of the Spalding Club* (Aberdeen, 1842), 2:lx.
17. Morer, 53; Brereton, in *Early Travellers*, 144; CH2/521/3, p. 97 (1599).
18. The elders ordered penitents 'to enter the place of repentance as soon as the minister comes to the pulpit' for this purpose: NLS ms 2782, f. 60.
19. CH2/716/2, f. 89; CH2/400/1, p. 117; *First Book*, 168–71. See also CH2/521/7, p. 413; CH2/636/34, f. 4; *SAKS* 1:6.
20. CH2/383/1 (1640), f. 8; SAU CH2 624/2, p. 5 (1594); CH2/523/1, f. 44.

should 'put no persons upon the pillar, because they mock at them, as the other kirks have also determined'.[21] The stool was a place of utmost seriousness, a reminder to those in the congregation of the pervasiveness of sin even in the most godly communities.

If a penitent's sin were known in more than one parish in a town, or in more than one community, the offender might be assigned to stools in several kirks for a single offence. This was most often the case with notorious sinners in urban settings with more than one parish, as in Aberdeen when James Kemp, who had defamed four fishwives as witches, had to 'sit in sackcloth on the pillar of repentance two several Sundays, the one in the new kirk and the other in the old kirk'. In similar fashion, Marion Walker of Temple had to 'satisfy publicly partly in Newbattle and partly in Temple parishes' because the slander of her fornication was known in both places.[22] More extreme cases were those of a well-travelled excommunicated catholic from Liberton who was obliged to 'satisfy the kirks of Glasgow, Stirling, Edinburgh and Liberton', or of William Baillie of Lamyngton, who for his notorious fornication in 1597 was required by the presbytery to 'stand and make my repentance in divers kirks within the bounds thereof', securing a testimonial of obedience from the minister of each kirk whose stool he occupied.[23] After John Schawe stabbed his pastor in Kilmalcolm, the Paisley brethren assigned him to the stools of all eleven parishes of the presbytery.[24] On rare occasions, one of the parishes knowing the offence might be eliminated from the list, or a single-stool repentance might be shifted to a parish distant from the offender's, as a matter of physical security: when Andro Clark killed a man in the course of a feud, his presbytery allowed confession 'in any kirk in Fife where he might be safest' from the relatives of the slain man.[25] In

21. NLS ms 2782, f. 60. The Ayr session in 1605 noted the understandable unwillingness of a penitent to appear on his assigned day, for shame 'because there was so many strangers in the town': AAC CH2/751/1, f. 18.
22. CH2/448/3, p. 11; CH2/424/1, n.f., 2 May 1592.
23. CH2/121/1, f. 26; NAS CH8/42. Ministers regularly provided signed testimonials attesting that repentance had been performed as ordered, generally when parishioners were moving out of the parish and needed to attest to the session of the new parish that they were in good standing in the kirk – e.g., CH2/198/1, f. 7v; CH2/4/1, ff. 10, 10v, 20; ML CH2/171/1, f. 5v.
24. CH2/294/1, f. 5v. This onerous form of repentance was supposed to reconcile him with his pastor and make him 'love him in all time coming in Christian love and brotherly charity'. The Glasgow presbytery in 1594 sent a cordiner (shoemaker) burgess of the city to five parishes for his well-published incest, another burgess again to five parishes in 1595 for toppling the communion table in a drunken rage on a Sunday morning (ML CH2/171/1, ff. 30, 64v).
25. SAU, CH2/277/1 (Newburgh), Box I, #8, pp. 367–69.

general, though, the stool where a penitent appeared was the one in his own kirk, 'in face of' his own neighbours.

The stool was elaborated over time. In the decades following the Reformation, many kirks constructed both a 'low stool' for lesser offenders (drunkards or quarrellers, for instance) and a 'high stool' for more serious or repeat offenders (like multiple fornicators or adulterers). In Perth, for instance, the elders decided in 1605 that the best way to repress the sexual sins that they were convinced were on the increase would be to 'ordain a more public place of repentance to be biggit [built] with all diligence, and in it certain degrees, that therein fornication and adultery may be distinguished and better discerned both by their place and habit'.[26] In 1617 they added another specialised stool, 'a chair of stone to be built in a public part [of the kirk] for setting of flyters and slanderers therein', to be paid for with flyters' fines.[27] The Elgin session also set aside for adulterers the highest part of a multi-levelled seat in an area 'near the choir door' where there were apparently several stools, and in 1591 they 'ordered a new stool to be built' for slanderers, lower than that for adulterers, in order to correct what they saw as overly 'severe and rigorous dealing' with slanderers hitherto.[28] The Dundonald minutes consistently distinguish orders to 'repent low' or 'repent high' and set fee schedules for the well-off 'to redeem the higher place'; in 1628 they allowed Marion Montgomery to repent her public drunkenness 'in the low place because she alleged she was not able to go up to the high place', suggesting that the high stool was something of a physical challenge.[29] Finally, the volume of disciplinary business conducted by active kirk sessions led to repeated enlarging and multiplying of the stools, which in their initial forms were simply too small and too few to hold the number of penitents before the congregations each sabbath. In urban parishes, it was not unusual for twenty or more people to perform public repentance on a single day.[30]

26. CH2/521/4, p. 57; cf. CH2/718/4 (1619), f. 9v; CH2/448/2, p. 8 (1602, a 'low stool' for ante-nuptial fornication; *SAKS* 2:793 (St Andrews' 'highest degree of the penitent stool' for adultery).
27. CH2/521/6, f. 89v. For flyting, see chapter 5, below.
28. CH2/145/1, ff. 25 (an adulteress in 1591 sent 'to the stool of repentance upon the highest degree of the southeastmost desk [bench] nearest the choir door'), 56 (a 'new stool in the northeast nook [corner] of the kirk').
29. *Dundonald*, 272, 258, 263.
30. Even in the tiny parish of Kinghorn, seven people sitting on the 'pillar' at one time in 1608 suggests that the pillar was in fact a long bench (CH2/472/1, f. 19v); cf. four fornicators at once in Innerwick (CH2/1463/1, f. 2). South Leith by the early seventeenth century generally had twelve to twenty penitents on the stool simultaneously (CH2/716/1, e.g., ff. 16v–18); Ayr averaged seven or eight (AAC CH2/751/1, ff. 14v, 16); Perth ten to twenty, including adulterers who appeared for twenty-six

The expense to which many parishes went to enlarge the stool or increase the number of stools graphically illustrates the centrality of penitential performances in the Reformed kirk.[31]

For a sin that did not quite merit sitting on the stool, a penitent might either stand at the foot of it, before the pulpit, or confess the offence from his own seat in the kirk. In Yester, for instance, a couple who had married in England (presumably in order to avoid the vetting required before banns were proclaimed in their own parish) confessed their offence publicly, but from their own seat; and the Dundonald session allowed penitents to confess from their own seats the sins of offering hospitality to gypsies and playing the trumpet on the sabbath.[32] The foot of the stool was the assigned place of confession for receivers of infamous persons in Newbattle and for sabbath drunkards in Boharm.[33] If in a single incident, two offenders bore different degrees of guilt, the exact place where they repented indicated the relative weight of their offence, as when the Perth midwife Marion Stewart concealed evidence of a bastard's paternity and had to stand at the foot of the stool and 'from that place confess her offence', while the mother of the illegitimate child she had delivered, as the more serious offender, had to sit 'upon the stool of repentance [to] confess likewise her offence, that they may both be examples to all

sabbaths (e.g., CH2/521/1, ff. 85–85v; CH2/521/3, ff. 55–74, 142–43; CH2/521/14, pp. 62, 146, 182–85; CH2/521/8/2, ff. 162v, 196). Brereton, in *Early Travellers*, 144, refers to stools 'capable of about six or eight persons'; during a sermon at Greyfriars 'there stood three women upon the stool'. Some sessions tried to avoid displays of acrimony on the stool by assigning quarrellers to different days (e.g., CH2/400, p. 151); most, however, tested their resolve to get along in future by seating them together. Parishes likewise varied on whether they put both partners in a sexual offence on the stool at once, Innerwick opting to separate them (CH2/1463/1, f. 1v), Dundonald (more typically) to present them in public together. In fact, in 1628 a man and both of the women with whom he had offended sat together on the stool – a recipe for disaster, one might think, though the minutes note no public eruption on this occasion (*Dundonald*, 243).

31. After five Lasswade parishioners crowded the stool at once, the parish invested 13s to add another stool to its collection: CH2/471/1, ff. 7, 67. The Menmuir elders in 1640 set aside 54s 'for bigging of the stool of the pulpit being two days work for two joiners', but found that it was not enough and added 13s 4d for materials and 5s to hire a barrow to move the stool into the kirk – suggesting that theirs was a substantial piece of furniture (CH2/264/1, ff. 26–27).
32. CH2/377/1, f. 60v; *Dundonald*, 259, 274. See also CH2/526/1, p. 32; CH2/523/1, ff. 20v, 43; and CH2/77/1, ff. 31v, 49v (a Culross case of cursing, the offender saying he 'would be content to serve the devil to have amends of James Huton').
33. CH2/276/1, f. 18; CH2/1115/1, ff. 8v, 9. cf. CH2/636/34, f. 35v; CH2/381/1, f. 20; CH2/326/1, pp. 2, 3; CH2/472/1, f. 13; *Dundonald*, 210; CH2/716/1, ff. 18v, 19; CH2/716/2, ff. 104v, 106v.

others'.[34] A Kinghorn couple convicted of fornication in 1608 were 'freed from the pillar' and only had to 'appear [standing] before the pulpit', but the fact that this was achieved at the considerable cost of £20 indicates the significance that contemporaries attached to the difference between sitting on the stool and standing at its foot.[35] The session of South Leith came up with an apparently unique alternative to the stool for one category of offenders: since couples who committed fornication 'under promise of marriage' thereby violated matrimony itself, they performed their repentance 'at the back of the marriage stool' rather than on the stool of repentance.[36] Clearly the place of repentance and the seat itself carried enormous weight in the moral and status hierarchy of the early modern community.

In time, the penitents' stool acquired such a degree of intrinsic meaning that it could become the weapon of choice in a feud. In 1631 the Dalkeith presbytery dealt with an extraordinary struggle in the parish of Temple that highlights the social meaning that had come to inhere in new, protestant church furniture. In March of that year, a newly widowed woman, Marion Boyd, Lady Temple, complained that Bessie Hutcheson had brought wrights to the parish church to demolish the pew built by Boyd's late husband for his family and use the wood to construct a new stool of repentance – a consummate insult to the memory of the deceased and the standing of his widow. With no immediate response from the presbytery beyond their agreement to investigate, Boyd took matters into her own capable hands. A few weeks after the offence (on Good Friday, the minutes report) and apparently with her minister's complicity, she entered the kirk, took an axe to the new penitents' stool and made a spectacular bonfire of it in the kirkyard. She then returned the kirk door key to the manse and had cakes and ale with the minister's wife. The minister reportedly had a good laugh out of it, remarking that Boyd's goodman would heartily approve; his own siding with one party, however, only divided his parish further. The session sent him out of their next meeting to determine what to do with their numerous penitents in the absence of a stool. Meanwhile the minister commissioned a new stool to be made out of wood from the seats occupied for the last half-century by another group of parishioners, men presumably on Bessie Hutcheson's side of the quarrel. When asked by the presbytery why he had thus contravened their order

34. CH2/521/2, f. 43v (1590).
35. CH2/472/1, f. 23v. The financially strapped session soon regularised this practice. See also CH2/521/2, f. 43v; CH2/521/6, f. 105 (only 20s in Perth); CH2/145/1, f. 4 (1585); CH2/400/1, p. 50.
36. CH2/716/1, ff. 11v, 13 (1605); for the marriage stool, see chapter 6, below.

to await presbytery visitation of the kirk to construct and place a new stool, he answered that there was such 'abundance of delinquents' in the parish that discipline required quicker action. They were not convinced and suspended him pending further examination. Extended investigation with numerous depositions from witnesses followed, but the presbytery had still not ruled on the case when the minister died in August and the affair was dropped.[37] The point here is that both the stool of repentance and the seat constructed by a prominent man had acquired in their physical substance layers of meaning that, if violated, could be used to express the profound rifts in the community. The dead man's seat was a statement of his 'honest reputation'; using its wood to build a penitents' stool placed him and his widow in the company of the ungodly, defamed and humiliated. The physical composition of the furniture had become a vehicle of protest and dissension. This was possible precisely because the penitents' stool itself had the power to communicate. So much for the notion that protestants succeeded in detaching power and signification from physical tokens.

For offences of varying seriousness, one might be required to sit for one, three or six sabbaths, or for adultery or 'apostasy' (catholicism) half a year or a whole year of sabbaths, for the duration of both the morning and afternoon services, from the end of the third (final) bell calling congregants to church until the end of the sermon. On the final sabbath of a series, the penitent recited an individual confession.[38] In Edinburgh, sinners were sometimes required to perform their repentance on Sunday, Wednesday, Friday and the next Sunday for a more compressed version of multiple 'satisfactions'.[39] A Sunday on the stool was more serious than

37. CH2/424/1, ff. 5v–16v. The minister's servant, Grissel Adamson, supplied Marion Boyd with the fire, and the minister himself had borrowed the kirk door key from the officer who usually kept it, allegedly so that he could escape the din of his children and do his sermon preparation in the kirk rather than at home. He 'ma[de] a laughter of it when he saw it [the stool] burning.' Division between town and landward is suggested by the fact that there were 'none of the town of Temple upon the session' (f. 10). Other complaints about the minister emerged in the course of the investigation, including his infrequent celebration of communion and his slander of another parishioner, to whom he was required to apologise in public (f. 13v).
38. E.g., CH2/521/4, pp. 62,146; CH2/523/1, ff. 26v, 44v (six months for adultery in Perth and Burntisland). There was little consistency across parish boundaries, however: the same offence in Elgin and in Aberlady brought only 'three several Lord's days' in the 1580s and 1630s, respectively (CH2/145/1, ff. 25–25v; CH2/4/1, ff. 10, 11v). For a variety of other multiple-sabbath repentances, see CH2/523/1, ff. 1, 10; CH2/145/1, f. 9v; CH2/400/1, pp. 74, 101, 102, 163.
39. NAS ms RH2/35/1, ff. 12, 21 (my fol.). Tuesday and Sunday were the usual pillar days in South Leith (CH2/716/1, ff. 72–72v).

a weekday appearance, presumably since attendance at a Tuesday or Thursday sermon was lighter, so that one would sit beneath the gaze of fewer of one's neighbours. The exception would be the Saturday preparation day before communion – a particularly appropriate day for penitential performance, since the theme of the sermon was sin and its effects, and the communion to follow celebrated forgiveness and reincorporation. Sessions regularly assigned special Saturday appearances on the stool during the communion seasons, especially the spring season formerly denominated Lent.[40]

Just as the place of penance could be negotiated, either for a fee or, as we shall see, because of unusual display of sorrow for sin, so both the number of days and the day itself were matters of discussion and occasional adjustment. When in 1608 George Griff of Kinghorn showed visible sorrow for his offence (having caused a riot in the kirk by opposing the banns of his erstwhile fiancée with another man), his sentence to the pillar on the sabbath was 'mitigated, that he come before the pulpit upon Tuesday and confess his fault'. A Falkirk couple likewise 'in all humility' confessing 'the filthy and wicked' sin of fornication, 'acknowledging their just demerit to be censured therefore with all rigour, nonetheless' petitioned successfully to have their six sabbaths in sackcloth reduced to the single Sunday required by the 'common form of single fornication'; the session was impressed at the language of regret for the sin in their petition, and the fact that they had decided to get married.[41] Attitude and promise of amendment made all the difference. It was insufficient for a Falkirk woman simply to ask for a two-week holiday from her multisabbath repentance; this the elders rejected out of hand. Petition could in fact be risky: when a Perth couple convicted of adultery in 1607 appealed for mitigation of their six-month sentence, the session not only denied their petition, it added three more sabbaths for their presumption.[42] It goes without saying that taking a break without permission brought severe reprisal. A day missed from the Mid-Calder stool required the penitent to 'begin of new again . . . as if they had not begun'.[43] The local economy, weather and the demands of one's vocation were factored in: penitential

40. E.g., CH2/400/1, pp. 94, 116; CH2/383/1, f. 14.

41. CH2/472/1, f. 26 (1608); CH2/400/1, pp. 130, 171. Burntisland fornicaters petitioned successfully to sit five rather than six sabbaths if they had meanwhile contracted marriage: CH2/523/1, f. 41; also CH2/521/3, p. 74.

42. CH2/400/1, p. 102; CH2/521/4, p. 146.

43. CH2/266/1, ff. 1, 6v; the session in 1610 ordered Margaret Alexander to stand two days for every day that she had missed (f. 12). In Elgin, Marjorie Anderson had to appear three Sundays for every one she had been absent in 1587; failing that, she was branded on the cheek and banished: CH2/145/1, ff. 10v, 16v.

performance could be deferred for fishermen or sailors at the beginning of the season until their return from the sea.[44] On the other hand, a contumacious offender might be barred from access to his livelihood until he had at least agreed to his sentence of repentance: the Aberdeen elders 'required the magistrates to charge the skipper of the ship presently bound to Dansken that he transport not' the merchant burgess Andro Duncan, who had sinned by failure to support his wife.[45] Finally, when we consider the punitive nature of being 'ordained to the stool', we ought not forget that a sentence passed in a Sunday session meeting was for the following Sunday, giving the offender a long week to dread the experience. Small wonder that the wealthy consistently tried to buy their way off the stool.

There were alternatives to the stool, and indeed to appearance before the congregation at all. Although very serious and public offences required public confession, a more private form of the penitential performance was available for those who had committed lesser sins, for very young and especially first-time offenders, for those whose offences were not generally known (having perhaps been discovered only by the sabbath visitors), or for individuals who voluntarily confessed sins that had escaped observation. Such offenders might be ordered to kneel before the elders in the session meeting place and confess their sin, 'craving God and the session mercy', producing some external signs of sorrow for sin, tears being the preferred indicator. Helen Duncan of Yester repented her fornication, which was not generally known, first before a visiting elder and her father, then before the session, where the clerk tells us, 'she sat down upon her knees in presence of us all in session and did pray God mercy with tears'. The elders decided there was then no need for her to repent in public.[46] Such actions were clearly preferable to sitting under the gaze of one's neighbours for several hours on a Sunday.

At the other extreme, offenders whose inner penitence was doubted, or who had snubbed their initial summons, often commenced their repen-

44. CH2/1142/1, ff. 78v (granting a Fraserburgh adulterer 'the liberty of his summer trade' before beginning his repentance), 95 (a deferral for sailors); CH2/716/1, f. 18v ('for going to his voyage') and CH2/716/2, ff. 13–13v ('to go over the water'); CH2/523/1, f. 4 (William Ramsay's 1602 'bill craving liberty to go to the sail before his full satisfaction for adultery', unsuccessful only because 'William is found to have committed fornication in Leith since he began to satisfy for adultery' and so was sent to the presbytery. Inclement weather could also be a factor, as when a Burntisland penitent managed to postpone a penance in Kirkcaldy for an offence committed there until weather permitted safe travel: CH2/523/1, f. 41, cf. 27.

45. CH2/448/2, p. 200.

46. CH2/377/1, f. 60v (1626).

tance by being warded (gaoled) for a period of time to bring them to a proper sense of their sinful nature. The Perth session set aside a chamber over the north door of the kirk as the 'ward of the fornicators'. Others warded sinners in the steeple, vault or vestry, or (with the magistrates' aid) in the town tollbooth or a 'house of correction', often on a diet of bread and water.[47] The penitentiary intent of incarceration is clear. When a Perth flesher (butcher) found working on the sabbath injured the kirk officer rather than submitting to discipline, the elders warded him specifically so that he would be 'brought to the knowledge of his offences and humbled truly for the same'. It worked. The following week the flesher 'with humility upon his knees confessed' his sin. In the same parish, when James Mar was 'brought forth of ward', he 'humbled him on his knees delivering that since he was warded he has been sore troubled in his conscience for concealing of the truth' about his adultery, 'and now by the motion of God's spirit having heavily displeased for his sin and willing to declare his public repentance therefore simply confessed that he committed the fearful crime.'[48] By the time they had spent a week or so in ward, with nothing but filth, vermin and hunger to distract them from the spirit's motion, most penitents found they had no trouble drumming up sufficient regret for their actions to demonstrate convincing penitence when they came to the stool.[49]

Another supplement to the stool for particularly egregious offenders

47. CH2/141/1, f. 47 (fornicators warded in the vestry of Trinity College kirk, Edinburgh for six weeks before three sabbaths on the stool, 1630); CH2/84/28, f. 2 (St Nicholas East, Dalkeith, also using its vestry for adulterers, 1610); CH2/448/2, pp. 14, 24, 28, 37 (adulterers in the vault in St Nicholas, Aberdeen); CH2/448/4, pp. 187, 190 (warding for 'uttering imprecations' and 'scandalous carriage'); CH2/521/1, ff. 36v (tollbooth), 76v (cf. 85v, fornicators warded 'every one of them in an sundry house' in 1582); CH2/472/1, f. 10v (steeple and tollbooth); CH2/716/1, f. 7; CH2/145/1, ff. 3v, 36 (contumacious adulterers, 'filthy language'); SAU CH2/624/2, p. 153; CH2/145/1, f. 146; and CH2/624/3, p. 24 (fornication). The Glasgow session in 1606 ordered a 'new ward to be made in Blackfriars steeple' (NLS ms 2782, f. 59v). For warding on bread and water, see CH2/521/5, f. 9 (forty days for adultery); CH2/716/1, f. 22v; NLS ms 2782, ff. 59–59v (the incarcerated paying for their own 'steepling' in Glasgow 8s each day or 20s for eight days – the bargain price).

48. CH2/521/3, pp. 205, 207 (1601); CH2/521/7, pp. 25–29 (1619); cf. CH2/521/8/2, f. 181v.

49. The Perth council in 1604 admitted the 'insufficiency of the ward' to be a cause of 'skaith and danger': PL ms B59/16/1, f. 90. Elspeth Blyth was 'near famished for want of entertainment' after a fortnight in ward in 1622, and a fornicator incarcerated in 1633 complained of 'such a multitude of rodents that he feared to have been destroyed by them', though the session thought he deserved what he got for his 'sinful life, contempt of God, and disobedience to the session': CH2/521/7, p. 350; CH2/521/8/1, f. 99v.

was the rather more evidently punitive use of jougs or branks. The branks (in England called a scold's bridle) was a sort of iron cage locked around the head with a forked protrusion designed to go into the mouth (see plate 15); the one used in St Andrews remains in Holy Trinity's vestry to this day; another still hangs near the south door on the wall of the kirk of Sorn in Ayrshire.[50] The jougs was an iron neck collar, sometimes with cruelly serrated edges and wrist manacles as well, which was often chained to the kirkyard wall near the gate (see plate 16), but sometimes to the wall of the kirk itself. In parishes like Stow, sabbath violators had to 'stand in the jougs . . . between the second and third bell' summoning worshippers, then go to the stool; in Anstruther Wester blasphemers did the same with the branks.[51] A Dundonald parishioner actually had to 'take the branks on his face at the kirk door and therewith to go through the kirk in his linen clothes to the public place of repentance', and the jougs in the Highland parish of Inveravon were located close enough to the stool for a penitent at the foot of it to be locked in.[52] The more usual location within the kirk was at the door.[53] We tend to associate both jougs and branks with secular rather than ecclesiastical use, and corporal punishment with civil rather than church courts. Clearly, however, enforced repentance and secular punishment overlapped, perhaps because of the overlap of personnel we have noted on session and town council. The St Andrews session went further with corporal punishment, ordering adulterers 'jougged,

50. Surviving branks and jougs can also be seen in the Museum of Scotland, and jougs still hang near the southeast door of the kirk of Weem, Perthshire.

51. CH2/338/1, ff. 1v, 7v, 8v (the latter case for hanging clothes out to dry on Sunday); SAU CH2/624/2, p. 12; SAU CH2/624/3, pp. 25, 32; CH2/472/1, f. 30; AAC CH2/562/1, f. 40; CH2/266/1, f. 51. Naturally people bought their 'relief from the jougs' or branks whenever possible (e.g., CH2/285/1, p. 5 – North Berwick, 1608, or SAU CH2/1056/1, f. 18 – St Monans, 1630). Scoonie assigned flyters to the jougs (CH2/326/1, p. 7); and a Dalkeith adulteress was put 'in the iron belt on Thursday' before coming to the stool on Sunday in 1610 (CH2/84/28, p. 2; cf. f. 53). In these cases, branks or jougs all seem to have been in or near the kirk; there are far more where the devices were clearly at the town's market cross (e.g., CH2/523/1, f. 12).

52. *Dundonald*, 203; CH2/191/1, f. 51 (this parish also had a branks in the kirk: ff. 14, 21, 42, 43). Scoonie's jougs were also attached to the kirk wall (CH2/326/1, p. 7); Elgin had 'jougs in the northwest nook of the parish kirk' (CH2/145/1, ff. 10–10v; cf. Mortlach, CH2/529/1, f. 7v).

53. This allowed penitents to be locked in for their sentence at the door during the ringing of the bells, as at Menmuir (CH2/264/1, f. 14v), Kirkwall (CH2/442/74, f. 7v), Tyninghame (CH2/359/1, f. 3), Brechin (Thoms, *Kirk of Brechin*, 59); and Dundonald (*Dundonald*, 238, 333). Menmuir seems to have had stocks at the door: CH2/264/1, ff. 20–20v – one who had shed blood fighting on a Sunday to 'be put into the stocks and remain in them on a sabbath at the most patent kirk door between the first and third bells'.

carted, and ducked' in the sea – in December, on which occasions 'the whole scholars and others, a great multitude of people . . . cast rotten eggs [and] filth' during the procession to the coast.[54] In any case, the frequency with which jougs and branks were prescribed by sessions in all parts of the realm, and their location in the kirk or kirkyard, suggest that we should regard these artifacts as ecclesiastical as well as civil implements to draw attention to the sin and instil greater regret in the sinner. Certainly jougs and branks provided another opportunity for the public display of the sinner and the setting apart (or, to use the anthropologists' term, 'dis-aggregation') of ungodly from godly, often in the kirk itself, but at least at the boundary between the sacred space of kirk and kirkyard, and the surrounding village or town – that is, at the kirkyard gate or the kirk wall or door.

* * *

Another medieval penitential tradition continued by protestants, in Scotland and elsewhere, was the costuming of penitents in linen or sack-cloth for the performance of their confessions (see plate 17).[55] Both fabrics were construed as humiliating, but there seems to have been a hierarchy, the more coarsely woven sackcloth being reserved in some parishes for more egregious offenders. Thomas Lamb of Perth was ordered to repent in linen for his violence towards a bailie in 1598, but a few weeks later Patrick Cunningham had to repent 'barefoot and in sackcloth' for his more serious violence against his own father.[56] In Yester, linen was routinely reserved for the lesser offences of slander and scolding, as opposed to

54. *SAKS* 2:793, 1594; CH2/472/1, f. 10v, a similar ordeal in Kinghorn.
55. For discussion of the gown pictured, Flora Johnston, 'Jonet Gothskirk and the "Gown of Repentance"', *Costume* 33 (1999), 89–94. I am grateful to Elizabeth Ewan for this reference.
56. CH2/521/3, pp. 55–56 (a 'rebellious child', Cunningham had 'put violent hands on [his father], struck and dang him with his knees'). Sometimes the costume is simply 'white sheets' – as in Boharm (CH2/1115/1, ff. 8v, 9); also CH2/521/6, ff. 11v, 119v; CH2/400/1 pp. 19, 50 (here used interchangeably with linen), 54 (fabric left to the kirk officer's discretion). Linen was usual in Dalkeith, Stow, Perth and Aberlady for fornication and adultery (CH2/84/28, f. 52v; CH2/338/1, ff. 19v, 44; CH2/521/1, f. 60v; CH2/521/4, p. 39; CH2/4/1, ff. 26, 33, 35v, 38v, and on 42v for consulting a 'cunning man'). The Perth presbytery prescribed sackcloth for failing to make prescribed repentance before taking communion, and for threatening ministers (CH2/299/1, pp. 290, 291); Monkton for relapse fornication (AAC CH2/809/1, f. 28v); Kirkoswald for pilgrimage to holy wells (AAC CH2/562/1, f. 40). Aberdeen's St Nicholas and Old Machar sessions required sackcloth for adultery and 'apostasy while abroad' (meaning resorting to catholic mass, generally while on mercantile voyages to Spain or Italy): CH2/448/2, pp. 11, 14; CH2/448/3, p. 6; CH2/1020/1, ff. 13, 41, 47, 57, following the orders of the General Assembly: *BUK* 1:159 (1569).

adultery or violence; in Jedburgh, linen was usual for sexual offences including adultery, but sackcloth was assigned for violence and bloodshed.[57] The hierarchy of sabbath breach is reflected in Glasgow's prescription of sackcloth for fighting on Sunday, linen for sabbath labour, and one's own gown for drinking during the sermon.[58] The Falkirk elders required repentance one Sunday in linen for superstitious pilgrimage to holy wells, but for a second such offence, three Sundays in sackcloth.[59] In some parishes the hierarchy of penitential garb was elaborated with the prescription of 'hairy cloth' for sins greater than those meriting sackcloth: in Elgin, where sackcloth was usual for adulterers, incestuous adultery required 'hairy cloth' (also prescribed once for 'playing on the great pipe' during a Sunday sermon, an act so offensive to the startled worshippers as to constitute blasphemy).[60]

By 1619 the Perth session found its stockpile of sackcloth gowns so worn from overuse that they had to order two new ones so that adulterers could 'appear in that habit at the kirk door and repentance stool every sabbath day by the space of half a year'. Parishioners apparently found penitential dress signally important to the wellbeing of the kirk: a North Berwick man donated 4s specifically for a new sackcloth gown, and in Morayshire a Boharm parishioner donated 2 merks to provide sackcloth.[61] The frugal Highland session of Inveravon found a sensible

57. CH2/377/1, ff. 67, 67v, 94v; CH2/198/1, ff. 7, 7v, 8v. In like manner, Kirkcaldy reserved sackcloth for adulterers, linen for lesser sexual offences or for parents of daughters left unsupervised at night (CH2/636/34, ff. 35v, 4v); cf. CH2/84/28 (Dalkeith), f. 52v. In other settings there is no discernible distinction between the meaning of the two fabrics: e.g., CH2/299/2, pp. 39, 40, 41, 52.

58. NLS ms Wod Oct. IX, f. 5. The Glasgow presbytery tended to order linen for fornication, sackcloth for adultery and incest: ML CH2/171/1, ff. 3v, 14v, 16v–17, 18v–19v, 30v, 58v, 64v.

59. CH2/400/1, pp. 194, 198; they almost always prescribed sackcloth for adultery, relapse fornication, slandering ministers or elders, and consulting witches (e.g., pp. 30, 33, 104, 123, 128, 132, 133, 163, 169). In 1623, their horror at a case of 'fourfold fornication with sundry women' is clear from their remarkable order for the sinner to wear 'an habit of sackcloth for the space of three years' in addition to paying £20 (p. 101). In 1605, the Burntisland session found its prescription of linen for an adulterer changed by the sterner presbytery to sackcloth (CH2/523/1, f. 16). For other uses of sackcloth, on the same general pattern, CH2/266/1, ff. 1, 35; CH2/191/1, ff. 9v, 14, 21, 42, 43; CH2/624/3, pp. 25, 27; CH2/326/1, p. 5; CH2/145/1, ff. 25–25v, 49v, 52v; NLS ms 2782, 60v; CH2/526/1, f. 1.

60. CH2/145/1, ff. 10–10v (1587, cf. sackcloth f. 25v), 37v, 42v, 48. 'Hairy cloth' may have been a fabric woven of flax with significant amounts of horsehair for strength. The elders could choose between 'hair or sackcloth' for slanderers (ff. 25–25v, 52v; CH2/145/5, f. 96v). The Glasgow session in 1647 purchased two new 'hair gowns' (NLS ms 2782, f. 60v). Brereton, in *Early Travellers*, 144, reported adulterers upon the stool 'during twelve months in a sheet of hair'.

61. CH2/521/7, p. 27; CH2/285/1, p. 23 (1658); CH2/1115/1, f. 13 (1637).

solution to the problem: they required Helen Bayne, for upbraiding the minister and his wife, to spend 3 merks to buy her own sackcloth. The Glasgow session adopted the same requirement for adulterers in 1607.[62]

People who had committed lesser sins, or who successfully petitioned the session for mitigation, were permitted to repent in their 'own clothes', or street clothes. In Dundonald, sabbath-violators could wear their own clothes, for instance, unless the sabbath broken happened to have been designated a fast day; then the session required linen. A Kinghorn couple convicted of fornication appeared on the stool in various kinds of dress to reflect the degree of each one's sin – 'he in sackcloth and she in her own habit' because, while it was the woman's first offence, the man was a relapsed offender.[63] In Edinburgh, the hierarchy of penitential garb was further refined by distinctions within the category of 'his own clothes': 'black gowns' or 'grey gowns' were required for those who had remained in the town when the queen's forces seized Edinburgh in 1574, for instance.[64] Those who not only stayed in the town, but also 'took plain part with the declared traitors, . . . assisting all their most wicked acts and enterprises as well in the demolishing and casting down of the buildings and houses of the said burgh as raising of fire within the same, and . . . shooting of great and small pieces indifferently in the faces of all without the fear of God or remorse of conscience' or who 'accepted armour and came in plain battle to shed the blood of their dearest brethren' had to repent 'dour clad in sackcloth'.[65] The degree of humiliation attached to sackcloth is also clear from petitions to be relieved of it. One of the Edinburgh offenders objected to it as too heavy a 'punishment in body and fame' for his sin, since, being in the midst of a 'deadly feud' with Archibald Ruthven, 'a man of great blood', he had remained in Edinburgh during the troubles for fear of his life and estate, as was 'well-known by many'. He insisted that he ought not be punished in such 'shameful manner as was used to wilful murderers and raisers of fire'; to go thus to the pillar would make him 'grievously and enormously hurt and evil done to and injustice'.[66] A Falkirk penitent paid the hefty sum of £10 'to be free of sackcloth'. And the Glasgow elders in 1586 had to admonish

62. CH2/191/1, f. 32; NLS ms 2782, f. 60v.
63. *Dundonald*, 60, 63; CH2/472/1, f. 27; cf. ML CH2/171/1, ff. 15v, 20v. A Lasswade parishioner's visible regret for 'putting hand to the minister's wife' in 1616 released her from penitential garb in favour of her own clothes: CH2/471/1, f. 13.
64. NAS ms RH2/35/1, ff. 2v, 8v, 15, 23v.
65. NAS ms RH2/35/1, ff. 7, 8v, 42 (also true for reconciled excommunicates – 50v).
66. NAS ms RH2/35/1, ff. 42v–44, 54v–55. The feud had begun four years earlier, in 1571, over a disputed marriage contract. The session concurred and permitted confession in his own gown, which he then gave to a poor man: *BUK* 1:323–24.

penitents not to remove the sackcloth at the kirk door after the service, but wear it 'from the kirk to their own house', the more thoroughly to achieve humiliation before their neighbours.[67]

In many parishes by the seventeenth century, the progression of a multi-sabbath repentance was marked by changes in dress. In Edinburgh, Trinity College kirk followed presbytery guidelines in requiring sackcloth on the first and last Sundays of the nine-week repentance for trilapse fornication, with the penitents' own clothing worn on the intervening sabbaths, creating a bookend effect to mark entrance into and reception from penitential status.[68] Elsewhere, repentance on the stool in one's own clothes for a set number of Sundays and in linen or sackcloth for only the final appearance highlighted the culmination of repentance, suggesting a steady heightening of sorrow for sin leading to the final catharsis in public confession and absolution.[69]

The meaning of clothing *per se* is graphically illustrated by the 1574 Edinburgh penance in which an elder, Robert Gurlaw, guilty of 'carrying away victual forth of this realm' during a time of shortage, thereby increasing the desperation of the poor, was required to confess 'clad in his own gown, and the same being performed and fulfilled . . . the said gown to be received from him and given to one of the poor.'[70] His gown constituted both a degree of humiliation for him when worn, and when given away, an act of charity that would help to make 'satisfaction' for his sin by redressing the offence he had committed against the poor of the parish. It carried the multiple meanings of penalty and gift, the latter a mechanism by which, having separated himself from the godly, he could be reunited with them.

67. CH2/400/1, pp. 134–35; NLS ms 2782, f. 61. For humiliation *per se* as a traditional part of penance, see M. Mansfield, *The Humiliation of Sinners: Ritual Penance in Thirteenth-Century France* (Ithaca, 1995).
68. CH2/141/1, f. 20v (1627); CH2/1463/1, f. 2.
69. CH2/400/1, p. 208. In Dysart the last four of an adulterer's twenty-six sabbaths of repentance were in sackcloth; his partner, being married, wore it for her last six (CH2/390/1, ff. 5–5v, 20v). The Edinburgh presbytery required the last of twelve Sundays in linen for a man who had seduced his servant 'in time of his wife's leprosy' (CH2/121/1, f. 28v), and Burntisland reconciled an excommunicate after six sabbaths on the stool, the last three in linen (CH2/523/1, ff. 25–25v). Stow departs from the norm in prescribing that the first rather than the last of a series of Sunday repentances for relapse fornication be in linen (CH2/338/1, f. 19v).
70. NAS ms RH2/35/1, ff. 5v–6. Further negotiation with the session allowed Gurlaw to confess 'in the marriage place after the sermon' rather than sitting under the scrutiny of the parishioners for the duration of the service on the penitents' stool, and to 'appear in cloak or gown as he shall think good', giving him a choice of what he would give away.

Often a penitent was required to wear a paper hat or other paper label on which the offence was written, as when a Kinghorn fornicator had to 'come to the kirk door barefooted with a pair of sheets about her and a paper upon her head with the cause wherefore she shall stand there written in it', or in South Leith when a father appeared on the stool in 1600 'with a paper on his head bearing this superscription, "for blasphemy and unnatural leaving his bairnes when he went to Flanders"'.[71] A 'mitre' or a 'capuch' on the head was the usual form of the label, but often a paper simply pinned to the penitent's gown would do. Thus a Falkirk adulteress wore 'sackcloth upon her and a paper upon her shoulder signifying her whoredome.'[72] The publicity function of the paper is clear in a 1591 instance, when the Elgin session dealt with a group of slanderers by ordering 'for the more public declaration of the offence, a paper be affixed on their breasts upon which shall be written the cause of their sitting [on the stool]'; in Ayr, Ninian Fleming in 1608 had 'his dittie [indictment] written in great letters above his head' for blasphemy'.[73]

Finally, undress was as important as dress. To be 'barelegged, barefooted, and bareheaded' was to exacerbate one's humiliation.[74] Exposing parts of the body usually unseen underlined the inappropriateness of the sinner's behaviour, an embarrassment to the godly community. Going bareheaded

71. CH2/472/1, ff. 26v (1608), 10v; CH2/716/1, f. 6v.
72. CH2/400/1, p. 147 (1627, Margaret Cuthbert's twenty-six sabbaths in sackcloth, three in linen). CH2/521/2, f. 7v prescribes a 'moyct or capuch', a woman's cap, 'having written on the margins thereof her fact and crime'; the Kirkwall and Elgin minutes use 'mitre' (CH2/442/74, f. 29v; CH2/145/1, ff. 32v, 52v, 56v; CH2/145/3, f. 173; CH2/145/5, f. 96v). The Kirkcaldy elders threatened Alison Muir in 1627 that, 'if she haunt men's company again' with 'slanderous behaviour', she should have her 'head shaved and a paper shall be put upon her head and she shall be made a public spectacle' (CH2/636/34, f. 102v). See similar rulings in Aberdeen, CH2/448/2, p. 24 (1603, repeat adultery); and Glasgow, NLS ms 2782, f. 60v (1602, pandering).
73. CH2/145/1, ff. 9v, 25, 32v, 52v; AAC CH2/751/1, f. 125; cf. the 'crown of paper' usual for relapsed fornicators in Aberdeen from the 1570s (CH2/448/1, pp. 4, 14, 107–09; CH2/448/2, pp. 11, 12).
74. CH2/145/1, ff. 4–4v, 9v, 10–10v, 49v, 51v, 61v (for fornication, overlaying an infant, adultery and incest, 1586–94); CH2/521/2, f. 87 (the porter's sabbath breach, 1593); CH2/141/1, f. 9 (adultery); CH2/400/1, pp. 19, 29, 33–34, 54, 118, 198 (fornication and adultery, disturbing the kirk in service time, and sabbath labour); *Dundonald*, 239 (reviling the session); CH2/1142/1, f. 109v and CH2/145/1, f. 4, CH2/472/1, f. 26v (fornication). See also CH2/448/1, pp. 14, 20; CH2/624/3, p. 24; CH2/1463/1, f. 2, AAC CH2/562/1, ff. 1–2; among many examples. Female fornicators came to the stool with heads covered in Perth (CH2/521/2, f. 72v; CH2/521/3, f. 10), but this was an exception to the rule (cf. *Canongate*, 11). Bare heads were also ordered for those who had remained in Edinburgh during the troubles: NAS ms RH2/35/1, ff. 2v, 11v, 42, 50v.

reduced one's status to that of a supplicant or a child (since adult men and married women or widows traditionally wore caps or hats).[75] It had the added advantage of guaranteeing greater physical exposure to the congregation. Perth was not alone in prohibiting the wearing of plaids on the stool. The kirk of Mid-Calder enacted a statute in 1604 that 'women on the stool must discover their faces that they might be known', and in Aberdeen a fornicator's plaid was to be

> taken from her by the kirk officer or his servant immediately before her upgoing to the pillar . . . because in times past the most part of women that came to the pillar . . . sat thereon having their plaids about their head, coming down over their faces the whole time of their sitting on the stool, so that almost none of the congregation could see their faces or know what they were, whereby they made no account of their coming to the stool . . . and thereby were made to persevere in their harlotry.[76]

In the Orkney parish of Kirkwall, the standard penalty for female fornicators was 'public repentance without a plaid', and in Glasgow 'women who appear in the pillar . . . and hold not down their plaids from their head, it shall not be esteemed as a day of their appearance.'[77]

The Innerwick session was as concerned with men's over-large 'bonnets' as with women's plaids: in 1608 they ordered the repentance of an adulterous couple, 'the man bareheaded and the woman her face discovered'.[78] Public visibility was absolutely essential to effective penance: without the embarrassment factor, appearance on the stool held no meaning and – if we take the Aberdeen judgment seriously – had no power to effect reformation of behaviour, either in the penitent or in the congregation. After all, part of the apologetic for public repentance was that it served as an 'example to others not to commit the like'.[79]

The physical implements with which sin had been committed, material

75. For the uncovered head as a sign of humiliation in another setting, see CH2/294/1, f. 1v, the 1602 case of a Paisley man who admitted seeking magical healing from a woman but denied 'any humiliation to have been made upon his knees to her or lifting his bonnet'.
76. CH2/266/1, f. 2v, showing that this experience of public humiliation was presumed to be corrective, not merely punitive; CH2/448/2, p. 305.
77. CH2/442/74, f. 7v; NLS ms 2782, f. 60.
78. CH2/1463, f. 2v.
79. CH2/141/1, f. 51; CH2/400/1, p. 86. The rite's presumed power to effect change, like that of the old sacrament of penance, is striking. In semiological terms, the signifier here became the reality it signified.

signifiers of sin, often served as props in the performance of repentance. An abusive wife who had wounded her husband 'in the head with a pair of tongs' had to 'pass barefooted, holding up the same tongs in her right hand above her head, through the streets' of Perth.[80] The right hand was understood as the active one, the one that had performed the wrong. Isobell Hird of Leith had to repent in sackcloth holding both the staff with which she had injured her husband and the napkin used to staunch his wound.[81] In Edinburgh, penitent feuders carried their weapons to the stool and, after confessing, cast them down to the floor. And when the Elgin saddler James Guthry threatened the town bailie 'with a drawn sword in his hand', the session made him 'stand three several Sundays in hairy cloth in the public stool of repentance and in presence of the congregation deliver the hilts' to the bailie; the sword was then hung on the kirk wall for three more weeks to 'declare the public offence committed'.[82] Guthry confessed his sin after the sermon, but the sword itself bespoke it even after he had finished. Props other than weapons also came into play: in the Highland parish of Inveravon, Alexander Mitchell repented in 1633 with a stalk of grain in his hand, for 'breach of the sabbath in shearing of corn', and Glasgow in the 1580s opted to continue the medieval tradition of adulterers carrying white wands.[83]

* * *

Penance was a choreographed as well as a costumed performance: physical posture and movement, in this as in any dramatic performance, helped to communicate the themes of the play. In this case it also reinforced for the actors the roles that they were playing and presumably the reasons for which they had been cast as they were. The penitent's body served to convey meaning on the penitential stage, where meanings could so easily be skewed (as with laughing penitents). Assigned posture and gesture were essential to the stability of the message.[84]

80. CH2/521/7, p. 315 (1622). The whole town being witness must have embarrassed husband as well as wife, perhaps intentional chastisement of a husband failing to control his household.
81. CH2/716/2, f. 93 (1613). In 1592, an Elgin woman 'for committing cruelty on her own person with a knife' went to the jougs, 'the said knife to be infixed in the tree beside her' – not a very therapeutic way of dealing with an attempted suicide, one would think, though perhaps it assuaged feelings of guilt that might have contributed to suicidal depression. Certainly it was used in other such cases: CH2/145/1, f. 42v; CH2/636/34, ff. 12v, 54v.
82. CH2/145/1, f. 37v (1592); CH2/121/1, f. 17v (a similar case in 1583).
83. CH2/191/1, ff. 18v, 19; NLS ms 2782, f. 61v (a common English practice rare in post-Reformation Scotland).
84. Clifford Davidson, ed., *Gesture in Medieval Drama and Art* (Kalamazoo, 2001), esp. chs

The usual posture for confession was of course kneeling, or 'sitting down upon the knees', whether before the session, the whole congregation or the particular person offended.[85] Kneeling was the posture assumed by the weak before the strong, the inferior before their betters. One who knelt in the presence of his neighbours felt tangibly the effects of sin on social standing: he was, for the nonce, in a morally subordinate position to the assembled community of the godly. In many session minutes, the terms 'humbled herself' and 'sat down upon her knees' are used interchangeably.[86] It might have been worse: in England, full prostration of penitents survived in some puritan congregations into the seventeenth century. There is no indication that the Scots followed suit, but they did retain other traditional gestures of apology and reconciliation, like shaking hands with an offended party, with the greater offender in a flyting incident, for instance, 'to take [the other party] first by the hand'.[87]

As important as gesture and posture was movement from one place to another during the course of repentance. While the penitents' seat beneath the pulpit was the central stage for the performance, both 'entry to the stool' and 'reception from' it were also very much part of the drama. Movement to and from the stage could speak as much to the audience as what happened on the stool. Performing repentance often began at the kirk door, the place of physical entry into the Christian community and one of those liminal sites beloved of anthropologists.[88] The Mid-Calder

1 and 5; Jan Bremmer and Herman Roodenburg, *A Cultural History of Gesture* (Ithaca, 1991); and Paula Backscheider, *Spectacular Politics: Theatrical Power and Mass Culture in Early Modern England* (Baltimore, 1993), esp. chs 5–6, inform this discussion. See also Charles Parker, 'The Rituals of Reconciliation: Admonition, Confession and Community in the Dutch Reformed Church' and Jennifer Selwyn, '"Schools of Mortification": Theatricality and the Role of Penitential Practice in the Jesuits' Popular Missions' in *Penitence in the Age of Reformations*, ed. K. Lualdi *et al*, 101–15, 201–21.

85. CH2/4/1, 7v; CH2/285/1, pp. 10, 12, 13; CH2/521/2, f. 12; CH2/521/6, ff. 116, 162v; CH2/521/7, ff. 4, 8, 25, 124, 200, 210, 212, etc; *Canongate*, 24; CH2/327/1, f. 10v; CH2/400/1, p. 11; CH2/377/1, f. 88; CH2/326/1, p. 4; CH2/266/1, f. 1; CH2/185/2, ff. 12v, 19.

86. E.g., CH2/145/1, f. 9v; CH2/471/1, ff. 8v, 13; CH2/285/1, pp. 9 (Sunday golfers 'humbling themselves on their knees'), 12.

87. Todd, 'A Captive's Story'; *Canongate*, 31, 32; CH2/523/1, f. 33; and see chapter 5, below.

88. CH2/448/1, pp. 14, 20; CH2/624/3, p. 24; NAS ms RH2/1/35, f. 50v. On the nature of the threshold in a rite of passage, see van Gennep, *Rites of Passage*, 81–96, 189, and, building on his work, Turner, *Ritual Process*, 94–130, coining the term 'communitas' to describe the nature of the 'in-between' state, a blend of 'lowliness and sacredness' marked by entry to a separated space by the 'threshold people'. Turner, *Performance*, 72–79, examines staging of the ritual process. Repentance being dramatically performed, the significance of its space in the kirk is helpfully illuminated by Marvin Carlson, *Places of Performance: The Semiotics of Theatre Architecture* (Ithaca, 1989).

elders specified that the ritual actually began not just *at* the door, but with the act of crossing the threshold, the penitent being to 'stand at the west kirk door *outwith* the said from the first bell, bareheaded, until the minister go into the pulpit, then to be conveyed between two elders to the public place of repentance'.[89] Doorways have multiple meanings and uses, but their use in ritual always marks a change in status. One came to the kirk door for the first time newborn and unincorporated into Christendom, and exited that same door after baptism a member of the Christian body. Its role in the penitential rite had similar theological import. A penitent entered unreconciled, but would eventually leave fully restored.

The elders carefully specified the time a penitent was to spend at the doorway before proceeding into the body of the kirk and eventually to the stool. This 'threshold time' was generally from the ringing of the first or second bell to the ringing of the third and last bell calling parishioners to Sunday worship. In other words, it was the period when most people would have entered the church, necessarily passing by and shaming their errant neighbour. Thus, in 1599 a Perth man, 'so beastly drunken' on the previous sabbath that he had missed both sermons, stood barefoot and in linen at the door from the second to the final bell to the sermon.[90] Adulterers, relapsed fornicators and consulters of witches in most parishes stood at the door a bit longer, from the first to the third bell. The Glasgow presbytery specified that an adulterer standing at the door 'for his horrible and fearful sins' must remain from the first bell 'till the people be upsit [seated in] the kirk'.[91] It is worth noting that penitents were invariably told to stand at the south door of the kirk in Perth. This is the door where on communion Sundays those with tokens entered; non-communicants came in at the north door.[92] Was this an effort to underline the contrast between the most godly and the sinner, or simply an assurance that the godly would

89. CH2/299/1, f. 8 (1608) (emphasis mine).

90. CH2/521/3, pp. 76–77 (cf. p. 88, drunkenness not on the sabbath bringing only a fine and repentance before the session); CH2/521/2, ff. 111v–12; CH2/471/1, f. 13. Attendance after the third bell was mandatory (e.g., CH2/448/1, p. 16), so that while parishioners started drifting in an hour early, there would presumably have been a rush at the end to avoid the fine for tardiness (see chapter 1, above).

91. ML CH2/171/1, f. 60v; CH2/141/1, f. 9; CH2/400/1, pp. 33, 54, 72, 123, 161; CH2/1463/1, f. 2; *Dundonald*, 33, 66, 67, 73; CH2/145/1, ff. 49v, 52v; CH2/716/1, f. 6v; CH2/442/74 (Kirkwall), f. 29v. When the Perth adulteress Sibilla Cochran, having appeared on the stool every Sunday for six months in 1607, appealed to the session to end her repentance, they prescribed three more sabbaths for good measure, but in a departure from the previous months of appearing on the stool only, told her at these appearances to stand 'first at the kirk door betwixt the second and third bell, and thereafter to come to the place of public repentance and so be received' (CH2/521/4, p. 146).

92. CH2/521/7, p. 23; CH2/521/8/1, f. 104v.

have the closest look at the penitent upon entering into that part of the kirk reserved for the obedient? Again, with the 'ward of the fornicators' in this parish located over the north door, a demand for penitent fornicators to enter the kirk at the south door would ensure a sort of penitential procession around the kirk, further increasing their visibility to the community.[93] For multiple-sabbath repentance, each Sunday before the last the penitent stood in the door again after the sermon, so that, as the Aberdeen elders stated it in 1568, 'they shall remain to be a spectacle to the whole people till all folks be past home and departed from the kirk.' It is clear that standing at the door while the congregation filed in and out was viewed as a heavy penalty: at St Cuthbert's, Edinburgh, in 1619, Andro Dod paid the impressive sum of an angel to be exempted from it.[94]

Beginning repentance at the kirk door was particularly appropriate when the door was where the offence had been committed. In 1594 two Perth men who had written 'infamous libels and slanderous tickets' and affixed them to the doors of the kirk on a communion Sunday, the better to render their enemies 'abominable both in the hearts and before the eyes of all men and women intending to communicate', had to repent at the 'kirk door where they affixed their infamous libel'. But in every case the time at the door functioned as a guarantee that most of the congregation would pass directly by the sinners and witness their humiliation at close quarters. Afterwards, penitents proceeded to the stool, where they sat or stood for the duration of the sermon. On the final sabbath of their repentance, they then confessed 'in the presence of the congregation', rising to do so if they had previously been seated, and finally, in the case of the Perth libellers, 'came down and ask[ed] the parties' pardon . . . whom they have ungodly traduced and unjustly slandered'.[95]

In some parishes movement to and around the kirk was more complicated. We have seen that the Perth wife's procession with tongs in hand

93. CH2/521/1, f. 76v.

94. CH2/448/1, p. 14; NLS ms 2782, f. 60; CH2/718/4, f. 16 – although this did not release Dod from two sabbaths in sackcloth on the pillar for his fornication. An angel, a gold coin minted in England, was in the sixteenth century worth about ten English shillings, or six Scottish pounds. D. Sibley, *Geographies of Exclusion* (London, 1995) discusses helpfully the complexities of space and social identification or rejection. On spectacle, see S. Lerer, '"Represented Now in Yower Sight": The Culture of Spectatorship in Fifteenth-Century England' in *Bodies and Disciplines*, ed. B. Hanawalt and P. Wallace (Minneapolis, 1996), 29–62.

95. CH2/521/2, ff. 100v–01. Examples of this movement could be multiplied: e.g., CH2/521/6, ff. 11v, 156v; CH2/472/1, f. 23v. One always stood to confess, even from one's own seat: CH2/145/1, ff. 49v, 74.

began with the trek from her house to the kirk; this procession from the house where the offence occurred to the kirk door was usual in other parishes for adultery as well as domestic violence.[96] Once arrived, penitents were often ordered first to stand at the door, then to move to the bell strings – the base of the steeple or bell tower – to stand for a prescribed period before progressing to the pillar, and after the sermon either back to the door or to the place assigned for confession. The processional nature of this movement was often enhanced, as we have seen in Mid-Calder, by assigning two elders to accompany the penitent. This 'convoy' was the usual practice for excommunicated adulterers in Perth, where the 'elders of every quarter' – that is, representing the whole parish – were assigned to the convoy, in Glasgow and Elgin for relapsed adulterers, in Aberdeen from a 1568 order standardising practice, and Edinburgh in the 1570s for the repentance of those who had taken up arms for the queen. Clad in sackcloth, they had to 'enter the kirk door and stand between the ringing of the bells till the whole people' had filed in, then be 'brought in by two of the brethren appointed and conveyed and sat in the public place till sermon end'. Then, on each repentance day (Wednesday and Friday as well as multiple Sundays) until the last, confession day, they were 'brought back to the same door by two of the elders', where they were to 'require the whole brethren that shall happen to come in and pass forth to pray for them that they might be remitted of their wicked offence', remaining in place at the threshold until 'the whole people be departed'. On the final sabbath of the term of repentance, the doorway appearance after the sermon was replaced by verbal confession from the stool and reception by the congregation. On that Sunday, the penitent, now finally reconciled, was restored physically to a place alongside her or his neighbours in the congregation, and could exit the kirk as part of the body, rather than separated from it and pleading at the door for intercession. The forgiven sinner no longer had to be 'convoyed' out between two of the godly, a foreign body infecting the body of Christ.[97]

This penitential procession in large parishes, with many penitents being escorted by deacons or elders, would have involved large numbers of

96. E.g., NLS ms 2782, f. 60v – a Glaswegian adulterer escorted from home to kirk by a deacon, 1586.

97. NAS ms RH2/1/35, ff. 2v–3, 7, 8v–9, 11v–12. In 1574 the session designated as a regular office two elders and two deacons 'to convey excommunicates to and from the kirk on sermon days' (f. 9). Examples from the other parishes listed include CH2/521/1, f. 43; CH2/521/2, f. 7; NLS ms 2782, f. 60v (Glasgow's 1586 provision that 'any other two honest men' could provide convoy if elders or deacons were unavailable); CH2/145/1, f. 52v; CH2/448/1, p. 20. See also CH2/400/1, pp. 97, 103; CH2/141/1, f. 9; CH2/1463/1, f. 1; CH2/472/1, f. 29.

people and taken a fair amount of time. It would have provided a dramatic visual display just before the sermon, and it surely spoke to its observers in a way no sermon could about the meaning of sin and godliness, about the threatening presence of agents or dupes of Satan in the midst of God's people and especially about condemnation and (finally) forgiveness. It was, as medieval penitential processions had been, a complex theology brought to visible, tangible life. Just as highly ritualised and formal, the Reformed penitential procession served to demonstrate dramatically the multiple aspects of the sin – against God and the kirk, the community of the godly, and against the individual slandered or assaulted, where this was the offence. The fact that mobility also enhanced display *per se* was a bonus.

Stopping points along the procession, like the place beneath the bell strings, had their own meanings, serving generally to recall the nature of the offence as well as to augment the exposure of the penitent. When James Gibson of Perth was punished for physically attacking Archibald Steadman in the kirk during Friday evening prayers, he had not only to stand 'barefooted in sackcloth at the south kirk door the next sabbath between the second and third bell' and to sit on the stool 'the whole time of the sermon', but also to move 'under the bell strings in the presence of the congregation and there confess his offence and crave God and Archibald Steadman and the whole congregation forgiveness'.[98] The bells had summoned Gibson to prayer with the rest of his neighbours. When he came to fight rather than pray, he separated himself from his neighbours. What more fitting site for his confession than beneath the bells that called the community together? The language of the bells was not entirely lost at the Reformation, then, despite restricted use of tolling to avoid 'superstitious' messages, like calling for prayers for the dead. The bells still did more than just announce the time: they carried a larger meaning, signifying the assembled godly standing together against sin, in this case violent sin, systematically excluding the ungodly until they had fully demonstrated repentance. Other processional pauses also used place to convey meaning. Robert Rickman's penitential procession the Sunday after he had disrupted a service in Mid-Calder with raucous misbehaviour took back him to 'the floor in that same part [of the kirk] where he disobeyed'. The place was a reminder of the sin; for how many observers did his repentance there serve also to cleanse a defiled space? Margaret Greiff of Elgin, who had 'suffered her bairn to be smothered through neg-

98. CH2/521/6, f. 118v (1617). Friday prayers not being required, the fact that Gibson attended the kirk then suggests that he was ordinarily one of the godly sort, for whom such public humiliation must have been doubly difficult.

ligence upon the night' in 1593, had to pause in her penitential procession in the place 'where the scholars sit under the great window', where the full light from the window would expose her sin fully and the school children in the loft would remind her and the parish of her own dead child.[99]

The final movement in the choreography of repentance, at the end of a prescribed term of appearances on the stool, was verbal confession and 'reception' again by the community of the godly into 'the bosom of the kirk', the traditional anthropomorphic image of the church being sensibly retained in the language of many parishes.[100] Other words chosen by the elders to record their decisions are likewise instructive: the Kinghorn session instructed a penitent to 'enter to the to pillar *to the intent she may be received* after the sermon'.[101] The pillar was not an end in itself; it was the avenue to restoration. The point brought clearly to light by the kirk session minutes is that the avenue was generally quite literal – physical movement back into the body of the kirk. Whereas after the earlier of multiple-sabbath appearances on the stool sinners had proceeded back to the kirk door where they had entered, again to withstand the embarrassing scrutiny of their now-departing neighbours, at the final sabbath they were 'received off', 'delivered off' or 'absolved off the stool'.[102] Their physical movement 'down from the stool' parted them at last from that dreaded item of furniture and situated them again into the physical space occupied by their more godly neighbours. On that final day after absolution, they were able to pass through the kirk door together with their fellow parishioners. They were no longer 'liminal people'; they had passed through the final stage of their rite of passage and in that transformative process been reincorporated into the larger community.[103]

* * *

99. CH2/266/1, f. 1; CH2/145/1, f. 52v. See Mary Douglas, *Purity and Danger: An Analysis of the Concept of Pollution and Taboo* (London, 1966) on the association of particular spaces with sin and purification.
100. E.g., CH2/472/1, f. 10v; CH2/523/1, f. 22; NAS ms RH2/1/35, f. 10; CH2/299/1, p. 63; CH2/264/1, f. 19; CH2/716/1, f. 37; NAS ms CH8/42 (a 1597 petition to be restored).
101. CH2/472/1, f. 26v.
102. This language is ubiquitous: e.g., CH2/471/1, f. 7; CH2/521/7, pp. 207, 211; CH2/1142/1, f. 100v, 102v, 106; CH2/276/1, f. 17; CH2/400/1, pp. 163, 184, 197; CH2/4/1, ff. 2v, 5, 28–28v; CH2/141/1, ff. 43, 47; CH2/523/1, f. 13.
103. Myerhoff, 109–17; Turner, *Ritual Process*, 105–10. In practice, if not in protestant theory, the ritual worked sacramentally to render 'metaphysically efficacious' that which it symbolised: Robert Scribner, *Popular Culture and Popular Movements in Reformation Germany* (London, 1987), 120–21.

Repentance was scripted as well as choreographed.[104] As we have seen, penitents standing at the kirk door before the prayers began often asked those entering the kirk for their prayers.[105] This was not the last of their speeches. Having sat in silence for the duration of the sermon, the individual on the stool then entered into a dialogue with the minister, 'answer[ing] the minister when he shall be called upon'. The dialogue included admonition by the minister, but at some point in the script the minister demanded an answer from the sinner beneath the pulpit. At his prompting, the sinner was to rise and answer, 'with his own mouth damning his own impiety'.[106] The proper response was in three parts – first, a confession of 'his wicked and filthy offences to the high offence of God and evil example to others'; then a 'hearty' request for forgiveness from 'God, the kirk and all whom by his evil example he has offended', and finally a 'promise by the grace of God to never do the like in no time coming hereafter'.[107] Where any uncertainty remained about the penitent's understanding of the sin or sincerity of sorrow, the dialogue between minister and penitent was expanded with an 'examination' which might entail quite specific questions about the offence and the penitent's attitude, and specifically 'whether he finds a hatred or displeasure of his sin'.[108] Since the session had already assessed the sinner's penitence, it must have been an embarrassment to the Anstruther Wester elders when in 1601 they had to censure a penitent after public examination revealed her 'counterfeiting repentance' on the stool.[109] If, however, the penitent gave correct answers to this 'trial of repentance', the minister responded with an exhortation 'to walk holily in time to come', and the penitent in turn uttered thanks for conversion.[110] Finally, the penitent addressed the congregation, asking to be 'received in their society again', as prescribed

104. On 'performative speech acts' and the semantic element of ritual, and particularly how it combines with pragmatic features, thought and action, see Tambiah, *Culture* 1–3, 129–41.
105. See the Edinburgh examples above, or CH2/145/1, f. 49v (1593).
106. *First Book*, 171; SAU CH2/276/1, p. 37; SAU CH2/624/2, p. 12; CH2/266/1, f. 1; CH2/145/1, f. 49v; CH2/185/2, f. 12v; CH2/1142/1, f. 4 (a fornicator admonished 'to call to mind and earnestly to weigh what weight of sin his pleasures of youth has brought him under', 1612). In cases of multiple-sabbath performances, the minister called for the oral confession on the final sabbath, the culmination of the series.
107. CH2/400/1, p. 50, offers two examples of the usual formula for confession; see also CH2/521/2, f. 12; CH2/377/1 (Yester), ff. 5v, 88; CH2/400/1, pp. 50, 118, 123; CH2/145/1, f. 4; CH2/338/1, f. 8v. *First Book*, 172.
108. E.g., CH2/4/1, f. 15; CH2/4/1, f. 28.
109. SAU CH2/624/2, p. 11; cf. NAS ms RH2/1/35, f. 10; CH2/326/1, p. 38 ('trials' in Edinburgh and Scoonie).
110. CH2/327/1, f. 8v; CH2/2/198/1, f. 6v; CH2/523/1, ff. 12–12v.; *First Book*, 171–72.

by the *First Book of Discipline.*[111] Edinburgh penitents asked to be 'received to the bosom of the kirk', having been 'by the spirit of God . . . reconciled with his true kirk' – a reminder to the congregation that where God had forgiven, the people could hardly refuse. Such speech in a liminal state has, as Turner puts it, ontological value: it 'refashions the very being of the neophyte.'[112]

The elders added to the text of the confession specifics appropriate to the sin. When Elspeth Gilmore of Westkirk in her preparation-day confession repented her absence from the kirk on Sundays, she had to 'profess herself sorry for the same' and promise 'to keep the kirk and times of God's public worship' and 'present herself to the sacrament of the Lord's Supper' the following Sunday.[113] Public utterance of this intention as part of her confession would presumably make it harder for her to renege on the promise of amendment. Clerks often copied into the minutes very detailed scripts, in the first person singular.[114] They routinely added to confessions of defamation formulaic phrases like 'false tongue she/he lied' (penitents here condemning their own slanderous tongues) and 'I know nothing but honesty of' the defamed victim. These codes survived from medieval practice to restore slandered reputations.[115] Where the offence was against correct doctrine, the script of the confession could be quite didactic, including specific statements of orthodoxy at the session's insistence. Thus, Aberdonians who had continued in or lapsed into catholic error had to pronounce and sometimes also subscribe a formal confession of faith in addition to admitting their sin of 'apostasy'. In Edinburgh, excommunicated catholics had to declare and subscribe detailed, set confessions that included vigorous condemnation of images, purgatory, pilgrimage, monastic vows, the pope and the invocation of saints; and a clear (if negative) protestant understanding of the sacraments, including the statement that the 'blasphemous idol the mass [is] not to be a sacrifice in propitiation for the sins of the quick and the dead, but rather the invention of man contrary to Christ.'[116] Finally, where the offence was

111. *First Book*, 171–72; CH2/383/1, f. 14; SAU CH2/624/3, pp. 12, 27; CH2/523/1, ff. 39–39v; CH2/400/1, p. 123; CH2/377/1, f. 88.

112. NAS ms RH2/1/35, f. 10; Turner, *Ritual Process*, 103.

113. CH2/400/1, p. 94. Robert Tomson's 1631 confession in Yester kirk, recited 'on his knees', included a list of his various sins before the promise of amendment: CH2/377/1, f. 88.

114. E.g., ML CH2/171/1, f. 54v (1595), a text to be uttered and subscribed before the whole congregation of the High Kirk of Glasgow; cf. ff. 5, 54.

115. CH2/448/1, p. 5; CH2/448/3, pp. 11–12, 38, 139; CH2/521/8/2, f. 169, for example. Chapter 5, below, offers fuller discussion of these formulae.

116. CH2/448/1, p. 20; CH2/448/2, p. 342. NAS ms RH2/1/35, f. 9v; cf. f. 50v (1574–75). Confessions of excommunicated catholics in the capital also routinely required a

sexual, as in the case of Harry Livingstone of Falkirk, the script would include not only the claim that he 'was sorry from his heart for haunting of all profane and wicked company, and specially . . . Elspeth Gordon', but also the vow – taken in this case 'with upholden hand' – never to be found in Elspeth's company in future and (for good measure) 'diligently and carefully [to] frequent and keep the kirk . . . and behave himself in such godly and Christian form of life in all times to come that by the grace of God he shall . . . redeem his former offence by walking in an holy sort of life.' The presbytery of Stirling approved this text as a promise 'to God and the world', and the world of Livingstone's fellow citizens would hold him to it.[117]

In the earliest stages of the Reformation, penitents were apparently authors of their own confessions of sin. In Edinburgh, for instance, those repenting either continued catholicism or a lapse into popery could at the appropriate time after the sermon 'speak with their own mouths what they desire' by way of public confession from the stool. The 1565 confession of an adulterer in the Canongate, recorded in the session minutes, illustrates how the penitent's script could function not only to indicate sorrow for sin, but also to inform and elicit sympathy from the audience. James Hert pointed out that 'It is not unknown by the whole here assembled how my wife departed forth of my house for such causes as is known, and remained from me the space of [paper torn] . . . into the which time God suffered me to fall and to be tempted, but of his mercy and goodness has caused me to acknowledge my sin.' He desired the congregation's forgiveness and emphasised the voluntary nature of his confession, 'offering myself willingly to repentance'. He finally pointed out that the difficult work of reuniting the family had already been accomplished: 'seeing I am reconciled with my wife in forgiving her trespasses against me and received her again to my house, and she also forgiven me, I trust in God your wisdoms will receive [me].' This was a highly successful performance: the congregation shortened his penance and received him straightaway.[118]

In other instances, penitents proved less reliable when allowed to pen their own confessions. The elders learned from negative experience. A Perth slanderer flagrantly misused his confession in 1617: appearing for his

statement affirming 'the great grief of our conscience' and the elders' 'gentle admonition' to win them back – the last a bit of self-advertisement by the elders who presumably wrote the text of the confession.

117. CH/400/1, p. 84. For confession of sins they found particularly egregious, sessions insisted on adding specific adjectives – 'filthy and abominable' being hands-down favourites: e.g., p. 123, for consulting a reputed witch.

118. *Canongate*, 20; see also *SAKS* 1:5.

last sabbath on the stool, Gilbert Robertson used the forum not to confess, but to defame his enemy further by an 'unadvised confession . . . otherwise than was enjoined him'. The session found that 'by his confession there [he] has not removed the slander from Margaret Johnston raised by him, but thereby has augmented the same.' They warded him while they rewrote his script. Under pressure from his cautioner, who stood to lose £100 if Robertson strayed from the prescribed form again, he appeared on the stool the following Sunday and 'there declared his repentance conform to the prescription aforewritten'.[119] Cirstian Leschman pulled the same trick in Falkirk, turning her confession on its head when she 'contrarily constantly abided by all the slanderous speeches she had formerly spoken in public in the kirk in presence of the whole congregation when she was required by the minister to have asked God, the congregation and all she had offended forgiveness . . . to the great aggrievement [aggravation] of her former offence'; her fine was increased by £5.[120]

Sometimes a script was prescribed for an earlier stage in the process, to elicit a confession of guilt before the session: when Thomas Baxter of Perth denied fornication after his partner had confessed and identified him, the elders ordered him to kneel and recite a carefully formulated prayer that God might 'inspire me with thy grace wherethrough I may be moved to confess the truth in the said matter of slander to the glory of God and my own salvation'. Unfortunately, having 'risen on his feet and being required to confess the truth . . . yet for all that he stood at an obstinate denial'. The elders subsequently ordered him to purge himself 'by his great oath upon the salvation and condemnation of his soul', but when he reached out to place his hand upon the Bible to swear, the minister had second thoughts and 'withdrew the Book from him and would not suffer him to swear'. Instead, the session 'knowing him by all good appearance to be guilty', ordered him warded until he should confess sincerely. The gaol again served as penitentiary: he confessed after three days in ward.[121]

119. CH2/521/6, ff. 115–15v. The bailie Andrew Conqueror was Robertson's cautioner (surety); clearly anxious about losing his money, he appeared before the session himself to denounce Robertson's perfidy.

120. CH2/400/1, p. 85 (as in Robertson's case, the cautioner paid, a total of £25). An Aberdeen fornicator adamantly refused to recite his confession when ordered, boldly leaving the stool despite an angry charge from the minister to stand and deliver. For his contumacy the session added a sabbath to his term of repentance (CH2/448/2, pp. 19, 21). See also CH2/266/1, f. 1, a Mid-Calder man's 'misbehaving words' and 'evil answer' to the minister, which got him warded until he would recite his lines correctly.

121. CH2/521/6, ff. 174, 175v.

* * *

Clearly, demeanour counted heavily in this process. Sessions needed to be convinced of sincere repentance by outward indicators.[122] The Aberlady elders accordingly ordered penitents not just to 'sit upon the pillar in presence of the whole people', but there to 'give signs of repentance'. They are typical of sessions everywhere in often defining the length of a penitential sentence in terms not of sabbaths but more vaguely, for instance: 'aye until the kirk be satisfied of his repentance' by some visible demonstration of sorrow, or as the *First Book of Discipline* prescribed, 'till open repentance appear manifestly in' the sinner. When Adam Schortus, who had violated a fasting Sunday, failed at this and 'gave not a sign of repentance as was ordered', he had to repeat his penance the following Sunday 'to give further and more pointers of repentance'.[123] The session minute books regularly record when penitents were 'received off' the stool that they had given 'great signs of unfeigned repentance'.[124]

The signs could take a variety of forms, including noteworthy gestures and postures of humility, particularly abject language of self-condemnation, voluntary rather than forced confession and especially the shedding of tears.[125] A fornicator in St Giles parish, Elgin, was allowed in 1585 to confess from his own seat rather than the pillar because of his extravagantly humble 'gestures of the body'. And Andrew Clark of Aberdeen found his situation much improved after 'bursting forth in tears' to signify he 'was sorry and penitent from his heart' for rebuking the minister in church on Sunday.[126]

Appropriate signs or tokens regularly brought mitigation or even remission of penalties. The Perth session, for instance, initially thought that the

122. Kirkoswald's first extant session book opens with instructions that penitents are 'required to give signals', and they enforced the rule consistently: AAC CH2/562/1, ff. 1v–2, 6v, 8v, 9–10, 18, 30, 32–32v, 37v, 39. See also ML CH2/171/1, f. 4v.
123. CH2/4/1, ff. 5, 7v, 8v, 9, 10v, etc. *First Book*, 172. Other examples of open-ended repentances in anticipation of 'signs' or 'tokens' include CH2/141/1, f. 9; CH2/1142/1, ff. 96, 103; CH2/338/1, ff. 17v, 44; CH2/400/1, pp. 34, 61, 116, 161, 163; CH2/266/1, ff. 1, 8, 35; CH2/1463/1, ff. 3v, 6; CH2/448/1, p. 7; ML CH2/171/1, ff. 3v, 54, 61; CH2/145/1, f. 49v; *SAKS* 1:29.
124. CH2/327/1, f. 42v; CH2/185/2, f. 19.
125. CH2/317/1, f. 10v; CH2/198/1, f. 8; CH2/141/1, f. 43; CH2/266/1, f. 1.
126. CH2/145/1, f. 4; CH2/448/2, pp. 108–09. Clark had 'stood up openly in presence of the congregation' to oppose Peter Blackburn's admonition to his friend William Allan – in dread, he admitted, of the sentence of excommunication to follow – and seized the documents of excommunication from the notaries. For the particular effectiveness of tears, see CH2/472/1, f. 17v; CH2/523/1, f. 29v; or CH2/521/7, p. 427 (tears supplemented by the penitent's prayer for 'God to strike him instantly to death if ever he' consulted a conjuror again).

adulterer Andrew Gray ought to be 'corrected in severity, yet because of his humble submission, they have mitigated his censure'. Patrick Graham's violence against another man on the sabbath brought the slight fine of 20s because he apologised 'on his knees penitent-like'; likewise Jean Dog found her sentence shortened in 1636 when she 'showed herself very penitent with shedding of tears for her folly'.[127] Particularly convincing outward behaviour could even free a sinner from the extreme penalties of excommunication and banishment from the community. In the Canongate, which encompassed Edinburgh's 'red light' district, convicted harlots were in general summarily banished from the town under threat of scourging and branding on the cheek; however, in 1564 two women, having admitted that they had borne children in harlotry, confessed so humbly 'of their own motive wills' that they were admitted to the penance of humiliation instead and permitted to remain in town upon promise of amendment.[128] The same session released a fornicator from ward and consented to baptise his bastard child 'by reason they have considered . . . his lowly submitting himself'. Likewise, in North Leith, Henry Ogill's slandering of an elder brought him a sentence of banishment, but by 'giving great signs and tokens of repentance' he had it diminished to public humiliation.[129] The same principle guided presbyteries.[130]

By contrast, when the Perth kirk officer reprimanded Margaret Mar for hiding her face on the stool, 'she uttered words against him in a bitter manner and extended her voice in such sort that she was heard through all the kirk in time of sermon, and so behaved herself uncomely', only to find herself warded for a week and required to repeat her repentance the following sabbath 'in a more humble manner'.[131] One would think that

127. CH2/521/4, p. 241. See also CH2/521/3, p. 207; CH2/521/6, f. 163v; CH2/521/7, p. 452; CH2/521/8/1, ff. 30v, 216; CH2/141/1, ff. 43, 47; CH2/338/1, f. 44; CH2/472/1, f. 8v; CH2/523/1, ff. 14, 17v.

128. *Canongate*, 10; cf. the more usual punishments ordered in another case heard on the same day, in which three prostitutes and their pimp were consigned to the branks in the market cross for three hours, then banished under pain of branding. None was said to have produced bastards; their penalties can only have been more severe than those in the earlier case because of involuntary confession and inadequate display of humility (pp. 7–8, 10).

129. *Canongate*, 21; cf. CH2/621/1, p. 363 (1605); CH2/523/1, ff. 29v, 31v (banishment).

130. CH2/327/1, f. 10v; CH2/121/1, f. 28 (Selkirk and Edinburgh presbyteries).

131. CH2/521/3, p. 97 (1599). She presumably complied, since she makes no further appearance in the record. The elders' action was in accord with the *First Book of Discipline*'s instructions (p. 169) to 'seek a further remedy' for those 'found stubborn'; gaol time allowed her to 'consider the dangerous estate' of her soul. Dundonald's session in 1612 ordered two women to 'make their public repentance again *more penitently* than they have done' (*Dundonald*, 231, emphasis mine).

penitents would be anxious enough to avoid or get off the stool that they would be willing to play the part, but clearly some balked at the pretence, rousing the sessions' ire. James Burnet of Fraserburgh paid the price in 1612 when his minister reported to the session that 'standing up before the congregation to give a confession of his sin, [he] had no grace thereto'. Burnet promised the elders that 'whatever oversight was in his former confession, he shall repair it again', only to find that the repair would require two additional sabbaths at the kirk door and upon the stool in penitent's garb, the first to confess his original fault, the second to admit 'his careless and jocund form of confession' the first time around.[132] In the same parish a fornicator found that her 'informal repentance' brought denunciation as an 'unpenitent whore'.[133] The duration of a penance could be changed from a specific number of weeks to an open-ended period for someone who misbehaved before the session or the congregation.[134] The ability to weep at will was a decided advantage for early modern sinners. In the most extreme cases of failure to produce 'signs', sessions could proceed to the most severe penalty, excommunication. This was the case in 1605 when Gilbert Keith appeared before the Aberdeen session for fornication and showed 'plain contempt' rather than sorrow when he 'rejoiced in his sin' and boasted of 'fifty more faults' of the like nature that he would be glad to describe from the stool. The elders heeded the warning and proceeded with the censures leading to excommunication.[135]

Sessions were often concerned that they might have misread 'signs'. They realised that people could easily feign outward tokens and so required 'trial of their penitence' by minister, elders, congregation or presbytery, depending on their level of uncertainty. In 1595 Glasgow's sessions began meeting with penitents on the day before their absolution to observe their signs, ordering the minister to absolve them 'as he finds them contrite'.[136] Presbyteries, not knowing penitents personally, often 'remitted to the congregation' such decisions. Selkirk presbytery 'after long trial of his repentance' decided to excommunicate John Simson as impenitent for slaughter in 1607; however, they referred many more such cases back

132. CH2/1142/1, f. 4v.
133. CH2/1142/1, f. 78v; cf. f. 94v. Presbyteries acted likewise. The Haddington brethren in 1597 found 'no tokens of repentance' or 'purpose to amend' in a relapsed fornicator, and told the minister to seek corporal punishment from the magistrate to elicit penitence (CH2/185/2, f. 6v); Aberdeen presbytery rejected repentance 'in a contemptuous and arrogant manner with foolish speeches' (CH2/1/1, n.f., 29 December 1608).
134. E.g., CH2/1142/1, f. 96; CH2/145/1, f. 49v.
135. CH2/448/2, p. 150. Keith finally gave in and repented.
136. CH2/327/1, f. 10v; NLS ms 2782, f. 61.

to sessions or pastors 'to be tried'.[137] In the case of Elspeth Tomson, who managed to produce tears, they accepted her sorrow but 'found [her] ignorant' of the full import of her sin (fornication) and sent her back to the session for enlightenment.[138]

* * *

The role of the congregation in a penitential performance was both audience and, though less obviously, actor. The rite must surely have appealed to the voyeuristic element present in most communities. A certain portion of the congregation may well have been lured to an otherwise distasteful sermon by the prospect of seeing their neighbours in white sheets compelled to admit their sexual escapades (and partners) or their drunken brawling. Might placement of this more titillating part of the service *after* the sermon have been a calculated move by the authorities to get people to stay the course?

The prurient element was substantial enough in many parishes to cause the elders to worry about the privacy of the session meeting. In parishes like Newburn, they found the eavesdroppers so numerous that they finally ordered that 'persons found standing near the windows or doors of the kirk during the time of session to hearken what was said and done there should pay for their disobedience 6s 8d.' In 1588 the Glasgow session found its own members altogether too busy leaking stories of people's sins to their interested neighbours; as a result they started requiring all elders to swear 'with uplifted hands' to keep session proceedings secret.[139] Quite apart from the lurid details of sexual abandon or familial violence that might be aired in the session but not necessarily from the stool, there was a myriad of other tantalising tales to be heard in the session's proceedings. The residents of Anstruther Wester who had not witnessed Margaret Ward's 'loose and light behaviour in dancing through the town with women and lasses in a ring' were naturally tempted to listen at the session

137. CH2/327/1, ff. 3, 4–5v, 8v, 37. Jedburgh presbytery, baffled by Hobbie Thompson's levity, returned him to the parish for further trial (CH2/198/1, f. 8; cf. f. 13v); as Haddington presbytery did with a 1597 adultery case, seeking the Pentland congregation's discernment of 'tokens of repentance' (CH2/185/2, f. 7). When the Newburgh session sent an adulterer to presbytery to make the determination, the brethren replied that 'he appeared outwardly to be penitent', but 'they could not otherwise judge, referring his heart to God' and his penalty to the session: SAU CH2/277/1, Box I, #8.

138. CH2/327/1, ff. 42v, 43v.

139. SAU CH2/278/1, p. 33; NLS ms 2782, f. 52v. The Aberdeen and Perth elders had the same problem; CH2/448/1, p. 13 (1568); CH2/448/4, p. 167 (1630); CH2/521/7, p. 90 (1619).

door for an account of it, or for the debate about whether Margaret Paterson, 'drinking with a stranger and vagabond' at night, had consumed ten pints of ale as charged or just the seven she admitted. In a pre-television age, with a largely illiterate populace newly deprived of many of its traditional festivities in the name of godly sobriety, one had to get one's entertainment where one could. So many were willing to pay Newburn's 6s 8d for the pleasure that the session had to repeat its order.[140]

In the more public setting, those penitents who played the clown on the stool may simply have been acting to their audience, either deliberately or as a result of being carried away by the exhibitionism of the ceremony they were assigned to perform. Thus, when the adulterer William Gillies found himself recalled by the Perth session in 1631 'for his misbehaviour on the stool yesterday in laughing where he should rather have wept', he blamed the audience: 'a neighbour having nodded his head to him moved him to smile.' The elders were not sympathetic to his excuse, and admonished him to act on the stool as if he had 'a sorrowful heart for the sin of adultery as he would procure the mercy of God'.[141] Less careless penitents would presumably have been all the more humiliated by taunting or smirking from the congregation. They looked instead for sympathy, the truly penitent joining with the more adept actors in producing tears for audience consumption. Clearly the experience of penitential performance was as various as its actors, their outward signs carrying more conflicting meanings than the reformers wished.

The congregation did not merely observe. They also took part in the action, both formally and informally. They might perform badly, as William Gillies's neighbour did, either by being inattentive or by actually disrupting the proceedings. Misbehaviour by members of the audience was a perennial problem and could actually result in their own sentence to public penance: when John Landray 'perturbed' a repentance service in 1579, for instance, the Perth session sentenced him to 'pass about the cross in linen clothes barefooted and bareheaded' on both preaching days, Thursday and Sunday, then 'come to the public place of repentance the time of the sermon, there publicly to confess' and pay a fine to the poor. Three more 'perturbers', apparently less disruptive, had only to repent from the stool on Thursday, but clearly the session wanted to establish early and definitively that proper sobriety was expected of the congregation. The audience might also err by leaving the kirk early. The North Berwick session complained in 1612 that many parishioners left before the blessing had been pronounced, and that some even ducked out when the

140. SAU CH2/624/2, p. 119; SAU CH2/278/1, p. 34.
141. CH2/521/8/1, f. 8.

sermon began and stood talking loudly just outside the door so that others could not hear.[142] Presumably the talkers would have gone home, had there not been an event after the sermon worth returning for – the confessions of their errant neighbours from the stool. Those who stayed for sermon and confessions but left before the blessing would have missed the last act of the penitents serving multiple sabbaths, standing by the kirk door as the congregation filed out. For the voyeurs, the oral confessions would have been the draw, but those of the audience who left early would have both reduced the humiliation of this last act, and missed out on that part of the didactic message intended for them.

The most important role played by the audience was the more formal and positive one of 'receiving' and 'absolving' the penitent from the stool at the end of the penance. In Reformed protestant theology it was for the congregation to determine when penitence had been sufficiently demonstrated. While they were generally represented by the session in this function, the assembled godly could act on their own, even to shorten a prescribed repentance. In the case of the Canongate adulterer James Hert, noted earlier, the congregation upon hearing his confession found Hert so obviously distraught by his sin that they feared for his sanity. In view of his 'great appearance of repentance come from the bottom of his heart, the *whole kirk* discerns willingly and heartfully to receive the said James . . . that he be not swallowed with desperation.' In setting the penance, the session had acted simply as representatives of the whole kirk, not as judges in their own right, and the congregation could amend their order at will. The latter were the final judges of what a penitential performance meant, and the decision could go either way. In Scoonie, when a slanderer in 1642 had stood in the jougs, paid 20s and confessed before the pulpit on her knees, it was the congregation who found her confession 'too small and limited', and sent her back to the session.[143] 'Receiving' is thus a highly significant enactment of the protestant principle of priesthood of all believers. At that moment in a penitential rite when before the Reformation a priest would have exercised the sacerdotal function of absolution, protestants looked to the assembled believers: Edinburgh penitents were 'to be received to the society of the kirk and obtain *their* absolution conform to the order and book prescribed', and in the Ayrshire parish of Kirkoswald, a penitent remained on the stool 'until the *congregation* receive[d] signals of his repentance' and decided absolution was in order. The passive voice in many of the session minutes for reception may be an indicator of the dispersal of responsibility for this act to

142. CH2/521/1, f. 27; CH2/285/1, p. 15.
143. *Canongate*, 20 (emphasis mine); CH2/326/1, p. 57.

all of the laity, rather than to clergy alone: in the Perth formulation, too, a penitent was 'received and absolved' by the 'whole kirk'.[144] Few parishes avoided the word 'absolution', as one might expect of a Reformed church virulently opposed to 'popish' language.[145] Most session minute books use it freely, but nearly always in reference to the congregation, reserving it to the minister or a commissioner from the presbytery only in the extreme case of reception of an excommunicate.[146] It was, in the end, the whole kirk that had to be 'satisfied' by the repentance for the sinner to be 'received into the bosom of the kirk and fellowship of the faithful'.[147]

The ritual and language of reception set specific roles to be played by the penitent, elders, minister and congregation. Following the dialogue between minister and penitent discussed earlier, the *First Book of Discipline* required the minister to turn from the penitent to the congregation, asking 'if they be content to receive that creature of God whom Satan before had drawn into his nets, in the society of their body, seeing that he declared himself penitent.' With a positive response, he exhorted the parishioners to receive the penitent as they desired God to receive themselves, thus reminding them that they, too, were forgiven sinners. Having ritually divided the sinner from the godly members of the community, both script and action now reunited them by emphasising their common identity as forgiven sinners. The elders and 'chief men' of the parish were then to take the penitent by the hand and 'one or two in the name of the rest were to kiss and embrace him with reverence and gravity, as a member of Christ Jesus.'[148] When one female excommunicate was received after repenting in Glasgow, the session ordered 'two elders to attend that day in the pulpit seat to take her by the hand in sign of her reception in the church'. In parishes like Markinch, where penitents were said to be

144. NAS ms RH2/1/35, f. 12; AAC CH2/526/1, f. 6v; CH2/521/6, f. 116v; CH2/521/7, pp. 207, 211. An Elgin penitent was received only 'if the elders *and congregation* find her penitent'; the parishioners were to judge 'tokens of repentance in her' (CH2/145/1, ff. 10–10v, emphases mine).
145. NLS ms Wod. Oct. IX, f. 3 for contemporary discussion of the term; Aberlady is an exception, opting for 'received' only: CH2/4/1, ff. 2v, 5, 28v.
146. CH2/266/1, f. 1v; CH2/191/1, f. 9v; ML CH2/171/1, ff. 3v, 18–18v, 30v, 53v, 54v–55 ('absolved by the clemency of the kirk'); CH2/529/1, f. 3v, though more usual in Mortlach is 'after humiliation received' (f. 10v). For clerical absolution, NAS ms RH2/1/35, 50v; CH2/121/1, f. 28; ML CH2/171/1, ff. 18v, 30v; NLS ms 2782, f. 61: excommunication coming generally from the presbytery, that body designated one of its members (usually the parish minister) to pronounce absolution.
147. NAS ms RH2/1/35, ff. 2v, 8v; CH2/299/1, p. 63.
148. *First Book*, 172.

'elevit [lifted] off the stool' at this point, it is easy to picture the elders literally raising the person by the hands from the place of humiliation and escorting them back into the midst of the godly.[149]

Sometimes the role of taking the penitent by the hand to receive him or her again was assigned to a member of the congregation who had been wronged by the offender – a graphic illustration of their personal reconciliation at the moment of the sinner's reconciliation to God and kirk. When the Aberlady elder William Thompson confessed in July of 1639 to bloodshed, having fired a musket at George Perth 'under cloud of night', his fellow elders deprived him of his office and assigned him nine months of repentance, but they gave a key role in his final act to his victim. After Thompson had 'sat upon his knees in presence of the whole congregation and craved of the whole parish and the said George Perth forgiveness', Perth 'in presence and audience of the whole people forgave him that offence, and in token thereof, took him by the hand' to receive him back into the community of the godly.[150] A posture of humiliation gave way to a gesture of friendship, raising Thompson to the physically upright position of an honourable member of the community. Much was hereby demanded of performers in the audience, however, and the results were not always so positive. In the same parish in 1642 the victim of slander played her role so badly that she wound up subjected to discipline in turn. Marion Taylor had successfully complained against David Baxter for slandering her as a witch; however, when he craved her pardon before the congregation as ordered, instead of forgiving him, she 'said in great fury and devilish disposition in presence of the whole congregation, "Lord, let never God forgive him", with many other wicked words.' This drama before the pillar turned on its head the message of forgiveness, charity and reincorporation that 'receiving' was to enact. The congregation being highly offended, the session sent Taylor to the pillar the following sabbath.[151]

The proper mode of receiving a penitent was with thanksgiving. The minister first gave 'public thanks unto God for the conversion of their brother and for all benefits which we receive of Christ Jesus' (again identifying sinner and congregation together as recipients of divine favour). Then the congregation followed suit. The Canongate clerk recorded that all the people 'gave thanks to God' after witnessing the apology of a

149. NLS ms 2782, f. 61; CH2/258/1, f. 12.

150. CH2/4/1, ff. 20, 27; cf. CH2/1142/1, f. 100v; CH2/521/1, ff. 60v, 119; CH2/521/2, f. 12; CH2/716/1; CH2/338/1, f. 7v.

151. CH2/4/1, f. 29.

drunken flyter in 1565.[152] The benediction that followed could thus include saint and sinner alike.

Once or twice a year, this message of reincorporation became even more dramatic when it was associated with communion. Whenever possible, sessions scheduled 'receiving again' just antecedent to a communion service, even if the prescribed length of a penance had to be cut short.[153] The South Leith session book is punctuated by annual lists headed 'Saturday before communion penitents received', or 'this day the Lord's supper was ministered; penitents received'.[154] Culmination of a repentance after the Saturday preparation-day sermon joined the penitent's particular humiliation with the more general seasonal humiliation (often combined with fasting) of the assembled congregation. Indeed, Andrew Gray recommended to his Glasgow parishioners that they ought all to assume penitential garb when truly repenting their sins before communion: 'Clothe yourselves in sackcloth and weep,' he told them in a sermon on how to achieve assurance of election.[155] The identity of sinner with congregation, all now properly humbled and forgiven, was dramatically displayed by corporate reception of often sizable groups of penitents at the end of the Saturday sermon – a living illustration of the sermon's usual theme of sin and forgiveness. Penitential performance was as communal an enterprise as the next day's sacramental meal, when restored penitents sat at the table with their neighbours, the hitherto divided community now again one body.

* * *

What are we to deduce from this evidence about how repentance was performed in Reformed Scotland? What does it tell us about how people understood the religious meanings of protestantism; about how the protestant community defined itself; about how individuals understood their relationships with their neighbours, with the larger realm of Christendom, with God? Ritual is designed to embody and enact meanings. Having now recognised that protestants, far from abolishing penitential ritual, retained and adapted it to suit their own purposes, what can we glean from the foregoing descriptions about what those purposes were and how they shaped a Reformed culture?

First, we must acknowledge that the meaning of the penitential rite *was* fundamentally religious. Too often historians, beguiled by the theories of anthropologists and sociologists, fascinated by the possibilities of their

152. *Canongate*, 24.
153. E.g., CH2/521/7, p. 24; CH2/191/1, f. 2v; CH2/264/1, f. 25v.
154. CH2/716/1, f. 23. See also CH2/716/2, f. 25v; CH2/562/1, f. 32.
155. Gray, *Sermons*, 80.

theoretical categories, have forgotten that the Reformation was the result of a quarrel about faith and salvation. Whatever social functions may have been served by a rite like making repentance – however it defined community, incorporated displaced individuals, marked transitions – it was first and foremost a demonstration of basic Christian beliefs about sin, repentance and divine forgiveness, and of basic Calvinist beliefs about the elect and the reprobate. It was genuinely humiliating, in a spiritual as well as a social sense. The penitent was not merely embarrassed before his neighbours, he was humbled – a virtuous stance – before God. It reinforced by public demonstration the division between the elect and the reprobate. Even if both appeared on the stool, those who appeared sorrowful enacted (and hopefully experienced) the proper attitude of the saint, while those who laughed or grumbled or railed, or who reappeared for multiple offences, suggested by their performance the presence of the damned in the midst of the saints. The fundamental dichotomy within the visible church, always vexing to Calvinist state churches, could not remain merely theoretical for Scots congregations as long as penitential rites were performed. The most troubling theological principles were literally made flesh before them, though the path to salvation was also made clear in ritualised display. The preachers' points about sin and sorrow, forgiveness and sanctification, were acted out after the sermon on the stage of the stool. And unless we write off as mere acting all the reported displays of sorrow by tears and demeanour, we must assume that individual sinners themselves processed through the agonies of doubt and despair about their spiritual standing as they went from doorway to bell strings to stool, underwent the tortures of conscience as they considered the words of the sermon and the minister's admonition, and emerged relieved of their guilt and comforted by their neighbours' physical embrace at the end of the process.

Some of the theological points made by penitential performance reinforced traditional beliefs, logically enough, since protestants and catholics ultimately shared more common ground than they occupied separate space. They shared the presumption that penitents ought to demonstrate regret, that they merited humiliation as a sign of their offence against God, and that their humiliation ought to be public as a sign of their offence against the values of the community. They shared the end of penance, the reincorporation of the sinner into a church built on divine forgiveness of the truly sorrowful. They shared hope for amendment. A penitent was sent to the stool 'to the *intent* he might be received', and petitions for absolution included the promise 'in time to become a new man'.[156] Protestants

156. CH2/472/1, f. 26v (emphasis mine); CH2/266/1, f. 1v.

even preserved the traditional catholic notion of a hierarchy of sins (rather contrary to the Reformed orthodoxy that all sin condemns) in the furniture of high and low stool; the clothing of black gown, linen or hairy cloth; and the distinction of single or multiple appearances. And one does wonder whether the rite communicated to those less inclined to introspective piety the message that acting out the external forms would do just as well – as it had with the old religion. Multivalency of the message communicated by the ritual may have troubled divines, but for many parishioners in the early generations of the Reformation, penitential ritual must have been a reassuring reminder of the past.

In Reformed as in catholic Scotland, the voluntary participation of offenders in a system of ritual humiliation is explained in part by the anxiety of offenders to be reconciled to the source of their spiritual solace. In Lent, and later in protestant 'days of reconciliation' or spring 'seasons of fasting and humiliation', penitents confessed and submitted to the discipline of bishops or sessions in order to be admitted to the spiritual consolation of communion, whether at catholic Easter or the protestants' annual or biennial celebrations. Were not reconciliation and communion in themselves powerful and effective rituals, it would be difficult indeed to explain the numerous voluntary confessions one encounters in session minutes. There was good reason for two Inveravon women in 1638 to jump the gun and present themselves to the stool on Sunday without the session's order: public repentance provided the one recognised mechanism whereby they could be rid of apparently overwhelming guilt over their sexual offences. A respectably married Aberdeen couple confessed sexual activity during a fast – clearly not the sort of sin that would ever have been discovered – presumably for the same reason. And Margaret Mitchell of Culross 'of her own accord made a pitiful confession of adultery' in 1631 because her reception of communion 'immediately after her fall', with the sin unconfessed, had caused her such 'great grief and trouble in mind' that she yearned to 'confess publicly to the effect to get relief therefrom if possible she might find it'.[157] Even foreign visitors from Reformed communities voluntarily submitted themselves to discipline: the Dutch skipper Hendrie Bredindick could easily have sailed away from Leith in 1613 rather than risking voluntary confession of drunkenness and fornication while in port, but warding 'during the session's pleasure' and an appearance on the pillar won him a spiritual solace that he obviously thought worth the trouble.[158] As many male as female fornicators sub-

157. CH2/191/1, f. 43; CH2/448/2, p. 267; CH2/77/1, f. 4. See also CH2/1142/1, ff. 4, 98 (voluntary admission of fornication with two men); CH2/521/1, ff. 80v–81 (confessing 'uncompelled', 1582); Blair, 68–69.

158. CH2/716/2, ff. 78v, 79.

mitted to public repentance lest their offspring be deprived of baptism, and they of communion. Rather than deny his child the sacrament, a male adulterer not yet revealed by the mother would come forward for penance, and couples who had offended without a resulting pregnancy or any other apparent discovery of the sin by the community nonetheless presented themselves before the session for discipline. In Lesmahagow, a man troubled by his antenuptial fornication actually complained that his minister assigned too easy a penance.[159] The rite 'worked', in other words, because of continued spiritual anxiety to purge oneself of sin and participate in what remained of the sacramental system.

Perhaps what we are seeing here would better described as a psychological phenomenon. Certainly the cathartic element in ritual served a perceived need in a culture where guilt was a central construct.[160] But however we explain it, the culture of early modern Scotland attached religious meaning to anxiety and prescribed a fundamentally religious solution to the problem. And the efforts described earlier to catechise and to continue religious education through sermon attendance surely mean that there was some popular understanding of that meaning *as* religious. Where such understanding was lacking, the elders incorporated education into repentance by requiring not only public humiliation, but also verbal instruction from the minister or designated elders.[161] They expended extraordinary effort in 'dealing with' penitents of all sorts, from sexual offenders to heretics, to bring them to a realisation of their sin and the meaning of repentance before admitting them to the stool. While their final actions may appear to us simply punitive, the minutes tells us that they believed sinners ought 'to be first handled and travailed with gently, if by any means possible they may be won'.[162] The Scoonie elders were

159. CH2/521/2, ff. 97v–98, voluntary confession by Robert Ross, who actually turned in to the elders a diary of his sins; and CH2/521/7, pp. 25–26, another diary of sin. For other examples of voluntary confessions by sexual offenders both male and female, and for their relatively equal distribution in performing repentance, see below, pp. 178–79, n. 187. NLS ms Wod. Fol. LXIII, f. 144v records complaint against the minister Robert Hamilton agreeing to marry the plaintiff 'without any public confession of fornication, for six dollars'.

160. This was as true for post- as for pre-Reformation society: Peter Marshall, 'Fear, Purgatory and Polemic in Reformation England' and David Gentilcore, 'The Fear of Disease and the Disease of Fear' in *Fear in Early Modern Society*, ed. William Naphy and Penny Roberts (Manchester, 1997), 150–66, 184–208; T.J. Scheff, *Catharsis in Healing, Ritual and Drama* (Cambridge, 1979) draws on cognitive dissonance theory (the higher the price paid, the more valued the experience) to explain the near-ubiquity of cathartic pain in effective (and affective) ritual.

161. CH2/521/1, f. 74; cf. Tambiah, *A Performative Approach to Ritual* (Oxford, 1979), *passim*, and *Culture*, 1–2 and ch. 4, on the combination of semantic and pragmatic features (thought and action together) in effective ritual.

162. CH2/383/1, f. 21; CH2/448/1, p. 20.

particularly troubled in 1640 by the possible heterodoxy of two women 'because we could not know the thoughts of their minds'. And in the face of Jonet Murray's erroneous belief, the Burntisland session combined 'serious dealing to bring her to remorse' with an order 'that she should be brought to the sermon every sabbath day by some elders'. When they eventually sent her to the presbytery, it was 'for the weal of her soul' and 'that she might be received again to this kirk'.[163] Reconciliation of the sinner to God, kirk and community was their ultimate aim, and it is important to remember that this was available even to people who had been banished and excommunicated: no excision from the community was permanent if repentance were finally achieved.[164]

Certainly, many penitents did understand the theological principles behind their acts of humiliation and repentance; it would be hard not to, given the number of hours people were compelled to listen to sermons about sin and forgiveness. Some took advantage of their grasp on the theology of penitence to ease their penalties: James Douglas, provost of Elgin, confessed fornication to the session in 1585, but pointed out that 'in respect repentance consisted not in the external gesture of the body or public place appointed for the same, but in the heart, of the which he had God and his own conscience giving him witness' (which they could hardly gainsay), he 'desired to keep his own place the time of preaching' and confess only before the minister. The elders granted 'his good meaning' and his petition. Of course, his 'good meaning' may have had less to do with their decision than his position in the town and his wealth: they seized the opportunity to make him 'declare his upright meaning' further by paying for glazing the kirk's north window.[165] Status along with a degree of theological sophistication reduced his penalty.

Putting historically religious meaning properly first, however, does not deny meanings with which sociologists or anthropologists would feel more comfortable. To be 'received again' had social (and economic) implications as well; offenders not received, but excommunicated, lost access not only to the spiritual comfort of the sacraments but also to participation in society and trade. The kirk regularly reminded householders not to receive or entertain (offer food and drink to) anyone excommunicated, whether

163. CH2/326/1, p. 36; CH2/523/1, ff. 23–25v. She finally repented and was received. The session dealt similarly with adulterers, probing for 'any sense or feeling of her sin' (f. 45), 'for the safety of his soul' (f. 43), before proceeding with a sentence to the stool. See also NAS ms RH2/1/35, f. 11v.

164. CH2/523/1, f. 21v; ML CH2/171/1, ff. 18–18v, 54–54v; CH2/716/1, f. 15v; NAS ms CH8/62.

165. CH2/145/1, f. 4.

for heresy or contumacy.[166] The penitential rite thus profoundly divided the community, physically separating offenders from their neighbours, marking them off by posture, dress and place. What van Gennep or Turner would define as its 'preliminary' stage materially displaced the individual from his or her previous status in the community into a location and an attire set aside for that one, divisive purpose. Crossing the threshold of the prescribed kirk door, standing beneath the bell strings, sitting on the stool, kneeling before one's victim, all placed the penitent in the second, 'liminary' stage of transition, a suspension between two states. Wearing sackcloth in that state eliminated the traditional status markers of dress and rendered the penitents as a group homogeneous, without rank, joined in passive reception of chastisement in preparation for a rebirth.[167] It is here in the standard anthropological version that the individual set apart is provided 'an experience of the sacred', in this case the judgment and condemnation of sin leading to divine forgiveness – the central spiritual experience of the Christian. Every stint on the stool was an enactment of that fundamental requirement for salvation, conversion by grace. But it was also a ritual definition of the community as exclusive of offenders against its defined norms, and inclusive of those who submitted to the authority of the group. Every reception from the stool, the third, 'post-liminary' stage, enacted the communal culmination of the ritual, restoration of the displaced person to the embrace – sometimes the literal embrace – of the community as well as God.[168] To the extent that offenders against the kirk's standards were also violating those regulations that maintained communal harmony, this three-stage process of separation, suspension and restoration served a transformative function to render the disruptive individual at least neutralised, but preferably so reformed in behaviour as to be able to contribute positively to the community. The begetter of a bastard was ideally received as a supporter of his child and husband of the mother; the drunkard as a sermon-goer; the slanderer reconciled and sworn to keep peace. Making repentance was a visual enactment at several levels of both social and metaphysical transformation.

Certainly, it enacted clearly the subordination of the individual to the larger community, with subordination understood not as merely static, but rather as a process by which the nonconforming individual was returned to defined normalcy. The suggestion of an earlier generation of historians that protestantism gave rise to modern individualism is given the lie by

166. E.g., SAU CH2/624/2, pp. 110–11, 151, 160.
167. Turner, *Ritual Process*, 95–103.
168. Van Gennep, ch. 6; Gluckman, 'Les rites de passage'; Turner, *Ritual Process*, 94–130, and *Performance*, 75–79; Myerhoff, 112–17.

Scottish penitential rites. The interests of the community of the godly, defined for practical purposes as coterminous with parish or town, must be served by the submission of the individual to the kirk's discipline, because individual sin brought divine wrath to the community. In God's eyes, culpability was always communal. The familiar history of ancient Israel, where failure to suppress sin regularly resulted in captivity and exile, was ever before the eyes of Scottish sermon-goers and left no room for tolerance of individual departure from defined norms. It was simply not an option that individual choices about what we so often designate as 'lifestyle' could be permitted to jeopardise the wellbeing of the whole community. The only choice open to a parish when an individual declined submission to the kirk was excommunication and expulsion from the bounds, with attendant loss of home, business and all social connections.

The individual's sins in the early modern period *were* the community's: the Perth elders in 1588 noted that those engaging in illicit festivity did so 'to the great grief of conscience of the faithful and infamous slander of the whole congregation'; every individual sin, said the Aberdeen elders, gave 'slander to this congregation'. Every conscience in the town was weighed down by the offences of a few, the sins of one being effectively borne by all in a complex doctrinal reversal of scapegoating. And only repentance properly performed could 'take away the slander'. The minister of Auchterderran explained that 'filthy livers within this reformed gate' must go to the stool to purge the whole community; God makes 'a conditional offer of sparing if any one would *perform*'.[169] It was simply not possible to separate an individual's guilt from the communal responsibility for godliness. In 1648, when the Innerwick elders discovered a troop of local soldiers who fought on the wrong side, they not only demanded public repentance by the soldiers of their 'sinful engagement', they declared a day of fasting and humiliation for the whole community 'with the paper containing the sins of the time' to be read and the Covenant renewed.[170] Certainly, God held all accountable for the sins of a few every time he sent plague or storms or dearth. It was in the midst of plague that the Perth session levied an unusually stern penalty on Elspeth Cudbert and George MacThane, 'apprehended in naked bed together in filthy fornication' on a communion and fasting Sunday. They were carted backwards through the town from the house where they had been apprehended to the market cross, in sheets and 'having paper hats upon their

169. CH2/21/5, f. 5 (my fol.); CH2/523/1, ff. 23v, 24, 25v, 30v, 34, 42, etc; NAS ms RH2/1/35, ff. 2–2v, 45; *Canongate*, 11; CH2/294/1, f. 3v; CH2/266/1, f. 1.
170. CH2/1463/1, f. 7v.

heads', warded until Sunday, then conveyed by elders to the stool – all specifically 'so that God of his mercy might remedy this intolerable plague from this town'.[171] The lesson is twofold: in the early modern era the distinction between individual and community was blurred at best, and the contemporary presumption was that everyone's welfare was at stake if sin were tolerated. This conviction surely helps to explain why people accepted the dictates and intrusions of the elders in their everyday affairs with remarkably little grumbling.

Penitents in the Scottish rite represented the community in another sense. Andrew Gray acknowledged a virtue in the humiliation displayed by sinners on the stool when he commended sackcloth to all the godly. Every Christian sat on the stool vicariously when one did, so that the penitent in sheets became a living icon in Reformed culture, with its focus on conversion as the central act of faith. The close proximity of audience and performer at the kirk door before and after the service also underlined the thinness of the division between them, given the pervasiveness of sin and everyone's vulnerability. Congregation and penitent were at once joined and separated by the threshold performance. Given, too, that the door was a means as much of egress as entry, the liability of every believer to the sin that might well expel her or him ultimately from the elect community was signified by the space itself. As the portals of catholic churches had been decorated by scenes of the final judgment or the mouth of hell, protestant threshold performances provided powerful living displays of theological precepts. They were both didactic and hortatory.[172] And they contained signals that united sinner and saint in the same plight, that not so much isolated as absorbed the individual in the corporate drama of salvation and damnation.

Offenders under discipline found their position within the social as well as the spiritual hierarchy of the parish defined by the penitential rite. In general, traditional hierarchy was firmly upheld. For instance, the well-born often had the option of buying their way out of the more humiliating aspects of the rite. For a substantial financial penalty, one could buy one's way off the stool, or purchase the right to wear a lesser form of penitential garb.[173] Masters regularly paid fines for their servants,

171. CH2/521/1, 116v. The fast that they violated had been declared to address the plague.

172. Myerhoff, 112, on liminal 'moments of teaching'; Carlson, *Places of Performance*; and Gillian Russell, *Theatres of War: Performance, Politics and Society 1793–1815* (Oxford, 1995), 17 *et passim* on social (or in this case theological) functions of 'performance, display and spectatorship'.

173. E.g., SAU CH2/1056/1, n.p. (St Monans, where 10s could buy freedom from the jougs for slander, but not from appearance before the pulpit); SAU CH2/624/1,

displaying both their own status and the servant's dependence.[174] The fact that sessions often forgave the fiscal penalties of poor offenders was both a matter of practical charity and a means of demonstrating the low status of the poor.[175] More often, if an offender could not afford a fine, the session called on the secular magistrates (themselves generally among the elders) to impose additional public humiliation outside of the kirk, at the market cross or on the cuckstool. The poor, like the young, underwent considerably more corporal punishment than their elders and social betters, regularly suffering the pillory or 'crosshead' because they were unable to pay a fine.[176] Sessions threatened children with the age-specific punishment of whipping or 'a palm on the hand', reinforcing the subordinate position of the child in the family and larger society (and perhaps the assumption that children's under-developed consciences would fail to produce the tears that beating could elicit).[177] The system thus served socially conservative functions.

At the same time, repentance in the Reformed tradition could undermine traditional hierarchy. The General Assembly ordered discipline 'without exception of persons' in 1562, and there are enough cases of the well-born failing to buy their way out to suggest that this message was the overriding one. Lairds and even lords who wished to demonstrate their support for the Reformed kirk often voluntarily submitted to public humiliation for their sins.[178] But others less willing succumbed to the

p. 5 (40s for private confession of slander to the session rather than on the stool, but with 'no redemption' for a second offence); AAC CH2/751/1, ff. 125, 131; CH2/523/1, ff. 33v, 37, 40, 41; CH2/521/6, f. 105; NLS ms 2782, ff. 59, 61v; CH2/400/1, p. 29; *Dundonald*, 289, 330; CH2/141/1, f. 14 (an adulterer's 'voluntary gift' of £30 12s 6d freeing him even from public admonition).

174. Among countless examples, SAU CH2/624/2, p. 157; CH2/359/1, f. 4v; *Dundonald*, 67.

175. E.g., CH2/448/2, p. 70 (1604, a penalty forgiven because the 'very penitent' sinner was 'but a servant and has no gear').

176. The Aberdeen elders ruled in the 1560s that, for swearing, people 'of poor degree' would be sent to the cuckstool, and the 'potent to pay silver' would be fined: CH2/448/1, p. 3; cf. CH2/523/1, f. 10v; CH2/472/1, ff. 18v, 19v; CH2/1173/1 (Kelso), f. 1v; CH2/145/1, f. 61v (trelapse fornicators 'not responsible in gear' banished from Elgin, 1594); NLS ms 2782, f. 59; *Dundonald*, 72; and in the Highlands, CH2/191/1, ff. 8, 9v, 12; CH2/529/1, f. 87.

177. CH2/448/1, p. 3; CH2/521/7, p. 388 ('insolent boys' playing during afternoon sermon 'threatened to be scourged, being young'); CH2/145/2, f. 23 (Elgin boys 'lashed' for playing during the sermon).

178. *BUK* 1:14, 41; Michael Graham, 'Equality before the Kirk? Church Discipline and the Elite in Reformation-Era Scotland', *Archiv für Reformationsgeschichte* 84 (1993), 289–309.

threat of suspension or excommunication just as their social inferiors did. The Perth elders dealt with Lady Errol in the same way they did anyone else who failed to come to sermons, 'proceed[ing] against her as a contemner [contemptuous] of the word'. Inveravon lairds got 'such censure for absence [from the kirk] as others shall do in like case'. And in Kirkoswald, Sir Alexander Kennedy avoided having to stand on the stool for his fornication only because of his sciatica; he still had to confess publicly from his own seat and pay the hefty penalty of £40.[179] Elite offenders might have to be referred to the higher power of the presbytery to enforce discipline, but they seldom escaped it entirely.

Nor did the elders and clergy escape, although they had some advantages. The elder William Dairsie went to the Anstruther Wester stool for fornication, but the amount of his fine was 'referred to his own discretion'. A Perth elder repented from his own seat for offering hospitality to papists in 1595; the same parish's reader, Henry Adamson, had to make his repentance and lost his licence to preach in 1621 for fornication. Aberlady's session required repentance of three elders between 1639 and 1643, depriving each of his office before imposing the stool.[180] Clerics were no more immune: the minister of Temple, for example, had to confess before his congregation and ask forgiveness of a man he had slandered, and William Wedderburn of Bathelny had to repent publicly for fornication.[181]

The sliding scale of penalties established by nearly every parish to allow for differences in ability to pay can also be seen as a levelling factor. Because an affordable penalty was available for all but the destitute, and the fines levied on the better sort were, as Belhelvie ordered, 'imposed proportionally to their estate' and so did not represent the mere 'slap on

179. CH2/521/3, p. 280; CH2/191/1, f. 46; AAC CH2/562/1, f. 33v. See also CH2/185/2, f. 12; CH2/145/1, f. 65 (Elgin's ruling that the 'common order be used anent the baron of Sanquhir for committing fornication', 1594); CH2/271/1, f. 85 (order of the bishop and synod of Moray that, where public repentance was warranted, ministers must not dismiss any man 'for the payment [of] his [financial] penalty how great soever it may be'); NLS ms Wod. Qu. XXI, ff. 256–57v (ladies disciplined sternly by the Edinburgh presbytery in the 1590s); CH2/390/1, f. 43 (excommunication of heritors); CH2/89/1 (Deer presbytery's order for the laird of Philorth to submit to his parish session's discipline, 1603). Repentance might even entail public apology to a wronged inferior: CH2/338/1, f. 30v.

180. CH2/624/1, p. 11; CH2/521/2, f. 139; CH2/521/7, p. 243; CH2/4/1, ff. 20, 27, 28v, 43, 44v (for bloodshed, sabbath breach and 'ill speeches'); cf. *Canongate*, 24; CH2/400/1, p. 63.

181. CH2/424/1, f. 13v; Spalding, 2:39. John Brand performed repentance in his parish for slander: *Canongate*, 13.

the wrist' that a standardised penalty might have, everyone was subjected in effect to the same system.[182] Although there are many examples of the poorest being subjected to physical punishment because of their inability to pay a fine, Menmuir was among many sessions that often remitted penalties altogether for poverty.[183] A young man playing ball on the sabbath in Perth, 'being a poor lad, [was] excused of his fine and only admonished', and the Dundonald session reimbursed half the penalty for sabbath breach paid by John Hendry of Crosbie 'considering his obedience [in borrowing the money to pay] and . . . poverty'.[184] And where sessions extended mercy in regard to public repentance, they did so often for rich and poor alike, the determining factors being degree of penitence, capacity of understanding and extreme poverty. Thus, the Scoonie elders required no performance of a 'poor simple shepherd lad' for holding a lamb for marking on Sunday since they did not believe he understood his offence, and the Jedburgh presbytery in a 1607 incest case simply admonished the offenders and asked the minister to try to 'bring them to some knowledge' since they 'were both half-souls [half-wits]'.[185]

Finally, there was a notable gender equality about kirk discipline. Both begetters and bearers of bastards appeared on the stool, generally together and for the same number of sabbaths. Session rulings against fornicators inevitably adopted egalitarian language – 'both of them to the like humiliation', 'as well for the man as the woman', 'he or she'.[186] Sampling of arbitrarily chosen years in a few parishes bears out the general impression

182. Belhelvie acted consistently on this principle: CH2/32/1, ff. 1v, 4v, 18, 20v–22. Perth levied fines according to 'quality, means and estate' (CH2/521/6, f. 105); they set for missing Thursday sermons in 1587 a fine of 10s 'for the poorer sort who are employed in handlabour', 20s for others (CH2/521/2, f. 6; CH2/521/6, f. 163v). Ellon ruled in 1607 that for sabbath breach a 'man of substance' must pay £6 13s 4d, a husbandman £4, a labourer 40s 8d (CH2/147/1, f. 7v; cf. NLS ms Wod. Oct. IX, f. 5v for Glasgow scales). South Leith set penalties for offenders 'according to their power' (CH2/716/1, f. 22v), as did Dalkeith (CH2/84/28, f. 74). Lasswade required for sabbath breach 6s 8d of masters of households and gentlemen, 4s 4d of 'yeomen', and 20d of servants; however, they declined to remit public confession altogether, contributions to the poor only reducing the length of repentance (CH2/471/1, f. 1).

183. CH2/264, f. 14v.

184. CH2/521/8/1, f. 47; *Dundonald*, 66; see also CH2/383/1, f. 19. In Highland parishes, fines could be paid in kind, 'a hen and a pot' or 'a mare and a sow' in Inveravon: CH2/191/1, ff. 24, 35.

185. CH2/326/1, p. 35; CH2/198/1, f. 14.

186. CH2/529/1, f. 53; CH2/226/1, f. 5; CH2/448/1, pp. 5–6, 10; CH2/1463/1, f. 1v; CH2/338/1, f. 2v; CH2/716/1, f. 1v (1597). St Andrews likewise required the same repentance of both parents when children were overlain, 'conform to equity': *SAKS* 2:766.

given by kirk session minutes that in fact the numbers of men and women prosecuted for fornication and adultery were roughly equal all over Scotland.[187] This is all the more remarkable given that pregnancy made sexual offence easier to spot in women than in men. Were Scottish midwives better than their counterparts elsewhere at eliciting the names of fathers from women in labour? Were the kirk visitors more diligent than we think, or neighbours nosier? Or perhaps Scottish sinners were so culturally attuned to penitential rituals by the second and third generations after Reformation that more of them voluntarily confessed? Where the records do show apparent inequities, they are often explained by simple delays in prosecuting men off at sea or fighting abroad.[188] To the degree that there were actual gendered inequities, they were in financial exactions, which tended to be harder on men than women – reasonably enough, since most men were better able to pay, given economic disparity.[189] Finally, when sessions allowed penitents to avoid public performance by 'acting themselves' – swearing generally upon their 'great oath' never to offend again – this option was generally open to servants, women and boys as well as men.[190]

Just as penitential performance defined the individual in relation to the larger community, so it defined the community itself in relation to God. That relationship was constantly petitionary on the part of the church, with performing repentance the most visible form of petition. The public humiliation of sinners, both as individuals and as whole congregations, was fundamentally propitiatory, arising from concern with sin angering God,

187. Sampled years for Falkirk (CH2/400/1) gave the following data for cases of sexual offence: 1618 (pp. 16–33): 30 men, 32 women; 1619 (ff. 33–52): 25 men, 23 women; 1621 (pp. 69–89): 32 men, 31 women; 1622 (ff. 89–109): 19 men, 20 women. For Dundonald (p. 203ff), the 1610 figures are 17 men, 18 women (only 6 of whom were pregnant as a result). Like results are found in Kirkcaldy (CH2/636/34, f. 11v *et passim*) and South Leith (CH2/716/1, ff. 26–42v (without exception listing male and female offenders together, 1611–42).

188. E.g., CH2/716/1, ff. 1v (1572), 12 (several cases where the male partner, 'gone to other countries', repented 'at his homecoming'); or CH2/448/2, p. 4.

189. E.g., CH2/338/1, f. 19v (£6 for a man, 20s for his partner, which he paid); cf. Innerwick's 1608 ruling for fornicators, £4 6s 8d and 'as much for the woman except in case of poverty' (CH2/1463/1, f. 1v), or NLS ms 2782, f. 59. The Newburn elders in 1633 reversed their earlier practice of fornicators' fines 'only exacted of men' and required women henceforth to pay half a dollar (SAU CH2/278/1, p. 35). Very often, the male partner paid both the penalties (e.g., CH2/400/1, pp. 22, 30, 56, 109, 156), but in Orkney the Kirkwall session required the 20s penalty for female fornicators (cf. 40s for men) to be paid 'out of her own hand' (CH2/442/74, f. 7v).

190. CH2/276/1, ff. 8v–9; CH2/1142/1, f. 102v; CH2/716/1, f. 10; NLS ms 2782, f. 61v; CH2/442/74, f. 26v; ML CH2/171/1, f. 44 (1595).

and with God's all-too-frequent response – punishing the individual with disease or accident, or the whole community with plague, pestilence, famine, earthquake or storm, 'spectacles of his wrath'. It was to avert divine wrath that sessions sent individual offenders to the stool, and that (in the communal version) the whole church periodically observed 'days of fasting and humiliation' in a form of group repentance to appease divine anger. The penitential rite was the place where the sacred and the profane came together at many levels. Individual repentance sought divine forgiveness from the stool; corporate repentance in a communal fast addressed the cosmic power that used snow and wind, disease and hunger to condemn sin. The wrath of God permeated both individual conscience and the health and wellbeing of burgh and landward, village and fishing fleet. Only visible, demonstrable repentance could address it effectively and avert natural disaster.

That the ancient ritual thus took on a semi-magical air seems not to have troubled the elders at all. Armed with plenty of biblical evidence of a vengeful divinity visiting the penalties of sin on the third and fourth generations, let alone the sinner's contemporary neighbours, they were able to provide the requisite theological grounds for a rite that both they and the sinners with whom they dealt hoped would have a practical effect. Thus, in 1612, two of the Fraserburgh elders themselves voluntarily confessed that they had 'highly offended God and slandered their calling in profaning the sabbath day and loosing their boat forth of the port, wherefore they acknowledged that the hand of God since had justly been against them to the great endangering of their lives . . . as also [on the positive side] that it was of the Lord his special mercy that they came safe to land.' They readily agreed, 'because their fault was public and they public persons', to 'confess their fault, and God his merciful deliverance before the congregation'. Tellingly, their penance was deferred 'because they were upon the head of their journey'.[191] Clearly these men thought the humiliation of penitential performance before those on whom they themselves usually sat in judgment was worth undergoing to ensure safe passage on their upcoming journey. However Reformed the language of their confession, the act itself was as propitiatory as a popish pilgrimage or, for that matter, a pagan sacrifice to vengeful gods.

In the context of natural disaster affecting the whole community, sessions routinely extended penance from the usual individual performance to a performance by the entire community. The Aberdeen elders construed the 'fearful earthquake' that rocked the town in 1608 as a clear 'document that God is angry against the land and against this city in particular for

191. CH2/1142/1, f. 2v.

the manifold sins of the people'. They accordingly proclaimed a 'solemn fast and humiliation', together with an order for 'the Covenant to be renewed by the whole people . . . by holding up of their hands all publicly before God'. With the plague that had surrounded the vicinity for some weeks finally attacking the town itself the following week, the fast begun in October was continued without abatement until January of the next year.[192] The flood of 1621 that inundated Perth and brought down the bridge over the Tay drove the session to order the congregation 'humbled all that week with fasting and prayer' and two sermons daily, with good results: 'God heard us that the water decreased.'[193] Ritual repentance had tangible benefits.

* * *

The ritual of repentance remained as mimetic as it had ever been before the Reformation – perhaps even more so, given the number of people involved and the rigorous enforcement of attendance by the audience. But of course there were differences. Communal 'receiving and absolution' diminished the sacerdotal element and elevated the laity to the position of authority previously occupied by the clergy. And protestant penance was embedded in sermon: it was a logistic performance, a miming of the words uttered by the minister, the words of the penitential psalms sung around the service, the words prescribed by the session for confession. But survival of this ritual in subtly altered and much expanded form demonstrates two principles that must inform any study of ritual in early modern Europe. First, it underlines the dynamic nature of ritual in history. Theories of ritual too often give us a static structure that makes no allowances for the changes that come with the passage of time and introduction of new ideas. Second, it clarifies the mimetic nature of protestantism. Ritual elements persisted, adapted to historical context, but still dramatic and weighted with meanings recognisable to their audiences. In the case of repentance, persistence and dynamism taken together served both to underpin the commonality of catholic and protestant concern with sin, separation and reconciliation (with God and community), and to undermine catholic clericalism, the 'superstition' of absolution and the theology of works co-operating with grace. The former was accomplished by continuity of practice and image (vestments, tears, symbols); the latter by sermonic context and the mechanics and language of 'reception' (by

192. CH2/448/2, p. 322, cf. pp. 72, 201, 316, 320, 340–41; CH2/448/1, pp. 10–11.
193. *Chronicle of Perth*, 22. A fast after the great snowstorm of 1635 likewise brought a 'gentle thaw' (p. 34). See also CH2/400/1, p. 95; CH2/472/1, f. 138; NAS ms RH2/1/35, f. 15v. For more on fasting and propitiation, see chapter 7, below.

session order or congregational direction, not priestly forgiveness). The former surely made the Reformation easier to accept for a population wedded to tradition; the latter was sufficient to convince the Reformers that dramatic performance had its place in a religion of the word.

Chapter 4

Profane Pastimes

The Reformed kirk has a reputation for vigorous repression of festivity hardly to be surpassed by any other protestant church. From the 1560s on, the authorities of the kirk from session to General Assembly waged a stern and unremitting campaign against the celebration of Yule, Easter, May Day, Midsummer and saints' days; against feasting at weddings and wakes; against Sunday sports and dancing – in short, against anything that might distract newly Reformed laity from the central protestant focus on the sermon, the Bible and the godly life of moral discipline and prayer. Their goals were both negative and positive. On the one hand, they were intent on quashing popish superstition, in part because they were convinced that its persistence helped to explain the recurrence of plague, famine and other divine judgments on the land. In a more positive sense, they were trying to clear the way for construction of that new vision of the good life that exalted word over image and stern self-discipline over ritual performance, and in which community cohesion was achieved by a shared protestant identity and the common goal of a devout and orderly society.

Modern observers generally credit their campaign with remarkable success; certainly the popular image of Scotland after the Reformation is grim and joyless – and with some reason. Days of fasting and humiliation nearly outnumbered the old saints' days and vastly outnumbered new days of thanksgiving, and official policy and legislation on the matter of festivity were exemplary for a Reformed nation. The *First Book of Discipline* in 1561 pronounced the feasts of Christ, the saints and the apostles to be popish inventions; and the 1575 General Assembly demanded civil enforcement of the ruling that 'all days that heretofore have been kept holy besides the sabbath day, such as Yule day, saints' days and such others may be abolished', with 'a civil penalty against keepers thereof by ceremonies, banqueting, playing, fasting, and such other vanities'. Having abolished celebration of Christmas, Easter and the other religious festivals, they then used the famine of 1578 as a spur to get the regent and Privy Council to abolish 'all kind of insolent plays as King of May, Robin Hood and such others in the month of May, played either by bairns at the schools or others'. By 1589 Patrick Blair could report that the old holy days had been so effectively abandoned that 'the common people do scarce know what day of the month or time of the year any of these days do happen.'[1] Their puritan counterparts in England could only look on in envy at these extraordinary accomplishments in the first generation of the Scottish Reformation.[2]

A closer examination of the deliberations and resolutions of General Assemblies, however, suggests that the picture of remarkable and early success of the protestant campaign against festivity may need correction. In fact, the flurry of 1570s resolutions against festivity seem to have been spurred by the reformers' recognition that, thus far, protestantism had made little dent in popular 'superstitious' celebration – or, for that matter, in clerical adherence to the old calendar. The context for the 1575 resolution against feast days was a complaint brought by the commissioner of Aberdeen that '*readers and ministers* in the country keep certain patron and festival days and on these days convene, pray and preach, and foster the people in superstition.' In 1577 the Edinburgh Assembly received a complaint about *ministers* who continued to celebrate communion on Yule, Lent, Pasch and saints' days 'to retain the people in blindness', and in 1579 the Assembly was asked, 'What ought to be done to such persons that after admonition will pass to May plays, *and specially elders and deacons and*

1. *First Book* 88–89, declared the 'holy days . . . that the papists have invented . . . utterly to be abolished from this realm'; *BUK* 1:332, 334, 339 (1575), 388 (1577); 2:407, 410 (1578). The 1578 Edinburgh Assembly called for a public fast along with abolition of May plays in light of the 'present famine', which they construed as divine punishment for 'increase in adultery, murder, sacrilege, sedition' and the disorder of May festivities (2:410). For Blair, LPL ms 3471, f. 48v.
2. Ronald Hutton's *Rise and Fall*; 'The English Reformation and the Evidence of Folklore', *P&P* 148 (1995), 89–116; and *The Stations of the Sun* (Oxford, 1996) demonstrate attempts by some English clerics and magistrates to abolish seasonal celebration other than Christmas and Easter, but there was no comparable national ecclesiastical legislation until 1643, when abolition of Christmas in England was the price of Scots military aid against the king. As the minister of Logie, Alexander Hume, opined in 1609, 'True it is that in England there is a begun Reformation . . . but as yet there remain some vestiges of idolatry and superstition, . . . [like] their observing of feasts, their fasting in the time of Lent, etc, which resemble the cicatrices of an evil-cured wound': *Wodrow Miscellany*, 1:581–82. The Scots in 1566 approved all of the Second Helvetic Confession *except* its allowance of 'the festivities of our Lord's nativity, circumcision, passion, resurrection, ascension' and Pentecost, which 'obtain no place among us, for we dare not religiously celebrate any other feast day among us than what the divine oracles have prescribed': *Zurich Letters*, ed. H. Robinson (Cambridge, 1842–45), 362ff.

others that bear office in the kirk?'[3] If even members of the kirk sessions continued to observe traditional feast days, it is hardly surprising that the laity did so as well.

The problem did not end with the resolutions of the 1570s. It was not until 1592 that the kirk finally convinced parliament to pass an act abolishing previous legislation 'for maintenance of superstition and idolatry', aimed especially at the 1551 act 'giving special licence for holding of Pasch and Yule'. And when in 1595, fully thirty-five years after the Reformation, the Assembly produced its own evaluation of progress to date, the scene they painted was not at all the one the reformers had intended. Instead they found

> superstition and idolatry maintained, which utters itself in keeping of festival days and bonfires, pilgrimages, singing of carols at Yule, . . . profanation of the sabbath, and specially in field time and harvest, and common journeying on the sabbath, and trysting, . . . exercising of all kinds of wanton games, . . . dancing, drinking and such like, . . . waiting [performance by waits or minstrels], and gluttony, which is no doubt the cause of this great dearth and famine, [along with] gorgeous and vain apparel, filthy and bawdry speeches, . . . a great number of idle persons without lawful calling, as pipers, fiddlers, songsters, sorners, pleasants, strange beggars, living in harlotry and having their children unbaptised, without any kind of repairing to the word [preached].[4]

The evidence of session minutes suggests that we cannot dismiss these complaints as merely an echo of the preachers' formulaic jeremiads; instead, the Assembly reflected accurately the experience of ministers and elders at the parochial level. A close examination of session books also gives us some indication of why revel remained a constant in their experience for so long, and at the same time why particular elements finally did succumb. The records suggest that the behaviour of the elders themselves had a great deal to do with the slow pace of reform on some fronts, but also that this behaviour may have been carefully calculated for ultimate protestant victory. We have seen that the sessions achieved remarkably quick progress on those fronts that really mattered to the reformers – doctrinal conversion and instruction by means of sermons. The elders were no fools; they chose their battles carefully, and with the priorities of

3. *BUK* 1:332, 389, 2:440 (emphasis mine). The response was that they should be debarred from the sacraments until they had satisfied the kirk's discipline, 'in special elders and deacons'; however, enforcement appears to have been negligible.
4. *BUK* 3:809, 874; *APS* 3:542.

the larger church and community in mind. And their actions went beyond repression: recognising the gaps that would be left when seasonal festivities and traditional rites of passage disappeared, they in practice tempered voluble disapproval with relative tolerance, until they had developed viable alternatives that would in the end redefine the festal culture of early modern Scotland.

* * *

Aberdeen's session books provide abundant examples of traditional 'profane pastimes' persisting for generations after the Reformation, particularly among the crafts guilds. Failing efforts by godly magistrates in May of 1562 and May of 1565 to stop the craftsmen's traditional holy-day processions and rituals, cordiners, websters, tailors and baxters were in the next decade repeatedly summoned before the session for keeping catholic holy days. The elders ordered the deacons of all of those crafts in February of 1574 to admonish their members to 'remove all superstition and occasion thereof in keeping of any holy day or any other festival days which were used of old time before, but to keep only the sabbath day . . . in preaching and prayers.' The craftsmen were rather given to spending Sundays working or in recreational activities like golf, bowls and kyles, for all of which sabbath occupations they were rebuked regularly into the next century. Their devotion (or at least abstention from labour) appears to have been reserved for the old saints' days. The elders had to repeat their 1574 admonition, in January of 1576, for instance, when they again charged the deacons of crafts to try their members for sitting idle on Yule Day, and the cordiners in particular continue to appear in succeeding January session minutes for offences like 'nightwalking', carding, dicing and 'extraordinary drinking' – Yuletide and New Year's recreations.[5] In 1577 several craftsmen were summoned before the session for having 'against the express command of the civil magistrates as against the minister's prohibition in pulpit' performed the 'Corpus Christi play upon Thursday the sixth of June last, . . . to the great slander of the church of God and dishonour of this whole town, because the play is idolatrous, superstitious and also slanderous'.[6] What is striking is how little change there was on the score of celebration in the next century. The town greeted royal

5. *Extracts from the Records of the Burgh of Aberdeen, 1398–1625*, ed. John Stuart (Aberdeen, 1844), 1:343–44, 459–60; CH2/448/1, pp. 30, 107; CH2/448/2, pp. 58, 85–86. The first extant session book has entries for 1562–63, 1568 and 1572–78; the second begins in October 1602.

6. *Miscellany of the Spottiswoode Society*, 2 vols (Edinburgh, 1844–45), vol. 11 July 1577; cf. the pre-Reformation order by the 1539 council *requiring* craftsmen, in this case litsters (dyers) to provide 'banners and pageants in the procession and plays on the

restoration of Christmas in the Perth articles of 1618 with more than a Nativity sermon.[7] A godly Aberdonian complained in 1643 that on 'good Yule Day [was] no work wrought in Old Aberdeen, . . . for all the thundering of their minister'.[8] Instead, shops closed for traditional holiday revels.

The long-standing association of crafts guilds with their patron saints, in Scotland as elsewhere, made their post-Reformation lot particularly difficult and helps to explain why they appear so often before the sessions of Aberdeen and other towns for 'superstitious' celebration of saints' and other holy days.[9] For their members to cease observance of their own saint's day entailed a loss of public identity, just as the loss of Corpus Christi processions, in which the guilds walked in order of their standing in the community, diminished the guild and undermined its corporate status in the town. But craftsmen were by no means the only violators of the kirk's order. Schoolboys and their parents constituted another category that challenged the abolition of traditional festivities in Aberdeen. Accustomed to closing the school on holy days, their master was still being admonished fourteen years after the Reformation to keep his students at work on Christmas Day and in the Easter season. He was told to 'give no play nor any privilege to their scholars in those days dedicated to superstition in papistry, but . . . retain them those days at their lessons, and if parents will stop their children from coming, they shall signify the same to the kirk.'[10] Yet future generations of schoolchildren remained adamant

festivals of Corpus Christi and Candlemas': *Annals of Aberdeen*, ed. William Kennedy (Aberdeen, 1818), 96–97.

7. At the king's insistence, though over strong objections from parochial clergy and the 1621 parliament, the Five Articles of Perth had in 1618 restored *religious* observance of Christmas, but not the 'profane' festivities associated with it. Many Scottish ministers declined to preach on Christmas Day anyway (NLS ms Wod. Fol. LXIX, f. 38v), and legislation after 1637 again abolished all observance of it until 1661. Christmas was again banned in 1690 when William and Mary gave the Scottish parliament its way, and it did not again become an official holiday until 1958, but the purely profane Scottish New Year's Eve, Hogmanay, remains the greater holiday.
8. Spalding, 2:176; cf. 2:107–08, 288 (the 1645 order that no one 'make good cheer or be merry according to the old fashion').
9. Allan White, 'The Impact of the Reformation on a Burgh Community: The Case of Aberdeen' in *The Early Modern Town in Scotland*, ed. Michael Lynch (London, 1987), 97; A.J. Mill, *Medieval Plays in Scotland* (Edinburgh, 1927), 247–53, and 'The Perth Hammermen's Play', *SHR* 49 (1970), 146–53.
10. CH2/448/1, p. 35. The grammar-school pupils had petitioned unsuccessfully for Christmas holidays in 1569; the session's action five years later suggests that parents had continued to ignore the authorities on this issue. See Alan White, 'Religion, Politics and Society in Aberdeen, 1543–1593' (Unpublished PhD thesis, Edinburgh, 1985), 277.

about the keeping of Christmas. In 1604 the boys violently seized control of the school in protest against attempts to control Yuletide celebration, 'keeping and holding the same against their master, with swords, guns, pistols and other weapons'. In 1612, another disorderly protest resulted in the expulsion of twenty boys, all gentlemen's sons.[11]

The town's university students likewise periodically protested the abolition of Yuletide observances, and not just in the decades immediately following the Reformation. While the 1618 articles had restored *religious* observation of Christmas, generally interpreted by the elders to mean a sermon on the day, the students seized on the opportunity for traditional profane celebration. As late as 1642, when a drummer and then a bell ringer were sent through Aberdeen to warn the citizens to 'keep themselves sober and flee all superstitious keeping of days' on Christmas Day (Sunday that year) and to open their shops and labor on Monday, 'the students fell upon the bellman and took the bell from him for giving such an unusual charge; so the people made good cheer and banqueting according to their estates and passed their times Monday and Tuesday both, for all their threatening.' That in the 1640s the prohibition of Christmas observance was regarded as 'unusual' surely suggests that the session's campaign against Christmas had in some measure failed. For the session, reform remained an elusive goal – literally so for the elder Andrew Cant, who disrupted the afternoon sermon on that Christmas Day in 1642 in fury at the more audacious students celebrating noisily just outside the kirk windows: 'hearing some noise in the kirkyard of bairns and people, he got up suddenly from his seat [next to the reader] . . . through the kirk and people goes he, and out at the door, to the great astonishment of the people in the Old Church, and when he came to the kirkyard, the bairns fled, but he chased them in to the New Kirk, whereat the people there was all feared.'[12]

Resistance to the abolition of Christmas and New Year celebrations was vigorous among all sorts of Aberdonians, especially when it came to Yuletide music, dancing and guising (the festive donning of costumes and masks for dancing and procession). Carolling was the particular offence of women in 1574, when fourteen were 'charged before the assembly for playing, dancing and singing of filthy carols on Yule Day at evening, and on Sunday at evening thereafter.' All admitted their fault and received admonition, but this mild censure failed to address the problem. The extant records of the Aberdeen session cease after 1578, but when they resume in the seventeenth century, we find the elders and minister still struggling

11. *Scottish Notes and Queries* 3rd ser., 3 (Aberdeen, 1925), 200.
12. Spalding, 2:107–08.

with the same problem. As late as January 1612 they denounced 'the superstitious observing of New Year's Eve by singing of idolatrous songs through all parts of this burgh'. They ordered that offenders thenceforth be apprehended by the magistrate and gaoled until they satisfied the session, and that an announcement to that effect be made 'by the handbell through the whole streets of this burgh one day or two before New Year's Day next to come'. Even those who merely kept the tradition of opening their houses and offering food to the 'songsters' were to be punished with the relatively heavy fine of £5.[13] The seventeenth-century session clearly recognised that their earlier, milder efforts had had no discernible effect. Yet the survival to the beginning of our own century of a traditional New Year's carol referring to giving food to the singers suggests that the draconian measures of 1612 may have had just as little impact:

> Rise up, guidwife, an' shak' yer feathers,
> Dinna' think that we are beggars;
> We are guid folks come to play,
> Rise up an' gie's oor Hogmanay.

With the refrain 'Hogmanay, Trol-lol-lay', protestant Scotland begins to look a bit less grim.[14]

Yuletide musical festivities included some even more offensive to the authorities than carolling, but still difficult to eradicate. In January 1577, four women 'with their accomplices' were tried for dressing as 'dancers in men's clothes under silence of night, in house and throughout the town'. The elders warned that if they offended again by cross-dressing and seasonal revelry they would lose all benefits of the kirk and be denounced from the pulpit. Again, though, mere warning made little headway against the problem. The early seventeenth-century register shows the practice passed down to the next generation. In January 1606, the session summoned a group of men – including of the craftsmen two litsters [dyers] and a baxter – who had gone 'through the town masked and dancing with bells on Yule Day last at night'. The session censured them and ordered that 'no man nor woman in this burgh about the superstitious time of Yule or New Year's Day, or any other superstitious time, shall

13. CH2/448/1, pp. 58–59, one man also offending; CH2/448/3, p. 90. Lutheran authorities in sixteenth-century Germany punished the same activity: Joel Harrington, '"Singing for his Supper": The Reinvention of Juvenile Streetsinging in Early Modern Nuremberg', *Social History* 22 (1997), 27–45.
14. Mary McLeod Banks, *British Calendar Customs: Scotland*, 3 vols (London, 1937–41), 2:45ff, includes several versions of this carol. 'Hogmanays' may have been biscuits made for New Year.

presume to mask or disguise themselves in any sort, the men in women's clothes, nor the women in men's clothes, nor otherwise, by dancing with bells, either on the streets of this burgh or in private houses, in any time coming.' Ministers issued warnings from the pulpit 'that none go through the town on New Year's evening singing any songs' under threat of prosecution as 'fosterers of superstition'.[15]

Despite the repetition of 'superstition' in these admonitions, the principal concern may have been with the wearing of disguises, and especially gender-inversion in dress. Masking of any sort, especially 'under cloud of night', created opportunities for sexual and even criminal misbehaviour less feasible were one's face clearly visible to neighbours. To the most vigorous of protestants, covering one's face, like performing a part in a play, was an inherently sinister act. It bespoke a fundamental dishonesty – a renunciation of one's own identity to take on that of another, in this case of a potentially mischievous and disorderly other. Donning the costume of the other sex, moreover, reflects the traditional association of winter festivities with misrule, or ritual inversion – a custom increasingly feared and opposed by both civil and ecclesiastical authorities all over Europe.[16] As David Cressy has recently pointed out, male transvestism in early modern England could be used to give men entry into female enclaves and provide enhanced opportunities for sexual dalliance.[17] Just as puritans railed against it there, so in Scotland elders and ministers perceived a turning of the gender hierarchy topsy-turvy, even for a season, as a clear danger to social order. Its setting in a popish season added fuel to the fire: Antichrist, the great deceiver, had long used the abandon of Yuletide to lead Christians away from the gospel and into superstition. And with a handy biblical injunction against cross-dressing (Deuteronomy 22.5), they were bound to prosecute it. But however they denounced it, and however sternly they admonished the revellers, traditional practice had a firmer hold on the popular imagination than the protestant ideal of gravity and honesty.

Festive transvestism was not restricted to seasonal celebration; it also occurred in Aberdeen in association with two rites of passage – marriage

15. CH2/448/1, p. 108; CH2/448/2, pp. 77–78.
16. Burke, *Popular Culture*. For examples of continental and English governments banning guisers for fear of crime, see Hutton, *Stations*, 12. In Scotland in 1508 a man was hanged for theft 'under guise of mumming': Mill, *Medieval Plays*, 30. Yet as recently as 1497 the king's court had paid Epiphany guisers in Aberdeen (Banks, 2:126).
17. Cressy, 'Gender Trouble and Cross-Dressing in Early Modern England', *JBS* 35 (1996), 438–65. Cressy sensibly argues against any particularly deep meaning in festive cross-dressing and its prosecution in England. Literary scholars, he says, have gone too far in reading into theatrical transvestism 'a sex-gender system in crisis' (p. 464).

and burial. Both had, of course, been sacramental occasions before the Reformation. In theory, they had now lost much of their former magnificence along with their sacerdotal elements, thanks to protestant legislation against extravagant feasting, procession and bell ringing.[18] As any anthropologist would predict, though, this loss was not easily accepted. In Aberdeen, resistance took the form of defiant feasting and cross-dressing at wakes and weddings, and of elaborate funeral processions, with some families even commissioning crucifixes to be carried in processions as late as 1618.[19] In 1576, for instance, Mage Moreson was made to pay a fine and make her public repentance for 'abusing of herself in clothing of her with men's clothes at the wake of George Elmisly's wife'.[20] And as with Yuletide masking, the generation of the Reformation bequeathed its defiance to the next, and to the one after that. In August 1605, the session summoned

> some young men and young women of this city for dancing through the town together this last week, the time of the bridals, the young men being clad in women's apparel, which is accounted abomination by the law of God . . . and the young women for dancing openly with them through the streets with masks on their faces, thereby passing the bounds of modesty and shamefastness which ought to be in young women . . . in a Reformed city.

In this case the session was concerned not only with gender-reversal, but also with mixed dancing, which was generally thought to lead to promiscuity – all the more likely when masks permitted anonymous misbehaviour. The matter was referred to the provincial assembly, which decided that cross-dressers of either sex or women dancing in the street in masks, 'disguised in such a wanton and unchaste form, in company with men', must pay a fine set by the session and make public repentance in the kirk,

18. *BUK* 2:431. Joel Harrington, *Reordering Marriage and Society in Reformation Germany* (Cambridge, 1995), 209–14, does point out that concern with extravagant wedding feasting crossed confessional bounds in Germany and had been legislated against since at least the 1470s; however, the focus of sixteenth-century reformers extended beyond traditional sumptuary regulation to the 'unchristian' nature of the celebration.
19. CH2/448/2, p. 72 (1604); CH2/448/3, p. 262 (1618), both prosecutions of artists for painting crucifixes to be carried in funeral processions, 'fostering . . . idolatry and superstition and introducing a dangerous example' (p. 72). In neither case was the painter punished. James Melville (1604) had a written order for his painting from a laird (who was not prosecuted); Alexander Pantoun (1618) claimed he had been reduced by poverty to painting on used boards with old religious paintings on the obverse.
20. CH2/448/1, p. 87.

second offenders wearing sackcloth. What is remarkable is that not only had this behaviour not been eradicated in the two full generations since the Reformation, but the synod's ruling shows that the authorities fully expected the offence to continue, and for individual offenders to repeat.[21]

In Aberdeen, the seasonal celebrations associated with May and Midsummer proved as difficult to abolish as those attached to the rites of passage and to Yuletide. The session had since the 1570s tried to end traditional 'vaguing [wandering] in the fields' in May and lighting bonfires at Midsummer and St Peter's Eve. They ordered the people in June 1577, for instance, to 'forbear superstitious days such as Midsummer Eve, Peter Eve and other days'. Specially targeted were the lighting of 'bone fires' on the latter two evenings – a customary practice in England as well as Scotland. Fires of animal bones were thought to dispel evil from the air, hence the 'superstitious' associations, but additionally these were scenes of feasting and drinking, into the wee hours.[22] It is worth noting that for bonfires to have their effect in Scotland at Midsummer, they would have to be lit after about 10.30 in the evening, so that the revelry around them would likely go on past midnight – a time inherently suspicious in the eyes of session and magistrates alike, given the misbehaviour that can go on 'under cloud of night'.

But Midsummer bonfire nights had another, eminently respectable aspect. They were also festivals at which social hierarchy and its attendant obligations were reinforced: the better sort lit fires at their gates, providing food and drink for their less prosperous neighbours and dependents. In England, the provider of summer fire and food might receive ritually a garland of greenery from a maiden of the poorer sort at the lighting of the fire as a sign of gratitude and deference.[23] Obviously, whatever implicit superstition and opportunity for illicit revelry they might provide, then, Midsummer bonfires also served important social functions. They reinforced the status of wealthy householders and extended benevolence and charity to the dependent multitude, and at the same time joined the elite with their inferiors in a common celebration of the summer's light and abundance, and the harmony of the civic community.

With such obvious social utility, summer bonfires proved even more

21. CH2/448/2, pp. 151–52. Harrington, *Reordering*, 213–14, finds German reformers' efforts similarly futile.

22. CH2/448/1, p. 116. St Peter's Eve is 28 June. Fires were also lit on the eve of St John the Baptist, 24 June. For England, Hutton, *Rise*, 37–38, 44, 51, and *Stations*, 25, 317.

23. Hutton, *Rise*, 38, 72. F. Marian McNeill, *The Silver Bough*, 2 vols (Glasgow, 1959), 2:89–90, notes an Aberdeen cleric setting a fire and offering a feast at his gate in 1745, but it is unclear whether this was a case of survival or revival.

resilient than Yule in the face of protestant zeal. However stern the 1577 order, we find that in early July 1608, nearly a half century after the Reformation, no fewer than fourteen men were prosecuted for 'setting on a fire . . . within the burgh on Midsummer Eve and Peter Eve, fostering thereby superstition'. They included the leading names of the town: Alexander Rutherford, the town provost, had 'a fire before his yett [gate] on Midsummer Even'; the wealthy Thomas Murray had one 'on the calsey [high street] before his stair', as did Gilbert Keith; John Toucht, a prominent merchant, was similarly charged, along with the burgess bailie, Thomas Menzies. Some of the accused blamed their children or servants for setting the fires and claimed (rather implausibly) never to have seen them. Menzies admitted that there was a fire before his gate, but insisted that it had been 'put on by bairns', and he stuck to his story when he was brought before the Aberdeen presbytery, blaming his son, 'a capped lad that did it'.[24]

Neither session nor presbytery was convinced; their responses, however, were decidedly feeble. The elders referred only two of the 1577 offenders to the presbytery, and the Midsummer bonfire was not the principal charge against either. In Menzies's case, a well-justified suspicion of popery was behind his being pursued to presbytery: he had communicated only once in three years and consorted regularly with excommunicated papists.[25] In the other case, Alexander Mortimer's fire-setting was aggravated by his 'injuring of Mr John MacBirnie, minister, . . . in taking his hat off his head and striking him on the face therewith' (perhaps his response to a rebuke for Midsummer revelry), and by his 'abiding from the sermons'.[26] All of the remaining offenders either confessed and

24. CH2/448/2, pp. 300–02; CH2/1/1, n.f., 24 February and 2 March 1609. 'Yetts' were iron gates often placed just inside the front door for additional security; they survive in towns like St Andrews, and there is a sixteenth-century one in the Museum of Scotland, Edinburgh. Proximity of the 'bonfire before his yett' to the householder's principal entrance would have reinforced the Midsummer message of hospitality. Only Thomas Gordon admitted being aware of the fire before his gate and failing to extinguish it (CH2/448/2, p. 301).

25. CH2/1/1, 24 February 1609. Menzies declined to appear before the presbytery when summoned; he finally came on 2 March and denied any involvement with the bonfire. He continued to trouble session and presbytery for suspect popery until May 1620 (CH2/448/4), when he was relaxed from excommunication for apostasy (to catholicism) and signed the Reformed articles of faith before the session.

26. CH2/448/2, p. 301. Mortimer (kinsman of the marquis of Huntly, Patrick Mortimer) also failed to respond to the session's summons; such contumacy was generally referred to presbytery. Gilbert Keith did report on 22 January to the bishop and session, provost, bailies and council of Aberdeen that he had performed his repentance as ordered on 18 January for a long list of sins *not* including bonfire-setting:

received light censures or were dismissed. The elders required no public repentance, and it is worth noting that they acted after the fact: no kirk officer went out on Midsummer or St Peter's Eve to douse the fires. One has to wonder how earnest the Aberdeen elders were in their desire to quash summer festivities. It is hardly surprising that their June 1647 minutes still record orders that 'there be no fires set on within the parish at Midsummer', and that they had to repeat the mandate in June 1648, when every elder resolved to 'take heed in their own bounds that there should be no Midsummer fires'. In June of the next year, a fire-setter when summoned insisted that he had offended in ignorance; however unlikely his claim, the session repeated the order once again in June 1650.[27]

The repetition of May offences engenders the same query about the session's real stance on festivities. Nearly every May saw a flurry of accusations against people who skipped afternoon sermons in order to wander the countryside, often taking along musicians and dancing along the way. That such 'maying' was a well-established Scottish tradition is evident from William Dunbar's 1490 poem of the 'mirth of May', with its vision of 'ane hundreth ladyes' gathered in green meadows with 'dame Venus, lufis mychti quene' and 'Cupide the king':

> And ewiry one of thir in grene arayit,
> On harp or lute full merily thai playit,
> And sang ballettis with michty notis clere,
> Ladyes to dance full sobirly assayit,
> Endlang the lusty rywir so thai mayit.

What is remarkable for our purposes is the post-Reformation (1568) echo of this work by Alexander Scott:

> And now in May to madynnis fawis
> With tymmer wechtis [tambourines] to trip in ringis
> And to play upcoil with the baqwis.

sermon absence, 'speaking against true religion', deserting his wife, breaking kirk windows, 'menacing' two elders, 'offensive behaviour towards the magistrates in the guild court', and 'misbehaving before the presbytery' (when brought before them on other charges – see CH2/1/1, n.f., 22 September, 6 October, 24 November, 16 and especially 29 December 1608, noting his 'contemptuous and arrogant manner'), CH2/448/2, pp. 341–42.

27. *Records of Old Aberdeen 1498–1903*, ed. Alexander Munro, 2 vols (Aberdeen, 1909), 2:27. 29, 33. The extant manuscript session book, CH2/448/4, skips from 1640 to 1660 at f. 269.

In May gois dammosalis and dammis,
In gardyngis grene to play like lammis.[28]

To the session's chagrin, Scott might easily have been writing about Aberdeen, where the sort of maying described by the poets continued well into the seventeenth century. On 8 May 1603, they finally decided to appoint a bailie and two elders to prowl the town on Sunday and 'search such houses as they think most meet . . . and chiefly that now, during the summer season, they attend . . . at the ferry boat and note the names of such as go across the river and over the countryside to Downie.' The next May they proclaimed a fast; in May 1605 they again posted an elder at the ferry to take down names; but May 1606 again saw numerous citizens 'passing over the water to Downie' during sermon time.[29] Three years later, the cases of Jaspar Mylne and William Stewart illumine the nature of Aberdonian maying: on 14 May 1609, the elders warned Mylne, the town's common piper, that they would deprive him of his civic office and banish him if he continued playing on May sabbaths and causing 'many others, both in this town and in Torrie, [to] profane the sabbath'. They issued the same admonition to Stewart, the fiddler, should he continue to 'observe his wonted superstition in playing and singing' the Sundays of May.[30]

The mayers' frequent destination of Downie was also significant: this was the location of an ancient spring or well on the south side of the Bay of Nigg, named for St Fithack (or Fiacre). The water of St Fithack's well were reputed to provide healing when drunk, if a piece of clothing were left as an offering (whether to the well, to a sprite inhabiting it or to the saint is unclear). Clearly this was the sort of superstition the elders were anxious to repress, yet as late as 1630 they were still dealing with crowds of parishioners venturing to the well on the first Sunday of May 'in a superstitious manner for seeking health to themselves or bairns'.[31] Taking a piper and a fiddler along provided the frosting on their

28. *The Poems of William Dunbar*, ed. Priscilla Bawcutt, 2 vols (Glasgow, 1998), 1:187–88, 'The Golden Targ', ll. 102, 110, 127–31; *The Poems of Alexander Scott*, ed. James Cranstoun (Edinburgh, 1896), 23–25, 'Of May'. The opening lines of the latter poem hint at what the elders may have seen as the most sinister aspect of maying: 'May is the moneth maist amene/ For thame in Venus service bene.'
29. CH2/448/2, pp. 25, 72, 134, 199–201. The last group prosecuted included the skippers of Futtie, their wives and children, three tailors and a bookbinder. Futtie villagers were again missing from the sabbath sermons of May and early June, 1608 (p. 297).
30. CH2/448/2, p. 357.
31. CH2/448/4, p. 166. For more on May pilgrimages to holy wells, see below.

forbidden cake. The maying that gave pre-Reformation England its appellation 'merry' was thus common in the northern part of the isle as well, and there it persisted for at least the first seventy years of Calvinist rule.

Critics may object that Aberdeen is not representative of protestantism's progress (or lack of it) in Scotland. Studies of the town in the first decades of the Reformation have demonstrated that Aberdeen joined the protestant cause only reluctantly and under considerable political pressure. The unevenness of its session register for the 1560s and 1570s may suggest that the session operated only irregularly before 1572, and even after it became firmly established, its members included several known catholics.[32] The mild censures it prescribed to revellers and its relative tolerance of bonfires and carollers may well reflect the persistence of more serious popish beliefs and practices in the town. And if the elders were not as wholly committed to instilling protestant culture as the reformers wished, they were further handicapped by the civil authorities on whom they depended to carry out pecuniary and physical penalties. The bailies had to be admonished in 1574 by the regent himself, before the Privy Council, for not enforcing the laws against 'superstitious keeping of festival days used of before in time of ignorance and papistry, and all plays and feasting at those times', along with images, organs and altars.[33] The latter objects disappeared in due course, but traditional celebration remained the province of the town's officials as well as of the disorderly servants and women, schoolboys, pipers and dancers whom they were supposed to be helping to transform into protestant saints.

By the turn of the century, however, historians have supposed that protestantism had finally made its mark even in this conservative town.[34] The most detailed recent treatment of sixteenth-century Aberdeen finds that protestant domination of council and session by the later 1580s enabled a more vigorous pursuit of the protestant reform programme, and that with the end of the Menzies provostship and the victories of protestantism nationally in the early 1590s, the Aberdonian Reformation was consolidated. Now the seventeenth-century session registers bring that assumption into some doubt, at least on the score of traditional festivity. Despite an active and regular session from 1572, the 'superstitious' culture of pre-Reformation Aberdeen was still very visible. Whatever the pro-

32. White, 'Religion', ch. 4 (141–86), and 'Impact', 87, 94–96, noting that, of four members of the Menzies family on the session in the 1570s, three were periodically accused of catholicism. Michael Graham, *The Uses of Reform* (Leiden, 1996), 115, identifies five catholics among thirteen elders in 1573.

33. CH2/448/1, pp. 58–59.

34. White, 'Religion', 178, 305, 317, 345. Graham, *Uses of Reform*, 125, dates Aberdeen's Reformation between 1578 and 1602.

nouncements of king and national assemblies, at the parochial level Scotland seems after all to have been slow to reform its pastimes.

★ ★ ★

What if we shift our focus to a different sort of town – one to all appearances vigorously protestant from the start? Perth provides a prime example. Having had its own protestant martyrs as early as 1543, the town proved ripe for the preaching of John Knox in 1559. Historians point to the remarkable iconoclastic rampage with which the townspeople responded to his sermon on 11 May of that year as evidence that Perth 'made the transition at once' to protestantism.[35] The town appointed the vigorous protestant John Row minister in 1560 and immediately set up sermons twice on Sunday and once on Thursday, along with a remarkable kirk session that was meeting thrice weekly by 1598 and four times a week by 1621.[36] We are told that Perth and its near neighbour Dundee, alone of Scottish towns, implemented the Reformation without any pressure from outside forces, and with every indication of enthusiastic popular support. The large numbers of communion tokens handed out by the elders lends credence to this judgment, given the doctrinal requirements for receiving a token.[37]

The minutes of Perth's kirk session, however, carry a message remarkably similar to that conveyed by Aberdeen's records about the persistence of popular festivities in the face of protestant disapproval. The citizens may have destroyed images and altars with alacrity in 1559, and quickly learned their Calvinist doctrine, but they retained Midsummer and Yule, bridal dancing and feasting at wakes, maying and Sunday piping as defiantly in Perth as in Aberdeen. And a close look at precisely how the session dealt with these offences helps to explain why this was possible in an otherwise thoroughly Reformed town.

Persistent winter festivities at Perth include the St Obert's Eve (10 December) play, which continued despite regular prosecution until 1587, and guising and cross-dressing at Yule and St Ives lasting well into the

35. Mary Verschuur, 'Merchants and Craftsmen in Sixteenth-Century Perth' in *The Early Modern Town*, ed. Lynch, 36–54, and her 'Perth and the Reformation: Society and Reform 1540–1560' (Unpublished PhD thesis, Glasgow, 1985); *Book of Perth*, ix, xi, 82. Perth's myriad monasteries and friaries, including Blackfriars, Whitefriars, Charterhouse and Greyfriars, along with nearby Scone Abbey and the forty-one altars and chapels of the town kirk of St John the Baptist, were all destroyed by the protestant mob.
36. See Introduction, n. 26, above, for frequency of Perth session meetings.
37. Michael Lynch, 'Scottish Towns 1500–1700' in *The Early Modern Town*, 19; CH2/521/7, p. 237, and chapter 1, above.

seventeenth century. St Obert was taken in Scotland as patron of the baxters (bakers), who had long maintained his altar in the town church before the Reformation. With the loss of that function, the baxters seem to have clung all the more fiercely to the celebration of their saint's day, beginning with the performance of a traditional play on the eve. We know little about the drama except that one of its actors was dressed in a 'devil's coat' and rode a horse in some sort of costume, and that it was accompanied with a torchlit perambulation of the town by guisers, dancers, pipers and drummers. The elders were scarcely fans of mummers in diabolic costume and were, like most town authorities of this era, leery of nighttime revels by masked men. They accordingly legislated against the play in November of 1574, but the first surviving volume of the Perth session minutes, for 1577, indicates that the act had at that point had little effect: on 16 December 1577 the session ordered the 'act made against superstition AD 1574 November 27th to be published on Sunday next, likewise all those persons that were playing Saint Obert's play the tenth instant to be warned to the assembly.' When they appeared, however, the elders merely scolded them and sent them home. Small wonder that, when December came around again, five more men summoned to the session confessed that 'superstitiously they [had] passed about the town on Saint Obert's Even disguised, in piping and dancing and torches bearing.' Again the elders simply admonished them and made them promise not to offend in future.[38] Three years passed before they again summoned 'sundry insolent young men' for 'playing of Saint Obert's play to the great grief of the conscience of the faithful and infamous slander of the whole congregation'; whether the players had desisted or simply gone underground in the meantime is unclear. But the 1581 session acted much more decisively than its predecessors. Meeting on Christmas Day, they ordered nine named men 'with all the rest' to be gaoled until they had each paid 20s to the poor; they were then to appear on the seat of repentance in the kirk during the next Sunday sermon. To insure against another repetition of the play, they specified double the punishment for a second offence, and then broadened the act to include 'all such idolatrous players and observers of suchlike superstitious days in times to come without exception.'[39]

In spite of this apparently stern order, December 1587 saw the baxters again performing the play. They were duly warded until they paid their fines and repented before the congregation, and the play never again

38. Banks, 3:194–95 (Obert is the French St Aubert, whose day is actually 13 December); CH2/521/1, ff. 5, 15v.

39. CH2/521/1, ff. 68v–69. Offenders who could not afford the 20s were to stand in irons on the Cross Head (the market cross) for two hours on market day.

appears in the registers.[40] But why was a fourteen-year campaign required to abolish it? Obviously the mild censures meted out in the 1570s delayed compliance, but even the 1580s acts lacked the severity that would have ensured proper behaviour: 20s Scots was not an outrageous fine for a member of the bakers' guild, and since one of their traditional corporate duties was charity towards the poor, who were after all the recipients of the money, they may well have seen the payment simply as performance of a worthy obligation. It is also not at all clear that having to repent publicly for upholding a popular tradition was perceived as a punishment rather than an opportunity for boasting. Finally, the session must have known that, while the baxters might have ceased their noisy processions in order to avoid future fines, they could easily have continued to perform the play in private. Yet there is no indication in the registers that they arranged to investigate this possibility, as we shall find them doing with other festivities, sending spies to note the names of the participants. Never had they disrupted the play itself; their actions were always taken after the fact (as the Aberdeen session had responded to bonfires). How intent were they, then, on ending this winter festival?

The same question must be asked about their prosecution of Yuletide celebration, which in Perth as in other Scottish towns extended well into January, even beyond the twelve days, and was by all accounts extravagant, disorderly and 'promiscuous' (involving women as well as men). Despite the early formal abolition of Christmas by General Assembly and parliament, the Perth session found it necessary to repeat again and again the order 'for suppressing Yule'. In 1592 the repetition itself was formalised when the session, recognising the 'abuses that fall out in the time of Yule . . . besides the evil example that it furnishes to landward parishes', ordered proclamation one month before each Yule of the order against it, 'in public, so none can claim ignorance'. That at this late date anyone could claim ignorance of the law against Christmas ought to be in itself enough to make us wonder whether the reformers' cultural revolution was not as mythical as Father Christmas himself. Nor did the citizens heed the repeated warning. In January of 1597, the baxters were in trouble again: this time William Williamson appeared before the session for selling the traditional celebratory 'great loaves at Yule, which was slanderous, and cherishing a superstition in the hearts of the ignorant', presumably both by setting apart the day as the papists had done, and by providing material for a Christmas feast.[41]

40. CH2/521/2, f. 14.

41. CH2/521/2, ff. 59, 114v. The Glasgow elders on 26 December 1583 required the town's baxters to give up the names of all those for whom they had baked Yule bread: Banks, 3:329.

As in Aberdeen, the turn of the century saw no change. When the Perth articles of 1618 reinstated Christmas and Easter sermons, the only objection came from the ministers and the presbytery; the return to Christmas religious observance by the laity was made apparently without a hitch.[42] As for broader Yuletide revelry in the new century, the Christmas and New Year season of 1620–21 saw the fleshers and skinners before the session nearly every week for neglecting sermons in order to engage in sports, dice and drink. Despite repeated warnings and admonitions, not until the season ended did they cease to appear regularly in the session minutes. Sometimes they even got their apprentices into trouble in the interests of holiday sport. On 8 January the apprentice skinner Robert Young tried to defend himself against a charge of profaning the sabbath by playing at the leads (pennystone) with his friends by complaining that 'John Lamb, skinner, his master, caused him bear his leadstones and play with him' and then to accompany him on a spree of drinking and dicing until three o'clock in the morning. The two finally got into a fight in which Robert was 'most shamefully abused . . . struck and dung down, and left for dead', perhaps for reprimanding his master. Yet when John Lamb appeared the next day, the elders merely admonished him 'to take heed to his ways in time coming' – little enough for his revelry having led, as the kirk authorities knew it would, to disorder and violence.[43] The same Yuletide season saw an instance of what may have been a resurgence of youthful misrule, when on New Year's Day a merchant appeared before the session complaining that several 'young professed knaves' had offended him by 'casting of their bonnets at him in the kirk this instant day'; these schoolboys were for their insolence 'taken to the grammar school and there scourged with Saint Bartholomew's taws', their youth and presumption ensuring that they would undergo severe punishment for just the sort of revelry that a few decades earlier was ritualised and condoned at Yuletide.[44]

Festive cross-dressing in the winter season seems to have been particularly difficult for the Perth session to abolish. Three couples appeared before the session in February 1609 charged with going 'through the town disguised with swords and staves' between 10 and 11 o'clock on the eve of St Ives, 'troubling and molesting their neighbours on the streets'; their

42. CH2/299/1, p. 81; CH2/521/6, f. 6 – John Malcolm, minister of Perth, dissenting from Easter sermons, although in the end he complied.

43. CH2/521/7, pp. 209–10; cf. pp. 200 (5 December), 205 (25 December, the session dutifully ignoring Christmas and going about their duties). Among repeat offenders was William Murray (p. 214).

44. CH2/521/7, pp. 207–08. Bartholomew's taws were a many-thonged whip named for the saint who had been martyred by flaying. One is displayed in the Perth museum.

defence was that they had 'no evil purpose or intention, but of merriness'. But their offence was the greater because one of the married women, having 'her hair hanging down and a black hat upon her head', departed from the usual habit of wives wearing their hair up and white-capped; and one of the married men wore 'a mutch [a woman's cap] upon his head and a woman's gown'. Their offence occurred, moreover, in time of pestilence, when penitential fasting would have been the appropriate activity. Unfortunately for the revellers, the town bailie (aptly named Constantine Malice) was one of the witnesses, and they were duly ordered to be warded all Sunday and then to repent the following Sunday in the kirk wearing the linen clothes of penitents and 'to be rebuked as dissolute and licentious persons in the presence of the whole congregation'. This is the most serious penalty we have yet seen actually carried out against revellers (particularly given the wretched condition of the gaol), but it may well be explained by the plague setting and by the potential for real violence presented by their possession of swords.[45] Other instances of festive disguise and transvestism, while roundly condemned, continued to be less vigorously punished. A man disguised in women's clothes went through the town 'in great profanity' on a December sabbath night in 1632, but was only admonished and made to repent privately before the session. A few weeks later, when 'a poor simple young fellow' profaned the sabbath by 'passing through the town with a woman's coat upon him', he responded that 'a neighbour's woman and he going for ale, the tail of her coat having fallen down from her, he took it up and put it over his head.' The session ordered him warded, but only for a few hours, and only because they doubted whether he would otherwise understand the gravity of his offence. Finally, in January 1634, the elders ordered a group of guisers to the stool of repentance on the following sabbath for exacerbating their offence with 'unreverent speech' and 'contempt in going after they were prohibited to do so'; however, it is clear that by this point they were seriously frustrated by their obvious lack of headway against Yuletide guising. There is a hint of desperation in their appeal for the presbytery to produce an act against 'such who disguise themselves in women's apparel and Yule and New Year's Mass as also being inhibited divers times would not desist.' The presbytery took them seriously and, 'in respect of the superstitious time, in respect of the habit against God's express word [in Deuteronomy] and Christian decency, which also may be the occasion of further wickedness and villainy, ordain[ed that] they make their public repentance in

45. CH2/521/4, pp. 182–84. On the condition of the gaol (the town tollbooth), PL ms B59/16/1, f. 90, and CH2/521/8/1, f. 99v.

sackcloth and be punished in their body and goods.'[46] The problem does appear to have abated somewhat after this ruling, although the rather abstemious note-taking of the new clerk of session after 1637 makes a firm conclusion impossible.

* * *

The problem of persistent spring and summer festivities in Perth was if anything more severe than in Aberdeen. Perth shared the struggle, common to most Scottish towns, to eliminate the Corpus Christi play in June, but this does seem to have disappeared finally after 1577.[47] Much more stubborn was the tradition of 'vaguing' and dancing in the countryside on spring and summer sabbaths, especially in May. Perth's persistent maying was complicated by the presence near the town of two 'holy wells' or springs that had traditionally been visited on the Sundays of May for the healing of 'back-gang bairns' (sick children), by a cave known as the Dragon's Hole in nearby Kinoull Hill that had likewise attracted May revellers by ancient custom (and still does), and by the proximity of Scone, which apparently hosted a series of spring and summer fairs known for their music and jollity. For all their professed Calvinism, the citizens of Perth dug in their heels when required to give up a form of maying that not only got them out into the countryside during the long-awaited season of extended daylight and relatively good weather, but also promised piping, dancing and good health for their children.

May visits to the Dragon's Hole clearly aroused the session's concern about promiscuity. It attracted young men and women, and pipers – always an unruly type, and in Perth individuals chronically in trouble for sexual dalliance.[48] Perhaps for this reason, once the session targeted Dragon's Hole festivities in 1580, they were soon brought under control. At least they disappear soon from the session minutes. In May 1580 the elders and minister ordered public announcement at the Thursday sermon by the minister and at the market cross by the bailies concerning 'passing to the Dragon Hole superstitiously', but whatever superstition they referred to seems not to have been uppermost in their minds. Rather they were worried 'that the resorting to the Dragon Hole as well by young men and women, with their piping and drums striking before them through the town, has raised

46. CH2/521/8/1, ff. 80, 83v, 124. The 1634 guisers appeared as ordered on the stool of repentance on 17 January. The Perth presbytery's response is CH2/299/1, p. 321.
47. CH2/521/1, f. 1v (1 July 1577) is the last recorded prosecution of citizens playing 'Corpus Christi's Play upon the sixth day of June last', the play being regarded as 'idolatrous, superstitious, and also slanderous'.
48. E.g., CH2/521/4, pp. 2, 44–45; CH2/521/7, pp. 330, 441. On the Dragon Hole, *Book of Perth*, 95, recounting May Day costumed processions gathering garlands of flowers and celebrating a legendary dragon slaughter on Kinoull Hill.

no small slander to this congregation, not without suspicion of filthiness after to follow thereupon.' The young people were to cease doing 'as they have done in times bygone, namely in the month of May', or pay a fine of 20s to the poor box and perform public repentance on the next sabbath. That fine, no great burden for an adult craftsman, was not so light for a young apprentice or servant, and it seems to have done the job. The next year the session got by with a repetition of the 'former act concerning the Dragon Hole' in April, along with a new order for 'no pastimes to be used through the town upon the sabbath, in special in the time of May'.[49]

That second order was clearly necessitated by the plethora of other festive and 'superstitious' May to Midsummer pastimes, which proved much more obdurate in the face of kirk opposition. The particular focus of the May 1590s sessions was upon sanctifying the entire sabbath, even the evening after the second sermon. On 3 May 1591 the session ordered 'all ungodly pastime to be discharged [avoided] that is used on Sunday at even after preaching . . . especially filthy and ungodly singing about the Mays', with a severe sentence – to sit first upon the cuckstool and then upon the stool of repentance, 'there to declare their offence and show their repentance for the same'. No such sentence appears to have been carried out, however, in that year or indeed in that decade. It may well have been that the bailies, who would have to enforce the cuckstool bit of the sentence, simply declined. The Perth session was not alone among Scottish towns whose civil officers neglected to implement orders they found unpalatable.[50] Perhaps in expectation of future leniency, then, customary maying continued. The next year the session determined to keep the town gates locked on Sundays to prevent people from 'passing to the pastime of Scone' during the afternoon sermon. Popular response was not compliant: a terrified town porter (gatekeeper) reported that a mob of angry citizens violently forced him to open the gate. The session instructed him thenceforth that 'if any go violently' he must report them to the elders whatever the danger to himself. Porters being more pliant than elders, however, the gates stayed open against orders in future, and prosecutions for maying continued. On 12 May 1600, five men confessed to having profaned the sabbath by 'travelling in the fields in time of preaching'; the elders rebuked them, but again without perceptible effect, since their offence continued.[51] Aggravating the problem was the fact that Scone's was not the only fair that lured would-be revellers from Perth.

49. CH2/521/1, ff. 37v–38, 56, 57v.
50. Among many examples of bailie reluctance to enforce the session's will, CH2/521/1, f. 114v.
51. CH2/521/2, ff. 49, 86–86v; CH2/521/3, p. 143. For repeat offences see, e.g., pp. 150–51, 226–27, 233, 274.

On 7 May 1604 the elders convicted David Chapman of profaning the sabbath by 'going to Ruthven to see profane and lascivious dancing'. Despite the rebuke, he apparently spread the word that the Ruthven fair was worth both the trip and the session's ire: the following week six more men and two women underwent the same censure, and the week after saw two more men admonished for the same offence.[52]

Even the young people who stayed in town on May sabbaths could not resist some celebration of the season: the 1604 session found the day profaned at 'even by lasses and young women singing, knocking [drumming upon the doors] and dancing lasciviously under stairs, to the great dishonour of God and slander of this congregation'. They admonished the dancers and ordered regular sabbath-evening visitation of suspect households by select elders 'for repressing of this profaneness', but the dancing seems to have continued all May, and throughout the summer. Finally, in September, the magistrates intervened and added a short gaol sentence to the session's 'sharp rebuke', and the session ordered masters of families to 'take heed to their children and servants' on Sunday evenings. Both this order and the place of their dancing suggests that the offenders were servants, and the magistrates doubtless took their action in the conviction that lascivious behaviour by servants would likely lead to financial burdens for the town in maintenance of bastard bairns.[53]

The celebrants of spring were not to be bowed. We find Perth's minister admonishing the congregation in 1617 'that none pass to Scone, nor vague in time of the sermons on the sabbath days', following the prosecution of seven men for 'vaguing to Scone'. One claimed that he went to visit his mother, 'that being known', but each nonetheless had to kneel before the session and declare his repentance, and to pay a fine of 20s to the poor. Yet just a few weeks later the session ordered 'admonition to be made the next sabbath that none of this congregation pass to the well of Huntingtower on the sabbath days, and likewise that no dancing be under stairs on the sabbath nights.'[54] The kirk was fighting a losing battle. In May 1618 no fewer than fourteen women visited the well at Huntingtower, and the following May three more women were found there and 'a great number of persons of this congregation were in Scone yesterday the time

52. CH2/521/3, pp. 318–21.

53. CH2/521/3, pp. 142–43, 318, 320, 321, 323 (4 June 1604, when the dancers were first prosecuted), 335–36 (3 September 1604, seven women confessing to 'under stairs dancing, singing and knocking upon doors, . . . [and] lascivious singing . . . for the which they were sorry'). The session ordered public announcement from the pulpit prohibiting dancing on sabbath eves.

54. CH2/521/6, ff. 83–83v, 91. Huntingtower is on the river Almond, about 3 km from Perth – a pleasant spring afternoon walk.

of the afternoon sermon'. The three women at Huntingtower in 1619, being servants, paid a reduced fine of 40d. The revellers in Scone, however, included citizens 'that are of good account', and since the number was apparently too large to make universal prosecution practical, some of these were summoned as an example and made to pay the penalties assigned by the parliamentary statute against sabbath-violation. But the session may have repented its own leniency in letting the others off, for a few weeks later they once again sent the bailies to summon a group of people who had 'passed to Scone the time of the afternoon's sermon'.[55]

Venturing into the countryside on May sabbaths was a pastime apparently ubiquitous in Britain, but visiting wells and springs, rarely mentioned in English court records, shows up very frequently in Scots session minutes.[56] It was a practice probably rooted in pre-Christian veneration of water, which early Christian missionaries incorporated into the Roman version of the faith by blessing the wells and associating them with Christ or the saints. The magical healing customarily associated with particular wells was simply transferred to their saints, one 'wishing well' (St Cyril's, near Loch Creran in Argyll) even producing enough income from the coins of petitioners to maintain a nearby chapel, where a priest prayed for the pilgrims' wishes to be granted.[57] By one estimate there were more than six hundred such wells in late medieval Scotland. The dates when wells were most frequently visited correspond to the beginnings of each 'raith' or quarter of the ancient Scottish year (May, August, November and February), but the waters were apparently thought to have their fullest power at Beltane, or May Day, and throughout the month of May.

55. CH2/521/6, ff. 137v, 138v; CH2/521/7, pp. 40, 50. On visitation of wells, see below.
56. Hutton, *Rise and Fall*, notes no such phenomenon in his exhaustive study of English pastimes, though Alexandra Walsham provides evidence of the practice in England: 'Reforming the Waters: Holy Wells and Healing Springs in Protestant England' in *Life and Thought in the Northern Church c. 1100–c. 1700*, ed. Diana Wood (Woodbridge, 1999), 227–56. In Scotland, well cults are rarer in Anglian Lothian parishes than in the Highlands, and the Uplands north of the Forth more recently (though by the later sixteenth century no longer) Celtic. The Celtic factor may explain frequent well pilgrimages in Wales, too: Francis Jones, *The Holy Wells of Wales* (Cardiff, 1992).
57. Glasgow cathedral was built over St Mungo's well; the kirk of Kilallan at the well where St Fillian baptised converts: E. Murray, *The Church of Cardross and its Ministers* (Glasgow, 1935), 2. J.C. Irons, *Leith and its Antiquities* (Edinburgh, 1897), 2:446 describes St Triduana's well, Restalrig; Banks, 1:161, gives examples of Christian wishing wells whose antiquity is suggested by discovery in the 1880s by a workman digging a drain at the back of a well near Culsalmond of a gold piece from James I's reign. See also Walsham, 228; V. Flint, *The Rise of Magic in Early Medieval Europe* (Oxford, 1991), chs 8–9; Janet and Colin Bord, *Sacred Waters: Holy Wells and Water Lore in Britain and Ireland* (London, 1985), ch. 2.

Certainly, May was the most convenient and pleasant time to go 'vaguing' in the fields to the wells, with both the weather and the daylight finally emerged from winter gloom and the pressures of the harvest season not yet come. Medieval pilgrimages to wells were joined eventually by fairs and markets, making the events even more festive.[58] After the Reformation, when Sundays became the only days free from work, the sabbaths of May, and especially the first one, nearest Beltane, presented the greatest challenge of the year to sessions intent on enforcing sermon attendance and eliminating ancient superstition. In Perth, it remained a challenge long after the town had supposedly been transformed into a Calvinist enclave.

The session minutes give us tantalising hints of what actually went on at visits to wells. First of all, the pilgrimages were made by groups rather than individuals, and particularly by groups of women. They were social events, generally accompanied by music and dancing, communal meals or picnics, and doubtless (in the session's collective mind) lewd and lascivious behaviour. Second, behaviour at the well was ritualised, making use of physical objects in a highly formalised way, to achieve a magical or miraculous end. And the traditional forms and representations were easily interpreted by the session as idolatrous.

The prosecution of several women in May 1618 for going to the well at Huntingtower illumines the nature of the 'idolatry'. The elders charged fourteen women and asked specifically if they had drunk of the well and whether they had left anything there when they left. They answered that they had drunk and had left 'some of them pins or pieces of their head-laces thereat', which the session found 'a point of idolatry in putting the well in God's room'. The elders opined that the women had 'ascribe[d] that to the foresaid well due to God only, as to think to get any help of it and give offerings thereto', and required the women to be 'humbled on their knees, declare their repentance therefore and promise never to do the like hereafter' and to pay a 6s fine. Clearly the session was anxious to dispel the popular belief that the well had magical power. A few years later, that popular belief led to a charge of witchcraft. Isabell Haldane confessed in 1623 that she had gone to the well of Ruthven and 'returned silent with water to wash' a sick bairn, having 'left part of the bairn's shirt' at the well. The child died after drinking some of Isabell's 'leaf brew', and since the woman was already in considerable trouble for admitting to con-

58. *Records of the Meeting of the Exercise of Alford* (Edinburgh, 1847), 415; Banks, 1:125–43; Jones, pp. 88–92 (Beltane in Wales). Hutton, *Stations*, 225 notes also that in pastoral areas, cattle were let out of their folds to pasture at the beginning of May, so that rituals to protect them against evil would have been especially appropriate at Beltane. While the registers contain no specific reference to well water being used for cattle, the connection might well have been made.

sorting with fairies and having second sight, her case was put to inquest.[59] Isabell was convicted and executed, and one would think that inclusion of the well in the list of her offences would have made the session take sterner measures against future May visitors. It did not, perhaps because the elders recognised that May pilgrimages to the well had social functions that rendered traditional association with magic generally innocuous. In the absence of set holy days when people could rest from their labour, get together with friends, walk the fields and share food, Sunday maying was bound to continue.

On the first May sabbath of 1624, another large and more diverse group of people ventured 'superstitiously to the Bank of Ruthven and Well thereof', this time more evidently for social as well as magical ends. Their trek was clearly a convivial affair. John Skinner (already known by the session as a 'nightwalker' for his noisy revelry after dark with the piper James Wilson the previous autumn) claimed that he had gone to the well with his wife only 'for recreation'. Henry, John and Gilbert Henderson and Gilbert's wife made the same claim, but the session was not mollified, perhaps because of John's 'excess in drinking with his complices' along the way, which suggests what sort of recreation was going on. John Patrick and Thomas Dulby likewise overindulged in drink. John Wylie and his servant were convicted with the rest despite their claim that they had 'passed not to the well, but went out in the morning for their pastime to Ruthven' and returned in time for both Sunday sermons. Either the session did not believe them, or it regarded sabbath 'pastime' as the real offence of all the maygoers. They also rejected Harry Crichton's excuse that he had gone to the well on the way to visit a friend who had been hurt, 'the contrary being tried'. The session was clearly convinced that these people were out to have a good time in May, but on the wrong day of the week and with too much alcohol to fuel the festivity. And the youth of some of their unmarried female companions doubtless aroused other anxieties in the elders: among those summoned to appear were five 'young lasses' who clearly had no business rambling the fields with the likes of John Skinner and John Henderson.[60]

59. Perth Museum ms 315; CH2/521/7, pp. 421, 430, and depositions against three witches, inserted into the back of the volume (16 May 1623); CH2/299/1, pp. 87–88; *Book of Perth*, 303–05. The three were put to an assize and burnt 18 July 1623. Belief in bringing spring water back to an ailing bairn in silence for more effectual healing was common: Banks, 1:125, and, in England, J.F. Champ, 'Bishop Milner, Holywell, and the Cure Tradition' in *The Church and Healing*, ed. W.J. Sheils (Cambridge, 1982), 153–64. On leaving pins or bits of fabric at the well, Walsham, 239–40.

60. CH2/521/7, pp. 489–93 (3, 4, 6, 10 and 13 May 1624), 432–39 for Skinner's background. The youth of four of the girls is suggested by the fact that they were

The cases of two of the other offenders suggest other problems with the trip to the well. David Chalmer admitted to being at the bank all Saturday night, suggesting that he held the traditional belief that, for a well's waters to have healing power, they must be drunk or bathed in before sunrise on Beltane. On the other hand, he may have had more nefarious purposes. When the maltman James Tyrie admitted that his daughter had been at the bank, he added that 'her plaid being wrest from her' while she was there, he had himself gone there on Sunday morning to retrieve it. Tyne's daughter must have made her journey, as Chalmer had, the night before, and if someone had really taken her plaid by force, the session (and her father) surely wondered about the circumstances. Being mentioned in the minutes not by name, but by relationship to her father, she was probably young and in any case an inappropriate night-time companion for Chalmer. But the alternative interpretation, that she had left her plaid as an offering to the well, would likewise have alarmed the minister and elders.[61]

The punishments meted out to this group of twenty-one people were varied. Most were simply admonished. The others, including Chalmer and the drinkers, paid fines ranging from 6s to 10 merks and repented on their knees before the session. As in earlier cases, none was required to make public repentance in the kirk as the General Assembly required; and never did the elders contemplate the statutory punishment – a ruinous £40–£100 for the first offence, death as an idolator for the second. They imposed significant financial penalties only on Skinner as a repeat offender on revelry charges and on Gilbert Henderson and his wife, who had snubbed them by failing to appear the first time they were summoned. Again, the session of this very protestant town treated profane pastimes rather lightly.[62]

The offence naturally continued. The volumes of session minutes covering 1624–31 are missing, but cases in 1632, 1633, 1634 and 1636 demonstrate continuity in the pastime. For a time, the elders' relative lenience

identified not by their own names, but as 'William Stone's two daughters, John Clayster's daughter . . . and John Lamb's youngest sister'. Pre-Reformation authorities also worried about sexual dalliance at wells: Lyndsay denounced those who visited wells 'under the forme of feynit sanctytude', but really to commit 'fowll fornication': 'Ane Dialog betuix Experience and ane Courteour' in *The Poetical Works of Sir David Lyndsay of the Mount* (Edinburgh, 1871), 324; cf. Alexander Scott on trysting in 'Of May', ll. 56–60. The Perth elders of May 1633 were unsurprised to learn of Jonet Reidheuch 'vaguing night and day through the fields with John Roth' in Beltane and 'abusing her body with him': CH2/521/8/1, f. 98.

61. Plaids were expensive: a Perth man purchased one for £5 in 1617: CH2/521/6, f. 78.
62. *APS* 3:212; CH2/521/7, pp. 489–93.

also continued. They dismissed John Garrock and his wife in May 1632 on their claim that they had passed by the 'profane well in the Bank of Ruthven' on Saturday on the way to visit his sick mother, and that they had returned in time for the Sunday sermons.[63] In 1633 they heard that 'great numbers of this congregation repair to Scone and the Bank of Ruthven', but they only repeated the earlier order against maying from the pulpit, taking no action against the contraveners. Only in 1634 did they finally begin to take a harder line. They started by sending out a spy, taking 2s from the kirk box on 20 May to pay 'the boy who passed to the Bank of Ruthven to note up the names of the persons that were at the said bank and well the last sabbath.' He reported that Katherine Anderson drank, filled a pint stoup (pitcher) with water to carry home to a sick bairn, and cut a piece of her head lace 'which she laid as an offering to the well'. In a sharp departure from previous sentencing practice, the elders ordered Anderson 'rebuked before the congregation for her superstitious, idolatrous form of doing at the well . . . in example of others not to do the like hereafter.' Isobell Quhyte used the same 'superstitious form' but had only to kneel privately before the session and declare her repentance. She may have appeared more 'humbled' than her companion. Others who 'neither drank thereof nor made any offering thereto' and 'hastened home to God's service' in time for morning prayers as well as the two Sunday sermons got off with simple admonition or repentance in the session house. None paid fines, and May revelry naturally continued. Two years later Janet Miller went maying on the sabbath, 'riding profanely on a horse, . . . making a great tumult in the town' and dancing with a group of women; she and the other women were 'humbled on their knees' to repent before the elders, but none received further punishment.[64] Small wonder that the profane pastimes of May persisted nearly eighty years after the Reformation.

Summer festivities were equally problematic. When Midsummer Day, a traditional fair day in the town of Perth, fell on a Sunday in 1593, the elders found it necessary to send 'John Jack, bellman, to pass through the town on Wednesday next and publicly intimate and proclaim that no market be made on the sabbath following, which is Midsummer Day.' Still, the searchers found the baxters on that Sunday during sermon time busily baking bread for sale at the fair.[65] In 1616 the session recognised that the

63. CH2/521/8/1, f. 55v. The couple probably would not have been summoned at all if they had actually made it to church on Sunday. It was absentees who were investigated.

64. CH2/521/8/1, ff. 96v, 137v–38. CH2/521/8/2, ff. 206–06v.

65. CH2/521/2, f. 78; they were only admonished, as were others for fishing and other country pastimes when the 1599 Midsummer Day fell on the sabbath (f. 80).

festive Midsummer Day fair of Perth attracted so many visitors to the town that the kirk might as well take financial advantage of the revellers: they ordered a special collection for church repairs on the Sunday immediately preceding Midsummer Day.[66] July saw another of the famous Scone fairs, always troublesome to the Perth session. In July 1605 they convicted the piper George Clerk of 'profaning the sabbath by playing into Scone' and 'sharply rebuked' but did not fine him.

By 1622 the problem seems to have grown, with numerous offenders occupying seven of the session's July meetings. Again, the elders acted with remarkable restraint, but details of the record explain why. The 1622 elders – practical businessmen that they were – finally decided to turn May and summer festivities to the kirk's pecuniary advantage. Among the revellers that year were citizens of considerable social standing, including one of the elders, the town bailie Andrew Conqueror, and his wife. Also among them was a group of savvy and well-off young women who devised a clever scheme to spare themselves the humiliation of appearing before the elders at all, by voluntarily offering a financial boost to the kirk's poor relief coffers in exchange for lenience. They sent a message to the session that they were 'ashamed to compear but are content to pay 12s each person and promise not to do the like hereafter'. The elders knew a good deal when they saw it. Delighted with the resultant windfall (not to mention the time saved), they decided that the benefits of this mechanism so outweighed the cost to sabbath observance that they would offer it as a regular option in future. On 22 July they ordered that 'those persons who are cited for passing to Scone on the Sabbath day and who are ashamed to compear before the session, if they will pay a penalty according to their estates and abilities, the session will accept thereof for their bypast fault.' They thus provided an easy way out for the wealthier revellers. Summer sabbath festivity effectively became a taxable entertainment. As for less well-heeled merrymakers, when George Ogilvy credibly explained that he had gone to Scone to seek 'some saddler work', and John Sym that he had gone 'to visit his sick bairn being in Scone in fostering', the elders just admonished them. They fined two other men who 'feigned excuse' (each 6s) and two women who travelled to Scone together (12s and 4s to allow for the difference in their ability to pay), and dismissed a man who claimed innocence and offered to pay 10 marks to the poor if anyone proved the contrary. All, except Sym, had to kneel and ask the session's forgiveness unless they had paid for exemption, and all fines were immediately distributed to the poor, whose names are listed.[67] In the

66. CH2/521/6, f. 40v.

67. CH2/521/4, p. 44 (July 1605); CH2/521/7, pp. 330–36 (July 1622).

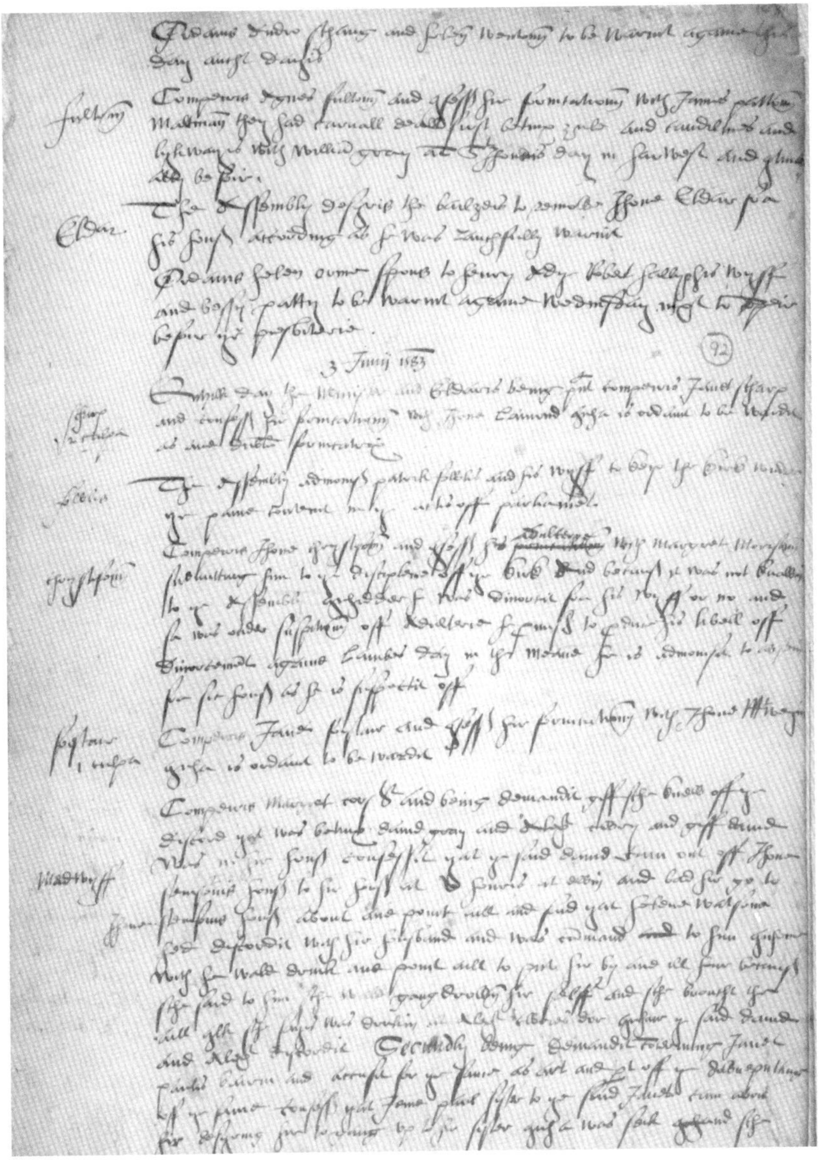

1. Page from the minute book of the Perth kirk session, June 1583, recording cases of fornication and adultery, discord and suspicious death of a child.

2. Pulpit of Parton kirk, Kirkcudbright, 1598.

3. Detail of the Parton pulpit's sounding-board canopy, with the text, 'Feir the Lord and honour his hous'.

4. (*left*) Sixteenth-century pulpit and reader's desk from Holy Trinity church, St Andrews, now in St Salvator's chapel. Note the sandglass attached to the reader's desk.

5. Pencaitland, East Lothian, pulpit with wrought-iron bracket for the baptismal basin, *c*. 1600.

6. Prestonpans parish church of John Davidson (1595–1604), with the Hamilton aisle projecting from the south front.

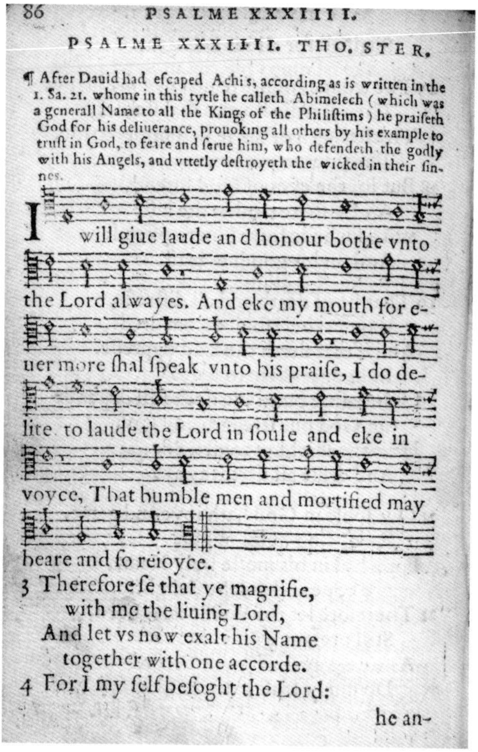

86 PSALME XXXIIII.

PSALME XXXIIII. THO. STER.

¶ After Dauid had eſcaped Achis, according as is written in the 1. Sa. 21. whome in this tytle he calleth Abimelech (which was a generall Name to all the Kings of the Philiſtims) he praiſeth God for his deliuerance, prouoking all others by his example to truſt in God, to feare and ſerue him, who defendeth the godly with his Angels, and vtterly deſtroyeth the wicked in their ſinnes.

I will giue laude and honour bothe vnto the Lord alwayes. And eke my mouth for euer more ſhal ſpeak vnto his praiſe, I do delite to laude the Lord in ſoule and eke in voyce, That humble men and mortified may heare and ſo reioyce.

3 Therefore ſe that ye magnifie,
with me the liuing Lord,
And let vs now exalt his Name
together with one accorde.
4 For I my ſelf beſoght the Lord:
he an-

7. Psalm 34 in the 1565 *Forme of Prayers*, Thomas Sternholde's metrical version. Note the explication of context before the psalm, its simple tune and common metre.

8. (*below left*) Communion cup, Rosneath parish kirk, Argyll, by John Mossman, 1586–96. This is the oldest known cup used by the Reformed kirk.

9. (*below right*) Communion cup by Thomas Cleghorn for Greyfriars kirk, Edinburgh, 1633, inscribed 'for the church of the southwest parish of Edinburgh', a mazer in design.

10. Communion bread plate, central medallion, by Thomas Kirkwood for Trinity College kirk, Edinburgh, 1633–35.

11. Penitents' seat, Holy Trinity Church, South Street, St Andrews, seventeenth century.

12. Penitents' stools, Holy Trinity Church, St Andrews, the 'cutty stool' variety, probably stood upon.

13. High penitents' stool, or 'pillar', from Old Greyfriars, Edinburgh.

14. Form for penitents from the kirk of Monzie, Perthshire.

15. Branks from Holy Trinity church, St Andrews.

16. Jougs attached to the kirkyard gate of Duddingston parish church.

17. Sackcloth from Calder kirk, 1646.

18. *Lowland Wedding*, after de Wet.

19. Melville desk, Burntisland parish kirk (St Colomba's), Fife, 1606.

20. Forbes loft, Pitsligo parish church (now in Rosehearty, Banff and Buchan)

21. Skelmorelie Aisle, Largs, Ayrshire, *c.* 1636, laird's loft over burial vault.

22–23. Mariner's lofts from Burntisland (St Columba's) parish kirk, Fife. Inscribed above: 'God's providence is our inheritance' and 'Though God's pouer be suffthinent [sufficient] to governe us, yet for mans infi[r]mitie he appointe[t]h his ang[e]ls to watche ovir us'.

24. Baxters' loft, Burntisland

25. Merchants' loft, Burntisland.

26. Joiners' loft from Dun parish kirk, with the legend 'God bless the joiners of Dun'.

27. Arms of Robert Montgomery and his wife, Margaret Douglas, Largs kirk, the pious sentiments rather overwhelmed by the family's heraldic images.

28. Anstruther Wester Kirk (now the parish hall), Fife, bas-relief illustrating Matthew 7.13, 'Enter in at ye strait get [gate]; it is the wyd get yat leds to perdition'.

29. Resurrection panel from the Lumsden painted gallery, Provost Skene's house, Aberdeen.

30. Sarcophagus monument of John Gordon, Anwoth parish church, 1635.

31. Memento mori on a seventeenth-century gravestone, Elgin.

32. Illustration from Zachary Boyd's awkwardly titled *1. Crosses 2. Comforts 3. Counsels Needfull to Bee Considered, and Carefully to Be Laid Up in the Hearts of the Godly, in these Boysterious Broiles, and Bloody Times* (Glasgow, 1643), sig. Ai, verso.

end, the system offered something for everyone: the poor were fed, the elders felt they had done their duty, and the merrymakers were able to retain their tradition at reasonable expense.

★ ★ ★

Seasonal festivities were not the only profane pastimes targeted by the Reformed kirk. Just as offensive to the Calvinist ministers were the 'superstitious' and disorderly customs associated with the sacraments, especially the now discarded sacraments of matrimony and extreme unction, but also the retained though simplified sacrament of baptism. We have seen that baptism continued, as before the Reformation, to be attended by large numbers of gossips who in the session's view mocked the sabbath, the seriousness of the sacrament, and the good order of the town with their drunkenness and unrestrained revelry.[68] Marriage feasts likewise tended to be extravagant and hard to control and had come under restrictive legislation early in the protestant era.[69] And the drunkenness at wakes was legendary. As with seasonal festivity, however, these customs continued long after prohibition, and the session only became heavy-handed when the degree of disorder grew threatening.

The reformers subjected wedding celebrations to the same sorts of constraints that they had attempted with gossipries. In 1581, the Perth elders, 'perceiving great abuse to ensue in contracts of marriage by the resorting and convening of many people with these parties who are to be contracted, wherethrough great perturbation not only is found in the assembly, but also in banqueting there', ordered that couples be 'convoyed with six persons every one of them of the nearest of their kin, and no more'. If they disobeyed, their banns were to be rejected. Even in the face of this threat, however, the elders found three years later that 'great abuse and slander has risen through the convening of great multitudes and banqueting in time of contract and banns.' They prohibited future contracts before the congregation and restricted them instead to the minister's chamber, in the presence of the minister, two elders and the couple's parents or two nearest of kin if the parents were dead. After the banns were given, no more than twelve 'nearest of kindred' could go before the congregation to ratify the contract. It is not clear how this division of the event into two parts was supposed to address the problem, but it seems

68. See chapter 2, above.

69. For 'festive excess' at weddings, and 'doles and dinners' after funerals in England, see David Cressy, *Birth, Marriage and Death: Ritual, Religion and the Life Cycle in Tudor-Stuart England* (Oxford, 1997), 350–55, 446–48, 435–38; on traditional matrimonial festivity in Germany, Harrington, *Reordering*, 206–14.

to have failed in any case. Prohibited bridal banquets continued the next year, even in time of plague, when there was all the more reason to circumscribe them.[70]

In 1591 the session tried a different sort of ploy. They ordered that before a marriage could be contracted, the couple had to appear before the minister and elders to offer a credible confession of faith, submitting to doctrinal examination on the grounds that the benefits of the kirk, including marriage, should not be given to 'infidels'. Genuine infidels being rather thin on the ground in Perth by now, the real goal of this ruling was presumably to lend a more religious and sober air to what had been an overly profane and festive occasion, and to reinforce the fundamental protestantism of the community by ensuring the orthodoxy of the kirk's communal foundation, the family. It was in effect an effort to transform the culture of bridals into something that was recognisably Reformed.[71] Still, the celebration of marriage with prohibited banqueting continued. After a 1586 ruling that designated Sunday morning as the only time when marriages could be celebrated, matrimonial festivity came under sabbatarian legislation. But even the 20s fine attached to sabbath profanation by the 1579 statute was deemed by some not too much to pay for a good time at an important rite of passage. Accordingly, well into the seventeenth century traditional celebration persisted. In 1623, for example, Andrew Hall was 'humbled on his knees' and paid 20s to the poor for violating the sabbath 'the day of the marriage of John Bennet, with dancing and minstrelsy, he and his colleagues'. And the clergy were as guilty as their parishioners: to celebrate his daughter's marriage in 1604, the minister Patrick Galloway happily accepted from the town council 'two puncheons of wine . . . and 50 merks to be laid out on such confections wet and dry as shall serve for the occasion'.[72]

The final rite of passage also occasioned customary feasting and disorder in Perth, in the form of 'lykewakes'. These all-night watches over the corpse entailed 'great profanities that customarily are used', and that the kirk had still failed to quell in the 1630s. In May 1631 the session summoned members of the council to meet with them and 'settle an ordinance about sobriety and godly exercises to be used at lykewakes' to replace the traditional 'profanities'. They were particularly concerned with the persistent playing of cruel practical jokes. Drunken attenders of wakes,

70. CH2/521/1, ff. 64, 98v, 111 (1580s). The General Assembly had ordered in 1562 that solemnisation of marriage be made by the simple Geneva order without excessive and popish celebration: *BUK* 1:30.

71. CH2/521/2, f. 55.

72. CH2/521/2, p. 1; CH2/521/7, p. 451; *APS* 3:138; PL ms B59/16/1, f. 91.

for instance, 'come at midnight to honest men's houses when they were upon rest and knock at their yetts', gaining entrance by 'declaring that certain special friends belonging to them have taken a sudden sickness tending to death, putting these persons at whose yetts they report these things under great fear, and causing them in a suddenty to rise forth of their beds to the visitation of those reported to be in the said sudden sickness, and find it but done in derision and mockery, tending to the offence of God and honest neighbours.' This custom may well have arisen as a way of ritually diminishing the emotional impact of a death by (rather perversely) emphasising the life of another. Like most 'profane pastimes under cloud of night', however, it did not go down very well with either the sleeping citizenry or the kirk session. In 1645 the General Assembly finally gave up trying to control the activities associated with these vigils and forbade lykewakes altogether. But such was the popularity of the custom that their order had to be repeated in 1701.[73]

* * *

Perth's early and archetypal protestantism, together with its very detailed and nearly complete session minutes for this period up to 1637, make it an ideal case study for the persistence of popular festivity long after the authorities had condemned them. The record of Aberdeen attests to the fact that Perth was not alone in the slow pace of its cultural Reformation. But the experience of these two sizable towns was repeated all over the country, in fishing villages and rural communities, in smaller towns and in the capital. A few examples will suffice here, but they could easily be multiplied.

Marriage feasts, like the excessive celebration of baptisms we saw in chapter 2, aroused the kirk's ire everywhere. The Edinburgh session's ruling 'inhibiting pompous convoy [procession] and riotous excess of banqueting the time of marriage' was repeatedly violated despite the imposition of public repentance on offenders from 1574. The elders were convinced that the imminent famine of that year was partly due to 'the unmeasurable intemperance of the air and water which . . . commonly follows riot and excess of banqueting' and so took severe measures against offenders, even when the celebration had not occurred on the sabbath. Still, the problem continued, with revellers sometimes visibly contemptuous of the session: a 1575 offender declared 'in great disdain and despite that he had rather be of the devil's kirk nor be of the kirk of this burgh' if he could not celebrate a wedding with traditional procession and feasting.[74] The

73. CH2/521/8/1, f. 16v; NLS ms Adv. 31.1.1A, f. 189.

74. NAS ms RH2/1/35, ff. 13v, 15v, 38v, 46. Parliament acknowledged the problem with the bridals act of 1581 (*APS* 3:221). Noble celebration continued to provide the

village of Dundonald in Ayrshire was similarly troubled, and in the university town of St Andrews, the 'scandal' of marriage feasts was exacerbated by performance of plays during weekday preaching times. The Moray synod dealt with fighting as well as drunkenness at bridals, and the Newbattle session in the 1620s found charivaris on bridal evenings getting out of hand 'in derision and scorning of many' with 'unseemly form[s] of doing'.[75] The Stirling presbytery in 1583 found 'great abuse and superstition used by sundry persons that come to parish kirks to be married in causing pipers and fiddlers [to] play before them to the kirk and from the kirk' and ordered that in future such offenders must be turned away from the church and not married until their behaviour was more circumspect. They stopped short of the Glasgow presbytery's efforts to ban bridals altogether; however, in 1593 they limited the amount that couples could spend on feasting in order to prevent gluttony and drunkenness, imposing heavy fines for disobedience.[76] This ploy was adopted by parishes throughout the realm, though it seems to have done more to fill the poor boxes than to curb matrimonial festivity.[77] Sessions from Duffus to Scoonie to Ayr forbade Sunday weddings 'because of the great conventions and resortings to dancings' and for 'eschewing of riotousness'; many also tried limiting the number of people in wedding parties.[78] But long after these efforts, in the little village of Auchterderran the minister John Chalmers traced divine wrath against the community to the 'profane feasts' at bridals, and

wrong model: the 1599 'Lentron' fast 'was stayed by reason of the banquet and marriage of the Earl of Sutherland and the Master of Forbes': NLS ms Wod. Oct. VII, f. 41.

75. *Dundonald*, 28, 236, the latter reporting 'tumult and trouble at the bridal' resulting in seven people being threatened with excommunication for contumacy. NAS ms RH2/1/35, f. 40v, reports the 17 February 1575 investigation by the General Assembly meeting in Edinburgh of the minister of St Andrews. See also *SAKS* 1:893–94, David Wemyss complaining to the session in 1599 that bridal dances had never been 'stayed before, and that the custom was kept at Raderny before any of the session was born' – for which he was gaoled. For Moray, CH2/271/1, p. 128; for Newbattle, CH2/276/1, ff. 8, 22. Similar cases in other parishes include CH2/266/1, f. 111; CH2/338/1, f. 7v.
76. *Stirling Presbytery Records 1581–1587*, ed. James Kirk (Edinburgh, 1981), 192; ML CH2/171/1, ff. 3v, 20, 26–26v, 27v, 29–29v, 31v, 33v, 58v, 61v.
77. CH2/84/28, ff. 54, 64v (St Nicholas, Dalkeith's fairly typical arrangement of 1615, limiting 'penny bridals to 10s each man, 6s 8d each woman, with a fine of £10 for disobedience and requiring a signed vow by the bridegroom to keep costs down, prohibit dancing and have all the guests in their beds by 10 o'clock); ML CH2/171/1, ff. 20v, 26v; CH2/718/4, f. 176.
78. CH2/96/1, f. 3v; CH2/326/1, p. 3; CH2/523/1, ff. 2v, 33; AAC CH2/751/1, ff. 134, 186v.

back in the environs of the capital, the suburban session of Liberton was still complaining about them regularly in the 1640s.[79] If the sessions' prohibitions represented the ideal, the reality was closer to the revelry depicted in de Wet's painting of a Lowland wedding, complete with piping and dancing (see plate 18).

As with marrying, so with burying. Although the *First Book of Discipline* required that funerary rites be simple and unencumbered with any 'ceremony heretofore used' other than committal to the grave with such solemnity that those present may 'hate sin, which is the cause of death', Perth was not alone in retaining the feasting that had traditionally preceded and followed funerals. And as at Perth, wakes were often accompanied by drunken misbehaviour. Several men were prosecuted in 1629 at Dundonald, for instance, for 'drinking to excess that day John Tailor's daughter in Arrothil was buried'.[80] South Leith's elders dealt with the same midnight summons to supposedly dying relatives that had troubled Perth, ordering warding for 'such insolence at lykewakes' in 1613; and the Burntisland session in 1609 sought the help of the council in 'discharging of lykewakes' altogether.[81] Death, now so little marked by ecclesiastical ceremony, required marking of some kind if the bereaved were to cope.[82]

As for seasonal celebration, Yuletide guisings troubled the Kirkcaldy, Tyninghame and Newbattle sessions in the 1610s and 1620s, Stow's and Kirkwall's in the 1630s, and Scoonie's into the 1640s. Indeed, the Scoonie elders remarked in 1630 that the problem in their parish 'never hath been taken order with as yet' – a remarkable case of neglect, given the importance of seasonal 'superstitions' to the first reformers. In Elgin, however, it continued despite quite evident efforts to quash it from at least the early 1590s. With great regularity in that decade they summoned sizable groups of young men and women for guising and piping during the season, sometimes with women's clothes 'damasked' about them and their faces 'blackened', one year to the music of 'a lad with them playing upon bones and bells'. They sentenced revellers sternly to fines and public repentance 'barefooted and barelegged in the kirk', yet after years of campaigning, 1599's Christmas season saw them censuring no fewer than twenty-five lasses, including a minister's daughter, for 'guising and piping, violing,

79. CH2/21/5, f. 11; CH2/383/1, e.g., ff. 18–19.
80. *Wodrow Miscellany*, 293; *Dundonald*, 274–75 (1629).
81. CH2/716/2, ff. 106v–07 (two women offending); CH2/523/1, f. 34. See also CH2/295/1, f. 40v.
82. R. Huntington and Peter Metcalf, *Celebration of Death: The Anthropology of Mortuary Ritual* (Cambridge, 1979), offers illuminating discussion of the relationship between bereavement and festivities surrounding death.

and dancing' in the kirkyard. Two decades later the futility of their efforts was demonstrated when five Yuletide guisers 'passed in a sword dance . . . in the kirkyard with masks and visors on their faces', while James Tailyour was 'playing on a trumpet to a number of lasses who were dancing'.[83]

Apart from guising, Yuletide processions, games and music proved obdurate in many parishes. The godly minister Robert Blair listed among the sins of his youth in the first decade of the seventeenth century his participation 'in a time of rioting (commonly called the holidays of Yule)', when, 'perceiving what liberty some elder than I took, to the end I might play the fool more boldly, I feigned myself to be drunk.'[84] Reformers complained to the regent in 1575 against the town of Dumfries for 'conveying a reader to kirk with tabret [small drum] and whistle to read prayers all the holy days of Christmas'. The pre-Reformation procession of Nativity images to the church during the season had been replaced by a procession only thinly disguised as protestant (with the reader at the centre) and still accompanied by festive instruments. The music could lead to other, even move dangerous revelry, like dancing. In 1596 at Logie a piper was summoned 'to answer for playing in the kirkyard of Lecropt to certain persons there convened on that day called of old Yule Day, whereby superstition is maintained'; he confessed having played 'on Andro Mitchell's green beside the said kirk to certain persons who danced there'. After public repentance at Lecropt and in his own parish kirk of Dunblane, he was enjoined not to play in future 'on the sabbath, Yule Day, Pasch Day, and the days called of old the saints' days, except at a noble man's table, under the pain of £10'. Yet the session had to summon the same piper again in 1608. The noble exemption was surely part of the problem. The Edinburgh presbytery on 26 December 1598

> being informed of the great abuse that has been in the king's majesty's house in the town of Edinburgh and other parts about the keeping of Yule has ordained that his majesty's ministers speak to his majesty that order may be taken with his house. And that the ministers of Edinburgh and the rest of the ministers about take order with their

83. CH2/636/34, e.g., ff. 24 (1619), 36 (1621); CH2/359/1, ff. 4–4v (1615–16, equating guising with cross-dressing); CH2/276/1, f. 8v; CH2/338/1, ff. 34v, 37v (guising 'at the Egyptians', or with gypsies, 1633); CH2/327/1, f. 18; CH2/442/74, f. 7v; CH2/326/1, p. 4. For Elgin, CH2/145/1, ff. 59–59v, 60v, 163; CH2/145/2, 28v; CH2/145/4, ff. 13v, 14v–15. See also CH2/266/1, ff. 7, 13v; SAU CH2/Crail/1, f. 2v.
84. Blair, 5.

> flocks by reason God's Word, the acts of the kirk and laws of the realm have damned the same.

The king was not amused.[85]

Neither, presumably, were the parishioners of Aberlady after the 20 December 1640 order that their elders must spy out each household in their assigned quarters of the village 'upon Friday next being Yule Day, that there be no superstitious feasting, but that all persons be at their work as at other times, and to report the same at the session the next Sunday'. The session of Culross followed suit in the 1640s – eighty years after Christmas had first been abolished – in view of the town's colliers 'keeping the Yule Day in feasting and drinking and abstaining from their ordinary work'. As it so happens, however, these townspeople were no fools: the minister reported to the session in December 1648 that he had visited all the families in his parish on the three 'chief superstitious days and had found them all working in their several houses, but was suspicious that some of them wrought no longer than he was present'.[86] The Slains and the St Andrews sessions in 1649 likewise ordered ordinary labour on Yule Day; in 1650, the latter session nonetheless had to summon several people for 'playing jolly at the goose' (revelry and feasting) on Christmas. In Elgin the minister searched people's kitchens on Christmas Day for the 'superstitious goose, telling them that the feathers of them would rise up against them one day'.[87] This session had legislated in the 1590s against Yuletide 'footballing through the town, snowballing, singing of carols or other profane songs, guising, piping, violing and dancing', but was still acting on it in the Decembers of 1617, 1618, 1626, 1629, 1630, 1631 and 1643. These repeated disciplinary actions only reveal the stubborn persistence among the populace of 'superstitious' pastimes 'expressly forbidden during the time called Yule'. In 1617 they compromised with popular demand by permitting the schoolboys a week's Christmas holiday, but such was the resultant festive disorder that the following December found them renewing the earlier order against 'casting of snowballs, hurling with stools on the streets' and 'women . . . clad in men's apparel' with the threat of a

85. Mill, 162; R Menzies Fergusson, *Logie* (Edinburgh, 1905), 2, 81; Banks, 3:234.
86. CH2/4/1, f. 30v, and also ff. 24v–25, conviction of a man and a woman for 'guising and dissembling themselves'. The penalty was public repentance and a civil penalty for contumacy. For Culross, CH2/77/1, f. 100 (1644); CH2/77/2, f. 17 (1647, repeating the order) and unfoliated entry for 31 December 1648.
87. Banks, 3:242; Wodrow's early eighteenth-century account of the actions in the 1640s of Murdoch McKenzie, in Banks, 3:226.

doubled penalty of 40s and warding for the first fault.[88] Their experience was typical of parishes from Ayrshire to Fife to Orkney.[89]

May and Midsummer plays and games likewise persisted. South Leith was still struggling to abolish the fleshers' 'May plays in Gilmerton' in 1619. In the Fife fishing village of Anstruther Wester, May games traditionally played in the kirkyard for the profit of the parish continued well into the seventeenth century with no objections. In May of 1610, the elders raked in 44s, 19 Irish two-penny pieces, and a penny when they broke 'the penny pig that the silver was put in which was gathered the time of playing at the ketch behind the kirk'; the minister, James Melville, used the profits of the games to help furnish the new kirk house and replenish the poor box. Clearly this pastime was sufficiently beneficial to the parish to make its abolition unwarranted, however 'profane' the activity. This only changed in the summer of 1611, and then not for religious reasons, but because damage to the fabric of the kirkyard suggested that the cost-effectiveness of the games had worn off. The session noted then 'how the kirkyard and kirk doors are abused and profaned many ways, specially by a multitude that useth commonly to play therein at the bowls, pennystone and such other pastimes, and by making water on the kirk doors' and decided to forbid any future recreational use of the kirkyard on pain of a 10s fine. The following year (1612) saw the yard 'become a jakes . . . and a stable for horses and beasts'; accordingly the session repeated the act 'against all them that shall play at any pastime or make water', with the additional banishment of horses and cattle from the kirkyard.[90] The important point is that the games themselves were not perceived as objectionable; only damage to the building and its yard brought them to an end.

Other May celebration likewise persisted throughout the Lowlands and southern Uplands. In Cranston, the session prosecuted thirteen men in May 1590 for performing plays about Robin Hood and the Abbot of Unreason on the sabbath. In 1625, the Lanark presbytery summoned a

88. CH2/145/1, ff. 59, 60v; CH2/145/2, quotation at f. 28v, f. 30; CH2/145/3, ff. 105v, 131; CH2/145/4, f. 102; CH2/145/5, f. 17; CH2/145/6, f. 81.

89. AAC CH2/809/1, f. 76 (Monkton, 1630); *Dundonald*, 69–70 (1605), 229 (Yuletide piping, 1612). In St Andrews, a 1575 fast was troubled when the magistrates declined to prohibit children and servants performing Robin Hood plays and games often associated with late Yuletide: NAS ms RH2/1/35, ff. 40–41; cf. *SAKS* 2:738–40, 808 (1592–95). CH2/258/1, n.f., 27 January 1633; CH2/472/1, f. 12; CH2/442/74, f. 7v (1636).

90. CH2/718/4, ff. 19, 21–21v (eight fleshers and six other men prosecuted); SAU CH2/624/2, pp. 107, 119, 129. See also Newbattle's and Dundonald's May pennystone (quoits) competitions in the 1620s: CH2/276/1, ff. 7v, 9; *Dundonald*, 248.

piper and six others 'for fetching home a May-pole and dancing about the same'. And the Elgin session disciplined nighttime May merrymakers in Spynnie Wood repeatedly in the 1620s and 1630s, and on 9 May 1628 ordered a kirk officer to 'go through the town with the bell intimating to each person . . . that shall be found in the Chanonrie kirkyard dancing or leaping or footballing, to pay a merk'.[91] In Ayrshire, the Dundonald session carefully examined people whose whereabouts at Beltane was unknown; they were particularly troubled by people who claimed to go off with the 'fair folk' who were thought to be abroad during May and at All Hallow's Eve.[92] In Peebles, May visitors to 'superstitious places' found the ministers of Stobo and Innerleithen, along with the bailies of Peebles and other appointed gentlemen, lying in wait to 'apprehend any who should come in pilgrimage . . . as had been the custom'; the authorities reported a group of men and women from Hawick, Selkirk and Minto to the presbytery in 1599. That their concern may not have been only with superstition is suggested by the 1571 order for 'half of the town to walk nightly till Beltane Even and the whole town to walk on Beltane Even, Beltane at even, and the morn after Beltane Day till they see what stay may come in the country for resisting of thieves'.[93]

May visitation of wells and sacred springs is ubiquitous in early modern session registers. The Stirling presbytery prosecuted thirty-eight people who visited Christ's Well near Falkirk for healing in 1583, and the Edinburgh presbytery of 1586 had to pass an act denouncing all 'persons passing pilgrimage to chapels or wells [or] . . . crofts or pieces of ground superstitiously reported to be consecrated to the devil [fairies?] under the name of the Good May'.[94] In Menteith, Christ's Well had attracted May pilgrims

91. CH2/424/1, p. 170; CH2/145/3, ff. 125v–26 (nine women, fourteen men and a piper 'dancing to Spynie on communion Sunday at even', May 1603) f. 190; CH2/145/4, ff. 95, 140; CH2/145/5, ff. 173, 182v. The wood visitors of May 1638 were warded.

92. *Dundonald*, 15 (May 1602 summons of Marion Or for 'professing herself to ride with the fair folk and to have skill'), 35, 51 (1604 prosecution of Jonat Hunter, who also claimed to be 'one that gaid [went] out with the fair folk' in May and thereby acquired healing powers.

93. CH2/295/1 (Peebles Presbytery), f. 39v; *Records of the Burgh of Peebles* (Edinburgh, 1872), 326 (25 April 1571). See also ML CH2/171/1, ff. 26v–28v, 52 (May 'piping and profane games' in Glasgow presbytery, 1594–95); *SAKS* 2:892–97 (Raderny May festivities, 1595); CH2/523/1, ff. 2v, 36v (Burntisland, 1602, 1609); CH2/327/1, f. 7 (May cross-dressing in Melrose, 1607); CH2/84/28, ff. 17v–18 (eighteen parishioners of St Nicholas East, Dalkeith, maying in 1611); CH2/338/1, f. 29v (Stow, 1630); CH2/264/1, f. 11 (May piping and dancing in Menmuir, 1635); CH2/77/1, f. 50v (Culross, 1636).

94. *Stirling Presbytery Records*, 115–16, 120, 135, 140, 147, 150; CH2/121/1, f. 9. The Stirling presbytery had denounced the practice in 1581 (pp. 4–5) to no avail; in 1583

despite repeated session denunciation since at least 1586. By May Day of 1624 the visitors had become so numerous that the Privy Council posted commissioners to wait nearby and seize and imprison them in Doune Castle; nevertheless, four years later Doune's and Falkirk's sessions were still prosecuting people for having 'passed in pilgrimage to Christ's Well on the Sundays of May to seek their health . . . idolatrously'. In desperation they set the severe penalty of three sabbaths' public repentance in sackcloth or linen plus payment of an enormous £20 fine for each fault, and those who could not pay were to be warded and fed on bread and water for eight days. The Moray synod campaigned against pilgrimages to wells 'from all quarters within this province' in the 1620s and 1630s. In 1631, Inveravon launched a campaign against the 'companies' that went 'in pilgrimage to chapels and wells', but the elders concluded that 'they could not delate one in particular because there were few in the parish that could purge themselves from going thereto' since 'this abuse had not been punished this long time bygone'. But longevity of the practice was by no means a Highland monopoly: the Kirkoswald well visitors still took their bairns and 'stayed there all night' in the 1630s. In the 1640s, Dunfermline and Culross toughened their strictures against 'song-singing and superstitious awe' at wells, and the 1649 General Assembly at Edinburgh, 'informed that some went superstitiously to wells denominate from saints', passed yet another ruling against 'holywell annuals', but to little avail. The Falkirk session rebuked a large number of parishioners in 1657 for travelling to the well at Airth to leave money or bits of cloth and bring water home for healing; and the Dunblane session as late as 1659 was prosecuting parishioners for 'carrying of water out of the superstitious well above Cullines'.[95]

Midsummer fires at St Peter's or St John's Eve continued nearly everywhere from the Reformation throughout the war years and the Cromwellian decade, and flourished thereafter along with other summer games and festivities. The Edinburgh session prosecuted August guising, cross-dressing and dancing in 1574, and the 1588 presbytery dealt with 'a

they sent members to take down names of well visitors and required public repentance. The ministers probably tended to construe as ground 'consecrated to the devil' the places where fairies were traditionally thought to emerge from their abodes at May Day (Beltane), returning on All Hallow's Eve: *Scottish Fairy Belief*, ed. Edward J. Cowan and Lizanne Henderson (East Linton, 2001).

95. Menteith visitors to Christ's Well had been prosecuted in 1586 as well: *Visitation of the Diocese of Dunblane and Other Churches 1586–89*, ed. James Kirk (Edinburgh, 1984), 12. Peebles presbytery also ordered brethren to wait at wells to apprehend visitors in the 1590s: CH2/295/1, f. 39v. For the Highlands, CH2/271/1, pp. 15, 20, 113; CH2/191/1, f. 7v. For Kirkoswald, AAC CH2/562/1, f. 39v. Other cases include CH2/77/1, f. 55; Banks, 1:147, 127, 158, 165; 3:41; and William Nimmo, *The History of Stirlingshire* (London, 1880) 1:281–82. The Falkirk pilgrims also 'had bread at the well', adding the picnic element.

great number of people within many of the kirks within the bounds who upon Midsummer even last set up bonfires to the fostering of superstition and evil example to others'.[96] The Dundonald session in 1602 ordered 'such as made bonfires this year to be pursued' and 'every master to correct his own hired [servants] who kindled bonfires this year, and to do the same before witness that the session may know it to be done . . . otherwise certifying them they shall be held as allowers of them.'[97] On 26 June 1655, the presbytery of Dingwall ordered the brethren to 'intimate to their congregations that they desist of the superstitious abuses used on St John's Day by burning torches through their corns and fires in their towns', but in June 1671 the presbytery ordered the 'Act passed in synod [of Ross] against Midsummer fires' repeated again to the congregations.[98] And sessions continued to rule regularly against a miscellany of other 'festival or saints' days sometimes named [for] their patrons' with banquets, dancing and 'vain superstitious songs' (the particular bane of Burntisland), or St Valentine's cards (the works of Ayr's 'maidens and makers of the rhymes and drawers of Valentines'), or Hallowe'en bonfires (a Fraserburgh 'pastime' in the 1610s).[99] Clearly presbyterian Scotland was not in practice the grim and joyless place of modern stereotype.

★ ★ ★

All this is not to say that the Scottish Reformation was undercut by the relative failure of the authorities to quash traditional festivities. The evidence suggests instead that protestantism may have succeeded in part *because* the sessions enforced their legislation against festivity lightly, flexibly and sporadically. Where a heavy hand might have strengthened the opposition to Reformed doctrine as well as discipline, the elders' sense of the inutility of quashing the useful and harmless allowed for a more gradual but secure cultural reconstruction. Traditional celebrations met real communal needs to recognise the stages of individual life and the passing of the seasons.[100] The protestant authorities would have been foolish not

96. NAS ms RH 2/1/35, ff. 14–14v (Jonet Cadye admonished for 'disguising herself in breeches and dancing in merry clothing'); cf. CH2/400/1, pp. 120, 176. For 'upsetters [builders] of bonfires', CH2/121/1, ff. 42v, 43v, 44v–45.
97. *Dundonald*, 20–21.
98. *Records of the Presbyteries of Inverness and Dingwall 1643–1688*, ed. William MacKay (Edinburgh, 1896), 268, 323; see also CH2/295/1, f. 44v.
99. CH2/523/1, verso of unnumbered title page, 1602; AAC CH2/751/1, ff. 14v, 16, 18; CH2/1142/1, f. 78v; cf. CH2/299/2, pp. 44–45; CH2/472/1, f. 1; SAU CH2/150/1 (Ferryport-on-Craig), f. 5v.
100. Van Gennep, 178–89. Andrew Pettegree has observed similar restraint by elders in the Netherlands: 'Coming to Terms with Victory: The Upbuilding of a Calvinist Church in Holland, 1572–1590' in *Calvinism in Europe, 1540–1620*, ed. Pettegree, A. Duke and G. Lewis (Cambridge, 1994), 176–79.

to have accepted this. In practice, the session minutes reveal them gradually subsuming old traditions into a new kind of festivity, with new ways of demonstrating individual and corporate status and communal cohesion in the face of both the linear and the cyclical passage of time. The seasonal communions discussed earlier, with their intensive preparation and performance rituals, are one example, providing a break from ordinary work schedules and opportunity for gathering with neighbours and friends. The introduction of political celebration and continuation of inoffensive sport, dancing and plays provide others; and even the dramatic and costumed rites of public penitence, the new 'seasons of fasting and humiliation', and the strict enforcement of sabbath observance all served to address the needs met by traditional 'popish' observance of holy times and seasons.[101] Rites of passage came to be marked by the public performance of examinations and the public reporting of deathbed pieties, while old icons were replaced by communion tokens, Bibles and psalters. In the end, the new protestant culture was as marked as the old by seasonal observances, ritual and costume, festival and song. Humans being what they are, there is a limited number of packages available to contain their meanings; the elders simply reconstructed the available containers along more protestant lines, taking their time about it, and exercising flexibility and restraint.

How self-conscious sessions like that of Perth were about their relative tolerance of festivity is unclear, but the sources do provide some hints. A favourite anecdote of John Malcolm, Perth's minister from 1591 to 1634, offers one of the most telling: 'My colleague William Cowper' (second minister 1595–1614), he said, 'often found fault with me for not going about into the people's houses on Yule Day to prevent their feasting, yet he accepted of a bishopric, and I continued minister at Perth.'[102] Malcolm (and presumably the elders who co-operated with him for so long) had a clear sense of his priorities, and repressing Christmas was not high on the list. Episcopacy, with its popish tyranny and disciplinary ineffectiveness, was in his view a much greater danger to protestant piety than a Yule goose or a Midsummer bonfire. For Cowper to renounce his earlier and vociferous presbyterianism to take a bishopric himself was to Malcolm the real scandal.[103] Correct church government and discipline – vastly more crucial to the establishment of protestantism – would be the easier to implement if the Yule goose were left on its spit. The way Malcolm spent his time is also telling. He visited families not to look for the goose,

101. For discussion of fasting seasons, see chapter 7, below.
102. NLS ms Adv. 31.1.1a, f. 258.
103. Cowper had signed the Protestation of 1606 against bishops.

but rather to catechise and examine.[104] His focus was on those devices that would serve to construct an alternative, protestant culture.

In the meantime, traditional revels continued to exert their appeal, and sessions continued to collect fines year after year from indulgers in profane pastimes. Some elders were simply remiss in their duty of repressing popish superstition; indeed, some regularly paid fines themselves for failing even to show up at session meetings.[105] But as we have seen, those who did attend and act against festivity seldom punished it vigorously enough to abolish it. Sufficiently severe mechanisms were available: parliament and General Assembly had authorised multiple sabbaths of public humiliation for sabbath breach (under which heading much of the prosecution came), and for a third relapse royal (not burgh) seizure of all the offender's goods was theoretically possible. But the Perth session never came close to this extreme, even with the most contumacious repeat offenders. Instead, their fiscal sense drove them to milk their more practical system of financial penalties for all it was worth. Finding that craftsmen, merchants and alewives were quite willing to pay a modest tax for the privilege of maying or carolling, particularly knowing that the fines went *ad pios usus*, they simply collected the fines and employed them to replenish their poor-relief funds and kirk-repair coffers. Often the very direct relationship between fine and kirk expenses is clear in the minutes: a sabbath-breaker of 1622 paid '6s penalty to John Brown's wife lying sick'. In 1631 Gilbert Henderson's fine (for calling the elders 'false knaves' and saying 'a turd for you all') was 'to be bestowed upon repairing of the faults of the kirk'. And when an apprentice slater who had behaved scandalously in the countryside in 1622 could not afford his fine, he was 'ordained [instead] to mend a hole of the body of the kirk in part payment of his penalty' and to be available for further roof repairs in future for the remainder.[106]

104. To be fair, Cowper preached five times each week in Perth. But it was Malcolm who redefined the pastoral duties of elders and minister. Within weeks of his arrival in Perth in 1591 he had introduced weekly visitation of the sick by elders and minister, doctrinal vetting of couples before marriage contracts were made, regular visitation of every household 'for their reformation and information in godliness', and weekly catechetical visitation of families by the elders for each quarter. In addition, he introduced Saturday morning prayers and a twice-annual review of every office-holder in the kirk: CH2/521/2, ff. 55, 57v, 58v, 70, 126v, 158.

105. E.g., CH2/521/2, f. 46 (bailies as well as elders fined 13s 4d for neglecting to report sabbath-breakers); CH2/521/6, p. 89; CH2/521/7, p. 378 (fines for non-attendance).

106. CH2/521/7, pp. 331, 349, 430; CH2/521/8/1, f. 25v records the penalty of the skinner Henderson, who was also one of the well visitors and was fined an amazing £100, which he duly paid. Perth was representative of other sessions in its distribution of fines to the poor: e.g., Kirkcaldy's 'Andro Auchinleck his 40s for his penalty received and given to Jonet Wilson to pay her housemeal' (CH2/636/34,

The session's willingness to mitigate public penances in exchange for a money payment has already been noted in the offer by wealthy offenders in 1622 to pay an increased fine to avoid public humiliation for May well-visiting – a goldmine that the elders were happy to exploit.[107] If this enabled the continuation of profane pastimes, so much the better for the kirk's fiscal well being. Only in cases where festivity degenerated into serious disorder, destruction of property or violence did the elders consistently depart from their cost-effective and generally palatable policy. Otherwise they denounced and prosecuted pastimes, but never disrupted revellers in the act or doused the bonfires or threw extra gossips out of the church.

In addition to treating forbidden revelry leniently, the Perth elders also declined to abolish all profane pastimes. Sports and dancing not on the sabbath or during proclaimed fasts were upheld, and even drew the participation of the elders. In 1624, for instance, the regular session meeting itself was cancelled because most of the elders were at a horse race.[108] Fairs likewise disrupted session meetings and even fasts: when the Perth presbytery proclaimed a week-long fast in June of 1621, they amended the dates because of conflict with the regular Midsummer fair, when 'holy action cannot be performed in such a solemn manner as is requisite'. When the 1623 session tried to reprimand a group of craftsmen for piping and making inordinate noise in the streets, they had to acknowledge John Skinner's objection that 'the like upon such occasion as he had has been used of before and no fault found therewith'. They explained that they had made an exception to their usual tolerance this time only because of the divine indignation against Perth indicated by the current famine and plague in the city (also noting that James Wilson's 'playing on the great pipe under silence of night' had resulted in the 'terrifying of neighbours as though either fire or sword had been within the town').[109] But a craftsmen's party with piping on a weekday was not in itself objectionable.

Neither was secular drama. The General Assembly in 1574 had forbidden 'clerk plays, comedies or tragedies upon the canonical parts of scripture', but they allowed that 'other plays, including profane, may be considered' as long as there was no sabbath performance. Accordingly, school plays were allowed after vetting, as in 1589 when the Perth elders

f. 25v). Surely this made the fine less painful for people convinced that charity was a virtue.

107. Other instances abound in the minutes: see chapter 3, above.

108. CH2/521/7, p. 484. Some were also at a burial in Scone. A 1621 statute decreed that horse-race winnings over 100 merks were to go to the poor: *APS* 4:613.

109. CH2/299/1, p. 62; CH2/521/7, pp. 432–41.

licensed a grammar-school play 'with the conditions that neither swearing, banning nor no scurrility be in it'.[110] Pageantry marked royal events like Anne of Denmark's coronation, when 'young boys with artificial wings at her entry [to Edinburgh] did fly towards her' to present the keys to the city, and 'at night the town was put full of bonfires'.[111] On special occasions public performances by members of crafts guilds even restored the extravagance of earlier costume, staging and dance. When the king visited Perth in 1633, the glovers' corporation built a floating stage upon the river Tay, where 'thirteen of our brethren of this our calling of glovers with green caps, silver strings, red ribbons, white shoes and bells about their legs, shewing rapiers in their hands . . . danced our sword dance with many difficult knots, five being under and five above upon their shoulders, three of them dancing through their feet and about them, drinking wine and breaking glasses.' Following this extraordinary performance, two tailors 'acted on the Water of Tay what they called a comedy, or spoke a poem in the way of dialogue' written by the bailie Andro Wilson. One 'personated the River of Tay', the other the town of Perth, and the drama served the multiple functions of entertaining king and people and attempting 'in a modest manner to solicit the royal favour for the building of a new bridge'.[112]

Political events in the decades following the Reformation produced not only a legitimate opportunity for occasional feasting and public revelry, but also, as in England, new calendar celebrations. The king's delivery from the Gowrie Conspiracy in 1600 and the Gunpowder Plot in 1605 produced new holidays on 5 August and 5 November – days of national thanksgiving to provide a bit of balance for all those fast days, and an opportunity to indulge in traditional revelry. In the month following the Gowrie Conspiracy 'there were bone fires set forth in Perth and all parts of the country for his majesty's deliverance from that treason'; thereafter, every year saw bonfires as well as sermons on the day.[113] The English bishop Joseph Hall remarked to a Scottish critic of English holy days that the Scots also celebrated the defeat of the Armada annually, and on that date as well as on 5 August and 5 November, 'the streets of your Edinburgh smoke with many thankful fires, and your Arthur's Seat [the

110. *BUK* 1:322–23; CH2/521/2, f. 27.
111. NLS ms Wod. Oct. VII, f. 19v.
112. NLS ms Adv 31.1.1a, ff. 242–43; cf. *Chronicle of Perth*, 33. Much of the old bridge had been destroyed by a flood in the winter of 1583, more fell in February of 1607, and in the great flood of 1621 it was completely destroyed and the townspeople were reduced to using a ferry to cross the river.
113. *APS* 4:213–14; LPL ms 3471, f. 129v; CH2/359/1, f. 2; CH2/285/1, p. 8; CH2/145/3, f. 179; NLS ms Wod. Oct. VII, ff. 42–43, 44v, 47v.

crags outside the town walls] flames with the bonfires of your triumph and exultation.' In addition, the citizens of Perth enjoyed occasional feasts for events like the 1598 visit of the queen's brother; or the royal visit of 1601, when 'there was a punchion of wine set there [at the market cross] and all drunken out'. At the king's accession to the crown of England, 'a bonfire was set forth in all Scotland', and bonfires were again lit when he was crowned, when Prince Charles returned from Spain in 1623, when he was married and when his French queen arrived in England in 1625. To mark the birth of the princess Elizabeth's first son, the people of Perth enjoyed 'bone fires, ringing of the bells, with other pastime' along with 'hearing of God's word and thanksgiving therefore'.[114]

Political festivities, while few, helped to address the popular craving for celebration. Together with surviving sports, dancing and fairs, not to mention disapproved-of but effectively tolerated 'profane' sabbath pastimes, they gave post-Reformation Scotland a very different appearance from that usually portrayed in the received version. When Hall, defending traditional festivity, asked his Scottish correspondent, 'Do not you think that those who took upon them the reformation of your church went somewhat too far and (as it is in the fable) inwrapped the stork together with the cranes . . . so violent was that holy furore of piety?', the Scot could quite justifiably have answered in the negative.[115] Reformed Scotland, if not as merry as we might like, was nowhere near as dour as its reputation would have it.

114. *Chronicle of Perth*, 3, 6, 8, 9, 11, 14, 24, 28; NLS ms Wod. Qu 20, f. 303v; Calderwood, *History of the Kirk of Scotland*, 7:628. For English parallels to the replacement of religious with political holidays, see David Cressy, *Bonfires and Bells: National Memory and the Protestant Calendar in Elizabethan and Stuart England* (Berkeley, 1989).

115. NLS ms Wod. Qu 20, f. 299v.

Chapter 5
Keeping the Peace

November 1567, The laird of Airth and the laird of Weems met on the high gate of Edinburgh and with their followers fought a very bloody skirmish where there was many hurt on both sides with shot of pistol.

3 June 1598, Robert Cathcart [was] slain [while] pissing at the wall in Peebles Wyndhead by William Stewart, son to Sir William Stewart. The same Robert Cathcart was at slaughter of the said Sir William Stewart before. . . . They that slays will be slain.

February, 1602, The laird of McGregor with four hundred of his name and faction entered in the Lennox, where he made spoilerie and slaughter to the number of sixty honest men besides women and bairns. He spared none.[1]

2 June 1613, Malcolme Troup and William Bien summoned for . . . mutual pursuit the time of [sermon] . . . with stones and clods, and . . . with drawn dirks.[2]

1637, complaint by Mr Robert Biggar, minister: on 26 January last Robert Creichtoune in Cairne . . . put violent hands in his person, buffeted and bruised him in diverse parts of his body, strake him on the head with a picked rod, shamefully nipped his cheeks, pulled his beard, and had almost killed him, were not with great difficulty he ran out at the door. But the said Robert followed him . . . hurled him out to a snow wraith [bank] and brake two ribs of his side, to the great effusion of his blood.[3]

19 August 1624, Patrick Levingston confessed his offence committed . . . by his cruel striking and blinding of John Levingston his son.[4]

1. NLS ms Wod. Oct. VII (diary of Robert Birrel, burgess of Edinburgh, 1532–1605), ff. 9v, 47v.
2. CH2/1142/1 (Fraserburgh kirk session), ff. 17–18.
3. *RPC* 6:467.
4. CH2/400/1 (Falkirk session), p. 133.

These terse entries from personal diaries, letters, and conciliar and ecclesiastical records of early modern Scotland reflect a violent society, in which towns and countryside alike were plagued with domestic violence, bloodfeud, and simple neighborhood quarrels escalating out of control – even on the sabbath.[5] Feud was not the least of the problems. The work of Keith Brown and Jenny Wormald comprises a heroic effort to revise our notion of feud by locating in the early modern period what cultural anthropologists like Max Gluckman have called 'the peace in the feud' – arguing that feud was structured to settle rather than exacerbate quarrels by defining the limits of vengeance and offering mechanisms like assythment (reparation) to restore peace. The fact remains, though, that these settlement devices offered peace *after* the feud, and then only for the wealthy.[6] Feud remained a bloody affair and a remarkably pervasive problem in the Lowlands as well as the Gaelic Highlands, towns as well as landward areas, and among all social orders, not just the magnates and lairds.[7] As for other forms of conflict, street brawls, assaults and domestic violence appear as ubiquitous and serious as feud. Contemporaries found the violence level unacceptable. Archbishop Spottiswoode lamented the 'bloods and slaughters daily falling out in every place', Samuel Rutherford the 'crying sins of the the land . . . blood touching blood'.[8] Parliament in 1587 noted the 'slaughter, blood, mutilation, shooting of hagbuts and pistolets' that occurred in kirks and kirkyards, and in 1592 they were still worried that 'divers persons for fear of their lives dare not resort to the preaching of the gospel' because 'cruelty and bloodshed are come to such an height within this land that . . . commonly all revenges and quarrels and deadly feuds are now execute[d]' there, even on Sunday.[9] The presbytery at Edinburgh in 1586 heard reports of weapons drawn and

5. Among many examples of sabbath 'tuilzing' or fighting, see *Dundonald*, 2, 16, 20, 23, 29, 41, 205, 210, 211, 214, 217, 225, 230, 231, 259, 289, 292, 329, etc; CH2/636/34 (Kirkcaldy), f. 86v.
6. Keith Brown, *Bloodfeud in Scotland 1573–1625: Violence, Justice and Politics in an Early Modern Society* (Edinburgh, 1986); Jenny Wormald, 'The Blood Feud in Early Modern Scotland' in *Disputes and Settlements: Law and Human Relations in the West*, ed. John Bossy (Cambridge, 1983), 101–44, 'Bloodfeud, Kindred and Government in Early Modern Scotland', *P&P* 87 (1980), 54–97, and *Lords and Men in Scotland* (Edinburgh, 1985); Gluckman, *Custom and Conflict* and *Politics*, ch. 5.
7. Brown, *Bloodfeud*, p. 7. Brown finds the Lothian/Fife crescent more peaceful than Ayrshire, Angus, Aberdeenshire and the Highlands; however, he concentrates more on the highest level of feud than on very local and small-scale quarrels.
8. John Spottiswoode, *History of the Church of Scotland*, 3 vols (Edinburgh, 1847–51), 2:465; *Letters of Samuel Rutherford* (Edinburgh, 1984, from the 1891 edn), p. 56.
9. *APS* 3:430, 544; among other provisions, this act refined Privy Council arbitration of feud.

blood shed during sermon time in Elgin parish, and the Edinburgh council in 1589 had to prohibit 'drawing of swords and shooting of pistolets' inside the high kirk.[10] After the laird of Leslie was 'hurt in the leg by a shot' in the course of 'some old roust betwixt' him and Sir Gilbert Menzies, an Aberdonian commented that the 'bearing and wearing of guns' bred 'much sorrow and mischief in this land'. In 1600, parliament passed an 'Act anent removing and extinguishing of deadly feuds', to deal with 'the great liberty that sundry persons take in provoking others to singular combat upon sudden and frivolous quarrels'.[11] Urban magistrates, local lairds and royal or ecclesiastical officials made what effort they could, but their resources were stretched thin by the demands of an expanding and well-armed population. Even school children were armed and dangerous: parliament complained in 1594 that students 'often incur great skaith [injury] and peril' by going into towns armed with 'swords, pistolets, and other weapons'; in September 1595 a grammar-school boy shot and killed an Edinburgh bailie during a student mutiny with the pistol he had brought to school (confirming the biblical precept that there is nothing new under the sun).[12] The Privy Council complained in 1582 that 'his majesty's good subjects over all his realm have been troubled heavily with bloodshed . . . to their great hurt and skaith' due to 'deadly feuds' and 'unnatural slaughters, bloodshed, barbarous cruelties', and the General Assembly demanded in 1596 that the 'flood of bloodsheds and deadly feuds' be addressed.[13]

One of the ways at the local level that such violence had been dealt with in medieval Britain was by arbitration of disputes before they erupted in physical violence. Arbitration was conducted by kin, by guilds and fraternities, in theory by parish priests especially during Lent, and in towns by councils, bailies or local notables.[14] At a higher ecclesiastical level,

10. CH2/121/1 (Edinburgh presbytery minutes), f. 17v; *Extracts from the Records of the Burgh of Edinburgh, 1403–1589*, 4 vols (Edinburgh, 1869–82), 4:539. We do not know how many of these quarrels might have been caused by contentious sermons, as happened in Calvin's Geneva: William Naphy, *Calvin and the Consolidation of the Genevan Reformation* (Manchester, 1994), 153–62.
11. Spalding, 2:96–97; *APS* 4:230; NLS ms Wod. Oct. VII, ff. 31, 35.
12. *APS* 4:70; NLS ms Wod. Oct. VII, ff. 28v–29. Perth prohibited all 'firing guns or pistols within the burgh . . . or four miles about' in 1605: PL ms B59/12/2, ff. 88v, 98.
13. *RPC* 5:248; *BUK* 3:874; *APS* 4:230.
14. Bossy, *Christianity in the West*; 'Blood and Baptism: Kinship, Community and Christianity from the Fourteenth to the Seventeenth Centuries', *Studies in Church History* 10 (1973), 129–43; *Peace* for a European overview; also articles in V.A.C. Gatrell, Bruce Lenman and Geoffrey Parker, eds., *Crime and the Law: A Social History of Crime in Western Europe Since 1500* (London, 1980); Sabean, Blood, 38–41, 47–54;

officials' courts heard defamation cases from their sprawling jurisdictions, but the concern here is with more immediate parochial arbitration.[15] Clerical intervention at that level was limited by the number of priests available; especially in an era when chantries and monasteries milked much clerical talent away from the parishes; by the cost and duration of suits in the church courts; and by the considerable geographical jurisdiction of the officials' courts. The officials who judged quarrellers and defamers were unacquainted with the individuals before them, ill-equipped to follow up on their judgments, and without personal investment in the harmony of a particular parish.[16] For the 1540s only one of the 221 cases initiated in

and Nicole Castan, 'The Arbitration of Disputes under the Ancien Régime' in *Disputes and Settlements*, ed. Bossy, 219–60. *Early Records of the Burgh of Aberdeen, 1317, 1398–1407*, ed. W.C. Dickinson (Edinburgh, 1957), 21, 154, 212, 282; *Extracts from the Council Registers of the Burgh of Aberdeen, 1398–1625*, 2 vols (Aberdeen, 1844–48), 1:331, 352; 'Extracts from the Records of the Burgh of the Canongate' in *Maitland Miscellany*, 2:290–301; and *Extracts from the Records of the Royal Burgh of Stirling*, ed. R. Renwick (Glasgow, 1887), 1:43, 83, reveal more punishment (mostly pillory or jougs) than mediation and settlement by burgh courts and councils, though there are examples of arbitration (e.g. PMAG ms 2/2, it. 35). See also David Maxwell, 'Civil Procedure' and A.M. Duncan, 'The Central Courts before 1532' both in *Introduction to Scottish Legal History*, (Edinburgh, 1958), esp. 414, 416 and 329–39; Peter Gouldesbrough, *Formulary of Old Scots Legal Documents* (Edinburgh, 1985), ch. 4; Brown, *Bloodfeud*, 48–58, 242–46; Wormald, 'Blood Feud', 115–19. Examples of guild mediation can be found in the *Gild Court Book of Dunfermline 1433–1579*, ed. E. Torrie (Edinburgh, 1986) and *The Perth Guildry Book 1542–1601*, ed. Marion Stavert (Edinburgh, 1993). For Scottish episcopal jurisdiction in pre-Reformation slander cases, which often involved mediation of quarrels, S. Ollivant, *The Court of the Official in Pre-Reformation Scotland* (Edinburgh, 1982), Introduction; and at the parish level, McKay, 113. For an English perspective see Catherine Patterson, 'Conflict Resolution and Patronage in Provincial Towns, 1590–1640', *JBS* 37 (1998), 1–25; Ian Archer, *The Pursuit of Stability: Social Relations in Elizabethan London* (Cambridge, 1991); J.A. Sharpe, '"Such Disagreement betwyx Neighbours": Litigation and Human Relations in Early Modern England' in *Disputes and Settlements*, ed. John Bossy (Cambridge, 1983), 167–87.

15. E.g., NAS ms CH5/3/1 (Lothian Official's court), ff. 309, 315, 333, 335; Elizabeth Ewan, 'Many Injurious Words: Defamation and Gender in Late Medieval Scotland' in *Scotland in the Middle Ages: History, Literature and Music*, ed. R. Andrew McDonald (Toronto, 2002). Slander and defamation cases were heard by bishops' officials and commissary courts, the latter into the 1580s. For early examples of parish-level intervention see Edinburgh University Library, Laing mss, Div. iii, no. 322. But defamation cases amounted to a minuscule portion of ecclesiastical court caseloads: Donaldson, *Scottish Church History*, 43–47. Procedures in officials' courts were expensive (McKay, 113), and as in English episcopal and archidiaconal courts the fees went to pay court officials: R.H. Helmholz, 'Harboring Sexual Offenders: Ecclesiastical Courts and Controlling Misbehavior', *JBS* 37 (1998), 258–68, 266.
16. Ian Cowan, *The Parishes of Medieval Scotland* (Edinburgh, 1967); Charles Haws, ed.,

the Lothian official's court is recorded as being submitted to arbiters.[17] And by the time problems came before an episcopal or archidiaconal court they had generally escalated to a degree of seriousness that entailed violence. In pre-Reformation Scotland, moreover, the clergy themselves were all too often participants in feuds and other violence.[18] Finally, the demise of religious guilds at the Reformation eliminated a whole other category of non-secular mediation of quarrels.

Reformed kirk sessions, however, provided a new parochial mechanism for conflict resolution. Their minutes allow us to examine precisely how that mechanism operated in a variety of parishes, and suggest that it was sufficiently effective to offer a partial explanation for the local success of protestantism in Scotland. They make it quite clear that we can no longer regard the Scots disciplinary system in purely negative terms – invasive and repressive, the elders just a meddlesome crew prowling the streets and peering in people's windows to ferret out innocent merrymakers. If that caricature were accurate, the relatively rapid implementation of the system and the high level of popular resort for peacemaking to sessions (by both quarrellers and their neighbours) would present us with a real mystery. Instead, the session minutes show the new structure of parochial government going far beyond overseeing repentance and trying to quell festival, and providing *positive* services to communities in systematically reconciling

Scottish Parish Clergy at the Reformation 1540–1574 (Edinburgh, 1972); Donaldson, *Scottish Church History*, 40–51; Ollivant, ch. 2, and pp. 142–45, 147–48; McKay, 98ff. Cf. Lyndsay's satire of *The Three Estates*, reflecting his own quite negative experience of the court of the official principal (in *The Poetical Works of Sir David Lyndsay of the Mount*). Parochial visitation by rural deans occurred at most annually, and only major cases travelled to the court of the bishop's official: *Statutes of the Scottish Church*, 276. There are examples of officials carrying out visitations, but only annually or at most twice a year. The courts themselves by the sixteenth century rarely moved about. While the officials' courts of Lothian and Dunblane met about the same number of days each year as the Perth session (220 or so, to Perth's 180–200 by the turn of the century), they were dealing with a widely dispersed population many times the size of Perth's, and with more than just the disciplinary cases that made up the bulk of the session's business – e.g., testaments, executry, teinds (Ollivant, 36, 48, 156).

17. Ollivant, 146, though surely more than this were informally arbitrated, leaving no record.

18. For feuding clerks and parsons, see McKay, 94ff. The fourteenth-century St Andrews statutes allowed travelling clerics to go armed with their 'whingers' (long daggers): *Statutes of the Scottish Church*, 70. Perhaps the most notorious example of a priest at the centre of a feud is the bloody affray in Elgin Cathedral in 1555 between William Innes, his thirty-two kinsmen and eight men-at-arms, and the prior of Pluscarden's stepmother's family, the catholic Dunbars, who failed to prevent the prior's murder on the altar steps: Robert Pitcairn, ed., *Ancient Criminal Trials in Scotland*, 3 vols (Edinburgh, 1833) 1:376.

enemies, reducing the violence level and restoring harmony when feud and other violence would otherwise be rife. It did so, moreover, by appropriating and expanding medieval traditions – specifically the guild and familial function of mediation, and the priestly function of formal Lenten reconciliation. As in the case of penitential rites, the elders did not eschew catholic tradition and rituals of reconciliation; they acted again on the general principle that a new theology and service would be more easily swallowed with a sauce of practical tradition.

* * *

Reconciling enemies was high on the kirk's agenda from the earliest stage of the Reformation. The General Assembly in 1581 sent out commissions to 'intervene for reconciling' feuding parties in the west, 'and others falling out in all their quarters, requiring them in the name of God and of the whole kirk to live in unity and peace with others . . . and not to give occasion by their division of slander, and open the mouths of the enemies to burden the Evangel with calumnies.' One of the questions they ordered to be asked at the regular 'trials' of pastors was whether 'he be careful to take all eyelifts and variances that fall out in the congregation'. Presbyters took the question seriously: at the 1583 visitation of Holyroodhouse, they found the minister 'negligent in . . . seeking of reconciliation among persons being at variance'. His apology is telling: he was concerned that reconciliation had actually been taking precedence over punishment of sin, especially in regard to the quarrelling women of the parish 'that by oft reconciling and without fear of punishment . . . were grown the more ready in daily flyting in the gate'. His answer also reflects some confusion about the relationship between the minister and a new parochial institution, the arbitration panel: the minister admitted negligence, but only in situations where he had not been 'chosen to be judge arbitral'.[19]

Holyroodhouse, the parish church of the Canongate, was among those that had 'taken order' soon after founding a session to offer regular arbitration of quarrels before they reached the level of violence by nominating four to six men to sit at least once a week, though sometimes as often as thrice weekly, for 'reconciling all those that they knew was at variance'. The minister instructed the congregation in December of 1565, for instance, that 'if there be any person or persons having any grudge of hatred or malice or any offence in his heart against his brother, that they . . . come on Tuesday in the morning at eight hours to the tollbooth

19. *BUK* 2:539; 3:992; NLS ms Wod. Fol. XLII, ff. 13–13v.

where four of the kirk shall be present to judge the offence, and . . . reconcile the same.'[20] When the visiting superintendent that year asked whether there was dissension in the parish, the elders simply pointed to their arbitration board, charging the assembled parishioners, 'if any [quarreller] has not come to the said four men, let them come on Saturday.' Similarly, in Burntisland 'certain of the elders' comprised a board established to 'travail diligently to reconcile such persons as are at variance'. Their guidelines said they were not to punish, but to draw quarrellers 'with lenience to agree with the [other] party, to the end they may live in peace in all time coming'.[21]

The Canongate parish combined with its permanent board occasional *ad hoc* mediation panels of 'brethren appointed by the kirk as judge arbitral to reconcile brother' as particular quarrels were brought to their attention. Thus, in 1565 the session persuaded James Mader and John Cowper to 'take two equal men to agree them' in their quarrel. They assigned an elder to each, with 'John Brand minister to be ourisman' (overseer and tie-breaker), and the three arbiters quickly settled the quarrel. They ended a dispute over a promise of marriage later the same year when 'both . . . parties referred them to two arbiters, who both being present, took the said matter upon them to discern instantly, the [disputants] John and Helen sworn to stand at their deliverance'.[22] Arbitration of this sort clearly had the advantage of speed.

Other parishes used such *ad hoc* panels for all arbitration not carried out directly by the session itself. In Falkirk, a 1620 action of slander brought by James Connor against John Gray was settled when 'the said parties are both content and consent . . . to submit themselves to the decision and agreement of four honest men to meet thereupon the morn and that they shall stand to the deliverance of the said men every of the said parties oblige themselves thereto under the pain of £10' – a bond to ensure that they would show up for and abide by the arbitration.[23] When two Anstruther elders utterered 'rash and sudden speeches' in 1613, the

20. NLS ms Wod. Fol. XLII, 13v; *Canongate*, 16, 17, 29, 31 (typical orders in the week before communion for the elders 'to reconcile brother with brother if there be any variance').
21. *Canongate*, 32; CH2/523/1, ff. 9, 10.
22. *Canongate*, 31, 25, 29. In another Canongate dispute over a marriage contract, Cristine Weddell having been told by her fiancé that he loved another, she declined to believe it and give him up unless he would repeat before the session 'that his heart was given to any other more than to her'; she was true to her word when he did so (p. 30), apparently believing it impossible for him to lie to the session.
23. CH2/400/1, p. 58. Arbitration by either the whole session or such appointed panels characterised Reformed churches elsewhere, too: e.g., Andrew Pettegree, *Foreign Protestant Communities in Sixteenth-Century London* (Oxford, 1986), 187, 193–97.

session 'desired both parties submit themselves concerning the said matter to the censure of the persons of the session' designated to arbiter, to which 'both parties agreed and submitted themselves and . . . reconciled'.[24] Sessions often allowed the quarrellers themselves to choose arbiters: in 1623 two Kirkcaldy women, 'having complained mutually upon each other, have each one of them chosen two men to agree the matter'; and two men quarrelling about the boundaries of their land went to the kirk rather than to a secular court, 'content to submit the matter . . . to six men, three chosen by every side, with full power to them to cognose in [investigate] the said matter and to decide thereunto.' The parties at odds handed the arbiters' names in to the session for approval, and the disputes were apparently settled straightaway.[25] Sometimes a few elders were designated to go out and find recalcitrant quarrellers to reason with them and 'travail . . . to reconcile' them, or the minister was appointed arbiter.[26] When James Robertson of Perth failed to communicate because 'there stands an jar [disagreement] between him and another person unreconciled', the session sent three elders to 'travail with him to be reconciled to the person with whom he is at variance', and in parishes across the country the minister (generally as ourisman) and small groups of elders regularly arbitrated quarrels.[27]

Most often, sessions functioned *per se* as arbiters. This was true not only for small parishes like Monifieth in Angus or Highland parishes like Inveravon, but also for large burgh parishes like Perth. There, in 1585, 'Robert Blakett and his faction were agreed by the minister and elders with Patrick Kay and his party', the two sides voluntarily bound 'to the decision of the minister and elders'; and in 1624 two groups of women in Perth agreed that their quarrel should be 'referred . . . to the arbitriment of the session'.[28] The Kinconquhar session turned noun to verb and

24. SAU CH2/624/2, p. 137.
25. CH2/636/34, ff. 51v, 38. Burntisland followed suit, e.g., CH2/523/1, f. 24.
26. *Canongate*, 16 (1565); CH2/521/7, p. 33 (a marital quarrel settled by the minister alone). In 1618, both Perth ministers, John Malcolm and John Guthry, arbitrated a dispute between a townswoman and the laird James Ross regarding a debt owed to her late husband: CH2/299/2, pp. 3–5, 20–22, 24–25, 38.
27. CH2/521/8/1, f. 95 (the Perth elders took the same action with John Lamb at the next meeting); CH2/326/1 (Scoonie), pp. 46–47; CH2/523/1 (Burntisland), ff. 14, 16, 24, 32v, 37v; CH2/424/1 (Dalkeith), f. 2v; AAC CH2/809/1 (Monkton), f. 10; AAC CH2/751/1 (Ayr), ff. 5, 7v; CH2/521/1, f. 21v; CH2/521/7, p. 476.
28. New Register House, Edinburgh, ms OPR 310/1, ff. 50v, 51v, 57v; CH2/191/1, f. 40v; CH2/521/1, ff. 21, 116; CH2/521/7, pp. 291, 510–11 (plaintiffs in this slander case, asked by the elders 'what amends they would have', only wished for the session 'amiably to reconcile them together'); CH2/521/8/1, f. 49v; CH2/521/8/2, f. 200v. For other examples of arbitration by full session, see CH2/621/1 (North Leith), pp.

'friended' those at odds'.[29] Resolution often came only 'after long reasoning', but with threats of punishment for the contumacious.[30] On rare occasions, a question involving slander had to be arbitrated with the aid of expert witnesses, as when the Perth session brought in two surgeons to decide whether bones buried in the laird of Tirsappie's kale yard were those of a bastard child killed by John Merton's daughter.[31] In all these arbitration modes, the elders were following a long-standing tradition of magnate kin, parliament and Privy Council in addressing feud or a quarrel that might engender feud at a much higher level.[32] The differences were that their arbitration was local and immediate, designed to forestall violence by addressing verbal dispute, and underpinned by a religious apologetic and an ecclesiastical enforcement mechanism.[33] The stated aim of the elders/arbiters was to get people to 'live together as becomes Christian neighbours', for reconciliation to redound 'to God's glory'.[34]

★ ★ ★

Arbitration either by an established panel or by the session itself occurred most regularly when quarrels were brought to the kirk's attention by flyting or by slander. Both have been seen as indicators of the disorderliness of early modern Scottish society. The kirk session minutes, however, suggest the opposite – that both functioned effectively as formal mechanisms to initiate mediation, to settle the quarrel rather than continue the disorder.

'Flyting', a term almost never found in early modern England, is sometimes simply translated as 'scolding', but in the Scots context it seems to

360–63, CH2/264/1 (Menmuir), f. 10v; CH2/442/74 (Kirkwall), ff. 18v, 32, 47v; CH2/699/1 (Longside), f. 1; AAC CH2/751/1 (Ayr), f. 5; CH2/77/1 (Culross), f. 4 (my fol.); CH2/716/1 (South Leith), f. 20 (a mediated land dispute); NAS ms RH2/1/35 (Edinburgh), f. 58v.

29. CH2/210/1, f. 2v.
30. CH2/326/1, p. 46; *Canongate*, 24–25.
31. CH2/521/8/1, p. 145. The slanderers of the girl were punished and Merton satisfied when the bones were found to be those of a twelve-year-old.
32. E.g., *APS* 3:360–62; 5:600 (1639); Brown, *Bloodfeud*, 242ff. It is worth noting that in some parishes, kin and kirk arbitration overlapped, as a glance at the numbers of Livingstones on the Falkirk session or Frasers on the Fraserburgh session suggests.
33. Of course, presbyteries also functioned as mediators, generally by designating a few ministers to arbitrate a particular quarrel: e.g., CH2/299/1, pp. 94–95 (a presbyter to 'ride to Redgorton to Harry Schaw's to agree him and . . . William Young'); or p. 317 (three brethren settling a parochial dispute over seating in the kirk); or CH2/185/1, ff. 3–3v (Haddington brethren mediating a lairds' feud); or CH2/294/1, ff. 6v, 8v–9v.
34. CH2/1142/1, f. 78; CH2/400/1, pp. 44, 31 (to act 'as becomes Christians'); cf. Menmuir's 'for keeping of good neighbourhood', CH2/264/1, f. 10v.

have been something rather more distinctive than our usual notion of scolding.[35] Certainly it brought a very distinctive response from the kirk. In general, flyting was mutual – with epithets exchanged on both sides; it was public, generally conducted in the street; and its language was formulaic and colourful – so much so that, unlike the scolding and defamation cases that dominated English church court agendas in the same period, it had excited the attention and imitation of the Scots makars (poets) from at least the fifteenth century. In Dunbar's 'Flyting of Dunbar and Kennedie' or Lyndsay's 'The Flyting of Montgomerie and Polwart' or Stewart's 'Flyting betuix the Soutar and the Tailyeour', the 'art' of flyting reached new heights, and made it into print.[36] But the makars' starting place, the actual flyting of the streets, had another distinctive feature, visible in the minutes of the kirk sessions after the Reformation: it constituted the first step of a recognised mechanism for conflict resolution at the local level. Dunbar and Kennedie did 'rais the Feynd with flytting', and modern literary scholars have called it 'an act of revolt, primitive and unashamed, against all socially-imposed restraint'; however, its real intent was the opposite – to force resolution by effectively summoning in the neighbourhood. When rancour is expressed in what amounts to a public ritual, the performance functions both as entertainment and as a plea to the neighbourhood for mediation.[37] Flyting in the context of readily available local arbitration serves as a means of avoiding feud.

35. The Aberdeen session distinguished between 'common skoldis' and 'flyttaris': CH2/448/1, p. 7. One of the rare uses in sixteenth-century English literature is in *The Gosynhyll Flyting*, a misogynistic rhymed comedy by Edward Gosynhill against 'femynye' whose first instalment, the *Schole House*, was published first in London in 1541. It borrows rather heavily from the *Fyftene Joyes of Maryage* of Antoine de la Sale (London, 1509) and the *A.C. Mery Talys* (anon., 1526). The first diatribe was answered by William Middleton as *The Prayse of All Women* (London, 1542); a second response appeared in the same year as *A Dyalogue Defensyve for Women*, attributed to Robert Vaughan. I am grateful to Leah Marcus for these references.

36. Priscilla Bawcutt, *Dunbar the Makar* (Oxford, 1992), 220–56, and 'The Art of Flyting', *Scottish Literary Journal* 10 (1983), 5–24; D. Gray, 'Rough Music: Some Early Invectives and Flytings', *Yearbook of English Studies* 14 (1984), 21–43. The *OED* defines flyting (from OE *flitan*, to quarrel) as 'a kind of contest practised by the Scottish poets of the sixteenth century, in which two persons assailed each other alternately with tirades of abusive verse.' Leah Leneman finds that formulaic flyting disappears from Scotland in the eighteenth century (private communication, July 1999).

37. Kurt Wittig, *The Scottish Tradition in Literature* (Edinburgh, 1958), cited approvingly by Kenneth Simpson, 'The Legacy of Flyting', *Studies in Scottish Literature: The Language and Literature of Early Scotland* 26 (1991), 503–14. Also useful on flyting is R.J. Lyall, 'Complaint, Satire and Invective in Middle Scots Literature' in *Church, Politics and Society: Scotland 1408–1929*, ed. N. MacDougall (Edinburgh, 1983), 44–63. Flyting bears some affinity in its ends to the Eskimo song-contests discussed by Gluckman, *Politics, Law and Ritual*, 303–14.

The publicity of flyting inevitably brought intervention by neighbours. It was staged in the streets, often in the calsey (high street), or at the booth door of a mercantile participant, or even in the kirk itself, during a sermon or even communion – the most public of any site and time.[38] When the records indicate how cases of street flyting came to the session's attention, the agency of neighbours is clear. It was they who 'raised the bruit', for instance, of Bessie Glass's 'skoffrie' of George Ruthven in Perth in 1592, 'greatly cried out against by the whole godly neighbours of this town'.[39] They could hardly have ignored it, given its public setting. When two Dundonald men 'cast words with each other', the bystanders brought them to the session and there 'verified in their faces that they would have been at the striking of each other unless they had been held', and in Fraserburgh it was six neighbours of George Paterson who in 1614 hauled him before the session for 'blaspheming' a woman.[40] Guidelines formally adopted by the Ayr session in 1605 specified that 'grossness and slander' about one's neighbours should be handled privately unless it had been 'revealed publicly either upon the High Street or before any witnesses except elders and deacons'; then it became a matter for the session to settle.[41] Most obvious to the 'whole neighbourhood' were the very numerous cases of flytings in the kirk in nearly every parish. It is simply not credible that quarrellers would have brought their arguments to such public view if they did not wish them to be brought to arbitration.[42]

The frequency with which clerks recorded the precise language of flyters offers another clue to flyting's importance in signalling the readiness of the quarrellers for resolution by outside mediators. The language is strikingly formulaic, both in substance and in structure. As in the works of the makars, street flyting abounds with demeaning references to physical appearance and to clan and ancestry, especially charges that one's forebears

38. CH2/359/1, ff. 1, 3 (flyting 'on the High Gate' with a large audience, 1615); CH2/383/1, f. 6v (1639 – flyting in church 'in time of divine service'); CH2/377/1, ff. 14, 66, 71v (scolding and 'riotous behaviour in the kirkyard on the sabbath', 1628), 72v, 89v (mutual slander during communion!); CH2/400/1, p. 56 (cordiners flyting on the High Street of Stirling), 131 (the calsey again), or 165 (a quarrel over seating in the kirk); CH2/521/7, f. 297; CH2/1142/1, f. 99 ('perturbing of the kirk in time of divine service' by 'railing against the minister' – a case referred to presbytery); *Dundonald*, 2; CH1/1173/1 (Kelso), f. 3.
39. CH2/521/2, f. 59v. CH2/400/1, p. 191 is similar.
40. *Dundonald*, 64–65; CH2/1142/1, f. 28v; CH2/521/8/1, f. 86v.
41. *Extracts from the Kirk Session Book of John Welch, 1604–1605*, ed. A. MacKenzie (Ayr, 1966), 50, including 'any rhyme or cokalane, . . . cartils and rhymes' posted against persons in the community as 'flyting'.
42. E.g., CH2/1142, f. 22; CH2/521/7, pp. 224, 304; CH2/521/8/1, ff. 175v, 176. In Yester, Bessie Miller 'flait with another honest man and said she cared not though the minister were standing by' (CH2/377/1, f. 97v, 1633).

or kin were immoral, diseased or criminal – a particularly powerful insult in a society where kin was even more important than rank or social standing.[43] Thus a Dundonald flyter flung at her enemy the charge that 'one of her forebears was burnt', presumably as a witch; an Aberdeen stabler called a maltman 'hanged man's get [progeny], and his father was hanged on an hill'; and Falkirk flyters routinely insulted their opponents' kin as 'gangorie' (afflicted with venereal diseases) or thieves.[44] One thinks of Kennedy charging Dunbar's forebears, 'generit betuix ane scho beir and a deill' (begotten of a she-bear and a devil), with treason (ll. 259, 307). Rude comments about physical deformity are conjoined with diabolical implications, as when Agnes Watson of Falkirk called Jonet Hunter 'thief, devil, lukinbrowit witch', or Agnes Williamson of Burntisland called Margaret Rowane 'foul slavering black buck-toothed harlot'.[45] Comparison with animals, real and mythical, abound in the streets as in the poets: Isobel Gib of Ellon called her enemy 'an drunken sow'; Elspeth Hutton called Isobel Garner 'firey dragon, . . . yellow gelding', Garner's response adding the diabolical element to her animals with 'old imp, fashioned harlot, serpent whom the devil had begotten' (though the more pedestrian 'drunken sow' remained the odds-on favourite animal reference).[46] The scatological

43. On the centrality of kin, Wormald, *Lords and Men*, 76–77, noting that surname was as important in the Lowlands as clan in the Highlands: this was not a peculiarly Gaelic phenomenon. Among many such references in Dunbar's 'Flyting of Dunbar and Kennedie', see ll. 257–64, 311–17: *Poems of William Dunbar*, 1:208–10.
44. *Dundonald*, 411; CH2/448/2, p. 335; CH2/400/1, pp. 93, 133. When it was 'verified to the [Aberdeen] session that' the maltman's father 'died in his bed and was honestly buried as an true honest poor man', the stabler had to repent publicly. See also SAU CH2/624/2, pp. 134, 111 (a woman called 'ill-gotten bitch' then calling her foe 'vagabond harlot, her mother a gyre carling, her brother lousy tailor'); CH2/523/1, f. 21; CH2/276/1, f. 12.
45. CH2/400/1, p. 38, cf. 294; CH2/523/1, f. 17v. 'Lukinfuttit' in *DOST* is 'webbed-footed'; the unfortunate Jonet Hunter seems to have had conjoined eyebrows, or perhaps a lowered brow. The elders made Agnes Watson apologise. In the Burntisland flyting the 'buck-toothed harlot' language is followed by hints as to the origin of the quarrel in inopportune placement of a haystack, perhaps on the wrong side of a boundary: Agnes Williamson continued her railing against Margaret Rowan, 'the devil blow thee in the air that built that straw stack', adding, 'if her goodman were dead she would not have so much as to piss over' and 'that he lived an uneasy life through her misbehaviour and that she was come of hinds'.
46. CH2/147/1, f. 2v; CH2/523/1, ff. 10, 17–17v, cf. CH2/1173/1 (Kelso), f. 1; and CH2/442/74, f. 26v. The wolf provided another frequently used animal label, as when a North Leith elder in 1605 complained that Henry Ogill had called him 'old false wolf carl' (CH2/621/1, p. 361) in a quarrel apparently springing from resentment of the elder's brother Patrick Scot as an exploitative landlord who 'had wracked all the poor ones on this side of the bridge'. In the Burntisland case, Garner and her ally Jonet Orrok added to their serpent label for Hutton 'that they should cut out her

element in the poets also derives from the streets: an Anstruther woman charged that her foe spent his time 'ly[ing] in his bed farting, breeding wiles and spending other men's women'; a Kirkoswald woman called her enemy a 'piss-bed'; and a Perth skinner railed publicly against the elders as 'false lownes [rascals], false knaves, a turd for you all'.[47] And again in both, flyters describe enemies as afflicted with particularly revolting diseases. A Smallburne webster complained that Agnes Mingell had called him 'evil-faced thief' and his wife 'gangorie thief . . . rotten and consumed with the gangore', and in Anstruther Wester Issobel Sibbald called John Thomson 'gangorie and crooked carl' and his daughter 'gangorie harlot who has the gangore dropping down her legs'.[48] One is again reminded of Dunbar, railing at 'cuntbittin crawdoun [poxed and craven] Kennedy' (l. 50). If the opponent were not tarred with criminal behaviour like thievery or witchcraft, or with disease, then idle occupation or duplicity for profit was usual – sorners, songsters, fiddlers, landlowpers and limmers providing the usual array, just as Dunbar's Kennedy delights in telling the 'lunatike, lymare, luschbald' to 'tak the a fidill or a floyte, and geste' (ll. 501, 507).[49]

The language of flyting is usually gender-specific, with women called harlots and witches, men thieves and mensworn (perjured); however, there are exceptions, as when a Falkirk man called another a harlot, or a

tongue and that they would her tongue were in their tails'. Two elders were charged to reconcile these flyters. Animal and diabolical references were often combined, as in 'witch bird' (CH2/523/1, f. 24).

47. SAU CH2/624/2, p. 144 (1614); AAC CH2/562/1, f. 34v; CH2/521/8/1, ff. 25–25v (before Henderson's booth), cf. f. 49v.

48. CH2/400/1, p. 80; SAU CH2/624/2, p. 134. Mingell had earlier (p. 81) complained successfully against the webster's wife for slandering her, 'saying she brake house and stall open and pulled stakes and . . . lay with sundry househusbands and three brothers'; the webster failed to prove his counter-charge. An Ayr woman called her enemy a 'glengorie hellion and deboshed thief' (AAC CH2/751/1, f. 131v). Other flytings involving venereal disease include SAU CH2/819/1, f. 27; *Canongate*, 64; CH2/276/1, f. 1v; AAC CH2/751/1, f. 131v. Leprosy is the other disease often included in flyting – e.g., CH2/523/1, f. 17 ('leper-faced harlot').

49. Cf. Dunbar, ll. 49, 63, 96, 120 – all references to idle entertainers, or ll. 187, 174–76 ('lyk to ane stark theif glowrand in an tedder') – examples of criminal labels. Sorning is begging with menace, landlowpers are vagabonds, limmers are rogues (*DOST*). Flytings charging thievery include CH2/191/1, ff. 6v, 13v; CH2/442/74, ff. 29v, 50; CH2/338/1, ff. 17v, 30v, 33; AAC CH2/529/1, f. 12; CH2/400/1, pp. 279, 294, 297, 325; CH2/276/1, f. 15 ('common thief and cornstealler'); AAC CH2/751/1, ff. 135, 136v. Among flytings that charge witchcraft, CH2/283/1, f. 17; CH2/400/1, p. 288 (a woman taunted for going 'withershins [backwards, or in a counter-clockwise circle] around her land' to secure her husband's health); CH2/448/2, pp. 90, 174–75; CH2/521/2, ff. 32v–33; CH2/390/1, f. 48; AAC CH2/529/1, ff. 18, 35. The combination 'thief witch' is also frequent: SAU CH2/150/1, f. 6v; CH2/264/1, f. 4v.

Kirkoswald woman attributed magical healing to a man.[50] There are also communities like Falkirk where women were actually rather more frequently insulted as thieves than men were, or like Kirkcaldy, where the figures are about equal.[51] And the combination 'thief and whore' was routinely applied to both sexes in a variety of parishes, both before and after the Reformation.[52]

Session minutes also reveal the highly formulaic structure of the language of flyting. Flyters generally flung insults in pairs or triads – 'theif and loun' or 'drunken jade carling' recurring plentifully in the Falkirk minutes; 'loun queane', 'witch carling' and 'evilfaced mensworne dog' in Kirkcaldy; 'bitch carling' and 'barren bitch' in Stow.[53] Pairs tended to be answered in pairs: when Elspeth Hutcheson of Falkirk called Jonnet Nore 'witch carling', Jonnet came back with 'thief huir'. And if one item in a pair is modified, the other also tends to be – 'common thief and gloming limb', for instance, or 'false harlot, poor queane'.[54] Frequent alliteration underlines the formulaic nature of flyting – 'drunken dog', 'doubly dissaving', 'blind bowther', 'burnt bitch', 'lipper loun', 'landlowper and landseller' occur among many other examples. Again, Dunbar comes to mind, with his 'skaldit [scabby] skaitbird and commoun skamelar [sponger]' (l. 37) or 'revin raggit ruke . . . scarth fra scorpione, scaldit in scurrilitie'

50. CH2/400/1, p. 43, cf. pp. 19, 26, 27, 63, 64, 80, 95, 124, 132, 160, 163, 165, 175; AAC CH2/529/1, ff. 18, 35. See also CH2/1142/1, ff. 22, 23v, 29, 77v, 79, 96; CH2/636/34, ff. 16–16v; CH2/326/1, p. 45.

51. CH2/400/1, pp. 28, 38, 40, 65, 80, 83, 124, 152, 157, 161, 176. In the four-year period sampled for Falkirk, August 1617–21, of 26 charges of thievery, 14 were brought against women, 12 against men. Of 7 charges of harlotry or sexual immorality, 5 targeted women, 2 men (e.g., p. 43). Tyninghame is another parish where more women than men are called thief: CH2/359/1, e.g., ff. 2v, 3. See also SAU CH2/624/2, pp. 111, 117, 118, 148, 169, 192 for women called thieves, SAU CH2/624/3, p. 19 for a man called a harlot. The Kirkcaldy session dealt with 6 cases of flyters calling their enemies thieves between 1615 and 1627, three each for men and women. The numbers are too small for one to make much of this, but they do reinforce the impression that gender specificity is by no means ubiquitous for this category. On the other hand, all the Kirkcaldy charges of witchcraft or whoredom were levelled at women (CH2/636/34, ff. 7–7v, 10–11v, 14v, 16–17v, 32v, 66, 68v, 80–84v, 90).

52. E.g., CH2/84/28, f. 30v (of a man in Dalkeith); CH2/400/1, pp. 28, 80, 161, 164 (of women in Falkirk), p. 98 (of a Falkirk man); *Dundonald*, 70; or CH 2/326/1, p. 39 (a Scoonie woman slandered as 'harlot and thief'); *Canongate*, 31; CH2/77/1, ff. 10v–11. For pre-Reformation examples, NAS ms CH5/3/1, ff. 324, 333.

53. Among many examples, CH2/400/1, pp. 96, 97; CH2/636/34, ff. 14v, 72, 80; CH2/338/1, f. 24; *Dundonald*, 296; CH2/523/1, ff. 10, 18, 28v; CH2/276/1, ff. 12, 16.

54. CH2/400/1, pp. 163–64, 51; CH2/326/1, p. 45.

(ll. 57–58).[55] Often the first item in a pair or list is expanded on in succeeding items – 'thief and a drawer of stakes', or 'thief and shoestealler'. A particular charge was often answered with the same charge returned in slightly altered language – so in Fraserburgh the insult 'common thief' brought a counter charge of 'stealer of gear'.[56] Repetition of words could serve to expand one insult into another in a list, as when Alexander Sadler of Aberdeen called William Goldsmith 'thief, thief's geitt, and witch's geitt', or when a Falkirk flyter called her enemy 'bleckint jade, landlowper, bleckint harlot, achieving a sort of bookend effect.[57] And flyters often employed puns, as when the Aberdeen skipper James Mar called the merchant Andrew Paul 'common witch and cum [born] of witches'. Finally, flyting often entailed deliberate redundancy in modifiers (like 'false liar') and repetition and restatement of themes in both pairs and lists (like 'false mensworne thief').[58] Literary scholars have commented on the poets' use of such devices for dramatic effect; in post-Reformation parishes, the drama in the streets effectively enlisted the community in the play and carried it to the kirk's stage for the next act.[59]

Sessions intervened quickly, in part because they were quite aware that verbal flyting and slander could lead to physical violence. The Aberdeen elders in 1562 prefaced their standard penalties for slander with the remark that murder originates in 'injurious and evil speech' and resolved to intervene when anyone 'injures and mispersons their neighbour with infamous and hateful words' so that 'the occasion of all strife and contention whereof slaughter and bloodshedding comes may be removed and avoided'. Experience bore out the principle: by 1592, the Anstruther Wester elders had confronted so many brawlers 'with drawn whingers' and flyters who 'put hands each one in another' that they promulgated an 'act anent injurious language thereby making provocation to strikes'. Their experience

55. CH2/400/1, pp. 114, 79, 118, 160; SAU CH2/624/2, p. 194, SAU CH2/624/3, p. 19; *Dundonald*, 296; CH2/621/1, p. 361; CH2/327/1, f. 20. Again, this phenomenon is traditional: NAS ms CH5/3/1, f. 309 records an earlier sixteenth-century example, 'crukyt carl'; Bawcutt, *Dunbar*, 220–56, and 'The Art of Flyting', 5–24.

56. CH2/400/1, pp. 11, 56; cf. *Dundonald*, 278–79, 292. CH2/1142/1, p. 99.

57. CH2/448/2, p. 219 (two bedesmen of St Thomas' Hospital); CH2/400/1, p. 175, cf. p. 144, a webster calling Cirstiane Lathangie 'witch carling and jade carling', or CH2/1173/1, f. 1. CH2/523/1, f. 13 records another 'bookend': 'thief, whore, and receiver of her gear'.

58. CH2/448/2, p. 249 (flyting at Paul's booth door, 1607); CH2/400/1, pp. 118, 132.

59. Bawcutt, *Dunbar*, 235–39, and 'A Miniature Anglo-Scottish Flyting', *Notes and Queries* 233 (1988), 441–44, notes some similarities to English and Latin invective traditions of the fourteenth and fifteenth centuries but remarks that Gaelic antecedents or parallels are absent; flyting was 'a striking phenomenon of Lowland Scots' (*Dunbar*, 236).

was echoed in parishes from Fife to the Highlands where 'ill words' led quickly to blows.[60] Sessions imposed stricter penalties when flyting entailed verbal threat of violence, like Margaret Murheid's public prayer that George Colby 'might be dung as small as meal', but too often it was the violence that followed flyting that brought kirk mediation into play.[61] The Fraserburgh session in 1613 intervened when William Towney's flyting with Janet Finley entailed his 'striking her, and that upon the sabbath day'; and two flyting bedesmen complained to the Aberdeen session of 'mutual injury by word and deed', including 'breaking of . . . William Goldsmith's head with a cane and wounding [him] therewith, riving of the hair of his beard' (to which Goldsmith responded in kind). When John Dickie of Corraith shouted at Simon Wallace, 'Away, false loun', Wallace raised his walking stick, Dickie parried with his sword hilt, Wallace's sons then entered the fray 'with drawn swords', and Dickie's 'complices' sprang to his defence, bringing flyting quickly to the level of violent feud – all in the kirkyard on a preaching day.[62] But sessions naturally preferred a more timely intervention to avoid such an outcome. Thus, when the Yester elders managed to reconcile Katherine Warnock and Robert Woundram after they had flyted during a 1631 communion service, they recorded their satisfaction that they had intervened 'to prevent greater harm to them both which might ensue thereupon'.[63]

Sometimes sessions managed to forestall even the flyting stage of a quarrel by taking preventive action when a dispute threatened to erupt. In 1635 Perth, much troubled by quarrels over seating in the kirk, was 'informed that Beatrix and Marry Rynds *intend* to make interruption to Nanse Clark, . . . their father's [new] wife, to sit in that part of the kirk where their late mother sat; therefore, for staying of that *intended* perturbation', the session appointed two elders to 'travail with the said Beatrix and Mary Rynds and their husbands to *dissuade* them from their said intention'. This event occurred in the wake of a violent incident three weeks earlier when two women quarrelling over placement of their stools in the kirk drew weapons, 'to the effusion of . . . blood'.[64] But the violent

60. CH2/448/1, p. 5; SAU CH2/624/2, p. 5, cf. 7, 11, 139; SAU CH2/1056/1, f. 9v; CH2/523/1, ff. 11, 13, 23, 47v; AAC CH2/751/1, f. 125v; *Dundonald*, 60, CH2/191/1, f. 52; CH2/276/1, f. 4; *Canongate*, 31, among many other examples.
61. CH2/400/1, pp. 50, 78. See also CH2/326/1, p. 36; CH2/1142/1, ff. 99v–100v; *Dundonald*, 2, 20, 207.
62. CH2/1142/1, f. 21; CH2/448/2, 12 October 1606; *Dundonald*, 20–21 (1602), cf. 59, William Wilson striking his enemy 'because he gave him ill words'. See also CH2/4/1, f. 27; CH2/326/1, p. 45; CH2/521/2, f. 84v.
63. CH2/377/1, ff. 89v–90.
64. CH2/521/8/2, ff. 169v, 166.

potential of the disgruntled stepdaughters was quelled by the session's intervention: we hear no more from the sisters. In an interesting Falkirk case, the session in 1621 dissolved a marriage contract but made the woman agree that she would 'at no time hereafter curse nor ban' her erstwhile fiancé 'nor no other woman he shall please to marry, but that she shall carry herself discreetly after a Christian and godly manner to him.' Here a potential stalker is forestalled.[65]

Sessions were particularly intent on mediating domestic conflict before violence ensued between parents and children, siblings or spouses.[66] In the little parish of Lasswade, for instance, they denounced a couple for open 'scolding and flyting', it being a particularly 'abominable thing to have such strife between honest married persons'; in a less public case they sent two elders to 'go and agree' a couple at odds that the session might not 'be any more troubled with them hereafter'.[67] The Dundonald elders in 1604 seized the opportunity when a woman was summoned for absence from church also 'to take up the debate between her husband and her and to settle them by the sight of honest men that they had chosen to that effect'. In Kelso, the session itself settled a quarrel between James Davidson and his two sisters, who had 'abus[ed] him with injurious words'.[68] In cases of domestic discord, sessions did not always uphold the hierarchy of parents over children or husbands over wives: investigating Margaret Cunningham's flyting 'betwixt her daughter and her', for instance, the Dundonald elders took into account that the mother was a 'common blasphemer', had cursed her daughter 'immediately after the communion', and that she had called one of the witnesses of the quarrel 'mensworn thief'. Identifying her as the problem, they dismissed the daughter but required the mother to stand for an hour on Sunday afternoon in the jougs in linen sheets and then declare her repentance. Peace

65. CH2/400/1, p. 78. For efforts to deal with actual stalkers, see chapter 6, below.
66. I take exception to Brown's assertion that 'in Scotland very little is known about violence in the home during the early modern period' because 'church court records show very little interest in domestic violence' (*Bloodfeud*, p. 17). Elders and ministers were in fact quite concerned about the problem, as the following chapter demonstrates in detail.
67. CH2/471/1, ff. 6, 12. In the former case, complicated by drunkenness as well as sabbath breach, the couple had to 'sit on the seat of repentance and make open confession of their fault before the congregation and pay 10s between them'. In the latter case, there is actually no earlier mention of the couple in the session minutes, suggesting the relative privacy of the quarrel and the elders' disinclination to bring to formal action anything that could be settled quietly. This also suggests that the cases reported in the minutes represent only the tip of the iceberg when it comes to kirk mediation of quarrels.
68. *Dundonald*, 65; CH2/1173/1, f. 1v.

was in this case more important than traditional hierarchy. In domestic conflicts as in any other, sessions identified 'flyting and fighting' as different offences and attempted to intervene quickly to prevent the former turning into the latter. In the 1593 case of Janet Dick of Perth, they intervened too late and had to punish her for 'flyting . . . especially with her husband, and . . . putting her hand on her husband to strike and ding him'.[69] But there are far more examples of timely intervention and 'travailing with' husbands and wives, parents and children, and siblings.[70]

Preventing violence was not the only end that could be accomplished by using the display of flyting to initiate arbitration. Women in particular seem also to have used it as a device to protect their sexual reputations and to forestall more serious criminal prosecution. Taking a quarrel to the session could produce the quick and early intervention that could preserve a woman from the much more dangerous charge of witchcraft or sexual offence. It had a preventive function in serving to nip in the bud irreparable damage to reputation or fatal pursuit for sorcery. A 1622 Falkirk incident illustrates the point.

Cirstiane Watson, wife of James Packok, a dirkmaker, first appeared before the Falkirk session in October of that year as the plaintiff in a slander case against John Dun, the kirk officer, who had apparently regaled his friends with a scurrilous story featuring Watson ruining the ale in Thomas Acton's pub. The story goes that when Dun and a large group of men and women were drinking there, Watson came to the door to ask to borrow some 'quickening' or wort, which Acton's wife, Cirstiane White, agreed to give her. The two went to the brewhouse, where the goodwife sought out her yeast mixture; when her back was turned, Watson 'took a leadgallon [container] which was standing by her and pissed in it and thereafter cast it in a wort stand or tub with small drink being in it'. The goodwife subsequently served the ale to the drinkers, to decidedly poor reviews. Dun insisted that he had actually witnessed the contamination of the ale before he reported it to the others.[71]

Now, as other entries in the session book make clear, Watson already had a local reputation for being a witch, capable of bringing on and healing illnesses and foretelling (and perhaps causing) accidents.[72] She had

69. *Dundonald*, 333–35; CH2/521/2, f. 84v. Lay/clerical hierarchy was also laid aside in cases of slander, as when the minister of Temple had to repent publicly for it: CH2/424/1, f. 13v.
70. For further treatment of domestic violence, see chapter 6, below. Among many other examples of domestic arbitration, see CH2/521/7, pp. 33, 76, 311; CH2/521/8/1, p. 53; CH2/621/1, p. 360; CH2/523/1, f. 10v.
71. CH2/400/1, p. 103.
72. CH2/400/1, pp. 105–08, 111–14.

to be careful lest her tenuous hold on respectability be lost, with potentially fatal consequences. Dun's attempt at a joke gave her the opportunity. If, as she anticipated, the session determined that Dun had unjustly defamed her, they would in the process provide for her a redefined identity as innocent victim of her neighbour's malice. Her darker reputation would be set in the context of the sort of village quarrel in which the epithet 'witch' was routinely flung about without anyone taking it seriously. If she could get the session to exonerate her in a clearly frivolous case, she would stand a much better chance in future when her enemies brought serious charges against her.

The session did indeed find Dun's story not credible. Perhaps they thought it odd that he had reported Watson's offence to his friends *after* they had drunk the contaminated brew! The elders pressed him relentlessly until he finally admitted that 'he saw her not do it' and that his story was a 'manifest lie made and forged by him against her'. They removed him from office, fined him and demanded public repentance in sackcloth – reducing him to a position much inferior to that of his poorer and female victim.[73] The very public outworking of the session's ruling effectively redefined Watson's character before the whole community. Reducing Dun's status elevated hers; condemning him labelled her the innocent.

When later in the month Watson found herself facing other enemies who charged her with witchcraft, she was in an excellent position to counter-sue with a complaint of slander against her accusers. Her suit took advantage both of the session's earlier exoneration of her character and of its labelling of her enemies on that occasion as ill-affected persons. The charge of witchcraft was brought by Margaret Davison, a servant, and Jonnet Buchanan, who happened to owe Watson payment for fourteen pints of ale. Buchanan, a contentious person convicted earlier of slander against an elder, William Livingston, seems to have been rather perversely motivated to bring the charge by an act of generosity on Watson's part: after Buchanan had repeatedly ignored her creditor's summons to her house to settle the debt she owed, Watson deduced that Buchanan must

73. CH2/400/1, pp. 103–04. They restored Dun to his office later in the year, but 1623 saw him 'accused for his filthy drunkenness and companying with such persons as is scandalous'. The elders fined and threatened to deprive him again, but half-heartedly, since they apparently had difficulty retaining an officer with their stingy salary scale (p. 114, Dun's 1623 efforts to negotiate a raise; the reader James Jonston also complained of the session's meanness, p. 112). Dun was only permanently removed in 1625, for 'drunkenness and evil disposition, . . . [and] the filthy scandal and bruit of adultery' – all despite 'sundry action of the session made for terrification of him and restraining of his lewdness' (p. 142).

be in dire straits and sent her a gift of 3s. Buchanan and her husband, David Livingstone, either thought the money cursed or found the gift an offence to his pride; Livingstone burned the purse in which it had been sent and returned the 3s and the price of the ale. Accepting charity from Watson may well have threatened their own place in the community's hierarchy. When Buchanan subsequently fell ill with a fever, she assumed the worst and asked Watson to come to her and lift the curse – yet another device to bring Watson's character into question. Watson sensibly refused, suggesting to Buchanan that she had brought the illness on herself by procuring an abortion. She asked 'if she had parted with the bairn she was with'; here we have the counter-charge usual in flyting. Watson did, however, offer a recipe for hot spiced wine; when Buchanan recovered she insisted that the drink was a potion and that it was witchcraft that had worked in her favour.

Watson's offence against Margaret Davison was a similarly misconstrued or perhaps resented act of generosity: Davison's request for a cure for her own illness (made at her mother's urging, based presumably on Watson's old reputation as a magical healer) brought from Watson the offer of a sack of grain, which Davison chose to interpret as bewitched. Watson was handicapped both by her old identity as a healer, and by the fact that she occasionally behaved oddly, or perhaps insultingly – failing to speak when greeted on the high street by Buchanan, for instance. The point to stress here is that she believed that she could have recourse to the session to resolve the neighbourhood disputes that carried such potential danger for her.[74] As it happens, the session decided that the seriousness of the charges warranted referral to the presbytery of Linlithgow, where Watson appeared on 15 January 1623, apparently undismayed. She chose to use the same aggressive method that had brought the initial intervention of the session and brought counter-charges against both of her enemies, calling Buchanan 'an infamous profane and ungodly person who had been brought up and haunted among witches' and Davison 'infamous and godless' and a fornicator who had 'passed to her mother's house and parted with a bairne'.[75]

The presbytery would have nothing to do with the case and determined that the session could very well handle what had now become something like a case of flyting, with the usual *pro forma* charges of witchcraft and bastard-bearing. Back in Falkirk, Watson collected an impressive

74. CH2/400/1, pp. 107–08, 111. Buchanan owed money to others in the community as well. She may also have resented that a loan of quickening from Watson on an earlier occasion proved defective when she tried to brew her ale (110–11).

75. CH2/400/1, pp. 112–13.

array of thirteen witnesses who 'deponed all in one voice that they knew nothing to her but honesty'; in the face of only one counter-witness, a friend of Buchanan's who thought that Watson had predicted his broken leg, Watson's case was made. The elders told Buchanan that if she really wanted to pursue a witchcraft charge, she should do so in the lord's court, and that if she declined to do so, she would be pursued for slander. They succeeded in calling her bluff, and she duly performed six sabbaths' repentance in sackcloth for maligning Watson. Margaret Davison suffered more than one might have expected for her slander, since she wound up convicted of fornication as well as consulting Watson *as if* she were a witch. She had to pay 50s and repent in the 'common form of fornicators' for the former offence and do additional public repentance in sackcloth six sabbaths for the latter.[76]

Obviously the session's principal concern in this case was not sorcery, but reputation – that vital but fragile feature of early modern life whose loss could be, in the case of a real charge of witchcraft, fatal. When this quarrel caused by resented generosity reached the level where it could be dangerous for Watson, her resort to kirk mediation served to prevent the more serious charge and restore, even create anew, a positive reputation for a woman previously the butt of village jokesters. Clearly not part of the village elite, this humble woman still benefited from an institution with a well-deserved reputation for fair mediation, in this case regardless of gender or social standing.

Such cases, with similar outcomes, could easily be multiplied.[77] Modern historians' interest in witch crazes should not blind us to the fact that contemporaries were well aware that interpersonal conflict very often lay behind charges of witchcraft.[78] Thus, the Dundonald session dealt in 1604 with charges of charming against Pet Lowry in light of the fact that his accuser had earlier impounded a stag of Lowry's that had 'destroyed his corn' and that the two had been 'discording therefore'; the week

76. CH2/400/1, pp. 113, 123.

77. The device also worked for men. The success of a Calder man's slander suit in 1609 freed him from the taint of 'using of charmes to cure the were evil [calamity thought to be caused by werewolves – a rarity in Scotland]': CH2/266/1, f. 11; cf. CH2/523/1, f. 26v.

78. CH2/400/1, p. 121. For two similar cases later in 1623, pp. 122–23, both requiring men who had requested magical healing of women reputed to be witches either to bring criminal suit or to pay the penalty for slander. Both took the latter course, and neither woman was investigated for witchcraft. One man did take out his ire on the kirk officer who had apprehended him, 'despitefully call[ing] him knave' and saying 'his wife was a thief and that she shall hang'. For this, both his £5 fine and his Sunday repentance for slander were doubled. However much trouble John Dun, the officer, had given the elders, he still got their protection.

following, when John Park was charged with having laid a sickness on David Dickie, they noted that for some time before, 'they were in a fray'.[79] In fact, the vast majority of witchcraft charges in kirk session books were answered by mediation of a quarrel rather than pursuit of presumed sorcery, and in nearly every case the individual bringing the charge of witchcraft was made to apologise to the woman (or more rarely the man) so labelled, even when the slanderer was male and of higher social status. In Falkirk, for instance, of six flyting cases between 1617 and 1627 where an enemy was called 'witch', only one of the cases was referred to presbytery for investigation; all, including that one, were treated as slander.[80] Kirkcaldy heard five cases between 1615 and 1627 in which women were publicly called witches; not one was prosecuted, except as slander.[81] In the midst of a real witch craze in 1626–27, the Dysart session punished any slander of witchcraft with unusual severity, given the serious outcome of criminal pursuit. And in Aberlady, even when a slandered woman refused to forgive her enemy when he apologised before the congregation, cursing him instead and behaving 'devilishly', the elders punished her for failure to reconcile, not for witchcraft.[82] The Aberdeen session satisfied four wives who had been slandered as witches, 'ruining their good reputations', by sentencing James Kemp to two Sundays on the pillar, 'the one Sunday in the new kirk, and the other in the old' (so that he was seen by the entire community), and at sermon's end on the second Sunday to 'come down in sackcloth before the pulpit, barefooted, and there in all humility sit down on his knees in presence of the whole congregation and there confess (as the truth is) that he has most unjustly and maliciously slandered the said persons and ask first God, and next the congregation, with the whole parties [all the women] slandered, pardon and forgiveness, and to say "false tongue he lied", or else be banished.'[83] To cause division in the community was clearly as much an offence against God and the town as against the women slandered – perhaps more so, given the order in which the apologies were prescribed. Taken altogether, the preponderance of session minutes reveal ministers and elders much less concerned with witchcraft than with restoring harmony in the community.

79. *Dundonald*, 58.
80. CH2/400/1, pp. 19, 38, 103, 111–12, 123–24, 144, 163; cf. *Dundonald*, 21 (1602).
81. CH2/636/34, ff. 7–7v (referred to the presbytery, which condemned the woman bringing the accusation as a slanderer), 16, 49, 50v, 52, 80.
82. CH2/390/1, ff. 42–47v, with a £10 fine, ten days' warding, and public repentance as the penalty for falsely charging witchcraft; CH2/4/1 (1639), ff. 29–29v.
83. CH2/448/3 (1609). Kemp reported having seen the women dancing at midnight in a pool with a platter of fish 'shining and glittering'; they had in fact been fishing and were dividing the catch.

The same preventive function of session arbitration could protect women from sexual defamation. When a woman charged with fornication in Falkirk claimed that her alleged partner had 'unjustly raised the bruit thereof and been the occasion of the scandal' against her, the session ordered her to bring a slander charge if she wished to avoid censure as a fornicator on his testimony. Another succeeded in demonstrating Thomas Callender's claim that he 'had ado with her in a chair' to be slander, for which Callender had to perform the six months' repentance in sackcloth usual for adultery (which was, after all, his own claim).[84] In this case, reducing the charge from fornication to slander would in itself be evidence that a quarrel rather than sexual offence was the issue; an innocent woman's best defence would be counter-suit before a body that placed a premium on conflict resolution.

* * *

Cultural anthropologists have taught us that, for arbitration to be successful, it must culminate in a public ritual of reconciliation that not only affirms the restoration of order but also offers some guarantee of future peace between the quarrelling parties.[85] Publicity, place, posture and language all play central roles in effective reconciliation rites.

The public nature of the final settlement of a quarrel has received appropriate attention in studies of high-level feud in early modern Scotland. The visible signing of bonds of manrent and payment of assythment after murder in the course of feud allowed both the parties involved and their neighbours to see that justice had been done; the attendant exchange of documents thus took place at the market cross or in the church 'in plain audience of the people'.[86] Publicity *per se* tended to ensure that the peace would be kept, since violating an agreement witnessed by the whole neighbourhood would bring charges of duplicity and undermine reputation. Kirk sessions followed suit in settling local quarrels, choosing the public venue carefully to ensure that all who had witnessed the original breach could also witness its mending. Thus, in 1589 in Perth, Margaret MacLaren (a burgess wife) had to kneel before Margaret Robertson, whom she had slandered, 'afore her own house, the place where she uttered the slanderous words' and crave her pardon in full view of all the

84. CH2/400/1, pp. 115, 297–98. The same course was taken with charges of theft. Of many examples, see pp. 127–28, where again the plaintiff declined to pursue his charge criminally.
85. Gluckman, *Custom and Conflict*, *passim*, and *Politics, Law and Ritual*, 183–207.
86. Wormald, 'Blood Feud', 123, quoting from an account of the 1561 reconciliation in Glasgow of the associates of Neil Montgomery of Langshaw and Robert, Lord Boyd.

neighbours who had heard her offence; the Deer presbyters routinely had slanderers repent both in their parish kirks and at the houses of those offended. Bessie Kinglassie of Perth in 1594 apologised to the elder who had rebuked her sabbath breach 'in the common street before his own yett', where she had railed at him. And after two wrights fought over their seats in St John's kirk in 1621 (with flyting references to one's late father), they had to repent 'in the wright's seat wherein they offended'.[87] Retracting evil words in the place where they had first been uttered has obvious symbolic value, but the practical element in such public apology is also evident in the 1586 case of John MacWalter and his spouse, Alison Bruce, often called for 'troubling their neighbours and especially for backbiting' two other couples. They had to apologise openly in 'the place where they made their offence', and the session specified that thenceforth their neighbours' 'bare accusation shall be a sufficient plea of conviction' for any future flyting and result in the couple's banishment. Publicity of offence brought both public humiliation and future public accountability: the considerable power of these neighbours for future conviction reflects contemporary perception that the offence was against neighbourhood as much as the enemy families. Here as elsewhere, kirk intervention seems to have worked – no more is heard from the couple.[88] Where the neighbourhood witnessed peacemaking, neighbours underpinned peacekeeping.

The central act in a ceremony of reconciliation was an apology, but one that acknowledged that quarrel or feud was the problem of the whole community, not just the offending parties, and an offence against God as well as neighbourhood. Here the considerable power of the kirk as spiritual authority came into play. The session represented divine displeasure at quarrelling, divine insistence on peace, divine retribution against disturbers of God's peace and, indeed, against their communities. The kirk's frequent calls to periods of fasting and humiliation contained the constant refrain that plague, famine and storm were the just deserts of communities that allowed dissension and violence in their midst. In every parish, the formula for reconciliation therefore demanded apology not only to the individual offended, but also to God and the community, generally in the kirk, 'in presence and audience of the whole people', as the Aberlady session ruled.[89] In Elgin after sitting on the stool, offenders craved pardon 'as well of the party offended and slandered as the congregation present'.[90] Place again played a symbolic as well as a practical

87. CH2/521/2, ff. 28v, 106; CH2/89/1, f. 6 (1603); CH2/521/7, pp. 224–26. See also CH2/621/1 (North Leith), p. 362; *Dundonald*, 459; CH2/523/1, ff. 4v, 16v, 19v; ML CH2/171/1, f. 28; CH2/1142/1, ff. 96–97.

88. CH2/521/2, f. 5.

89. CH2/4/1, f. 27.

90. CH2/145/1, f. 9v, 'General Act anent Slander', 1587; *Dundonald*, 383, 404, 406–07, 413.

role: apology to God and community was most efficiently made in the kirk itself, on the stool for audition by the whole congregation, then at the offended party's place in the nave.[91]

The language of apology could be as formulaic as flyting itself. In Aberdeen, the medieval formula for self-condemnation as liar was retained for slanderers and flyters, who were made to ask forgiveness before the congregation and the offended party saying, 'False tongue she/he lied', in addition to paying a fine *ad pios usus*.[92] In every parish, the elders made flyters restore the sullied reputations of those they had slandered by saying, 'I know nothing but honesty of this woman' or man. This formula functioned in cases of local quarrel much as assythment did in larger-scale and violent feud, to 'make the scathis hale' (heal the injuries).[93] Assigned scripts included 'promises by the grace of God never to commit the like hereafter'. The Canongate's text ran: 'Brother, I confess I have offended you, and therefore I desire you to forgive me, that we may live together as godly brethren, casting from us all hatred.'[94] And frequently language of oblivion was incorporated: Canongate arbiters required reconciled quarrellers 'to forgive the other and to embrace charity as becomes the members of Jesus Christ, where instantly the one forgave the other and promised never to call to mind any bypast offences.' In a 1565 case, not only were the quarrellers themselves to declare oblivion, but the session declared 'in the name of the whole rest of the kirk that they [the session] had utterly forgiven, remitted and *forgot* all kind of offence done, . . . and that no faithful should call it to mind, and if any did, they should be reported to have offended the whole kirk.'[95] Oblivion was in effect mandated as a device to help mend the breach.

Gesture and posture reinforced the message of reconciliation and, in the prescribed public setting, underpinned future adherence to the settlement.

91. E.g., CH2/1142/1, f. 100v, where Hew Peit was made to 'come down from the stool and crave the said Cuthbert's pardon' for 'upbraiding' and threatening him with a knife. See also CH2/326/1, p. 7; CH2/383/1, f. 6v.
92. CH2/448/1, p. 5. For a second offence the culprit was sent to the cuckstool; for the third, he or she was banished. Among countless other examples, see CH2/448/3, pp. 9–11, 38, 132. The formula 'fals tong scho leit' (false tongue, she lied) had been used in borough as well as ecclesiastical courts for centuries: Elizabeth Ewan, '"Tongue You Lied": The Role of the Tongue in Rituals of Penance in Late Medieval Scotland', paper read at the International Medieval Congress, Kalamazoo, Michigan, May 2001.
93. E.g., CH2/521/8/1, f. 24; *Dundonald*, 384 (swearing 'that nothing was true that he had spoken of her'); Wormald, 'Blood Feud', 131, citing the fifteenth-century *Liber Pluscardensis*.
94. CH2/400/1, p. 97; *Canongate*, 61 (1567).
95. *Canongate*, 13, 17. See also AAC CH2/809/1, f. 10, Monkton's 1617 order that the parties 'greet each other by taking them by their hand, and all matters in controversy between them to be buried in oblivion'.

Flyters took it in turn to kneel before each other in physical expression of penitence for their offence against the other.[96] They knelt before the session in physical expression of sorrow for their offence against the kirk and God. In many cases they were made to face the assembled congregation on Sunday morning to apologise for offending the community, standing for a slight quarrel, 'sitting down upon their knees' for a more disruptive or vituperative one. George Smyth of Falkirk 'in all humility and signs of obedience prostrate[d] himself upon his knees and asked God, the said Robert [Rayne, whom he had cursed] and all whom he by his example offended, forgiveness.'[97] Reconciled flyters shook hands or (in the Perth formula) 'in a friendly manner took each other by the hand' in physical expression of restored trust. Burntisland quarrellers demonstrated that 'they are mutually agreed in all points' by 'joining hands in sign and token thereof'.[98] If the flyting had involved threat of violence by one of the parties, the prescribed gestures of apology were modified to show the unequal levels of offence. Thus, in Perth, when Henry Adamson hurled epithets at Thomas Wilson and Wilson responded with a threat to 'throw [twist] his nose', the elders ordered 'that the parties be reconciled, [but] because that the said Thomas' offence [threatening violence] is thought to be greatest, the session ordain [him] to crave the said Mr Henry Adamson's pardon, which he did, and they took [each] other by the hand.'[99] In one-sided cases of slander, the offender likewise knelt before the other, and then rose for the two to shake hands in sign of pardon granted. It is worth noting, too, that this procedure was followed in disregard of gender and social standing, as we have already seen in cases of witchcraft accusation in the course of flyting. Where violence had accompanied flyting or domestic disturbances, the weapons used were brought into the ceremony, the Edinburgh presbytery in 1586 ordering quarrellers, 'having in their hands the weapons wherewith they did the injury', to confess 'in the presence of the whole people and cast down their weapons' in a dramatic ritual of repentance and reconciliation.[100] Finally, the ceremony often

96. CH2/523/1, ff. 16v, 19v; AAC CH2/751/1, f. 14v; CH2/84/28, ff. 5, 6v, 48; and many other examples. The act of paying penalties to the poor box, equal amounts from each party for a mutual offence, also underpinned the even-handedness of the session and the agreement of the parties: SAU CH2/1056/1, f. 19v.

97. CH2/400/1, p. 129; Smythe had said 'Hell be his winning' to Rayne, a merchant; cf. p. 63, and *Dundonald*, 325, 326.

98. CH2/521/8/2, f. 169v; CH2/523/1, f. 12, cf. ff. 11v, 14, 14v, 17v ('joining hands'), 33 ('shaking hands'). See also *Dundonald*, 261; CH2/145/1, f. 1; CH2/716/1, f. 20; CH2/276/1, f. 16; CH2/210/1, f. 2v; *Canongate*, 31–32, 70.

99. CH2/521/7, p. 417 (1623).

100. CH2/121/1, f. 17v; CH2/32/1, ff. 29, 33.

ended with the parties' promise to get along in future being 'writ in the session book . . . to remain a perpetual memorium'. The act of writing in that very important book had acquired the power to bind action: 'touch of the pen' or 'putting their hands to the [clerk's] pen' became the gesture that embedded in memory the pardon of past wrongs. Here is evidence, from the Highlands to the Borders, of the traditional gesture of an illiterate society – shaking hands – being reinforced by one of a culture now centred on the written word.[101]

Food and drink often had a place in reconciliation rites. When two Perth factions in 1585 were 'agreed by the minister and elders', Patrick Kay as head of the more violently offending faction drank to the health of his erstwhile foes in presence of the session.[102] The 'awaytaking' of 'a certain variance and discord' between two Perth baxters got out of hand in 1599 when their ceremonial meal 'entered on Wednesday before noon and continued [with] drinking till the even and . . . on the morn again' to the following night, when Thomas Richie was 'so drunken . . . that he cannot walk or convey himself upon the streets', which the session found 'very slanderous'; however, drinking 'to the end they might agree' was clearly a traditional part of reconciliation.[103] Where flyting and feuding had been particularly rife in a community, a communal meal in a public setting served as the final stage in cementing arbitrated peace. At John Welch's 1590 arrival in strife-ridden Ayr, he 'made it his first undertaking to remove the bloody quarrellings', often interposing himself physically 'betwixt two parties of men fighting, even in the midst of blood and wounds, . . . and so little and little he made the town a peaceable habitation.' The peace was the better kept because, 'after he had ended a skirmish amongst his neighbours and reconciled these bitter enemies', he placed a 'table upon the street and there brought the enemies together, and beginning with prayer he persuaded them to profess themselves friends and then to eat and drink together, then last of all he ended the work with singing a psalm.'[104] This was a striking echo of the communion ritual, but the meal itself was a mechanism used in secular settlement of feud at a higher level: James VI reportedly feasted newly reconciled magnates in Holyrood before making them process the Royal Mile holding hands with their enemies. And at the 1597 public reconciliation of Huntly and Errol, after a public fast, mutual confession before the

101. CH2/266/1, f. 2 (1604); CH2/191/1, f. 52 (1640); CH2/276/1, f. 7v.
102. CH2/521/1, f. 116.
103. CH2/521/3, p. 101; CH2/523/1, f. 22 reports a similar incident in Burntisland in 1605.
104. *History of . . . Reverend John Welch*, 5.

pulpit, reception by ministers and town officials, communion and two sermons, an extraordinary street party cemented the reconciliation, with musicians and maskers, sweetmeats and confections, and wine 'in great abundance' provided on a covered table at the market cross.[105] What the kirk added to the secular tradition was extension to social orders below the nobility, and of course the religious element, with psalms and prayer in Welch's case, fasting, sermons and communion in the Huntly case. Welch's feast as a public act of sharing, echoing the ecclesiology of communion, bound the church's spiritual seal with a visible, tangible performance before the assembled community (in the street) to make it impossible for those reconciled to violate the peace in future without loss of faith as well as face.

None of these reconciliation rituals was particularly innovative in the sixteenth century.[106] The point is simply that, in peacekeeping as in penance, the Reformed sessions recognised the utility of traditional ceremony, place and position, and appropriated them, expanding their application and resorting to them with a regularity and frequency not available to most earlier courts or individuals. It is also worth noting that the reconciliation ceremony was itself negotiated and designed to fit the circumstances. Sessions were flexible, reducing fines or omitting the most public performance of apology, for instance, if the offended party were satisfied without it.[107] In 1605, when Henry Ogill of North Leith could not pay the fine for calling his pastor 'false old wolf carl and false thief carl' and an elder 'landlowper and landseller', his 'great signs and tokens of repentance', with the consent of the two men offended got his penalty reduced to public apology on the sabbath in the kirk. And the Falkirk candlemaker John Bownd, 'in respect of his poverty and that the party offended by him and he is agreed', was forgiven payment of his penalty upon promise of amendment'.[108] Penalties were routinely mitigated for poverty.[109] Consultation with plaintiffs about fines and settlements was

105. NLS ms Wod. Oct. VII, f. 18; *Spalding Miscellany*, 2:lx–lxii (letter from the Aberdeen lawyer Thomas Mollison to a friend in Edinburgh, 28 June 1597). I am grateful to Jenny Wormald for this reference. The earl of Huntly went on to ask 'the ministry to intercede for his reconciliation with the earl of Moray's friends for his slaughter' (lxi).

106. E.g. McKay, 113; CH5/2/1, ff. 269, 334. Dunbar has Kennedie vow, 'thou sall cry *cor mundum* on thy kneis. . . . And thou sall lik thy lippis and suere thou leis' (ll. 393ff). The *Flyting* was printed in 1508, composed probably in the 1490s: *Poems of Dunbar*, 2:427–29.

107. E.g., CH2/521/2, f. 28v.

108. CH2/621/1, pp. 361–63; CH2/400/1, p. 93; cf. pp. 134, 152, 161. See also CH2/523/1, f. 46v, mitigation requested by the offended party.

109. E.g., CH2/400/1, pp. 58, 86, 92.

usual, though the question was often simply referred back to the original arbiters: two Perth plaintiffs in 1624, asked 'what amends they would have, . . . referred the same to the arbitriment of the session', who 'reconcile[d] them together' by having the offenders 'crave forgiveness of the offended and in sign of their reconciliation together take each other by the hands'.[110] As usual, the focus was not on punishment so much as penitence; pecuniary penalties seem to have mattered less than apologies and promises of reform, and money often came into the equation only as a 'caution' against future misbehaviour. When fines were levied in a flyting case, they were imposed on both sides; being contributed directly to the poor, they appear much more akin to medieval penitential acts of charity than fiscal penalties.[111]

Finally, prescribed reconciliation ceremonies made use of face-saving devices – essential in a society finely attuned to insult. For a settlement to work, it had to be perceived as fair to both parties, but it had also to avoid so humiliating one party that he or she could construe it as grounds for continued or even expanded feud. When the Falkirk merchant John Leisthmen complained in 1623 against the weaver Adam Russell 'for abusing and wronging of him in the kirk upon Sunday last' by throwing him 'violently out of his own seat in the church' and calling him names, he found abundant witnesses to prove his case, so that Russell was fined £5 and made to repent publicly. But the same witnesses pointed out that Russell's action was no reason for Leisthmen's response of 'casting away his bonnet . . . and making turbulence in time of sermon', so Leisthmen was also made to repent publicly at the same time, though not to pay a fine.[112] The even-handedness of such decisions ensured the subsequent compliance of both offenders: neither had motivation for retaliation against an inequitable judgment or loss of face. In Yester, the party who began a flyting was made to pay 20s to the poor, the one who responded only 13s, but neither got off entirely, lest the other begrudge the settlement.[113]

110. CH2/521/7, pp. 510–11. Another example of settlement negotiated with the offended party is CH2/299/1, pp. 62–63, where the Perth presbytery sought to prevent feud by making sure that the rape victim and her mother were satisfied; the offender still had to deal with the civil courts.

111. E.g., CH2/326/1, p. 7; CH2/521/8/1, p. 24; CH2/377/1, f. 5v. In an exception to this rule, Alexander Young's £5 fine for slandering John Russell was counted against Russell's £40 debt to Young: CH2/400/1, p. 107. Contrast pre-Reformation ecclesiastical courts, whose fines tended to enrich the court officers (above, nn. 15–16).

112. CH2/400/1, pp. 116, 75 (an assault victim made to repent for unwisely keeping company with the other man knowing him to be drunk); *Canongate*, 31 (slander victims admonished not to give 'occasion nor injury to' their abuser in future).

113. CH2/377/1, f. 14.

The same principle applied to spousal reconciliation. In a 1608 Aberdeen abandonment case, the elders admonished Archibald Boyd and made him promise to return to his wife, Agnes Gray, and support her. But the couple then shook hands in acknowledgment that 'all bygone faults and oversights were buried and put in oblivion *on either side*, promising by God's grace to keep a good duty *either of them to the other* in time coming'. The language recognises the two-sided nature of the problem and saves face for the more sternly punished. The elders' even-handedness is also evident from the second part of the reconciliation: the week after Boyd's promise, they summoned the couple again, this time for Gray to do her part and be 'publicly admonished by the moderator in name of the whole session' to refrain from ungodly company and the 'society of her who loves not her husband and desires his hurt or skaith, whose names her husband will delate [declare] to her in quietness [privacy], and that she will be an obedient wife . . . and do her duty in humbleness in all respects as becomes a loving wife to her husband.' She gave her oath in turn, and we hear no more from the couple. Boyd was the first to be reprimanded, but he could hardly take umbrage at being singled out when his wife was so sternly reprimanded in the same setting. It is also noteworthy that the session avoided expanding the quarrel by keeping private the names of Gray's troublemaking companion, a woman who apparently had her own quarrel with Boyd.[114] What we have in all these cases is not so much punishment as penitential conciliation.

* * *

Kirk arbitration of quarrels was generally successful in part because it contained follow-up procedures and built-in preventive measures. The advantage of a sizable group of local men over an individual priest or a

114. CH2/448/2, pp. 256–57, 280. There is more to this particular story of domestic rift and mending. While Boyd's refusal to support his wife was the first offence acknowledged in the prescribed reconciliation, Gray's offence was actually the more serious: when her husband had returned from a voyage to Danskyn the previous summer, presumably after a long absence, Gray had got a friend, James Gordon, to bar him from entering their home, 'holding him violently at his own door and noways suffering him to enter within the same', swearing that 'he should never be a husband to her, and a blanket should never cover them'. His subsequent failure to live with and support her seems to have been her choice, not his, which the session in August 1607 had recognised by having Gray warded. In the intervening five months, they had managed to bring the couple back together, however, and rather than undermine the settlement by singling out Gray, they allowed her to save face by requiring her husband's performance first. Public acknowledgment that there was some fault on both sides (perhaps Boyd was away longer than necessary?) allowed both to retain their pride.

distant court is here readily apparent. Sessions could provide effective oversight of the community because they apportioned out 'quarters' or subsections of the parish to designated elders. While a priest might take months to make the rounds of all of his parishioners, elders dividing the work could make frequent visits. Among the objectives of their visits were to assure compliance of quarrellers with their promises of amendment, to gather information from neighbours about new quarrels, and to hear individual confessions.[115]

The other mechanisms for prevention they adopted from secular courts: offenders were usually made to 'act themselves', or take a formal oath before the session, not to offend in future. If they did, they would be bound to pay a sizable sum of money, with compliance insured by a cautioner. Thus, in 1626 the Yester elders required two flyters to promise that if they quarrelled publicly again, the one who began the flyting would pay 40s to the poor and 'both of them to make satisfaction in the kirk'; Perth flyters promised to pay £10 if they offended again 'by word nor deed'; and in Dundonald John Hunter and Robert Dickie 'voluntarily and of their own proper consents acted themselves to live in peace and quietness together hereafter under the pain of £5' for whoever broke the peace first.[116] The amounts to be forfeited varied by parish and often in accord with the social status of the offender.[117] In view of the threat of feud, the act often extended to kin: in 1618 David Livingston and Samuel Burne of Falkirk bound themselves, 'their wives, bairnes and servants that in case that they are any of them be found at any time hereafter to trouble or molest either by flyting, scolding, or evil carriage of themselves towards [the] others', failing to act 'as becomes Christians, that . . . they shall pay the sum of £10'.[118] If repeat offenders could not afford their penalty, the cautioner was held responsible, suggesting that cautioners probably

115. CH2/4/1, f. 26, for example.
116. CH2/377/1, f. 57v (though the session was flexible enough to depart from this rule when holding two notorious flyters equally responsible for future disturbance was regarded as a more likely deterrent – 'if Margaret Hunter and Bessie Kirkawell be found flyting again that both shall be alike guilty whomever beginneth and shall be alike punished': f. 52v, 1627); CH2/521/8/1, f. 49v; *Dundonald*, 23 (cf. 326, flyters agreeing that if they offended again they would stand in the branks for two hours in lieu of a fine that they presumably could not afford; or 412, two couples promising to pay '40s, every one of them, if they were found to flyt and brawl one with another'). See also CH2/521/1, f. 6v; CH2/1142/1, f. 18v; CH2/400/1, pp. 31, 129, 147.
117. In the first half of the seventeenth century the usual fine in Aberlady was 1 dollar (CH2/4/1, f. 18v); in Falkirk £20 (CH2/400/1, p. 83).
118. CH2/400/1, p. 31. The flyting had actually been conducted by the wives of the two, Jonet Buchanan saying that Burn 'held his house with a den of whores and thieves,

took some responsibility for keeping the peace lest their own cash be forfeited – an additional follow-up mechanism. Repeaters would naturally not be able to find cautioners and so would be banished from the community.[119]

The best witness to the relative effectiveness of kirk arbitration of quarrels is simply the frequency with which people resorted to the sessions. People brought their quarrels to the elders even knowing that they would have to pay penalties for their own part; the fact that they would be financially poorer for the effort did not diminish the value of arbitration. People were willing to pay for the service. So popular was resort to sessions for arbitration that in many parishes they replaced some of the more traditional mediators, like crafts guilds or fraternities. Thus, when two cordiners in Falkirk quarrelled in 1619, they brought their dispute not to their guild, but to the session; two Perth wrights did the same in 1621, as did two dyers in Ferryport-on-Craig in 1640; and Glasgow's session handled quarrels among the armourers.[120] And many cases that might have gone to the civil authorities were instead brought to the session or its arbitration boards for mediation, as in the 1565 Canongate case in which a poor man's sow was killed by his neighbour: clearly the poor man expected justice from the appointed arbiters.[121] So overburdened were sessions with such mediatory duties that most began imposing heavy fines on people who brought complaints against their neighbours that they could not prove by witnesses. In Dundonald a false charge of slander cost 12s, and the amount had to be consigned to the treasurer before the elders would even hear the case; the penalty for conviction of slander was only slightly more, 13s 4d. In Glasgow both plaintiff and defendant had to consign 26s 8d before their case would be heard; whoever lost would forfeit the money. Crail's elders in 1618 complained that they were 'daily molested with complaints of slander' and so would require 20s consigned by plaintiffs in case of false accusations, and a uniform punishment of two hours in the jougs or £3 for those convicted. And the Falkirk session began its first extant session

and that there was a man in his house that lay with both his daughters'. Janet Archibald, Burn's wife, returned that Buchanan was a 'landlowper, common whore and thief' (p. 28). There are many other examples, as f. 10, Patrick Grindlay and James Alexander in 1617 'inact[ing] themselves for them, their wives, bairns and servants that neither of them should molest [the] others with slanderous speeches, every party . . . under the pains of 100 merks to be uplifted from the party offender by the minister and session of Falkirk, and to be employed *ad pios usus*.'

119. CH2/400/1, pp. 89, 160. There was a sliding scale of cautions, as of initial penalties (e.g., p. 92).

120. CH2/400/1, pp. 52, 56 (an unsuccessful arbitration); CH2/521/7, pp. 224, 304; SAU CH2/150/1, f. 4v; ML CH2/171/1, f. 29v (a 1594 case referred to presbytery).

121. *Canongate*, 17.

book with a case of two families 'molest[ing] each other with slanderous speeches', and a blanket act ordering that no complaint of slander would be heard without the plaintiff consigning cash or a bond (presumably for less well-heeled plaintiffs).[122] Yet even with fair and oft-repeated warning of the cost of groundless suit, people resorted to the session in steady or increasing numbers.[123] It probably helped that consigned funds, like penalties for flyting or other offences, went not to cover court costs and enrich its officers, but *ad pios usus* (by the sixteenth century, it was a code phrase for action that traditionally had spiritual merit). The utility of kirk arbitration was enhanced by the utility of supporting poor relief, which was after all another mechanism to ensure communal stability in unsettled times.[124]

The recidivism rate was low: it is rare to find the names of reconciled parties appearing in later flyting, slander or domestic violence cases, and rarer still to find people banished from a community for 'constant flyting'. This may be due in part to some parishes' strenuous punishment of people who refused to reconcile or repeated their flyting. In Dundonald, such individuals had to appear in the public place of repentance in white sheets and pay more substantial fines than first offenders.[125] Dysart's elders were given to gaoling recalcitrant quarrellers together for three days in the kirk steeple. Forced to cohabit in close and grim quarters, they would hopefully sort out the problem among themselves. But they were also warned that they were 'not to be heard again' under 'pain of a month's warding'. Their three days would have given them a fair taste of what that would be like.[126] Whatever the means, the recidivism rate stands as a tribute to effective kirk resolution of quarrels.

122. *Dundonald*, 282, 416, 419, 427; the penalty in Falkirk was much higher, £5: CH2/400/1, pp. 7, 27, 28, 81, 83. NLS ms Wod. Oct. IX, f. 6; SAU CH2/Crail/1, f. 2; cf. CH2/442/74, f. 23v (12s in Kirkwall); CH2/191/1, ff. 6v, 38v; CH2/32/1, f. 33.
123. E.g., the figures for the four years before and after the Kirkcaldy session ruled that 'whosoever shall complain upon his neighbour some slander . . . and proves not shall satisfy . . . by giving an pecunial sum' (CH2/636/34, f. 23v, 1618) are comparable (13 before, 11 after).
124. E.g., CH2/285/1, p. 12. In the Highlands, Inveravon departed from the norm by dividing forfeited funds between the slandered (for 'bloodwyt', the penalty for bloodshed in feud settlement) and the poor: CH2/191/1, f. 38v.
125. *Dundonald*, 332, 336, 410, but in these cases the flyting was also aggravated by (respectively) offending a local notable; using 'most unnatural, filthy and unwomanly words (language apparently unfit to be copied into the record earning Bessie M'Ald an hour in the branks, barefooted and in linen with 'a paper on her brow' defining her offence, repentance in the kirk, and a heavy £10 fine); and communion absence.
126. CH2/390/1, ff. 6, 51.

The clusters of cases arbitrated just before the twice- or thrice-yearly communions in many parishes suggests that an additional reason for popular resort to the sessions was their effective adoption of that familiar and comfortable pre-Reformation season of penitence and reconciliation – Lent. As we have seen, the Reformed parishes' 'days of reconciliation' just before the two-Sunday communion services served much the same purpose in the community as Lent. Before each communion in the Canongate, there was from 1564 an 'exhorting of the whole neighbourhood to mutual peace and love, whereby the celebration of the Holy Communion might prove the more religious, to the glory of God and comfort of the whole people', and a gathering of 'the whole brethren and honest neighbours' to 'remove all eyelifts' or misunderstandings; on these occasions arbitration boards sat to reconcile particular quarrels.[127] Parishes from Dron to Fraserburgh, Burntisland to Dalkeith, followed suit, regularly 'ordering the elders to [go to] parties at variance if any be to the end they may be concorded before the communion.'[128] Certainly people took seriously the traditional charge to reconcile with their enemies before receiving communion. Being 'at variance with [one's] neighbour' served frequently as an excuse for missing the sacrament, though such claims were carefully investigated by sessions and in the end were never acceptable: two Burntisland cases dealt with on the same day in 1604 resulted in arbiters being appointed to settle one quarrel, but the other non-communicant being rebuked and punished when his claim of being 'at variance' with his neighbour was 'found to be frivolous'.[129] The Dumfries elders typically ruled that 'in no case [did] hatred excuse absence', since 'means for reconciliation' were available, and they applied the principle to lairds as to their dependents, and to 'deadly feud' as to lesser conflict.[130] Communicating without reconciling was, of course, severely punished.[131] When William Fairly in Edinburgh 'obstinately refused' to take the prof-

127. *Dundonald*, 24; CH2/122/1, ff. 1v–2; *Canongate*, 16–17, 257.

128. CH2/93/1, f. 19v; CH2/1142/1, f. 78v; CH2/523/1, quotation at f. 18v, cf. 16v, 38–39; CH2/84/28, f. 60; CH2/718/4, f. 12 (reconciliation day before each of the four-Sunday communions in St Cuthbert's, Edinburgh).

129. CH2/523/1, f. 12v. Among other examples, see NLS ms Wod. Oct. IX, f. 5v; CH2/523/1, f. 12v; *Canongate*, 16, 24; SAU CH2/624/2, pp. 124–25; CH2/400, pp. 167–68 (three couples 'absent from the table of the Lord because of malice'); *Dundonald*, 40, cf. 257, an exception granted to a man travelling to Ireland and willing to reconcile, but with a less compliant adversary.

130. CH8/54/1a, ff. 1–1v; likewise CH2/294/1, ff. 1v, 3; CH2/716/2, ff. 80v, 95.

131. Grissell Thomson had to pay 20s or 'give signs of repentance the next sabbath from the public place for presuming to approach to the Lord's Table, being at variance with John Wallace in Gatesyd and his family unreconciled': *Dundonald*, 335; cf. 406, 410.

fered hand of his enemy in a 1574 reconciliation ritual, insisting that he 'could not remit the gorge of his heart, . . . the kirk suspended the said William from all participation of the benefits of the said kirk in time coming until said reconciliation.'[132]

* * *

How much of the contrast that has been noted here between medieval and Reformation practice may also apply to that between the English and Scots situations – the difference lying perhaps more in number than in kind – is up for discussion, but several notable differences between the two protestant realms in how the ecclesiastical courts dealt with discord help to illumine the Scottish development and suggest the impact that a particularly zealous Calvinist reform movement with local discipline by sessions could have on the larger culture. Of course, English archidiaconal and consistory courts heard an abundance of scolding and defamation cases.[133] But the latter vastly outnumber the former: the *mutual* slander of flyting constitutes a relatively small minority of English archidiaconal cases, and of these a preponderance seem to have been not staged on the street, but more privately exchanged. Second, while English scholars tell us that arbitration of quarrels went on, records of specific cases are actually rather rare.[134] Sampling a four-year period for the archdeaconry of Chichester and a twelve-month period for Taunton turned up not a single case of

132. NAS ms RH2/1/35, f. 29v, 1574.
133. The latter dominated the business of many early modern English church courts. In the most recent study of local attempts to control disorder in England, Marjorie MacIntosh, *Controlling Misbehavior in England 1370–1600* (Cambridge, 1998) defines 'scolding' as not necessarily including mutuality; it includes the category of 'back-biting' (pp. 9, 61). She reports (via personal communication, March 1999) that she has found no instances of arbitration in her studies.
134. Gowing, *Domestic Danger*, 36–37, but citing only Sharpe; Sharpe, *Crime in Early Modern England* (London, 1984), 45, *Defamation and Sexual Slander in Early Modern England* (Borthwick papers 58, 1980), and '"Such Disagreement betwyx Neighbours"', 167–87; Martin Ingram, 'Scolding Women Cucked or Washed: A Crisis in Gender Relations in Early Modern England?' in *Women, Crime, and the Courts in Early Modern England*, ed. J. Kermode and G. Walker (Chapel Hill, 1994); *Church Courts, Sex and Marriage in England, 1570–1640* (Cambridge, 1987), 33, 111, 318; and 'Communities and Courts: Law and Disorder in Early Seventeenth-Century Wiltshire' in *Crime in England*, ed. J.S. Cockburn (Methuen, 1977), 125–27; Houlbrooke, 275–79 *et passim*; Richard Helmholz, *Select Cases on Defamation to 1600* (London, 1985). Susan Brigden, *London and the Reformation* (Oxford, 1989), 28, does note informal pre-communion peacemaking. I do not wish to deny that arbitration went on in England, only to remark that it is rarely recorded by comparison to the Scots session minutes, that there is no indication of regular or formal boards or arbitration, and that the precise role of the courts themselves in the process is nowhere clear.

arbitration in either, and Ralph Houlbrooke finds no effort to reconcile quarrelling spouses in his York sources.[135] We have no record whatsoever of regular parochial arbitration panels, and clerical mediation is generally only self-reported.[136] The records suggest at least a very significant difference in degree, regularity and formality of arbitration in the church courts of the two realms. The English courts generally addressed quarrels with punishment rather than efforts to reconcile.[137] Third, and helping to explain the differences already noted, most recorded quarrels in England were handled not at the parish level, but in a higher court far distant, where judgment was rendered by officers who did not know the quarrellers and were ill-equipped to sort out causes, exercise flexible intervention and enforce reconciliation. Indeed, a startling feature of many archdeaconry and consistory court records is the number of times the presenting churchwarden has to admit that he 'knoweth not the names' of the combatants and can only report that a quarrel occurred.[138] Fourth, the English canons of 1604 only mandated annual presentation of disciplinary cases, reasonably enough, given the size of archdeacons' jurisdictions: the archdeaconry of Taunton included several towns of moderate size and 157 parishes and chapelries.[139] A related problem for England was the length of time for a case to be brought to conclusion – on average in York, nine months, and the attendant expenses of suits in church courts.[140] Contrast the quick judgments rendered by Scots elders. In England, too, common-law courts competed with the church courts in a way unknown to the northern realm, where civil and ecclesiastical courts co-operated and indeed (given the composition of the sessions) often overlapped.[141] Finally,

135. *Act Book of the Archdeacon of Taunton*, ed. C. Jenkins (Taunton, 1928), 1623–24; *Churchwardens' Presentments . . . Archdeaconry of Chichester*, ed. Hilda Johnstone (Lewes, Sussex, 1947), sampling 1621–25; *Depositions and Other Ecclesiastical Proceedings from the Courts of Durham* (London, 1845), yields the same result concerning arbitration. Houlbrooke, 68.

136. E.g., Richard Baxter, *The Reformed Pastor* (orig. 1656, repr. Edinburgh, 1974), ch. 3.

137. McIntosh, 63. Fines were usual in English local courts, although the cuckstool or tumbrel was often used for female scolds.

138. *Churchwarden's Presentments . . . Archdeaconry of Chichester*, e.g., p. 31: 'we cannot certainly certify their true names', or p. 48: 'whose names I know not'.

139. *Act Book of the Archdeacon of Taunton*, 10.

140. Ronald Marchant, *The Church under the Law: Justice, Administration and Discipline in the Diocese of York* (Cambridge, 1969), 65; Richard Wunderli, *London Church Courts and Society on the Eve of the Reformation* (Cambridge, Mass., 1981); C. Haigh, 'Slander and the Church Courts in the Sixteenth Century', *Transactions of the Lancashire and Cheshire Antiquarian Society* 78 (1975), 1–13; Gowing, ch. 2.

141. Ingram, *Church Courts*, 295. Common-law courts may have attracted the bulk of the defamation cases because of the fiscal benefits to plaintiffs of their policy of recompensing the slandered.

the exceptions to these generalisations about England tend to be towns like Northampton or Colchester or Dedham, where godly laymen and puritan ministers joined together to form something very like sessions in the 1570s and 1580s. Before their bishops suppressed them as 'Genevan', these bodies did occasionally offer arbitration of notorious quarrels at the parochial level.[142]

Could a partial explanation for what many now see as the relatively slow pace of protestant progress at the popular level in much of England be the decision there not to adopt a system of parochial administration like Scotland's, capable of restoring disrupted communal harmony quickly and effectively? Of course, a still-feuding society may have had a correspondingly greater need for such an expanded peacemaking process (although it should be said that whether one regards Scotland or England as the more violent early modern society depends largely on whether one is a Scottish or an English historian).[143] Again, a feuding society had ready to hand mechanisms of mediation and 'caution' that the kirk could adopt. But there is also an ecclesiological aspect to all this: disharmony within the parish brought 'slander' to the whole community; so concord reflected the congregation's fundamental identity as the body of Christ and in the process underpinned the covenant theology so central to Scottish divinity. In the activities of the sessions, the practical and the theological went hand in hand.

In any event, at the end of the day the kirk was peacemaker, precisely because it maintained and expanded the reconciliation function and mechanisms of medieval church and guild, at the most local level, cheaply and quickly. Had the reformers banished religious guilds without replacing one of their most vital functions, mediation, they surely would have been markedly less successful. Instead, they expanded that function to make it available to any member of the community, without cost unless the cause were frivolous or the quarrellers found slanderous. Even then, the fines were reasonable, were often levied on a sliding scale, could be paid in instalments, and went directly into the poor-relief coffers. And with dozens of laymen as involved in mediation as the ministers in each community, the service was considerably broadened compared to what the medieval church could offer. When Reformed ministers and elders threw out the

142. E.g., Byford, 322; W.J. Sheils, *Puritans in the Diocese of Peterborough 1558–1610* (Northampton, 1979), 120–21; or most obviously, the Dedham classis (presbytery), *The Presbyterian Movement in the Reign of Queen Elizabeth as Illustrated by the Minute Book of the Dedham Presbyterian Classis, 1582–1589*, ed. R.G. Usher (Camden Society, 3rd ser. 8, 1905), 71.
143. Wormald, 'Blood Feud' and Brown, *Bloodfeud*, both question the received (English) version. Brown, 14, suggests that persistent feud may have displaced other kinds of violence.

popish bath water, they were careful to keep not only the baby, but also some bath toys to keep it happy. They selected several of the most constructive for communal harmony and took them over with Calvinist zeal, making the kirk as mediator essential to the peace of the community.[144]

144. Bossy's claim (*Peace*, 78–100) that Reformed theology made no logical room for peacemaking is clearly given the lie by the Scottish record.

Chapter 6

Church and Family

The household as seminary of church and commonwealth was a sixteenth-century commonplace that gave the kirk all the backing it needed to intervene in every aspect of family life. From the foundation of Reformation, the new protestant authorities traced sin and error, 'all enormities' in kirk and realm, to the ill-government of families. More positively, they found hope for the eventual establishment of Christ's kingdom in Scotland in the agenda they set for the reformation of family life, to make 'the family to be a Bethel, or the house of God'.[1] As agents of this agenda, they proceeded to regulate and discipline sexual behaviour with unprecedented vigour, to oversee preparations for marriage and to intervene when marriage relationships were reported to be going sour. No family quarrel was too petty for them to mediate; no sexual dalliance was too private for their prying to expose and punish it; no absent father went unsought; no mother-in-law's complaint remained uninvestigated. Sessions were relentless in their pursuit of fornication and adultery, bastard-bearers and begetters, and the 'lewd livers' who might so easily fall into that category. Anything that might lead to scandalous behaviour in violation of matrimonial chastity or pre-marital abstinence they condemned out of hand, whether 'mixed dancing' or visits to the Dragon Hole with a piper. Session books from every parish are dominated by cases of fornication and adultery, with occasionally lurid accounts of couples caught in the act, abundant depositions by suspicious neighbours or witnesses, and vigorous grilling of suspects about times and places.

There are two important facts to note about this state of affairs. First, the Reformed kirk did not invent this role for itself; it simply maintained the medieval church's jurisdiction over matrimony and its violation, a long-standing ecclesiastical bailiwick. If protestant sessions were more

1. *Familie Exercise*, sigs A3v, A4v–5v *et passim*; *BUK* 3:873–74; Margo Todd, *Christian Humanism and the Puritan Social Order* (Cambridge, 1987), ch. 4; Harrington, *Reordering Marriage*, ch. 2.

comprehensive and vigorous in enforcement than their priestly forebears, it was more a function of their regular, frequent and readily accessible local court sessions than any difference in jurisdictional definition.

Second, and more important, there was a positive aspect to much of the kirk's involvement with the family. We must not let the elders' manifest preoccupation with fornication distract us from either its intended result – avoiding the problems of single-parent households where poverty almost invariably accompanied bastardy – or from the other important aspects of their involvement in family life. They did much more than harass the promiscuous, and much of it was quite constructive. In fact, the sessions operated in relation to family life much like a combination of modern social welfare agency, marriage counselling service and police domestic violence unit. They provided genuine social services to families in need by intervening in spousal abuse and other domestic assault, curbing stalkers and sexual predators, investigating child neglect and abuse, enforcing child support by absent fathers, seeing to the economic sustenance of abandoned spouses, fostering orphaned or foundling children, assisting single fathers of infants by securing nurses, and keeping an eye out for mistreatment of elderly parents. In short, they used their mandate to foster Christian families to underpin positive as well as negative intervention. In the process, they won a well-deserved reputation as problem-solvers. The willingness of large numbers of people actively to seek the elders' help with their own and their neighbours' family crises is only the most obvious testimony to their effectiveness.

Of course, the sessions would not have expressed their functions in this arena as social services. Their objectives were on a higher plane. It was the new church's conviction that the family was seminary of the church that drove its involvement not only with families in trouble, but also with those getting on quite well, or even just starting out. In addition to continuing medieval ecclesiastical jurisdiction over sexuality, they developed new forms of intervention in families in the interests of the all-important word. When couples appeared before their sessions to ask their banns of marriage to be pronounced, the elders were interested not only in whether they had already ventured into 'carnal deal', but also in how well they grasped the fundamental teachings of the Reformed faith so that they could pass along correct religious knowledge to their future progeny. Established families received regular visits from elders to ensure ongoing religious 'exercise' in their domestic seminaries.

The two forms of family intervention were not unrelated. The social services guaranteed the measure of peace and physical security needed before instruction could be successful. A child ill-fed or maltreated was in no position to absorb the word, hence the elders had perforce to be equally concerned with physical and spiritual nourishment. Spouses at odds and children abandoned or hurt also brought scandal upon the community – an invitation to divine judgment by storm or pestilence as well as to disrepute for the protestant gospel. Elders/magistrates most concerned with the parochial expense of maintaining bastards thus had no problem finding a religious apologetic for oversight and discipline of sexuality. In the end, though, the programme made possible by that theory had constructive results for both the disorderly and the theologically ignorant. It was both practical and catechetically effective. As with arbitration of quarrels, then, the kirk's family policies and their relatively efficient execution help to explain the protestant cultural revolution in Scotland.

* * *

A new household was properly founded with a marriage, so it was here that the elders began their systematic oversight of domestic life. They mandated that marriage not be contracted privately, undermining the authority of parents. Young people who 'have their heart touched' and wish to marry ought rather to 'give honour to their parents' by 'open[ing] unto them their affection, asking their counsel and assistance, how that motion, which they judge to be of God, may be performed'. On the other hand, the kirk roundly condemned marriage for gain rather than affection, even if the father's authority were thereby undermined: 'If the father, friend or master gainsay their request, and have no other cause than the common sort of men have, to wit, lack of goods and because they are not so high-born as they require', the couple could go to the minister and ask him 'to travail with their parents for their consent, which to do they are bound'. Then, even if the minister were unsuccessful, 'after sufficient admonition to the father' the minister could 'enter in the place of parents' and grant their marriage. 'For the work of God ought not to be hindered by the corrupt affections of worldly men', even when those men were fathers.[2] This was the theory – and a remarkable one for the time, attributing romantic love to God and elevating it over the authority of parents by putting the kirk *in loco parentis* in disputed cases. If implemented, it would surely have put marriages on a surer foundation than the

2. *First Book*, 192–93. Much of this development can be found across Europe and owed something to humanist thought; it was certainly part of the Calvinist agenda everywhere: Todd, *Christian Humanism*, ch. 4; Harrington, *Reordering Marriage, passim*; Jeffrey Watt, *The Making of Modern Marriage: Matrimonial Control and the Rise of Sentiment in Neuchâtel, 1550–1800* (Ithaca, 1992); Thomas Max Safley, *Let No Man Put Asunder* (Kirksville, 1984).

traditional dictates of profit and convenience. How well did the theory play out in the parishes?

Cases like that of Agnes Adamson and George Tomson of Belhelvie suggest that it was fully implemented. When Agnes's father objected to their proposed match in 1624, the session required him to 'give in the reasons why he protested and objected against the said marriage'. He did so, but the elders found his reasons insufficient and let his daughter follow her heart. In the interests of love and concord, they also supported children who, having bowed to parental pressure to contract a marriage, wanted to back out when they discovered how incompatible the spouse-to-be was. Always worried about long engagements, the Burntisland session in 1605 summoned Helen Anderson and John Tod in 1605 to ask them why they had not yet solemnised their marriage, long since arranged. Tod was willing to go ahead, but Anderson had changed her mind, having found Tod 'to be a waster insofar that he has spent all that he had'; not only did she have no affection for him, she had no intention of letting him squander her own estate as well. The session found her convincing 'and therefore pronounce[d] her free'. In gratitude for this narrow escape she 'gave of her own free will 40s *ad pios usus*'.[3] The Perth session acted likewise in the face of a very influential burgess, Alexander Peblis, when in the early 1630s both his son, Oliver, and his daughter, Isobel, opted out of the marriage contracts he had made for them in order to marry people more to their liking. They acted 'with mutual consent' of the contracted parties (children thus did have the power to abjure a contract if both parties agreed), but such was Peblis's power in the burgh that the presbytery had to be brought in to impose the session's decision on him, after the brethren appointed to 'deal with him' had failed to bring him around to his children's positions.[4] Absence of affection also sufficed for Marie Hutson, who told the Kirkcaldy session that she 'cannot find it in her heart to marry Matthew Prett', and Marion Giffert, who told the Liberton elders that her long engagement to Ronald Forrester had driven her to conclude that 'marriage was hell'. The sessions sensibly released both.[5]

3. CH2/32/1, f. 9; CH2/523/1, f. 19.
4. CH2/299/1, n.f., 5 September 1632 (Isobel), 15 May 1633 (ff. 97v, cf. 123v, Oliver). In the end, Isobel married a Perth burgess in the parish kirk, but the minister of Scone proclaimed Oliver's banns in the parish of Early, perhaps to avoid the dissension of another disputed marriage in the town church.
5. CH2/636/34, f. 4v (1614); CH2/383/1, f. 9. There are similar cases in Ellon (CH2/147/1, f. 13, 1607) and Perth (CH2/521/2, f. 76v, 1593). On the other hand, the Liberton session thought another couple an inappropriate match but found them so infatuated 'that there was no way' to part them, so they ordered 'perfecting of the promise of marriage passed betwixt them' (CH2/383/1, f. 12v).

The kirk's regulation of marriage obviously overlapped very considerably with the family's. Not only could the elders override a father's veto of marriage partner, they could also act in the stead of an offended father by, for instance, ordering a 'shotgun wedding' to deal with bridal pregnancy.[6] In marriage negotiations, they often acted to uphold parental objections to a proposed bride too young to marry, or to a young man too immature to take on the responsibility of a family. The South Leith session in effect wreaked a father's vengeance on his daughter's suitor/seducer by negotiating the excommunication of Robert Naper of Edinburgh 'for enticing William Trumbull's daughter and marrying her after an unlawful manner and contrary to her father's will, she being within twelve years of age'. This action may not have helped the new couple very much, but it did serve to underpin the authority of the bride's father. The Aberdeen elders acted in a more timely manner when in 1605 they voided a marriage agreement in support of the father of an apprentice cordiner who was still a minor and clearly not in a position to marry.[7] The Glasgow presbytery sensibly declined permission for Helen Bar to marry James Annan in 1594 'in respect the said James is in great debt' – nipping in the bud the family discord that, then as now, so often sprang from financial difficulties. And the Perth session refused in 1595 to let Thomas Cargil marry until he had repented the tomfoolery of his youth, being 'a fool and profane sporter', guising and cross-dressing, 'playing the counterfeit man'. Such juvenile behaviour was bad enough in adolescents; it should hardly characterise the head of a family.[8] Youth *per se*, however, seems not to have been a bar to matrimony: Perth on one day in 1618 witnessed the marriages of four 'honourable personages . . . being all four but pupils not exceeding twelve years old' with the assent of the session; in the same year Perth's minister married the master of Sanquhar and the daughter of a Yorkshire knight, 'neither of the parties exceed[ing] thirteen years of age'. In these cases, the kirk upheld the authority of families of considerable property and influence in the burgh.[9] But the parents'

6. As in Kirkcaldy, CH2/636/34, f. 7, where marriage was for the man effectively a penance for fornication. For a general treatment of early modern marriage in Scotland, see T.C. Smout, 'Scottish Marriage' in *Marriage and Society: Studies in the Social History of Marriage*, ed. R.B. Outhwaite (London, 1981).
7. CH2/716/1, f. 21; CH2/448/2, p. 138.
8. ML CH2/171/1, 28 January 1594; CH2/521/2, f. 127v.
9. CH2/521/6, f. 154; *Chronicle of Perth*, 19. These arrangements were carried out in spite of a 1600 General Assembly ruling that boys under fourteen ought not be married (twelve for girls) – a ruling enforced in Fife (*BUK* 3:953; *SAKS* 1:299). *First Book*, 194, explains, however, that the main reason for this ruling was that the partners should be mature enough to understand and affirm protestant doctrine; presumably these

consent counted for naught when the kirk's principal interest – fostering of correct doctrine and godly behaviour – was at stake. Thus, the Inveravon session refused to allow William Stewart to marry Helen Lesh 'in respect the woman did neither frequent the kirk nor communicate' and so was ill-suited to instruct a new family in doctrine and godly conduct.[10]

Effective networks of kirks within a presbytery or synod – a phenomenon that set Scotland's apart from other national Reformations – also put sessions in a good position to investigate the appropriateness of proposed partners from other parishes. James Boyson's experience is illustrative. In 1606, his pastor refused to marry him without a testimonial of his good behaviour from his former parish of Jedburgh; the message that came back was that he had committed adultery in the burgh seven years earlier, but had duly performed his repentance and behaved well since. Whether that testimonial sufficed to reassure his prospective bride's family, the record does not say.[11] But with a system like this in place, suspicious families had no need of private investigators to verify the suitability of their children's partners.[12]

Sessions worried that too long a delay between contract and solemnisation of a marriage in the kirk would lead to fornication, so they introduced a policy to ensure close oversight of the betrothal period and to punish financially a couple's failure to marry within a specified period of time, generally forty days. In the sixteenth century, this usually involved appointment of a 'cautioner' who would be held liable for any failure, to the tune of £10 in Perth by the 1580s.[13] Clearly it was in the cautioner's best interests to keep a close eye on the young people during the weeks before their marriage. After the turn of the century, however, sessions like Falkirk's found promises to marry so 'oft frequently broken', making it 'a continual act to pursue the cautioners' to pay the fine, that a more efficient mechanism was needed. They began requiring couples to make an

children had performed their examinations acceptably. They were doubtless the children of substantial citizens anxious to settle marital property arrangements. The usual age at first marriage for Scottish women was, as in Western Europe generally, in the mid- to late-twenties: *Women in Scotland c. 1080–c. 1700*, ed. Elizabeth Ewan and Maureen Meikle (East Linton, 1999), 225.

10. CH2/191/1, f. 9v. The session relented when Stewart paid a substantial bond and secured caution that she would reform.
11. CH2/198/1, f. 7v.
12. Marriage outside the church was possible but uncommon before the 1660s: Smout, 'Scottish Marriage', 204–36, presents the alternatives as 'illegal but valid'. This difference between Scottish and English legal systems may help to explain the greater success of ecclesiastical regulation of marriage in the northern realm.
13. CH2/521/1, ff. 4v, 98v; SAU ms 30451, ff. 4–4v.

advance deposit of money or valuables with the kirk officer as a pledge for accomplishment of the marriage within the forty days. Failure meant forfeiture of this 'pund'. Refusal to proclaim a couple's banns without it ensured that the money would come to the kirk's hands with no need for collectors to go to the trouble of tracking down recalcitrant cautioners – a system so evidently practical that sessions everywhere adopted it.[14] Usual deposits ranged from a half-merk in Dysart to £5 in Inveravon, with only a few burgh parishes aspiring to Perth's extravagant £10.[15] In Highland parishes it was often a sword, targe or plaid. Inveravon's elders ordinarily required a sword from the man's family, a plaid from the woman's. They were not overly rigid in imposing this system, returning a sword to a bride's father in 1640 despite failure of his daughter to marry within forty days, since it was 'not in his daughter's fault why the promise of marriage did not hold, seeing the man was diseased, not meet for marriage'. But for another couple they insisted on two targes to ensure that both partners would have learned the creed in time.[16] Sessions routinely kept the deposit if there were unexcused delay beyond forty days, if failure of the doctrinal examination required postponement, or if 'carnal deal' were suspected in the interval.[17] Since forfeitures went to the parish poor box, people anxious to avoid the elders coming to their doors for 'voluntary' contributions to the poor (as they did when the box ran dry) had a strong pecuniary as well as moral and religious motivation to keep watch over the betrothed in their midst and to report any suspicious behaviour to the session.

The kirk's concerns with marriage were doctrinal as well as moral, so they went to great lengths to set matrimony firmly within the context of the word. In the first generation of Reformation, Perth's elders had set up what came to be the norm in burgh parishes and the ideal throughout the land for pre-marital instruction and examination. They were dismayed in 1578 to find parishioners requesting proclamation of their banns 'almost always to be ignorant and to misknow the causes why they would marry; therefore, the assembly ordained all such folk to appear before the reader for the time . . . to the effect he may instruct them in the true knowledge of the causes of marriage.' By 1581, those to be married came to the kirk the evening before requesting their banns 'to be tried of the

14. CH2/400/1, p. 82; CH2/1463/1, ff. 1–1v; CH2/390/1, f. 1; CH2/624/2; CH2/716/1, f. 22v; CH2/471/1, f. 3; CH2/521/6, f. 108v; SAU CH2/Crail/1, f. 2v.
15. CH2/390/1, f. 1 (half a merk); CH2/1463, f. 1 (2 dollars); CH2/400/1, p. 82 and SAU CH2/Crail/1, f. 2v (both £5); CH2/191/1, f. 11 (£5 or an item of value); CH2/521/6, f. 108v and CH2/716/1, f. 21 (both £10).
16. CH2/191/1, ff. 51v, 52v, 54.
17. CH2/1463/1, ff. 1–1v; CH2/521/1, ff. 4v; CH2/400/1, p. 82.

minister and some elders' to make sure not only that they understood the protestant apologetic for matrimony, but also that they had sufficient command of their catechism to be able to instruct their own children when the time came. This was, after all, a major objective of family formation. Those unable to give a detailed confession of faith were 'not to be married till they learn to do the same'.[18] Other parishes followed suit, requiring as a matter of course demonstrable knowledge of the creed, ten commandments and Lord's Prayer. Those unable to perform in Glasgow were by a 1588 act of session 'declared unworthy to be joined in marriage and further censured' – reasonably enough, since they were obviously supposed to know their catechism anyway.[19] The examination at betrothal simply provided yet another checkpoint in the parish's regular catechetical programme. The couple's appearance for 'booking' their banns also provided an opportunity for the minister, reader or designated elders to offer 'exhortation to abstinence and holiness of life', as the Anstruther Wester session mandated.[20] Finally, it was a chance to ferret out closet catholics: one of the charges against Archbishop Patrick Adamson of St Andrews was that he had married the earl of Huntly 'without the confession of his faith'.[21]

The final solemnisation of marriage was also a logocentric event – hence its celebration in the setting of public worship. There were many reasons for the kirk to legislate against private marriages, and against marriages outside the home parish. In practical terms, together with proclamation of banns on each of the three preceding Sundays, it allowed public scrutiny of the parties in time to report impediments, like previous marriage in a neighbouring parish, or 'rumour of fornication', which would require public repentance before marriage.[22] More important,

18. CH2/521/1, ff. 9, 57; CH2/521/2, ff. 55, 81. The general guideline was *First Book*'s order that marriage not be offered to people unable to give an account of their faith (p. 196).
19. NLS ms 2782, f. 41. Other examples include Liberton (CH2/383/1, f. 18) and St Andrews (*SAKS* 1:439). Innerwick profited from ignorance by raising its 2-dollar pund in 1608 to £5 where they suspected it (CH2/1463/1, f. 1).
20. SAU CH2/624/2, p. 141 (1614).
21. LPL ms 2014, f. 186v (1591).
22. AAC CH2/751/2, f. 14v: In Ayr, a man off 'on his journey or voyage by sea or land' could until this 1622 act of session have a private marriage; now he had to marry 'immediately after divine service in the choir'. Clearly *First Book*'s mandated public solemnisation following three Sundays of banns (pp. 195, 197) was unevenly enforced in port towns. For synodal affirmation of the need for banns, see SAU ms 30451, f. 4. 'Informal marriage', without banns, was punished severely: Trinity College imposed a £30 fine in 1627 (CH2/141/1, f. 14). Sessions consistently punished marriage outside the home parish, in part because of the concomitant loss of oversight (e.g., CH2/400/1, p. 163).

requiring that marriage be solemnised 'in the face of the congregation' or 'in open audience of the kirk' affirmed the communal nature of the faith and the necessity of congregational participation in the rites of a church holding to the priesthood of believers.[23] It was, in short, an ecclesiological statement. Arguably the most important reason, however, was to ensure that the sermon and the additional ministerial admonition prescribed by the *Book of Common Order* for matrimony would surround and define the action. Accordingly, not only must marriage be public, it could only be celebrated on preaching days. Glasgow set aside Sunday afternoon 'before the sermon', adding later 'at sermon time Sunday and weekdays' but specifying that marriage should never be celebrated at mere reading of prayers.[24] The Edinburgh presbytery regarded the sermon as so essential to proper foundation of a new family that they disciplined ministers who married parishioners without it.[25] The wedding sermon could be a major production, as when Whittinghame's minister, Alexander Douglas, wed Agnes Merser in 1615, inviting a guest preacher to officiate, with 'nearly all the parishioners present'. On the other hand, it could be a 'short discourse about the nature and reasons of matrimony' (the usual triad of reproduction, avoidance of fornication and 'mutual comfort'), and 'a short harangue setting their duty afore them' just before the blessing of the couple at a weekday preaching service.[26] In either case, marriage was inaugurated by the word, the defining feature of protestant culture.

This is not to say that there was no ceremony involved in matrimony, however intent protestants were on abandoning 'vain rites, signs and traditions'. The protestant liturgy prescribed a 'form of marriage' with set prayers.[27] Place remained important. Pre-Reformation betrothal had been before a priest, and matrimony began at the 'wedding door' of the kirk.

23. *BUK* 1:192 (1571), and 1:393 (1581); *First Book*, 195–97. Public solemnisation in the home parish also had financial benefits, since the couple's fees to the kirk officer formed an important part of his stipend, and wedding offerings aided the parish poor. Perth accordingly forbade parishioners marrying in nearby Kinoull as 'prejudicial to the poor of this burgh', though it sold exceptions for £3 (CH2/521/8/1, f. 122).
24. NLS ms 2782, f. 41v (1584, relenting in 1633 to permit marriage at prayer services with payment of 19s); CH2/521/1, f. 105 (Perth ordering marriage 'in time of sermon'). Kilconquhar's session in 1637 blamed Sunday morning weddings for absences from afternoon sermons after searchers 'found a great number of those who were at David Quhyt's [morning] marriage drinking in John Ireland's, and . . . slaying a sheep in the midst of the hall' during the afternoon sermon. Ireland claimed that they had missed the sermon because 'their dinner was not finished'; if mutton were on the menu, their dinner may not yet have begun. He was disciplined for sabbath breach: SAU CH2/210/1, ff. 6–6v.
25. CH2/121/1, ff. 14, 16 (1586).
26. CH2/359/1, f. 3; Morer, 64–65.
27. *Forme of Prayers and Ministration of the Sacraments*, 93–100.

After the Reformation, the couple to be contracted came to the minister's chamber with their parents and two elders to witness the contract, and then 'with twelve of their nearest kindred' appeared 'in presence of the whole session to ratify the contract'.[28] And just as baptism moved at the Reformation from the kirk door to the pulpit, so the place of matrimony shifted from the door to a designated place 'apart from the rest of the company' near the pulpit, where the kirk officer was 'to place the couple on the stool of marriage'. Gesture and dress continued to matter, even in the absence of traditional material objects associated with marriage. The minister after his discourse directed the couple 'to join hands without using the ring'. And seventeenth-century brides with their hair 'very artificially plaited' went 'bareheaded to church and for all the wedding day, but then covered'.[29]

We have seen that festivity continued to be associated with marriage, and while the kirk certainly tried to curb the excesses of this merriment – as much for sumptuary and economic reasons as for religion's sake – they also recognised the appropriateness of marking the event. Thus they forbade marriage during fasts, knowing that abstinence would go by the board in favour of celebration, but at other times permitted feasting and dancing – though within strictly defined guidelines. The Glasgow elders required marriage feasts to be scheduled at noon, not at night; forbade 'superfluous gatherings' and limited the cost of banquets; and prohibited 'dancing openly on the street or beating of drums at marriages'. The Fife synod likewise banned 'in the day of their marriage any piping or fiddling or any such light vanities in open streets, about market crosses or any other common place', or processing to church 'having bagpipes playing before them'. But they did not attempt to abolish feasting, piping or dancing within doors.[30] And, as seventeenth-century genre painting suggests,

28. McKay, 100, 106; CH2/521/1, f. 98v; CH2/636/34, f. 21v; CH2/471/1, unnumbered folio at the beginning of Lasswade's book; *SAKS* 2:544 (St Andrews' 1584 requirement for contracting in the council house on Wednesdays, but before the ministry and parents). An exception to the rule, Aberdeen in 1568 barred the clergy from contracting of marriages, presumably to avoid confusion of matrimony with the tradition of handfasting, which allowed cohabitation without marriage: CH2/448/1, p. 15; Charles Rogers, *Social Life in Scotland* (Edinburgh, 1884), 103–04, noting an order six years earlier for those handfasted to marry immediately.

29. CH2/521/3, p. 213; Morer, 64–66; CH2/448/1, pp. 15–16 (marriage 'upon the stool afore the desk, conform to the use of Edinburgh and other kirks'; NAS ms RH2/1/35, f. 5v; *Early Travellers*, 140 (Sir William Brereton's 1636 account of Scottish dress).

30. NLS ms 2782, f. 41v (Glasgow acts of 1583, 1592, 1604 and 1625); SAU ms 30451, f. 5v. See also *SAKS* 1:341 (St Andrews' attempts to control newlyweds and their guests 'after supper insolently, in evil example of others, perturb[ing] the town with

sessions' efforts to abolish street dancing and piping (see plate 18) were in any case not particularly effective.[31] When burgh sessions like Perth's found in the 1580s that many of their labouring parishioners were 'marrying landward' to avoid the expense of town weddings, lacking funds 'to buy them clothes, nor to make bridals', they required them to marry in the burgh kirk on weekdays, when expectations for display seem to have been lower. Their explicit aim was to keep matrimony under their strict oversight to ensure proper instruction, examination and admonition; however, their orders implicitly recognised the continuing tradition of festive bridals.[32] If matrimonial ceremony was simpler than it had been, and festivity rather more restrained, nonetheless neither element disappeared entirely from Reformed celebration of marriage.

* * *

The kirk's regulation of marriage did not stop with formal solemnisation. Ministers and elders fully realised that this was only the beginning. For a truly Reformed family life to be established, continued supervision of married couples would be necessary. If the minutes of kirk sessions are any indication, they were as aware as modern marriage counsellors of the myriad difficulties that beset the husband–wife relationship, from simple disappointment or interfering relatives to financial stress or the depredations of alcohol. Determined to keep families together, they never hesitated to involve themselves in spousal quarrels or to investigate cases of apparent abandonment; moreover, they acquired a sufficiently good reputation as counsellors and reconcilers that parishioners willingly resorted to them in great numbers, either on behalf of neighbours or relatives, or to settle their own disputes. In extreme cases, victims of spousal abuse, both verbal and physical, found in the sessions a quick, relatively sympathetic and generally practical response to problems that required advisory and hortatory as much as punitive address. Matrimony was the kirk's proper

running therethrough in minstrelsy'), and CH2/1026/1, n.f., 7 June 1579 (Holy Rood, Stirling, prohibiting 'all public dancing and plays in the gates of the burgh on the day of the marriage', with a £10 fine – the inclusion of plays indicating another aspect of bridal festivity).

31. This painting by Jacob de Wet or one of his school dates from the second half of the seventeenth century. Sir William Bruce brought de Wet from Holland to paint the ceilings of Holyroodhouse. His only genre painting is this wedding scene, which appears as *Highland Wedding* in a 1724 inventory of Sir John Clerk of Penicuik: MacMillan, 79–80. The Museum of Scotland calls it *Lowland Wedding* or *Country Dance*.

32. CH2/521/1, f. 105; Stirling's session and council forbade bridals outside the burgh because of their inability to control landward festivities: CH2/1026/1, n.f., 1 December 1608.

jurisdiction, but in any case the sessions offered a better alternative than burgh or barony courts because their primary objective was restoration, not retribution. The formula adopted by Perth's clerk in recording marital difficulties brought to the session in the 1580s is telling: 'The minister and elders having respect to the good love and amity that should be betwixt a man and his wife, especially between Alexander Paterson and Jonet Duncan his spouse, appoints [three elders] to confer with them and make them to agree.'[33] Parochial sessions also had the advantage over secular courts in their established mechanisms for intensive counselling (or 'dealing with') and long-term oversight and enforcement.

Examples abound of couples voluntarily bringing their marital problems to the elders, sometimes separately, to complain about each other, but often together. Andrew Nune and Agnes Leslie of Aberdeen are typical: they came to the Aberdeen session in 1604 'mutually complaining about the misbehaviour of the other', each apparently hoping that the session 'after the hearing of both parties' would identify the other as the offender. Instead, and again typically, the elders identified fault in both parties and, after long dealing with the couple to get them to recognise the fact, admonished both to behave themselves 'lovingly and dutifully each towards the other in time coming and to put in oblivion all bypast grudges on either side'. To add teeth to the admonition, they also warned that the first to break the concord would be 'severely censured'. In Perth, 'great enmity having risen between Robert Rutherford and Jonet Morice his wife, and each of them having given in complaints against the other', the elders found their behaviour 'very unkindly between a man and his wife' and 'laboured to reconcile them together'. They finally got Rutherford to 'consent to adhere to his wife and entertain [materially sustain] her as becomes [a husband] . . . conditionally if she would bring home the gear she took forth of their house' during their last quarrel. She in turn consented to act as a Christian wife 'if he do his duty towards her, whereupon each of them in presence of the session made mutual promise to the other' – a ritual conclusion to a lengthy negotiation.[34] Admonitions 'to live Christianly and to keep order in his own house' or 'to adhere Christianly and peaceably among themselves' were underpinned with threats of censure from the pulpit; what is noteworthy is that, even knowing this, couples still had recourse to the kirk. With any luck, private settlement in the session house would work, and the embarrassment of

33. CH2/521/2, f. 11v *et passim*.
34. CH2/448/2, p. 73; CH2/521/7, p. 33. In ritually finalising an agreement, couples often 'acted themselves' to maintain harmony, 'putting their hands to the pen' of the notary to record their promise, as in the 1625 Newbattle case of Henry Wardlaw and Jonet Aitken: CH2/276/1, f. 7v.

public admonition could be avoided.[35] The kirk's ultimate objective was always to prevent separation and strengthen marriage.

Reconciliation involved a balance of investigation, negotiation, counsel and admonition, arrangements for supervision, and the threat, if not the execution, of punishment for future failures. The treatment of the first two was as a rule quite even-handed. The elders knew it takes two to tango, and never heard one party's complaint without then listening carefully to the other. Their orders reflect this. The Glasgow presbytery, asked to investigate the proposed divorce of Christiane Graham, Lady Hilsyt, from Sir Walter Levingstone, prevented the split in favour of her promise to be obedient 'if it please her husband to have her as his spouse' and his 'willingly to resort and adhere to dame Christiane Graham his lady and do the duty of a husband to her': each had to grant something to the other.[36] Elgin's session found in a 1587 investigation of William Hendry's complaint that his wife, Jonet Vaus, 'refuses the duty of marriage to him' that she had good reason, since 'she feared the danger of her life at the hands of the said William'; they censured both and required each to have a caution for future adherence and restraint from violence. When David Greffyt's wife complained of his adultery, the Inveravon elders took just as seriously his explanation that his wife 'had no will to abide with him and cannot serve him as his wife'; they punished him for his sexual offence but also required 'his wife to adhere to him, otherwise he is not bound to sustain her'.[37]

Of course, there were times when the fault did, indeed, lie so much more on one side than the other that the session condemned the offender out of hand and either threatened or prescribed condign punishment – generally in the case of errant husbands.[38] The Selkirk brethren had no

35. CH2/523/1, ff. 9v, 10; NLS ms 2782, f. 62.

36. ML CH2/171/1, ff. 50v, 55. The Capsie session resorted to the presbytery to settle discord between lairds and their wives. See NAS ms RH2/1/35, f. 36 for a similar Edinburgh settlement.

37. CH2/145/1, f. 11v; CH2/191/1, f. 45 (1635). Anstruther Wester's elders likewise sympathised with James Crichton, who in 1626 'declared he could not keep house' with his wife, Margaret Paterson, 'because of her wickedness and evilness', which her neighbours verified: SAU CH2/624/3, p. 15 (1626); the case went to presbytery, whose records for the 1620s do not survive.

38. ML CH2/171/1, f. 22 (the magistrates to proceed against a man if he would not 'do the duty of a faithful husband to her'); SAU CH2/624/3, p. 35 (Andro Dasone to 'adhere to his wife and keep company with her or else to leave this congregation'); CH2/327/1, ff. 9–9v (an adulterer in Langnewton threatened with excommunication for 'continuing in evil manners'); CH2/448/2, p. 5 and CH2/716/1, f. 21v (deserting husbands warded in Aberdeen, threatened with prosecution for adultery in South Leith).

sympathy for the Kippelaw feuer Nicholas Halywell, who claimed that he was too poor to 'bide together' with his spendthrift wife; finding 'no such impediment', they required him to 'do his duty to her' or be excommunicated, noting in addition that he had earlier fallen into adultery while away from his wife and had best avoid another temptation by reuniting.[39] Examples where the wife was singled out as the sole offender are more unusual, but they did occur.[40] In adultery cases, even if one spouse had committed violence against the other's partner, the elders prosecuted only the sexual offender. Thus, when Jonet Aitken of Newbattle caught her husband offering Jonet Tor 20s and a pair of shoes for sex (which 'he deponed they would have soon done'), she attacked Tor and hauled her husband before the session; the elders ignored Aitken's violence against Tor but required public repentance of her husband. Again, the Burntisland elders traced William Stevenson's 1611 knife attack on James Fathie over 'a little jealousy that he had against him with his wife, Isobell Ivet', to Ivet's flirtatious ways, so she was the one 'sharply rebuked' and ordered 'to behave herself as is becoming her sex with modesty, not to wander about, but to keep at home, and not to abuse her husband by word or deed'. They put Ivet in the charge of a neighbour, Marge Peacock, who was to report any future suspicious behaviour – an example of the follow-up procedures that sessions devised to ensure compliance.[41]

The process of sorting out what was really going on in a marriage and bringing the couple around to a settlement could be quite lengthy and require some effort by the minister and elders in 'dealing with' or counselling the couple. The minister Robert Blair recorded spending two days and a night counselling 'a gracious woman married to a gross churl' in his congregation before the unfortunate woman 'achieved victory' and returned to her spouse.[42] And Perth's minister John Malcolm dealt

39. CH2/327/1, f. 9; cf. CH2/1/1, n.f., 22 September 1608. A feu was a heritable lease of land in exchange for a fixed annual rent, unlike the English leasehold in which there was no permanent transfer of land: Margaret Sanderson, *Scottish Rural Society in the Sixteenth Century* (Edinburgh, 1982), 142.
40. CH2/521/6, f. 96v; CH2/390/1, f. 40; CH2/523/1, f. 46.
41. CH2/276/1, f. 7v; CH2/523/1, f. 46; cf. CH2/521/1, f. 73 (1582). St Andrews appointed set times for spouses to report back to them their compliance – e.g., Andro Lummisden to 'adhere in bed and board within forty-eight hours and let the minister and elders know'; to double-check, they also required a report within a week from the wife and 'others their neighbours': *SAKS* 1:28.
42. Blair, 105–06. Blair was at the time a widower with three children, but no one seems to have looked askance at his time with this woman. He recorded that she was so desperate that she preferred death to life with her husband. One wonders whether this marriage merited his effort or her devotion. There is no indication that Blair conferred with the husband, but this may be because the man was recalcitrant and gave the minister no 'victory' to record.

'thrice . . . to reconcile the strife between' a couple in his parish before turning over the abusive husband to the session upon his stubborn insistence that his wife 'justly deserved whatever he did to her'.[43] The Paisley case of Agnes Ralston and John Logan, begun by Ralston's petition 'craving adherence of the said John', continued from February through to the end of April 1603 before a settlement was reached; in other cases sessions saved time by imposing binding arbitration.[44]

In many cases the fault lay not so much with either partner in the marriage as with family friends or other relatives, particularly mothers-in-law. James Mill complained to the Canongate session in 1566 that his mother made life miserable for his bride, 'calling his wife bare-assed whore' and 'other sundry injurious words.' The elders appointed 'two honest amiable men for their agreement', with 'the whole kirk to be ourisman', which seems to have done the trick, for the couple do not again appear in the records. In 1587, Elspeth Cudbert of Perth located the source of her marital problems less in her husband than in his friend Malcolm Denis, who 'entertained her husband in his house and suffered him not to come to his own house neither night nor day, nor to entertain his wife and house as he should do, which was found to be very evil done.' The session ordered Denis to leave Cudbert's husband alone to get on with the more important relationship with his wife.[45] Elders were aware that wives struggling to keep their husbands' affections ought to be able to count on the church's help, lest they resort to more nefarious means: Katherine Bras of Bog Kirkland considered another option when in 1595, 'a discord falling out between her and her . . . husband, he became hard and outward to her'. When Pet Lowry, an 'expert leech', found her 'lying in her yard dreary and sorrowful for that cause', he 'offered to her to cause her husband love her as well as ever he did if she would give him 40s therefore'.[46] If the choice were session intervention or a love potion from the local charmer, the elders' duty was clear.

It was often abandoned wives who initiated kirk involvement in family problems. Sometimes their petitions, like those of abused spouses, were

43. CH2/521/8/1, f. 53. The elders had him warded in the tollbooth overnight, but they also found his wife guilty of 'despiteful misbehaviour towards her husband'. The Kirkcaldy session in 1628 spent weeks sorting out the troubled marriages of Walter Creighton and John Herd: CH2/636/34, f. 108.

44. CH2/294/1, f. 7v; *Dundonald*, 65; CH2/521/2, f. 11v; ML CH2/171/1, f. 52.

45. *Canongate*, 48, 63 (another such case, both spouses and the wife's mother all found 'criminable the one to the other' and made to 'ask each other's forgiveness there instant'); CH2/521/2, f. 6v.

46. *Dundonald*, 57–58. She was too poor to take him up on the offer of a love potion. She voluntarily reported the affair to the session nine years later, by which time she was a widow.

simply the required prelude to divorce proceedings, possible after the Reformation in commissary courts for those with the wherewithal to pursue them.[47] But more often, petitioners seem to have genuinely sought reconciliation, 'both at bed and board'.[48] In part, this could be attributed to the loss of face attached to abandonment, for men as well as women. In many cases, financial dependency was the issue, so that petitions asked for 'entertainment' as well as 'adherence'. But a preponderance sought restoration of the spousal relationship, knowing that the session would also provide continued supervision to ensure that an errant spouse would not only 'adhere', but also 'keep a loving and dutiful behaviour towards her' in future.[49] The elders were in fact the regular resort of women whose absent husbands were seeking divorce in the commissary courts but who did not for their own part wish to dissolve the marriage. When William Rantoun sued Elizabeth Geddy for divorce on grounds of adultery in 1560, she turned to the St Andrews session to restore her sullied reputation as well as her marriage. Insisting that he had trumped up the adultery charge just to be rid of her, she asked the session to be 'the instrument of a mutual love between my husband and me'. The elders duly investigated, obtaining more than twenty depositions from witnesses on both sides, and, after concluding that she was innocent, proceeded to attempt restoration of the relationship by ordering him to treat her 'in bed and

47. On divorce and the jurisdiction of commissary courts, see David B. Smith, 'The Spiritual Jurisdiction 1560–64', *RSCHS* 25 (1993), 1–18, 'A Note on Divorce for Desertion', *Juridical Review* 51 (1939), 254–59, and 'The Reformers and Divorce', *SHR* 9 (1912), 10–36; R.D. Ireland, 'Divorce, Nullity of Marriage and Separation' in *An Introduction to Scottish Legal History* (Edinburgh, 1958), 82–89. Initial resort to parochial courts provided the documentation of desertion or other grievance necessary to commence divorce proceedings, with violation of an adherence order or a conviction for adultery serving as grounds for divorce. The fact that the commissary courts handled such acrimonious aspects of separation as property division left sessions free to focus on the pastoral side. For pre-Reformation divorce (really separation, since remarriage was not permitted), see J.D. Scanlan, 'Husband and Wife: Pre-Reformation Canon Law of Marriage of the Officials' Courts' in *An Introduction to Scottish Legal History* (Edinburgh, 1958), 69–81; Ollivant.
48. CH2/448/2, pp. 6–7 – Margaret Wood's March 1603 petition after her husband, Alexander Brodie, had left her and 'got his entertainment in Effie [Robertson]'s house' for several years, which the Aberdeen elders found 'suspicious'. They eventually banished Robertson but allowed Brodie to remain in town after repenting his adultery, in order to maintain his marriage (p. 62, February 1604). Adherence in bed as well as board was frequently demanded by wives as well as husbands on grounds that the Form of Marriage specified that neither had power over their own bodies; being by marriage 'knit together', neither could decline sexual intercourse without grounds.
49. E.g., CH2/448/2, pp. 73, 80.

board as becomes a husband'.[50] While the record indicates no particular effort at counselling the troubled couple, simply by rehabilitating Geddy's good name in the community the elders provided a service to her, and if her husband had been genuinely suspicious, their investigation may have calmed his fears. With no more hope of divorce, moreover, he would have acquired some motivation at least to work towards an accommodation with his wife. The protestant kirk, unlike its catholic forebear, was willing to offer divorce, but only in cases demonstrably irreconcilable or physically dangerous to one partner, or when abandonment was of many years' duration and appeared irreversible. Rather, elders and ministers devoted considerable time and effort to reconciliation, even following the adultery of one or both spouses.

Abandonment in some cases may in itself have been a call for help by troubled spouses. It drew to the Burntisland session's attention the trouble between Archibald Nicholson and his wife, Isobell Kimbell, in 1603. When the couple were summoned to account for their 'separating themselves from each other, being married persons', Kimbell declared that she was 'willing ever to dwell with her husband and that the default was on his part'; the fact that Nicholson granted the point and readily agreed to the elders' order to 'adhere' in future suggests that their rift was not deep and perhaps just needed a bit of outside attention to mend it. They did not again appear before the session.[51]

Other abandonment cases were more complicated. Christiane Alan of Falkirk complained of her husband's absence rather late in the day, after he had not only left her, but also committed bigamy. They had married eleven years before, but the relationship disintegrated straightaway. He quickly 'disposed her goods and thereafter deserted her maliciously and did never resort to her again till now, when he acknowledged that he had married another wife.' Still, the session managed to pressure him into a promise 'under the pain of death never hereafter to bear company with Jean Murray whom he last married' and to 'adhere to' Alan; he agreed to public repentance and banishment from the town if he failed to remain faithful ('pain of death' being his own addition to the promise). The session departed from the norm for adulterers in imposing no financial penalty, presumably to spare the innocent wife, already despoiled of her goods, and

50. *SAKS* 1:18. Cf. the similar case of John Scott and Jonet Murray, *SAKS* 1:437–39, 441–42, culminating in Scott's repentance for slander, kneeling before his wife in the kirk and saying, 'False tongue thou lied' with 'his own tongue in his hand'. Michael Graham, 'Women and the Church Courts in Reformation-Era Scotland' in *Women in Scotland*, 187–98, also notes this case; he argues effectively that women often used the sessions to defend their interests. See also CH2/77/1, f. 10v.

51. CH2/523/1, f. 9.

to avoid putting the refounded marriage at risk by undermining the couple's solvency.[52] Other sessions accompanied 'adherence' orders with threats of excommunication and provisions for offending spouses periodically to reappear before the elders to report their obedience.[53] Burntisland 'sharply threatened' banishment to get Geillis Loquhory to return to her husband, John Glen, in 1605; Glen had promised to 'do anything the session will enjoin to him' to get his wife back, which may have swayed her as much as the threat did. They concluded an agreement before the session by 'joining their hands' as a sign of mended union. When the elders checked two weeks later, however, Glen had failed to take his wife back, claiming that he could not safely do so without 'a warrant that she would not put violent hands on him'. Finding his fear well-founded, they 'sharply rebuked' Loquhory and extracted her promise to 'behave herself dutifully unto him as becomes'. After further exhortation, the couple again 'joined hands and departed in peace', this time with no further recorded relapse. When Aberdeen's follow-up procedures revealed failure to adhere, they got the bailies to imprison recalcitrant husbands in the kirk vault or steeple and threatened contumacious wives with dunking.[54] But sessions rarely resorted to such heavy-handed measures unless gentler efforts had repeatedly failed.

The distinctive networks among Scots parishes enabled a tracking system for deserting spouses that made resort to the church a sensible option for the abandoned. When Jonet Balmanne reported to the Burntisland elders that her husband, James Anderson, had left her and 'remained in Ayr this two or three years bygone and has neither called nor sent unto her' as he had promised, they simply had their clerk write to the minister of Ayr and have him 'enjoin the said James to return back to his own wife'. The Dron session sent two of their number to speak with a neighbouring minister in like circumstances, and the Glasgow brethren regularly facilitated such communications among parishes in the presbytery.[55] With such a system in place James Turnbull of Perth had no luck trying to justify his adultery in 1622 by explaining that his wife, Bessie Pringill, 'without any cause on his side, has deserted from him the

52. CH2/400/1, pp. 276–77 (1635). Obviously the fact of bigamy indicates that parochial oversight of matrimony was uneven; it was still possible in the 1630s to find Scottish parishes that did not enforce the requirement of a testimonial. Bigamy itself was punished in secular and commissary courts; the latter's records for this case are not extant.

53. CH2/145/1, f. 4 (1586).

54. CH2/523/1, ff. 22; CH2/448/2, pp. 6–7, 12, 14, 62.

55. CH2/523/1, f. 9; CH2/93/1, ff. 23–23v (my foliation); ML CH2/171/1, ff. 32v, 45 (also communicating with other presbyteries about deserting spouses).

space of two years bygone'; the elders just wrote to their counterparts in Cupar, where she had gone, to have her sent back 'to be confronted together and examined for knowing in whose default their non-cohabitation was'.[56]

Given the loss of face entailed by abandonment, one would expect that the family of the abandoned spouse would be the logical body to turn to for help in such cases, and doubtless relatives did such service rather than submit the family name to further opprobrium by getting the kirk involved. Duncan Robertson, whose sister Violat had been abandoned by her husband, Thomas Dundy, succeeded in 1579 in getting a case already before the Perth session remanded to the family 'under hope of agreeance'; unfortunately, the elders resumed jurisdiction a month later after the family had clearly failed. To Violat Robertson's complaint that Dundy had left her 'destitute of all succour, took her goods and gear, and would not entertain her', Dundy explained that she had been unfaithful to him on Yule Day of 1577, when she 'passed beyond the burgh and there abused her[self] in piping and dancing and pollution of her body'. The elders found this a credible complaint – attesting again to the survival of raucous Yuletide celebration; however, Dundy failed to prove his claim and was ordered to 'entertain her in bed and board . . . as becomes a faithful husband unto his lawful wife, under pain of excommunication'.[57] Given that this husband was so anxious to separate from his wife that he was willing to pay the price for slandering her, we have to wonder how happy an arrangement this would have been, but at least as a result of the 'entertainment' ruling, Robertson was assured of financial support.

In other cases sessions despaired of reconciling couples and granted separation, but they nearly always performed the useful service of ordering material sustenance of the wife, particularly if she were maintaining dependent children or if, like Bessie Gibson of Perth, she were 'an aged sickly infirm woman'. Gibson won 'a weekly help for relief' from her husband, to be enforced by the town bailie. So did Marion Layng, the 'spouse leprous' of James Mitchell of Balmour. This was a difficult case, sent on to the Glasgow presbytery in 1594. The brethren thought it reprehensible that Mitchell abandoned Layng in her sickness, but they could hardly require very close adherence to a woman with a highly contagious disease. They decided to call in the neighbours to ask what they 'think better be done between the said James and Marion'. In the end,

56. CH2/521/7, p. 303. The session still punished Turnbull's adultery. They did not record the conclusion of the case, and Cupar's records for this date are not extant.

57. CH2/521/1, ff. 14–15v, 17v–18 (case continuing from October 1578 to February 1579, and culminating in Dundy's admonition before the congregation).

all agreed that Mitchell need not live with his wife, but he must support her, 'the minister to see this put to execution, and the neighbours to them to testify to that effect'. In Mortlach, John Roy had to agree to sustain his wife and secure a cautioner to ensure that, if he failed, he would give 'half of all his goods to the proper use of Elspeth More his wife' – the usual settlement in a formal separation, which was within the judicial provenance of the session.[58] The hope implicit in separation orders was usually that in time the couple might be reunited. Thus, when the Glasgow session arranged an annual allowance to the wife in a 1635 separation, they noted that the couple were 'content to separate one from the other *till God send more love into their hearts*'. Of course, sessions also issued support orders to husbands who had not separated from their wives, but whose wives had reported them for failure to 'entertain'.[59] Sessions may have been composed entirely of men, but they were not insensitive to the needs of women.

* * *

The most serious instances of marital discord with which the sessions dealt were those involving spousal abuse. These are strikingly numerous in many minute books and must have taken a significant amount of time; however, nowhere do elders seem to have been daunted by the problem. They took on the challenge even of these most extreme cases, seeking resolution and restoration of the relationship, and always recognising that their continued monitoring would be required for the process to work.

If the minute books are any indication, domestic violence was rampant in early modern Scotland. Charges of 'dinging', 'striking' and 'misusing his wife' – all too often 'to the great effusion of her blood' – recur with appalling frequency.[60] Details recorded in depositions can be chilling. When the wife

58. CH2/521/7, p. 471; ML CH2/171/1, f. 30v; CH2/529/1, f. 10v (1625). Preventing a wife's destitution was obviously in the best interests of kirk and community, since otherwise they would have to add her to the poor rolls. The kirk granted separations, which unlike divorces did not permit remarriage, presumably because they allowed for the possibility of reunion. CH2/448/1, p. 14, records another failure to reconcile.
59. NLS ms 2782, f. 41v (emphasis mine); CH2/636/34, f. 56v. For negotiation of alimony payment schedules, see CH2/448/2, p. 131.
60. In the tiny parish of Burntisland, there were eight cases of spousal violence in just the first five months of 1604: CH2/523/1, ff. 9v–11. See also CH2/448/2, pp. 32, 80, 102, 105–06, 136; CH2/472/1, f. 21v; CH2/258/1, f. 23v; CH2/276/1, ff. 1v, 6, 69; CH2/716/1, ff. 9v, 12v; CH2/716/2, f. 92; CH2/621/1, ff. 358, 362; CH2/751/1, ff. 3v, 11v, 185v; CH2/CH2/521/3, pp. 316–17; CH2/521/7, p. 92; CH2/521/8/1, ff. 53, 109; CH2/521/8/1, f. 225; *Dundonald*, 248, 257, 330, 380; AAC CH2/751/1, ff. 8v, 10v – among many other examples.

of an adulterer, David Gray, in 1582 ventured to reprove him for his infidelity in the presence of their neighbours, 'he came home immediately thereafter and bound her hands and feet and took the stenchal off a window and laying her on the sill, brake her legs, arms and shoulder, which she showed before the assembly, and neighbours testified.' Gray's partner in adultery, Helen Watson, was victim of his violent temper as well. When the elders sent to seize the couple for their renewed adultery in 1584 found her 'at home in her bed lying in the brewhouse, being full of blue and bloody strokes', she told them that 'David did it because he got not his will of her'.[61] John MacWatter of Perth admitted 'abusing of his wife' for doing a poor job of keeping his accounts, 'striking her with hands and feet, and pursu[ing] her with a drawn whinger, and lately hurt with a knife on the shoulder'.[62] A merchant burgess of Aberdeen, in an altercation with his wife, Bessie Gordon, 'wound[ed] her in the head to the effusion of her blood in great quantity'; another in the same burgh 'ofttimes in his rage and fury . . . abused [his wife, Katherine Thornton] by many extraordinary forms of dealing, as by giving her strikes, both blood and bla [bruise], cutting off her vesture, burning the same in the fire, with many other oppressions and cruelties which the said Katherine is ashamed to report', including 'unnatural forms of dealing', not to mention taking her goods and leaving her destitute 'and her bairns . . . in great misery' when he went off to England.[63]

The violence could go in the other direction as well. Recorded instances of husband abuse are remarkably numerous, given the loss of face that a man in this society would have suffered in making complaint of

61. CH2/521/1, ff. 82v, 104. The elders learned 'by report of neighbours' that Gray and Watson had been cohabiting for some time. The elder Dyonisius Conquerer agreed to serve as Gray's caution at £100, a sum he lost when in 1584 the watch found Gray and Watson 'in his naked bed' and sent them to an assize, 'lest that otherwise by any longer winking at their wickedness, God in his justice plague both us and you with the rest of this city, as miserable experience has begun to teach us' (f. 106v). They were executed in January 1585 'on the gibbet beneath the cross foreanent her mother's yett': CH2/521/1, f. 107.
62. CH2/521/3, pp. 316–17. The elders found him 'a profane man many ways' but got him to repent and agree to 'live in concord with his wife'.
63. CH2/448/2, pp. 80, 102 (1604). Thornton's husband, William Allen, not only 'converted all his lands, gear and moyen in sums of money in defraud of his said spouse', but also 'of mere malice, he has served and registered an inhibition against her, that no person shall lend or let her anything on her credit' (pp. 105–06; the case continues pp. 112, 131, ending in separation with payment of alimony). Abusive husbands often seized or destroyed their wives' clothing (cf. CH2/521/7, p. 92, for instance), perhaps to prevent them appearing in public to seek help. Other notorious Aberdeen cases include Elspeth Dalgarne's near-blinding at her husband's hands (CH2/448/2, p. 136, 1605), and Peter Sewan's 'unmerciful dinging of his wife' and insistence to the session that 'it behoved him to break her arm' (CH2/448/3, p. 74, 1611).

victimisation by his wife.[64] His own humiliation would be all the greater if his wife had to undergo public repentance, as Issobel Hird of South Leith did, on Sunday in the kirk and Monday for two hours in the jougs 'for scolding, drunkenness and putting hand in her husband and causing him blood by braking of a staff upon him'.[65] The abuse must have been severe indeed for the victim to submit to his neighbours' inevitable criticism for failure to rule his household well. Here we have implicit testimony to the effectiveness of church discipline as a preventive: surely men would not have submitted their cases to the elders were the kirk's solutions not reputed to end violence.[66]

Of course, there were also many cases of mutual abuse. The Mid-Calder session dealt in 1609, for instance, with the 'continual strife and debate between Alexander Anderson' and his wife; the Canongate elders in 1566 with a wife 'casting at [her husband] with her hands, stones and dirt' but swearing that she had 'greater cause to complain upon him, for I dread bodily harm of him'. They ruled 'both culpable', as the Perth elders did the skinner William Robertson, his wife, and their daughter-in-law, finding that 'he struck and dang them, and they him, with crying and shoutings to the great dishonour of God's holy day'.[67]

Domestic violence, then as now, was very often fuelled by alcohol. Phrases like 'convict in drunkenness in striking his wife', 'drunken and abusing his wife' and (in cases of mutual violence) 'drunkenness and open misbehaviour the one towards the other' or the order 'him and her to abstain from fighting and drinking' recur regularly in the minute books.[68] Sessions investigating charges like John Young's, that 'when he goes out she [his wife] shames him', frequently uncovered evidence that the plaintiff's own drunkenness was what actually brought on the shaming.[69]

64. E.g., CH2/621/1, p. 359 (1605); CH2/521/1, f. 26; CH2/521/2, f. 66; CH2/521/7, p. 315; CH2/718/4, f. 10v; *Dundonald*, 233; CH2/448/2, pp. 256–57, 280.
65. CH2/716/2, f. 97v. She repented in sackcloth, holding the staff. Marion Anderson repented in Govan in 1593 in linen for having 'dung her goodman' (ML CH2/171/1, f. 10v); cf. NLS ms 2782, f. 62; CH2/521/2, f. 66; CH2/191/1, f. 39 (the jougs for husband-beating in Inveravon).
66. I have not found instances of repeat offences by wives, although there are (rare) instances of husbands appearing before the sessions for repeating their abuse, and generally being banished for recidivism: e.g., CH2/621/1, pp. 358, 362.
67. CH2/266/1, f. 10; *Canongate*, 38 (the case initiated by the husband); CH2/521/8/2, f. 225.
68. In Burntisland (CH2/523/1), for instance, see ff. 10v, 11, 12v, 16v, 17, 19, 19v, 21v, 23–23v, 39v, 44v, etc. Among examples from other parishes, see CH2/716/2, ff. 92, 97v; AAC CH2/751/1, ff. 3v, 11v; CH2/471/1, f. 5v.
69. CH2/523/1, f. 10v. They discovered from their own records that Young, a habitual drunkard, had been in trouble for fighting ten years before and so prescribed abstinence.

Drunken misbehaviour towards a spouse could bring the kirk officers themselves into danger as they attempted to intervene physically(taking on a role of modern police forces), as when David Loudon of Ayr, interrupted by a deacon while beating his wife, threatened to 'have a mends of him'.[70] While the kirk sessions did not often order abstinence from ale or *aqua vitae* (whisky), they certainly recognised a connection between alcohol and violence, in the home as on the streets. As William Cowper told his parishioners, drunkenness is 'both a sin and a mother of sins'; Zachary Boyd gave his auditors the pithier 'If thou would be a man of health, be not a drinker of healths'.[71] Accordingly, they often ordered restraint in its consumption as part of a marital settlement. Only in extreme cases like those of Henry Blau and John Young of Burntisland (both publicly fighting with their wives after drinking) did the session prescribe complete abstinence as the means to 'live Christianly in concord and amity with his wife'.[72] A husband's drunkenness did not necessarily excuse a wife's misbehaviour, however: when Matthew Young was rebuked for 'striking his wife, drinking, banning, swearing, [and] blaspheming', he complained that his wife drove him to it, since 'whether he drink or not, she calls him drunken'. Upon further investigation, the elders were convinced by the couple's neighbours that their abuse was mutual, in words and blows, and ordered 'both to amend' or be banished.[73] On the other hand, when John Hunter told the same session that he had struck his wife in his drunkenness because she 'invited him with ill words' and would only amend 'if she behave herself more quietly', the elders found no evidence of her fault and so reproved him alone.[74] Generally even-handed in their treatment of husbands and wives, they realised that in some cases the fault lay in one spouse.

The kirk was remarkably forward-looking in its recognition of verbal as well as physical abuse. Where else in the sixteenth century do we find the church actively punishing injury 'by *word* or deed', or 'misusing her *by word*

70. AAC CH2/751/1, f. 3v (1604).
71. Cowper, 347–48; Boyd, *Balme*, 81, concluding the charge to 'drink soberly', though not to abstain from drink. See also *First Book*, 166–67; *BUK* 1:284 (1573).
72. CH2/523/1, f. 10v, ordering that in case Blau lapsed, he would pay 40s, and in addition sending an elder 'to admonish his wife and exhort her to these things' – presumably to concord, since she was the one who complained about his drinking. Young was threatened with banishment.
73. CH2/523/1, ff. 10v, 23v, 27v (1604–07).
74. CH2/523/1, f. 23; cf. ff. 16v, 19v, 21v. Where Burntisland's elders after investigation (generally by inviting the depositions of neighbours) could not agree on who was at fault, they sent the couple out of the room to vote on the ruling (e.g., f. 39v).

against the duty of a loving husband'?[75] John Hunter's wife may not have used ill words against him, but Margaret Ross of Aberdeen's tongue was thought to have driven her husband 'to ding her', so the Aberdeen elders balanced his imprisonment and public repentance with her admonition 'never to offend him by word in time coming'.[76] Geillis Henryson appeared before Burntisland's session both for 'reproachful words spoken to her husband and casting stones at him'.[77] But evil speech was not the exclusive province of women. The Ayr elders sought to prevent verbal taunting of a wronged wife by her adulterous husband, Thomas Bowman, when they ordered him 'not to name the name of the said Agnes [his paramour] to his wife under pain of £20 unforgiven [not to be reduced on any grounds], and his wife's oath to serve for a sufficient proof of this act' – the latter provision giving power of oversight to the wife, specifying for the record that they would believe any report she made.[78]

The kirk attempted to prevent recurrence of spousal abuse by punishment or threat of punishment, by seeking and addressing the causes of family discord, by providing rituals of reconciliation and by giving oversight of compliance.[79] Identifying the cause of the problem was clearly a priority. Ayr's elders ordered Thomas Bowman not only 'to abstain from striking of his wife, flyting or chiding with her', but also 'to forbear the company of Agnes Bryce privately or publicly, also in eating or drinking or any manner of fellowship with her': they presumably hoped that if any suspicion of infidelity could be avoided, perhaps the couple would get along. Tracing the violent discord in William Robertson's household to a disruptive daughter-in-law, the Perth elders ordered her to move out.[80] And we saw in the previous chapter the care with which the Aberdeen session sorted out the problems of Archibald Boyd, too long away at sea,

75. CH2/448/2, p. 80; CH2/716/1, f. 9v (emphases mine); cf. CH2/191/1, f. 39; AAC CH2/751/1, ff. 7v, 12.
76. CH2/448/2, p. 32. The couple had come to the session voluntarily with 'mutual complaint'. On the other hand, the Perth bell-ringer's wife calling him 'Turkish man' was not taken as sufficient justification for his 'dinging his wife and knocking her kerchief off her head publicly in sight' of the neighbours (CH2/521/8/1, p. 109).
77. CH2/523/1, f. 10v. She claimed to have been throwing stones at another man, not her husband (one imagines the elders rolling their eyes), and was simply 'admonished to love her husband and to live Christianly with him'.
78. AAC CH2/751/1, f. 185v (1610).
79. Ministers also preached against wife-beating, though perhaps not often enough: e.g., Robert Rollock, *Lectures upon the Epistle of Paul to the Colossians* (London, 1603), 347: 'Is it lawful for a man to strike his own flesh?'
80. AAC CH2/751/1, f. 185v; CH2/521/8/2, f. 225 (1637). They also ordered all three warded one day and acted husband and wife to behave themselves in future. The couple does not again appear in the records.

and Agnes Gray, who consorted with his enemies and had him thrown out of their house when he arrived home.[81]

Threats of punishment for repeated offence worked wonders to quell domestic violence. Couples often formally 'acted themselves' not to offend again, promising to pay a heavy fine if they did.[82] Sometimes, though, a mutual promise of concord seems to have been all the couple wanted from the kirk's mediation: when the Canongate baxter George Stene and his wife, Jonet Mordo, voluntarily brought their violent quarrelling to the elders' attention, they 'heartily were content' to receive admonition that 'if any of them both commit such crimes in time coming, they shall be put out of the kirk as wicked-doers'. Each saw the threat as protection against the other. Bessie Gordon of Aberdeen got a more tangible guarantee when the kirk dealt with her abusive husband: 'for her greater security hereabout', they decreed that if he 'ding or strike her' again, he must pay £100 – not to the poor, as was usual, but 'to the utility and behalf of the said Bessie'. If he beat her again, at least she would have the wherewithal to sustain herself without him in future.[83] Use of a cautioner to ensure payment of the fine, as in the case of other quarrelling, allowed oversight of the misbehaver by someone other than the elders, and the significant amounts of money owed in case of relapse must have given offenders pause.[84] Where the abuse was not physical, an offender could act himself under pain of censure rather than a fine, as Hendrie Nicoll of Leith did in 1612, formally signing a promise to 'lead a peaceable life with his wife'. Nicoll also promised to come to sermon and communion in future – indicating the connection the elders saw between sermon attendance and general good behaviour.[85] Oversight, as we have seen, could be provided by the offended spouse, the cautioner or the neighbours. Ayr's elders reconciled a couple in 1604 with provision for 'the byremen and women to witness which of them began the fley [flyting]' and to report them; the community took on responsibility to guard the marriage.[86] And

81. Above, chapter 5, n. 115; CH2/448/2, pp. 256–57, 280.
82. AAC CH2/751/1, f. 185v; CH2/266/1, f. 10; CH2/716/1, f. 9v.
83. *Canongate*, 38; CH2/448/2, p. 80 (1604). By contrast, one who 'refused to be enacted to live Christianly' was sent to the presbytery or the magistrates: CH2/276/1, f. 69 (1624).
84. Nanse Anderson of Perth found too little safety in her husband's caution 'that he should not abuse her': she fled to her mother's house in 1619 'for fear of her life', only to have the session threaten to banish her unless she reunited with her husband, on grounds that his caution (ordered by the presbytery) should suffice to prevent renewed violence: CH2/521/7, p. 92. They may have been right, since we do not see the couple again before the session.
85. CH2/716/2, f. 81.
86. AAC CH2/751/1, f. 7v.

although Perth's session declared a wife's violence 'more against the law of God' than a husband's, it must be granted that the punishments and enforced agreements they prescribed were comparable.[87]

It is difficult to gauge the success of kirk intervention in domestic discord. A couple's absence from subsequent session minutes is probably telling; however, if continued domestic violence escalated, the abuser may have appeared instead before a criminal court. Or the couple could seek divorce, from the session until 1564, and thereafter from the newly established commissary courts, although this was expensive and prohibitively time-consuming for most people, since commissary courts were not local.[88] What is more important for our purposes than counting up the outcomes (supposing that were possible) is the overwhelming evidence of the kirk's ready assumption of responsibility for marital stability, its central role in what we ordinarily assume would have been a matter for the magistrates, and its evident commitment to regular and active involvement in marriages that we would identify as dysfunctional, with full co-operation of couples and communities. Violation of any member of a family by another was abuse of a divinely ordained institution that the kirk was intent on protecting, and while sessions pronounced and enforced punishments, they also sought the repentance, conversion and reconciliation that would surely in at least some cases have served the cause.

Divorce was never the preferred end. To grant it at all was to emphasise the importance of affection and fidelity to the marriage relationship; if these were lost, the marriage in protestant eyes was reduced to a sham. When this happened and divorce was granted, however, the kirk manifested the event ceremonially before the parish just as any other rite of passage. In 1585, for instance, the vicar of Inchenan publicly represented

87. CH2/521/2, f. 66 (1592). Jonet Dick for 'putting hands on her husband to strike and ding him', however offensive to the divinely ordained gender hierarchy, was like any male offender fined 13s 4d and assigned public repentance. It is interesting that her husband served as her caution. Did he really have the power in this relationship to enforce the session's ruling?

88. A systematic tracing of cases in the records of other courts would be useful, but it is beyond the scope of this study. On establishment of the commissary courts, see *BUK* 1:19, 34; *RPC* 1:152; Smith, 'Spiritual Jurisdiction', 1–18. The central commissary court was in Edinburgh; the inferior commissaries sat in large burghs. For examples of divorce cases heard by kirk sessions, see *SAKS* 1:18–27 (the Rantoun–Geddy cases discussed above), 50–59 (a case refused by the Kirkcaldy session in 1560 but heard by the St Andrews session); Pitcairn, *Ancient Criminal Trials*, 1:460; CH2/448/1, unfoliated acts of December 1562. For commissary divorces, NAS ms Registers of the Edinburgh Commissary Court Decreets, CC8/2 series, e.g., CC8/2/1, ff. 46, 72; or the registers of Hamilton and Campsie Decreets, CC/10/2, including a few orders of adherence and orders for solemnisation as well as divorces.

the divorce of two of his parishioners by 'putting him out at one kirk door and her at another, and so gave them a bill of divorce'.[89] But this was a ritual demonstration of failure. In Reformed Scotland, it was a failure of the kirk as well as the couple.

* * *

The kirk's regulation of sexual behaviour in general, too often dismissed as merely authoritarian and repressive, aimed ultimately at firm establishment and maintenance of marriage and family. The campaign against fornication reduced the likelihood of single-parent families, with their concomitant poverty and dependence on the parish.[90] It was also intended to establish patterns of fidelity that would keep the marriage together and provide examples of godly behaviour for the rest of the community. Sessions acted on behalf of the sanctity of matrimony in other situations as well, including intervention in cases of rape and incest, and in what we would call stalking. Co-operating with criminal prosecutions, they also served to keep at the forefront the religious dimension of these offences, reminding the community of the divine ordination of the family.

Courtship could be fraught with danger in a setting where both neighbours and authorities were constantly on the lookout for signs of fornication. A Dysart case of suspected 'carnal deal' in 1619 makes the point. Only after multiple deponents indicated that they had seen the couple 'sundry times kiss together, but no more' or that they had only seen the couple together during the evening at visible outside locations and 'never saw them kiss together nor no other unlikely [suspicious] thing between them' were the unfortunate young people dismissed, and even then with admonition to behave themselves.[91] Kilconquhar's elders declared that where there was any suspicion of illicit association, the persons involved must be warned that the next report of 'company-keeping', however innocent in appearance, would be treated as actual fornication.[92] Such scrutiny may seem excessive, but it served to protect the

89. NLS ms 2782, f. 41v.
90. The campaign itself has been treated elsewhere at sufficient length (see, for example, Graham, *Uses of Reform*, and for a later period, Leah Leneman and Rosalind Mitchison, *Sexuality and Social Control: Scotland 1660–1780* (Oxford, 1989), and their 'Acquiescence in and Defiance of Church Discipline in Early-Modern Scotland', *RSCHS* 25 (1993), 19–39. Here the focus is on aspects of sexual regulation that have received less attention from historians.
91. CH2/390/1, f. 3v.
92. CH2/210/1, f. 3v (1637). Even if committed 'under promise of marriage', antenuptial fornication brought public repentance and a fine: e.g., CH2/400/1, p. 130; CH2/716/1, f. 12; CH2/471/1, f. 3. Couples in this situation were often ordered to proceed straightaway to marriage as well: CH2/141/1, f. 53.

reputations both of the Reformed community and of the individuals involved. Scotland's notable success at reducing bastardy rates by the early seventeenth century did indeed give the Calvinist realm a name for sexual restraint.[93] As to the benefits for individual reputation, it behoves us to remember that this was a culture in which loss of sexual reputation could mean a serious decline in marriageability, especially for women – hence the ready resort of single women to the session when they had been slandered as unchaste. The elders responded quickly to any 'vaunting of sin', as when Kirkwall's elders confronted a man whose penchant for 'kiss and tell' behaviour threatened the good name of a young woman with whom he had been seen, or when South Leith's assigned public repentance to William Wilson for 'vaunting and bragging that he committed fornication with Jonet Greig'.[94] The Perth elders were guarding the good name of a female servant when they ordered Andrew Moncrief to move her out of his house 'in respect of her beauty and of her being delicately clad and none being in household with them but they two, which are great allurements to him to be enamoured of her'. Even though he claimed 'that his heart is otherwise disposed and that no such fleshly lust is in him', they thought the 'comely young woman' too vulnerable – to public disapproval if not to her master's 'folly'.[95] Young male servants living in the households of powerful women also drew their intervention. Lady Burgh objected when the Perth session ordered her to move Alexander Drummond out of her house: 'Who can hinder me, a gentle[woman], to hold a servant to serve me and to do my errands?' But she protested in vain. In the face of 'public slander of him resorting to her night and day', the elders demanded that as long as she lived singly she 'have women servants only'.[96] In other instances, such orders could protect mistress as well as servant, as cases of rape by male servants attest.[97] Where fornication had

93. Rosalind Mitchison, *Lordship to Patronage: Scotland 1603–1745* (London, 1983), 9; Leah Leneman and Mitchison, *Girls in Trouble* (Edinburgh, 1998), and *Sin in the City* (Edinburgh, 1998).

94. CH2/442/74, f. 34v; CH2/716/2, f. 75 (1611). Wilson had to repent as a fornicator even before there was any evidence that actual fornication had occurred (f. 78v).

95. CH2/521/8/1, f. 55. They dismissed the case only when they learned that he was about to move to Rogorton.

96. CH2/521/8/1, ff. 55v, 59. Even after she 'purged herself' (swore that there was no 'carnal deal'), the elders remained adamant – perhaps for good reason, since Alexander was found in her house again several months after she had promised to send him away (ff. 59, 65).

97. *Dundonald*, 30. Mitchison, *Lordship*, 85, remarks that the frequent exhortation for women not to live alone because of the 'scandal' it might provoke also served to protect isolated women from sexual assault.

been committed, but 'under promise of marriage', sessions investigated the alleged promise carefully and if they found it convincing either compelled the man to marry his otherwise shamed partner, or if he refused, denied him the possibility of marrying anyone else.[98] While this policy did not do much to salvage the woman's reputation, at least it put the man at a punitive disadvantage and would have served as a stern warning to other men tempted to promise marriage too lightly.

There were other vulnerable groups over whom sessions watched, including the daughters of parents known to be sexually promiscuous and fosterers of such behaviour in others. The Perth session confronted mothers as panders of their own daughters, and even mothers who arranged *ménages à trois* for themselves and their daughters – a 'fault and foul bruit more abominable and worthy of punishment' than most of the offences with which they had to deal.[99] In both these and more ordinary cases of sexual exploitation and misbehaviour, sessions got apparently enthusiastic co-operation from parishioners watching out for the young people of their neighbourhoods: while elders as sabbath searchers or visitors of their quarters did sometimes catch fornicators in the act, it was much more often neighbours who reported offences to them.[100]

Individuals concerned with their own reputations often had recourse to the session when relationships disintegrated and their erstwhile partners declined to let go. John Honnet complained to the Falkirk session in 1618 that Jonet Henderson was stalking him and fuelling rumours of 'slanderous behaviour'. He was 'continually troubled . . . by the said Jonet's frequenting and haunting the places and company where he resorts' and asked the elders to intervene 'so that he might be free of her company in time to come' – an end achieved by their demand that she repent in the kirk and act herself to stay away from him in future.[101] In Edinburgh, Robert Dickson's stalker was more frightening: he reported that after a brief adulterous affair with Elizabeth Vans, when 'he would have left her,

98. CH2/716/1, f. 10, a 1602 South Leith case in which the proof of the alleged promise was 'referred to Margaret [Jameson]'s oath'. When she 'held up her hand and swore' before the session and James Hill, 'he would not deny' it – a testimony to the inherent power of oath-taking, by women as well as men.

99. CH2/521/7, pp. 209, 211, 212; CH2/521/8/2, ff. 180v, 183v. The Kirkcaldy case of Margaret Auchmentie and her daughter also hints at the mother pressing her daughter into prostitution: CH2/636/34, f. 85. Offenders were generally turned over to the magistrate for banishment.

100. E.g., CH2/400/1, p. 172 – William Gib and Katherine Monteath 'deprehended and taken out of their bed by the minister and some of the elders' in Falkirk; cf. the more usual circumstances of neighbours reporting a man entering and leaving a woman's house at odd hours when her husband was in Stirling: CH2/400/1, p. 277.

101. CH2/400/1, p. 23 (1618).

yet [he] could not do it for her impudencies and importunities'. For five years after their fling he found himself 'not able to dispose either of his affections or of his body' because of her constant harassment and interference with his other relationships. And she was potentially dangerous: 'She would wait sundry times on him at my lord Reidhon's closehead with a great knife in her hand and put it to his throat and threaten him therewith if he kept not company with her.'[102] He willingly confessed his adultery and underwent public repentance; it was a small price to pay for the session to stave off his stalker's potentially fatal attraction by extracting from her an oath to stay away from him, and requiring her public humiliation for both adultery and 'plaguing' Dickson.

Strict control of sexual behaviour could prevent worse sin. Sessions were particularly concerned with abortion and infanticide by single mothers. Elspeth Elliott admitted voluntarily to the Liberton session that 'she had used all means to obtain a drink to destroy the fruit of her womb, thinking thereby to have concealed the sin of fornication'; far better in the elders' view that she and her partner (both of whom were sent on to the Edinburgh presbytery) should have been prevented from committing fornication in the first place.[103] Sessions relied on midwives to report not only the names of fathers whose bastard children they delivered, but also any attempt by a mother to kill an inconvenient newborn.[104] They received reports from midwives who had prevented newborns being smothered or passed off as foundlings or belonging to someone else.[105] They also grilled midwives who failed to report credibly the cause of death of an illegitimate child, sometimes with shocking results. The

102. CH2/141/1, f. 22v. This case was simultaneously before the secret council. Dickson asked that it be remanded to the session since 'he found himself guilty' of adultery, which in the secular court might 'cost him his life', given statutory definition of adultery as a capital offence. He appealed to the church court in part with his suspicion that Vans had 'used sorcery against him', which the session quickly dismissed.

103. CH2/383/1, f. 3. See also CH2/521/6, f. 41v, rumour of Margaret Moncreiff's concoctions to 'destroy the bairn in her womb'; and NLS ms 15948, p. 327 (a similar case reported by Sydserf, 1636).

104. E.g., SAU ms 30451, f. 7v; CH2/716/2, f. 36v. Midwives elicited paternal identity from women in labour on the assumption that they were in that state unable to lie, and with the threat of withholding assistance until the name was forthcoming. Mothers who still refused to reveal the paternity of their base-born children were banished: e.g., NLS ms Wod. Fol. XVI (Edinburgh Southeast parish register), ff. 2v–3, 4v, 21v–22, 23, 24–24v.

105. E.g., CH2/521/5, f. 3. Margaret Moncreiff took the latter course when she 'brought a howling bairn' to a neighbour (f. 5v, 1611). Perhaps it was her own experience with discipline for bastard-bearing that inspired her to concoct and distribute potions to procure abortion (CH2/521/6, f. 41v).

Kirkcaldy midwife Margaret Halkhead admitted after long questioning in 1620 that a single mother, Elspeth Henny, had paid her to keep still and not call in the neighbours to witness the birth of a 'bairn to another wife's husband, and that Elspeth put her hand upon the bairn's mouth and put it down'. When Halkhead protested, '"Lord, Elspeth, how canst thou commit such a cruel deed as that", she answered that she had seen the like done before in Edinburgh by a servant woman and the bairn put in a closet', upon which Halkhead agreed to bury the child. Stillbirths without witnesses were treated as probable infanticide: Helen Truemaiden(!) of Kirkcaldy, 'having brought forth a dead bairn (as she affirms) without witnesses' was put in the jougs and then banished under threat of being scourged and branded if she returned.[106]

Obviously many of the sexual offences addressed by the kirk were also criminal: to infanticide and serious domestic violence we can add rape, incest and sodomy. In all such cases the sessions worked in tandem with secular courts but never relinquished their particular jurisdiction over any sexual misbehaviour as a violation of matrimony. Sodomy and incest are rare in the minute books, homosexuality being difficult to detect and grounds for incest having been reduced by the Reformation's elimination of many catholic definitions of prohibitive consanguinity; however, they do occur. The Glasgow session required public repentance of a parishioner in 1593 just before he was executed for buggery; the magistrates put his severed head on the town battlements. And the South Leith session excommunicated William Geddes 'for the ravishing of Dean Dick's boy' in Edinburgh before he went on to the criminal courts.[107] They hoped that public discipline would both bring the sinner to penitence before he faced his maker, and send a message to the rest of the congregation. Incest they punished variably. The Jedburgh brethren believed a couple of cousins when they claimed that they had been unaware of their nearness of blood when they married; they just separated them. The Culross elders, however, turned John Young and his mother, Janet Ferguson, over to the criminal courts for 'lying in naked bed within the sheet' together. Refusing to acknowledge and repent 'the crime of carnal copulation', they were sentenced to exhibition at the market cross and then banished.[108]

106. CH2/636/34, ff. 30 (Henny was banished; Halkhead repented but lost her licence), 108.
107. NLS ms 2782, f. 65.
108. CH2/198/1, ff. 5v, 6v; CH2/77/1, f. 11v. The Dundonald elders also dealt vigorously with a brother and sister who 'nightly lie together . . . in naked bed' (*Dundonald*, 206–08); as did the Kirkoswald elders with John McIlmorrow and his stepdaughter, who 'confessed their abominable sin of incest' and underwent six months of public repentance barefoot and in sackcloth (AAC CH2/562/1, f. 1, 1620).

Rape appears more often in the minutes and reveals the all-male sessions at their least enlightened, since they often punished the victim as well as the perpetrator for fornication, and their usual solution to the problem was to pressure the victim to marry her attacker.[109] The elders' presumption of willing fornication often held sway even over detailed descriptions of the use of force. Jonet Mar, wife of John Patoun of Pitmarthly, recounted that Harry Schaw had 'ravished her against her will in his barn when she was getting straw to fill her bairn's cradle. He staked [locked] the door, and wrestling with her, she got a grip of his dirk [and] almost drew out the same, [but] he thrusting it in again bled her hand and made a great wound into it.' Their inbred suspicion was fed by the fact that the attack had occurred seven years before and Mar, like many rape victims, had not reported it.[110] But in the course of telling about the attack, Mar herself also made a startling confession of 'the sin of adultery committed by her' when she was raped, and she agreed to perform public repentance. She seems to have accepted the presumption of her time that any sexual activity outside of marriage entailed guilt by every participant, however unwilling. So did Helen Kennedy of Falkirk after John Drummond, 'forcing her against her will, commit[ted] fornication with her in the Lades Myln'; despite his admission of 'intending to enforce and put hand in the said Helen', both attacker and victim were banished for twenty days from the town.[111] Kennedy and Mar are testimony to the effective indoctrination of women as well as men by authorities more intent in such cases on finding guilt than offering comfort or justice. It is no wonder that we also read in the minutes of heroic struggles against rape and gratitude to bystanders who intervene. Jonet Ingram of Reding was fortunate indeed in the outcome of her 1618 encounter with John Livingstone, laird of Castlecarie. She told the Falkirk elders that he 'dealt with her that he might lie with her, and because that she would not consent to his wicked desire, he violently cast her down and struggled with her to have forced her and pressed to stop her mouth with his hands to hinder her from crying.' Fortunately, Agnes Bellendyne was passing nearby and 'heard the said Jonet crying murder'. Bellendyne sent for help, which arrived in the nick of time, Livingstone 'above her struggling with her and she crying for help'. But for Ingram's strength, her screams, and

109. This practice was the norm on the continent as well: Ulinka Rublack, *The Crimes of Women in Early Modern Germany* (Oxford, 1999).

110. CH2/299/1, pp. 80, 96. The crime would never have come to light if Schaw had not told 'Catherine Weymes his harlot who bore him two bairns in fornication' and who then told Grissel Saunders, who told her husband, who decided to pursue the case before the kirk.

111. CH2/400/1, p. 20 (1618).

the help of her neighbours, she might well have been judged guilty of fornication.[112]

Marriage of victim to rapist was often at the behest of the family, presumably anxious to dispose of a woman no longer as marriageable as a virgin would have been. It was Margaret Lander's father who brought her to the Edinburgh presbytery in 1588 'desiring the presbytery to take order' with Francis Mowbrie, 'who had forced and lain with the said Margaret before Fastingseven last in open fields far from any town, she under cloud of night coming from Edinburgh home to her father's house'. The order he sought was for Mowbrie now to marry his daughter, and two of the brethren were accordingly sent to 'travail with Francis and his father' to this end. The Dundonald session similarly pressed the widow Bessie Lin to 'agree upon some purpose of marriage' with her servant/rapist George Wright.[113] So did the Perth presbytery, again at the family's urging, in a notorious abduction case when William Stewart 'under cloud of night violently ravished and [took] away Elizabeth Henryson . . . from her mother's house in the Southgate of Perth, assisted by accomplices all in armour'. Neither kirk nor families seem to have given much thought to what sorts of marriage they were demanding, especially from the perspective of the unfortunate wives. At least in Elizabeth Henryson's case the presbytery asked for a formal statement of her 'good will and assent' to the settlement, though the records do not indicate the parental pressure that may have been brought to bear. Of most interest to the authorities was the 'testification produced that her mother and her brother who were offended with the said fact are yet [now] satisfied'.[114] If family honour were assuaged by the marriage, preventing the likelihood of feud, the kirk's greater aim of peace was achieved. In the contemporary ordering of priorities, a young woman's happiness counted for little in the face of family honour and social concord. Cases of enforced marriage after rape, however, are an exception to the rule that the kirk sought happy marriages and harmonious families to foster true religion.

★ ★ ★

We have seen that the elders targeted spousal violence in their campaign to reform family life and achieve concord within households. They were

112. CH2/400/1, pp. 171, 174 (the order for Livingstone's apprehension and warding). Even the Dundonald widow raped by her servant was convicted of fornication; his sin being the composite of 'fornication *and forcing* her thereto', only he had to perform public repentance (*Dundonald*, 30, 33, emphasis mine).

113. CH2/121/1, ff. 40v–41; *Dundonald*, 30.

114. CH2/299/2, pp. 58, 60–68, 70–73 (1620); quotations at 58, 62, 73.

just as cognisant of other forms of domestic violence. Sibling quarrels are especially numerous in the minute books. Where these involved verbal abuse only, or blows without injury, they were addressed with the same mechanisms as other flyting and slander or 'fechting and tuilzeing [fighting]' cases, with public apology and promise of amendment, and offending individuals rarely reappear in the records.[115] Where they involved more serious physical violence, sessions worked in tandem with criminal prosecutors to add religious condemnation to secular punishment, but they also attempted reconciliation.[116] It was not enough for James and William Gavelok of North Leith, 'either of them accused for striking the other', to be fined and warded by the bailies; the elders required that they publicly confess and then saw to it that they 'were reconciled together' and 'acted themselves never to be found doing the like again'.[117] A session's careful investigation of a case could relieve burgh magistrates of much of their burden, as when Andrew Hannay of Dundonald admitted that he had struck at his brother John, but John 'alleged him to have done more': it was the session's collection of witnesses that proved John's case (Andrew 'invading his brother, . . . making five sundry onsets upon him') so that appropriate punishments could be prescribed. But reconciliation was always the principal aim, to the end that even after fratricide, a penitent offender who had escaped the ultimate criminal punishment could be 'received again' by the kirk.[118]

Resident in-laws presented a special problem for early modern families. We have seen that where they interfered with husband–wife relations,

115. E.g., CH2/448/3, p. 138 (one sister calling another witch and being set the usual 'false tongue' formula); CH2/1173/1, f. 1v (a Kelso man complaining of 'his two sisters for abusing him with injurious words); AAC CH2/751/1, f. 135 (Bessie Neving 'for calling her sister Margaret whore and lowne'); CH2/716/1, f. 5v, and SAU CH2/624/3, p. 17 (flyting sisters in Leith and Anstruther Wester); CH2/77/1, f. 10 (a quarrel over which sister got credit for placing the father's gravestone in Culross). CH2/442/74, f. 34, illustrates the importance of the kirk taking seriously charges of 'injurious words' by one brother against another: the Kirkwall cordiner John Stenhger was so angry at his brother that he charged him before the session with being a 'nightwalker and drunkard' who did not 'lie nightly in his parents' house'; only because the charge could not be proved by witnesses (including the brothers' parents) did James Stenhger avoid prosecution as a probable fornicator; the elders only censured him. The parents must have been mortified at their now public inability to keep order among their own children, but better to have the session intervene than to have the brothers resort to violence.

116. CH2/636/34, f. 29 (two Sundays' public repentance added to John Paton's secular punishment for killing his brother).

117. CH2/621/1, p. 360. The brothers were warded until they paid their £3 fine; perhaps this shared experience encouraged them to mend their quarrel.

118. *Dundonald*, 329; CH2/636/34, f. 29.

the elders ordered them out of the household. But sessions also addressed violence against dependent in-laws, vigorously punishing abuse and working for reconciliation. The Perth elders, convinced in 1584 by three witnesses of Walter Bog's 'cursing and biting of his mother-in-law to the effusion of her blood', made him repent 'as if he had been an adulterer or a homicide' and publicly crave her pardon both in the kirk and 'in the common vennal [lane] where he committed the offence'. They approved the parallel action of the magistrates 'for punishing his person civilly in respect his offence and fault were judged by the Book of God heinous and worthy of death', but his repentance and craving of pardon in the kirk both underlined the religious dimension of his violation of family order, and paved the way to a reconciliation.[119] His father was made his caution 'that he not molest her by word or deed hereafter' under threat of both father and son being subjected to ecclesiastical and civil censures. A family problem was thus returned to paternal oversight, but now with the kirk as ultimate recourse and judge.

Assaults by adult children against their parents fall into a separate category, violating the fifth commandment and horrifying a society that rooted obedience to magistrates in the subordination of children to parents. Verbal assaults brought intervention in hopes of preventing escalation, and as often as not ended in corporal punishment by the magistrates as well as humiliation in the kirk.[120] But physical attacks appear all too frequently in the minutes as well. In some cases parents sought the session's help with an out-of-control teenager – by no means a peculiarly modern problem. The father of Patrick Cunningham had to admit to the Perth elders in 1598 'that his son was a rebellious child unto him, and that he had put violent hands on him, struck and dang him with his knees'. Unable to deal with a child physically stronger than himself, he had to rely on the authorities; what is significant is that he came to the elders rather than the magistrates. The two groups as usual co-operated, as the father perhaps anticipated, warding the boy for a week and ordering his

119. CH2/521/1, f. 99v. See *Dundonald*, 418, for investigation and vigorous prosecution of Robert Wyllie of Coraith for 'struggling and casting down his goodmother to the ground and taking her plaids from her'. CH2/523/1, f. 9, and CH2/636/34, f. 107v record similar cases in Burntisland and Kirkcaldy, civil and ecclesiastical authorities working in tandem.

120. E.g., CH2/84/28, ff. 23–23v (parents in Dalkeith, St Nicholas parish, trying to forestall their teenaged son's 'swearing and disobedience to his mother' from developing into something worse); CH2/390/1, f. 35 (George Smyth 'abusing his mother both in word and deed'); CH2/276/1, ff. 1v–2 (Newbattle cases of 'banning his father' and disobedience of parents, requiring offending boys to 'crave their parents' mercy'); CH2/636/34, ff. 33, 70v (cursing of parents leading to jougs and public repentance).

repentance barefoot and in sackcloth. This may have been as humiliating for father as for son, but it elicited sufficient 'signs of repentance' for reception again by the congregation, and there is no indication in the session minutes of a subsequent lapse.[121] The same session later had less success in bringing to repentance Patrick Steel, whose father reported that he had 'invaded him with a dirk wherewith he intended to have stricken him if he had not kept him close in his house, and because he could not get his will of him, he sticked [stabbed] his father's horse and broke up his father's malt loft doors and took forth malt and gave to his horse.' The session, 'highly incensed', found the boy impenitent for what were clearly criminal as well as religious offences, and turned him over to the magistrates in hopes that corporal punishment would do the trick.[122] Only the extreme act of excommunication by Burntisland's session brought Jonat Murray around after she attacked her father and would have 'shot him over [knocked him down] had not his wife kept him [safe].' In the course of her assault, Jonat reportedly said to her father, 'In spite of your heart [desire] I shall have [my will] of you'.[123]

In all of these cases, the victims reported the sin to the elders; however, there were cases where the victim was apparently afraid to bring a complaint, lest session intervention not suffice and worse abuse follow. In such cases, though, neighbours could generally be relied upon to alert the elders to a problem. It was a neighbour who reported to the Ayr session in 1604 two brothers who 'cruelly dang and blinded' their mother 'and had almost broken their mother's arm'.[124] The mother in this case readily confirmed the report. The Dundonald session, however, hearing a neighbour's report of John Bryand's 'masterful striking of his father', had to order the reluctant father to accuse his son so that they could formally proceed against him. A similar summons by the Ayr elders of Helen MacFairsen's father upon a report of her 'dinging of her father' resulted in her absolution when he 'purged her of the challenge by his oath'.[125] In such cases, one hopes that the neighbours who had brought the family to the kirk initially would continue to keep an eye on the suspected children.

121. CH2/521/3, f. 56.
122. CH2/521/8/2, f. 181v. There is no evidence apart from silence that their ploy worked.
123. CH2/523/1, f. 23v (1606). Jonat refused initially to repent, though 'heavily exhorted' and publicly admonished; after excommunication she did submit (f. 24). We are not told what she wanted from her father.
124. AAC CH2/751/1, f. 6. The brothers were 'given up' to the session by William Ranken, whose name is not on the book's lists of elders.
125. *Dundonald*, 63; AAC CH2/751/1, f. 126 (1608).

Instances like this also remind us that the domestic violence we see in court records, then as now, is the tip of the iceberg. Reports of violence against parents abound, in parishes from Ayrshire to Fife, the Borders to the Highlands.[126] Elgin was so frequently troubled that the session in the 1590s passed a set of blanket acts against 'dingers or misusers of their parents'.[127] For every instance we read about, how many went either unreported or denied by frightened victims?

Sessions were all the more anxious to convert such offenders because their acts were 'unnatural' as well as ungodly.[128] So was failure of adult children to support elderly and infirm parents, another significant category of family problems taken on by the kirk. Among the first acts of the Aberdeen session in 1562 was the requirement for grown children to sustain poverty-stricken parents; the elders warned that the children of any such parents found begging would straightaway be excommunicated. The Perth session was rather less quick to resort to the ultimate censure; they appointed two elders to 'speak with John Ruthven, merchant, about the entertainment of his mother' in 1587, apparently with good results.[129] The Dundonald session did likewise in 1610 when they heard that John Findlay was 'not entertaining his father as his duty required'. Their interview with the old man revealed the neighbours' reports to be accurate and they ordered Findlay *fils* to provide his father with 'entertainment of meat and cloth, with testification [that] if he fails he should be pursued and proceeded against with the censures of the kirk'. This case is especially interesting because the son proved recalcitrant, and the session did pursue, ordering him a month later 'to furnish his father a cloak and sark [shirt] within eight days' and the month after that to give 'to his sustenance the sum of four merks money . . . while the session be further advised'. Finally,

126. AAC CH2/751/1, ff. 6, 17v; AAC CH2/562/1, ff. 3v, 30; CH2/390/1, ff. 35v, 51v; CH2/636/34, ff. 8v, 71 (Duncan Budge abusing his mother by 'biting her nose'), 85; CH2/141/1, f. 28; CH2/145/1, ff. 5v, 29v, 32v; CH2/198/1, f. 8; CH2/400/1, f. 98v. Often, as with other sorts of domestic violence, attacks on parents were fuelled by alcohol: e.g., SAU CH2/624/2, p. 145; CH2/400/1, f. 10; CH2/1026/1, f. 2; CH2/276/1, ff. 1v–2, 10. Of course, sessions also intervened in quarrels between parents and their adult children where the fault lay on the other side (*Dundonald*, 335).

127. CH2/145/1, ff. 29v, 32v. They ordered the clerk to summon 'honest and discrete persons to give delation' of the 'dingers' and warned that offenders would do time in the jougs wearing a paper mitre describing their actions 'at the tree next the [market] shambles'.

128. CH2/198/1, f. 8 (Hobbie Thomson striking his own mother, 'unnatural misbehaviour'); CH2/400/1, f. 98v (the 'most unnatural abuse' of a woman striking her mother), for example.

129. CH2/448/1, p. 4; CH2/521/2, f. 11v.

Findlay 'faithfully promised and thereupon gave his hand to the minister' to 'amend the wrongs done to his father' and to satisfy the kirk 'for the slander given by him thereby'. The session, still suspicious, continued for several months to visit the father for progress reports.[130] They thereby provided a social service unavailable from any secular source, and badly needed in an age when veneration of the elderly was no more evident than in our own day.

★ ★ ★

The perennial problem of child neglect and abuse naturally drew sessions' intervention in the interests of the next generation of the Reformed congregation. They received an abundance of complaints and pleas for help. In them, they found, as modern social-service caseworkers do, that abusive husbands are often abusive fathers as well, and that alcohol all too often plays a role.[131] They found that women as well as men abused their own children. Fathers unable to curb their wives' violent tempers in the home resorted to them, as when Geilles Finlayson's husband reported that she 'of barbarous cruelty wilfully broke her own bairn's thigh bone'. Unless a child's life seemed to be in imminent danger, sessions generally joined with magistrates in giving stern admonition and warning at the first offence, though sometimes with disheartening results, as when Patrick Levingstone confessed to the Falkirk elders 'his cruel striking and blinding of John Levingstone his son after that he was directly inhibited by the magistrate not to do the same'.[132] Of course, child abuse was the more difficult to curb when preachers told parents that their duties to children included 'frequent beating of them'.[133]

Mysterious deaths of young children drew the elders' attention particularly when there had been three or more in succession in a family. Such suspicious circumstances might never have reached the criminal courts had not sessions initiated investigation. The Newbattle elders were struck that

130. *Dundonald*, 203, 205–06. See also CH2/400/1, f. 45 (two Falkirk brothers 'exhorted to work diligently in their lawful callings and to support the necessity of their mother', rather than spending all their time in the alehouse). Sessions also disciplined children for not sheltering aged parents: e.g., CH2/141/1, f. 28, Isobel Crawford putting her mother 'forth of the house oftentimes', according to the deposition of her neighbour, Elspeth Muir.
131. CH2/521/3, p. 87 (1599 complaint by David Jackson and his mother against his father, who 'misused them many ways' and was 'given to drunkenness and fighting'; the elders sent him to the magistrates.
132. CH2/521/6, f. 2 (1615); CH2/400/1, p. 133 (1624, the elders imposing public repentance and a fine on Levingstone; the civil penalty is not recorded).
133. Cowper, 484.

three children had died in Isobel Gorlay's care in the 1610s, all 'sudden' (that is, unexpectedly), but all witnessed by her husband, who saw the last two 'die in his arms'. Unable to decide whether all were accidental, or whether there had been collusion by the parents, they decided to send the case to the magistrates, assembling their own notes and depositions to provide the documentary grounds for a criminal case. The same session was more certain of what happened when a child in Isobel Marchell's custody was injured after falling off a table, she 'not witting because she was in her drunkenness'. This time the elders opted not to alert the magistrate, but simply ordered her never again to drink excessively while caring for children. They gave her another chance since the child was not 'disjointed' by the fall, but warned her that they would be on the lookout for future carelessness.[134] As we have seen, it was hard to hide from the elders. The ever-watchful kirk was in this instance, as in so many others, the first line of defence for vulnerable children.

Death by smothering – generally, 'overlaying' when a parent rolled over onto an infant in the night – was the verdict in many cases of unexpected child death. Since early modern children often slept in their parents' beds for warmth, however, it was difficult to ascertain whether the cause of such deaths was accidental. Multiple smothering deaths in the same family tended to erase doubt, however. Thus, Marjorie Anderson of Elgin, unable in 1587 to prove the 'death of her two bairns to have been without violence and smothering', was forced to admit that 'she had by her negligence killed two bairns being in bed with her'. The elders found this 'odious' rather than merely negligent, and fearing that 'being unpunished it shall be occasion to others to neglect their maternal duty' (which suggests that they thought the problem likely to be widespread), ordered her to the stool in sackcloth, barefoot and with a paper mitre, and after her repentance banished her from the town. Fatal overlaying was so common in Glasgow that session and presbytery in 1586 and 1592 passed acts that 'smotherers of children be punished as adulterers', and the session in 1594 established a 'place of [repentance for] smotherers to be above the pillar near the new-built wall'.[135] And when the mother of a child whose death was unexplained became pregnant again, the elders kept a closer

134. CH2/276/1, ff. 19–19v, 16. Marchell's drinking partner, William Reid, turned her in; both case records include depositions from several neighbours.

135. CH2/145/1, f. 8v; NLS ms 2782, f. 62. Both women and men appeared on this new penitents' seat for 'art and part in smothering' children. St Andrews punished both parents in smothering cases 'in equity': *SAKS* 2:766 (1593). The Fife synod also passed a general ruling for the punishment of 'suppressors of their children and bairns', requiring public satisfaction barefoot, bareheaded and in sackcloth: SAU ms 30451, f. 7.

than usual eye on her – even across parish lines if she had moved, by communicating their fear to their counterparts in the new parish.[136]

Sessions investigated not only abuse, but also neglect. This was often the failure of single parents like the Leith labourer George Carr, who abandoned his young children to take a job in Flanders, or John Thomson, who left his 'young little one' to go off to work each day and 'suffered the young thing to lie under stairs, and it has been seen lying objected to wind and wet'. In such cases, the elders' solutions tended to be practical: they garnished Thomson's wages, designating half for a caregiver, Jonet Gardner, 'to sustain his boy'.[137] Patrick Bannatyne of Kirkcaldy, a recipient of parish alms found 'entertaining his daughters slanderously' (not feeding them), lost both the alms and his children, who were fostered out to more responsible parishioners. On the other hand, when the Edinburgh weaver William Gillespie in 1575 took his six-month-old child along to beg for sustenance after his wife's death, the session took pity and provided 20s from the poor box to get a nurse for the baby so that Gillespie could abandon begging and get on with his weaving.[138] For young children to be seen begging brought 'scandal' upon the Reformed community. The Ayr session accordingly disciplined John McMurchsie, 'who has sent his bairn with an Irish woman to beg', and ordered him either to 'take his own bairn within his house' or separate from 'the wife and bairn both' – suggesting that the neighbour who reported the case may have done so at the behest of McMurchsie's wife, unable to prevent her husband sending the child away with the beggar as long as she was living in his household.[139]

Sometimes the father who failed to support his children was simply a ne'er-do-well like Alexander Gibson, whose mother-in-law denounced him as living 'an idle, wastrel, non-Christian life, not providing for his family'. Her own nagging had failed to reform him, and indeed brought her into danger: 'he menaces her with words, saying he will put a knife under her shoulder.' Sensibly, she took the problem in 1606 to the Burntisland session, which appointed three elders to 'take trial' and meanwhile admonished Gibson to do his duty. The exhortation did not sway

136. CH2/521/7, p. 217 (Langhill and Perth sessions watching 'a most wicked and vile woman' suspected of murdering her first child, 1621).

137. CH2/716/1, f. 6v; CH2/521/7, p. 342 (1622). Thomson's weekly wage, 6d 8/12 sterling, was 'withdrawn from him' and divided to provide for the child.

138. CH2/636/34, f. 85 (1626); NAS ms RH2/1/35, f. 34.

139. AAC CH2//751/1, ff. 10v, 12 (he opted to keep the family together); cf. SAU CH2/624/2, p. 194, a weaver exhorted to 'defend [prevent] his bairns from begging in time hereafter'; and *SAKS* 2:833, a 1597 order for John Diplein to entertain his daughter 'in God his fear, and sustain her from begging'.

him; three months later his mother-in-law again complained, now of his 'oppress[ing] her cows and sheep, threatening to break up her kists [chests containing possessions]' if she did not stop chastising him for neglecting his children. This time the session sent him to the civil magistrates, who apparently had no better results. Three years later, the persistent mother-in-law again complained about 'his drinking night and day and spending all'; to his counter-complaint that they should 'cause her hold her peace', the session returned an order for him to stop drinking and be a good father or be publicly admonished from the pulpit – a threat that finally seems to have achieved the desired effect. The fact that the children's grandmother repeatedly resorted to the session serves as testimony to contemporary perception that the elders could be centrally important (if a bit slow) in such a process.[140]

A father who sincerely wished to support his children but had fallen on hard times could expect concrete help from the session. The Anstruther Wester elders in 1616 loaned to the single father John Wilson 'to pay his bairns' board £3', which he promised to repay 'the first hire he get'. Likewise, James Christie received 6s weekly from the Kirkcaldy session 'for sustaining of his young bairn', but significantly 'with this condition – that if he sustain it not well, he shall forfeit it'.[141] The session declared its intent to follow up on his behaviour, to ensure that he was proving a responsible parent.

Too often, though, intervention came too late. Margaret Watson not only left her two bairns unbaptised, but 'one of them she suffered to perish and starve for hunger in the lodges infected with the pest'; impenitent, she was in 1585 excommunicated by the minister 'at command of the session' of Perth. The same elders four years later found Violet Broun penitent when, 'after long inquisition heard and taken of her negligence and sloth towards her young infant', she 'of herself freely confessed that the bairn perished through her negligence'; they received her again after repentance in linen on the stool.[142] Evident sorrow for sin was certainly the preferred outcome; not only did it relieve the session of having to find someone to foster any surviving children, it also kept the mother, as

140. CH2/523/1, ff. 27, 28v, 45v (1606–10).
141. SAU CH2/624/2, p. 162; CH2/636/34, f. 11v. Sessions often paid for nursing of one or both twins of poor parents: e.g., Thoms, *Kirk of Brechin*, 37; CH2/32/1, f. 27v.
142. CH2/521/1, f. 110v; CH2/521/2, f. 22v; cf. f. 58v (1592 case of the tailor's wife Helen Henry and the 'sudden departure of her infant bairn' through negligence); Thoms, *Kirk of Brechin*, 26 (a cottar of Windyedge repenting his 'barbarous and inhuman fact in exposing a sick boy out of his house in this cold season, who shortly thereafter died' – in fact, leaving him outside the door of the alehouse when he went in to drink).

a member of the congregation, subject to the systematic oversight that could prevent irresponsible behaviour in future.

Other children suffered poverty because of the neglect of an absent parent, generally a father. Poor mothers brought this complaint to the elders, and more often than not, with good results.[143] Sessions took full advantage of their presbytery connections to locate absent fathers and of magistrates to help force them to sustain their offspring, either by making payments to the mother, or by taking custody of the child. In 1606, for instance, Barbara Asteane had recourse to the Aberdeen session when, after five years of marriage and her being 'great with child', her husband, the merchant burgess Andro Duncan, 'passed to the east parts to reside and be altogether free of her entertainment'. She asked the elders 'at least to cause him give her of his substance and goods whereon to entertain her and her bairn aye until it shall please God to mould his heart to give adherence', but if 'he cannot be moved', to compel him to return her dowry and ask the magistrates to 'arrest not only his person, but also his goods . . . until she be satisfied in some measure'. They were happy to comply, requesting the magistrates to charge the skipper of his ship, bound for Danskyn, to refuse him transport; though he apparently could not recover his affection for her, he was compelled to support her and their child.[144]

Sessions included children conceived in fornication and adultery in their oversight of support, negotiating settlements acceptable to both parents.[145] This was a service that in some cases forestalled another form of domes-

143. E.g., AAC CH2/751/1, ff. 6, 124; CH2/636/34, ff. 10, 56v; CH2/523/1, f. 47v.

144. CH2/448/2, p. 200 (two ministers had earlier 'privately admonished' Duncan, but to no avail). See also CH2/521/2, f. 5v; CH2/636/34, f. 32v; CH2/400/1, pp. 42, 286; CH2/521/1, f. 4 (warding to enforce support).

145. E.g., CH2/400/1, pp. 78, 101 – both cases in which the mother renounced her claim of the father's promise of marriage 'providing she get satisfaction for upbringing' of the child. In the first, Mitchell Grindlay was ordered to pay 20 merks within six weeks and 'free her of all sustaining and expense necessary to be bestowed upon the upbringing of the bairn' and at Lammas 'he shall receive the said bairn of her hand and entertain him in meat and clothing in all time coming upon his own charge'. This was a fairly standard settlement, and one with the added advantage of the mother's agreement not to 'curse nor ban the said Mitchell nor no other woman he shall please to marry', guarding against harassment. Mothers of means could be ordered to provide partial support: e.g., CH2/400/1, p. 41 (a female caution insuring the mother's compliance). See also CH2/521/1, f. 94; CH2/521/2, f. 4; CH2/521/8/2, f. 209v. A father's being abroad or away fishing did not excuse him from his duty: George Broun of Leith was permitted to go to Flanders in 1600, but only having left 'his brother Daniel Broun to do for the bairn [his illegitimate child with Margaret Tod] as if myself were present till his return again to Scotland': CH2/716/1, f. 7v.

tic disorder – harassment of former lovers, and even violent attacks on their new wives by destitute mothers. Marion McGillichrist, for instance, brought to the Inveravon session in 1634 her complaint that Marie Dow 'her husband's former party had stricken her in her own house, . . . striking and blooding' her. The elders sent Dow to the jougs, but also sympathised with her explanation that she had gone to McGillichrist's house 'to seek meat from the father of her bairn . . . for sustaining of his bairn'. 'Considering her case, [they] modified her penalty' and ordered the father 'to pay £5 for her penalty and supply new victual to the said Marie for the sustentation of her bairn, a half boll at Hallowday, and the rest at Candlemas'. From his unfortunate new wife, who seems to have had her own funds, they took 'the rest of his own failure' (his back payments to Dow). One wonders whether this might have been their response to her failure to get her husband to supply Dow adequately in the first place. Had Dow earlier come peacefully to ask for her child support and been repulsed by McGillichrist? Reformed sessions were called upon to deal with some very tricky cases, and while their records leave tantalising gaps, there is enough evidence to demonstrate that they performed a difficult and much-needed service to families in need.[146]

When disputes arose later about whether each party was doing what had been required by a support settlement, it was the session that mediated the dispute and adjusted the arrangement where necessary. The quarrel of Patrick Hall and Margaret Heart of Falkirk is typical. This couple in 1619 'submitted themselves to the decree and sentence of the session about upbringing of the bairn begotten in fornication between them. With one voice they agree[d] Margaret should keep and foster the bairn herself and Patrick shall deliver to her £5 quarterly for his part.' If Margaret found that she could not nurse the child, Patrick's contribution would be increased to include two-thirds of a nurse's fee. Six months after this settlement, however, Patrick returned to the session complaining that Margaret was not doing her part by paying the other third of the nursing

146. The McGillichrist/Dow case is CH2/191/1, ff. 19v–20v. CH2/521/7, pp. 311, 313, is a similar 1622 case of a Perth woman harassing her child's father after having once been prohibited by session order; she promised to desist only 'if he will provide nourishment to his child and relieve her thereof'. The elders thought this reasonable and sent two to 'travail with' him and secure his agreement to board the child so the mother could go into service. See also CH2/266/1, ff. 5–5v, a new wife in Mid-Calder even less sympathetic than McGillichrist: when Jonat Hathorne found her husband's former lover and her child at her door asking for 'sustentation of the said bairn', she beat both 'the poor woman and bairn', for which she paid a heavy price in public humiliation and fines, and which drew the elders' attention to her husband's neglect of duty as well.

costs; he requested that the child be boarded with the nurse for the next quarter, with his payment to Margaret to be given directly to the nurse. This plan worked for a year, but early in 1621, the child no longer in need of a nurse, Patrick asked for Margaret to be charged with custody for the first quarter of the following year (perhaps while he settled his own financial and domestic affairs), after which he would assume 'all charges and care of the bairn forever after'. Margaret, having by this time 'fallen in fornication' with another man, jeopardising her place as a servant, was unable to offer a stable household for the child, so the session agreed to this temporary custody arrangement. Patrick then ceremonially 'in presence of the session delivered his bairn to Margaret . . . to be kept and entertained by her for the space of thirteen weeks' and presented his caution for resuming custody thereafter and 'free[ing] her from all further charges'. Ritual delivery of the child in the session house signalled that the elders would hold Margaret responsible for the child's welfare during her brief remaining custody.[147]

Session intervention in a family's pecuniary affairs was by no means always effective. The system worked better for younger than older children: the Perth elders unburdened themselves of 'two poor bairns of the late John Canye' in 1635 by giving them 'the session's token to wear upon the breast of their clothes' – that is, permitting them to beg. And their penchant for punishing people with fines could wreak havoc on the dependents of an offender: when William Murray complained that he had no money to pay his 40s fine 'for his sloth to bide and work in his calling, and for his drunkenness' since he lacked funds even 'to entertain his life, wife and bairns', the Perth elders stubbornly warded him – ensuring that he remained out of work. Only when a week later his wife appeared and reported that she had 'laid her plaid in pledge of a merk and besought [them] to accept it and let her said spouse be relieved out of ward' did they relent.[148] It seems not to have occurred to them that now the wife would go cold so that her husband could do his job; like modern economic sanctions imposed by nation states for political reasons, the sessions' pecuniary fines may have hurt the innocent more than the intended target.

Still, for all their shortcomings, limits of vision and outright failures, sessions did take seriously their calling to transform families into harmonious, Christian 'seminaries', and in this they recognised fully the fundamental necessity of material wellbeing. The superabundance of prescriptive literature about godly household formation that poured from early modern presses would count for naught if children were left unfed and

147. CH2/400/1, pp. 52, 58, 72–74.
148. CH2/521/8/2, f. 200; CH2521/7, pp. 215–16 (Murray was a weaver).

unsheltered. This brings us to the final category of needy children whom they served in practical ways – the orphaned and abandoned. The kirk was the foster-care agency of early modern Scotland. It was the sessions to whom foundlings were brought, who investigated abandonment, and who located and vetted foster care for deserted children.

Desperate parents generally abandoned children where they would be found and cared for (hence the term 'foundling') – at the yett of a wealthy householder, for instance.[149] Perhaps the 'northland woman' who in 1622 left her nine-month-old in the chamber of a Perth schoolmistress while she was in the kirk at sermon time hoped that her child would remain there to be educated.[150] Rarely do we hear of infants being left in the open – like the Highland child 'going wild in the sands between Irvine and Ayr' and turned over in 1604 to a Dundonald elder by a travelling charmer; or the baby 'laid in a hole and the earth above it, found by the shepherds, living' that a passing elder, Ninian Drummond, quickly baptised and then presented to the Perth presbytery 'to try if they can find any women in their parishes suspicious of such a thing'.[151] Sessions and presbyteries did investigate abandonment, assigning searchers to 'report their diligence' to locate deserting parents.[152] But they gave the greater part of their attention to locating nurses for infants and foster parents for young children, going to great lengths to secure funds and schedule payments to the fosterers.[153] Funds came variously from the fines of

149. AAC CH2/562/1, f. 39v; CH2/294/1, f. 11v; CH2/266/1, f. 27v; Thoms, *Kirk of Brechin*, 26, 37. The usual term in the Scots records is 'foundbairn' or 'fundling bairn'. On the history of abandonment, John Boswell, *The Kindness of Strangers: The Abandonment of Children in Western Europe from Late Antiquity to the Renaissance* (Chicago, 1998); Linda Pollock, *Forgotten Children: Parent–Child Relations from 1500–1900* (Cambridge, 1983).

150. CH2/521/7, p. 327: the mother, 'a simple damsel [with] no means to pay for the bairn's fostering', quickly 'departed away', so the session found a nurse to keep the child.

151. *Dundonald*, 59 (1604); CH2/299/1, p. 313. There was also a case in Anstruther Wester in 1588 of travellers to Pittenweem finding 'an infant being a lass bairn in an acre of beans, . . . lying above the bankhead' and turning her in to the session for fostering: SAU CH2/624/1, pp. 32–33.

152. E.g., CH2/294/1, f. 11.

153. NAS RH2/1/35, ff. 24v, 60 (support for a foundling boy including school fees); CH2/377/1, f. 80v; CH2/521/7, p. 214; CH2/266/1, ff. 27v–28v; SAU CH2/624/3, p. 51; CH2/141/1, ff. 20–20v (budgets for clothing as well as food and lodging); CH2/636/34, ff. 44v, 48 (weekly or quarterly payments specified). Whole pages of Anstruther Wester's first extant session book are devoted to accounts and schedules of such payments to sustain foundlings: SAU CH2/624/1, pp. 32–33, a foundling fostered by the webster, David Saltar, with quarterly payments of 40s plus clothing allowances.

fornicators and adulterers, voluntary contributions, the poor box, door-to-door collections by the elders for a particular case, and *ad hoc* rates imposed on a sliding scale and collected by elders or deacons.[154]

Sessions provided for the fostering of orphans as well as foundlings. Sometimes these were children who had been maintained for some years *gratis* by relatives or family friends who now found themselves no longer able to meet the cost.[155] In other cases, the session sought a foster family straightaway upon the parents' death, providing for school fees and apprenticeship of boys old enough for these courses.[156] Older orphans sometimes submitted their own petitions for assistance: David Craig, 'a poor boy, fatherless and motherless', requested help of Perth's session in 1598, for instance, 'desiring them for God's cause to give him some support to put him to a craft'. He was bound apprentice to a tailor, who got £10 'to learn him the tailor craft'. The same session some years later gave 13s 4d to 'a poor chapman boy' on his own after his pack was stolen; another furnished a horse to carry 'a small boy . . . to his friends'.[157]

Finally, sessions sometimes found parents to be so deficient in godliness that they removed the child to a foster family. The Edinburgh elders in 1575 found Hew Lander so sinful that he was not fit to raise his own infant; admonishing and threatening him with excommunication, they proceeded also to remove his child and have him 'baptised out of the hands of James Nycolson, writer', who would 'bring up the bairn in true fear and knowledge of God'.[158] In Dalkeith, the brethren were horrified to find 'a bairn surnamed Douglas of seven years of age as yet unbaptised, the parents being fugitive'; they appointed a godly householder to 'receive the said child to baptism' and instruct him as the parents ought to have done. And when impenitent adulterers were banished from godly com-

154. CH2/266/1, ff. 27v–28v (funds from fornicators' fines); CH2/264/1, f. 6 (Menmuir's tax scale, the lowest payment 12d, cottars paying 2s, and 'gentlemen according to their desires to help the bairn's first quarter's board'); CH2/521/7, p. 214 (elder collection 'to put the bairn in nourishment'); NAS RH2/1/35, f. 31 (a foundling girl put on the Edinburgh poor rolls).

155. CH2/266/1, f. 4 (a Mid-Calder grandfather seeking to limit his responsibility for his son's child to one year); CH2/424/2, f. 8 (a friend whose 'parent left the bairn in her hands' five years ago, 'she not being able to keep it any longer'; CH2/141/1, f. 43 (an elder sister 'who has spent her own means in sustentation . . . of her sister by the space of a year'); CH2/264/1, f. 6 (an elder brother doing the same, but having 'nothing himself . . . and the bairn without their help would perish for want').

156. CH2/141/1, f. 41v; *Dundonald*, 267.

157. CH2/521/3, p. 41; CH2/521/6, f. 52v; CH2/266/1, f. 109.

158. NAS RH2/1/35, ff. 56–56v (Lander may have been a catholic); cf. NLS ms 2782, f. 39v.

munities like Leith and Edinburgh, their children were 'fostered in the town' by families more likely to sustain them and to see them, if they came 'to years of discretion, . . . instructed in the heads of religion'.[159] Such fostering arrangements were in some cases, like that of Hew Lander, intended to help bring the father around; however, in others, they ended in adoption of the fostered child by a householder who 'promised to bring up the same' in the fear and admonition of the Lord.[160]

⋆ ⋆ ⋆

The elders' evident concern with religious upbringing of children in fostering cases brings us full circle, back to their overarching purpose for intervening in family life in the first place – their identification of families as 'seminaries of church and commonwealth'. Lest this survey tempt us to think of the Reformed kirk in relation to the family as simply a social welfare agency, let us conclude with the final recurring family-related item in the minute books, 'family exercise' of religion. Family harmony in its turn served the even greater cause of instilling the principles of the gospel into the next generation, specifically by means of an organised, disciplined, regular and rigorously enforced round of family discipline, prayers and catechism.

The Reformed church's early ruling that children must be 'brought up by their parents in the true religion of Jesus Christ' was for many not easy to implement, particularly in the first generation of protestantism, when the doctrine was as new to parents as to their children.[161] Recognising the need, ministers like John Davidson of Prestonpans and John Craig of Aberdeen produced for their parishioners instructions for 'exercising yourselves and your families in reading and practising' true religion.[162] The culmination of generations of such handbooks of domestic prayer and

159. CH2/424/1, n.f., 4 May 1592; CH2/716/1, f. 12v (1604); CH2/141/1, f. 17v (1627); *Canongate*, 63 (1567).
160. NAS RH2/1/35, f. 31v, the 1574 adoption of a child whose mother, still living in the town, was 'ordinary poor' and had had her child in fostering for several years – a good indicator that she was in the elders' judgment unable to care for him properly.
161. *BUK* 1:176; *First Book*, 90–91; *BCO* 139. Preachers repeated the refrain: e.g., Cowper, 484.
162. John Davidson, *Some Helpes for Young Schollers in Christianity*, 132–67, quotation at 134; John Craig, *A Short Sum of the Whole Catechism*, ed. T.G. Law as *Craig's Catechism* (Edinburgh, 1883). Davidson's work was commissioned by the Haddington presbytery for 'the unlearned' who must 'reform their houses and use prayers at morn and evening, with reading of scriptures after dinner and supper'. The presbytery ordered every minister to 'visit their houses and see whether it was so or not': CH2/185/1, n.f., 10 March 1596.

catechism would come with the 1639 publication of the authorised *Familie Exercise; or, The Service of God in Families*, a 'great help to king and commonwealth, whereof families are the seminary'. Sessions like Aberlady's ordered in the year of this volume's publication that it be acquired by every family in the parish 'with all expedition'.[163] It set forth a catechism in 'plain and easy' language; recommended either *ex tempore* or set prayers (the latter for the 'rude and weaker' sort unable to 'conceive a prayer' on their own) for morning, evening and mealtimes; gave instructions for fasting and humiliation either in the face of public calamities or for 'the private distress of the family'; required regular psalm-singing and reading of the scriptures by the father or mother; and made parents the first line of discipline by demanding their 'admonition, reproof and correction of such faults as are proper to be censured' after 'diligent observing and watching over' the behaviour of their children and servants.[164]

The sessions kept householders to these requirements. Perth's elders in 1592 finding an abundance of 'enormities in families' obliged themselves to more regular visitation of 'every particular household and family within this burgh for their reformation and information in godliness, . . . to admonish to the use of prayers at morning and evening, at meals and meat hereafter, with psalms [and] with other godly practices', and entries for the decade following indicate that they maintained their resolve.[165] The elders of Ballincrieff at every visitation of their quarters investigated whether 'the worship of God be advanced and set up in their families, and . . . report[ed] thereof to the session'; those of Mid-Calder who set out 'to try who uses to exercise in their families' were able to report that only 'some few' failed to do so.[166] Presbyteries and synods enforced the order on any sessions that seemed reluctant.[167] And the elders themselves were to model the correct behaviour by holding family worship in their own households, as the Innerwick session put it, 'that they may give good example to all the families within the parish and may with more boldness reprove the neglect thereof and delate the condemners of the same

163. *Familie Exercise; or, The Service of God in Families* (Edinburgh, 2nd edn, 1641), sig. Av verso; CH2/4/1, ff. 22v–23.

164. *Familie Exercise*, sigs Avi–Aviii verso. A properly done 'family humiliation' could involve a whole day of prayers and Bible-reading: Blair, 65.

165. CH2/521/2, f. 58v; ff. 126v, 158 (weekly visits to 'know what profit and progress their people make in Christianity').

166. CH2/4/1, ff. 25v, 30v (failure of an elder to make such visits brough a 4s fine); CH2/266/1, ff. 110–110v. See also CH2/191/1, ff. 50–50v, 'anent families service'. Ministers like Patrick Forbes of Corse urged family religious exercise on the king's household, too: NLS ms Wod. Fol. LVIX, it. 7.

167. CH2/299/1, p. 379; CH2/271/1, ff. 128, 132.

within their own bounds.'[168] Godly proprietors like the laird of Careltoun refused to lease holdings to families who failed to exercise household religion, and punished lax tenants in their own courts.[169]

When searchers found families falling short of their standards, they 'severely censured' them, just as they did fathers who failed to bring their wives, children and servants to sermons and so were 'the more suspicious to be authors of . . . ungodly behaviour in their families'.[170] In serious cases of parental failure to teach, discipline and model correct behaviour, they held parents responsible for the sins of their children. Recognising that 'little children must partly follow the example of their parents', and 'specially fathers of families', the Ayr session opted to have irreverent children's parents 'punished for them' in cases of 'fearful and horrible cursings and bannings' where the parents had 'not repressed them', and declared that 'the weight shall be imputed to their parents or masters whose bairns or servants shall be found guilty' of 'playing in the streets . . . on the sabbath day'. The Lasswade elders likewise ruled that a father who had failed to act as pastor and session to his family 'shall be counted guilty' of his children's sins 'and satisfy as the offender should have done'.[171]

It made good sense for elders intent on establishing a pure kirk to devote this time and attention to its most basic building block. The family rather than the church was the primary guard against error and sin, the first teacher of truth and guide to righteousness. The extent to which the culture of protestantism came to permeate Scottish society in the generations following Reformation was due in large measure to the elders seizing authority over that foundation stone of the Christian edifice and re-forming the family into an agent of the protestant gospel.

If in the process the sessions became willy-nilly a much-needed agency of social welfare and domestic policing, so much the better for the good name of the Reformed kirk. The connection between doctrine and discipline was logical: it served the larger purpose of protestantism for elders to intervene whenever household disorder, neglect or violence made godly instruction and guidance impossible at that level. It was an added bonus if, in the course of their intervention, they served the needs not only of orthodoxy, but also of the weakest members of the community – children, poor single parents and the dependent elderly. Sessions may not

168. CH2/1463/1, ff. 9, 10v.
169. Wodrow, *Analecta*, 1:71. The laird also gathered his tenants and led them to church each Sunday.
170. *Dundonald*, 269; CH8/54/1a (Dumfries); CH2/141/1, f. 12v; SAU CH2/624/2, p. 5.
171. AAC CH2/751/1, ff. 19v–20; AAC CH2/751/2, f. 4v; CH2/471/1, f. 3v; cf. CH2/390/1, f. 16v, and NLS ms 2782, f. 62v.

have eliminated domestic violence or paternal abandonment, but they seized the initiative with a zeal and comprehensiveness beyond the vision or capacity of the pre-Reformation church. In the course of their intervention, they also protected the rights and dignity of women to an extent that belies our traditional association of Reformation with narrow patriarchalism. Admittedly short-sighted by modern lights, they flew in the face of contemporary attitudes and inequities with their demonstrable awareness of the physical and fiscal realities of spousal abuse, sexual exploitation and missing child support, and with their allowance to women of a role in leading household religion, at least in the absence of their husbands.[172] Theirs was, in short, a culturally transformative role. Their fundamental presumption that conversion ought to turn around behaviour, as well as belief, truth and righteousness going hand in glove, made the family the base camp of the cultural revolution that we call protestantism.

172. 'The mistress of the family hath a special hand' in leading household religious exercises, according to the *Familie Exercise* (sig. Bii), and James Melville, *A Spirituall Propine of a Pastour to his People* (Edinburgh, [1598]), 18.

Chapter 7

Sacred Space, Sacred Time

The pre-Reformation church offered myriad avenues by which ordinary folk could approach the holy and expect to be heard. The veneration of a saint, especially on the saint's day, brought intercession and protection in time of crisis. Guild patronage of altars served both to cement the unity and identity of the members and to secure the guardianship of the saint to whom the altar was devoted, and whose day would be celebrated by guild processions, masses, mystery plays and banquets. Pilgrimage to holy sites, chapels and sacred wells, depositories of relics and witnesses of earlier miracles, could guard one's soul after death, reducing years in purgatory. The fifteenth-century flourishing of devotion to Mary, to the passion and to the eucharistic sacrament in cults of the Holy Blood or Corpus Christi brought the lowliest lay person into the presence of the divine by means of the arts that it fed and the holy days set aside for celebration.[1] The collegiate chapels that sprang up in impressive numbers from the fifteenth century – at least fifty founded from 1400 to 1550 – provided votive masses for the departed, together with an opportunity for the wealthy families who built them to define their status in terms of piety as well as lineage and substance.[2] Burial in the church's most sanctified space – the closer to the altar, the better – displayed status by association with holiness and, together with obits for the dead, did some good for souls in purgatory.[3]

1. Galbraith, 'The Middle Ages', 20–21, 24–25; Fitch, 'Search for Salvation'; McKay, 'Parish Life'; Cowan, *Medieval Church*, 170–92; Mill, *Medieval Plays*, 247–53 and 'Perth Hammermen'; *Book of Perth*, 59; Michael Lynch, 'Scottish Culture in its Historical Perspective' in *Scotland: A Concise Cultural History*, ed. Paul H. Scott (Edinburgh, 1993), 28–29.
2. I.B. Cowan and D.E. Easson, *Medieval Religious Houses: Scotland* (London, 1976), 213–30; Easson, 'The Collegiate Churches of Scotland', *RSCHS* 6 (1938), 193–215 and 7 (1939), 30–47; Ian Cowan, 'The Early Ecclesiastical History of Edinburgh', *IR* 23 (1972), 20–21; Sanderson, *Ayrshire*, 14–15; Cowan, *Medieval Church*, 174, 176; Lynch, 'Scottish Culture', 30.
3. Spicer, '"Rest of their Bones"'; Colvin, *Architecture and the After-Life*; Gordon and

The church physically presented to its members a visual display of the holy in the devotional context of the mass, with candle-lit altars, lavishly embroidered vestments, brightly painted and gilded furnishings and icons: it was sanctified space.[4] Close association with the holy could bring practical results: a fisherman or sailor off to the dangers of his season at sea could pray to St Andrew or St Brendan for protection; a woman in childbirth could seek the aid of St Margaret; a host of local native saints was available to comfort, guard and sustain petitioners in stressful circumstances.[5]

For the most zealous of the reformers, this panoply comprised superstition at best, idolatry at worst. Accordingly, the iconoclasm associated with the Reformation in Scotland was sweeping, the formal abolition of holy days and saints' festivals unequalled in any other protestant realm, as we have seen.[6] To leave no doubt about their position on these matters, the elders of Perth had their clerk inscribe into the minute book in 1587 their exclamatory condemnation of all 'superstitious rites and ceremonies, from which the Lord preserve us!'[7] In practice, however, what modern historians have labelled desacralisation, even here in the most extreme of Reformed settings, was not quite what we have supposed.[8] Human needs, individual and communal, being what they are, the kirk would not have

Marshall, *Place of the Dead*, 1–16; *The Obit Book of the Church of St John the Baptist, Ayr*, ed. James Paterson (Edinburgh, 1848); Fitch, 54; McKay, 99, 110–13; Cowan, *Scottish Reformation*, 4, 62.

4. McRoberts, *Medieval Church of St Andrews*, 68–71; Galbraith, 17–32; MacMillan, *Scottish Art*; Howard, *Scottish Architecture*, 168–205; Hay, *Architecture*.
5. McRoberts, *Medieval Church*, 63–120; McKay, 105–09; Irons, 1:299, 2:446–47 (St Triduana's well to cure blindness); David McRoberts, 'Scottish Sacrament Houses', *Transactions of the Scottish Ecclesiastical Society* 15 (1965), 33–56 and 'The Rosary in Scotland', *IR* 23 (1972), 81–86; Lynch, 'Scottish Culture', 15–46; Cowan, *Scottish Reformation*, 6–8.
6. McRoberts, 'Material Destruction', 415–62; Irons, 1:299, 2:466–67 and *BUK* 1:5 (on the fate of Restalrig, 'razed and utterly cast down' in 1560 as a 'monument of idolatry'); LPL ms 3471, f. 31; Cowan, *Scottish Reformation*, 99–101, 189–92 and *Regional Aspects of the Scottish Reformation* (London, 1978), 13–14, 17. The iconoclasm reported with glee by contemporary reformers like Knox is increasingly confirmed by local studies like Sanderson's (*Ayrshire*, 68), though the 1641 parliament still saw a need for an 'Act for abolishing monuments of idolatry' (*APS* 5:351).
7. CH2/521/2, f. 12v (on the occasion of several Scots catholic clerics returning from Spain). They condemned all ceremonies that 'bring men under the thralldom of idolatry and ignorance of the true knowledge of Christ our Saviour revealed to us in his word'.
8. A point made well for Lutheran Germany by Robert Scribner, although he grants 'a weaker and more ill-defined form of sacrality' in protestant tradition: 'Reformation and Desacralisation: From Sacramental World to Moralised Universe' in *Problems in the Historical Anthropology of Early Modern Europe*, ed. R. Po-chia Hsia and R.W. Scribner (Wiesbaden, 1997), 75–92, quotation at 76.

found it possible to desacralise its space or time completely, even if its authorities had wished to do so, particularly in such temporal proximity to medieval traditions of the holy. But Scottish elders and ministers were not, after all, the secular beings that modern Western people consider themselves to be; they were arguably not even our intellectual ancestors in inclining towards that secularised view of the cosmos so often, and so erroneously, associated with the early modern period. Theirs was still a world created and regulated actively by the divine, in which some times, some places, were simply closer to God than others, and in which the secular found its meaning in the sacred. They treated the space of kirk and kirkyard with reverence as holy ground; its furnishings, from Bible to pulpit to communion boards, won a respect not accorded to ordinary books or tables. The times that they set aside for 'holy observance' – sabbaths, communion preparations, fasts and feasts – were sacrosanct, so that sin committed during those times was greater and merited a more severe penalty than the same sin on an ordinary day. They believed profoundly in divine interference in human affairs, and in the possibility that human communication with the divine could affect that interference, for good or ill. For all their condemnation of 'popish superstition', they maintained a steadfast conviction that wizards and witches, fairies and demons, angels and ghosts, populated the same world that they did, and that visions, dreams and even audible divine voices provided guidance in the conduct of their lives.

Why, then, do so many suppose them to have been less inclined to sanctify space and time than their predecessors? In part, it is because we misconstrue much of what they did with buildings, images, days and seasons. The iconoclasm that deprived their churches of statues of saints and paintings of biblical scenes in favour of whitewashed interiors looks to us like a secularising move. Even more, filling the churches with pews and galleries constructed by guilds and wealthy families and decorated with their arms and symbols of their trades and crafts gives us a very secularised impression of how they defined themselves. And above all, the abolition of holy days other than Sunday, paring down festivity and quite considerably increasing the number of days in the year devoted to labour, has moved historians of a certain bent to claim both secular modernising of the society and capitalisation of the economy for the Reformed tradition.[9] But all these changes have multiple, and often internally conflicting, meanings. There is, without question, a tension in the way Reformed churches were decorated and time was used. If we explore that tension as it was

9. Gordon Marshall, *Presbyteries and Profits: Calvinism and the Development of Capitalism in Scotland, 1560–1707* (Oxford, 1980).

manifested in kirk session minutes, we will find that it was one in which a notion of the sacred continued to define individual and communal identity and make sense of a cosmology still ordered principally by divinity rather than human reason.

★ ★ ★

The Scottish post-Reformation was an era of pew-building. Kirk session minutes are cluttered with petitions for permission to construct 'seats' or 'desks' – pews with attached lecterns and sometimes canopies – for members of eminent families.[10] There are countless petitions from guilds to erect 'lofts' or galleries of seats for their members.[11] Subsequent petitions asked to enlarge or improve seats.[12] Clearly there are practical reasons for this phenomenon. Protestant sermons were lengthy, unlike the mass, which was easily stood through. Petitioners asked for seats 'for more commodious hearing of the word', or because there was otherwise 'little room and evil ease in hearing the word', and a lectern for Bible and notebook made good sense for a householder responsible later for examining his charges on the sermon's content.[13]

There were also social reasons, though, and it is these that lend credibility to the secularisation argument. A prominent family's desk could be a sumptuous affair. Decorated with the owner's name, heraldic devices, and botanical or geometric designs, even the more modest served to display its occupants' eminence in the community (see plate 19).[14] The more elaborate could be elevated over a family burial vault and incorporate stairways from the kirk floor or separate outside entrances, and

10. NAS ms CH8/153; CH2/699/1, f. 16v; CH2/400/1, pp. 35, 188, 197, 316; CH2/636/34, ff. 13, 35v; CH2/383/1, ff. 9v, 14v, 15; CH2/276/1, p. 33; CH2/716/1, ff. 1, 14, 15, 18; CH2/521/1, f. 68v; CH2/390/1, ff. 16, 23–24, 25v; NLS ms 2782, ff. 30v–31; CH2/442/74, ff. 31v, 39, 45–46, 49.

11. The Anstruther Wester session received them in one year alone from the wrights, smiths, masons and timbermen (CH2/624/3, p. 15), as did Burntisland in one year from the wrights, smiths, coopers and masons (CH2/523/1, f. 37v). See also CH2/472/1, f. 27v (wrights); CH2/523/1, f. 7v (sailors); CH2/716/1, f. 21v (timbermen); CH2/521/1, f. 69v CH2/521/3, p. 86 (tailors); CH2/390/1, ff. 25v (baxters), 51 (mariners); CH2/400/1, pp. 14, 15 (merchants and maltsters).

12. CH2/383/1, f. 15; CH2/390/1, f. 27; CH2/338/1, f. 26; NLS ms 2782, f. 30v; CH2/400/1, p. 316.

13. CH2/400/1, pp. 14, 188; CH2/472/1, f. 27v; CH2/523/1, f. 7v; CH2/521/4, p. 155. For similar developments in England, see Kevin Dillow, 'The Social and Ecclesiastical Significance of Church Seating Arrangements and Pew Disputes, 1500–1740' (Unpublished DPhil thesis, Oxford, 1990).

14. The Melville desk in Burntisland (see plate 19) displays the arms of Sir Robert Melville and his wife, Dame Joanna Hamilton, and dates from 1606. See also NAS CH8/153, the Banff merchant William Gordon's petition to erect a 'pen-desk' for his family, to be 'decorated with his name and arms'.

heated retirement rooms – eloquent affirmation of social status (not to say conspicuous consumption) in a place where all one's neighbours had to put in an appearance at least weekly (see plates 20–21).[15] The laird of Corstorphine in 1631 petitioned the Dalkeith presbytery for permission to build a 'loft foregainst the pulpit from the west end to the third pillar inclusive', and 'for his entry thereto, that he may have a door off the kirkyard, providing it hurt not the fabric of the kirk, or otherwise he shall make a stair in the west end thereof. And for entry to the people to the rest of the loft he shall make another stair in the east end thereof on his own expense, which loft of his he seeketh for himself and his tenants'.[16] Clearly, elite pew-building radically altered church interiors. Some families were powerful enough to get a previously public kirk door reserved for their exclusive use in proceeding to their seat: the Dysart session in 1623 ordered that the 'east kirk door be condemned to all parishioners except to the house of Sinclair and to the mistress and her folks'.[17] Construction of new doors, stairways, lofts and seats was at the petitioner's expense, and the right to an individual or family seat was, for a fee, a heritable property.[18] The more eminent the family, the more room for their tenants and the better the location of the seat, proximity to the penitents' stool being a preferred place (suggesting again the attraction of the penitential performance to the rest of the congregation).[19]

Guild lofts served much the same purpose, displaying both social status

15. Howard, 186, 199–203; Gifford, *Fife*, 170 (describing the Dunfermline Aisle, 1610, in St Bridget's, Dalgety Bay).
16. At the same time three other lairds all appeared before the presbytery 'to arrange for the design of their places', the laird of Arniston requesting 'the rest of the loft foregainst the pulpit designed for him and his tenants', which the brethren thought 'too much bounds'; they let him build in part of the loft: CH2/424/2, f. 15v. In Stow, John Hoppringill of that Ilk asked to extend his present seating space, promising that it 'should not be prejudice to no person nor troublesome to any': CH2/338/1, f. 26 (1631).
17. CH2/390/1, f. 14v.
18. CH2/521/1, f. 68v (the 1581 Perth order to build 'upon their own expenses'). For inheritance of seating, see CH2/442/74, ff. 31v, 39; CH2/390/1, f. 23v; CH2/400/1, p. 177; NAS CH8/153 – though special permission had to be sought for a relative not specified in the original deal to sit in the seat, even in the absence of the person usually occupying it: CH2/400/1, p. 202. In South Leith, William Logan could build a seat for his mother only on condition that 'none of her posterity claim title to the seat without licence of the session', the elders retaining power over this indicator of social status 'for the avoiding of all inconveniences that may fall out' (CH2/716/1, f. 1, 1597). Falkirk's elders brokered deals for transfer of seats as property, as when Alexander Livingstone appeared formally 'to give over possession' of his seat to James Monteath and his heirs: CH2/400/1, p. 177.
19. Among other requests to build 'beside the repentance stool', see CH2/390/1, ff. 20, 23; CH2/442/74, f. 47. CH2/424/2, ff. 9, 15, typically specifies room for tenants.

and the communal identity of the members of a trade or craft. Their facings were carved and brightly painted with emblems of the guild – ships for mariners, a sheaf of wheat or a baker's paddle for baxters, balances for merchants in Burntisland, for instance (see plates 22–25). The way to carry on a quarrel with another guild in this parish was in fact to deface the enemy guild's gallery front, as the maltsters did to the baxters in the 1620s – clear testimony to the loft as an affirmation of identity and standing. Dangling over many a sailors' loft, as in the Ayr kirk, was a model ship, carrying on a Dutch tradition and doubling the identity markers in the kirk for that guild.[20] The joiners of Dun added to the tools of their trade on their gallery front a petition for divine blessing (see plate 26). The ambitions of guilds could lead to conflict with sessions over the right to define space. Glasgow's deacons of crafts in 1591 tried to claim all the choir lofts as the guilds' exclusive domain; while the session overruled them in defence of its own liberty to grant what seating petitions it would, the fact that space was thus claimed by the craftsmen testifies to the perceived relationship between corporate identity and space in the kirk.[21]

A visitor to an early seventeenth-century Scottish church had no difficulty seeing the social structure of the community in the arrangement of seats. A 1629 traveller to Selkirk observed, 'The hammermen and other tradesmen have several seats mounted above the rest, the gentry below the tradesmen in the ground seats; the women sit in the high end of the church, within the choir; . . . my lord Buccleugh's seat is the highest in the church, and he hath a proper passage into it at the outside of the vaulted porch.'[22] Even after parishes began constructing seats for more ordinary people at parish expense – for schoolboys and women, for instance – the placement and decoration of lairds' and guild seats set them visibly apart from the less privileged.[23] The elders of Kirkwall ensured that

20. Gifford, *Fife*, 112; Howard, 194.
21. NLS ms 2782, f. 30v.
22. C. Lowther, *Our Journal into Scotland* (Edinburgh, 1894), 15.
23. For women's seats, see CH2/390/1, f. 52 (a 1629 order for 'honest women to keep their ordinary seats in time of preaching'); NLS ms 2782, f. 31 (1586 use of old pulpit stones to be laid 'in ranks for the women to sit upon'); SAU CH2/624/3, p. 29 (Anstruther Wester charging women 20s for each seat). Some wives sat with their husbands (CH2/390/1, f. 27, or CH2/276/1, p. 33). Kirkwall, Perth, Dysart and Glasgow were among parishes constructing seats for school children: CH2/442/74, f. 47; CH2/521/1, f. 68v, 1581; CH2/521/2, f. 90v, 1594; CH2/521/7, p. 141 (a 1620 warning against boys creating 'tumult or perturbation at their coming and sitting down in their seats'); CH2/390/1, f. 1 (a 'fore face' to be added to the scholars' seat); NLS ms 2782, f. 66 (grammar-school boys sitting in the reconstructed rood loft). Other special seats were built for the minister's family (CH2/636/34, f. 105v, 'of wainscott'; SAU CH2/624/2, p. 141) and magistrates and bailies (CH2/390/1, f. 27; NAS

the community's hierarchy would remain evident in the kirk with a 1629 act to avoid the 'great incivility and undecentness of the baser sort among the people, . . . who being sat down in the chiefest seats of the kirk would not rise up to give place unto their betters and superiors', even though it was commonly known that the galleries above the new doors were intended for 'great men, strangers, or elders of the session'. Persistent violation of this order by a cordiner, a merchant and a tailor suggests that the spiritual equality represented by communion seating might have got out of hand in this Orkney parish; if so, the session's equally persistent punishment of the trio worked to nip in the bud any social levelling that protestantism might have implied.[24] The presumption that seating corresponded to status was shared by English visitors to Scottish churches, though their ignorance of the penitents' stool could lead to confusion. Fynes Moryson in 1598 recorded a rare instance of raucous hilarity in St Giles, Edinburgh, when 'a gentleman, being a stranger, and taking [the penitents' stool] for a place wherein men of better quality used to sit, boldly entered the same in sermon time, till he was driven away with the profuse laughter of the common sort.'[25]

The elders provided quality control for construction of seats, generally designating 'kirkmasters' to approve plans, ensure that proper timber was used, place some limits on decoration and oversee the construction.[26] Sessions went to great lengths to keep construction sufficiently uniform and restrained to avoid distracting attention from the preacher, and to prohibit elaborate canopies or elevation that blocked people's view of the pulpit. This could be tricky when prominent families were involved, and especially when rivalries between important lairds were being fought out in the space of the church. In Kirkwall, the elders had to remove the seat of Sir James Stewart, laird of Mains, for 'keeping of peace and quietness and good order both in kirk and country' when a quarrel arose over its prominent placement.[27] Sessions sometimes referred questions of

CH8/153). Kirkcaldy in 1620 gave a blanket order for 'plenishing of the kirk with seats': CH2/636/34, f. 33.

24. CH2/442/74, ff. 6, 33, 35–36. The Perth council voted in 1602 to lock the lord's seat in St John's kirk to prevent students entering the seat reserved for gentlemen: PL ms B59/16/1, f. 25.

25. *Early Travellers*, 83–84. Laughter may have been more frequent in Elgin, whose elders in 1641 passed an 'act against laughing in the kirk': CH2/145/6, f. 32.

26. CH2/521/1, f. 69v.

27. CH2/442/74, f. 49v. For similar cases in other parishes, see CH2/636/34, ff. 102v (a 1628 dispute between the laird of Bogie and John Whytt about Whytt's canopy); CH2/390/1, f. 23v (resulting in removal of 'the foreast (front corner on the east side) part of David Wemyss' seat', 1625).

precedence to the higher court of presbytery, as when Kingsbarns's elders, fearing 'great troubles should arise' from the 'great discontentment' of two gentlemen desiring seats in the same space, 'did put it off to the [presbytery] visitation of the kirk' so that the visiting brethren could settle the matter 'in a more calm . . . way'.[28] But for the most part they stuck firmly to the rule that the pre-eminence of sermon and sacraments required even the great to allow a clear view of the pulpit and open passage to the tables. Sessions limited the width of a portioner's seat in Newburn, forbade Sir John Wanshope of Niddrie from erecting a seat 'prejudicial either to the lights of the [Liberton] kirk [blocking the window] or seats already built', and warned a Falkirk heritor that his seat must be 'no further in length out upon the church floor than the seats already built upon the other side of the church beneath the loft'.[29] And they did not hesitate when their conditions were violated to order removal of the offending structure: when the 'decorations from the head' of Wanshope's seat did indeed block the light from the window behind it, the Liberton elders declared that he could either 'remove the entire cover [canopy] of the seat' or 'lose his seat and room'.[30]

28. SAU CH2/819/1, p. 14 (1640); cf. f. 31, and CH2/424/2, f. 13v – William Murray of Newton settling a quarrel with the laird of Womett by asking presbytery to determine whether the latter's new seat would 'prejudge him of the sight of the pulpit' by 'sight[ing] the same'. Three brethren of the Perth presbytery had to settle a quarrel in the parish of Forteviot when Laurence Chapman complained 'that his seat was removed out of the ancient place whereof he and his predecessors had been in possession many years and the laird of Innermay's seat put in, who was but a new entrant': CH2/299/1, p. 317 (1633).
29. CH2/276/1, p. 33; CH2/383/1, f. 9v; CH2/400/1, p. 188 (Harry Grindlay, awarded 'the bounds of a double desk'). See also CH2/442/74, f. 45 (three or four Kirkwall elders to 'take a vision of the place' requested by a petitioner to 'try if it might be conveniently done without offence or stop to the service of communion to stay the entry and passage to the table or pulpit'). Perth acted against wrights who erected 'divers seats for private persons wrought and set in the kirk . . . without the knowledge and licence of the ministers and elders first had thereto' (CH2/521/8/2, f. 218).
30. CH2/383/1, f. 17v: he removed the projecting decorations from the canopy and so was allowed to retain it, but he had to shorten the seat as well. Grindlay in Falkirk also had his seat inspected after construction: CH2/400/1, p. 197. And the Kirkcaldy elders ordered Matthew Anderson's 'footgang that is before his seat to be removed' and announced that, in future, 'whosoever shall make any alteration in the kirk by up-putting or downtaking any work in the kirk except they acquaint the minister and the bailies therewith shall pay £10 and make satisfaction therefor publicly' (CH2/636/34, ff. 109–09v) – an order also adopted by Glasgow's session in 1604 (NLS ms 2782, f. 30v). The Moray synod ordered the minister of Rothiemay's desk removed from the choir because 'the passage and room of the kirk is impeded and hindered therefor': CH2/271/1, p. 132.

The proprietary value of seats as status markers made them very often a cause of quarrels and even violence in the kirk. Even common seating for women, and for that matter the space in which a parishioner, by arrangement with the session, placed the stool she brought with her to church, had sufficient status value to cause riot when violated. The Perth elders in 1600 were so disgusted at a 'difference . . . fallen out between some honest women of the town for particular and proper seats in the kirk' that they ordered all seats 'appertaining to women to be demolished and taken out of the kirk for avoiding of such slanderous strifes'. Requiring women to bring their own stools, however, did not solve the problem, as the 'stool wars' of the 1630s attest. In 1634 the elders appointed the kirk officer 'to have a care that every honest woman's stool be not removed forth of the place wherein they are accustomed to stand' after a 'contention between the widow of the late James Gall and Thomas Inglis's spouse for their seats in the choir in setting of their stools'. A few months later they had to deal with Elspeth Kettle and Barbara Stewart after Kettle 'raised Barbara off her stool, violently pulling it from her and striking her on the side of the head with her knife' and Stewart responded by jabbing Kettle 'with a needle in the ears to the effusion of her blood'.[31] The difficulty with common space and common seating seems to have been that it failed clearly to demarcate who had precedence when there was not enough room for everyone. In a culture that found order in strict maintenance of hierarchy, the results could be disastrous, both for the harmony of the community and for the authorities themselves. In Anstruther Wester, Lawrence Dischington was so distraught at not being thought worthy of a place that he 'violently broke the principal seat of the kirk and gave unto sundry of the elders many injurious languages' – an attack on the seat of the privileged to protest lack of a seat for himself.[32]

Other quarrels, often violent, arose over questions of inheritance, over limited space in guild lofts or over construction jointly funded by a group of individuals with the understanding that they would take it in turns to sit in the pew. John Suord of Falkirk incited a small riot in 1620 by 'troubling, molesting and holding [his brother and another man] out of their seat in the kirk upon the sabbath day . . . notwithstanding that they are partners with him of the said seat'. Suord protested that 'he did it upon reason that he could not get payment of the parties of the expense and charges . . . for building of the said seat'. The session admonished the trio to sort it out themselves and share quietly in future or else 'sit in the common forms' (public benches) and relinquish their seat to 'others more peaceable'.

31. CH2/521/3, p. 135; CH2/521/8/2, ff. 145, 162; cf. CH2/636/34, f. 13.
32. SAU CH2/624/2, p. 143.

Threatened with what would clearly entail loss of status, they settled their financial arrangements and worked out a schedule for sharing the seat.[33] Fortunately, in most disputes over seating, physical violence was directed against furniture rather than people. Angry parishioners removed the names of their rivals from their seats, defaced and demolished pews, and as we have seen in Temple parish, even symbolically attacked their enemies by reconstructing seats of honour into stools for shaming penitents.[34]

The close identification of guild membership with seating in the kirk is clear from disputes over whether non-members could ever be permitted to sit in guild space, even when it was not occupied fully by the members. A complaint brought to the Perth session by a newly elected deacon, Patrick Robertson, against the baxter John Ferguson illustrates both the proprietary interests of guilds in kirk seats and the session's power to uphold the status of its own diaconal officers. Robertson objected that when he had tried to occupy a vacant place in the baxter's pew the previous Sunday at the second bell to the afternoon sermon, Ferguson 'gave him a repulse and would not suffer him enter', causing great disruption to the service. Ferguson defended himself by explaining that he was 'enjoined by his deacon of craft to suffer none to enter in their seat until the brethren of the craft were first placed', and there remained a half-hour before sermon time for all the baxters to come. As it happened, the elders considered the kirk deacon's office so important that its violation took precedence over the insult to guild privilege: they warded Ferguson for having 'disgraced the said Patrick'. In a later ruling, the elders again subordinated guild rights to comfortable audition of the sermon when they told the skinners that they could lock the door of their seat on weekdays, but if space permitted 'it be patent to honest men to sit in it the time of God's service'.[35] Obviously, there was a tension between the interests of the whole kirk and the privileges of guilds, with suits and negotiations producing not altogether satisfactory compromises in the end. But to presume, as the received version has it, that the Reformation's elimination of parish fraternities and guild-sponsored altars 'made the creation of community more difficult' is to ignore the opportunity presented by the pew.[36]

33. CH2/400/1, p. 68 (Suord also paid a £5 fine). For an inheritance dispute, see CH2/521/8/2, f. 178v (protesting non-kin sitting 'in the seat in the kirk wherein his late mother sat'). For a 'loud quarrel' between two wrights over seating in their gallery, CH2/521/7, pp. 224–26.
34. CH2/636/34, f. 15v (removing the name plate); CH2/147/1, f. 35v (act again 'altering, demolishing or breaking' seats); CH2/424/2, ff. 5v–17, 19, and chapter 3, above, for Temple.
35. CH2/521/8/2, ff. 217, 219v.
36. Goodare, 174.

Granted, protestantism hindered traditional guild activities. Quite apart from abolishing saints' festivals, the Canongate elders in 1566 stopped craftsmen convening their corporations on Sundays, as they had time out of mind, lest they stay away from church to drink. It behoves us, however, to take seriously the significance of the protestant alternative for guild cohesion and display. The Canongate session told guildsmen to assemble and come as a group to the kirk for 'hearing of God's word . . . as they would be judged members of Jesus Christ'.[37] Processing into the kirk together, sitting massed in their own clearly labelled gallery before the captive audience of their perforce sabbatarian neighbours, guildsmen declared both their corporate identity and their piety as clearly as ever they had in earlier processions or festival pageantry.

It is significant that the status battles represented by stool wars, whether by guilds, individuals or families, were fought out within the church. Plaintiffs were intent on defining their corporate identities and privileged status in that context by using material objects that were religious in their association with hearing the word preached, but that also obviously contained layers of social meaning in their construction, design and placement. Without question, seats in the kirk were an opportunity for display of status for families, a tangible demonstration of corporate identity and cohesion for guilds, a symbolic weapon in feud or rivalry – in short, a tangible representation of the social structure of the early modern Scottish community. Visually dominating the interior of the kirk by the early seventeenth century, outstripping in number and bulk all other items of furniture in the building, they naturally lead us to conclude that in material terms, the kirk had become a vehicle of secular display.

Such a conclusion, however, begs a number of important questions. Consider the medieval predecessor of the protestant church building – a clutter of icons, side altars, funerary monuments, paintings and coloured windows. How did those furnishings function in the traditional scheme of things? Who paid for them, and how do we know? What messages did they convey to their observers? Of course, they had religious functions, the doctrine of purgatory being perhaps the most important engine of artistic production in the later Middle Ages. But so did pews in the protestant scheme, with its long sermons as the focus of worship. And just as the meaning of the seat for protestants was not exclusively religious, so the message conveyed by the furnishings of the pre-Reformation kirk had been multivalent. Why do portraits of patrons appear in altarpieces and stained-glass windows, if not to draw the observers' attention to the patron's status, to the wealth that paid the artist as well as to the piety of

37. *Canongate*, 54.

the donor, to the influence of the individual able to mould literally in his own image the fabric of the parish church? Is such a portrait less a signature on the image than the name plate on a seventeenth-century desk, claiming effective ownership, if not of the object itself, then of its benefits and meanings? Was depiction of the deceased on a medieval funerary monument necessary for the fate of that person's soul in the next world, or just a proclamation of her or his family's standing in the community for all posterity? Who in a medieval parish was unaware of which altar had been funded by the baxters or the cordiners? Who chose the saints to whom those altars were devoted, if not guildsmen announcing their own corporate identity to the community by elevating their chosen spiritual patron? When maltsters or merchants or mariners processed on their saint's day with their images and relics, perhaps producing a pageant or play along the way, was the focus of the audience less on the dramatic display of guild status and corporate wealth than on the saint being venerated? In other words, before as after the Reformation, the interior of the church was the slate on which the prominent inscribed their names, and where corporations defined themselves in relation to the larger body of the community.

After as before, they did so *not* in secular terms, but using holy space and religious language to explain who they were. Just as the guildsmen of the fifteenth century organised themselves around their saint by constructing and maintaining an altar, so their sixteenth-century counterparts defined themselves as a divinely protected corporate entity by decorating their lofts with entwined images of their secular occupations and the angels who watched over them, as we have seen in Burntisland. Just as their predecessors processed with their relics, so they came to the kirk each preaching day *en masse* to sit prominently displayed before their neighbours in the place reserved for religious observance. Just as medieval guilds had maintained their altars, so long after the Reformation their corporate descendants were still ordered as 'possessors of altarages to put up their lights in the kirk and to put upon the Sunday a two-penny candle' in winter.[38] Just as wealthy donors a century earlier worked their images and arms into devotional art, so prominent men's seats in the protestant kirk displayed heraldic imagery and, in the burial vaults so often beneath their lofts, portraits in stone of their families. Was the kirk thereby rendered an arena of secular display? Of course. But this was no more so after the Reformation than before, and in neither age was it devoid of an essentially sacred underpinning. The choice to display status in the kirk demonstrates an ineluctable truth about the span of centuries surrounding the

38. CH2/521/1, ff. 64, 84v (1581–82).

Reformation: individual, family and corporate identity in early modern as in medieval Scotland was defined in fundamentally religious terms. The early modern is no more an age of secularism than an age of individualism.

★ ★ ★

Protestants defined the physical space enclosed by the kirk walls as 'God's house', a 'temple', a 'house of prayer and spiritual exercises' and so a sacred space.[39] Like their catholic forebears, the authorities in the Reformed kirk accordingly demanded particularly reverent behaviour in that space and punished misbehaviour there more vigorously than elsewhere. The Dysart session, for instance, announced in 1619 that 'to do any offence in God's house' would bring the draconian penalty of warding and £40.[40] Sessions continued an age-old campaign against physical defilement of the space. If for every medieval condemnation of 'pissing against the kirkwall' we find dozens in the session minutes, it is only because there are fewer extant sources for the pre-Reformation; the same goes for the ongoing struggle to keep dogs from defiling the church.[41] The sessions' frequent punishment of violence within the kirk's walls cannot be taken to indicate less popular reverence for the building than had existed before, when medieval clerics had often 'to reconcile a church polluted *sanguinis . . . effusione* [by bloodshed]'.[42] And to the extent that costly repair and improvement of a building indicates regard for the sanctity of its space, as anthropologists tell us it does, then both the decrepitude of many of the medieval buildings inherited by protestants and the regularity of individual and parochial expenditure on painting, pointing, glazing, masonry and bell-foundry should correct our misapprehensions about protestants and

39. E.g., CH2/390/1, f. 1; CH2/521/4, pp. 22, 74.
40. CH2/390/1, f. 1.
41. CH2/442/74, f. 30; CH2/521/2, f. 56; NLS ms 2782, f. 30v (ruling explicitly against 'abus[ing] the sanctuary by pissing at the kirk walls'); CH2/84/28, f. 10v; SAU CH2/624/2, p. 129 (against 'making water in the kirkyard'). CH2/636/34, f. 102 reports the rather unusual offence of 'pissing in the kirk upon sabbath last in time of sermon' – a public offence that the tailor William Gray denied in vain, since two witnesses deposed that 'they saw the place wet'. Orders against dogs in the church include CH2/390/1, f. 1; CH2/521/1, f. 115v; CH2/146/2, f. 155 (dogs and vagabonds). SAU CH2/624/2, f. 134 bans storing 'gear or timber' in the Anstruther Wester kirk. For pre-Reformation examples of the same problems, see McRoberts, *St Andrews*, 71, 75; Sanderson, *Ayrshire*, 21–22; Cowan, *Scottish Reformation*, 4.
42. CH2/716/1, f. 16v; CH2/526/1, f. 3; cf. Donaldson, *Scottish Church History*, 223; McKay, 85, 97; Cowan, *Medieval Church*, 171; *APS* 3:544; A. Grant, *Independence and Nationhood: Scotland 1306–1469* (London, 1984), 207–09.

holy buildings.[43] They were at least no more remiss than their catholic forebears. And many remind us of the medieval communities that devoted their labour and funds to erecting holy buildings. William Cowper found confirmation of his calling to Bothkenner in Stirlingshire, where the kirk at his arrival was without 'door, nor window, nor seat, nor pulpit, nor any part of a roof', in his parishioners' enthusiasm to repair without compulsion not only the nave, but also the choir, 'which of due should have been done [paid for] by the parson'. Nor were they 'content to have built it only, they adorned it within and without, not inferior to any other church of such quality round about it.'[44] English visitors were surprised to find Scottish burgh churches 'tiled and well enough furnished', and some 'fairer churches for in-work than any I saw in London', with 'seven great bells, . . . many candlesticks, . . . the finest seats I have seen anywhere and the orderliest church'.[45]

Decoration of sacred space certainly was more abstemious after the Reformation than before, what with protestant objections both to the principle of veneration of saints and to any visual depiction of biblical figures (with the notable exception of protective angels), lest they become objects of worship in place of God. But protestants had their own icon in the text of the Bible. They accordingly decorated the place where the word was preached, if not with images, then at least with expensive fringed cloth, highly carved pulpits, and coloured (generally green) surround walls.[46] Even more significantly, they decorated the kirk building and its

43. CH2/147/1, f. 13v; CH2/338/1, ff. 5v, 12v, 15v, 29v, 38, 41; CH2/390/1, ff. 23, 41v; CH2/283/1, ff. 11v, 34v; CH2/258/1, n.f., 7 May 1637 and 20 December 1637; CH2/1115, f. 3v; CH2/264/1, ff. 14–15; CH2/442/74, f. 38; CH2/266/1, ff. 34, 36v; NLS ms 2782, ff. 29, 31v; CH2/191/1, f. 32v; New Register House, Edinburgh, ms OPR 310/1, f. 54v. Jane Hubert, 'Sacred Beliefs and Beliefs of Sacredness' in *Sacred Sites, Sacred Places*, ed. D. Carmichael, J. Hubert, B. Reeves and A. Schanche (London, 1994), notes that maintenance of a site set apart as sacred or 'pertaining to the gods' requires physical care, like repair, as well as ceremonial care for the spirit housed in the space (pp. 11, 16). Still, pre-Reformation neglect and abuse of church buildings was rife: Hay, 18–19.

44. Cowper, 4. The parishioners who were 'stented', or taxed, to pay for such work were also consulted about its design: the minister William Fraser, for instance, reported to the Moray synod that he had 'convened his parishioners . . . to consider how to build the old and ruinous foundation' (CH2/271/1, f. 11, cf. f. 13, Inneravon).

45. Morer, 53; Agnes Mure Mackenzie, *Scottish Pageant 1625–1707* (Edinburgh, 1949), 100 (quoting a 1629 visitor).

46. CH2/636/34, f. 107v; NLS ms 2782, f. 31; CH2/390/1, f. 39 (a pulpit to be improved 'with wainscott work'); CH2/521/7, p. 71 ('so much of the great pillar that is above the pulpit [to] be coloured green according to the draft and pattern . . . devised by the painter who would undertake the said work and to make it excellent and durable, whereof the colours would be costly').

furnishings with the word itself. The Parton pulpit, built in 1598, displays on its sounding board the admonition to 'fear the lord and honour his house' (see plate 3), an incorporation of protestant meaning into material object just as a catholic altarpiece incorporated meaning in its images. 'Fear God, 1623' is inscribed on the east gable of the Upper Largo church, together with the initials and arms of Peter Black, who paid for the exhortation in stone; Robert Montgomery's 'The Lord is only my support/ Only to God be Laud & Gloir' is rather overshadowed by the brightly painted and much larger arms that accompany it in Largs (see plate 27), but both Black and Montgomery show how display of worldly status and family piety combined to decorate protestant churches with the word.[47] On a larger scale, the ceiling over the Skelmorelie Aisle in Largs, an overpowering status symbol, is painted with texts from the Geneva Bible, along with figures of the four seasons and the coats of arms of the tribes of Israel (see plate 21).[48] The text of the ten commandments was painted on kirk walls, in Scotland as in its protestant neighbour to the south, but favourite texts accompanied by illustration could also be incised into both exterior and interior walls, as with Anstruther Wester's text of Matthew 7.13 carved into the kirk wall together with the image of the wide gate leading to destruction (the destination clear in the flames enclosed by the gate), the narrow to salvation (see plate 28). Family pews sported biblical texts and pious ejaculations as well: the Sandilands of Torphichen decorated their 1595 pew in Mid-Calder with 'The Lord is my shepherd, I shall not want. Psal. XXIII.1. I live in Christ', along with their family arms.[49]

Images were not entirely lost in the logocentric décor of the new kirk. We have seen that the coastal parish of Burntisland had its mariners' galleries painted with images of ships and angels as well as prayers for protection (scc plates 22–23). That same church displays on its walls and gates the image of an anchor, inverted to point heavenwards, to the final haven and ultimate source of spiritual shelter. These are petitionary images, visual prayers for protection at sea, rather than objects of adoration. But they are images nonetheless, and indeed, like icons, emblems of efforts to address

47. Black's inscription is on a carved panel about halfway up the gable. Montgomery's includes his initials and those of his wife, Margaret Douglas, dated 1636. Quite protestant prayers were carved into interior walls of churches like Kirkmaiden, where the arms and initials of Patrick Adair of Alton and his wife accompany their petition, 'O God, make me to hear in faith and practice in love thy holy word and commandments; thou only art my support. God, make me thankful. 1618': John Gifford, *The Buildings of Scotland: Dumfries and Galloway* (London, 1996), 388.
48. Spicer, '"Defyle Not Christ's Kirk with your Carrion"', 149–69.
49. Hay, 196–97.

the divine in his own house. They may not seek the intercession of a saint, but they still materially represent the petitioners' recognition that here, in holy space, they might be heard with particular clarity.[50] The images on walls, lofts and pews were also brightly coloured – contrary to the drab image we usually conjure up for early modern Scottish churches. Burghs often bore the cost of painting, as in Ayr where the accounts of 1598 and 1613–14 include 'dressing and colouring of the lofts in the kirk'. The Edinburgh session paid for 'painting and colouring' Greyfriars in 1621, and in 1647 the Tron Kirk ceiling was painted by John Sawers at a cost of £200.[51] The act of colouring (and paying for it) itself declares a conviction that material representation in sanctified space is weighted with meaning; indeed, that it has its own potency.

There are rare survivals of more traditional religious imagery both in post-Reformation churches and in private homes. In some cases the latter provide evidence of persisting catholicism; however, one of the most striking examples – a whole gallery of painted panels depicting the life of Christ from annunciation to ascension in Provost Skene's house in Aberdeen – was commissioned in the 1620s by a vigorous protestant who would later take up arms for the Covenant in the Bishops' Wars (see plate 29).[52] Clearly, not all Reformed parishioners were willing to forgo the spiritual stimulus or comfort of religious art, even if they risked discovery of 'superstitious monuments' in their domestic chapels. The Glasgow presbytery in the 1590s was dismayed to discover painted crucifixes 'in many houses, . . . which is likely to breed a corruption and to turn the hearts of the ignorant to idolatry'; they also acknowledged the persistent popular belief behind the problem, 'that their houses cannot be happy or blessed but where the crucifix is'. It turned out that there were two painters 'secretly kept in the houses of Glasgow painting the crucifixes', and apparently making a good living at it.[53] Parish churches also retained a surprising number of images. Glasgow's elders in 1593 destroyed images their

50. Cf. Hubert, 'Sacred Beliefs', 9–19, and Carmichael, Hubert and Reeves, 'Introduction' in *Sacred Sites*, 1, 3. Many of the authors in this collection of essays by sociologists psychologists and anthropologists demonstrate that the significance of sacred sites can transcend such cultural changes as religious conversions.

51. Hay, 216.

52. The 'Painted Gallery', executed when Matthew Lumsden owned the house (1622–44), includes ten painted panels of the life of Christ and emblems of the Five Wounds: *Provost Skene's House* (Aberdeen, for the City Council, 1994), 14–15. There are also pre-1638 images in Mary Somerville's house in Fife, including Mary, the Apostles and a head of Christ: MacMillan, 57, 70.

53. *Maitland Miscellany*, 1:420; E. Murray, *Church of Cardross*, 30; *Records of Inverness and Dingwall*, 1 ('an idolatrous image called St Finian kept in a private house' burned by the ministers of Inverness at the market cross after a Tuesday sermon in 1643).

searchers found in a chapel in the Irongate, but their next major campaign in 1641–42 uncovered many 'superstitious pictures and crucifixes' – some in the private homes they inspected, but three in the High Kirk, including depictions of the Five Wounds and the Holy Lamb. The parish kirk of Grandtully still has a Last Judgment painted in the 1630s.[54] While these survivals are rarities, they do point to some ongoing notion of space set aside for visual stimuli to an experience of the divine. There was not, after all, an absolute consensus about the need to abolish religious images.

Protestant retention of church names is another survival hinting at the multiple layers of meaning in physical space, and the futility of trying to abolish traditional associations of saints with places. Edinburgh's High Kirk remained St Giles, Burntisland's St Columba's, Perth's St John's, long after images and feast days of those saints were banned; nor was there ever any discussion of abolishing the names. Indeed, the burgh of Perth was still called 'St Johnstoun' long after the Midsummer feast of the Baptist had been condemned, so central to urban identity was the name of its ancient patron.[55] This should not surprise us. Studies of place and collective memory have shown that place names do more than delineate space.[56] Space is defined and labelled by its occupants, but in turn, and over time, it comes to define human identity, so that its name becomes part of the meaning of the community that inhabits it. If the space accumulates sanctity as well, loss of a traditional name would be all the more traumatic. Whatever the dangers of associated idolatry, then, Scotland's parishes retain to this day their sacred names, an unthinking but culturally effective compromise by the reformers.

All this is not to deny that a variety of 'profane' activities also took place in the kirk. In parishes without school buildings, pupils received their lessons there.[57] Ministers' children played in kirk as well as kirkyard, and parish money-making schemes included games in the kirkyard.[58] But as with display of status and corporation in pews, this phenomenon simply continues medieval tradition rather than being a peculiarly protestant

54. NLS ms 2782, ff. 30, 43–43v; MacMillan, 80.
55. E.g., LPL ms 3471, f. 39v (Patrick Blair, 1589); CH2/390/1, f. 57 (1630).
56. Robert Tittler, *The Reformation and the Towns in England, c. 1540–1560* (Oxford, 1998), ch. 13; Keith Basso and Steven Feld, eds, *Senses of Place* (Santa Fe, 1996), esp. 91–135 (Feld, 'Waterfalls of Song') and 230–57 (Charles Frake, 'Pleasant Places, Past Times, and Sheltered Identity in Rural East Anglia'); Anne Buttimer and David Seamon, eds, *The Human Experience of Space and Place* (New York, 1980); Saul Kripke, *Naming and Necessity* (Harvard, 1980).
57. CH2/424/2, f. 16v; CH2/521/4, p. 22 (Perth's scholars' disputations in the kirk, only forbidden in 1605).
58. CH2/424/2, ff. 7v–8; SAU CH2/624/2, p. 107.

departure from earlier notions of sacred space.[59] Some 'profane' activities, moreover, continued in the kirk for religious reasons. Medieval notaries had set up their tables in the church 'so that the sacred character of the place would add its own sanctity' to legal transactions, divine witness rendering agreements harder to break. Time out of mind, redemption money was counted out at the altar for the same reason. Should we be surprised that in the 1570s – long after altars, icons and relics had been removed – debts were still being redeemed in St Andrews cathedral at the place where the altar of St Catherine had been located?[60] Space acquires meanings that will not go away at a preacher's order, especially space long set aside for divine oversight, where generations believed that violators of truth and honesty would inevitably draw God's wrath. Most persistent, and thoroughly condoned by ministers and sessions, was the tradition of regarding oaths taken in holy places in the kirk as particularly binding, or as indicating incontrovertible truth. When the Canongate elders in 1567 thought that one of their own number, Cuthbert Ferguson, was lying about his wife's communion attendance, they ordered him to repeat his testimony under oath 'in the kirk in the morning after sermon . . . as his conscience will dictate'; then they would believe him. Even so improbable a testimony as that of a Monkton couple admitting 'being in the naked bed with each other but deny[ing] carnal action' was taken for verity when they 'purged themselves' by oath in the kirk.[61] There was a clear presumption that lying was more difficult, if not impossible, in a sanctified place, where the divine presence was so immediate as to preclude falsehood.

The kirkyard also constituted holy space, as continuation of the medieval campaign against grazing, tilling and storing lumber there attests. Sessions seem to have been no more successful in this endeavour than their catholic predecessors, but they certainly tried to preserve the sanctity of the burial ground.[62] Their efforts included prevention of excommunicates and suicides being buried in holy ground, specifically because they should not be allowed to pollute the company of the faithful

59. Donaldson, 223; McKay, 85, 112–13; *APS* 2:245.
60. Sanderson, *Ayrshire*, 21–22; NAS, Protocol Book of James Nicolson, f. 103; McRoberts, *Medieval Church*, 69, 83.
61. *Canongate*, 68; AAC CH2/809/1, f. 26v; cf. CH2/529/1, f. 74v.
62. E.g., CH2/171, f. 29v; CH2/400/1, p. 117; CH2/191/1, f. 21; CH2/266/1, f. 28v; CH2/84/28, ff. 10v, 16, 37; SAU CH2/624/2, pp. 129, 189; CH2/326/1, pp. 1–3, 7; NLS ms 2782, f. 31v; NLS ms Wod. Oct. IX, f. 5; CH2/442/74, f. 21v; *SAKS* 2:755. Even the kirkyard walls were protected by sessions' acts, as in Perth's 1579 mandate that websters desist drying their cloth on Greyfriars walls: CH2/521/1, f. 16. For medieval parallels to these efforts, see McKay, 112–13; *APS* 2:245.

departed: they must be 'no participant of their company when they are dead' any more than 'when they were living' – an interesting indicator of the presumed society of the deceased in sanctified burial space, and of the power of the reprobate dead to defile the communion of saints.[63] They also continued ancient tradition in punishing 'all speaking evil of the dead, or casting up the faults of the dead, who have suffered for their demerits, to the living'. Such 'despiteful speech against the dead' got Isobel Perk sentenced to the market cross of Fraserburgh (for saying of William Burnshaw, 'the devil raise him up and make him a gouge in a door because he owed her a debt'); it brought public repentance in the kirk for Glaswegians.[64]

The real innovation that Scots reformers attempted in regard to interment of the dead relates explicitly to their understanding of sacred space: they banned 'burial within kirks and suchlike erecting of tombs' there, on grounds that the kirk was a house of prayer and preaching, and not, as the papists had made it, a 'cairn of dead men's skulls'.[65] But this was the view from the study, not the pew. There is surely no louder testimony to continued lay reverence for sacred space, and perhaps the benefits that burial there could confer on the soul, than the utter failure of this effort in the face of popular insistence on kirk burial, and its eventual transformation into yet another fundraising device. Prosecutions abound for 'violent breaking of the kirk floor and burial of his bairn within the same' or 'breaking the kirk floor divers times and burying of his children', pointing to the psychological need of the bereaved, especially parents, for some sense that their loved ones were provided with a material indicator of spiritual wellbeing after death.[66] Burial in a holy place is a

63. SAU ms 30451, f. 6. See also CH2/521/1, f. 86v, Perth's 1582 order for William Sawyer, 'who drowned himself at the head of the smithy in the Water of Tay' not to receive 'the burial appointed for the faithful'.
64. NLS ms 2782, f. 62; CH2/1142/1, f. 103v (Perk's exact phrase was 'ane skethie to ane duir becaus he was awane hir deit').
65. The initial 1581 Assembly order had to be repeated four more times by 1643 (1588, 1597, 1638). As early as 1573, the Assembly asked the council to ban kirk burial, but to no avail until 1610: *BUK* 1:280, 378, 388; 2:603, 733; 3:937. *RPC* 8:425 (but with an exception for either 'heritable right' or payment of a £40 fine); *First Book*, 201. William Birnie (minister of Lanark in the 1590s), *The Blame of Kirk-Buriall, Tending to Cemeteriall Civilitie*, ed. W.B.D.D. Turnball (Edinburgh, 1833), ch. 11. See also *SAKS* 1:452; *Visitation of the Diocese of Dunblane*, 3, 14, 30. For pre-Reformation practice, see McKay, 110–13; Sanderson, *Ayrshire* 15–16; Paul Binski, *Medieval Death: Ritual and Representation* (London, 1996).
66. CH2/400/1, pp. 127 (Dr William Callendar the offender in 1624), 177v, 179v; CH2/299/1, p. 297 (1632); CH2/521/2, ff. 28v, 29; Mark Smith, 'The Presbytery of St Andrews 1586–1605' (Unpublished PhD thesis, St Andrews, 1985) (an edition of

nearly ubiquitous human mechanism to assuage grief and deal with the fear of death and uncertainty about the afterlife; obviously it would not easily be abolished, even by the most zealous Scottish divines.[67] Of course, burial inside the kirk was also a traditional status marker, making elimination of the practice even more difficult.[68] The elders took the easy way out and made a profit while they were at it. As in the case of festivities, they opted to exhibit their flexibility about unpopular rules by systematically allowing them to be broken for a fee. Initially this was articulated as a penalty for the offence of 'breaking the kirk floor', but sessions quickly adjusted to heavy demand for kirk burial by shifting their language from that of punitive fines to straightforward fee schedules announced before parishioners might be tempted to sneak into the kirk and excavate graves themselves. Sessions across the realm collected small fortunes for their poor boxes, with fees ranging from 40s to £100 depending on proximity to the pulpit or the east end of the kirk (significantly, where the high altar had stood before the Reformation) and the social standing of the deceased. They also required annual payment of 'burial silver' to keep the body in place.[69] Clearly laypeople regarded interment in the most sacred space of the kirk as worth considerable financial sacrifice and commitment over time, the annual payments in fact reminiscent of the expense of those pre-Reformation commemorative masses, the 'months minds' and obits on the anniversary of a death.[70]

the St Andrews presbytery minutes), 189–91, 197, 207, 259–60; CH2/121/1, ff. 8, 20v (Edinburgh presbytery's efforts to stop burial in Holyrood, 1586–87); NLS ms Wod. Oct IX, f. 17 (1640 complaint that the choir of Erskine was 'pitifully abused by burying the dead within' at gentlemen's insistence on their hereditary rights.

67. Huntington and Metcalf, *Celebrations of Death*; Duffy, 313–14, 340–41.
68. Spicer, '"Rest of their Bones"', 173.
69. CH2/521/3, p. 278 (50 merks for a laird's burial, 1603); CH2/521/8/2, f. 226v (£100 for 1637 burial of Lady Stormouth's mother in the kirk's east end); CH2/141/1, f. 36 (£40 for the Countess of Drinlannach, 1628); SAU CH2/Crail/1, f. 3v (£40 in the 1610s); CH2/4/1, f. 13v (20 merks for a place near Aberlady's east door); New Register House ms OPR 310/1, f. 58; CH2/390/1, ff. 6, 10, 13v; CH2/191/1, ff. 11 (collection of 'law silver' or 'burial silver' in Inveravon), 28 (£5 in 1635); NLS ms 2782 (40s for 'lairs in the High Kirk', 1593, but 'more for persons of quality', rising to £50 in 1616); *BUK* 1:272–73, 294 (a Mauchlin case where John Hamilton and friends threw aside the communion table to bury Sir William Hamilton of Sanquhar in the kirk – obviously as near the protestant version of the altar as possible). The Canongate elders in 1565 tried to democratise the privilege of kirk burial, with the church 'either to be used generally that desires, or else prohibited and refused to all, that no exception of persons be made therein' (p. 16), but the demands of hierarchy and display undermined this resolve.
70. Sanderson, *Ayrshire*, 15–17; Spicer, '"Rest of their Bones"', finds 'the desacralised burial of the Reformed Church . . . failed to provide the reassurance' that the

The complex meanings of spaces in the kirk emerge sharply from the Inveravon case of William Gordon. Unable to afford kirk burial, but determined to bury a beloved relative in a space both holy and socially exalted, Gordon sneaked into the kirk and buried the corpse under the desk of Patrick Stewart of Kinnochlon, who duly complained to the elders. The latter found it a 'great fault' and ordered Gordon to exhume the body and pay a £20 fine – more than the cost of kirk burial in the first place. The ensuing discord required presbytery intervention. In view of Gordon's apparent poverty, the brethren directed the session to pay for exhumation, but Gordon bore a heavier cost to his reputation when the body was reburied in a space freighted with all the wrong meanings – beneath the penitents' stool. When he finally complied with the presbytery order and performed his public repentance, he did so standing over the corpse he had vainly tried to honour.[71] The authorities clearly recognised the profound meanings embedded in the physical space of the kirk.

The most affluent parishioners went beyond mere indoor burial and petitioned sessions for permission to erect funeral monuments, which preachers might condemn as vain, but sessions like South Leith's regarded as 'a thing both comely and honest'. They granted licence to Jeremie Lyndesay to build a tomb for his wife on the south side of the kirk wall in 1603, inaugurating a flurry of monument-building in that kirk that culminated with a 1612 licence for a laird to bury his wife beneath a tomb 'the breadth of four kists [casket-widths] of the wall . . . to be a heritable burial place to him and his posterity' – in exchange, of course, for a substantial gift to the poor box. The Kirkcaldy elders in 1628 granted a petition from the lairds of Raith and Bogie to enlarge their monuments.[72] Monuments at burial sites in the kirk could be grave slabs set into a wall, like that of Sir William Bruce of Earlshall (d. 1584) in Leuchars, with its carved coat of arms and the inscription 'Here lies of all piety a lantern bright, Sir William Bruce of Erlishal, knight'. They could be brasses, like that of Regent Moray in St Giles, Edinburgh (1570), with the images of Religion and Justice, or the Mynto monument (1605) in Glasgow cathedral. Many were arched altar tombs, an abundance surviving from the later sixteenth century in Tarves, Banff, Kirkcudbright and Greyfriars,

bereaved needed (p. 178), despite his awareness of exceptions to the rule against kirk burial. He may have underestimated how routine these exceptions were. On obits, Cressy, *Birth, Marriage and Death*, 398–402; Duffy, 461–62.

71. CH2/191/1, ff. 57–58.

72. NLS ms Wod. Qu. XX, ff. 148v–49v ('Ane funerall speech generall'); CH2/716/1, f. 11; CH2/716/2, f. 77; CH2/636/34, f. 102v.

Edinburgh.[73] They could include life-sized figures of the deceased, together with the usual *memento mori*, like Agnes Lindsay's (d. 1635) in Leuchars or the much more elaborate 1630 monument to Sir George Bruce of Carnock in Culross abbey kirk (1630), with its recumbent effigies of Bruce and his wife and the kneeling alabaster figures of their children.[74] They could even be massive, free-standing sarcophagus monuments dominating the centre of the church, like that to the mother and wives of John Gordon of Cullindoch erected in 1635 in Anwoth kirk, with the Gordon arms and high reliefs of skeletons, crossbones, hourglass and open book, and the words 'memento mori', lest observers somehow miss the point. The striking thing about this monument is the amount of space it occupied in the small church. It must have obscured a view of the pulpit for some, but it sent its own message about sin and death (see plate 30).[75] But the most elaborate kirk burial places were the purpose-built burial aisles that proliferated after the Reformation and gave rise to the 'T-form' so characteristic of protestant kirks when the long wall of the nave was broken to add a wing to the building (see plates 6, 21).[76]

Clearly these monuments were social status markers for the family survivors, but their location in the sacred space of the kirk, in clear violation of the General Assembly's orders but with full approval of sessions, suggests the survival at the local level of traditional associations between sanctified space and spiritual identity as well, albeit in Reformed guise. The inscriptions to John Gordon's second wife on the Anwoth monument proclaim her protestant piety, asking observers not to pray for her soul, but to admire and by implication imitate her upright life: 'Ye gazers

73. The Forbes of Tolquhon monument at Tarves (1589), the Ogilvy (1580) monument in Banff, and the Thomas Maclellan monument at Kirkcudbright (1597) are particularly noteworthy sixteenth-century examples; an abundance from the following century are discussed by Hay, 205–09.

74. Gifford, *Fife*, 308; cf. 311 (Old Scoonie Parish Church monuments), 417 (Ferryport-on-Craig monuments), 41 (St Leonard's 1590 monument to Robert Stewart, Earl of March and the Wilkie monument of 1611; the Pitcairn monument of c. 1585 and the William Shaw monument of 1602 in Dunfermline abbey; and Bruce's in Culross abbey).

75. Described well by Gifford, *Dumfries and Galloway*, 101–02, though viewing this very large monument in the kirk allows one to see how overwhelming its presence would have been to the congregation.

76. Spicer, '"Defyle Not Christ's Kirk with your Carrion"', 149–69, title quoted from Sir James Melville's mausoleum at Collessie in Fife; Howard, 176, 198–207; Gifford, *Dumfries and Galloway*, 37, 101; Gifford, *Fife*, 35, 59, 170, 207, 257, 274, 417. The architectural term 'aisle' is used in Scotland to refer to a projecting wing of a church, often transeptal, intended for use by a guild or landed family for special seating and/or a burial vault.

on this trophy of a tomb, send out one groan for want of her whose life was born on earth and now is in earth's womb. Lived long a virgin, now a spotless wife. Church keeps her godly life, this tomb her corpse, and earth her famous name.' His mother's 1612 inscription is her self-description: 'Walking with God in purity of life, in Christ I died and ended all my strife. For in my soul, Christ here did dwell by grace; now dwells my soul in glory of his face.' These are impeccably protestant sentiments, and placing them on the tomb allowed the Gordon family a sort of preaching role to future generations. The tomb thus bespeaks protestant innovation. But it does so in a completely traditional cultural context, in which the illiterate observer might well have perceived a harking back to the function of older tombs, whose legends asked aid for the soul's well-being after death. Such likely confusion was the reason for the General Assembly's prohibition of kirk burial, and for that matter of funeral services with prayers, reading or singing that 'are not only superstitious and vain, but also are idolatry'. The *First Book of Discipline* granted that 'things sung and read may admonish some of the living to prepare themselves for death', which was all very well, 'yet shall some superstitious think that singing and reading of the living may profit the dead.'[77] The reformers thus recognised that the 'ceremony heretofore used', together with the monuments they had tried so hard to keep out of the kirk, had multivalent meanings for a congregation that included 'ignorant' as well as 'godly'. The material culture of protestantism that emerged from the sessions' flexible (not to say cavalier) administration of the Assembly's policy willy-nilly allowed for the inevitable variety of interpretations drawn from pious proclamations carved with images into sacred space. Gordon paid for proclamation of his mother's thoroughgoing Calvinist orthodoxy and evident assurance of her election, but in a less protestant mode he also wanted her remains physically ensconced in the holiest ground available, under her image in stone. Is display of social status a sufficient explanation for this desire? Had there been no continuing association in people's minds between burial and the place of the soul, would not even the social value of kirk interment have abated? And whatever Gordon's intentions, would not many of his neighbours have taken a more traditional, 'superstitious' view of the meaning of the images he provided – as, indeed, the reformers had predicted? These are ultimately unanswerable questions, but in view of the clear failure of the General Assembly prohibition

77. *First Book*, 199–201; *BUK* 1:43, 280, 378, 388; 2:603, 733; 3:937; *SAKS* 1:452. There were also practical reasons to prohibit burial in the kirk: the Edinburgh council ruled against it in 1561 for the 'savour and inconveniencies that may follow thereupon in the heat of summer': *Records of the Burgh of Edinburgh*, 3:106.

of kirk burial in the face of popular demand, they are surely worth asking.

The end result in any case was that both elaborate imagery and religious symbolism persisted in monumental art after the Reformation. Far from austere, church interiors continued to display image as well as word in stone and wood, and brightly painted to boot, as both the material of surviving monuments and textual evidence tell us. Zacharay Boyd chided his Glasgow congregation for 'striv[ing] by artifice to make the grave pleasant by painted and carved stones' when in fact human effort comprised 'but a painted destruction'. The monuments of burgh churches, however, suggest that he was whistling in the wind.[78]

When people did accede to the Assembly order and bury their dead in the kirkyard rather than the kirk, they were still seeking interment in traditionally 'holy' ground, and they still indulged in the same highly decorated image-making in gravestones as their social betters inside the kirk, and for the same combination of religious and social reasons. Clearly parishioners thought it important to label the holy ground where a body was buried with images of death and resurrection, and with pious admonitions and indicators of the deceased person's godliness. People went to great expense to do so, the costs being recorded when they petitioned the session for licence to erect a stone.[79] For that matter, they went to some expense just to get the kirk officer and gravedigger to bury the body: this was not a service free to all comers, although sessions did try to keep costs under control and prevent their officers from 'exacting of extraordinary prices for burial' and even, in a notorious Falkirk case, holding decomposing bodies hostage during price negotiations.[80] Clearly burial in holy ground mattered, though it was more than a matter of piety. Relatives also wanted the community to recognise who had gone to the expense of providing grave and stone. The Culross session had to settle a quarrel between two sisters in 1631 when one removed her father's stone without session approval and replaced it with one that had only her own and not her sister's name on it as donor. The sister found this such a public insult to

78. Boyd, *Balme*, 211; Howard, 204, discusses evidence for full polychromy of the monuments.

79. E.g., CH2/400/1, pp. 119 (20s for licence to a cordiner to put a stone in the kirkyard 'whereby it may be designed as a burial place for himself'), 316 (£3 for a stone in a rather better location), 154 (unexplained refusal of a licence to William Murheid, 1626). Sessions paid for their ministers' gravestones: CH2/636/34, f. 101v.

80. CH2/400/1, p. 114 (1623). Sessions paid for common mortcloths and biers, and for shrouds and other burial costs for the parish poor: e.g., CH2/471/1, f. 67; CH2/266/1, f. 28v. Highland interments tended to be in clan rather than kirk burial grounds; however, these were no less sacred places.

her filial piety that she was only satisfied when the elders ordered her name to be inscribed on the new stone as well.[81] For a combination of religious and social reasons, then, monuments proliferated remarkably in seventeenth-century Scottish kirkyards. When Sir William Brereton visited Edinburgh and saw the multitude of 'very fair tombs and monuments erected in memory and honour of divers merchants and others' in Greyfriars kirkyard, he predicted (correctly, as modern visitors can attest) that if the trend continued, 'in the revolution of a short time the whole wall will be most gracefully adorned with tombs'.[82]

The images on gravestones throughout the seventeenth century were abundant and entirely traditional. Like interior monuments, they often included life-sized images of the deceased.[83] Standard *memento mori* like skulls and hourglasses (see plate 31) are ubiquitous.[84] Just as the grotesques in medieval churches reflected fear of death and purgatory – the terrifying and emotionally wrenching effects of sin – so the images in stone of post-Reformation kirkyards reinforced the same message in precisely the same way. In funerary monuments the negative images of traditional religion survived outside the kirk just as penitential rites did inside. The words of many sermons, as we have seen, painted the same picture, and just as graphically, drawing the same emotional response; what is striking is that for all the reformers' denunciation of images, when sin and death were the subjects, visual images survived to sustain the words. While this is most evident in kirkyards, we find sin and mortality visually represented even in published illustrations of sermons by preachers of the most impeccably Calvinist credentials (see plate 32).[85] Pictures, in

81. CH2/77/1, f. 10; cf. f. 18v, an order for inspection of gravestones set up without leave. The Bruce vault in Culross typically proclaims itself 'provided by George Bruce of Carnock, his eldest son' (Gifford, *Fife*, 149).

82. *Early Travellers*, 146 (1639).

83. E.g., the Agnes Lindsay stone at Leuchars, or David Martin's at Auchtertool, both 1630s.

84. Charles Rogers, *Monuments and Monumental Inscriptions in Scotland*, 2 vols (London, 1871–72), gives parish-by-parish descriptions of funerary monuments; Willsher, 'Scottish Graveyards', analyses images like winged soul effigies and notes that it will be harder to argue from such artifacts in another generation, given the rate at which these mostly sandstone monuments are disintegrating. Typical stones are those of John Fairfoul (d. 1626) in Anstruther Wester, with its cartoon-like skull, hourglass and arms; or of Thomas Bourlay (d. 1641) and his parents and children in Old Scoonie, Leven, with its skulls and a thin skeleton. For analysis of English monuments of the same era, Nigel Llewellyn, *The Art of Death: Visual Culture in the English Death Ritual c. 1500–c. 1800* (London, 1991).

85. Illustrations in printed sermons are admittedly a rarity. The ones that exist are often aimed at focusing attention on sin and death, like this one in Zachary Boyd's *1. Crosses 2. Comforts 3. Counsels Needfull to Bee Considered, and Carefully to Be Laid Up*

Reformed Scotland as in every culture, reveal the central concerns of a society; we do not need to read sermons to know what troubled early modern Scots protestants.

Tolling bells for the dead, before the Reformation a call for prayers for their souls in purgatory, was like kirk burial a practice condemned by protestants but clearly surviving in the parishes. Allegedly bell-tolling met the practical need to announce the death of a neighbour. But the elaborate levels of tolling set up by sessions, with differential fees for more or less ringing, must have been read at least by the 'ignorant' as an affirmation of spiritual benefits attached to the ringing, as of old. In Brechin, quite apart from the ringing of a handbell through the town to announce a death, ringing of the great bell at a funeral cost £1 6s 8d, 'doubling the bells' by ringing both great and small bells cost £2 – an auditory parallel to the fee hierarchy for kirk burial, £10 for the aisles and transepts, £20 for the nave.[86]

Finally, a burial service of sorts also survived, again despite prohibition. To guard against 'superstition, idolatry, and whatsoever hath proceeded of a false opinion', the *First Book of Discipline* prohibited both 'prayers over' the dead and 'funeral sermons, [which] shall rather nourish superstition'. Instead, a small 'honest company of the kirk, without either singing or reading, yea without all kind of ceremony heretofore used', and without the minister, were to convey the body to the grave. Only after interment did the *Forme of Prayers* permit the minister to 'make some comfortable exhortation to the people touching death and resurrection'.[87] In practice,

in the Hearts of the Godly, in these Boysterous Broiles, and Bloody Times (Glasgow, 1643), sig. Ai verso.

86. Thoms, *Kirk of Brechin*, 21, 45; cf. NLS ms 2782, f. 32; Bodleian ms Rawl. C.584, p. 115 (noting retention of tolling in practice); ML CH2/171/1, f. 3v (Glasgow presbytery trying to limit bell-ringing, 1593). LPL ms 3471 (Patrick Blair, 1589), ff. 40v, 47, notes Scots antipathy to tolling as 'dangerous', bodies 'carried to the grave . . . in dumb manner', but Morer, 67–68, later observed death announced first by handbell and cryer, and a second time to indicate when people could attend the body to the burial ground, processing in rank and gender order, women at the end. See also CH2/266/1, f. 28v. Perth provided its bellringer with a new coat, breeches, shanks and shoes in 1622 for 'more decent discharge of his service': CH2/521/7, p. 313.

87. *First Book*, 200–01; *Forme of Prayers*, 112; *BUK* 3:939. Morer, 66–67, reported Scottish burials without the minister, 'whom they will have so far from popery concerning the dead, that he must not be concerned with interring the corpse, and is seldom seen at their most solemn funerals'. The *First Book* also voiced concern that ministers might 'have respect of persons, preaching at the burials of the rich and honourable, but keeping silence when the poor and despised departeth, and this with safe conscience cannot the minister do. For seeing that before God there is no respect of persons, . . . whatsoever they do to the rich in respect of their ministry,

however, formal funeral services continued. The form used in Montrose in the 1580s included a sermon, prayers and hymns, and Knox himself was among those to preach funeral sermons. The General Assembly was still struggling in 1597 to prevent large processions and 'pictures or images be[ing] carried around in burials'.[88] Funerals for important people attracted large gatherings and, as we have seen, the 'profane pastimes' that sessions never quite managed to wipe out included wakes.[89] When fundamental human need is at issue, as in the most stressful time surrounding the death of a loved one, both ritual and art thus preserved tradition in the service of comfort to the bereaved. The genius of the Scottish Reformation at the local level was the willingness of sessions to compromise with instructions from above, to negotiate solutions that would both address the social and psychological needs of parishioners and maintain a sufficiently protestant guise to further the Reformed agenda.

* * *

Contemporary critics of Scottish protestants complained that they 'keep no holy days', having abolished both saints' days and the feasts celebrating the life and resurrection of Christ.[90] Defenders of the Reformation, however, could claim that they actually had greater regard for sacred time than did their popish foes, for three reasons. First, they adhered rigorously (not to say rigidly) to the biblical mandate to keep the sabbath holy, banning on all twenty-four hours of that day any 'profane' activity whatsoever, unlike catholics who allowed dancing, games and feasts on Sunday. Second, by abandoning set days 'invented' by human agents rather than divinely ordained in scripture, they actually increased reverence for Sunday by eliminating false competition. Finally, they could point to the fact that they did observe other holy days than the sabbath, but with biblical precedent. These were days designated either as feast or fast, and set aside not because of any artificial calendrical tradition, but because on particular

the same they are bound to do to the poorest of their charge' – that noble, early Reformation sentiment that so rarely survived in practice (p. 201).

88. 'Forme and Maner of Buriall Used in the Kirk of Montrois' in *Wodrow, Miscellany*, 291–99. Knox preached at the burial of Regent Moray in Edinburgh: Calderwood, *History of the Kirk of Scotland*, 2:525–26. *BUK* 3:939. NLS ms Wod. Qu. XX, ff. 148–50 is a model funeral oration; the 1625 eulogy for Robert Boyd of Trochrig is in the *Bannatyne Miscellany* 1:283–98.

89. *RPC* 7:315 (funeral of Adam Menzies's son in Durisdeer, 1607); *APS* 4:626. For lykewakes, see chapter 4, above.

90. Sir Anthony Weldon's 1617 judgment after a visit to Scotland, in *Early Travellers*, 101. Critics pointed to the Calvinist theory that all times are equal: NLS ms Wod. Fol. XXVII, f. 10.

occasions they understood God to have spoken to the kirk, just as he had to the children of Israel, for good or ill, and to have demanded time set aside for a response. God spoke in famine, war, tempest and plague – direct divine judgments – or more positively in good harvest; both required answers from the kirk, in repentance or thanksgiving. Fast and feast were sacred times, in other words, just as the kirk was sacred space: they were points of conjunction between human and divine.

Scottish sabbatarianism was a legend in its own time, caricatured by an English visitor in 1617 as 'a preaching in the forenoon and a persecuting in the afternoon', a time when 'they stop their ears if you speak of play'. They 'hold it above reach, and God willing, I shall never reach for it,' quipped Sir Anthony Weldon.[91] But the Scots' strictness was nothing if not a veneration of time set apart by divine commandment for holy exercise. Cowper explained to his Perth congregation the difference between the sabbath and the papists' feasts: 'no king or church can make a holy day', but only God who 'sanctified the seventh'.[92] Any activity apart from sermon attendance, catechism, prayer, reading and discussion of scripture was sabbath breach, an offence directly against God as well as kirk and community. We have seen that sessions punished even the most innocuous activities, including 'breaking the sabbath day in feasting' in Kirkcaldy, 'playing at the football on the fasting Sunday' by 'the boys of Newbattle', or 'running a race in time of sermon' in Edinburgh.[93] They dealt with offences like quarrelling, drunkenness or bloodshed on Sunday much more severely than if they had been committed on weekdays, 'in respect it was upon a sabbath'.[94] Indeed, the language of condemnation often makes the sabbath breach more serious than 'dinging of his neighbour' – the day more sacred than the neighbour's skin. The Mid-Calder session convicted James Gilbertson of 'breaking the sabbath by striking of Marion Anderson a poor woman upon . . . a fasting day' – the day providing the bookends to what we would consider the more serious sin. An Edinburgh woman likewise sinned by 'abusing God's day' in striking her neighbour on Sunday, and Thomas McQuin of Kirkoswald was 'convicted of break of the sabbath in striking John Muir his servant'.[95] The sabbath

91. *Early Travellers*, 100–01.
92. Cowper, 8.
93. CH2/636/34, f. 7v; CH2/84/28, f. 27v; CH2/718/1, f. 2v.
94. CH2/447/74, f. 27. See also CH2/400/1, pp. 77, 335; CH2/390/1, f. 7v; CH2/338/1, f. 10; CH2/264/1, ff. 14v, 20–20v; ML CH2/171/1, f. 26v; CH2/141/1, ff. 4v, 6, 38v–39, 41; CH2/636/34, f. 28; CH2/718/1, ff. 4, 7v.
95. CH2/266/1, f. 50; CH2/141/1, f. 38v; AAC CH2/562/1, unfoliated entry for 29 May 1626. See also CH2/716/1, f. 82v; *Dundonald*, 29, 225, 231; CH2/636/34, f. 32; CH2/400/1, p. 335; CH2/264/1, f. 20v.

was effectively personified, almost deified, and made the greater victim in such cases.

The entire sabbath was to be kept holy, 'from the rising of the sun to the downpassing thereof'. Boharm extended the definition to forbid farm labour even after sunset, and Dysart included the Sunday hours 'under night' in its requirement of particularly circumspect behaviour on the holy day.[96] During communion seasons, festive behaviour was forbidden on Saturday evening as well, and for the week between the two communion Sundays, Glasgow's elders in 1587 ordered excommunicates to stay indoors, 'their house closed till they be absolved'.[97] Such orders go beyond the alleged aim of encouraging sermon attendance. There was an almost magical quality about the twenty-four hours, an almost superstitious fear of even seeing the excommunicate during the holy time. But there was a pay-off to the strictness: a sabbath properly observed was a time when 'manifestations of God' will come 'after hot exercises or a scorching heat in the conscience', and 'the soul will win into Christ's bosom.'[98] This fits the classic definition of a holy time, a day set apart by specific acts for a more immediate communication with the divinity than was possible at any less sacred time.

The other protestant holy days were fasts for repentance and communal 'humiliation' – self-abasement before a holy God, and feasts 'for solemn joy and thanksgiving'. Like the sabbath, both required 'cessation from ordinary trades, both before and after noon, so the people might frequent the assemblies', with their sermons. Also like the sabbath, they extended from morning to evening, to be 'kept holy unto the Lord in the nature of an extraordinary sabbath'.[99] And they facilitated contact and communication with God.

Feasts were something of a rarity in early modern Scotland. As Zachary Boyd explained to his Glasgow congregation, they are not so beneficial as fasts because 'a feast is made for laughter, which will not admit the company of so grave meditations. Laughter will not suffer the living to lay his end to his heart.'[100] One wonders how much laughter would have been heard at what was always called 'solemn thanksgiving', focused mainly on a sermon.[101] Parliament's order for Gowrie Day thanksgiving

96. CH2/400/1, p. 133; CH2/1115/1, f. 5; CH2/390/1, f. 3.
97. CH2/716/2, f. 106v; NLS ms 2782, f. 61v; *Dundonald*, 307.
98. Folger ms V.a.415, f. 81v.
99. Cowper, 8; Alexander Henderson, *The Government and Order of the Church of Scotland* (Edinburgh, 1641), 25–26.
100. Boyd, *Balme*, 231.
101. The days were not specifically named. The names of pre-Reformation feast days survived, but now just to indicate calendrical date, as when clerks record a bairn

'in all time coming' describes the celebration as a day of 'public preaching, prayers, and solemn thanksgiving' when 'all work, labour and other occupation which may in any sort distract the people from the said godly exercise and thanksgiving yearly upon the day foresaid shall be forborne and abstained from.'[102] Thanksgivings offered relaxation, then, but not a lot of jollity.

Days of thanksgiving were generally slated for the end of a particularly good harvest season, to indicate corporate gratitude for 'God's great bounty in the abundant and seasonable harvest' or for the 'seasonable weather sent by the Lord for collecting of the fruits of the ground for sustenance of man and beast'.[103] They could be set for celebration of political or military victories as well, or for Gowrie or Gunpowder Plot Day, or the end of a plague outbreak, and there was a spate of them in January 1639 'for the Lord's sensible blessing upon the proceedings of the General Assembly'.[104] All such 'blessings' were construed as direct communication from God. Unlike old saints' festivals, celebrated on arbitrarily set dates regardless of whether God at that moment had a positive or a negative message in play, Reformed feasts were designed to be direct responses to divine communications – truly sacred times because initiated by divine activity.

Unfortunately, God seems to have communicated much more judgment than blessing on early modern Scotland, if the preponderance of fast over feast days is any indication. The Scots were the only Reformed church to prescribe a liturgical fasting order, *The Ordour and Doctrine of the Generall Faste* (1565, from 1587 incorporated into the *Book of Common Order*).[105]

got 'twenty days before Fastingseven, born five days before Martinmas' or a fornication 'at Hallowmas' or a payment due 'between now and Yule' or work to be done 'against Pasch' or by Whitsun: e.g., CH2/716/1, f. 9; CH2/716/2, ff. 48, 70, 81, 82; CH2/191/1, ff. 3, 9v, 15–15v, 42v; NLS ms 2782, f. 15. Law courts also retained 'Yule' vacation until 1639 (*APS* 5:595).

102. *APS* 4:213–14.

103. CH2/424/2, ff. 1, 23; CH2/359/1, f. 3v; CH2/145/3, f. 12. Trinity College parish held a thanksgiving feast every November from 1626–31: CH2/141/1, ff. 10v, 34v, 35v, 51.

104. E.g., CH2/4/1, f. 33; CH2/145/6, f. 28 (military victories). SAU CH2/210/1, f. 13; CH2/285/1, p. 8 (5 November). NLS ms Wod. Qu XXI, f. 258 (after a 1607–08 pestilence); CH2/264/1, f. 21 (General Assembly). Cromwell's death occasioned one, too: Wodrow, *Analecta*, 2:150.

105. Ian Hazlett, 'Playing God's Card: Knox and Fasting, 1565–66' in *John Knox and the British Reformations*, ed. Roger Mason (Aldershot, 1998), 176–98, quite appropriately judges Scotland 'in the vanguard of the fasting tradition until the eighteenth century', with 'more fasting (including abstinence as a civil requirement) in Scotland after the Reformation than before it' (181–82). The *Ordour* is discussed 180–83. *BCO* 150–91. See also Charles McCrie, *The Public Worship of Presbyterian*

Public fasts were proclaimed for the whole realm by the General Assembly or by king, council or parliament.[106] They were ordered even more frequently for localities by sessions, presbyteries, synods and bishops.[107] The duration of a fast varied from one day to several weeks or, in times of severe stress, months – something that was never true of thanksgivings. Aberdeen's fast in the severe winter and plague season of 1608–09 lasted from early October to 15 January.[108] Extended fasting seasons could include Sundays or particular weekdays only, or every day of the week.[109] Protestant fasts were supposed to be scheduled not at

Scotland Historically Treated (Edinburgh, 1892), 122–25, and William D. Maxwell, *A History of Worship in the Church of Scotland* (London, 1951), 108–09.

106. SAU ms Hay Fleming Box 53, it. ii, p. 55 from the back (my pagination) notes a preacher's explication of private (by families or individuals) and public fasts. Fasts throughout the realm include CH2/141/1, ff. 30, 32 (May and August, 1628, by royal proclamation); *BUK* 2:410 (1578 General Assembly order); LPL ms 3471, f. 26v (Privy Council and ministers, 1586); CH2/145/1, f. 70v (Assembly, 1594); and CH2/258/1 (April 1640, parliament and Assembly). For other Assembly fast orders, see Calderwood, *History*, 2:317, 324, 486 (empowering superintendents and provincial commissioners to call fasts); 3:384; 4:304–05, 676, 682–83; 5:179, 278, 737; 6:113–16. Parliament and the king also declared non-religious fasts, mainly to protect the fishing industry and regulate animal husbandry: *APS* 3:40, 353, 453; 4:70 (1567 ban on eating flesh Wednesday, Friday and Saturday, 'for the common weal', reaffirmed in 1584, 1587 and 1594 in view of 'great dearth of all manner of fleshes' and specifically applied to 'the time of Lent', defined in 1594 as 1 March to 1 May); PL ms B59/16/1, f. 70 (royal proclamation of fish days enforced by Perth's council, 1603).
107. Examples of presbytery proclamation of fasts include CH2/299/1, pp. 70 (for the 'second Sunday in Lent'), 76, 86, 298, 317, 330, 343, 362, 365–66; CH2/299/2, pp. 113, 298, 330; CH2/198/1, ff. 5–6; CH2/636/34, f. 39v; CH2/294/1, f. 1; CH2/424/1, n.f., 20 January 1591; ML CH2/171/1, ff. 16v, 51, 251; CH2/327/1, f. 43v; NLS ms Wod. Qu. XX, ff. 281–83 (by bishop and presbytery, 1627). CH2/271/1, p. 113 is a synodal proclamation; Inveravon's in 1632 was proclaimed by the bishop (CH2/191/1, f. 12). Session orders for fasts include CH2/145/1, f. 65v; CH2/266/1, ff. 51v, 111v; CH2/636/34, ff. 51, 65; CH2/400/1, p. 314; CH2/448/1, pp. 36, 73; CH2/448/2, pp. 72–73, 100–13, 316 (after conference with the magistrates), 320–21, 326–37; CH2/448/3, pp. 36–38, 180, 340–42; CH2/472/1, ff. 138–38v; CH2/145/1, f. 36; AAC CH2/562/1, ff. 3, 30, 31v; CH2/264/1, f. 9; CH2/521/2, ff. 12v, 56v; CH2/521/3, p. 334; CH2/521/7, p. 250; CH2/521/8/1, p. 147.
108. CH2/448/2, pp. 316–38; p. 201 records the beginning of a fast lasting several weeks in June and July of 1606 for 'inundation of wets likely to rot the corn', with Sundays the designated fasting day each week. By contrast, p. 37 records a single-day fast for Michaelmas, 1603; p. 72 records a one-week fast in May 1604 'in respect of the imminent danger of the plague of pestilence'.
109. The Glasgow presbytery in 1595 clarified that the week-long fasts they ordered were to be 'two Sundays and all the weekdays': ML CH2/171/1, f. 51. Aberdeen's fasts were usually 'every Sunday and preaching day': CH2/448/3, pp. 340–42. Edinburgh in May 1628 designated a fast 'to begin upon Sunday the 18th day of May instant,

arbitrarily set times in the Christian calendar, as in the days of popery, but only for extraordinary occasions; Calvin ordered them only 'if either pestilence or famine or war begins to rage . . . in order that by supplication the Lord's wrath may be averted'.[110] But there were, in fact, predictable fasting seasons, especially in late winter/early spring (formerly Lent) and for the duration of the harvest season. The former was often a time of severe weather, particularly troublesome for those who made their livings at sea, but in practice the idea of Lent was not a problem for sessions or even presbyteries: the Perth presbytery explicitly designated a 1622 fast for 'the second Sunday in Lent'. The latter season was surely the most anxious of the year, when blight or storm could mean dearth, and warm weather fostered plague. There is no better reminder that early modern Scotland was an agrarian society than the regularity with which the kirk prescribed 'solemn fast [to be] kept all the sabbaths in harvest'.[111]

Fasts obviously entailed abstaining from meat, strong drink and physical pleasure. They were the only times when the kirk approved temporary sexual abstinence for married couples, the better to focus their attention on prayer and humiliation.[112] As we have seen, fasting did not mean complete abstention from food, though sessions often fined people for eating meat or drinking in alehouses, and the Dundonald session summoned those found 'at bread and cheese' as well as 'beef and other meat'. A 'temperate diet' of small drink (ale) and bread or oatmeal generally served.[113] Hunger was less the point than simply avoiding physical gratification and overindulgence. As the preachers explained, 'prayers are sluggish while the belly is full. A full belly maketh the spirit lumpish.'[114]

to continue the next Wednesday thereafter following and to the end and be concluded upon Sunday thereafter following the 25th day of May instant, in all the kirks of this burgh both before and after noon': NLS ms Wod. Fol. XVI, f. 35.

110. Calvin, *Institutes* vol. 4, chs. 12, 14–21, pp. 1241–48.

111. CH2/299/1, pp. 70 (Lent), 76, 86, 298, 317, 330 (August 1634, for fear of 'destruction of the fruits of the ground by violent tempests of wind' – a presbytery fast extended for two weeks more by the Perth session), 343, 362, 365, and 366 are all presbytery calls for January or late summer fasts. Other Lenten fasts include CH2/145/3, f. 185, CH2/521/8/1, f. 160v. Among other harvest fasts are CH2/636/34, f. 39v (for the quotation); CH2/472/1, f. 138v (October 1593); CH2/141/1, ff. 19v, 30, 32; CH2/1142/1, f. 21. For more on timing of spring fasts with Lent, see chapter 2, above.

112. *Forme of Prayer*, 95–96 – though couples were warned not to make the period of separation overly long; CH2/448/2, p. 267 for discipline of offenders.

113. *Dundonald*, 61, 73, 77 (1605 permission to eat meat for a pregnant woman who had already fasted for several days and feared that 'without greater hurt to her health she could not fast any longer', provided she ate 'with temperance'); NAS ms RH2/1/35, f. 30, *BCO* 152, 169, 178. For food regulation, see A. Henderson, *Government and Order*, 25–26 and chapter 2, above, n. 34.

114. Boyd, *Balme*, 201; Struther, 49, 60. An anonymous early seventeenth-century manu-

'Gorgeous apparel' was forbidden on any day of a fasting week, William Struther commending 'coarse and base' dress to keep the mind on things heavenly and demonstrate the humiliation required by sin.[115] Fasts also required desisting from 'any kind of games' and from labour, at least for the duration of the central event of every fasting day – gathering at the kirk for prayers and a sermon on repentance. The order given by the Edinburgh elders in 1628 is typical: they instructed parishioners during the fast to 'abstain from their ordinary callings the said day and to repair every one to their own parish kirks before and afternoon in most humble and devout manner to put up their prayers to almighty God that he might be pleased to avert his most fearful judgments in the threatened agonies against us for our sins.'[116]

That fasts were understood as holy time is evident from vigorous prosecutions of less than reverent or abstemious behaviour on designated days, and especially for absence from the fast sermon. Eating meat or drinking on a fast day in Ayr brought fines of 40s for a first offence, £4 for a second, and £6 for a third; Perth punished a second offence with repentance in sackcloth as well as a hefty fine. Ordinary sermon absence was punished by sessions, but absentees on fast days in Glasgow were sent to the presbytery. And in Kinconquhar, men caught drinking during fasts made public repentance and paid the doubled penalty of 'a merk because it were a fasting sabbath and day of humiliation, which should have been wholly spent in fasting and prayer, and not in surfeiting and drunkenness'.[117] (The elders may also have feared the effects of drinking on an empty stomach, which got Thomas Dougall in trouble in 1605 when drinking after fasting all day 'took him by the heart and ran in his head, that he wist not what he said'.[118]) Fasting days were set aside to commune with a wrathful God; if God, being effectively petitioned to attend, then witnessed disregard and outright sin on the day, surely he would be the more incensed and harder to appease.

What most distinguished protestant from catholic fasts, apart from

script in the Wodrow collection joins 'whippings' with fasting as 'corporal and voluntary punishments of the body [that] are made means of procuring the soul's health' and are appropriately called by 'the word penance'; however, I have not found other Scottish discussion of auto-flagellation in connection with fasts or repentance. The same document finds it 'superstitious to think the first day of Lent more fit for repentance than other times': NLS ms Wod. Fol. LXIV, f. 269.

115. *BCO* 178; Struther, 61.

116. *BCO* 178; CH2/141/1, f. 32.

117. AAC CH2/751/1, f. 2; CH2/521/2, f. 128v; ML CH2/171/1, ff. 51v, 58; SAU CH2/210/1, f. 16. See also CH2/521/1, f. 54 (the elder Constantine Malice disciplined for marrying on a fasting day); CH2/32/1, f. 30; *Dundonald*, 59, 64, 73; CH2/338/1, f. 16; CH2/448/2, p. 197.

118. CH2/716/1, f. 12v.

their supposedly circumstantial rather than seasonal scheduling, was the centrality of the sermon. The *Book of Common Order* recommended that fast sermons be longer than usual, though not 'so tedious that it should be noisome to the people': three hours for the morning sermon, two for the afternoon were thought adequate.[119] Even weekday fasts required one or two sermons, and long fasting seasons placed a real burden on preachers. Glasgow's fasting weeks in 1603 set sermons each day of the week in both the High Kirk and the New Kirk; Aberdeen's session routinely ordered 'public preaching twice every day' for its fasting weeks; and Edinburgh's ministers found themselves so exhausted 'by reason of the public fast appointed' in 1588 that they petitioned presbytery for extra preachers. When Menmuir observed a fasting sabbath 'for the extraordinary weather and tempests', the regular Sunday session meeting was cancelled in favour of an additional sermon, and in Perth and Aberdeen 'the people kept church all day' during fasts.[120] Fasting days also required private prayer and family 'humiliation'. Edinburgh's elders in 1628 explained to their charges that the best preparation for the fast sermon was in fact for 'all the intervening time of before the fast [to] be religiously spent . . . in their own private devotions and religious exercises to the effect their own fast may be the more solemnly celebrated'.[121]

Its logocentric nature ought to have sufficed to prevent any confusion of the protestant fast with its popish competitor; however, ministers still exerted some effort to explain that theirs were not the fasts 'abused by papists', but were efforts to subdue the flesh 'without superstition' and not 'for custom, nor for the day', which was 'plain superstition'.[122] Sessions and presbyteries vigorously prosecuted identifiable catholic fasts, like that in 1595 kept by Archibald Legat, who observed 'superstitious rites or days, in abstaining from certain meats upon certain days, to the offence of the godly'.[123] But it was one thing to claim the days were not superstitious, and quite another to abolish traditional associations, particularly given the

119. *BCO* 178.
120. CH2/121/1, f. 44; ML CH2/171/1, f. 251; CH2/448/2, p. 320; CH2/264/1, f. 9; Spalding, 2:42. For the strain of extra fast sermons on overburdened Perth preachers, see CH2/521/7, pp. 250–52; CH2/299/2, p. 113.
121. NLS ms Wod. Fol. XVI, f. 35, 'certifying the contraveners they shall [be] exemplarily punished at the will of the magistrates'; Struther, 69.
122. Cowper, 611–12; *BCO* 151, 168–72.
123. ML CH2/171/1, f. 54v. On Knox's efforts to rebut the catholic argument that protestant fasts reintroduced the doctrine of efficacious works, see Hazlett, 194; however, the author does not attempt to examine how fasts were perceived by the laity and whether Knox's argument would have had any effect with people who had a rather different and entrenched view of fasts.

temporal juxtaposition of spring fasts with Lent, and also the quite evident purpose of fasts, which had not changed with Reformation.

Fasts were efforts to appease the wrath of God displayed in natural and occasionally political disaster. The reasons given for declaring a fast directly reflect the principal causes of anxiety in early modern society. Fear of pestilence and of dangerous weather rivalled threats to the harvest as the most frequently cited causes of a fast – hardly surprising in an age of extremely high mortality, even among the young, when failure of a harvest or destruction of the fishing fleet by storm or an outbreak of epidemic disease could devastate communities. Contemporary chronicles are a laundry list of horrors that make the fear palpable. For Perth, 1590 saw plague 'among the bestial', 1599 'great dead amongst the people', 1605 'great pest', August 1606 'blood, fire and the pest come in, which continued till May thereafter', 1608 again a pest 'wherein died young and old five hundred persons' – about a tenth of the population. In 1622 there was 'universal sickness in all the country as the like has not been heard of'; in the burgh 'no family in all the city was free of this visitation'. And apart from plague, recurring storms destroyed parts and eventually all of the vitally important town bridge in 1583, 1607 and 1621; a 'great wind' in 1609 'blew down the stones of the mantle wall of the kirk in time of sermon and terrified the people'; floods put people in 'peril of drowning' in 1615, and in 1621 an 'inundation of water like in no man's remembrance was seen', people 'wet in their beds and wakened with water to the waist'. Earthquakes terrified people in 1597, 1608 and 1614; 'deadly storm of frost and snow' in 1615, 1624 and 1635; dearth in 1614, 1616, 1621 and 1623. No wonder that, with the divine signal of a solar eclipse on 'mirk Saturday' in 1598, the parish added to its call for a fast a flurry of witch-burnings, and that the 1621 floods had people 'humbled all that week with fasting and prayer, twice preaching every day' in a way that 'moved the people to cry'.[124]

Fast orders from sessions convey a sense of the desperation the authorities felt in the face of disasters they could not control, and their conviction that their only recourse was appeasement of divine wrath. There was never any question about the cause of the disaster. The Aberdeen elders presumed in 1610 that it was God 'punishing this city by his visitation of the young children with the plague of the pox', and sending heavy rains at the same time 'causing corn to rot on the ground and dearth [to]

124. *Chronicle of Perth*, 3, 5, 7, 9, 10–12, 14–18, 22–24, 26, 34 *et passim*: the list goes on, disasters dominating all other subjects in the chronicle. The years co-ordinate with the Perth session and presbytery fasting dates noted above. The 1635 snow is also noted (CH2/521/8/1, ff. 161v–62) because mortality among the poor drove the session to distribute additional relief in clothing and fuel.

follow'. They had known in 1608 that it was because 'sin and impiety abound in this city' that 'God is threatening the city by the plague of pestilence'. They responded with a one-week 'public fast and humiliation' that they extended in stages from early October through to January, with two sermons daily on weekdays and sabbaths, 'in respect God cease[s] not to threaten this city by his visitation'. Each continuation order recorded a worsening of the disaster, tracking progress of the plague from Glenburgh, twelve miles from Aberdeen, to 'Torrie beyond the water being already infected' in the fourth week, and recording with horror on 9 November 'the fearful earthquake that was yesternight . . . to be a document that God is angry against the land and against this city in particular for the manifold sins of the people'. At this point they added to the ordinary observation of the fast an order for 'the covenant to be renewed by the whole people, both ministers, magistrates and Commonalty, with God, by holding up of their hands all publicly before God in his sanctuary' – holy words uttered in a holy space in the holy time of fast to appease God's evident wrath.[125] Just as bonfires could cleanse evil from the air and offerings to wells cured illness, so communal fasts and Covenant-swearing could avert snow and wind, plague and famine.

Aberdeen is typical in regarding natural disasters as 'evident tokens of God his wrath kindled against this country for sin', as the Paisley presbytery put it, and in presuming that 'plague of . . . man and beast' was inevitable 'if it be not prevented by sincere repentance' by means of public humiliation and fasting, 'that [God] may remove from [us] his said anger'. Use of fasts as a preventive, 'for the averting of the judgments threatened by God', was of course preferable to fasting in response to disaster already present, and was usual if plague had already been detected in towns not far distant, or if the weather were unsettled at harvest time.[126] Hope of averting ill obviously explains the numerous winter and harvest season

125. CH2/448/3, p. 36; cf. 180 for a 1615 fast; CH2/448/2, pp. 316, 320, 321, 322 (Covenant order), 325–27, 331; 72–73 records another (1604) fast 'in respect of the imminent danger of the plague of pestilence wherewith this burgh is threatened, the towns of Edinburgh and Leith being already infected, . . . and the burghs by south having begun their public humiliations already.' Mullan, *Scottish Puritanism*, 191–92, notes the 1596 'exercise of renewing' the covenant conjoined with fasting in several parishes; cf. Innerwick's 'fast kept, Covenant read' in 1648: CH2/1463/1, f. 7.

126. CH2/294/1, f. 1 (1602); CH2/521/8/2, f. 162. The Perth session also announced a January 1635 fast during a 'plague of frost and snow . . . threatening destruction both of man and beast, if it be not prevented by unfeigned repentance' (CH2/521/8/1, f. 160v). See also CH2/271/1, p. 113, Moray synod declaring a fast 'for begging of a blessing from the heavens', 1639; CH2/299/1, p. 330, Perth presbytery in 1634 noting famine in the north and Isles, 'tokens of his present wrath and imminent judgments upon us in these parts', and calling for a fast lest 'destruction of the fruits of the ground by violent tempests and wind' strike further south.

fasts. But many disasters could not be foreseen; still, fasting might avert one calamity being heaped on another, as in Aberdeen's earthquake atop plague. Zachary Boyd preached that God's judgments are '*like* earthquakes, which might make all hearts to quake', but sometimes they actually *were* earthquakes, and hearts had best be driven to spiritual quaking if more of the real thing were to be avoided.[127]

Fasts were also proclaimed for political and military causes, to seek preservation of the king (from the 'imperilling of our king's good person . . . by Bothwell' in a 1592 order, for instance), victory in a war (particularly a religious war, as in 1639 to rescue the godly Scots 'from spiritual and bodily slavery' to the English), or an end to persecution of co-religionists in Europe (as in the 1628 Edinburgh fast for 'the distressed estate of La Rochelle' and 'distress of God's church everywhere in all Europe').[128] The authorities presupposed that God directs all events in human experience, whether 'natural' or political, meaning that each one was a message, if it could only be properly interpreted. They ordered fasting at all levels, from household to realm, to aid that understanding. The *Familie Exercise* gave heads of households the duty of interpreting divine messages for their families, 'to shew and set forth the works of God, and to direct and order the times and manner of [family] humiliation' in response to providential warnings.[129] God's displeasure was without exception earned by human sinfulness, as calls for fasts made clear with extensive lists of reasons. Kinghorn's elders, for instance, ordering fasting in 1593 in light of 'decay of godliness and piety', 'increase of papistry, great increase of atheism and ignorance, oppression, bloodshed, incest, adultery and other such crimes', 'falling from our former zeal', 'oppression and thralldom of the kirk, 'entertaining of papists' even in light of 'conspiracy universal by the papists in all Europe against Christians to put in execution the commands of the blind council of Trent', 'universal oppression and contempt of the poor', and 'the danger wherein the king's majesty stands through company resorting about him by whom it is feared he be corrupted in religion and manners'. No one, even the leaders of church and state, was omitted from this list of offenders who brought on the 'heavy hand of God plaguing us . . . with scarcity and death and . . . extraordinary drought'.[130] Sin brought

127. Boyd, *Balme*, 6.
128. CH2/424/1, n.f., 20 January 1591/92; *Diary of Sir Archibald Johnston of Wariston, 1632–1639*, ed. George Morison Paul (Edinburgh, 1911), 45; CH2/141/1, ff. 19v (for 'success to the king's navies and armies' in 1627 'against the enemies of God's kirk'), 30, 32; NLS ms Wod. Fol. XVI, f. 35; CH2/521/2, f. 56v (1592, for the Reformed kirk of France, 'presently in trouble'); ML CH2/171/1, f. 16v (November 1593, 'during the time of the confusion within this country').
129. *Familie Exercise*, sig. Bi verso.
130. CH2/472/1, f. 138. The fast was ordered to last for three weeks.

calamity, 'our sins are the cause of all our plagues'; humiliation and repentance by means of fasting, prayer and sermon attendance were the only sensible response.[131]

That humiliation was given a ritual form (fasting), in sacred time (a season of repentance), and on sacred ground (in the kirk). It was precisely the same sort of propitiatory activity that had gone on before the Reformation, and for that matter in most religious cultures in times of stress. It was no more 'superstitious' than other ritual uses of sacred time and space – external actions to indicate an internal state – to appease a wrathful deity. But it is difficult to see how it was any less so, either.

★ ★ ★

There were other ways to approach and appease the Almighty besides observing holy times or standing in sacred space. There were also, as there had always been, holy words. In the form of oaths and vows, these had particular power to contact the divine, to call down blessing or judgment. An oath taken with the proper language – designated a 'great oath' in the minutes – was taken as truthful because, if it was broken, judgment would be sure to come. A curse could operate in the same way, though condemned by the church. Petitionary prayer, the approved way to seek blessing, in protestant guise ought to have operated on its own; what is significant for our understanding of how Scots protestants contacted the sacred in the midst of the mundane is the frequency with which they accompanied prayer with a vow as a mechanism to secure divine blessing in particularly stressful circumstances. The vow constituted a quite separate and identifiable set of sacred words, binding the speaker to an action in exchange for the benefit sought.

Vows appear most often in session minutes as acts of desperation by seafarers in the midst of storm. Patrick Anderson, for instance, came to the Perth session in 1601 'to pay and give that to the poor which in his last voyage, being in danger, he had freely vowed' (a new bed in the hospital). James Kinloch recounted to the same session in 1635 that when his vessel was 'by tempestuous stormy weather drowned upon the crags of Norway, wherethrough he and the remainder of persons in the ship were in extreme danger of their lives, together with the loss of ship and goods', he made 'a solemn vow by God that if it shall please God to deliver him of this danger, that he should give to the hospital of Perth . . . twenty-six dollars for declaration of his thanks to God for the said benefit'. By the time he had got the money together, he had moved to London; still, he

131. Boyd, *Balme*, 25.

took the vow seriously and sent a notary to deliver it.[132] Among his shipmates on what must have been a harrowing voyage from London, Robert Pitcairn also 'vowed if God spared him and brought him home again in safety, he should give 300 merks to the poor' (which he did, in two instalments); Andrew Duff gave a dollar of his vow; and Dougall Johnston reported his vow of £300, though the clerk noted that, not being resident in Perth, he could not be held accountable by the elders – God alone could hold him to his pledge.[133] Examples could be multiplied, particularly from coastal fishing and mercantile towns. In 1591 Anstruther Wester received 'the master of the Marie Katrin', who having gone aground on a voyage from England, made good on a 30s vow for his own safety, despite loss of his ship. The Elgin merchant William Guthrie in 1621 gave the kirk six glass windows, 'which he avowed to do in his danger in peril in the seas'. And in 1620 John Donaldson and his brother 'at their return from their sea voyage' offered the Brechin elders £4 4s for the poor without reporting danger – perhaps as much a precautionary payment as a thanksgiving, for the next season the brothers were not so lucky. In 1622 John paid another £4 'in remembrance of God's mercy done to him about this time twelve months in delivering him safe with his life out of that ship cast away beside Stanhyve, wherein many of that company were perished.'[134]

Other forms of danger could provoke similar vows. The Edinburgh merchant John Trotter in 1627 paid £20 6s to the poor of Trinity College after recovery from a serious illness. And in the midst of the 1621 flooding of the Tay in Perth, 'many made vows for their safety'.[135] The words

132. CH2/521/3, p. 174; CH2/521/8/2, f. 190v. Kinloch, clever fellow, managed to combine this payment for divine protection with an annuity for an aged kinswoman by asking that the income from 20 dollars of his payment be paid out twice yearly to her. Since she was already resident in Perth's hospital, the session accepted this charitable annuity as a donation *ad pios usus*.

133. CH2/521/8/1, ff. 129v–30, 148v. Other Perth examples include CH2/521/7, p. 174; CH2/521/8/1, ff. 32, 60–61 (five merchants jointly vowing 110 merks and putting 40 merks down upon their return from sea).

134. SAU CH2/624/1, p. 29; CH2/145/3, ff. 174, 13v (three merchants 'troubled on the sea, who since God relieved them they gave to the poor £5' in 1613); Thoms, *Kirk of Brechin*, 46. See also CH2/141/1, f. 44; CH2/718/4, f. 9 (a Leith servant sending his pledge by courier from London after his safe arrival); SAU CH2/624/2, ff. 137, 140 (fishermen returned from Norway offering £7, 1613). We probably ought to read the naming of ships as yet another use of holy words for protection. The Perth owners of the 'ship called the Grace of God' seemed genuinely surprised when her crew fell ill in 1602: PL ms B59/16/1, ff. 34–35.

135. CH2/141/1, f. 13; *Chronicle of Perth*, 22. The Fife minister Alexander Wedderburn offered a different sort of pledge when he 'entered into a very solemn vow to preach Christ more than ever he had' after surviving a dangerous fever: Wodrow, *Analecta*

they uttered were costly in material terms, but they were vows for which the speakers were convinced God would hold them accountable, and the gains they would hopefully garner in the form of protection from physical danger were worth the investment. The preachers might insist that prayer alone sufficed to communicate with God, but in perilous times resort to traditional mechanisms at least offered comfort.

As for oaths, the sacred space in which a 'great oath' was generally uttered was, as we have seen, one of its sources of power. But the words themselves had intrinsic potency as well. They were easily given a protestant veneer: rather than swearing by a saint or on a relic, a Reformed parishioner swore 'upon her salvation and damnation' in Kirkwall, or 'by his salvation and condemnation' in Glasgow.[136] But sometimes they remained remarkably traditional – and remarkably cognisant of the sanctity of the material space in which they were sworn: 'I take all the persons of the blessed trinity to witness, I take angels and saints above the throne to witness, I take the *stones and timber of Bothwell kirk* to witness,' a Glasgow preacher swore.[137] Veracity was ensured by such words, whether uttered by a woman or a man, great or lowly. Thus, while Janet Moorhead happily denied committing slander even before the Falkirk session, when she was asked to swear her innocence, 'being informed of the nature of an oath, [she] refused' and so was convicted.[138]

The sinful counterpart of holy words was curses and maledictions, which the sessions vigorously punished. Both ordinary folk and elders took curses very seriously. It was two of James Rysyde's drinking buddies who turned him in to the Ayr session in 1605 for 'cursing himself, praying the devil to take his soul' when he was 'in his drunkenness'; they feared the power of his words to damage his soul; a neighbour of Christiane Stirling did likewise upon hearing her 'cursing both her body and soul'. Ayr's session punished swearing 'by the holy name of God or by the wounds of Christ', a recurring problem, as both popish superstition and blasphemy.[139] Maledictions like Jonnet Murray's 'cursing and banning of' William Livingstone in Falkirk, and 'specially for her lately beseeching God's malediction might come upon him and all his', drove her victim to complain because he was convinced her words had the power to hurt him; whether the elders found cause for his fear or simply found her a

2:331. Calling payment of a vow 'thanksgiving' protestantised it in theory; however, this language is often missing from session minutes recording vows.

136. CH2/442/74, f. 26v; NLS ms 2782, f. 61v.

137. Folger ms V.a.415, f. 47v (emphasis mine).

138. CH2/400/1, p. 281, 1636; cf. CH2/1142/1, f. 102v; CH2/716/1, f. 10; CH2/442/74, f. 26v.

139. AAC CH2/751/1, ff. 12, 14, 134; CH2/751/2, f. 3v.

cause of discord, they fined her £5 and made her repent before the congregation.[140] Burntisland's session likewise disciplined Matthew Young for cursing Kathleen Wilson with 'God let never sea nor salt water bear her nor hers above' – a terrifying curse in a fishing community. John Keir complained to the same elders when Margaret Dawson 'begged God's maleson word [curse]' that his ship and crew 'should not come home', though perhaps in part because she spoke before witnesses, hurting his efforts to recruit sailors. Such maledictions were so frequent in this parish that the session passed an act in 1602 against 'cursing of neighbours, . . . wishing them to perish by sea'.[141] If oaths were holy words, curses were not merely mundane, but evil.[142] Like George Adamson's 'blasphemous speech against the omnipotence of God in removing of the storm of snow and frost' in Belhelvie in 1624, they had the power to call down divine wrath on the whole community if not quickly punished.[143] This was not a society that took snow, frost or maritime storm lightly; words were taken seriously, as vehicles by which God or Satan might be called to act.

If the holy language of the vow was a way to secure protection from illness or storm, and that of the oath a device to determine truth, the risk that either might smack of superstition was worth taking in a society living precariously near the edge of disaster. The kirk did well to approve such sacred speech, if only to guard against that other language so often used to secure supernatural aid, the charm. We need to keep in mind that early modern Scotland was a realm of competing religious cultures, including not only the protestant/catholic rivals, but even more dangerous, the surviving pre-Christian culture of fairies, sorcery and charming. In times of stress, failure of protestant prayer and vows to secure protection could all too easily drive desperate parishioners to those other sacred spaces, holy wells and fairy mountains, or to their local charmer for charms or incantations.

Sessions regularly had to deal with parishioners who sought, in particular, healing for themselves or their sick children from people who claimed

140. CH2/400/1, p. 114.
141. CH2/523/1, ff. 18, 28v–29, 1.
142. It is worth noting, however, that although their intent was evil, the curses were not actually diabolic: they called on God's maleficent will, rather than on the devil.
143. CH2/32/1, f. 10v. Adamson was apparently attempting a joke: he claimed that he 'only said that if the storm continued, he would not be able to pay his farm [rent], seeing it is not the Lord's custom to cause corn [to] grow but [by] labouring'; the elders, however, were not amused at what they regarded 'heinous blasphemy, . . . words to import a perilous meaning' and ordered him to kneel and repent. Similar 'idle naming of God' was held responsible by the St Monans elders for 'most fearful and terrible judgments' threatening their village in 1641: SAU CH2/1056/1, n.f.

to have acquired their potions or charms from the fairies. John Gothray, bane of the Perth presbytery, told a fairly typical story. He reported being 'taken away by the fairies in a harvest evening and among them got kindness of a little lad who called himself his brother and showed him how he himself was taken away by them, being but a month old'. Having stayed with the fairies for some time, he was released with a gift for his trouble, in the form of healing power, renewed periodically by visits from 'that little lad who comes to him once in a month and shows him such and such herbs and tells him for what use they serve'. He concocted potions with water from a holy well, taken while 'distracted of his wits and speechless' by 'putting his hand into the well' and removing 'three things like plums' named 'one health to my body, another health to my mind, the third saving my soul [surely blasphemous], and those three he swallowed and thanked God three times'. To ensure that his potions would work, he prescribed for his clients a 'fast from all blood for a year' together with the magic words, 'I take all ills that God took and forsook all ills that he forsook.'[144] This combination of age-old fairy lore with Christian traditions of fasting and three-part incantations or trinitarian utterances clearly appealed to ordinary folk anxious for healing however they could get it, for stories like Gothray's are common the realm over. The fairies created charmers for sick cattle in Dundonald, for sick people in Falkirk, for ailing bairns in Perth; and everywhere there was enthusiastic resort to the healers despite session harassment.[145] Three-part charms and incantations include Isobel Hervie's 'Three bittes has thee bitten, evil heart, and evil eye, evil tongue; almost three thy bytt will be, Father, Son and Holy Ghost', learned from a mysterious 'wayfaring man' in Kirkcaldy, and used elsewhere in Fife and the Lothians. Other charms echo traditional catholic prayers, like Jonet Black of Perth's 'These sores are risen through God's work and must be laid through God's help. The mother Mary and her dear Son, lay these sores that are begun'.[146] The Perth elders surely understood the vital folk

144. CH2/299/1, pp. 377–78, 380–82. Aggravating his problems was his reported boast 'to the lads' that 'he could charm a woman from childbearing'. Gothray may have been a real miscreant: he also confessed 'he gave a bairn a spoonful of drink and the bairn [a lass] lay with him all night'.

145. *Dundonald*, 10, 51, 64, 277, 306; CH2/400/1, p. 91; CH2/521/7, inserted folios, unnumbered, at end of volume; PMAG ms 315; CH2/264/1, f. 6v; CH2/338/1, ff. 16, 25 (fairies ordering combined use of south-running water and the perfectly orthodox 'God keep her' as a charm to heal sick bairns); CH2/285/1, pp. 12–15; CH2/390/1, ff. 34v–35 (Katherine Hey, a healer who 'gave out that she used to go with the fairy folk'); CH2/185/1, ff. 23v–24v, 27v (1597); CH2/285/1, f. 5.

146. CH2/636/34, ff. 26v, 27, 28–28v; cf. CH2/390/1, ff. 22–22v (the same charm for a sick horse, repeated thrice by Elspeth Makie and 'learned at her goodmother

alternative to orthodox seasons of fasting when they called for a fast against plague in 1635: they resolved on a simultaneous censure of the local charmers.[147]

Early modern belief in witches, sorcerers and charmers has been read as protestantism's failure to meet the propitiatory needs of congregations, given its scaled-back mechanisms – prayer directly to God, but no holy water or saints.[148] If this is so, however, it points to a similar failure of catholic mechanisms, for recourse to charming and cursing, holy wells and fairies, was certainly not new in the sixteenth century. They were remnants of pre-Christian beliefs, and they characterise not only medieval Scotland but, in one form or another, many societies without scientific means to provide healing or weather prediction or insurance against flood or chemical guards against crop blight. Scottish fairies lived under mountains, seized people unexpectedly, made them live in their dominions for a time, and released them with potions; in southern Africa, Shona *njuzu*, spirits who lived beneath the water, lured people to their realms as well, and later released them with bags of medicine or horns of oil to become *nganga*, healers.[149] There is a substratum of such folk belief all over the pre-scientific world, condemned by all sorts of Christians who nontheless find that they must live with a certain amount of it.

The Scottish elders who censured folk healing seldom went further than

Margaret Eisle'); CH2/521/8/1, f. 55v. In Markinch, Janet Broun charmed two people with the words, 'Our Lord forth said his foal's foot sore, Our Lord down lighted his foal's foot righted, saying flesh to flesh, blood to blood, thorn to throne in our Lord's name': CH2/258/1, n.f., 17 March 1644. CH2/185/1, f. 27v records Helen Porteous saying the creed and Lord's Prayer in Latin as part of a charm used with water from St Ann's well for healing in 1597, taught her 'by a poor man that said he used to go with the Jews'. Cf. CH2/338, f. 19 (also incorporating the Lord's Prayer); CH2/327/1, ff. 40–40v (prayer to Our Lady in an incantation). There were material charms, too, like John Hodge's horn of a living ox, turned in to the North Berwick session clerk in 1610: CH2/285/1, pp. 9–10, 12.

147. CH2/521/8/2, f. 162. Charming could also be used for other ends than healing. Charmers like the merchant Alexander Fraser of Kynboge provided 'trial of theft by writing of certain persons' names on pieces of paper and casting them in water accounting that person guilty whose name did sink' (CH2/1142/1, ff. 103–03v).

148. Thomas, *Religion and the Decline of Magic*, ch. 3.

149. Michael Gelfand, *The Spiritual Beliefs of the Shona* (Gweru, Zimbabwe, 1977); Gelfand, S. Mavi, R.B. Drummond and B. Ndemera, *The Traditional Medical Practitioner in Zimbabwe* (Gweru, 1985); and C. and P. Kileff, eds, *Shona Customs: Essays by African Writers* (Gweru, 1992). Christians in Mozambique and Zimbabwe had just as much trouble as Scottish sessions trying to abolish these psychologically useful superstitions.

that. However insistently preachers tried to associate it with diabolic power, sessions rarely did more than admonish and hardly ever charged healers with witchcraft.[150] Even with a 'great number of charmers, consulters and persons delated' in Dalkeith presbytery in 1630, 'simple charmers and consulters' seeking healing, and even 'witches without practice' – that is, those who had not harmed anyone – were simply bound to abstain in future.[151] The elders recognised charmers as part of a rival religious culture which would retain its own vitality as long as life was as precarious as it was for early modern people.[152] They focused their real efforts on providing alternative, orthodox mechanisms to seek divine

150. Boyd, *Balme*, 207, preached that 'Satan makes men believe that he can heal diseases also with words which we call charms'. The Perth session and presbytery told the 'superstitious people' who took sick children to the mill and put them in the flapper 'with some such other unlawful ceremony' for healing that this practice was 'a lesson of Satan' (CH2/521/8/1, f. 160; CH2/299/1, p. 337). But even when Helen Birrell of Kirkcaldy dealt with a 'black man come into . . . her house with cloven feet' (CH2/636/34, f. 85), or Bessie Thomson of North Berwick sought her child's health from the devil (CH2/285/1, p. 29), their respective sessions, like Perth's, did not bring witchcraft charges. Admittedly, the formal charge was expensive for the parish, given costs of the commission against the accused and of sustaining her in gaol while awaiting trial: CH2/636/34, ff. 36v, 38v–39 (27 merks for warding Alison Dick in 1621, plus cost of the commission).

151. CH2/424/1, n.f., 28 October 1630; CH2/424/2, f. 1 (6 November 1630). Other presbyteries and sessions also distinguished between healing or efforts to heal, and cursing or doing harm – maleficium, and rarely did more than admonish the former: e.g., CH2/390/1, ff. 20v–21, 22–22v, 27–35, 47–47v, 56v–58; CH2/338/1, f. 19; CH2/258/1, n.f., 31 December 1643, 17 March 1644, and pp. 13–15 (charming changing to witchcraft when maleficium – sickness, and a cow going dry – was reported; as also for a potion gone wrong in Selkirk, CH2/327/1, ff. 40–40v). Cf. CH2/400/1, pp. 103–14 (Cirstiane Watson's case, referred to 'my lord's court').

152. It is worth remembering that even for the educated, divines included, this was a world populated by ghosts and other spirits, as well as fairies: Brown, *Early Travellers*, 157 ('spirits' in Carick cave); Blair, 8 (a ghost at the College of Glasgow, which Blair found 'never troubled nor terrified [him] a whit'); Wodrow, *Analecta*, 1:101 (angelic appearances); Louise Yeoman, 'Archie's Invisible Worlds Discovered – Spirituality, Madness and Johnston of Wariston's Family', *RSCHS* 27 (1997), 156–86. Belief in fairies proved irrepressible throughout the seventeenth century, as the Robert Kirk of Aberfoyle attests – *The Secret Commonwealth* (Edinburgh, 1691) – perhaps because it was not particularly associated with Catholicism, and unless practitioners of fairy magic harmed people, the sessions tended to discipline them lightly, if at all. The often associated phenomenon of 'second sight', particularly in the Gaelic Highlands, was similarly persistent, and in practice as lightly punished; indeed, as we shall see in the following chapter, it became an attribute of some presbyterian ministers under the rubric of a prophetic gift of God. For a general treatment, Hilda Davidson, ed., *The Seer in Celtic and Other Traditions* (Edinburgh, 1989), esp. chs 1–3, 6.

healing, good harvest, protection from storm, or victory in battle, even if they had to borrow them from earlier catholic practice, with accompanying adjustments to their theoretical bases and outward forms.

★ ★ ★

Holy space, time and language, in early modern Scotland as in every religious culture, facilitated a relationship with the sacred that in turn provided the underlying principles ordering both human society and the natural world in which it was set. A notion of holiness that is not merely intellectual or ethereal, but local, temporal, and ritualised, enables humans to make sense of it all. It allows them to see in the ordering of desks in the kirk a divine prescription of social hierarchy, to read harvest failure, plague and storm as communications from heaven. It facilitates recognition of a cosmological order in which they have a place and, significantly, in which they have access to supernatural power through ritual acts, words uttered in places designated abodes of the gods on earth, and physical demonstrations of piety.[153] Access requires purity – achieved in this particular culture by stern discipline as well as the corporate humiliation of fasts. And in a society thus shriven, it worked. Even within a theological system that eschewed apotropaic magic as a rejection of the divine in favour of superstitious practice to avert evil, it achieved enough results – in comfort, if not in actual dissipation of storm or pestilence – to allow a mild but increasingly general condemnation of the rival counter-culture of fairies, healing springs and potions. For most, the trappings of customary magic, along with traditional sacred objects like holy water or relics, may have gone by the board; however, they were effectively replaced by the word itself – the sacred book around which were organised sermons, sacraments and rituals of appeasement in fasts and public repentance. But the replacement – the protestant cultural revolution – was effective precisely because its structure retained a material, temporal and ritual framework for the sacred. As the current revision of anthropological structuralism has it, 'the ready structuralist notion of *plus ça change* . . . is a very historical idea. The past, it says, is always with us.' Marshall Sahlins's precept, that 'history is organized by structures of significance', is a reversible one: structures of significance are reorganised by history, in Captain Cook's Hawaii for him, and in post-Reformation Scotland for us. Sahlins concludes that 'the great challenge to an historical anthropology is not merely to know how events are ordered by culture, but how,

153. M. Eliade, *Patterns in Comparative Religion* (New York, 1958); Bossy, 'Holiness and Society'.

in the process, the culture is reordered', how 'the reproduction of a structure become[s] its transformation'.[154] The material culture of the Reformed kirk, artifacts as well as texts, has allowed us to take on that challenge.

The persistence of holy words, time and space, like the persistence of festivities, was a practical mechanism by which sessions eased the transition from catholic to protestant culture. They managed to achieve change within continuity by gradually shifting language and external form – a sacrosanct pulpit for a diminished altar, decoration with word rather than image alone, heightened sabbatarianism in lieu of saints' days. But they did not in the process ignore the very real needs of people living in difficult times, or of a population long accustomed to defining its social hierarchy and corporate existence in a religious context. The historiography that associates the Reformation with desacralisation is given the lie by the physical space and material culture of kirk and kirkyard, and by the kirk's holy times, holy words of oath and vow, holy actions of fast and sabbath observance. Protestants replaced the imagery they destroyed with physical display of scripture or with images centred on the word, like those bas-reliefs illustrating biblical texts on kirk walls, and with the construction of elaborate pews both for display of status and more 'commodious hearing of the word preached'. They replaced the artistic elaboration of side altars to saints often maintained by guilds with guild lofts or galleries decorated with both craft emblems and propitiatory imagery. The accompanying action, particularly by mariners, was the very traditional offering of vows in exchange for divine protection during one's voyage – vows carefully made good upon return in substantial payments to the poor box. Guilds may have lost their patron saints and festival days at the Reformation, but they maintained a clear presence in the kirk. Kirkyards remained as before places to display images of both death and angelic guardians, with increasingly elaborate monuments to celebrate the status of the deceased person's family. What is crucial is that all these efforts to define identity, of guild or family, remained closely associated with sacred space. Both space and time, moreover, were used to affirm contact with the divine and to petition for sustenance and preservation. This transformed culture was emphatically not desacralised.

154. Sahlins, *Historical Metaphors*, 8, 67 ('what began as reproduction ends as transformation'; indeed, 'one may question whether the continuity of a system ever occurs without its alteration, or alteration without continuity'). See also his *How 'Natives' Think*. Cf. the anti-historical structuralism spurred by Ferdinand de Saussure, *Course in General Linguistics*, tr. Wade Baskin (New York, 1966, orig. 1915).

Chapter 8

Old Priest Writ Large: Clergy and Laity

John Milton's judgment that 'new presbyter is but old priest writ large' was at once profoundly true and fundamentally flawed. Milton wrote of the ecclesiastical polity of early seventeenth-century Scotland that was now to be imposed on his own England in the midst of civil war.[1] His condemnation was rooted in resentment of the authority usurped initially by a sacerdotal priesthood and then to an even greater degree and even more egregiously, in his view, by presbyterian ministers wielding inordinate power over both secular authorities and individual consciences. Their power, underpinned and executed by the sessions, was indeed very real and rightly alarming to one who sought to guard some freedom of belief for 'consciences that Christ set free'. But Milton may have underestimated the degree to which clerical power in protestant Scotland was also circumscribed by the laity. Ministers were beholden to their own parishioners for their jobs, to a degree that few old priests ever were. They were called by congregations and had their subsequent performance vetted regularly by the whole parish. Presbyteries took seriously parochial complaint about ministers, whom they could require to 'satisfy' their congregations – sometimes with public repentance – or suffer dismissal. Ministers were constrained to co-operate with the lay elders, who outnumbered them on the session and who carried out the system. And both ministers and the elders who worked with them to enforce discipline suffered verbal abuse and physical assault by offended laity. They had to watch their step.

On the other hand, Milton was right about the similarity of new

1. 'On the New Forcers of Conscience under the Long Parliament' in *The Works of John Milton*, ed. F.A. Patterson (New York, 1931), 1/1: 71. The poem condemns the 'classic Hierarchy', 'plots and packing wors then those of Trent' by which 'Men whose Life, Learning, Faith and pure intent/ Would have been held in high esteem with Paul/ Must now be nam'd and printed Hereticks/ By shallow [Thomas] Edwards and Scotch what d'ye call.'

presbyter to old priest in ways that he may not have recognised fully. The power of Scottish ministers lay not only in the force that their sessions could bring to bear to compel individual profession and behaviour, but also in the identity of preacher with prophet in the Reformed tradition. The preacher's command of the all-important authority for protestant belief, the Bible, made him more than a mere functionary in the kirk. It gave him a pipeline to the divine will upon which his parishioners came to depend, and which the elders could draw on to underpin their own authority. The upright living enforced on ministers gave them an aura of sanctity. By the seventeenth century, particularly charismatic preachers had acquired reputations as visionaries, prophetic dreamers and even miracle-workers. They attracted followers who hung on their every word and wrote accounts of their lives that can only be described as hagiographies. Milton might have gone much further: many new presbyters were more like old saints than old priests.

The resultant tensions between lay and clerical authority, between fear and resentment of clerical discipline on the one hand and admiration of clerical sanctity on the other, and between spiritual authority based on the word and one rooted in clerical claims to visions and miracles, will unavoidably complicate our definition of protestant culture. But they lay the groundwork for the continual negotiations that comprised it. What emerged was a culture neither anticlerical nor clericalist, but one in which ministers could function as both awe-inspiring conduits to the divine will and lay-controlled functionaries as need and constituency dictated. Ultimately, it was one in which a lay spiritual elite was able to claim near-clerical status, either as elders or as imitators of the most visionary clerics, effectively broadening the category of 'saints' to a larger and more inclusive one than had obtained before while still retaining a religious authority structure with real control over discipline and belief.

* * *

Protestant clergy had obviously lost the sacerdotal identity of the medieval priesthood at the Reformation. In the new scheme of things they were not intercessory; their words no longer transformed communion elements into blood and body; they had passed the power of absolution back to their congregations. To the degree that these protestant objectives had been accomplished, Milton was certainly wrong. Perhaps less evidently, however, his judgment was skewed by the fact that Reformed ministers were in a very real sense subject to their own parishioners.

Lay control of clergy was by no means unknown before the Reformation, of course. It was clearest in burghal appointments of town chaplains and in the power of lairds over the chaplains of their collegiate foundations. The Linlithgow council had determined the hours and duties of their parochial chaplains, and the Dundee council had held contractual control over the chaplains they hired for the town.[2] But lay-appointed chaplains accounted for only a segment of medieval clergy – those occupied largely with saying masses for the dead; those controlling them, moreover, were few and great. By contrast, the first General Assembly appointed congregational election of all parish ministers, elders and deacons 'in the public kirk' with a 'premonition' the Sunday before election day so that objections to nominees could be raised by any parishioner who cared to speak up.[3] Certainly these 'elections' were carefully controlled by the parish elite; still, general approbation of the community was required before a minister was called to a parish.

Securing congregational approval involved public performance by the would-be minister in the form of preaching.[4] Only if the congregation then found the candidate 'a young man in whom there is appearance of good gifts' did they send a commission to ask the presbytery to appoint him their minister. It was 'the parishmen', or at least the better sort among them, who called the minister based on their 'good experience of him'; their delegates communicated to presbytery or bishop 'in name of the whole parishioners' that they 'find themselves edified by his doctrine' and accordingly called him to serve their parish.[5] Those of Cramond in 1588

2. Cowan, *Scottish Reformation*, 61–63; P. Symms, 'A Disputed Altar: Parish Pump Politics in a Sixteenth Century Burgh', *IR*, 42 (1991), 133–36; McKay, 88–89; Sanderson, *Ayrshire*, 13, 15.
3. *BUK* 1:5.
4. The candidate was pre-approved by the presbytery on the basis of his performance there of 'exercises' on assigned theological topics or biblical texts. Admission to exercise before the presbytery generally came after private examination by established ministers.
5. CH2/299/2, pp. 35–38 – 1619 call of Archibald Moncrieff to Dollar after the congregation had heard him preach several times and sent two delegates to the bishop of Dunkeld (*Fasti* 4:196); and of James Lyons to Collace after his 'comforting them with preaching of the word', adding that they, the parishioners, were also the ones who had sacrificed to build a manse. In Mid-Calder after a 1604 congregational meeting reported no objections to Robert Gilmore's specimen sermon, 'the lord and whole gentlemen in the barony convening appointed' delegates to the presbytery 'and in their names consent to the said Mr Robert's admission'. The extent of parochial democracy in the process was limited, then, to veto power; the actual call came from the parish elite in the name of the rest: CH2/266/1, f. 2v. CH2/1026/1, ff. 11v–12, records the 1598 election of their successors by the elders of Holyrude, Stirling, but the congregation assembled to confirm the vote, 'that they be not defrauded of their consent'. They could 'oppose or declare any reasonable fault' in the proposed elders and if necessary put 'others more godly and famous . . . in their place'. See also CH2/390/1, f. 31 (Dysart's judgment of William Spittal 'his doctrine to be orthodox, good and

protested the Edinburgh presbytery's attempt to translate to the capital their minister, Patrick Simsone, precisely because it was they, not the presbytery, who had chosen him in the first place: 'our minister was received at our entreaty' and 'God has settled our love and affection towards him, likewise his towards us'.[6] William Cowper as bishop of Galloway in 1614 refused to nominate his replacement as minister of Perth, instructing the congregation to meet and 'advise upon the man whom ye would have to supply his room. . . . I have no other intention but to admit to that ministry the man whom after advice ye find fittest for you. Enjoy your privilege in God's name.'[7] By the same token, the laity could reject a candidate they found wanting. Even the illiterate could weigh in on a veto, as in Neilston in 1595, when 'certain of the parish, . . . partly with their own hands for them and their tenants, and partly by John Dunlop, notary, . . . appeal from the judgment of the presbytery of Glasgow about the admission of Mr Andro Law to be minister at Neilston.'[8] This was an unsuccessful protest; however, when the parish elite were fully behind the opposition, presbyteries found themselves hamstrung. When the lady of Pitcur opposed Andro Forrester's appointment to Collace, no amount of cajoling by brethren of the Perth presbytery could change her mind: Forrester arrived at the kirk to preach a specimen sermon only to find the door locked against him.[9]

Once in place, the minister was still periodically reviewed by the congregation, often at the regular presbytery visitation, but sometimes on the parishioners' own initiative, quite apart from presbytery or superintendent. From the 1560s, the Canongate elders reguarly ordered 'trial to be taken of the life and conversation and doctrine of the minister', with questions about each area directed to the assembled parishioners in the minister's

sufficient' after his trial sermon); CH2/521/7, p. 298 (1622 Perth council and session commending a new assistant minister); CH2/89/1, ff. 7–8v (Thomas Ries called to Longmay, Deer presbytery, after six months of preaching in the parish).

6. CH2/121/1, ff. 10v, 32v, 38v, 40, 42 (quotations at 10v and 38v); see also CH2/299/2, p. 327.
7. Letter to the town of Perth, 26 April 1614, *Chronicle of Perth*, 15–16; PL ms B59/16/1, f. 6 (council objections to Cowper's translation from Perth).
8. ML CH2/171/1, f. 56v. The presbytery 'found him apt, having heard him teach and having testimony of the presbyteries of Hamilton and Paisley', so they admitted him to the position; however, they were clearly not opposed by all or even a majority of the parish. He remained at Neilston until his death in 1639, succeeded by his son in 1632; however, the son, John Law, was deprived for inefficiency in 1649: *Fasti* 3:157.
9. CH2/299/2, pp. 55, 59. The presbytery complained to the archbishop of St Andrews, and Forrester was installed in the parish in 1620. In the end, however, the lady's judgment proved right: Forrester died in 1631 'covered with debt and infamy', to be succeeded by a distant member of the family of Pitcur (*Fasti* 4:199).

absence; from at least the 1570s, all four Edinburgh ministers were periodically sent out of the assembly so that the congregation could raise objections to their lives or doctrine. Aberdeen's ministers in the 1570s underwent 'such trial . . . by the whole kirk' before each communion, in a meeting where 'liberty was publicly proclaimed in pulpit who would give in accusation against any of them that they should appear this day and they should be heard'. The ministers generally got good reviews, but occasionally some chiding is recorded.[10] The authors of the *Second Book of Discipline* hoped to forestall parochial complaint by ordering elders to 'take heed to the like manners, diligence and study of their ministers'. If they found him 'worthy of admonition, they must admonish him; of correction, they must correct him; and if he be worthy of deposition, they with consent of the kirk and superintendent, may depose him.'[11] This responsibility, or right, constituted real lay power over clergy, and one that continued to be exercised very regularly in parishes throughout the realm. English visitors recorded parochial 'trial' of ministers, elders and deacons annually in the 1630s, 'so that if any just exception can be made against them, they may be put by that office and others elected.' Perhaps this is what another English observer meant when he described the Scottish settlement as 'their anarchy here established'. For some, this 'lay and popular government', the invention of 'firey young and green heads of little experience . . . assisted by the simplest men in their parishes', laid 'all honour aside'. Such condemnation, caricatured as it is, is eloquent testimony to the power of ordinary laypeople in Scots ecclesiastical polity.[12]

Congregational vetting of the ministry was routine at presbytery, superintendent's and episcopal visitations of parishes, when first the minister, then the elders, and finally the deacons were removed so that the assembled parishioners could voice freely any objections they might have to their service.[13] The visitors posed set questions, first to the session and then to the larger congregation, about the minister's 'conversation',

10. *Canongate*, 16, 32 (the congregation reporting in 1565, 'We have nothing to lay to his charge, neither for life nor doctrine, but praise God of the same'); NAS ms RH2/1/35, ff. 29–29v, 54, 62 (noting a few complaints); CH2/448/1, pp. 17–18, 28–29.
11. *Second Book*, 176.
12. Brereton (1636), in *Early Travellers*, 144, though in fact annual replacement of elders or deacons, common in the first generation of the Reformation, was by then rare. The critics are Robert Naunton, writing in 1589 in defence of episcopacy (LPL ms 2014, f. 168) and Patrick Blair (1589, LPL ms 3471, f. 31v). An example of the procedure for deposition is the case of Paul Methven, *BUK* 1:31.
13. CH2/121/1, ff. 7, 43v; CH2/424/1, n.f., 2 February 1592 (Musselburgh), 2 March 1592 (Carington); CH2/146/1 (Ellon), ff. 15–15v; CH2/185/1, f. 30; CH2/185/2, f. 8v.

doctrine, exercise of discipline, administration of catechism and sacraments, visitation of the sick, and government of his family. The Haddington visitors quizzed parishioners about Alexander Forrester in 1597 in hierarchical order, 'beginning at my Lord Seton and so forth to the rest'.[14] The Glasgow presbytery delayed a 1597 visitation because there was 'no intimation of it last Sunday' to alert the parishioners to prepare their objections or praise of the minister. At Rothiemay, the visitors prefixed their questioning of the elders in 1640 with an oath, demanding that they 'hold up their hands to God and swear as they should answer to God at the great day to declare the truth in every thing that should be asked of them concerning the minister.' The elders 'answered nothing but good' in this case, adding that Alexander Innes preached at convenient times every week, catechised regularly and effectively, governed his family well, visited the sick and had 'no fault in his life and conversation'.[15]

Usually the questions produced positive responses like those of the Rothiemay session, or the Mortlach parishioners, who 'did all in one voice uplift hands approving' William Forbes in 1641, or the St Cuthbert's congregation, who in 1619 replied that they 'knew nothing but praise of God for' their minister. But congregational review was not merely a rubber stamp on the status quo. A group of Monimail parishioners in 1585 reported to their visitors that their minister, Patrick Adamson, 'altered his ordinary text on Sunday morning 25 December' in order to preach a nativity sermon, in violation of the kirk's abolition of Christmas, and that he had maligned 'the flock of St Andrews' – the godly of the neighbouring parish. Here the complainers were more advanced in Reformed practice than their minister.[16] The visitors of St Cuthbert's got an earful in 1586 when they asked about the minister: parishioners reported that he left the kirk door open for days on end, allowing beasts to enter; baptised children begotten in adultery; 'inveighed against them that came not to his doctrine, declaring them disobedient to kirk and king'; left town without permission; committed slanderous libel against members of the congregation; and overstepped his bounds as a searcher, having 'entered in other men's houses at his own hand'. The Edinburgh presbytery was

14. CH2/529/1, f. 81v; CH2/185/2, f. 8v (finding 'nothing to accuse him of either in life or doctrine').
15. NLS ms 2782, f. 57 (at the visit, 'inquisition made among the sessioners about the life, etc of the ministers' first, and then the congregation was queried); CH2/271/1, p. 128.
16. CH2/529/1, ff. 81v–82; CH2/718/4, f. 12; SAU unnumbered ms, St Andrews presbytery/1, ff. 5v, 6v. The presbytery appointed arbiters to settle what was apparently a quarrel within the congregation between defenders and opponents (led by the minister) of Andrew Melville.

appalled and ordered James Daish to 'satisfy' his congregation by public repentance and to correct his behaviour.[17] George Sempill's Killellan parishioners in 1603 reported him a rumour-monger, spreading 'odious lies and slanderous calumnies' of 'sundry honest famous gentlemen in the country' known 'manifestly to be altogether untrue' and sufficiently disruptive of the peace to 'renew a deadly feud amongst the great men in their fields'. The Paisley presbytery agreed with their 'great misliking' of him, judging him 'a great hinderer to the work of God . . . and instrument of debate and schism'. They deprived him and forwarded the parishioners' complaint to the General Assembly.[18] Less serious was the offence reported to the Haddington visitors in 1589 that a minister who was otherwise satisfactory had preached rather too many sermons on the same passage and might be urged to 'teach upon another text, which was concluded should be done'.[19] Examples could be multiplied, but the clear message of this data is that the laity had real power over their ministers, extending even to getting them dismissed.[20]

Never was this more abundantly clear than in 1638–39, when parishioners throughout the realm rose up against ministers who had with episcopal support adopted English-style ceremonies, Arminian doctrine and finally the new prayer book – anathema to the style of worship and doctrine that had been in place since the 1560s. In the General Assembly's processes against the ceremonialists, it was parishioners' complaints

17. CH2/121/1, ff. 3, 5.
18. CH2/294/1, ff. 6–7v, 11–11v, 12–12v, 13v, 18v, 20v; LPL ms 3471, f. 130v. The plaintiffs seem to have been well within their rights: when the presbytery sent Robert Henderson to offer a trial sermon for the parishioners to consider him as Sempill's replacement, Sempill (spelled Symple in Paisley's record) and his wife made the rounds of the parish to spread 'malicious and open slandering of' Henderson as having 'neither soundness nor method in doctrine', and seeking 'planting of the said kirk in his own favour'. The parish eventually settled on John Cunningham, but presbytery arbitration was required for the property settlement between him and Sempill. Ultimately the presbytery sought letters of horning against Sempill as a breaker of the peace.
19. CH2/185/1, f. 30.
20. Other examples of lay complaint at ministerial reviews include ML CH2/171/1, f. 26v ('sundry of the godly being offended with the misbehaviour of Mr Andro Hayt' of Glasgow for 'leaving his charge'); CH2/424/1, n.f., 2 March 1592 (complaint against Lucas Housie, for 'not repairing of their . . . kirk'; CH2/185/1, f. 25v (David Adisone of Pencaitland reporting that his pastor, James Gibson, had 'invaded him cruelly of his life' and 'cut his cloak in sundry places'); NLS ms Adv. 29.2.8, f. 179 (congregation of Clerkington's letter to Dalkeith presbytery against Alexander MacGill, 1593); CH2/89/1, f. 15 and *RPC* 7:381, 678 (Thomas Bisset of Peterhead 'relieved of his charge'); CH2/154/1, September 1613, and SAU ms 30451, f. 6v (a Fife minister 'evil disposed to teach upon the sabbath' after drinking in Perth every Saturday).

that provided the fuel.[21] They wrote letters, made depositions and sent delegates to their local presbyteries and synods with messages to send on to the Assembly. Elgin's provost, John Hay, was the town's delegate to the Moray synod, but his commission made it clear that he spoke 'in name of the rest of the council and commonalty thereof and in the name of the parishioners of Elgin' when he objected to the minister John Gordon's neglect of Tuesday sermons; his carelessness of session meetings, now reduced 'partly through negligence and partly through obstinacy' to monthly rather than twice-weekly meetings; and his having taken unauthorised vacations two or three times a year, deserting 'a very populous congregation'. His parishioners also found him 'in private discourse and conversation both scandalous, profane and irreligious'; some heard him joke that 'he would say mass in the forenoon and preach in the afternoon, . . . that he would teach heresy to his auditors and make them recall it as orthodox doctrine.' Like the Edinburgh uprisings at the first reading of the prayerbook service, these numerous and detailed complaints reveal a high degree of lay involvement in doctrine and the direction of worship, and a strong presumption that it was the people in the pew who held power over the form of the service.[22] But session and presbytery minutes from the sixteenth century reveal that this presumption was not just a function of the heady days of the Bishops' Wars; it was fundamental to being a protestant in early modern Scotland.

Lay people also brought complaint about their ministers to the session, without waiting for a presbytery visitation or a public review. The Perth burgess and erstwhile elder Alexander Peblis did so in 1619, 'taking exception against the doctrine delivered by John Guthry, minister, last sabbath afternoon', though the hearing he received was not very sympathetic. He 'alleged the minister had slandered him and his house of sorcery and consulting therewith by turning the riddell' (spinning a sieve on the point of a shears, popularly thought to predict the future or locate lost goods). Peblis thought this an attack *ad hominem*, since apparently everybody in town knew that riddell-turning was going on in his house. The elders, however, noted that the sermon had not mentioned him by name. Together with the other minister, John Malcolm, they upheld 'in one voice that the doctrine was general and necessarily followed on his text'.[23] The

21. NLS mss Wod. Fol. LXI, it. 99; Wod. Fol. LXII, its 1–2, 22, 24–26, 43; Wod. Fol. LXIII, its 1–2, 4, 6, 54, 63–68, 70–71.
22. CH2/271/1, pp. 107–10; NLS ms Wod. Fol. LXVI, it. 26 (report of the earl of Stirling to Balcanquhal about the 'great tumult').
23. CH2/521/7, p. 65. Alexander Peblis of Chapelhill, probably the son of the elder Oliver Peblis, became an elder himself and would be provost several times between 1628 and 1638. See also CH2/521/2, f. 34 (1589 prosecution of Violet Brown for 'turning

point here is that a layman was free to bring the objection, and lay elders had authority to render judgment on the minister. In other cases, parishioners used less formal ways to communicate disapproval, voting with their feet in Ayr in 1636, for instance, when the minister insisted on kneeling at communion: 'the people all left the church and departed, and not one of them stayed, only the pastor alone.' Objections to Edinburgh ministers in the 1590s took the form of rhymed libels.[24]

Quite apart from formal parochial review or informal criticism of the minister, the laity exerted control over the kirk in a variety of other ways. Most obviously, they wielded the power of the purse. Even quite popular ministers had trouble collecting their stipends from penny-pinching heritors and burgesses; those who had offended their charges could be forced out of the pulpit by simple non-payment of salary.[25] And, of course, the kirk's important defining feature of discipline was exercised principally by lay elders. Without 'assistance of the gentlemen', there 'is no discipline in the kirk', as the Perth presbytery found of Kilspindy in 1620.[26] It was lay elders who searched, reported infractions, tried and sentenced; and lay magistrates and bailies were the ultimate enforcers. The Innerwick session included 'my lord's bailie or office continu[ing] with the minister and elders for good order in matters of discipline within the lordship', and Perth's elders voted in 1616 to make the provost and bailies *ex officio* session members, so essential was their enforcing function.[27] Ministers were

of the riddle with shears, a point indeed of witchcraft and devilry against God's word, and that for wanting of a crown of a young man within her house' – she allegedly sought a lost coin by magic); CH2/390/1, f. 9 (riddle-turning in Dysart); *Dundonald*, 34; and James VI, *Daemonologie* (1597), ed. G.B. Harrison (Edinburgh, 1966), 12.

24. Brereton, in *Early Travellers*, 156 (reporting on a visit to Ayr); NLS ms Wod. Fol. L, it. 71.
25. John Malcolm of Perth in 1633 'regrets the ungrateful dealing of the council towards him' in withholding his stipend; it took weeks of complaining to get partial payment: CH2/521/8/2, ff. 87v, 104v. And this was not the first time: in 1618 he had complained of non-payment 'now by the space of a year bygone': CH2/521/6, f. 124v. For the Perth council's financial dealings with his predecessor John Row in the 1570s, and Malcolm and William Cowper 1601–03, see PL mss B59/28/7, B59/28/12 and B59/16/1, ff. 5–6, 8v, 18v, 21v–22, 37v–38, 42; and PMAG ms 345. The Haddington presbytery had to send delegates to the local lairds to secure adequate provision for Thomas Greg at North Berwick: CH2/185/2, f. 20v.
26. CH2/299/2, p. 71. See also CH2/1463/1, f. 1; and Cowper's 1612 'common head' before the Perth presbytery on 'ruling elders conjoin[ing] with pastors': NLS ms Wod. Fol. XXVII, f. 2v.
27. CH2/1463/1, f. 1; CH2/521/6, f. 66v – an act made following complaint (f. 58v) that Charles Rollock and other bailies were dilatory in carrying out their duties and attending session meetings as non-members.

constrained to co-operate with their sessions if they wanted to do anything at all: in Lasswade, a 1615 act of session (in which the minister was presumably outvoted) prohibited him even giving funds from the poor box to a hungry stranger without the session's agreement. The real power lay in the hands of lay elders. Merchants, cordiners, baxters, smiths, skinners, cutlers – each, however mundane his occupation, had the same vote on the session as the minister, and together they considerably outnumbered the clergy.[28] Finally, both ministers and elders had to co-operate with town councils in matters ecclesiastical. In Perth, the minister and elders could not even stop the appointment of a new reader in the face of council support in 1636; the reader was admitted 'without consent of minister and elders' and installed by the council, the provost (Alexander Peblis, who had his own history with the session!) ceremonially delivering 'the Bible and Psalm book in his hands'. Interestingly, one elder, George Bisset, wore two hats in this instance and 'dissented to his admission as elder, and after consented as councillor'. Gordon Donaldson's conclusion that town councils and rural heritors ran the kirk is perfectly justified from the evidence of session minutes.[29]

Finally, the doctrine of a priesthood of all believers gave rise to lay-conducted prayer meetings and exercises 'for mutual edification, . . . conference, prayer, singing of psalms' and even 'exhorting of the scriptures read'.[30] The ministers were forced by their own doctrine to grant that lay preaching could, with God's blessing, convert, since even private men might have the gift of prophecy. Their own insistence that the laity acquire theological understanding likewise required them to admit that 'the people publicly before all the congregation' can 'propound questions, move doubts, and argue with their ministers'.[31]

* * *

If lay elders in the name of the parish exerted the most direct control over ministers, the elders themselves occupied an at least semi-clerical status that at once conferred spiritual authority on them and subjected them to congregational review. The judgment of historians that elders fell

28. CH2/471/1, f. 5v; NAS ms RH2/1/35, f. 19v (1574) lists occupations of Edinburgh elders. See also Introduction, n. 23, above.
29. *Chronicle of Perth*, 35; Donaldson, *Scottish Church History*, 226.
30. NLS ms Wod. Qu. XXIX, it. 19 (1642 instructions for meetings of laity for Christian fellowship); CH2/146/1, f. 20; Blair, 93 (twice-weekly voluntary prayer meetings at Blair's house); Mullan, *Scottish Puritanism*, 129.
31. NLS ms Wod. Fol. LXIV, ff. 267, 268v, citing 1 Cor. 14, although the anonymous author thought the gift of prophecy rare among the laity. He granted that it became useful if the minister were ill. One can almost hear his sigh of relief at the observation about congregations arguing with ministers that this practice was 'seldom used in any church amongst us'.

more on the clerical than the lay side of the divide is surely correct. While the *First Book of Discipline* called for annual election of elders, the *Second Book* in 1578 made the office a lifelong appointment and a 'function spiritual, as is the ministry'.[32] Sessions, technically elected by the parish, became self-perpetuating in practice. Elders nominated replacements for those who had died or wished to retire from the onerous duty, the congregation simply approving or rejecting the nominees.[33] Elders went through an initiation ceremony akin to ordination, taking public oaths with hands uplifted to perform their duties diligently and, like ministers, adhere to the highest standards of Christian life and conversation, to 'give good example in their own person and in governing their own families'.[34] They attended presbyteries, synods and General Assemblies, though not in proportion to their numbers on sessions.[35] At home, they exercised many pastoral duties: aside from discipline, they catechised, counselled the spiritually anxious, visited the sick and dying, and even heard parishioners' confessions.[36] Like the minister, they occupied a special seat in the kirk, generally before the pulpit.[37] William Cowper acknowledged their call to 'labour in the word', since they had an 'internal call of the Holy Spirit

32. Donaldson, *Scottish Church History*, 227; *Second Book*, 192; *SAKS* 1:77, 127, 196–99, 205.
33. E.g., CH2/1026/1, f. 11v (1598); CH2/390/1, f. 14v (1623); CH2/521/1, f. 84; CH2/521/8/2, ff. 115v (discipline of a man for refusing to accept office), 259. In St Andrews, election was by free burgesses, the rector and regents of the university, and the town council, from a slate nominated by university and council (*SAKS* 1:2).
34. Quote from SAU CH2/624/2, p. 2, where the the session comprehensively described the duties of elders both in terms of their own behaviour and towards those to whom 'the Lord has given them the charge, . . . reproving all loose profane and dissolute behaviour, . . . see that the people were on the word when the exercise of it is offered, . . . to visit the families allotted to them, and to assist . . . pastors in visitation and in catechism and examination to prepare the people to the Lord's supper' as well as to exercise discipline in the session. See also *Second Book*, 175–76. For ceremonial induction of elders, see CH2/264/1, f. 4v; CH2/338/1, f. 39; SAU CH2/624/2, p. 109; SAU CH2/624/3, p. 6; CH2/390/1, f. 15; CH2/471/1, ff. 8, 11; *SAKS* 2:905; CH2/523/1, f. 32; CH2/141/1, f. 13; CH1/1463/1, f. 9v; CH2/521/1, f. 96; CH2/4/1, f. 16; CH2/191/1, f. 60; CH2/1026/1, f. 12.
35. CH2/264/1, f. 20; CH2/400/1, pp. 309, 323; CH2/266/1, ff. 2–2v, 47v; CH2/716/2, f. 13v (1609); CH2/4/1, ff. 16v, 19, 22v; CH2/191/1, ff. 48v, 53, 53v, 54v; CH2/93/1, f. 22v; AAC CH2/562/1, f. 38v. Most lay elder delegation to presbyteries was from 1638 on, although there are some earlier examples. On lay membership of General Assemblies, see Cowan, *Scottish Reformation*, 125–28.
36. Examples of auricular confession to elders include CH2/4/1, ff. 26, 31v. Typical of their counseling function is the 1609 South Leith session order for two elders to visit Elspeth Barclay 'who is troubled in spirit, to take an honest comfort to her and . . . to see what help friends will make to her': CH2/716/2, f. 12v. For other regular duties, see SAU CH2/624/2, p. 2; CH2/521/2, f. 70; CH2/521/3, p. 177.
37. CH2/442/74, f. 6; CH2/141/1, ff. 16v, 28v, 53.

by the gifts'.[38] Theirs was thus an anomalous position; they illustrate both lay control over the ministry and the nearly clerical status that elevated a significant group of laymen to spiritual power, though subjecting them to the same parochial trials as ministers.

Like ministers, elders were vetted first by the rest of the session, then by the assembled congregation at initial appointment and at periodic reviews.[39] In Burntisland, for instance, the 1605 reviews began with 'every elder of the session being put apart and tried by the rest'. 'Election was of the whole former members' in this case, but elders still had to be 'admitted publicly in the congregation, and to that effect, an edict [was] to be served next [sabbath] day if any person has to object against their life and conversation.' On election Sunday, the minister ceremonially 'called thrice by the kirk door if any person or persons had anything to object'.[40] The Canongate went through this process twice- or thrice-yearly from at least 1564, 'for stopping of slanderous mouths which move oft-times by rage of Satan to backbite and slander those that bear office in the kirk of God'; if 'every man shall have liberty to speak' against errant elders before every communion, the respectability of elders who survived the vetting would be assured, and the slander removed. In this parish the initial election of elders seems to have given the congregation more than just the power of veto, each parishioner's vote recorded by 'every one standing in order as they were wanted'.[41] A regular 'censure' of elders went on in every parish, though generally less frequently in rural areas and as time went on.[42]

38. NLS ms Wod. Fol. XXVII, f. 2v, expounding on 1 Tim. 5.17, 'gifts' referring to 1 Tim. 4.16 and 2 Tim. 1.6.
39. CH2/529/1, f. 81v; CH2/718/4, f. 12; CH2/448/1, pp. 28–29; NAS ms RH2/1/35, ff. 29–29v, 54, 62v; *SAKS* 1:1; Brereton, in *Early Travellers*, 144. For the prescribed form, see 'The Ordour for the Electioun of Elderis and Deaconis in the Privie Kirk of Edinburgh', John Knox, *Works*, 2:151ff; *BUK* 1:5; *Second Book*, 174–79 (establishing in its 'common and free election' a system for nomination from the floor of the congregation, in case 'any man know other of better qualities within the kirk than these that be nominate', that they might 'be put in election, that the kirk may have the choice' (p. 174), though I find no indication in session minutes that this occurred).
40. CH2/523/1, ff. 21v, 47 (the procedure followed every three or four years: 31v, 32).
41. *Canongate*, 5, 26, 48, 71.
42. E.g., CH2/521/2, f. 57v; CH2/1463/1, ff. 1v, 10; CH2/4/1, ff. 16–16v, 23, 50v–51; CH2/471/1, f. 8; CH2/147/1, ff. 3–3v, 42v–43; CH2/338/1, ff. 39–39v; CH2/636/34, ff. 5v, 23, 29, 35; SAU CH2/624/2, pp. 109, 162, 182–83; SAU CH2/624/3, p. 5; CH2/390/1, ff. 14v–15, 34v; NAS ms RH2/1/35, ff. 19v, 21; CH2/141/1, ff. 12v, 24v, 36v, 44v (Trinity College, Edinburgh, nominations and initial trial conducted by provost and bailies, council, deacons of guild and the minister, Thomas Sydserf, before presentation to the congregation, from 1627. Many of these men were also elders, though).

Like ministers, elders were very often criticised at these reviews. And for them as for the preaching clergy, serious complaints could result in non-election or deprivation. Examination of a prospective elder in Innerwick revealed a 'public scandal' that transformed the man's election into a trial; in Kirkcaldy, when a parishioner in 1625 objected that an elder already in place was 'not meet to bear office in the kirk in respect he had slain a man with his own hands', the trial that ensued produced letters of horning (outlawing) demonstrating the elder 'unfit to brook office in the kirk'.[43] In South Leith, William Fourd was in 1597 'put off the session for consulting a warlock in Newcastle', and the session in 1613 had to punish both a harlot and her customer – the elder John Mattheson, now 'forfeit of his eldership'.[44]

Parochial trial often revealed lesser offences, of course. These variously brought admonitions from minister or fellow elders, or fines – especially for dereliction of duty.[45] John Greir was suspended but not dismissed from eldership for 'ill speeches and rough words in presence and audience of the [Aberlady] session' – a hint that session meetings could be acrimonious affairs. Robert Gurlaw managed to keep his place on the Edinburgh session after being disciplined by the General Assembly for 'buying and charging of certain victuals forth of the realm' during a dearth, giving 'occasion of slander, being an elder'.[46] Sessions had to set fines for elders who worked on the sabbath during the preaching, failed to search their quarters as assigned, swore, slandered their neighbours and failed to keep the session's secrets – surely a serious temptation in communities that thrived on gossip.[47] A parochial review in St Cuthbert's parish in 1619 brought a different sort of complaint, of overzealous performance of duty:

43. CH2/1463/1, ff. 9–10; CH2/636/34, ff. 75v–76. The elder Thomas Sibbald produced a letter showing him relaxed from the horn, but the thoroughly alarmed session referred the matter to presbytery (f. 76v).
44. CH2/716/1, f. 1; CH2/716/2, f. 100; cf. *BUK* 1:14, 98; *Canongate*, 24, 32, 43, 62. *Second Book*, 179, describes procedures.
45. Fines for absence from session meetings are a feature of most session minute books: e.g., CH2/84/28, f. 46; NAS RH2/1/35, f. 50; CH2/400/1, p. 146; CH2/636/34, f. 6; CH2/390/1, f. 55v; CH2/276/1, f. 68; CH2/326/1, p. 6; CH2/716/1, f. 24 (fines for elders 'who go to any pastime when they should be present at the session'); CH2/716/2, f. 36v; CH2/1463/1, f. 1v; CH2/141/1, ff. 12v, 19v; NLS ms 2782, f. 52v. *Canongate*, 70, illustrates the reproving of an elder (Hendre Kinlok) found at a regular review to be 'slothful in executing his office', an offence oft-reported and unsurprising, given the demands of eldership on men who had jobs to do. Fines were small and perhaps just regarded as expenses of office-holding. The payoff – status, power and demonstrable piety – seems to have kept most elders on task most of the time.
46. CH2/4/1, f. 43; NAS ms RH2/1/35, ff. 4v–6.
47. CH2/338/1, ff. 4v, 6v, 15v, 18, 19v, 24, 18, 19v; NLS ms 2782, f. 52v.

there the congregation 'knew nothing but praise of God' for their elders, 'but desired there to be no walkings now [as] they have done in this bypast, and visit the bounds' – that is, they had endured quite enough surprise visits by the searchers and thought regular, announced visitations of the quarters would suffice. The elders had no objection, doubtless being themselves rather weary of the process.[48]

What all this evidence attests to is the preponderance of power held by laity over their clergy, whether preaching ministers or semi-clerical elders, in post-Reformation Scotland. Milton's critical gaze only skimmed the surface of what was going on in the kirk; had he read the session minutes, he might well have reconsidered his old priest, even writ small, in favour of Gordon Donaldson's conclusion that the Reformation went a 'long way to eliminate the distinction between clergy and laity altogether and vest authority in the community or congregation, of whom the minister was merely the chosen delegate'.[49]

* * *

Viewed from another perspective, however, kirk session minutes suggest that Milton was more accurate than he knew, though for reasons that he probably would not have admitted. Modern scholarship has revealed that, whatever the claims of medieval clergy for reverence from their flocks, old priests were not always either revered or obeyed by their parishioners. They were in some cases – burgh chaplains and collegiate priests – as much subject to the more prominent laity as post-Reformation preachers were to the 'better sort' among their congregations. Their lay patrons kept their pay low and often in arrears, and told them what to preach or what services to say. Lay reformers roundly criticised their failures.[50] And the victims of their efforts at discipline, or the parties to feud that they denounced, verbally and sometimes physically abused them – even to the point of bloodshed and murder.[51] The notorious murder of Prior Robert Montrose in 1393, Alexander Stewart's sacking of Elgin cathedral after his excommunication for adultery in 1390, or the 1421 attack on a subprior in St Andrews cathedral on Palm Sunday eve by an excommunicate probably represent only the tip of the iceberg, considering how little survives of medieval ecclesiastical records. We do know that medieval clergy were permitted to

48. CH2/718/4, f. 12 (1619).
49. Donaldson, *Scottish Church History*, 226.
50. Sanderson, *Ayrshire*, 12–13, 15–20, 30, 33; McKay, 88–89, noting that priests without manses could be boarded on as many as fourteen different neighbours; Symms, 133–36.
51. Sanderson, *Ayrshire*, 33.

carry weapons when they travelled, given the likelihood of physical assault even in the face of their clerical attire.[52] Attacks on priests were *ad hominem* as well as *ad officium*; most should not be taken to indicate anticlericalism *per se*. But the stranglehold on lay conscience and behaviour that Milton attributed to catholic clergy was more rhetorical than real; certainly it was not significant enough to offer protection to the priesthood. And the Reformation does not appear to have changed the situation.

It is hardly surprising that not everybody liked their ministers in the new kirk. The good minister, after all, 'praises the forwardgoer [and] prays [for] the backlyer', but he also 'purges the refractory'.[53] All too often, those backlyers, far from exhibiting reverence for their chastising minister, sought revenge, in either verbal denunciation or physical attack. The former was naturally the most common. Marion Anderson of North Leith pronounced 'curses and malesones [maledictions] upon the pastor and his family, without any offence done by him or any of his to her' in 1605, but an earlier entry in at the session book reveals that she had been punished for adultery. It was after he had been admonished for playing golf in sermon time that Thomas Anderson offered 'presumptuous speeches' to the same minister, and Elspeth Kob's 'railing on her pastor John Black' of Menmuir occurred in the course of his 'dealing with herself' for her sins.[54] The Perth flesher William Rynd had been found guilty of slander against Violet Robertson when he, 'in great madness and fury, without regard of God, the holy place where he stood, or due regard and reverence of his said pastor, with great oaths, vows and attestations uttered these speeches, "that if the act of slander . . . were not extracted [from the session book] and given him, he [the minister] should either stick or be sticked [stabbed] before even, and he should put the said Violet in a seething caldron.'[55]

The great were just as likely as the lower sort to malign their ministers after receiving reproof: Margaret Ker, Lady Yester, was summoned to the Haddington presbytery by her minister, William Hay of Lochans, for 'injuring him in words by giving him the lie thrice when he admonished her of her duty'. It seems that when he had asked about the religion of

52. McRoberts, *Medieval Church*, 75; A. Grant, *Independence and Nationhood*, 207–09; *Statutes of the Scottish Church*, 70. On the eve of the Reformation, Elgin cathedral was the site of 'Bloody Vespers', when William Innes of Innes with thirty-two of his kinsmen and eighty men-at-arms attacked the prior of Pluscarden at the altar steps in the course of a feud: Pitcairn, *Ancient Criminal Trials*, 1:376; McKay, 97.

53. NLS ms Wod. Qu. XX, f. 137; cf. Bodleian ms Rawl. C.584, p. 113.

54. CH2/621/1, ff. 356, 360; CH2/264/1, f. 6v.

55. CH2/521/7, p. 75. He exhibited no remorse for this 'outrageous and unreverent behaviour'.

her steward, she 'answered laughingly that he was of the religion of the French crown'. Failing to see the humour, Hay chided her for this 'taunting and scornful answer', as well as for tolerating a catholic servant, upon which she turned from joking to scornful speech against him. The presbytery duly censured her.[56]

George Blyth, in trouble in Dysart for skipping sermons, refrained from verbal abuse in response but played a practical joke on his minister when he gave him a forged summons to appear before the bishop of St Andrews. His minister, who rushed off to St Andrews in some trepidation, was emphatically not amused. Glaswegian revellers in 1586 were likewise creative in their protest at clerical discipline: on St Thomas eve (20 December) at midnight they 'went through the town with pipers, &c. and laid a dead horse to the minister's yard'. After a time in gaol without meat or drink, they repented from the pillar.[57] In Kinghorn, a rash of such ministerial abuse broke out at the same time that the minister was apparently conducting an especially vigorous perambulation of his parish to rebuke parishioners for swearing and profane pastimes – including some bawdy horseplay by John Gray's wife, 'being in the fields and taking a horse band and knit it to her belt with the one end between her legs and got on upon another woman as if she had been a man.' A minister who went around systematically disrupting his parishioners' play, however off-colour, should not have been surprised at one's 'pray[ing] to God to close his minister's mouth'.[58] The victims of kirk discipline resented clerical imposition of a uniform sobriety on a community with a still quite diverse notion of what constituted acceptable behaviour. The Leith session in 1614 heard Hendrie Nicoll reject their authority altogether since 'we desired no man to dwell beside us but such men as ourselves', which was quite true.[59] The push for a uniform code of godly behaviour was bound to

56. CH2/185/2, ff. 18–18v.
57. CH2/390/1, f. 39v; NLS ms 2782, f. 43.
58. CH2/472/1, ff. 34–35v. Among many other instances of verbal abuse of ministers by their disciplinary 'victims', see CH2/1142/1, ff. 98, 102 (George Cormack, under censure for fornication); CH2/276/1, p. 37 (David Wilson, admonished 'for night drinking, feasting, quarrelling and blaspheming', then 'upbraided the minister to his face while he was doing his office lawfully as moderator'); CH2/299/1, p. 291 (George Fillan of Tibbermuir, perhaps chafing under his minister's restrictions on wedding festivity when in 1632 he uttered 'evil words to the minister on the day of his marriage', threatening to 'put a dirk through his cheeks'). See also AAC CH2/809/1, f. 26v; CH2/96/1, f. 8v; NLS ms Wod. Qu. XXI (Hamilton presbytery, 1596), ff. 54v–55; CH2/327/1, f. 46v; NAS ms RH2/1/35, ff. 24, 25v–26, 43v–44, 47v–48; LPL ms 3471, f. 38.
59. CH2/716/2, f. 80v. Nicoll was before the session for a variety of offences but finally repented and promised to 'receive the sacraments with the rest of the congregation and . . . lead a peaceable life with his wife' (f. 81).

create at least as much lay opposition as the most sanctimonious medieval clericalism.

Some verbal attacks on ministers were protests on behalf of friends, relatives or fellow guildsmen who had been subjected to ministerial censure. John Lockie of Mertoun 'upbraided the minister' after a sermon in which he understood the preacher to have called his daughter a whore.[60] A Perth dyer who uttered 'vile, slanderous and abominable speeches against' the minister, 'to wit, that the said Mr William [Cowper] was a false common thief and that he should have been hanged, . . . and that he should improve him in the scriptures', explained that he was angry because Cowper 'shewed no pity to the poor man that was in ward' – probably his fellow dyer, Robert Blair, recently gaoled for slander. When the Perth session in 1601 left it to the council to discover the authors of an 'infamous libel' against Cowper, posted on his yett, the council immediately summoned the 'guild brethren to enquire of them if they knew the authors', which, as it turns out, they did. It seems the fleshers were tired of having their brethren disciplined for merrymaking.[61]

Parishioners who found themselves the targets of condemnation in their ministers' sermons, even if they were not mentioned by name, often had recourse to verbal attack. Cowper brought a successful slander charge against Robert Keir in 1607, producing as his witness the parish treasurer who had tried to collect from Keir his allotted payment for the minister's coals. Evidently in high dudgeon, Keir had responded to the collector, 'Mr William preached against me the last [sabbath] day. . . . The Devil a penny I'll pay for [his] coals.'[62] When a group of men in the same parish perceived John Guthry's sermon against superstition and fortune-telling as a personal attack, they responded with verbal criticism and threats, aggravated by refusal of hat-honour – a serious insult in early modern society. Thomas Young admitted his minister's charge that 'he has met him divers times since [the sermon] on the calsey [high street] and would not discharge that civil duty of salutation as became him to do towards his pastor', which Guthry found a 'provocation, to tempt his pastor by his want of particular duty, pass[ing] by him without using any kind of reverence'. Both minister and session were 'highly offended that he should

60. CH2/327/1, f. 73. His daughter, Helen, also had trouble restraining her tongue, 'miscalling the session' after 'she was provoked by the words of some one of the elders that made her say he lied, whereupon the minister was angry and put her forth.' She was sent to the presbytery, which instructed her session to 'try the woman's whoredom' while they punished her contempt for the ministry.

61. CH2/521/3, pp. 341, 347–48; PL ms B59/16/1, ff. 14–16 (the crafts to punish the culprits further after their apology to Cowper).

62. CH2/521/4, pp. 115–16. The elders sent Keir to the presbytery – the usual course when ministers were slandered.

have so far misregarded his pastor and provoked him to ire'. Young apologised for the slight, but insisted that 'it was not the duty of the pastor to charge his people with witchcraft, sorcery, [or] turning of the riddell, and to utter calumnies against his flock.' The elders, unswayed, were about to censure him when Guthry forgave him: having brought the charge in the first place, he now gained points for mercy. But he clearly thought it important to bring some action in order to nip in the bud the tendency of parishioners to malign preachers of unpopular messages. Another of Young's cohorts, William Rynd, paid a 10-merk fine for threatening the minister with physical violence. Threats were naturally treated more rigorously than other forms of verbal assault, given the frequency with which they were carried out; still, they abound in the minute books.[63]

There are instances of principled abuse, physical as well as verbal, springing from conscientious objection to bishops, for instance, in the case of Margaret Cleland's 'casting stones at the bishop of Galloway' in 1638. Cleland had plenty of company in that contentious time, though from at least the turn of the century some parishioners had been using alleged sympathy with episcopacy to slander their ministers. The Perth litster William Hay maligned William Cowper by proclaiming before witnesses that if Cowper were 'passing to England to London, ere he came home [he] would wear a surplice and a four-nooked [cornered] bonnet' (which prediction eventually proved correct).[64] Thomas Anderson of Perth, on the other hand, objected to his minister's presbyterianism in 1584 and interrupted the sermon to say so, 'calling his minister a drunken man'.[65] There are surprisingly numerous instances of parishioners standing and interrupting sermons and prayers, supposedly to disagree with the teaching, but often because they had endured quite enough denunciation of their sins. Thomas Elphinson of Calderhall objected to his minister's criticism of the political order, interrupting him to shout 'that he could not sit and hear a man so rail against the kirk and state'. But Andro Jameson was hied before the Selkirk presbytery 'for upbraiding the minister in pulpit and interrupting him in his sermon with many opprobrious words' in sheer despair at the incessant 'thundering judgment against him'; he shouted that 'he had enough of that and would not hold his tongue, . . . away with

63. CH2/521/7, pp. 78–79, 80 (both men friends of the riddell-turning Alexander Peblis); cf. CH2/327/1, f. 20 (Ralph Askin in 1608 threatening to 'put a whinger into' his minister, Alexander Symson, though one witness heard him qualify the threat with 'if he were no a minister').

64. CH2/400/1, p. 301; CH2/521/3, pp. 347–48. The prescient Hay claimed to have 'said that part in jest'. Although Cowper signed the 1606 Protestation, he did indeed later accept a bishopric.

65. CH2/521/1, f. 101v.

him [the preacher] and ban we all ye.' His dramatic condemnation of too much preaching on sin got him excommunicated.[66]

Another sort of principled verbal riposte sprang from frustration at ministerial corruption that had not been dealt with by session or presbytery. Margaret Key of Kinghorn railed against her minister because he was 'both judge and party' in a slander case against her and her husband.[67] The Fife synod had to discipline a minister for stealing the 'poor folks' silver'.[68] And clerical corruption in the parish of Temple may have been one cause of the infamous stool-burning episode there: the minister Thomas Copland was eventually found by the Dalkeith brethren to be a malicious slanderer of his own parishioners, but not in time to spare William Jordan punishment for threatening that 'he should have a sword in the kirk' to deal with the minister's verbal destruction of his reputation. It took multiple accusations of slander from others in the parish, and eventually the minister's confession, to convince the presbytery that Copland probably merited the verbal abuse and threats that had come his way.[69]

Many records of verbal abuse of ministers do not directly indicate either ideological motivation or response to disciplinary action, though ministerial censure of either the offender or a family member may well have occurred long before, or be unrecorded in the session book. One ought not to argue from silence, but it is easy to imagine perceived insult festering over time, aggravated by every sight of the minister, and finally

66. CH2/266/1, f. 119 (the elders approved Mr Semple's 'preaching freely against the sins of the time' and thought Elphinson 'did exceedingly scandalise the people of God'); CH2/327/1, ff. 72v–73. The Selkirk presbytery summoned Thomas Markie in 1608 for what may have been a similar sentiment: in the midst of his minister's prayers of confession, 'he openly spake to the minister and bade him pray for himself' (f. 21). Of the numerous instances of irate parishioners disrupting services to rail at ministers, most unfortunately do not indicate the cause of the outbursts: e.g., CH2/32/1, f. 4; CH2/1142/1, ff. 94v, 97v, 99.

67. CH2/472/1, f. 31v (1608). She 'said she was in Kinghorn before him and would be in Kinghorn after he would be in heaven', effectively claiming greater authority than her newly arrived minister since she was an old-timer in the community.

68. He also took penitents' fines 'and converted the same to his own use': SAU ms 30451, f. 6v. The Perth presbytery in 1623 forbade ministers henceforth serving as cautioners to quell talk of their milking that system for profit: CH2/299/1, p. 87.

69. CH2/424/1, ff. 4v, 12v, 13v. Copland had reported falsely to Jordan's master that he had stolen oats from him, but unable to produce a witness (apparently his master was absent), Jordan could not prove the slander since 'an accusation against a brother . . . should not be received without witness' – a judgment that must have fed popular suspicion that presbyteries furthered clericalist privilege. Copland was eventually suspended for admitting that he had slandered another man of bribery in Edinburgh and Dalkeith 'out of anger and passion'; he had to repent publicly everywhere he had offended and before the synod.

erupting in slander or violence. But some angry encounters were probably matters of personal discord having nothing to do with doctrine or discipline. We shall never know what motivated Jonet Russell's 'imprecations against the minister' of Kingsbarns, or what possessed George Livingstone and three of his friends, one a minstrel, to come after midnight to the house of the minister of Gullane, Thomas Makquhue, 'he lying diseased in his bed', and play 'a whistle and tabron at his doors, dinging up his chamber window and [making] such perturbation in their drunkenness as efflayed [caused pain to] his head by reason of the sudden and unlooked for noise they made'.[70] Drink accounted for railing in many cases, as when the weaver John Hynde criticised his minister's dress, 'uttering disdainful speeches against Mr John Guthry, minister, in saying that he . . . wanted the webster's handywork', explaining that 'in his rough humour after drink he spoke it and not of any disdain of his pastor', to whom he apologised on his knees.[71] Emotional distress following bereavement may have explained why in 1594 Walter Bower cried 'God his malediction' on his minister, John Coupar, praying 'the devil make him quit of the kirk and a pastor'. Bower apparently blamed his wife's and his mother's recent deaths on food or drink sent to his house by the minister. He threatened that 'he should either have Mr John Coupar slain or he him, that Mr John was a help of Walter Bower's wife's death' – words that he repented when he was hauled before the Glasgow presbytery.[72] But all such harassment is evidence at least that new presbyters were not revered by everyone.

Some parishioners were so angry with their ministers, whether as clerics or as men, that they moved beyond verbal to physical abuse. The ministers who complained so often about 'combats with wicked men' knew whereof they spoke, and they spoke not just metaphorically.[73] Alexander Mortimer of Aberdeen was so furious with his minister in 1608 for

70. CH2/819/1, p. 26; CH2/185/1, f. 12. See also CH2/390/1, ff. 27, 35v, 37, 38; AAC CH2/562/1, f. 32; NAS RH2/1/35, f. 8; CH2/521/1, ff. 43v–44; CH2/400/1, pp. 62, 66, 147; CH2/294/1, ff. 1v–2v, 3v; CH2/327/1, ff. 10v, 18, 20; CH2/191/1, f. 31; CH2/424/1, n.f., 23 March 1592; CH2/621/1, p. 355.

71. CH2/521/7, p. 215; see also CH2/448/1, p. 35.

72. ML CH2/171/1, ff. 44–44v. One deponent heard Bower say, 'the offering that Mr John Coupar sent was the cause' of his wife's death; another heard him 'thank Mr John Coupar of his mother's death'. Because of the death threat, the presbytery sought numerous depositions in this case.

73. This is a constant refrain in ministers' sermons and autobiographies, doubtless in part asserting fulfilment of the biblical principle that the godly are persecuted: CH2/521/3, pp. 347–48; Boyd, *Balme*, 202; Rollock, *Select Works*, 1:393, 407; Blair, 39–40; *History of . . . Reverend John Welch*, 2–9, 21–29.

denouncing his Midsummer bonfire that he resorted to 'taking his hat off his head and striking him on the face therewith'. Much more seriously, the Glasgow burgess Archibald Legat, excommunicated for having 'railed against the pastors of the truth to bring the word thereby in contempt', responded to the minister dealing with his heterodoxy in 1582 by 'putting hand unto the violent invasion of Mr John Howson'. The Inveravon session denied marriage to a man who had drawn a sword on his minister, 'offering him injury'; perhaps he was having difficulty passing the doctrinal requirement for matrimony.[74]

The unfortunate Mr William Young of Redgorton, far from being Milton's powerful new presbyter, paid the price in his person for disciplining Harry Schaw for the rape of Janet Mar. He recounted his tale to the brethren of the Perth presbytery:

> Working among the stock of his own glebe in a solitary and quiet place called the How of the Park, at his meditations in quiet and sober manner, looking for no evil to have been done or said to him by any person, . . . Harry Schaw of Perth, having conceived a deadly hatred against [him] . . . for citing him before the presbytery of Perth, . . . of set purpose, provision and forethought felony, violently invaded and pursued him of his life, having in his hands a rung with a long dirk or else a dagger.

The minister, 'seeing him in a rage and threatening him of his life, ran away', but Schaw gave chase, shouting, 'Thy feet shall not bear thee from me', and Mr Young, 'an aged man and fearing he should have felled him with the rung, cried many times, "God's mercy"', to no avail. Harry overtaking him 'asked him what he said of him to the presbytery . . . and commanded him to swear that he should never speak of him again to the presbytery or by the blood of Jesus he should presently die.' Young was finally rescued 'by some poor men that came from shearing of their corns' and heard his cries, but the irrepressible Schaw 'immediately thereafter . . . made vaunt of his doing to his own shearers' and boasted that 'he had caused the minister [to] swear and cry many times, "God's mercy".'[75]

There were certainly cases where physical assault of a minister targeted him as an individual rather than as a clergyman. John Forrest in 1585 lay

74. CH2/448/2, p. 301; ML CH2/171/1, f. 54v; CH2/191/1, f. 51.

75. CH2/299/1, pp. 91–92, 94–95. Schaw ultimately repented in linen in the kirk of Rogorton. The presbytery sent John Guthry of Perth to 'teach and receive' and 'agree him' with Young, but Schaw never suffered the civil penalty provided by James VI's eleventh parliament for violence against ministers, forfeiture of all movable property, half to the minister, half to the crown.

in wait for his minister, Thomas Douglas, for three hours after his sermon and 'at a convenient place pursued and invaded him and drew his blood, and except certain persons had intervened, the said Mr Thomas had been in danger of his life'. But when the session of St Andrews charged him with slander against the kirk for his attack, 'he could not understand that he had committed in any ways slander against the same notwithstanding he had offended the said Thomas.' His attack was on Thomas as a person, not a minister, because 'the said Mr Thomas had offended him' in a matter not related to the kirk. Still, crimes like this one, together with robberies of ministers and burglaries of manses, do suggest a less reverential attitude towards ministers than Milton presumed, at least among the more disorderly sort of the population.[76] In the rough and ready Highlands, Andro Dow Fraser told the Moray synod in 1624 that he could not serve his parish without better protection from the local lords because 'by unknown persons of the Highlands he had lately sustained harm in his body and had been despoiled of his goods'. The roads to Inveravon were so dangerous in 1631 that the minister could not even make it to church on Sunday, 'being hindered by James Stewart, who while he was coming to the kirk on the sabbath day being accompanied with a number of lawless renegades, beset the way so that he could not pass by to the kirk without some disaster or harm of his life.' And the minister of Boleskin reported to the presbytery of Inverness that he could not stay in his parish, lacking 'security for his life or goods, his house being lately seized upon by Lochabber robbers, himself threatened with naked swords and drawn dirks at his breast, his money and household stuff plundered.'[77]

To the extent that elders shared with ministers a clerical identity, they also found themselves subject to verbal and physical attack by disgruntled fellow parishioners. Resentment of discipline was obviously a frequent motivation, as it was for assault on ministers. Marion Cock's sentence to the Liberton jougs was 'for breaking of the sabbath and abusing of the sessioners for reproving her', for instance; in 1581 Duncan Drummond of Fraserburgh 'abused' an elder 'when he charged him'; and Thomas Arthur of Kirkoswald uttered 'fearful and horrible speech in praying God let never the sun [rise] upon one of the elders who delated him last'. In Burntisland Walter Angus's 'injurious words' about the elders arose from his resentment at their judgment against his wife in a flyting case in 1603,

76. SAU unnumbered ms St Andrews presbytery/1, ff. 3, 4v–5; cf. Spalding, 2:28–29 (William Chalmer, minister of Skeyne, 'robbed and spoiled both moneys and other goods' by 'some lymmers').

77. CH2/271/1, p. 4; CH2/191/1, f. 5; *Records of the Presbyteries of Inverness and Dingwall*, v, 5. Other examples of violence against ministers and their families include CH2/294/1, ff. 5–5v; CH2/471/1, f. 13.

and John Black's a few months later came after an elder intervened in his wife-beating. Margaret Ward's slander of the Anstruther Wester elder William Dairsie followed his delation of her for 'loose and light behaviour in dancing through the town with women and lasses in a ring', which she said came 'of envy' – Dairsie apparently being a sober fellow; she maligned him by saying that 'he said he would ding her and therefore she durst not go east nor west', but relented and knelt in apology before the session for 'misreporting him'.[78] Examples of 'unreverent carriage' before the session abound, as do recorded rebukes for 'reviling the elder that found fault with her'.[79] The Fraserburgh elders were so often assaulted that their session book includes a statement that such persecution must be expected as part and parcel of the office: elders were 'exhorted to take in patience that as the best reward to be looked for at the hands of a faithless generation for pains faithfully taken unto the Lord's ministry'. For elders as for ministers, suffering persecution could in fact be interpreted as a sign of election. When Jesus himself was crucified, how could his true followers expect better? Suffering conferred status among the godly.[80]

Some assaults on elders were in effect tax revolts. Two elders collecting for the poor at the kirk door of Menmuir in 1638 found themselves 'cast . . . into the boards upon the ground' with 'all violence and thrusting' by two men. And an Edinburgh elder making a door-to-door collection for the poor in 1628 was greeted by a woman who said 'that she had rather give him a tow to hang him'.[81] It is unclear whether these angry parishioners resented being pressed for a 'voluntary' contribution, or whether they distrusted the honesty of the collectors. Certainly some elders were, as Gilbert Henderson of Perth charged, 'false knaves', in for the take. Sessions often enough decreed that the poor box must have two keys, kept by two different elders, with the box itself held by a third, and that the session should check the accounts of those responsible for collection and distribution, so that one wonders how much they trusted each other.[82]

78. CH2/383/1, f. 9 (1640); CH2/1142, ff. 98, 99–99v, 100v; AAC CH2/562/1, f. 34; CH2/523/1, ff. 9, 12v, 42; SAU CH2/624/2, p. 119.
79. CH2/636/34, ff. 20, 29; CH2/338/1, ff. 7v, 14, 17v, 24; AAC CH2/562/1, f. 18; CH2/390/1, f. 50v (William Givin slandering the Dysart session, 'saying that there was among them that had done greater faults than ever his wife did' after she was summoned for flyting); SAU CH2/624/2, p. 127; SAU CH2/624/3, p. 22; CH2/716/2, f. 95 (cf. ff. 80v, 97 – case of John Thomson); CH2/400/1, pp. 48, 50.
80. CH2/1142/1, f. 2. Other examples of verbal abuse of Fraserburgh elders in response to discipline include the cases of Christiane and Janet Dewy (f. 23) and James Burnett (ff. 96v, 99).
81. CH2/264/1, f. 18; CH2/141/1, f. 26v.
82. CH2/521/8/1, f. 24v; CH2/400/1, p. 146; CH2/147/1, f. 172; SAU ms 30451, f. 6v (one key to the minister, one to an elder). Mortlach typically required that all the elders sign the parish accounts: CH2/529/1, f. 80.

Their fellow parishioners often suspected something was up. Marion Cunningham 'called half the session [of Ayr] mansworn in distributing [to] the poor folk' in 1621, and James Thomson of Dundonald claimed that 'there was not an honest man in the session'. It was difficult and risky, though, to bring a specific charge against an elder: the Dundonald session in 1636 mandated that anyone charging an elder or deacon with slander must pay the significant fine of two merks if the case were not proved. On the other hand, the elders recognised that there might well be grounds for charging corruption and so included a provision that if an elder or deacon were convicted, he should pay double the usual penalty.[83]

Anecdotes about corrupt Scottish elders delighted English critics of presbyterian polity. In 1589 William Bruton gave a London friend 'an example of the consistorial government in Scotland' that may or may not have been based in fact, but that surely reflected and perhaps fed distrust of sessions. According to the story, an elder in an unnamed parish, jealous of a merchant's wealth, persuaded the minister and session to excommunicate him on charges of 'excessive banquetings and drinking of wine when he entertained his friends, who would have been contented with less costly entertainment'. As Milton would have expected, when he appeared before the session, the members 'would not utter by whom he was accused'. Meanwhile the elder, 'who had begun in malice, procured certain lewd persons to repair to the merchant's house and to break up his shop and to rifle the same and also his house of all they found convenient to be carried away.' Returning home to find that he had been burgled, the merchant in all innocence reported the theft to the elder, seeking justice and indicating that he would do what was necessary to have his sentence of excommunication lifted in order to 'have law and right against those that had taken away his goods' (an excommunicate being deprived of the benefits of civil society, including law enforcement). The canny elder, however, used the kirk's teaching on charity to block his efforts: 'What? Will you be restored to the congregation to the end you might be revenged? You must have charity and forgive all that is past, or else you are not fit to be a member of Christ's church.' The unfortunate merchant was caught between a rock and a hard place. He could not be restored unless he would forgive the loss of all his goods, 'and so fearing they would take away his life also, he came into England and so to London', where he doubtless found a warm reception from the likes of Milton.[84]

83. AAC CH2/751/2, f. 7; *Dundonald*, 239, 409.

84. LPL ms 3470, f. 107. Archibald Gilmore in 1619 attempted a sort of false-arrest charge against the Falkirk session, claiming that they had trumped up a charge of selling drink in sermon time of 'envy and malice'; however, his failure to control his wrath

New elders, like old priests, also suffered *ad hominem* attacks, and many of the references in the minutes to bitter verbal and physical assault without a corresponding mention of the perpetrator being under discipline must have fallen into this category.[85] Attacks on the whole session without a notation of discipline may indicate disapproval of the system itself, or a more generalised distaste for authority. This may explain Lawrence Dischington's symbolic act of destruction in Anstruther Wester, where he 'violently broke the principal seat of the kirk and gave unto sundry of the elders many injurious languages and called them all evil men'.[86] When all is said and done, though, what we are left with is a sense that popular perceptions of the clergy had changed less than one might have thought with the Reformation – except insofar as the category of clergy was now expanded to include their fellow disciplinarians on the session. That portion of the community not particularly inclined to the sobriety and rigorous piety required by the kirk – whether lairds and ladies or the baser sort – treated their ministers as their catholic counterparts had their priests. The medieval statute allowing clerics to bear arms in self-defence would best have been maintained against the 'violent hands' that 'so long had troubled the peace' of their successors.[87]

* * *

If the irreverence of some people for the clergy demonstrates continuity with the pre-Reformation, so does the rapt veneration of others. There had always been a portion of the parish that revered the priesthood, along with friars and monks and the panoply of saints who periodically sprang

in their presence ruined his case. He 'in a most impudent and scandalous manner in presence of the whole session sat down upon his knees and most execrably swore by his ten bloody banns that he should complain to the judges for the manner of the minister and elders' and 'in a great passion as a madman void of all wit and judgment avowed by sundry terrible oaths that . . . he should do an evil turn.' The session turned him over for civil judgment to the lord of Linlithgow and required public repentance: CH2/400/1, pp. 48, 50.

85. CH2/32/1, f. 14; CH2/523/1, f. 9; CH2/276/1, f. 2v; CH2/521/1, f. 60v. There were also practical jokes on elders, as on ministers, that may have been retaliatory either for discipline or for a personal offence: Robert Griene took a page from George Blyth's book and 'caused the clerk summon David Gray', a Stow elder, 'to appear before the session by a forged token from the minister' in 1627: CH2/338/1, f. 8v.

86. SAU CH2/624/2, p. 142 (1614); cf. CH2/400/1, p. 299; AAC CH2/751/1, f. 131v; CH2/471/1, ff. 11–11v (servants in 1616 railing, 'The devil take the elders, session and altogether'); CH2/521/6, f. 4v; CH2/141/1, ff. 41, 54v; CH2/716/2, f. 77; CH2/327/1, f. 42; CH2/400/1, p. 132;

87. CH2/521/1, f. 60; CH2/191/1, f. 1 (elders of Inveravon reporting that they will now, in 1631, do a better job of keeping the kirk and exercising discipline since 'now he who so long had troubled their peace was apprehended').

from their number. Clerical visionaries – prophesying hermits, miracle-working nuns, ascetics who heard the voice of the Virgin, not to mention priests who by their sacred words transformed bread to flesh in the mass or made holy the water of baptism – had long inspired the awe and even emulation of the devouter sort of laity. With protestantism's campaign against 'superstition', invocation of saints, and sacerdotalism, and for a devotion centred on the word read by a priesthood of all believers, it is reasonable to expect that this attitude towards the clergy would have gone by the board. Giving the laity control over clerical appointments and demission, and abandoning the doctrine of apostolic succession and the rigamarole attached to episcopal ordination, ought to have reduced the protestant ministry to the level of mere functionaries in the kirk and obviated any notion of 'holy men'. But it was not so. First, the survival of a highly ceremonial induction of ministers maintained ritually an exalted position for them, corresponding to the singular importance attached to their principal function – preaching – for the fate of their auditors' immortal souls. Second, and perhaps more surprisingly, Scottish clergy retained the roles of prophet, visionary and saint in an age when, in the perception of laity and clergy alike, miracles had by no means ceased.

The received version has it that the traditional ceremony of ordination 'was eschewed at the Reformation' with the demise of apostolic succession through bishops.[88] The term is not used in the *First Book of Discipline*, which demanded only 'public approbation of the people and declaration of the chief minister that the person there presented is appointed to serve that kirk'. Acknowledging that 'the apostles used the imposition of hands, yet seeing the miracle is ceased, the using of the ceremony we judge is not necessary' and might encourage superstition.[89] In fact, however, while the ceremony installing a new minister was no longer in the hands of a bishop, it was no less ritualised, and many of the same gestures and symbols remained intact, surely implying to viewers many of the same meanings that had inhered in traditional ordination rites. The imposition of hands, formally restored by the *Second Book of Discipline* in 1578 for 'the separation and sanctifying of the person appointed of God and his kirk', had in fact not fallen out of use. And it still signified a transfer of spiritual power, now preceded by 'fasting and earnest prayer' and with the bishop's hands replaced by those of brethren from the presby-

88. Kirk, *Patterns*, 159.

89. *First Book*, 96–97, 102, the miracle reference to the supernatural transferral of power akin to the miraculous healing also achieved by laying on of hands in the apostolic era, or to the apostolic succession that gave to Catholic bishops authority to ordain – a presumption unwarranted by the scriptures in the protestant view.

tery (the protestant bishop often among them in those periods when episcopacy had been reimposed by the king).[90] Cowper told the Perth presbytery in 1612 that the minister receives the 'power he has gotten . . . by that imposition of the hands of the presbytery according to the word and practice of the kirk primitive'.[91] If the bishop's claim to power had lain in apostolic succession, the presbyters' lay in their demonstrated command of scriptural knowledge and orthodox doctrine. They were the ones who had 'well tried and found qualified' the man now elected to a parish.[92] But the representation of power transferred by one authority to another was the same physical sign that it had always been. Installation of a minister was by 'solemnisation . . . decently executed', in the presence of presbytery commissioners, after the always-central sermon, and with movements carefully ordered to affirm the verbal elements asserting his divine vocation. When Andro Maky was ordained to Gullane in 1597 by commissioners from the presbyteries of Edinburgh, Dalkeith, Dunbar and Haddington – as impressive an array of authority as any medieval bishop would have provided – the preacher after the sermon 'demanded him being risen up to come to the place appointed for his public receiving, there to describe his call', engage in a dialogue with the preacher about the 'gravity and weightiness of this charge', and 'vow solemnly by holding up of his hand before God and his kirk' to discharge his office faithfully, 'beseeching the Lord if he violate any part of that promise with knowledge that the present day's work [that is, the ceremony of ordination] should be a witness of his condemnation'. Ritual *per se* was thus personified. The preacher then 'descended out of the pulpit and after he had incalled upon the name of God, . . . Andro being humbled upon his knees was admitted to the office of the ministry by laying of the hands of the whole brethren present according to the order. After which ceremony the said Mr Andro being ready to be delivered to that people as their pastor',

90. *Second Book*, 65–73, 180. The 'hands of the eldership' was construed earlier to apply to a group of ministers and elders drawn from neighbouring congregations; by 1582 it meant presbyters: Cowan, *Scottish Reformation*, 184. Robert Blair was ordained by the bishop of Down and Connor, John Livingston by the bishop of Raphoe, both of whom joined with other presbyters in laying on hands: Blair, 59; *Select Biographies*, ed. W.K. Tweedie (Edinburgh, 1845), 1:141. The bishop of Orkney, directed by commissioners of the General Assembly, joined nineteen other men in the South Kirk of Leith to admit David Lyndsay 'in name of the whole session as pastor, . . . received by a certain number of the elders': CH2/716/1, f. 22.

91. NLS ms Wod. Fol XXVII, f. 1v, though with the attendant ritual to 'warrant he has enjoyed the approbation of [the] flock by the upholding of [their] hands': both hand actions were important. Cowper cited 'laying on of the hands of the company of the elders' in 'the kirk of Ephesus . . . which is the ceremony of ordination' (1 Tim. 4.14).

92. *Second Book*, 180; NAS ms CH8/39.

he addressed them briefly. A dialogue between preacher and congregation followed, the preacher asking the people assembled 'if they would be content to avow and accept of the said Mr Andro . . . and would promise all due obedience to him', and 'the whole people consenting and most willingly agreeing by a uniform voice and gesture of holding up of their hands as they were required testifying the same'. Finally, the 'principal men in name of the whole people' stepped forward and 'received the said Mr Andro . . . by the hands'.[93] The new importance of the laity in calling their own minister is clear in the ceremony, but the motions of hands conferring power, hands upheld in solemn vow, hands receiving the minister also indicate the very real authority that still inhered in a duly ordained cleric.

The words of Andro Maky's testimony about his calling also served to sanctify his clerical status very powerfully by describing what was in effect a direct communication from God – the sort of thing that set a saint apart from ordinary believers. Asked to tell his new flock 'what the Lord had declared to his conscience', he answered 'that since he came to ripeness of years and the Lord gave him any judgment to discern between good and evil, he found his heart ever inclined to the ministry and so inclined that it could not be withdrawn therefrom without violence to his conscience.' He asked God for 'an inward warrant thereof' and received 'never greater assurance of God's mercy or of the remission of his sins in the blood of Christ nor had of the calling of God to the work, . . . protesting before him that knew the secrets of all hearts that neither honour nor commodity nor any other particular in the earth moved [him] thereto save only the said calling of the Lord, together with the zeal he had of his glory and edifying of' the people. Asked in what seems to have been the usual formula of the Haddington presbytery 'if he thought himself able by his own style [ability] to discharge that calling, [he] answered that he knew the burden to be great because the care of every soul in that congregation was committed to [him] in such sort that if any perished in his default, their blood was to be required at his hands', so he would 'not run to the said calling in his own name', but only with God's help. Asked, finally, how he proposed to carry out his office, he promised to do so 'without any partiality, although he should incur the hatred of the people, although his life should come in hazard therefore' – which certainly happened with other ministers, as we have seen. His final speech presented the condition upon which he accepted his new charge, 'that they would

93. CH2/185/2, ff. 25v–26. This installation was the culmination of 'two years trial of Andro Maky's doctrine and conversation' (f. 23v); he succeeded his infirm father in the position.

faithfully one and all promise obedience to *the voice of God in his mouth*'.[94] Most ordinations are not so completely described in presbytery minutes as those of Haddington ministers, but accounts like this one serve well to indicate the surviving ceremonial that enabled Scottish clergy to retain something of the spiritual status of old priests, and the remarkable claim of the ministers to speak for God – that is, in effect to intercede between less gifted believers and God.[95] No wonder a critic of the *Second Book of Discipline* in 1585 worried about the potentially popish message of the rite: 'If the power [of a minister] be immediately of God, what [do] ministers' inaugurations serve?' Might not the imposition of hands 'be called a sacrament' by the ignorant?[96] Elaborate ceremony naturally created confusion about whether the rite itself might be the potent agency.

The power of ministers, most evident in preaching, was evinced in other ways as well. While the elders were essential for discipline, there were generally no session meetings when ministers were absent.[97] The place reserved for the minister in the kirk was sacrosanct, the Fife synod ordering none 'to take upon hand to preach or teach in the pulpit but such as are admitted ministers. . . . All other exhorters and readers stand in some other place depute to them to use the execution of their offices.'[98] Ministers pronounced excommunication. They also publicly prayed and offered 'intercession unto God for the conversion of' the one excommunicated.[99]

94. CH2/185/1, f. 25v (emphasis mine).
95. Other descriptions of ordination ceremonies, with imposition of hands, raising of hands in vows, and receiving by hand, include CH2/383/1, f. 3; CH2/521/7, p. 303; CH2/448/3, pp. 229–30; CH2/266/1, f. 3; ML CH2/171/1, f. 56v; *Chronicle of Perth*, 5. The letter of admission of William Stirling to Badernock, entered into the Glasgow presbytery minutes, ML CH2/171/1, f. 34v, offers a particularly detailed description of his ordination, noting delivery of 'the book of God called the Bible unto his hands', and 'requiring all the parishioners and inhabitants of the said parish to obey him as the lawful pastor of their souls with such reverence and obedience as it becomes them to do to their pastor', presbytery ordering 'inhibitions to all [who] stop or trouble him in peaceable being'.
96. NLS ms Adv. 29/2/8, ff. 128–28v, concluding, 'vocation or calling and promotion by name of a minister is required, albeit . . . it is said that they have power immediately of God, so it appears *impositio manuu[m]* ministers not.'
97. CH2/521/5, f. 31; CH2/521/8/2, f. 143; CH2/191/1, f. 22v.
98. SAU ms 30451, f. 5v.
99. E.g., NAS ms CH8/62, f. 2; CH2/147/1, f. 27v, *SAKS* 1:203–05, 266–76; CH2/1026/1, f. 6. Either session or presbytery formally excommunicated, though the minutes suggest that it was most usually a presbytery act (NAS ms CH8/64, Borthwick; CH2/89/1, ff. 5–6 (Deer presbytery); NLS ms Wod. Qu. XXI, f. 258v (Hamilton presbytery). It was never an act solely of the minister, lest episcopal usurpation of this power be reintroduced, but ministers pronounced: ML CH2/171/1, f. 56; CH2/185/2, f. 30. For the theory, see *Second Book*, 165, 185. The *First Book* gave the

And it was most often ministers in the presbytery, having presumably enhanced capacity for 'understanding and evidently seeing many evident tokens of God his wrath kindled against this country for sin' who took it upon themselves to interpret those tokens and call respondent fasts.[100] One sermon notebook records dutifully that 'what is entrusted to ministers differs from that of private professors'; ministers being 'ambassadors, viceregents' of the divine 'therefore act authoritatively'.[101]

Ministers even provided auricular confession, not as a requirement, of course, but as one noted, 'it is very expedient that in heavy anguish of mind a sinner for the obtaining of comfort should sometimes confess his faults (whereby the mind is disquieted) to some pious men, especially to the preachers of the word.'[102] This was particularly important for those on their deathbeds, and surviving accounts show ministers hearing deathbed confessions and offering comfort sometimes, though more often severe criticism, probing for further sins or for the state of the (likely hypocritical) heart, and withholding comfort until a state of sufficiently elevated anxiety attests to genuine contrition.[103] While extreme unction was rejected by the reformers, deathbed communions acted as a substitute. Some ministers 'scrupled to be employed in that service' that smacked so of the catholics' last rites, but presbyteries supported the continuity of practice,

power of excommunication to 'the minister and consent of the ministry and commandment of the kirk' (p. 170); cf. *BUK* 1:75, 195, 284, 385; NLS ms Adv. 29.2.8, f. 127, excommunication only 'by advice and consent of the eldership'.

100. CH2/294/1, f. 1.

101. SAU ms Hay Fleming Box 53, it. ii, p. 30.

102. NLS ms Wod. Qu. XXIX, it. 19. The author does add that 'private men' can both teach each other and hear confessions. Catherine Anderson probably regretted having 'in private . . . confessed [fornication] . . . to the [Burntisland] minister' in 1606, since he promptly turned her over to the session; perhaps he thought public repentance more likely than private to ensure her contrition: CH2/523/1, f. 25. Auricular confession to minister or an elder was commended by the Aberlady session, CH2/4/1, f. 31v; reported to the Haddington presbytery, CH2/185/2, f. 3 (1596, laird of Stirling's deathbed confession of adultery).

103. *The Last and Heavenly Speech and Glorious Departure of John Viscount Kenmuir* (Glasgow, 1712). The unfortunate Kenmuir was attended on his deathbed by the thoroughly aggravating Samuel Rutherford, who so viciously condemned him for his sin in leaving the last parliament to avoid voting against ceremonies in the kirk 'for fear of incurring the indignation of my prince and loss of further honour' (p. 7) that his deathbed proved the site of agonising distress rather than comfort. Far from encouraging the sick and penitent man to hope for heaven, Rutherford 'read unto him the first eight verses of the sixth to the Hebrews, and discoursed to him of the far ongoing of reprobates in the way of heaven, and of their taste of the good word of God, and of the virtues of the life to come, and yet are but reprobates', then moved on to describe the 'everlasting burning' for which he was headed. He did eventually inspire enough signs of repentance from the weeping Kenmuir to relent and offer comfort.

instructing Gormock's minister to accede to Patrick Butter's request to serve his son who, 'lying deadly sick in this town, earnestly desired the sacrament of the communion of the Lord's supper to be ministered to him being now at the point of death'. The brethren found this 'a godly and reasonable' desire.[104]

Clerical status won ministers preferred treatment in ecclesiastical courts, as it had for their catholic predecessors, if to a lesser extent. The violent Harry Schaw was vigorously prosecuted for assaulting his minister, but his rape of Janet Mar – clearly a violent act which she struggled to resist – was treated as adultery by both parties. Mar, a laywoman, did not get the protection of the law that the cleric, William Young, did.[105] And parishioners charging Thomas Copland of Temple with slander found that the plaintiff's oath that would have convicted a lay offender had to be supplemented by witnesses to support a case against a 'brother'. The principle was that maligning a minister constituted assault on the word preached and had best be sorted out with special care.[106]

The preachers themselves showed no reluctance to incorporate exaltation of their own estate into their sermons. John Chalmers's anonymous auditor in 1624 noted down in his sermon book his definition of ministers as heirs of the apostles whose parishioners 'would be apostates and inexcusable' if they 'reported not in godly upholding him'. Ministers were God's 'messengers', his 'prophets, the substance of their preaching' sent directly from heaven. His notes on a later sermon record that ministers have 'extraordinary callings and gifts and affairs, as had Moses, Elias, Baptist, Jeremiah and other prophets. So had our first reformers.' At a Kirkcaldy sermon in 1625 he described John Gillespie as 'God's minister to them in his person'; and from a Dunfermline sermon he learned that preachers as prophets provide 'remarkable sentences against the day of need', and particularly in 'these apostate and corrupt no less than dangerous days'.[107]

104. CH2/299/1, p. 81; cf. CH2/185/2, f. 3; NLS ms 2782, f. 14 (1593 Glasgow session act for those with 'sick folk' in their households to 'come to the ministers and they to pray for them and visit them and comfort them').

105. CH2/299/1, pp. 81–84, 88–89 for the attack on Mar, 91–92, 94–95 for that on Young.

106. CH2/424/1, f. 5.

107. CH2/424/1, ff. 5v–16v. Cf. CH2/448/2, p. 7; SAU CH2/21/5, ff. 7, 11v, 12, 64, 68, 92. Notes like these permit the presumption that similar sentiments in published sermons were actually received in the pew. See, e.g., Boyd, *Balme*, 8, 67–68, 180, 183, 187, 202; Rollock, *Select Works*, 292, 407, 415. James Melville, in a dreadfully alliterative poem on Rollock's death, called him 'divine doctor dearest', 'peerless preacher, . . . painful pastor' and informed his Edinburgh parishioners that it was 'his words, his warks, his wayes, his vertues gar [enabled]/ Thee [to] get this gaine of great felicitie', putting Rollock almost in Christ's place: *Certaine Sermons upon Severall Places of the Epistles of Paul Preached Be M. Robert Rollok, Minister of the Evangell of Jesus Christ at Edinburgh* (Edinburgh, 1599), sigs Ai–A8v.

Zachary Boyd's parishioners heard him describe preachers as heirs of St George: 'Let no man wonder that Satan raiseth slanders upon preachers. This maketh the dragon often to stretch out his tail that hereby he may sweep down the lights of the world, which shew unto us the way of salvation.'[108]

Insofar as elders shared clerical status, they, too, garnered a special reverence from their fellow parishioners, though they fell short of the category of prophet. Assaults on them may have been numerous, but they were in nearly every case (excepting those in which verbal attack proved to be legitimate complaint) vigorously punished, as was contumacy. A Dundonald fornicator in 1604 actually had to perform a more serious repentance for his contumacy than for his sexual offence, standing 'at the kirk end . . . in his linen clothes for his disobedience' to the session, and the next Sunday 'in his own clothes for fornication'. Dysart's session ordered in 1621 'if any craftsman be disobedient to the voice or decree of session or presbytery, that no honest man receive again them either in their house or in any service.'[109] Elders, as 'watchmen, visitors and attenders upon the manners, life and conversation of the people', had real power, and this extended even outside their parish bounds, given the requirement of a 'testimonial' from one's own session to settle in a new parish.[110]

It is the power of preachers as 'prophets', though, that compels a closer look at precisely what clerical status signified in the culture of protestantism. The term (προφήτης) in its technical sense meant to the reformers simply preachers, interpreters of the will of God in sermons, speaking for God as Old Testament prophets had to the people of Israel, more often than not in judgment. But of course there was a popular meaning as well, connecting preachers with supernatural powers of telling the future, not to mention other miraculous potential. Both sorts of prophecy won extraordinary popular followings for particularly charismatic preachers. Andrew Gray of Glasgow 'was exceedingly followed', so that on communion Sundays 'the Outer Church was so thronged that there was no getting near the door; and within the confusion was so great [that] several persons were brought out sick and fainting'; people able to take notes on his sermons kept them 'preserved as a precious relict of him' – a sort of textual icon. (Should we re-examine sermon notebooks as protestant reli-

108. Boyd, *Balme*, 202. He was a bit more self-deprecating in his *Exposition of the Epistles of Saint Paul*, in *Selected Sermons*, ed. D.W. Atkinson (Aberdeen, 1989), 10–11: 'Say not, O the preacher! O the wonderful man! . . . but say rather, God is mighty in the man. Look over the man and gaze upon God'; but he still calls ministers 'God's interpreters' (p. 11).

109. *Dundonald*, 64; CH2/390/1, f. 7. See also CH2/1463/1, f. 1; CH2/521/1, f. 117v.

110. *SAKS* 2:762–63; CH2/716/1, ff. 2, 4.

quaries?) We know that 'multitudes of all ranks would have crossed several ferries every Lord's day to hear' Robert Bruce; 'yea, they came both from Ross and Sutherland' when Bruce was in Inverness. One aspiring prophet travelled 140 miles from Glasgow to visit that 'ancient heroic servant of Christ' and found that 'in my return, I also met with sweet passages of divine providence, some being drowned in rivers about that same time, and others killed by robbers': Bruce's visitors had special, divine protection, just like those who had ventured on pilgrimage of a different sort a century earlier to venerate a relic.[111] The veneration in which godly laypeople held their ministers was palpable. Samuel Rutherford complained that he served a congregation 'like hot iron, which cooleth when out of the fire'; yet when he was deprived for opposing episcopacy in 1626, a deputation of his parishioners travelled with him from Anwoth to Aberdeen to support him.[112] When William Cowper died in 1618, so beloved was he that 'it was thought for grief that the wives of Edinburgh came in to him and showed to him his own books', a distinctively protestant display of relics.[113] English observers remarked that Scots

> have so great a veneration for their ministers . . . that notwithstanding their natural roughness and perhaps rudeness to other sorts of travellers, these persons' [clerics'] coats are a sufficient protection and passport . . . which respect is grounded on a principle that they have, that should they in the least injure such a man, they must not expect to prosper all the days of their life. Highlandmen themselves . . . reverenced gownmen to a degree not much short of superstition.[114]

Surrounding the great preachers, there was in fact a prophetic aura that easily sustained near-superstitious reverence from Scot and Gael, rude and well-born alike. Their hortatory pronouncements edged over into the other definition of prophecy, supernatural knowledge across the bounds of time and place, derived from privileged association with the divine that conferred other extraordinary powers as well.

Among the ministers were men who saw visions, heard the voices of both God and the devil, foretold the future and worked miracles. The

111. Wodrow, *Analecta*, 2:364; Gray, v. Blair, 39–40.
112. Rutherfard, *Letters*, 6, 12, 43.
113. *Chronicle of Perth*, 3. Even less-renowned preachers had no trouble getting testimonials from their sessions that they 'never knew anything to him but soundness in doctrine, zeal and uprightness in discipline, . . . to the great comfort of them and the whole inhabitants of their whole town': CH2/716/1, f. 4 (1599); CH2/448/3, p. 351 (1620).
114. Morer, 7.

stories told about them constituted a Golden Legend for the Reformed kirk. They lived in a world populated by angels, who were, at least to them, visible and audible. Samuel Rutherford's childhood in fact began with angelic deliverance from a well into which he fell as a four-year-old: he reportedly told his distraught parents when they found him safe and sound at the well's edge, 'There was a bonny young man pulled him out by the hand. There was nobody nearby at the time, and so they concluded it was no doubt an angel.'[115] They saw visions that gave them glimpses of the future – of the nation, the kirk, themselves or others – and provided guidance in their decision-making. One spent the night praying in the snow in 1637, 'wrestling with the bishops' in his vision or imagination, and the following morning correctly predicted their downfall within a year. Cowper was directed to accept his call to Perth by a vision of the town 'in my thoughts in the night', when 'there seemed a man to lead me by the hand to a little pleasant city in a plain valley on a river's side' with all the features of Perth: 'such a sight I got of it in that vision as afterward I saw with my eyes.' The man (an angel?) led him 'a long time up and down the streets of that town', and when he woke he found he was facing the southwest, where the burgh lay.[116] Such ministers fit quite naturally into the Gaelic tradition of 'second sight', blurring lines of orthodoxy in the popular imagination, but underpinning reverence for the ministry.[117] Andrew Cant recounted a prophetic vision in 1638, when he had two sons at the Aberdeen college:

> he was looking out at his chamber window, which looked towards the [market] cross, and saw about two hundred, as [he] guessed, of the children of the town, all in white, singing and playing most melodiously, and his two sons on the head of them; and in a very little [time] after, the smallpox came to the town, and his two sons and multitudes of other children were carried off by them.

(Second sight was as much a curse as a blessing.) In addition to angels and the soon to be deceased, devils and ghosts also appeared to ministers, though Robert Blair boasted that he 'saw only one ghost [which] never troubled nor terrified [him] a whit'; he concluded that ghouls and devils

115. Robert Wodrow collected these stories into the *Analecta*, 1:57, noting that the minister James McDougal also received 'the ministry of angels'. Another angelic vision is reported at 1:101, this time bringing a message of condemnation to the minister of Montrose.

116. Wodrow, *Analecta*, 1:59; Cowper, 4; see also *Select Biographies*, 108 (Patrick Simsone's apparitions).

117. Hilda Davidson, *The Seer in Celtic and Other Traditions*, 1–24.

appear only with God's permission, to teach a lesson about their subservience to God.[118] James Ruatt told his Bothwell congregation that it was at times of especially good communication with God that he encountered 'the devil, frowning', to whom he had simply to say, 'Then coo thou devil, I'll never do thy bidding.'[119]

Ministers also reported hearing voices during their prayers. 'The Lord, by these speaking dispensations, says it to me,' Robert Blair told his friends to explain his decision to move to France – though in the event, it seems he misunderstood the voice, since he found shipboard life with uncouth Highlandmen too much to bear and not far out of Leith left the ship. (His cause was not helped by his decision to 'rebuke them for swearing and cursing', at which one 'pulled out his dirk, vowing to stab him'.) When storms arose during a likewise abortive voyage to America in 1635, the sailors so trusted Blair's voices that they referred their inclination to turn back to the preacher, who 'did fall into a fit of fainting or a kind of swarf [swoon], but shortly recovering, he was determined to be of their mind' (his severe seasickness probably explaining both the swoon and the inclination to return). John Welch's wife reported that she heard him praying aloud, pausing for God's responses. And James Ferguson reported an 'audible voice or . . . strong impression, he knew not' that he would not die during a particular outbreak of plague despite physical contact with people who were infected. The voice told him the day and hour of his eventual death, and his friends reported he 'died precisely at that day and hour'.[120]

Ministers' prophecies could be terrifying. Those sermon critics tempted to show their displeasure during the preaching might have taken warning from the story of one of John Welch's auditors, who

> cast a loaf at him when preaching. Mr Welsh [sic] stopped and told them he knew not the person that had done so, but he was persuaded there would be more persons at that person's death than there were hearing him preach that day; and everybody knows what a confluence there was at Philip Stainfield's execution, for murdering his father, and this Philip was the person that thus mocked Mr Welsh [sic] in his youth.

On the other hand, ministers could be the source of miraculous blessing as well as fatal curses. When the popular preacher of Cramond, Patrick

118. Wodrow, *Analecta*, 2:374; Blair, 8.
119. Folger ms V.a.415, f. 84v.
120. Blair, 151–52, 143; *History of . . . Reverend John Welch*, 9; Wodrow, *Analecta*, 1:67.

Simsone, lay dying in 1619, 'all the people fearing his hasty departure thronged in, . . . great multitudes from all parts of landward and the town, to be blessed of him, whose hands, albeit weak, they would have laid upon their heads – to men, wives, bairns, rich, noble and all others, which he did with great contentment, so far as he could speak.' Known for his prophetic utterances, his blessings were presumed as effective as those of the priests and saints whose paths, however disapprovingly, he and his fellow ministers trod.[121]

The preachers, like saints of old, were reputed miracle-workers. Blair's followers were convinced that he healed the sick and exorcised demons. They found him undismayed when one of his parishioners claimed that Satan had visibly appeared to him and 'stirred him up to stab' Blair in exchange for 'a great purse full of silver'. The man warned him that 'often . . . my whinger hath been drawn and kept under my cloak to obey his commends' and admitted that he often 'fell a-crying and lamenting', 'exceedingly terrified' at the devil's claim, "On Hallow-night I shall have thee, soul and body, in despite of the minister and all he will do for thee."' But Blair took the man's disorder (and the devil's challenge) in his stride. He ordered an elder to convene the people of the village to pray and sustain him during the night he agreed to stay in the house of the distraught man. There, said Blair, 'I prayed with and exhorted him, sang a psalm over and over, mixing prayer and singing till towards the morn, when he defied Satan and his works, and recovered and behaved better.' Satan never again troubled him, and Blair presumably got a good deal of credit for healing a man not altogether in touch with reality. As a result, it was the easier some years later to credit him with 'conjuring a lying spirit' that caused 'pangs like convulsions' in Lochlearn. As minister in St Andrews, he dramatically released a young ministerial candidate from a covenant with the devil signed with his own blood. This time he summoned a prayer meeting of the whole presbytery, attended by the youth, 'overcome with fear and terror'. 'In time of his [Blair's] prayer, there came a violent rushing of wind upon the church, so great that they thought the church should have fallen down about their ears, and with that the youth's paper and covenant drops down from the roof of the church among the ministers!'[122]

121. Wodrow, *Analecta*, 1:64 (Welch), 101–07 (Simsone). For other prophecies like Welch's, see 1:132 (John Walwood), 133 (Richard Cameron), 156 (George Gillespie) and 2:3 (Patrick Warner). Welch's name is variously spelled Welsh or Welch in contemporary records, often in the same document.

122. Wodrow, *Analecta*, 1:84, 103–04; Blair, 67–68, 88. The 'possessed' parishioner may simply have been an alcoholic, since Blair also 'showed him the horribleness of his

Blair's miracles pale next to John Welch's. Quite apart from his many prophecies, which 'made the people begin to think Mr Welch was an oracle', that he 'walked with God, and kept close with him', Welch won renown for raising the dead. He was living in France when a young Scottish gentleman fell ill and died in his house, at least 'to the apprehension and sense of all spectators'. Sure that he was 'no more but a carcass', they bought a coffin and prepared to dress his body for burial. Welch, however, asked them to wait for twenty-four hours. The next day, they drew the minister's attention to 'the weather being extremely hot' and asked to bury the body straightaway; Welch made them wait two more days. When 'his friends perceived he believed the young man was not really dead, but under some apoplectic fit', they called doctors who 'pinched him with pincers in the fleshy parts of his body and twisted a bow-string about his head with great force'. No signs of life being forthcoming, 'the physicians pronounced him stark dead', but Welch 'fell down before the pallet and cried to the Lord with all his might for the last time . . . till at length the dead youth opened his eyes and cried out to Mr Welch, whom he distinctly knew, "O Sir, I am all whole but my head and legs", and these were the places they had sore hurt with their pinching.'[123]

People who knew Welch's reputation must have thought twice before insulting him, since his power over life and death worked both ways. To one 'popish young gentleman' who made fun of his godly discourse at a dinner party in Edinburgh castle, Welch announced, 'observe the work of the Lord upon that profane mocker' and 'immediately [he] sank down and died beneath the table, but never returned to life again, to the great astonishment of all the company.' And it was after Welch prophetically denounced the episcopal ministers in Edinburgh that Patrick Galloway 'died easing himself upon his stool'. People who were good to him prospered; those who criticised him inevitably suffered; he could predict the plague and identify those whose prayers would stop it. It is hardly surprising that some parishioners 'were so bold as to call him no less than witch'. Others, however, described him as one might a medieval saint, 'a type of Christ', though the recorder of this sentiment notes that it was 'an expression more significant than proper'. But what is a saint without a nimbus? Welch even managed this: 'One night as he watched [prayed and meditated] in his garden very late, and some friends waiting upon

ignorance and drunkenness'. The seminarian admitted he had done a deal with the devil in despair of coming up with his own trial sermon for presbytery, being 'very unfit'. Satan, 'a man in black on the road who claimed to be a minister', gave him a sermon that he could memorise in exchange for a promise to perform unspecified service in future. Wodrow heard the story from one John Glasford of Stracathro.

123. *History of . . . Reverend John Welch*, 26–27; Wodrow, *Analecta*, 1:35–37.

him . . . one of them chanced to open a window towards the place where he walked and saw clearly a strange light surround him, and heard him speak strange words about his spiritual joy.'[124]

The preachers who reported their own prophecies and miracles, visions and voices, knew the danger of their claims. Cowper was quick to defend himself from the inevitable charges of 'the superstition of either papists or anabaptists'. He granted that 'there is no revelation now of doctrine or new article of faith to be sought in dreams', but insisted that God, 'who sleeps not, can given warnings to the souls of his servants when their bodies are sleeping'. But if the venerable Mr Cowper saw visions and heard voices, it must have seemed a bit much to the erstwhile elder and provost Alexander Peblis to have the Perth ministers criticise his practice of riddell-turning to see the future.[125] Here, within the session of a thoroughly Reformed town, we see an active competition between two systems of relating to the supernatural, two rival religious cultures. It should hardly be surprising that charmers, diviners and fairy healers drew a numerous following among the people and often escaped lightly when pursued by sessions. The line between divine and diviner was a fuzzy one. With ministers seeing the future and raising the dead, it was natural for the parishioners of Libbermuir to presume their minister's co-operation with a local witch. With Samuel Rutherford boasting that God controlled the weather on his behalf when he was summoned to High Commission but 'the sea and winds refused to give passage to the bishop of St Andrews', it was reasonable enough for the Dundonald parishioners in 1605 to hold that the late minister of Kilwinning had controlled the weather of Ayrshire.[126]

All this takes us back to the perilous nature of early modern life, in which people were desperate to know the future, to discern the divine will in time to avert disaster, to secure some modest control over their uncertain world. How much support could a minister have garnered from his anxious parishioners if he had *not* claimed the sort of power that Cowper or Blair or Welch did? This was not an age in which cool reason could often prevail; protestantism could only have achieved victory in its cultural revolution by embracing a certain amount of what we might call superstition, disguising it, if thinly, in Reformed garb. To rebaptise magic as miracle was to give the protestant clergy a fighting chance in the post-

124. *History of . . . Reverend John Welch*, 4, 10, 22–24; Wodrow, *Analecta* 1:3–4, 8, 12–13, 29–30.
125. Cowper, 4; CH2/521/7, p. 65 (1619); n. 23, above.
126. CH2/299/1, pp. 87–88; Rutherford, *Letters*, 53; *Dundonald*, 75–77.

sacerdotal system that now obtained in a still precarious world of storm and pestilence.

Their visionary aspect certainly helped ministers to win a devoted following. The more extraordinary a preacher's prophecies, the more likely he was to gain what one might as well call 'groupies', often women, who sought out their pastors constantly, followed their counsel blindly, found no fault in them, unwaveringly supported them in times of trouble and, most significantly, emulated them.[127] Like the holy men of an earlier era, the ministers inspired visions and miracles among their lay followers, spawning a whole second tier of saints with remarkable access to supernatural power. When Samuel Rutherford's indefatigable correspondent Marion M'Naught complained of 'deadness' and 'want of the bestirring power of the life of God', he promised her that she would hear the voice of God. Even the most unlearned claimed such distinction: John Broun heard the voice of the devil in warning, but also saw Christ physically present at communion. And at the other end of the social spectrum, Lord Geddart 'was first turned serious by a dream wherein he had a most lively representation of hell and saw some of his old bon-companions there.'[128] Female prophets abounded in the seventeenth century. The godly Janet Scoular, who 'had somewhat of the discerning of spirits', had the same fortune-telling capacity of one who had 'gone with the fairies', but she claimed her gift was from God and she used it to help her minister decide which woman he should marry, and to predict troubles for the kirk – a recurring refrain in both lay and clerical prophecies, and likely enough in those times of episcopal persecution of the godly ministry. When she heard two ministers preach, 'she said, "They preached well, but wanted the bonny thing" (so she termed grace), and the one fell in fornication and was deposed, the other [fell] into adultery.' The minister who recorded her prophecy was quick to add, 'this was when they were probationers, and three or four years before any miscarriage, or anything tending that way.' Women in childbirth predicted which of their children would be saved. The marquis of Argyll's wife told her husband in the 1650s that he would in due course lose his head – which, after the king's return, he did.[129] Lay visions and dreams, like those of ministers, also served to offer comfort in

127. Mullan, *Scottish Puritanism*, 148–50, 156–58, 168–70.

128. Rutherford, *Letters*, 38; Wodrow, *Analecta*, 1:70, 63.

129. Wodrow, *Analecta*, 1:60–61, 71, 67. For more on female prophesying, see Louise Yeoman, 'Covenanting Prophetesses' in *'Fantasticall Ymaginations': The Supernatural in Scottish Culture* (East Linton, forthcoming). For a glimpse of the catholic parallel, see Kent Emery, 'The Story of Recusant Women Exiled on the Continent' in *Analecta Carthusiana*, 130, 118–34.

trying times: Robert Wodrow told a story recounted by his grandmother about a time of 'famine and mortality in the land' when some of her fellow parishioners 'saw a young child about seven years old lying and dying by a dyke-side [beside a wall], which could not but move their pity', when the child rose and 'looking up cheerfully towards heaven, clapping its hands, making a tripping or dancing motion with its feet, they heard it cry, . . . "I see heaven! Lamb's days forevermore!" And with that it presently fell down and died.' At another such time, 'a young boy about four years of age . . . one day went to the door and presently returned to his mother in a kind of a rapture: "O! Mother, come to the door, and see Christ!"' When the mother followed him, she saw no one, but her child insisted, 'I saw Christ and he bade me come to him!' Soon afterwards the child fell ill and died.[130] Such visions might seem grim and unsatisfactory to us, but in an era of very numerous child deaths, they at least served to comfort bereaved parents with the assurance that their children were likely to have gone to heaven. A religious settlement that barred the miraculous and the prophetic would not have served so well. And one in which the godliest laypeople could not have hoped to follow in the paths of their clerical masters in the realms of fortune-telling and heavenly voices would have been too constraining. If presbyters were new priests, the priesthood of all believers extended even their most remarkable spiritual powers to the laity in a way that provided for their needs.

* * *

The ministry of Reformed Scotland, at once spiritually exalted, with powers that in another setting would be called magical or shamanistic, and at the same time strictly circumscribed by lay authority in the kirk, in the end served much the same function as the kirk's flexible condemnation of festivities, or maintenance of penance in expanded form. It combined real protestant innovation with enough elements of continuity to meet parishioners' needs for the comfort of a connection with the divine that was tangible, audible, visible and participatory. In the protestant clergy's combination of rational, text-based discourse in the new mode, with fervent homiletics, and visions, prophecies and miracle-working, we see reflected the multivalent religious culture of early modern Scotland. The ministry offered something for everyone. The simple and the profane needed some dramatic connection with supernatural power to deal with the uncertainty of their lives. The godly and biblically literate sought intellectual understanding of the protestant scheme, the religion of the word. And all needed an emotional outlet, a cathartic experience in the

130. Wodrow, *Analecta*, 1:114–15.

process of defining themselves as elect. The clergy needed to be both powerful and constrained by the word, both spiritually authoritative and circumscribed by the new lay priesthood. Had they not managed to be all things to all men, they would hardly have brought off the cultural revolution entailed in replacing an iconic with a logocentric religion.

Conclusion

A Puritan Nation

There has been a good deal of scholarly interest of late in the vexing problem of Scottish identity and how one might seek its historical roots.[1] It is a dangerous search, terms like 'character' and 'identity' being all too often confused with caricature and stereotype. What we tend to mean by those terms, however, is really culture – that accumulation of values, meanings, and ways of expressing and transmitting them that distinguishes a particular people from others. The identity of a group is, in effect, its culture. And fortunately, the search for cultural definition can be conducted on rather firmer ground, since things must be said and written down, constructed and enshrined, for them to be effectively inculcated.

That the kirk was after the Reformation a central defining element of Scottish culture (or if you will, national identity) is beyond debate. It was the kirk that wrought the profound cultural change that has given us a Scotland characterised (and caricatured) by abstemious self-restraint, sober but affective piety, unrelenting sabbatarianism, highly visible and rigorous social discipline, and a militant conviction of the rightness of the Calvinist cause against all enemies. It has given us the Scotland of the psalter, free of 'hard English terms and harsh phrases', and of the Covenant – a nation bonded by religious conviction, ready to take up arms for a set of meanings that a century earlier would have made no sense to any

1. Michael Lynch, 'A Nation Born Again? Scottish Identity in the Sixteenth and Seventeenth Centuries' in *Image and Identity*, ed. Dauvit Broun, R.J. Finlay and Lynch (Edinburgh, 1998), 82–104; Lynch, 'National Identity in Ireland and Scotland, 1500–1640' in *Nations, Nationalism and Patriotism in the European Past*, ed. C. Bjorn, A. Grant and K. Stringer (Copenhagen, 1990), 123–34; William Ferguson, *The Identity of the Scottish Nation: An Historic Quest* (Edinburgh, 1998); Keith Brown, 'Scottish Identity in the Seventeenth Century' and Jane Dawson, 'The Gaidhealtachd and the Emergence of the Scottish Highlands' in *British Consciousness and Identity*, ed. Brendan Bradshaw and Peter Roberts (Cambridge, 1998), 236–58, 259–300; Roger Mason, 'Imagining Scotland' and 'The Scottish Reformation' in *Scots and Britons*, 3–13, 161–86.

but a tiny group of religious radicals.[2] It has given us a people determined to claim their own ground as an elect nation distinct from a pitiably half-Reformed neighbour infected by popish ceremony and corrupted by sin undisciplined.

If Scotland's protestant cultural transformation was revolutionary, the mechanisms by which it was achieved we have found to be measured, flexible and comprehensive – and all of these precisely because its agents, the sessions, were local. Sabbath-breakers were censured not by an episcopal agent or an emissary from some far-off authority, but by their neighbours. These were men who knew their circumstances, shared many of their inclinations, and knew when to look the other way or to slap offenders on the wrist rather than come down hard on them. Child-beaters and railing spouses were admonished by the same men who would observe their subsequent behaviour and note both evidence of reform and lapses into old ways. They knew the family history well enough to discern the difference between an innocent victim and a provoker of violence, and to evaluate both sides of a discordant relationship. Being part of the community, they knew where a child could be safely fostered, and where to find a neglectful parent. Quarrels were ritually mended in the face of the neighbourhood, not in a distant court, and so were more likely to remain so, both for the sake of reputation and because the elders/neighbours would be keeping an eye out. Yuletide guisers or Midsummer merrymakers could be sternly fined and humiliated or merely chided, depending on whether they were known to be fundamentally disorderly and potentially dangerous, or just out for an uncharacteristic lark to break the tedium of a regulated life. And where the system's demands had to be modified – to meet the needs of the bereaved for holy space, or to address the anxieties of those in dangerous occupations for talismans and charms – who better than the elders to grant a lair in prohibited space or an image in the kirk? Where enforcement was local, distinctions could be made and exceptions admitted to guard against the regimen becoming truly repressive, and to ensure that it functioned constructively for the community. The system required local knowledge and discriminate oversight. But for the institution of the kirk session, the transformation it achieved would have been neither so dramatic, nor so durable.

Dramatic change relies on drama itself. For too long we have struggled to understand the Scottish Reformation as a rejection of ceremony and image, when it was instead a restructuring of both along protestant lines. The phenomenon has been hard to see, let alone sort out, because we have limited our sources. We have been so intent on the works of divines and

2. *Bannatyne Miscellany*, 1:240; Mullan, *Scottish Puritantism*, 171–207, 285–317.

official pronouncements from the national or at best presbytery level that we have failed to recognise that religious change happens (or not) in the pew. One must go to the parishes to see how prescription played out in the lives of the people. We have done so by using session minutes as an opportunity to interview the natives. When we approach this long-past culture as one would an unknown tribe, in an alien world with its own meanings and expressions; when we seek from the evidence of outward signs, gestures and ritual the order of those meanings; then that order in fact begins to come clear. Granted, we are still hampered, as an anthropologist in the field is, by our own preconceptions. As historians working with texts and artifacts rather than living people, we are further hindered by mediated testimony. But these impediments are no more insurmountable than those confronting anthropologists who must decide when their subjects are lying or distorting to win favour or keep secrets, or whether their access to all the perspectives of the tribe in question is being mediated or impeded by the authorities. We now know much more about our natives than we ever knew before, and they in turn have told us more about the Reformation than we have ever known. Taking their local witness in session minutes together with the material culture they have left us, we now have a Reformation more complex than the textbooks have offered, ridden with tension and contradiction, but for all that more credible than the received version and certainly more illuminating of the larger population's multivalent perceptions and receptions of the new ideas.

We can now recognise the 'frames of meaning' within which early modern Scots lived out their lives as a necessarily complex melding of pre-Christian and catholic survivals with new assumptions, made possible in large part by the printing press and rising literacy. If the earnestly protestant English visitor Sir William Brereton could in 1636 proclaim that the 'greatest part of the Scots are very honest and zealously religious, . . . very sound and orthodox', it was in no small measure because of the balance the kirk had managed to achieve between the 'theatrical pomp' that they so feared and the word and discipline by which they were convinced the 'kingdom of Satan might be brought under'. The flexibility with which sessions carried out their discipline, the rituals they retained, and the additional services they offered to their parishioners really had achieved a transformation of traditional culture. As the ministers themselves put it in 1618, 'other kirks abroad . . . have not been favoured with [our] measure of reformation; . . . the Lord hath been more liberal to us and requireth of us that we give example and encouragement to them to aspire to our perfection.'[3]

3. *Early Travellers*, 147; NLS ms Wod. Fol. XXVII, ff. 23, 24v (letter of the particular kirks to the kirk in Edinburgh); CH2/424/1, n.f., 4 May 1592.

Chief among those 'other kirks' was, of course, England, the perennial foil for Scottish self-definition, and in this case self-vaunting. Andrew Hunter, writing from Leith in 1586 to an English friend, boasted that 'the kingdom of Satan in this country [Scotland] is even at an end'. But he did so in order to 'comfort the brethren of England. Desire them not to be discouraged for . . . their disappointed expectations.'[4] So dramatic was the thoroughgoing Reformation of Scotland, English puritans might take hope for their own halfway job. Scotland could provide the model.

Hunter's position was not unreasonable. In view of the official settlement, it is arguable that Scotland within a couple of generations of Reformation was not merely protestant. It was a puritan nation. Its strict sabbatarianism was a standard (and unattainable) part of the English puritan agenda.[5] Its discipline was the envy of puritans to the south, banned as they were by bishops and queen from implementing classes and consistories on the Genevan/Scottish model.[6] Its piety, judging from sermons and sermon notebooks, fasts and family exercise, was exemplary of puritan affective religion, compulsive self-scrutiny and doctrinal rigour. It was controlled, as John Tawle reported to a correspondent in London in 1590, by 'they of the puritan sort', defined by archbishop Patrick Adamson of St Andrews as 'earnest and zealous, who can abide no corruption' (including his own).[7]

English puritans need not have adopted presbyterian polity to emulate this model.[8] Scotland's ecclesiastical government kept bishops in place at the Reformation, installed a few semi-episcopal 'superintendents', had episcopal authority restored by the king in 1584, and even after legal recognition of presbyteries in 1592 operated *de facto* a system of presbytery within prelacy admirable to moderate puritans in England. Bishops like William Cowper served as 'perpetual moderators' of presbyteries.[9]

4. LPL ms 3471, f. 21v. The 'brethren' were Scots clerical exiles in England as well as their English puritan sympathisers.
5. J.H. Primus, *Holy Time* (Macon, 1989), chs 7–8. For a more sanguine view, Kenneth Parker, *English Sabbath*, chs 4–6.
6. Richard Baxter's proper 'parish discipline' (over against what the 'diocesans' did) was precisely the practice of Scots sessions: *Reliquiae Baxterianae* (London, 1696), 32.
7. LPL mss 3471, f. 57, 2014 (1591), f. 190v.
8. Polity is not a necessary part of the definition of 'puritan': Peter Lake, 'Defining Puritanism – Again?' in *Puritanism: Transatlantic Perspectives on a Seventeenth-Century Anglo-American Faith* ([Boston], 1993), 3–29; Lake, 'Puritan Identities', *Journal of Ecclesiastical History* 35 (1984), 112–23; Patrick Collinson, *Godly People* (London, 1983); Todd, *Christian Humanism*, ch. 1.
9. David Mullan, *Episcopacy in Scotland: The History of an Idea 1560–1638* (Edinburgh, 1986); Donaldson, *Scottish Reformation*. A 1586 act modified the 'Black Acts' of 1584 to permit presbyteries to operate together with bishops; in 1610 episcopal authority was restored again, albeit with presbyteries retained.

More important than presbytery or bishops was the kirk's parochial administration – the one that counted for most people. This was thoroughly Genevan in rigour, personnel and co-ordination with a larger network – whether or not there happened at the moment to be bishops in view. As people in the parishes experienced it, the Reformed religion's polity above the level of the session was very nearly irrelevant. Certainly few lay people thought beyond the presbytery, or cared what the moderator's title might be. Rulings by 'bishop and presbyery' or 'bishop and synod' recur in minute books with no hint of controversy or local objection.[10] A few contemporary radicals, more obsessed with presbyterianism and episcopacy than any of the laity and surely most of the clergy, have for centuries led historians a merry chase, distracting us from what religion may have meant to its ordinary practitioners with their inordinate, often well-nigh exclusive focus on polity.[11] Turning away from Calderwood's cohort and towards parochial records has thus revealed very different concerns and in practice an agenda that would have greatly pleased English puritans like William Perkins or Richard Rogers, Brilliana Harley or Lucy Hutchinson. The Scottish kirk, in the settlement it established, was of the hotter sort.

Of course, this is not to say that every individual Scottish parishioner was a puritan. We must keep in mind that for 'puritans' to exist at all, they must have a group of recognisable 'ungodly' to measure themselves against and, more important, to corral into the kirk for sermons and to subject to discipline, on the supposition that there could well be some elect among them, and that holy writ had in any case commanded it. It is hard to fathom how puritans would have occupied themselves without the ungodly multitude as objects of their ongoing reforming endeavours. After all, protestantism is all about evangelisation and conversion, and its toughest Calvinist version was never so presumptuous as to claim omniscience about who was elect and who was not. Proclamation of the gospel was not something they had a choice about, and an orderly community made proclamation easier.

The enforcers of the discipline, moreover, had diverse motives for their service on sessions, some not altogether religious, or protestant. One thinks of those catholic elders in Aberdeen – many must simply have seen the practical advantage of rigorous moral oversight, imposed on an otherwise disorderly society. The culture of protestantism, or of the puritan nation, is in anthropological terms a structure designed to serve human needs by

10. E.g., CH2/145/3, f. 12; and throughout presbytery minutes like CH2/299/1 and CH2/294/1, and synod minutes like CH2/271/1.
11. David Calderwood chief among them, *History of the Kirk of Scotland*; Row, *History of the Kirk of Scotland*.

defining and reifying human relationships with each other as well as with the gods. What we must recognise is that cultural structures contain an array of meanings, understood somewhat differently by individuals whose aims, anxieties and relationships were not quite identical with those of their fellows. The structure, in other words, contained multivalent meanings, but it co-ordinated them into a cogent whole that could both address individual issues and unify a diverse community. The genius of Scottish protestantism was its incorporation of jokers on the stool, sailors beset by fears, bereaved parents and status-conscious lairds into the same larger, unified cultural construct as the godliest sort. What is most significant is that the *system* the authorities in Scotland fostered was emphatically puritan. As it developed and achieved the extraordinary pervasiveness and rigour that we have seen in the session minutes, its message, the meanings it embodied and enacted, redefined the culture of protestant Scotland as what any English puritan would have recognised to be the ultimate goal of the self-defined saints.

The degree to which Scots religious culture thus became distinctive in contrast to non-puritan England is revealed graphically in a 1619 exchange in London between King James and the Edinburgh bookseller James Cathkin. The immediate dispute was about church attendance on holy days, but the larger issue that emerged was the yawning chasm between English and Scottish protestantism. For all that Cathkin claimed his religion to be the same as the king's, his explanation that he had not been at church on Christmas 'because, sir, holy days have been cast out of *our kirk*, and has [sic] even been preached against since ever I can remember, and we have been taught that it was superstitious to keep them' drew a vehement denial from the king: 'The devil take you away, both soul and body! For you are none of my religion. . . . Ye are worse than Turks and Jews! I can never get an order of this people of Edinburgh. . . . The devil rive their souls and bodies all in collapse, and cast them in hell. . . . Farts on you and the session of *your kirk* both!'[12] This from a king raised in that kirk. If the Scots retained sufficient hope for progress of England's slow Reformation that they claimed common religious ground and offered encouragement to neighbouring puritans, English authorities had a clear sense of the cultural revolution that had happened in Scotland and of the deep fissure that the Tweed now represented. From their perspective, the Scots' religious identity made them as much 'other' as Jews and Turks.

12. *Bannatyne Miscellany*, 1:197–216, 'A Relation of the Imprisonment and Examination of James Cathkin', pp. 197–216, quotations from 202–03, 206 (emphases mine). Cf. NLS ms Wod Fol. XXXI, it. i, reporting popular conviction by 1618 that Yule was 'will-worship, superstition' and an impetus 'to all sorts of excess and profanation'.

Where James's son failed to see the extent and power of the difference and attempted 'ecclesiastical imperialism' in the 1637 Service Book, Scottish eyes were sufficiently opened to their own religious otherness that they would seize upon that other distinctive feature of their religious culture, the covenant, to band themselves together for war.[13]

Cathkin was not wrong, however, to posit common ground with English protestants, given that the English 'hotter sort' were after precisely what the Scots would fight for in 1638, though they joined the fray later.[14] Why had their church not achieved it? Why would even the puritan revolution of the 1640s and 1650s not manage it?[15] Quite simply, England lacked kirk sessions, the vital network of local agents so well placed to undermine the old ways, profoundly reorient religious practice and administer the new discipline systematically. But this begs a larger question. Why were sessions established in Scotland but not in the Scottish king's other Calvinist realm? We have seen that sessions were not *per se* incompatible with bishops; had English bishops been as pliant as the Scots' during the time they were re-established, they might have overseen sessions as well as presbyteries or superintendents did. Indeed, puritan-controlled towns in England came remarkably close to the Scots model.[16]

A crucial difference was that in Scotland, sessions had powerful patrons, even in conservative towns and in the countryside where most people lived. The men with power – lords and lairds, substantial burgesses and landward proprietors – had a need for the sessions' services that was not so pressing in England. There, where power had been effectively centralised for centuries, and where an efficient system of JPs had carried out the royal will since the fourteenth century, enforcing a common law and administering a relatively uniform code of order throughout the realm, it was less clear that there was a vacant slot for the sessions to fill. In comparatively decentralised Scotland, however, long plagued with royal

13. John Morrill, 'A British Patriarchy?', 209–37; Mullan, *Scottish Puritanism*, chs 6–8.
14. Dawson, 'Anglo-Scottish Protestant Culture'.
15. Christopher Durston, 'Puritan Rule and the Failure of Cultural Revolution 1645–1660' in *The Culture of English Puritanism 1560–1700*, ed. Durston and Jacqueline Eales (New York, 1996), 210–33; Derek Hirst, 'The Failure of Godly Rule in the English Republic', *P&P* 132 (1991), 33–66.
16. Mark Byford, 'The Birth of a Protestant Town' in *The Reformation in English Towns 1500–1640*, ed. Patrick Collinson and John Craig (New York, 1998), 23–47, and 'The Price of Protestantism'; David Underdown, *Fire from Heaven: Life in an English Town in the Seventeenth Century* (New Haven and London, 1992); Paul Slack, 'Poverty and Politics in Salisbury, 1597–1666' in *Crisis and Order in English Towns*, ed. Peter Clark and Slack (London, 1972), 164–203; W.J. Sheils, 'Erecting the Discipline in Provincial England: The Order of Northampton 1571' in *Studies in Church History* 8, ed. James Kirk (Oxford, 1991), 331–45.

minorities and weak monarchs, and without an effective system of JPs until the later seventeenth century, there was a crying need for a mechanism to impose order and uniformity in the localities.[17] What the heritors found in the sessions was an idea whose time, in Scotland, had come. The timing was the more fortuitous because it coincided with the expansion of small proprietorships resulting from the feuing movement: an emerging category of new landholders anxious for a greater voice in administering local affairs found a natural outlet for their ambitions in kirk sessions.[18]

With a cogent theory already worked out in Geneva, sessions were first established in Scottish burghs, where they adopted many of the time-tested procedures of burgh and guild courts, and then provided a model readily adaptable to the landward surrounding urban centres, and later to the more distant countryside, eventually even to the Highlands and Isles. The burgh model proved flexible, adjusting demands and mechanisms to local custom; borrowing ancient Scots devices of oath-taking, bonding and arbitration; even (though slowly) adopting Gaelic elements in the Highlands.[19] But

17. JPs were established in Scotland by an act of 1609 but were not effectively in place until the end of the century. Heritors had traditionally been responsible for their own tenants, cottars and servants in quite independent feudal courts of barony and regality, leaving lesser proprietors, lairds and 'bonnet lairds' (owner-occupiers who worked their own lands) dependent on private justice. Heritable jurisdiction was not abolished until 1747.
18. Feuing was a movement well underway in the fifteenth century in which substantial holders exchanged what amounts to a hereditary leasehold (a 'feu', without parallel in England) for ready cash. It transformed a rural economy, in which it was rare (compared with England) for small plots to come onto the market. In Scotland, a larger percentage of the population had access to some land (cf. England's large wage-labour population), but a much smaller portion held their own heritable property. For feuing and its social implications, see Sanderson, *Scottish Rural Society*, 64–107; and Ian D. Whyte, *Scotland before the Industrial Revolution* (London, 1995), 98, 107, 150–58. A systematic comparison of English and Scots law, tenure and ecclesiastical structures is beyond the scope of this study, but would surely repay the effort.
19. Donald Meek, 'The Reformation and Gaelic Culture: Perspectives on Patronage, Language and Literature in John Carswell's Translation of "The Book of Common Order"' in *The Church in the Highlands*, ed. James Kirk (Edinburgh, 1998), 37–62 (noting adoption by the reformers in the west of not only Gaelic language and rhetoric, but also greater deference to the ecclesiastical authority of secular magistrates, or chiefs); Dawson, 'Calvinism in the Gaidhealtachd'. It is not hard to see a model for presbyteries in the Conventions of Royal Burghs that commenced in the later fifteenth century, meeting four times yearly. Session adoption of burgh court procedure (summons to compearance, depositions, cautioners, sentence and fining conventions, record-keeping) is clear from a glance at the burgh and guild court books, e.g., *The Gild Court Book of Dunfermline*; *The Perth Guildry Book*; PL ms B59/16/1; PMAG mss 2/2, 4 (Tailor Incorporation minutes, 1530–1734).

flexibility never overwhelmed the common, defining features that made sessions effective components of the larger network of presbyteries and synods, able to enforce a common culture – a new common identity – of protestantism. In the process of promoting the religion of the word, they maintained order and reduced local violence, circumscribed the sexual misbehaviour that had long troubled the authorities, and even provided the basis for a system of poor relief that included the strict oversight of behaviour and prohibition of idleness mandated by the English system. Quite aside from their immediate religious goals, sessions had achieved a virtual golden age of peace in the eyes of one admittedly starry-eyed Scot in 1625: 'Our commons have turned their swords into scythes, our burgesses rest under the shadows of the green trees, our Borders have left their violent riding, our Highlands their thieving, our Isles their traitorous murdering', all under the oversight of the elders.[20]

The heritors found a variety of their immediate practical needs satisfied by the institution. By giving the sessions oversight of the poor and responsibility to collect 'voluntary' charity, they avoided the heavy rates of the English poor laws that (given less broadly disbursed land ownership in Scotland) would have burdened them disproportionately.[21] By letting the sessions settle disputes and punish the disorderly, they were able to reduce the burden of their own exercise of justice for their dependants. By sitting officially on the session, as they did, they had a voice whenever they wanted it, but much of the drudgery – searching, and 'dealing with' offenders – they could leave to other elders. They could be confident that the session would maintain their authority: business of political import was routinely cancelled if 'the gentlemen heritors' or 'the master men were absent, at whose returning they would do as becomes', as the Dron clerk wrote.[22]

At the same time, by distributing power (with its attendant status) broadly among the elders, they could rest assured that the work would be taken on more or less willingly. We have seen that all sorts of people, even the great, submitted to kirk discipline, sometimes to demonstrate their own protestant piety and respectability, or perhaps to underpin by their own example the authority of a body that served well their ambitions for a more orderly society. A session's millers and skinners thus bore real authority. But we have also seen that this inclusiveness did not particularly under-

20. NLS ms Wod. Qu. XX, f. 141.
21. Rosalind Mitchison, *The Old Poor Law in Scotland: The Experience of Poverty, 1574–1845* (Edinburgh, 2000), 1–21.
22. CH2/93/1, f. 24. Menmuir always included the lairds in meetings for 'keeping of good neighbourhood': CH2/264/1, ff. 10v, 13v.

mine hierarchy, the status of the great still displayed in the fabric of the kirk – seats, arms, monuments – as well as their power in the session, and now more than ever free from the threat of clerical domination. English critics might condemn the settlement as 'their anarchy here established', but it was clearly more established than anarchic, both for its disciplinary victims and its beneficiaries.[23] As a Glaswegian preacher pronounced, 'The imaginary cords that seem to fasten men to heaven have tied things here below surer together than any other obligation.'[24] The distinctive features of Scots land tenure, law and politics thus created both a need for and a receptivity to the new institution of sessions that England lacked, with disastrous results for the religious ambitions of English puritans.

When division between the two realms finally came in 1637–38, it was over an issue easily construed as a frontal assault on Scottish identity – the forcible introduction of an English-style liturgy by bishops not of Cowper's ilk, but shaped by Laud's efforts to minimise predestinarian theology and restore ceremonies.[25] Opponents of the established, arguably puritan kirk, they were ecclesiological aliens in that kirk, and perceived as agents of foreign corruption. At the centre of the National Covenant was the Scottishness of a now established puritan culture, a culture that embraced the nation in its network of sessions and presbyteries, that imposed a remarkably uniform discipline on the visibly ungodly, that had come, over time, to define Scotland. Looking at that Covenant from the perspectives of those who raised their hands and swore it in the local kirks has taken our attention away from the theological intricacies of an inclusive ecclesiology at odds with a predestinarian soteriology over which so much ink has been spilt, and has focused it instead on the ordinary believers' understanding of themselves as part of a chosen people ready to do battle for what had become so absolutely central to their identity.

That identity, and the melding of old and new that achieved it, were as confusing to contemporary observers beyond Scotland's borders as to modern historians. As one Englishman put it in the 1630s, 'We consider the Scottish affairs as country people do the moon. Some think it to be

23. An oxymoronic judgment by Robert Naunton in 1589: LPL ms 2014, f. 168.
24. Folger ms G.a.11, p. 65.
25. Mullan, *Scottish Puritanism*, 224–43, finds little outright Arminianism in Scotland and he is probably right, but the complaints brought in the 1630s against ceremonialists like Maxwell, Sibbald and Forbes do include their theological positions on free will. Morrill, 'Ecclesiastical Imperialism', 209–37, argues that imposition of the service book was an effort at congruity across the border rather than Anglicisation of Scottish religion, but contemporary Scots would have found the distinction artificial: *Scotland's Supplication and Complaint*; and the parochial complaint in NLS mss Wod. Fol. LXI–LXIII.

no bigger than a bushel, and others (contrariwise) imagine it a vast world, with strange things undiscovered in it.'[26] But as Clifford Geertz has reminded us, a culture is not the monolithic entity we might prefer to fill our small, predetermined categories; it rather consists in 'the faults and fissures that seem to mark out the landscape of collective selfhood'. The culture of protestant Scotland, like any other, is comprised by 'the recurrence of familiar divisions, persisting arguments, standing threats, the notion that whatever else may happen, the order of difference must be somehow maintained'.[27] When we acknowledge the diversity that received protestantism in sixteenth-century Scotland – Gaelic and Scots, rural and urban, elite and unlearned, male and female, pious and worldly – together with the amalgam of tradition and innovation that so remarkably joined them in a visible, covenanted protestant identity, those 'strange things undiscovered' begin to make better sense, and the kirk to look a bit less like the moon.

26. Foger ms G.a.11, p. 65.
27. Geertz, *Available Light*, 249–50.

Bibliography

Part I: Manuscript Sources

National Archives of Scotland, Edinburgh (General Register House)

CH2-prefixed manuscripts (kirk session minute books unless otherwise noted)

1/1	Aberdeen presbytery	1598–1610
4/1	Aberlady	1632–45
21/5	Auchterderran sermon notes	1613–28
32/1	Belhelvie	1623–41
37/1	Bolton	1640–83
39/1	Botriphnie	1627–83
77/1	Culross Abbey kirk	1629–46
84/28	Dalkeith (St Nicholas)	1610–17
89/1	Deer presbytery	1602–21
93/1	Dron	1632–82
96/1	Duffus	1631–48
100/1	Dunbarney	1602–31
121/1–3	Edinburgh presbytery	1586–1607
122/1–3	Canongate	1613–49
122/76	Canongate (collections)	1647–1750
122/181	Canongate	1564–67
141/1	Trinity College kirk, Edinburgh	1626–38
144/1	Elgin presbytery	1635–51
145/1–6	Elgin kirk	1584–1643
146/1	Ellon presbytery	1597–1607
147/1	Ellon kirk	1603–04
154/1–2	Fife synod	1610–57
185/1–3	Haddington presbytery	1587–1627
191/1	Inveravon	1630–49
198/1–2	Jedburgh presbytery	1606–44
242/1–2	Linlithgow presbytery	1610–32
258/1	Markinch	1626–46
264/1	Menmuir	1622–1701
266/1	Mid-Calder (St John's kirk)	1604–49
271/1	Moray synod	1623–44
276/1	Newbattle	1616–28
283/1	Newton	1630–40

285/1	North Berwick	1608–16
294/1–2	Paisley presbytery	1602–47
295/1	Peebles presbytery	1596–1624
299/1–2	Perth presbytery	1618–47
326/1	Scoonie	1626–40
327/1	Selkirk presbytery	1607–19
338/1	Stow	1626–46
359/1	Tyninghame	1615–50
377/1	Yester	1613–43
383/1	Liberton	1639–78
390/1	Dysart	1619–42
400/1	Falkirk	1617–40
424/1	Dalkeith presbytery	1582–1630
442/74	Kirkwall (St Magnus), Orkney	1626–49
448/1–5	Aberdeen (St Nicholas)	1562–1638
450/1	Edinburgh General Kirk	1574–75
471/1	Lasswade	1615–37
472/1–2	Kinghorn	1581–1647
521/1–8/1–2	Perth	1577–1642
523/1	Burntisland	1602–67
529/1	Mortlach	1623–54
553/1	Inverness presbytery	1632–44
621/1	North Leith	1605–42
636/34	Kirkcaldy	1614–45
699/1	Longside	1620–33
716/1–3	South Leith	1597–1642
718/1–4	St Cuthbert's, Edinburgh	1586–1629
722/1–5	Stirling presbytery	1581–1640
1020/1	Aberdeen (Old Machar)	1621–39
1026/1	Stirling (Holy Rude)	1597–1614
1115/1	Boharm & Dundurcas	1634–52
1142/1–2	Fraserburgh	1612–61
1173/1	Old Kelso	1622–47
1463/1–2	Innerwick	1608–95

CH1/5/7	Andrew Melville verses
CH1/5/115	Thomas Burns notebooks
CH1/25	John Lawrie letter
CH8/39	presentation letter for David Barclay, 1590
CH8/41, 42	miscellaneous ecclesiastical documents
CH8/54	Dumfries, 1606
CH8/62	excommunications, Dumfries, 1611–20
CH8/64	excommunication, Borthwick parish, 1615
CH8/69	Alex Inglis accounts, 1623
CH8/87	letters of Zachary Boyd, 1632–37
CH8/113	confession of Margaret Nimmo
CH8/153	petition to erect a desk
GD/1/395/6	notes on Andrew Ramsay sermons, 1614–42
GD/16/46/25	address by James Cunningham, minister of Cumnock, to Council, 1637
RH2/1/35	Edinburgh General Kirk, 1574–75

NAS, Edinburgh (New Register House)

OPR310/1	Monifieth kirk session, 1560s	

Mitchell Library, Glasgow

CH2/171/1–2	Glasgow presbytery	1592–1608

Ayrshire Archives Centre, Ayr

CH2/562/1	Kirkoswald	1617–60
CH2/751/1–2	Ayr	1604–21
CH2/809/1	Monkton	1615–45

St Andrews University Library

CH2-prefixed manuscripts

Crail/1	Crail	1604–84
150/1	Ferryport-on-Craig	1640–74
210/1	Kilconquhar	1637–53
277/1/Box 1/8	Newburgh	1629–97
278/1	Newburn	1628–87
316/1	St Andrews	1638
548/1	Monimail	1631–44
624/1–3	Anstruther Wester	1578, 1587–93, 1598–1605
819/1	Kingsbarns	1630–48
1056/1	St Monans	1597–1640
ms 30386	Sermon notebook, seventeenth century	
ms 30451	Fife synod, undated	
Hay Fleming Box 53, it. ii	manuscript sermon notebook and commonplace book, seventeenth century	
unnumbered ms	St Andrews presbytery	1585–1605, 1641–56

National Library of Scotland, Edinburgh

Advocates mss

29.2.8	church documents, including papers of the bishop of Dunblane, 1620s; Melville letters; excerpts from St Andrews presbytery minutes, 1596–97; draft on teaching of the catechism in Edinburgh, 1581; 1593 complaint from congregation of Clerkington
31.1.1–1a	transcription of excerpts from Perth kirk session minutes, with comments by James Scott
33.7.23	history of the College of Edinburgh to 1647, Thomas Craufurd

Wodrow mss

Fol. XVI	Southeast parish of Edinburgh, session register 1626–38
Fol. XXV	church documents, 1631–51, including Wilkie/Balcanquhal correspondence
Fol. XXVII	church papers, 1612–92, including William Cowper discourse before Perth presbytery, 1612
Fol. XLII	correspondence of Andrew Melville, William Cowper, John Hume, 1613–20s; 1583 presbytery visitation of Holyroodhouse
Fol. XLVIII	sermons 1638–43
Fol. L	rhymed libel against the ministers of Edinburgh, 1592
Fol. LXI	church documents, 1549–1638, including process against James Forsyth, minister of Kilpatrick, 1638

Fol. LXII	1638 processes against David Mitchell, George Hannay, Thomas Forrester
Fol. LXIII	1639 processes against Arminian ministers
Fol. LXIV	observations concerning Lent, conversion, repentance
Fol. LXVI	episcopal correspondence; Balcanquhal papers
Fol. LXIX	church documents, correspondence of Lord Binning
Oct. VII	diary of Robert Birrel, burgess of Edinburgh, 1532–1605
Oct. IX	church documents, 1585–1688, including extracts from Paisley presbytery minutes
Oct. XXVI	catechisms, examinations, synod exercise, sermon notes, 1634–51
Oct. XXVII	papers of Thomas Wylie, minister of Fenwick, 1552–1653
Quarto XIV	autobiography and diary of James Melville, minister of Kilrenny
Quarto XX	church documents, 1584–1634, including the reader's service; Boyd letters, 1629; sermon notes
Quarto XXI	church documents, 1560–1606, including excerpts from minutes of Hamilton and Edinburgh presbyteries, 1595–1606
Quarto XXIX	sonnet by Lady Culross to John Welsh, 1606; Rutherford letters; John Livingstone correspondence
Quarto LXXXIV	papers of John Fergushill, minister of Ayr, 1564–1633
Quarto C	papers of John Brown, minister of Wamphray, 1620–75

Other NLS mss

2782	Glasgow session records
15948	Sydserf papers

A.K. Bell Library, Perth

B59/12/2, 9	Perth burgh court and council records	1543–1685, 1580–87
B59/16/1	register of acts of the Perth council	1601–22
B59/28/7–21	documents concerning ecclesiastical finances	1577–1617

Perth Museum and Art Gallery

ms 2/2/35–43	Perth convener's court book	1560–1632
ms 86/12	kirk receipts, fragments of session book	1583–99, 1692
ms 315	transcriptions of witchcraft cases	1623
ms 345	documents concerning ministerial pensions	1589–96

Folger Shakespeare Library, Washington, D.C.

ms V.a.415	anonymous seventeenth-century sermon notebook, Bothwell
ms G.a.11	Robert Naunton's 'Answer to a gentleman of Norfolke concerning the Scottish business', 1639

Lambeth Palace Library, London

ms 2014	Robert Naunton, 1589
ms 3470	William Bruton letter, 1589
ms 3471	letters to Canterbury concerning Scottish ecclesiastical affairs

Bodleian Library, Oxford

Rawl. C.584	anonymous Scottish commonplace book, early seventeenth century

Part II: Printed Primary Sources

Act Book of the Archdeacon of Taunton, ed. C. Jenkins, Taunton, 1928.

Acts of the Lords of Council in Public Affairs, 1501–04, ed. R.K. Hannay, London, 1934.

Ancient Criminal Trials in Scotland, ed. Robert Pitcairn, 3 vols, Edinburgh, 1833.

Annals of Aberdeen, ed. William Kennedy, Aberdeen, 1818.

Bannatyne Miscellany, I, Edinburgh, 1827.

Baxter, Richard, *The Reformed Pastor*, Edinburgh, 1974 (orig. 1656).

———, *Reliquiae Baxterianae*, London, 1696.

Birnie, William, *The Blame of Kirk-Buriall, Tending to Cemeteriall Civilitie*, ed. W.B.D.D. Turnball, Edinburgh, 1833.

Blair, Robert, *The Life of Mr Robert Blair, Minister of St Andrews, Containing his Autobiography from 1593–1636*, ed. Thomas M'Crie, Edinburgh, 1848.

The Books of Assumption of the Thirds of Benefices: Scottish Ecclesiastical Rentals at the Reformation, ed. James Kirk, Oxford, 1995.

The Book of Common Order of the Church of Scotland, Commonly Known as Knox's Liturgy, ed. George Sprott, Edinburgh, 1868.

The Book of Perth, ed. John Parker Lawson, Edinburgh, 1847.

Boyd, Zachary, *The Last Battell of the Soule in Death*, Edinburgh, 1629.

———, *The Balme of Gilead*, Edinburgh, 1633.

———, *1. Crosses, 2. Comforts, 3. Counsels Needfull to Be Considered and Carefully to Be Laid Up in the Hearts of the Godly, in these Boisterous Broiles, and Bloody Times*, Glasgow, 1643.

———, *Selected Sermons*, ed. David W. Atkinson, Aberdeen, 1989.

Bruce, Robert, *Sermons*, ed. William Cunningham, Edinburgh, 1843.

———, *The Mystery of the Lord's Supper: Sermons on the Sacrament Preached in the Kirk of Edinburgh in A.D. 1589*, London, 1958.

The Buik of the Kirk of the Canagait 1564–1567, ed. Alma B. Calderwood, Edinburgh, 1961.

Calderwood, David, *Resolutions for Kneeling*, Edinburgh, 1619.

———, *The History of the Kirk of Scotland*, ed. Thomas Thomson and D. Laing, 8 vols, Edinburgh, 1842–49 (orig. 1678).

Calvin, John, *Institutes of the Christian Religion*, ed. John T. McNeill, tr. Ford Lewis Battles, Philadelphia, 1960.

Charters, Statutes and Acts of the Town and Senatus, 1582–1858, ed. Alexander Morgan, Edinburgh, 1937.

The Chronicle of Perth: A Register of Remarkable Occurrences, Chiefly Connected with that City, from the Year 1210 to 1668, ed. James Maidment, Edinburgh, 1831.

Churchwarden's Presentments . . . Archdeaconry of Chichester, ed. Hilda Johnstone, Lewes, Sussex, 1947.

Craig, John, *A Short Sum of the Whole Catechism*, ed. T.G. Law as *Craig's Catechism*, Edinburgh, 1883.

Cowper, William, *Workes*, London, 1629.

Craufurd, Thomas, *The History of the University of Edinburgh from 1580 to 1646*, Edinburgh, 1808.

Davidson, John, *Forme of Familiar Instruction and Examination of Rude People . . . Practised in the New-Erected Kirk of Salt-Prestoun* in *Three Scottish Reformers*, ed. Charles Rogers, London, 1876.

———, *Some Helpes for Young Schollers in Christianity, as They Are in Use and Taught, Partly, at the Examination Before the Communion: & Partly in the Ordinarie Catechisme Every*

Sabbath-Day, in the New Kirk of Salt-Preston (1602), in *Three Scottish Reformers*, ed. Charles Rogers, London, 1876.

Depositions and Other Ecclesiastical Proceedings from the Courts of Durham, London, 1845.

A Directory for the Publique Worship of God, London, 1644.

Dundonald Parish Records: The Session Book of Dundonald, 1602–1731, ed. Henry Paton, n.p., 1936.

Early Records of the Burgh of Aberdeen, 1317, 1398–1407, ed. W.C. Dickinson, Edinburgh, 1957.

Early Travellers in Scotland, ed. P. Hume Brown, New York, 1970 (orig. Edinburgh, 1891).

Extracts from the Accounts of the Common Good of Various Burghs in Scotland, Relative to Payments for Schools and Schoolmasters . . . 1557–1634, Miscellany of the Maitland Club, Edinburgh, 1840.

Extracts from the Kirk Session Book of John Welch, 1604–1605, ed. A. MacKenzie, Ayr, 1966.

Extracts from the Records of the Burgh of Aberdeen 1398–1625, ed. John Stuart, 2 vols, Aberdeen, 1844–48.

Extracts from the Records of the Burgh of Edinburgh 1403–1589, 4 vols, Edinburgh, 1869–82.

Extracts from the Records of the Burgh of Edinburgh, 1604–1626, ed. M. Wood, Edinburgh, 1931.

Extracts from the Records of the Royal Burgh of Stirling, ed. R. Renwick, Glasgow, 1887.

Familie Exercise; or, The Service of God in Families, Edinburgh, 2nd edn, 1641.

The First Book of Discipline, ed. James K. Cameron, Edinburgh, 1972.

The Forme and Maner of Examination befoir the Admission to the Tabill of the Lord, Edinburgh, 1581.

The Forme of Prayers and Ministration of the Sacraments, Used in the English Church at Geneva and Approved and Received by the Churche of Scotland, . . . With the Whole Psalmes of David in English Meter, Edinburgh, 1565.

Gild Court Book of Dunfermline 1433–1579, ed. E. Torrie, Edinburgh, 1986.

Gray, Andrew, *Select Sermons . . . Including Three Sermons Preached at the Celebration of the Lord's Supper at Bothwell, as also Exhortation and Discourses at Serving of Tables at the Communion at Kirkliston*, 2nd edn, Falkirk, 1792 (orig. 1649).

Hamilton, Patrick, *Catechisme*, ed. Alexander F. Mitchell, Edinburgh, 1882.

Henderson, Alexander, *The Government and Order of the Church of Scotland*, Edinburgh, 1641.

The History of the Life and Sufferings of the Rev. John Welch . . . Minister of Ayr, with Some Prophetical Letters Wrote by him when Prisoner in Blackness, Falkirk, 1780.

James VI, *Daemonologie*, ed. G.B. Harrison, Edinburgh, 1996, orig. 1597.

Johnston, Archibald, *Diary of Sir Archibald Johnston of Wariston, 1632–1639*, I, ed. George Morison Paul, Edinburgh, 1911; II, ed. D.M. Fleming, Edinburgh, 1919.

Kirk, Robert of Aberfoyle, *The Secret Commonwealth*, Edinburgh, 1691.

Knox, John, *Works*, ed. D. Laing, 6 vols, Edinburgh, 1846–64.

Livingstone, John, *Autobiography*, in *Select Biographies*, I, ed. W.K. Tweedie, Edinburgh, 1845.

———, *Sacramental Discourses* in *Sermons Delivered in Times of Persecution*, Edinburgh, 1880.

Livingstone, William, *The Conflict in Conscience of a Dear Christian, Named Bessie Clarksone, in the Parish of Lanark*, Edinburgh, 1632.

Lowther, C., *Our Journal into Scotland*, Edinburgh, 1894.

Major, John, *History of Greater Britain*, Edinburgh, 1892.

Melville, James, *A Spirituall Propine of a Pastour to his People*, Edinburgh, [1598].

———, *Diary, 1556–1601*, ed. G. Kinloch, Edinburgh, 1829.

———, *Autobiography and Diary of James Melville, Minister of Kilrenny*, ed. Robert Pitcairn, Edinburgh, 1842.

Milton, John, *Works*, ed. F.A. Patterson, New York, 1931.
Minutes of the Synod of Argyll, 2 vols, Edinburgh, 1943–44.
Miscellany of the Maitland Club, vols I–II, Edinburgh, 1832–40.
Miscellany of the New Spalding Club I, Aberdeen, 1890.
Miscellany of the Spalding Club, 5 vols, Aberdeen, 1841–52.
Miscellany of the Spottiswoode Society, 2 vols, Edinburgh, 1844–45.
Miscellany of the Wodrow Society, ed. D. Laing, I, Edinburgh, 1844.
Morer, Thomas, *A Short Account of Scotland*, London, 1702.
The Obit Book of the Church of St John the Baptist, Ayr, ed. James Paterson, Edinburgh, 1848.
The Order and Doctrine of the Generall Faste, appointed be the Generall Assemblie of the Kirkes of Scotland (1565), reprinted in *The Book of Common Order of the Church of Scotland*, Edinburgh, 1868.
Original Letters Relating to the Ecclesiastical Affairs of Scotland, ed. D. Laing, 2 vols, Edinburgh, 1851.
The Perth Guildry Book 1542–1601, ed. Marion Stavert, Edinburgh, 1993.
The Poems of Alexander Scott, ed. James Cranstoun, Edinburgh, 1896.
The Poems of William Dunbar, ed. Priscilla Bawcutt, 2 vols, Glasgow, 1998.
The Presbyterian Movement in the Reign of Queen Elizabeth as Illustrated by the Minute Book of the Dedham Classis, 1582–1589, ed. R.G. Usher, Camden Society, 3rd ser., 8, 1905.
Records of the Burgh of Peebles, Edinburgh, 1872.
Records of the Diocese of Argyll and the Isles 1560–1860, ed. J.B. Craven, Kirkwall, 1907.
Records of Elgin, ed. W. Cramond, 2 vols, Edinburgh, 1903.
Records of the Kirk of Scotland, ed. Alexander Peterkin, Edinburgh, 1838.
Records of the Meeting of the Exercise of Alford, Edinburgh, 1847.
Records of Old Aberdeen 1498–1903, 2 vols, Aberdeen, 1909.
Records of the Presbyteries of Inverness and Dingwall 1643–1688, ed. William MacKay, Edinburgh, 1896.
Records of the Synod of Lothian and Tweeddale, 1589–96, 1640–49, ed. James Kirk, Edinburgh, 1977.
Register of the Ministers, Elders and Deacons of St Andrews 1559–1600, ed. D.H. Fleming, 2 vols, Edinburgh, 1889–90.
Register of Ministers, Exhorters and Readers, and of their Stipends, after the Period of the Reformation, Edinburgh, 1830.
Register of the Privy Council of Scotland 1545–1625, ed. J.H. Burton and D. Masson, 1st ser., 14 vols, Edinburgh, 1877–98; ed. D. Masson and P. Hume Brown, 2nd ser., 1625–43, 7 vols, 1899–1906.
Reports on the State of Certain Parishes in Scotland Made to His Majesty's Commissioners for Plantation of Kirks . . . 1627, Edinburgh, 1835.
Rollock, Robert, *Certaine Sermons upon Severall Places of the Epistles of Paul*, Edinburgh, 1599.
———, *Lectures upon the Epistle of Paul to the Colossians*, London, 1603.
———, *Select Works*, ed. and tr. William M. Gunn, 2 vols, Edinburgh, 1844–49.
Row, John, *The History of the Kirk of Scotland*, ed. D. Laing, Edinburgh, 1842.
Rutherford, Samuel, *Christ Dying and Drawing Sinners to Himself*, Edinburgh, 1647.
———, *Joshua Redivivus, or Mr Rutherfoords Letters*, ed. Robert McWard, Edinburgh, 1664.
———, *Fourteen Communion Sermons*, ed. Andrew Bonar, Glasgow, 1877.
———, *Letters*, Edinburgh, 1984 (from the 1891 edn).
Scotland's Supplication and Complaint Against the Book of Common Prayer (Otherwise Laud's Liturgy), ed. David Hay Fleming, Edinburgh, 1927.

The Scots Confession, 1560, ed. G.D. Henderson, Edinburgh, 1937.
The Second Book of Discipline, ed. James Kirk, Edinburgh, 1980.
Select Biographies, ed. W.K. Tweedie, Edinburgh, 1845.
Spalding, John, *The History of the Troubles and Memorable Transactions in Scotland and England from 1624 to 1645*, ed. James Skene, 2 vols, Edinburgh, 1828–29.
Spottiswoode, John, *History of the Church of Scotland*, 3 vols, Edinburgh, 1847–51.
Statutes of the Scottish Church, 1225–1559, ed. D. Patrick, Edinburgh, 1907.
Stirling Presbytery Records 1581–1587, ed. James Kirk, Edinburgh, 1981.
Struther, William, *Scotland's Warning; or, A Treatise of Fasting*, Edinburgh, 1628.
Visitation of the Diocese of Dunblane and Other Churches, 1586–89, ed. J. Kirk, Edinburgh, 1984.
Welch, John, *A Reply against M. Gilbert Browne Priest*, Edinburgh, 1602.
———, *Forty-Eight Select Sermons*, Glasgow, 1771.
Wodrow, Robert, *Biographical Collections*, Edinburgh, 1834.
———, *Analecta; or, Materials for a History of Remarkable Providences, Mostly Relating to Scotch Ministers and Christians*, 4 vols, Edinburgh, 1842–43.
———, *Selected Biographies*, Edinburgh, 1845.
Zurich Letters, ed. H. Robinson, Cambridge, 1842–45.

Part III: Secondary Sources

Aldis, H.G., *A List of Books Printed in Scotland before 1700, Including those Printed Furth of the Realm for Scottish Booksellers*, Edinburgh, 1973.
Archer, Ian, *The Pursuit of Stability: Social Relations in Elizabethan London*, Cambridge, 1991.
Backscheider, Paula, *Spectacular Politics: Theatrical Power and Mass Culture in Early Modern England*, Baltimore, 1993.
Bakhtin, Mikhail, *Rabelais and his World*, tr. H. Iswolsky, Cambridge, Mass., 1968.
———, *Speech Genres and Other Late Essays*, tr. V.W. McGee, Austin, 1986.
Banks, Mary McLeod, *British Calendar Customs: Scotland*, 3 vols, London, 1937–41.
Bannerman, John, 'Literacy in the Highlands' in *The Renaissance and Reformation in Scotland*, ed. Ian Cowan and Duncan Shaw, Edinburgh, 1983, 214–35.
Bardgett, Frank, D., 'Dilapidation of Church Property in Angus after 1560', *IR* 40 (1989), 2–23.
———, *Scotland Reformed: The Reformation in Angus and the Mearns*, Edinburgh, 1989.
Barry, Jonathan, 'Keith Thomas and the Problem of Witchcraft' in *Witchcraft in Early Modern Europe*, ed. Barry, M. Hester and Gareth Roberts, Cambridge, 1998.
Basso, K. and S. Feld, eds, *Senses of Place* (Santa Fe, 1996).
Bawcutt, Priscilla, 'The Art of Flyting', *Scottish Literary Journal* 10 (1983), 5–24.
———, 'A Miniature Anglo-Scottish Flying', *Notes and Queries* 233 (1988), 441–44.
———, *Dunbar the Makar*, Oxford, 1992.
Beale, J.M., *History of the Burgh and Parochial Schools of Fife*, Edinburgh, 1983.
Bell, Catherine, *Ritual Theory, Ritual Practice*, Oxford, 1992.
———, *Ritual: Perspectives and Dimensions*, Oxford, 1997.
Binski, Paul, *Medieval Death: Ritual and Representation*, London, 1996.
Bord, Janet and Colin, *Sacred Waters: Holy Wells and Water Lore in Britain and Ireland*, London, 1985.

Bossy, John, 'Blood and Baptism: Kinship, Community and Christianity from the Fourteenth to the Seventeenth Centuries', *Studies in Church History* 10 (1973), 129–43.

———, 'The Social History of Confession in the Age of the Reformation', *Transactions of the Royal Historical Society*, 5th ser., 25 (1975), 21–38.

———, 'Holiness and Society', *P&P* 75 (1977), 110–37.

———, 'The Mass as a Social Institution 1200–1700', *P&P* 100 (1983), 29–61.

———, *Christianity in the West 1400–1700*, Oxford, 1985.

———, *Peace in the Post-Reformation*, Cambridge, 1998.

———, ed., *Disputes and Settlements: Law and Human Relations in the West*, Cambridge, 1983.

Boswell, John, *The Kindness of Strangers: The Abandonment of Children in Western Europe from Late Antiquity to the Renaissance*, Chicago, 1998.

Bremmer, Jan and Herman Roodenburg, *A Cultural History of Gesture*, Ithaca, NY, 1991.

Brigden, Susan, *London and the Reformation*, Oxford, 1989.

Bristol, Michael, *Carnival and Theatre*, New York, 1985.

Brown, Keith, *Bloodfeud in Scotland 1573–1625: Violence, Justice and Politics in an Early Modern Society*, Edinburgh, 1986.

———, 'The Laird, his Daughter, her Husband and the Minister: Unravelling a Popular Ballad' in *People and Power in Scotland*, ed. Roger Mason and Norman Macdougall, Edinburgh, 1992, 104–25.

———, 'Scottish Identity in the Seventeenth Century' in *British Consciousness and Identity*, ed. Brendan Bradshaw and Peter Roberts, Cambridge, 1998.

Burke, Peter, *Popular Culture in Early Modern Europe*, New York, 1978.

———, 'The Repudiation of Ritual in Early Modern Europe' in *The Historical Anthropology of Early Modern Italy*, Cambridge, 1987, 223–38.

———, *History and Social Theory*, Ithaca, N.Y., 1992.

———, *Varieties of Cultural History*, Oxford, 1997.

Burns, Thomas, *Old Scottish Communion Plate*, Edinburgh, 1892.

Buttimer, Anne and David Seamon, eds, *The Human Experience of Space and Place*, New York, 1980.

Byford, Mark, 'The Birth of a Protestant Town' in *The Reformation in English Towns 1500–1640*, ed. Patrick Collinson and John Craig, New York, 1998.

Bynum, Caroline Walker, 'Introduction: The Complexity of Symbols' in *Gender and Religion: On the Complexity of Symbols*, ed. Bynum, S. Harrell and P. Richman, Boston, 1986, 1–20.

———, *Fragmentation and Redemption*, New York, 1991.

Cameron, J.K., 'The Refoundation of the University in 1579', *The Alumnus Chronicle of the University of St Andrews* 71 (1980), 3–10.

Cant, R.G., 'The New Foundation of 1579 in Historical Perspective', *St John's House Papers* 2, St Andrews, 1979.

Carlson, Marvin, *Places of Performance: The Semiotics of Theatre Architecture*, Ithaca, NY, 1989.

Castan, Nicole, 'The Arbitration of Disputes under the Ancien Régime' in *Disputes and Settlements: Law and Human Relations in the West*, ed. John Bossy, Cambridge, 1983.

Champ, J.F., 'Bishop Milner, Holywell, and the Cure Tradition' in *The Church and Healing*, ed. W.J. Sheils, Cambridge, 1982.

Cheape, Hugh, 'The Communion Season', *RSCHS* 27 (1997), 302–16.

Chibbett, Michael, 'Sung Psalms in Scottish Worship' in *The Bible in Scottish Life and Literature*, ed. David Wright, Edinburgh, 1988, 140–54.

Clark, Stuart, *Thinking with Demons: The Idea of Witchcraft in Early Modern Europe*, Oxford, 1997.

Cochran-Patrick, R.W., *Records of the Coinage of Scotland*, 2 vols, Edinburgh, 1876.

Coffey, John, *Politics, Religion and the British Revolutions: The Mind of Samuel Rutherford*, Cambridge, 1997.

Collinson, Patrick, *Godly People*, London, 1983.

———, *The Birthpangs of Protestant England*, New York, 1988.

———, 'Elizabethan and Jacobean Puritanism as Forms of Popular Religious Culture' in *The Culture of English Puritanism 1560–1700*, ed. Christopher Durston and Jacqueline Eales, London, 1996, 32–57.

Colvin, H., *Architecture and the After-Life*, Yale, 1991.

Connerton, Paul, *How Societies Remember*, Cambridge, 1989.

Cowan, Edward J. and Lizanne Henderson, *Scottish Fairy Belief*, East Linton, 2001.

Cowan, Ian B., 'The Five Articles of Perth' in *Reformation and Revolution*, ed. Duncan Shaw, Edinburgh, 1967, 160–75.

———, *The Parishes of Medieval Scotland*, Edinburgh, 1967.

———, 'The Early Ecclesiastical History of Edinburgh', *IR* 23 (1972).

———, *Regional Aspects of the Scottish Reformation*, London, 1978.

———, *The Scottish Reformation: Church and Society in Sixteenth-Century Scotland*, London, 1982.

———, *The Medieval Church in Scotland*, ed. James Kirk, Edinburgh, 1995.

——— and D.E. Easson, *Medieval Religious Houses: Scotland*, London, 1976.

Cramond, W., *The Church and Priory of Urquhart*, Edinburgh, 1899.

Craven, J.B., *History of the Church in Orkney 1558–1662: Bishops Bothwell, Law and Grahame*, Kirkwall, 1897.

Cressy, David, *Literacy and the Social Order: Reading and Writing in Tudor and Stuart England*, Cambridge, 1980.

———, *Bonfires and Bells: National Memory and the Protestant Calendar in Elizabethan and Stuart England*, London, 1989.

———, 'Gender Trouble and Cross-Dressing in Early Modern England', *JBS* 35 (1996), 438–65.

———, *Birth, Marriage and Death: Ritual, Religion and the Life Cycle in Tudor-Stuart England*, Oxford, 1997.

———, *Travesties and Transgressions in Tudor and Stuart England: Tales of Discord and Dissension*, Oxford, 2000.

Cullen, L.M., T.C. Smout and A. Gibson, 'Wages and Comparative Development in Ireland and Scotland, 1565–1780' in *Economy and Society in Scotland and Ireland 1500–1939*, ed. Rosalind Mitchison and Peter Roebuck, Edinburgh, 1988, 105–16.

Dalgleish, George and Stuart Maxwell, *The Lovable Craft*, Edinburgh, [1987].

Davidson, Clifford, ed., *Gesture in Medieval Drama and Art*, Kalamazoo, 2001.

Davidson, Hilda, ed., *The Seer in Celtic and Other Traditions*, Edinburgh, 1989.

Davis, Natalie Zemon, *Society and Culture in Early Modern France*, London, 1975.

———, 'The Sacred and the Body Social in Sixteenth and Seventeenth-Century Lyon', *P&P* 90 (1981), 40–70.

———, 'Charivari, Honor and Community in Seventeenth-Century Lyon and Geneva' in *Rite, Drama, Festival, Spectacle: Rehearsals Toward a Theory of Cultural Performance*, ed. John J. MacAloon, Philadelphia, 1984, 42–57.

———, *Fiction in the Archives*, Cambridge, 1987.

Dawson, Jane, '"The Face of Ane Perfyt Reformed Kyrk": St Andrews and the Early Scottish Reformation' in *Studies in Church History 8: Humanism and Reform: The Church in Europe, England and Scotland, 1400–1643*, ed. James Kirk, Oxford, 1991, 413–36.

———, 'Calvinism in the Gaidhealtachd in Scotland' in *Calvinism in Europe 1540–1620*, ed. Andrew Pettegree, Alastair Duke and Gillian Lewis, Cambridge, 1994, 231–53.

———, 'Anglo-Scottish Protestant Culture and Integration in Sixteenth-Century Britain' in *Conquest and Union: Fashioning a British State 1485–1725*, ed. Steven G. Ellis and Sarah Barber, Harrow, Essex, 1995, 87–114.

———, 'The Gaidhealtachd and the Emergence of the Scottish Highlands' in *British Consciousness and Identity*, ed. Brendan Bradshaw and Peter Roberts, Cambridge, 1998.

———, 'The Protestant Earl and the Godly Gael: The Fifth Earl of Argyll (c. 1538–73) and the Scottish Reformation' in *Life and Thought in the Northern Church c. 1100–1700*, ed. Diana Wood, Woodbridge, 1999, 337–64.

Delumeau, Jean, *Sin and Fear: The Emergence of a Western Guilt Culture, 13th–18th Centuries*, tr. Eric Nicholson, New York, 1990.

Donaldson, Gordon, *Accounts of the Collectors of Thirds of Benefices 1567–1572*, Edinburgh, 1949.

———, 'The Post-Reformation Church at Whithorn: Historical Notes', *Proceedings of the Society of Antiquaries of Scotland* 85 (1950–51), 126–28.

———, *The Making of the Scottish Prayer Book of 1637*, Edinburgh, 1954.

———, *The Scottish Reformation*, Cambridge, 1960.

———, *Scottish Church History*, Edinburgh, 1985.

———, 'A Backward Nation?' in *Scotland's History: Approaches and Reflections*, ed. James Kirk, Edinburgh, 1995.

Douglas, Mary, *Purity and Danger: An Analysis of the Concept of Pollution and Taboo*, London, 1966.

Duffy, Eamon, *The Stripping of the Altars*, New Haven, 1992.

Duncan, A.M., 'The Central Courts before 1532' in *Introduction to Scottish Legal History*, Edinburgh, 1958.

Dunlop, A. Ian, 'Baptism in Scotland after the Reformation' in *Reformation and Revolution*, ed. Duncan Shaw, Edinburgh, 1967, 82–99.

Durkan, John, 'Education in the Century of the Reformation' in *Essays on the Scottish Reformation 1513–1625*, ed. David McRoberts, Glasgow, 1962, 145–68.

———, 'Education: The Laying of Fresh Foundations' in *Humanism in Renaissance Scotland*, Edinburgh, 1990, 123–60.

——— and James Kirk, *The University of Glasgow 1451–1577*, Glasgow, 1977.

Durston, Christopher, 'Puritan Rule and the Failure of Cultural Revolution 1645–1660' in *The Culture of English Puritanism 1560–1700*, ed. C. Durston and Jacqueline Eales, New York, 1996.

Easson, D.E., 'The Collegiate Churches of Scotland', *RSCHS* 6 (1938), 193–215, and 7 (1939), 30–47.

Eliade, M., *Patterns in Comparative Religion*, New York, 1958.

Emery, Kent, 'The Story of Recusant Women Exiled on the Continent' in *Analecta Carthusiana* 130, 118–34.

Ewan, Elizabeth, 'Many Injurious Words: Defamation and Gender in Late Medieval Scotland' in *Scotland in the Middle Ages: History, Literature and Music*, ed. R. Andrew McDonald, Toronto, 2002.

———, and Maureen Meikle, eds, *Women in Scotland, c. 1100–1750*, East Linton, 1999.

Fawcett, R., *Scottish Architecture from the Accession of the Stewarts to the Reformation, 1371–1560*, Edinburgh, 1994.

Ferguson, William, *The Identity of the Scottish Nation: An Historic Quest*, Edinburgh, 1998.

Fergusson, R. Menzies, *Logie*, Edinburgh, 1905.

Finlay, Ian, *Scottish Gold and Silver Work*, n.p., 1956.

Flinn, Michael, ed., *Scottish Population History from the Seventeenth Century to the 1930s*, Cambridge, 1977.

Flint, V., *The Rise of Magic in Early Medieval Europe*, Oxford, 1991.

Forrester, Duncan and Douglas Murray, eds, *Studies in the History of Worship in Scotland*, Edinburgh, 1984.

Foster, Walter Roland, 'A Constant Platt Achieved: Provision for the Ministry 1600–1638' in *Reformation and Revolution*, ed. Duncan Shaw, Edinburgh, 1967, 124–40.

———, *The Church before the Covenants*, Edinburgh, 1975.

Galbraith, James, 'The Middle Ages' in *Studies in the History of Worship in Scotland*, ed. Duncan Forrester and Douglas Murray, Edinburgh, 1984.

Gatrell, V.A.C., Bruce Lenman and Geoffrey Parker, eds, *Crime and the Law: A Social History of Crime in Western Europe Since 1500*, London, 1980.

Geertz, Clifford, 'Religion as a Cultural System' in *Anthropological Approaches to the Study of Religion*, ed. Michael Banton, London, 1960.

———, *The Interpretation of Cultures: Selected Essays*, New York, 1973.

———, 'Centers, Kings and Charisma: Reflections on the Symbolics of Power' in *Rites of Power: Symbolism, Ritual and Politics since the Middle Ages*, ed. S. Wilentz, Philadelphia, 1985, 13–38.

———, *Available Light: Anthropological Reflections on Philosophical Topics*, Princeton, 2000.

Gelfand, Michael, *The Spiritual Beliefs of the Shona*, Gweru, Zimbabwe, 1977.

———, S. Mavi, R.B. Drummond and B. Ndemera, *The Traditional Medical Practitioner in Zimbabwe*, Gweru, Zimbabwe, 1985.

Gennep, Arnold van, *Rites de passage*, Chicago, 1960, orig. 1909.

Gentilcore, David, 'The Fear of Disease and the Disease of Fear' in *Fear in Early Modern Society*, ed. William Naphy and Penny Roberts, Manchester, 1997.

Gibson, A.J.S. and T.C. Smout, *Prices, Food and Wages in Scotland 1550–1780* (Cambridge, 1995).

Gifford, John, *The Buildings of Scotland: Fife*, London, 1988.

———, *The Buildings of Scotland: Dumfries and Galloway*, London, 1996.

Gittings, Clare, *Death, Burial and the Individual in Early Modern England*, London, 1984.

Gluckman, Max, *Rituals of Rebellion in South-East Africa*, Manchester, 1952.

———, *Custom and Conflict in Africa*, Oxford, 1955.

———, 'Les rites de passage' in *Essays on the Ritual of Social Relations*, ed. Gluckman, Manchester, 1962.

———, *Politics, Law and Ritual in Tribal Society*, Oxford, 1965.

Goodare, Julian, *State and Society in Early Modern Scotland*, Oxford, 1999.

Gordon, Bruce and Peter Marshall, eds, *The Place of the Dead: Death and Remembrance in Late Medieval and Early Modern Europe*, Cambridge, 2000.

Gouldesbrough, Peter, *Formulary of Old Scots Legal Documents*, Edinburgh, 1985.

Gowing, Laura, *Domestic Dangers: Women, Word and Sex in Early Modern London*, Oxford, 1996.

Graham, Michael, 'Equality before the Kirk? Church Discipline and the Elite in Reformation-Era Scotland', *Archiv für Reformationsgeschichte* 84 (1993), 289–309.

———, 'Social Discipline in Scotland, 1560–1610' in *Sin and the Calvinists: Morals Control and the Consistory in the Reformed Tradition*, Kirksville, Missouri, 1994.

———, *The Uses of Reform: 'Godly Discipline' and Popular Behavior in Scotland and Beyond, 1560–1610*, Leiden, 1996.

———, 'Women and the Church Courts in Reformation-Era Scotland' in *Women in Scotland c. 1100–c. 1750*, ed. Elizabeth Ewan and Maureen Meikle, East Linton, 1999, 187–98.

Grant, A., *Independence and Nationhood: Scotland 1306–1469*, London, 1984.

Grant, James, *Old and New Edinburgh*, Edinburgh, 1880.

Gray, D., 'Rough Music: Some Early Invectives and Flytings', *Yearbook of English Studies* 14 (1984), 21–43.

Greenblatt, Stephen, *Renaissance Self-Fashioning*, Chicago, 1980.

———, *Shakespearean Negotiations*, Oxford, 1988.

———, *Learning to Curse: Essays in Early Modern Culture*, New York, 1990.

Haigh, Christopher, 'Slander and the Church Courts in the Sixteenth Century', *Transactions of the Lancashire and Cheshire Antiquarian Society* 78, 1975, 1–13.

Harrington, Joel, *Reordering Marriage and Society in Reformation Germany*, Cambridge, 1995.

———, '"Singing for his Supper": The Reinvention of Juvenile Streetsinging in Early Modern Nuremberg', *Social History* 22 (1997), 27–45.

Haws, Charles H., ed., *Scottish Parish Clergy at the Reformation 1540–1574*, Edinburgh, 1972.

Hay, George, *The Architecture of Scottish Post-Reformation Churches 1560–1840*, Oxford, 1957.

———, 'The Late Medieval Development of the High Kirk of St Giles, Edinburgh', *Proceedings of the Society of Antiquaries of Scotland*, 107 (1976), 242–60.

Hazlett, Ian, 'Playing God's Card: Knox and Fasting, 1565–66' in *John Knox and the British Reformations*, ed. Roger Mason, Aldershot, 1998, 176–98.

Helmholz, R.H., *Select Cases on Defamation to 1600*, London, 1985.

———, 'Harboring Sexual Offenders: Ecclesiastical Courts and Controlling Misbehavior', *JBS* 37 (1998), 258–68.

Henderson, G.D., *The Founding of Marischal College, Aberdeen*, Aberdeen, 1947.

Henderson, J.M., *Scottish Reckonings of Time, Money, Weights and Measures*, Historical Association of Scotland pamphlet, ns, no. 4, [Edinburgh], 1926.

Hirst, Derek, 'The Failure of Godly Rule in the English Republic', *P&P* 132 (1991), 33–66.

Horn, D.B., *A Short History of the University of Edinburgh*, Edinburgh, 1967.

Houlbrooke, Ralph, *Church Courts and the People during the English Reformation 1520–1570*, Oxford, 1979.

Houston, R.A., 'The Literacy Myth? Illiteracy in Scotland, 1630–1760', *P&P* 96 (1982), 81–102.

———, 'Literacy and Society in the West 1500–1850', *Social History* 8 (1983).

———, *Scottish Literacy and the Scottish Identity: Illiteracy and Society in Scotland and Northern England 1600–1800*, Cambridge, 1985.

———, *Literacy in Early Modern Europe*, Cambridge, 1988.

Howard, Deborah, *Scottish Architecture: Reformation to Restoration 1560–1660*, Edinburgh, 1995.

Hsia, R. Po-chia, *Social Discipline in the Reformation*, London, 1989.

Hubert, Jane, 'Sacred Beliefs and Beliefs of Sacredness' in *Sacred Sites, Sacred Places*, ed. David Carmichael, J. Hubert, B. Reeves and A. Schanche, London, 1994, 9–19.

Huntington, R. and Peter Metcalf, *Celebration of Death: The Anthropology of Mortuary Ritual*, Cambridge, 1979.

Hutton, Ronald, *The Rise and Fall of Merry England: The Ritual Year 1400–1700*, Oxford, 1994.

———, 'The English Reformation and the Evidence of Folklore', *P&P* 148 (1995), 89–116.

———, *The Stations of the Sun*, Oxford, 1996.

Ingram, Martin, 'Communities and Courts: Law and Disorder in Early Seventeenth-Century Wiltshire' in *Crime in England*, ed. J.S. Cockburn, Princeton, 1977, 110–34.

———, *The Church Courts, Sex and Marriage in England 1520–1640*, Cambridge, 1987.

———, 'Scolding Women Cucked or Washed: A Crisis in Gender Relations in Early Modern England?' in *Women, Crime, and the Courts in Early Modern England*, ed. J. Kermode and G. Walker, Chapel Hill, 1994.

Ireland, R.D., 'Divorce, Nullity of Marriage and Separation' in *An Introduction to Scottish Legal History*, Edinburgh, 1958, 82–89.

Irons, James Campbell, *Leith and its Antiquities*, Edinburgh, 1897.

James, Mervyn, 'Ritual, Drama and the Social Body in the Late-Medieval English Town', *P&P* 98 (1983), 3–29.

Johnston, Flora, 'Jonet Gothskirk and the "Gown of Repentance"', *Costume* 33 (1999), 89–94.

Jones, Francis, *The Holy Wells of Wales*, Cardiff, 1992.

Karant-Nunn, Susan, *The Reformation of Ritual: An Interpretation of Early Modern Germany*, London, 1997.

Keith, R., *An Historical Catalogue of the Scottish Bishops*, Edinburgh, 1824.

Kertzer, D., *Ritual, Politics and Power*, New Haven, 1988.

Kileff, C. and P., eds, *Shona Customs: Essays by African Writers*, Gweru, Zimbabwe, 1992.

Kirk, James, 'Polities of the Best Reformed Kirks: Scottish Achievements and English Aspirations in Church Government after the Reformation', *SHR* 59 (1980), 22–53.

———, 'The Jacobean Church in the Highlands, 1567–1625' in *The Seventeenth Century in the Highlands*, Inverness, 1986, 24–51.

———, *Patterns of Reform: Continuity and Change in the Reformation Kirk*, Edinburgh, 1989.

———, 'The Scottish Reformation and the Reign of James VI: A Select Critical Bibliography', *RSCHS* 23 (1989), 113–55.

———, '"Melvillian" Reform in the Scottish Universities' in *The Renaissance in Scotland*, ed. A.A. MacDonald, M. Lynch and I. Cowan, Leiden, 1994, 276–300.

———, ed., *The Church in the Highlands*, Edinburgh, 1998.

Kripke, Saul, *Naming and Necessity*, Harvard, 1980.

Lake, Peter, 'Puritan Identities', *Journal of Ecclesiastical History* 35 (1984), 112–23.

———, 'Defining Puritanism – Again?' in *Puritanism: Transatlantic Perspectives on a Seventeenth-Century Anglo-American Faith*, [Boston], 1993.

Lawson, John Parker, *The Book of Perth*, Edinburgh, 1847.

Leneman, Leah and Rosalind Mitchison, *Sexuality and Social Control: Scotland 1660–1780*, Oxford, 1989.

———, 'Acquiescence in and Defiance of Church Discipline in Early-Modern Scotland', *RSCHS* 25 (1993), 19–39.

———, *Girls in Trouble*, Edinburgh, 1998.

———, *Sin in the City*, Edinburgh, 1998.

Lenman, Bruce, 'The Limits of Godly Discipline in the Early Modern Period with Particular Reference to England and Scotland' in *Religion and Society in Early Modern Europe 1500–1800*, ed. Kaspar von Greyerz, London, 1984.

Lerer, S. '"Represented Now in Yower Sight": The Culture of Spectatorship in Fifteenth-Century England' in *Bodies and Disciplines*, ed. B. Hanawalt and P. Wallace, Minneapolis, 1996.

Lewis, I.M., *History and Social Anthropology*, London, 1968.

———, *Religion in Context: Cults and Charisma*, Cambridge, 1986.

Llewellyn, Nigel, *The Art of Death: Visual Culture in the English Death Ritual c. 1500–c. 1800*, London, 1991.
Lualdi, Katharine Jackson and Anne T. Thayer, eds, *Penitence in the Age of Reformations*, Aldershot, 2000.
Lyall, R.J., 'Complaint, Satire and Invective in Middle Scots Literature' in *Church, Politics and Society: Scotland 1408–1929*, ed. N. MacDougall, Edinburgh, 1983, 44–63.
Lynch, Michael, *Edinburgh and the Reformation*, Edinburgh, 1981.
———, 'The Origins of Edinburgh's "Toun College": A Revision Article', *IR* 33 (1982), 3–14.
———, 'From Privy Kirk to Burgh Church: An Alternative View of the Process of Protestantisation' in *Church, Politics and Society: Scotland 1408–1929*, ed. Norman Macdougall, Edinburgh, 1983.
———, 'National Identity in Ireland and Scotland, 1500–1640' in *Nations, Nationalism and Patriotism in the European Past*, ed. C. Bjorn, A. Grant and K. Stringer, Copenhagen, 1990.
———, 'Scottish Culture in its Historical Perspective' in *Scotland: A Concise Cultural History*, ed. Paul H. Scott, Edinburgh, 1993, 15–46.
———, 'Preaching to the Converted?' in *The Renaissance in Scotland*, ed. A.A. MacDonald, Michael Lynch and Ian Cowan, Leiden, 1994, 301–43.
———, 'A Nation Born Again? Scottish Identity in the Sixteenth and Seventeenth Centuries' in *Image and Identity*, ed. Dauvit Broun, R.J. Finlay and M. Lynch, Edinburgh, 1998.
———, ed., *The Early Modern Town in Scotland*, London, 1987.
MacDonald, A.A., 'Passion Devotion in Late-Medieval Scotland' in *The Body Broken*, ed. MacDonald, H.N.B. Ridderbos, and R.M. Schlusemann, Groningen, 1998, 109–32.
MacDonald, Alan R., 'David Calderwood: The Not So Hidden Years, 1590–1604', *SHR*, 74 (1995), 69–74.
Macfarlane, Alan, *The Family Life of Ralph Josselin*, Cambridge, 1970.
———, *Witchcraft in Tudor and Stuart England*, London, 1970.
MacKenzie, Agnes Mure, *Scottish Pageant 1625–1707*, Edinburgh, 1949.
MacKenzie, William Mackay, *The Scottish Burghs*, Edinburgh, 1949.
MacMillan, Duncan, *Scottish Art 1460–1990*, Edinburgh, 1990.
MacQueen, John, *Humanism in Renaissance Scotland*, Edinburgh, 1990.
Makey, W.H., 'The Elders of Stow, Liberton, Canongate, and St Cuthbert's', *RSCHS* 8 (1970), 155–67.
———, *The Church of the Covenant*, Edinburgh, 1979.
Mansfield, M., *The Humiliation of Sinners: Ritual Penance in Thirteenth-Century France*, Ithaca, NY, 1995.
Marchant, Ronald, *The Church under the Law: Justice, Administration and Discipline in the Diocese of York*, Cambridge, 1969.
Marshall, Gordon, *Presbyteries and Profits: Calvinism and the Development of Capitalism in Scotland, 1560–1707*, Oxford, 1980.
Marshall, Peter, 'Fear, Purgatory and Polemic in Reformation England' in *Fear in Early Modern Society*, ed. William Naphy and Penny Roberts, Manchester, 1997.
Masani, R.P., *Folklore of Wells, being a Study of Water-Worship in East and West*, Bombay, 1918.
Mason, Roger, 'Imagining Scotland' in *Scots and Britons: Scottish Political Thought and the Union of 1603*, ed. Mason, Cambridge, 1994.
———, 'The Scottish Reformation and the Origins of Anglo-British Imperialism' in *Scots*

and Britons: Scottish Political Thought and the Union of 1603, ed. Mason, Cambridge, 1994, 161–86.

———, *Kingship and the Common Weal*, East Linton, 1998.

———, ed., *John Knox and the British Reformations*, Aldershot, 1998.

Maxwell, David, 'Civil Procedure' in *Introduction to Scottish Legal History*, Edinburgh, 1958.

Maxwell, William D., *A History of Worship in the Church of Scotland*, London, 1951.

McCrie, Charles G., *The Public Worship of Presbyterian Scotland Historically Treated*, Edinburgh, 1892.

McCusker, John J., *Money and Exchange in Europe and America, 1600–1775: A Handbook*, Chapel Hill, 1978.

McIntosh, Marjorie, *Controlling Misbehavior in England 1370–1600*, Cambridge, 1998.

McKay, Denis, 'Parish Life in Scotland 1500–1560' in *Essays on the Scottish Reformation 1513–1625*, ed. David McRoberts, Glasgow, 1962.

McMillan, William, *The Worship of the Scottish Reformed Church 1550–1638*, London, 1931.

McNeill, F. Marian, *The Silver Bough*, 2 vols, Glasgow, 1959.

McNeill, Peter G.B. and Hector L. MacQueen, *Atlas of Scottish History to 1707*, Edinburgh, 1996.

McRoberts, David, 'Material Destruction Caused by the Scottish Reformation' in *Essays on the Scottish Reformation 1513–1625*, ed. David McRoberts, Glasgow, 1962.

———, 'Scottish Sacrament Houses', *Transactions of the Scottish Ecclesiastical Society* 15 (1965), 30–56.

———, 'The Rosary in Scotland', *IR* 23 (1972), 81–86.

———, ed., *The Medieval Church in St Andrews*, Glasgow, 1976.

Meek, Donald, 'The Reformation and Gaelic Culture: Perspectives on Patronage, Language and Literature in John Carswell's Translation of "The Book of Common Order"' in *The Church in the Highlands*, ed. James Kirk, Edinburgh, 1998, 37–62.

Mill, A.J., *Medieval Plays in Scotland*, Edinburgh, 1927.

———, 'The Perth Hammermen's Play', *SHR* 49 (1970), 146–53.

Mitchison, Rosalind, *Lordship to Patronage: Scotland 1603–1745*, London, 1983.

———, *The Old Poor Law in Scotland: The Experience of Poverty, 1574–1845*, Edinburgh, 2000.

Moore, Sally, *Law as Process*, London, 1987.

———, *Anthropology and Africa: Changing Perspectives on a Changing Scene*, Charlottesville, Virginia, 1994.

Moore, Sally and Barbara Myerhoff, eds, *Secular Ritual*, Assen, 1977.

Morrill, John, 'A British Patriarchy? Ecclesiastical Imperialism Under the Early Stuarts', *Religion, Culture and Society in Early Modern Britain*, ed. Anthony Fletcher and Peter Roberts, Cambridge, 1994.

———, ed., *The Scottish National Covenant in its British Context*, Edinburgh, 1990.

Morris, Ruth and Frank, *Scottish Healing Wells*, Sandy, 1982.

Muir, Edward, *Civic Ritual in Renaissance Venice*, Princeton, 1981.

———, *Mad Blood Stirring: Vendetta and Factions in Friuli during the Renaissance*, Baltimore, 1993.

———, *Ritual in Early Modern Europe*, Cambridge, 1997.

Mullan, David, *Episcopacy in Scotland: The History of an Idea 1560–1638*, Edinburgh, 1986.

———, 'Women in Scottish Divinity, c. 1590–1640' in *Women in Scotland c. 1100–c. 1750*, East Linton, 1999, 29–41.

———, *Scottish Puritanism 1590–1638*, Oxford, 2000.

Munchembled, Robert, *Culture populaire, culture des élites*, Paris, 1978.

Murray, David, *Legal Practice in Ayr and the West of Scotland*, Glasgow, 1910.

Murray, E.G., *The Church of Cardross and its Ministers*, Glasgow, 1935.
Myerhoff, Barbara, 'Rites of Passage: Process and Paradox' in *Celebration: Studies in Festivity and Ritual*, ed. V. Turner, Washington, D.C., 1982, 109–35.
Naphy, William, *Calvin and the Consolidation of the Genevan Reformation*, Manchester, 1994.
——— and Penny Roberts, eds, *Fear in Early Modern Society*, Manchester, 1997.
Nimmo, William, *The History of Stirlingshire*, 2 vols, London, 1880.
Ollivant, Simon, *The Court of the Official in Pre-Reformation Scotland*, Edinburgh, 1982.
Ortner, Sherry G., *Sherpas through their Rituals*, Cambridge, 1978.
Parker, Charles, 'The Rituals of Reconciliation: Admonition, Confession and Community in the Dutch Reformed Church' in *Penitence in the Age of Reformations*, ed. K. Lualdi *et al*, Aldershot, 2000.
Parker, Geoffrey, 'The "Kirk by Law Established" and the Origins of "the Taming of Scotland": St Andrews 1559–1600' in *Sin and the Calvinists: Morals Control and the Consistory in the Reformed Tradition*, ed. Raymond Mentzer, Kirksville, Missouri, 1994, 158–97.
Parker, Kenneth, *The English Sabbath*, Cambridge, 1988.
Patrick, Millar, *Four Centuries of Scottish Psalmody*, London, 1949.
Patterson, Catherine, 'Conflict Resolution and Patronage in Provincial Towns, 1590–1640', *JBS* 37 (1998), 1–25.
Pettegree, Andrew, *Foreign Protestant Communities in Sixteenth-Century London*, Oxford, 1986.
———, 'Coming to Terms with Victory: The Upbuilding of a Calvinist Church in Holland, 1572–1590' in *Calvinism in Europe, 1540–1620*, ed. Pettegree, A. Duke and G. Lewis, Cambridge, 1994, 160–80.
Pollman, Judith, *Religious Choice in the Dutch Republic*, Manchester, 1999.
Pollock, Linda, *Forgotten Children: Parent–Child Relations from 1500–1900*, Cambridge, 1983.
Primus, J.H., *Holy Time*, Macon, Georgia, 1989.
Provost Skene's House, Aberdeen, 1994.
Purser, John, *Scotland's Music*, Edinburgh, 1992.
———, 'Music' in *Scotland: A Concise Cultural History*, ed. Paul Scott, Edinburgh, 1993.
Rattue, James, *The Living Stream: Holy Wells in Historical Context*, Woodbridge, 1995.
Robertson, J.D., *A Handbook to the Coinage of Scotland*, Chicago, 1968.
Rogers, Charles, *Monuments and Monumental Inscriptions in Scotland*, 2 vols, London, 1871–72.
———, *Three Scottish Reformers*, London, 1876.
———, *Social Life in Scotland*, Edinburgh, 1884.
Ross, John M., *Four Centuries of Scottish Worship*, Edinburgh, 1972.
Rublack, Ulinka, *The Crimes of Women in Early Modern Germany*, Oxford, 1999.
Russell, Gillian, *Theatres of War: Performance, Politics and Society 1793–1815*, Oxford, 1995.
Sabean, David, *Power in the Blood: Popular Culture and Village Discourse in Early Modern Germany*, Cambridge, 1984.
Safley, Thomas Max, *Let No Man Put Asunder*, Kirksville, 1984.
Sahlins, Marshall, *Historical Metaphors and Mythical Realities: Structure in the Early History of the Sandwich Islands Kingdom*, Ann Arbor, 1981.
———, *How 'Natives' Think: About Captain Cook, for Example*, Chicago, 1995.
Sanderson, Margaret H.B., 'Some Aspects of the Church in Scottish Society in the Era of the Reformation, Illustrated from the Sheriffdom of Ayr', *RSCHS* 17 (1970), 81–98.
———, *Scottish Rural Society in the Sixteenth Century*, Edinburgh, 1982.
———, *Ayrshire and the Reformation: People and Change, 1490–1600*, East Linton, 1997.
Saussure, Ferdinand de, *Course in General Linguistics*, tr. Wade Baskin, New York, 1966, orig. 1915.

Scanlan, J.D., 'Husband and Wife: Pre-Reformation Canon Law of Marriage of the Officials' Courts' in *An Introduction to Scottish Legal History*, Edinburgh, 1958, 69–81.

Scheff, T.J., *Catharsis in Healing, Ritual and Drama*, Cambridge, 1979.

Schmidt, Leigh Eric, *Holy Fairs: Scottish Communions and American Revivals in the Early Modern Period*, Princeton, 1989.

Scottish Parish Clergy at the Reformation 1540–1574, ed. Charles H. Haws, Edinburgh, 1972.

Scribner, Robert W., *Popular Culture and Popular Movements in Reformation Germany*, London, 1987.

———, 'Ritual and Popular Belief in Catholic Germany at the Time of the Reformation' in *Popular Culture and Popular Movements in Reformation Germany*, London, 1987, 17–48.

———, 'The Impact of the Reformation on Daily Life' in *Mensch und Objekt im Mittelalter und in der frühen Neuzeit*, Vienna, 1990, 316–43.

———, 'The Reformation, Popular Magic, and the "Disenchantment of the World"', *Journal of Interdisciplinary History* 23 (1993), 475–94.

———, 'The Historical Anthropology of Early Modern Europe' and 'Reformation and Desacralisation: From Sacramental World to Moralised Universe' in *Problems in the Historical Anthropology of Early Modern Europe*, ed. R. Po-chia Hsia and Scribner, Wiesbaden, 1997, 11–34, 75–92.

Selwyn, Jennifer, '"Schools of Mortification": Theatricality and the Role of Penitential Practice in the Jesuits' Popular Missions' in *Penitence in the Age of Reformations*, ed. K. Lualdi *et al*, Aldershot, 2000.

Sharpe, J.A., *Defamation and Sexual Slander in Early Modern England: The Church Courts at York*, Borthwick papers no. 58, 1980.

———, '"Such Disagreement betwyx Neighbours": Litigation and Human Relations in Early Modern England' in *Disputes and Settlements*, ed. John Bossy, Cambridge, 1983, 167–87.

———, *Crime in Early Modern England*, London, 1984.

Sheils, W.J., *The Puritans in the Diocese of Peterborough 1558–1610*, Northampton, 1979.

———, 'Erecting the Discipline in Provincial England: The Order of Northampton 1571' in *Studies in Church History* 8, ed. James Kirk, Oxford, 1991.

Sibley, D., *Geographies of Exclusion*, London, 1995.

Sider, G., *Culture and Class in Anthropology*, Cambridge, 1986.

Simpson, Kenneth, 'The Legacy of Flyting' in *The Language and Literature of Early Scotland*, ed. G. Ross Roy, Columbia, SC, 1991, 503–14.

Slack, Paul, 'Poverty and Politics in Salisbury 1597–1666' in *Crisis and Order in English Towns*, ed. Peter Clark and Paul Slack, London, 1972.

Smith, David B., 'The Reformers and Divorce', *SHR* 9 (1912), 10–36.

———, 'A Note on Divorce for Desertion', *Juridical Review* 51 (1939), 254–59.

———, 'The Spiritual Jurisdiction 1560–64', *RSCHS* 25 (1993), 1–18.

Smith, Lesley M., 'Sackcloth for the Sinner or Punishment for the Crime? Church and Secular Courts in Cromwellian Scotland' in *New Perspectives on the Politics and Culture of Early Modern Scotland*, ed. John Dwyer, Roger Mason and Alexander Murdoch, Edinburgh, [1982], 116–32.

Smout, T.C., 'Scottish Marriage' in *Marriage and Society; Studies in the Social History of Marriage*, ed. R.B. Outhwaite, London, 1981.

———, ed., *Scotland and Europe 1200–1850*, Edinburgh, 1986.

Snow, W.G.S., *The Times, Life and Thought of Patrick Forbes*, London, 1952.

Spicer, Andrew, '"The Rest of their Bones": Fear of Death and Reformed Burial Practices' in *Fear in Early Modern Society*, ed. William Naphy and Penny Roberts, Manchester, 1997, 167–83.

———, '"Defyle Not Christ's Kirk with your Carrion": Burial and the Development of Burial Aisles in Post-Reformation Scotland' in *The Place of the Dead: Death and Remembrance in Late Medieval and Early Modern Europe*, ed. Bruce Gordon and Peter Marshall, Cambridge, 2000, 149–69.

Stevenson, David, 'Scottish Church History 1600–1660: A Select Critical Bibliography', *RSCHS* 21 (1982), 209–20.

———, *King's College, Aberdeen, 1560–1641: From Protestant Reformation to Covenanting Revolution*, Aberdeen, 1990.

———, *Scotland's Last Royal Wedding*, Edinburgh, 1997.

Symms, Peter, 'A Disputed Altar: Parish Pump Politics in a Sixteenth-Century Burgh', *IR* 42 (1991), 133–36.

Tambiah, Stanley Jeyaraja, *A Performative Approach to Ritual*, Oxford, 1979.

———, *Culture, Thought and Social Action: An Anthropological Perspective*, Cambridge, Mass., 1985.

Tentler, Thomas, *Sin and Confession on the Eve of the Reformation*, Princeton, 1977.

Thomas, Keith, *Religion and the Decline of Magic*, New York, 1971.

Thoms, D.B., *The Kirk of Brechin in the Seventeenth Century*, Perth, 1972.

Thomson, Duncan, *Painting in Scotland 1570–1650*, Edinburgh, 1975.

Tittler, Robert, *Architecture and Power: The Town Hall and the English Urban Community*, Oxford, 1991.

———, *The Reformation and the Towns in England, c. 1540–1560*, Oxford, 1998.

———, *Townspeople and Nation: English Urban Experiences 1540–1640*, Stanford, 2001.

Todd, Margo, *Christian Humanism and the Puritan Social Order*, Cambridge, 1987.

———, 'A Captive's Story: Puritans, Pirates, and the Drama of Reconciliation', *The Seventeenth Century* 13 (1997), 37–56.

Turner, Victor, *The Ritual Process: Structure and Anti-Structure*, Chicago, 1969.

———, *Dramas, Fields and Metaphors: Symbolic Action in Human Society*, Ithaca, N.Y. 1974.

———, *From Ritual to Theater: The Human Seriousness of Play*, New York, 1982.

———, *The Anthropology of Performance*, New York, 1987.

———, ed., *Celebration: Studies in Festivity and Ritual*, Washington, D.C., 1982.

Tyacke, Nicholas, ed., *England's Long Reformation, 1500–1800*, London, 1998.

Underdown, David, *Fire from Heaven: Life in an English Town in the Seventeenth Century*, New Haven, 1992.

Verschuur, Mary, 'Merchants and Craftsmen in Sixteenth-Century Perth' in *The Early Modern Town in Scotland*, ed. Michael Lynch, London, 1987, 36–54.

de Vries, Jan, *European Urbanization 1500–1800*, London, 1984.

Walsham, Alexandra, 'Reforming the Waters: Holy Wells and Healing Springs in Protestant England' in *Life and Thought in the Northern Church c. 1100–c. 1700*, ed. Diana Wood, Woodbridge, 1999, 227–56.

Watt, Jeffrey, *The Making of Modern Marriage: Matrimonial Control and the Rise of Sentiment in Neuchâtel, 1550–1800*, Ithaca, NY, 1992.

White, Alan, 'The Impact of the Reformation on a Burgh Community: The Case of Aberdeen' in *The Early Modern Town in Scotland*, ed. Michael Lynch, London, 1987.

Whyte, Ian, *Scotland before the Industrial Revolution: An Economic and Social History* c. *1050–* c. *1750*, London, 1995.

———, *Scotland's Society and Economy in Transition*, New York, 1997.

Willsher, Betty, 'Scottish Graveyards', *Proceedings of the Society of Antiquaries of Scotland* 118 (1988), 322–23.

Wittig, Kurt, *The Scottish Tradition in Literature*, Edinburgh, 1958.

Wormald, Jenny, 'Bloodfeud, Kindred and Government in Early Modern Scotland', *P&P* 87 (1980), 54–97.

———, *Court, Kirk and Community: Scotland 1470–1625*, London, 1981.

———, 'The Blood Feud in Early Modern Scotland' in *Disputes and Settlements: Law and Human Relations in the West*, ed. John Bossy, Cambridge, 1983, 101–44.

———, *Lords and Men in Scotland*, Edinburgh, 1985.

Wright, David F., '"The Common Buke of the Kirk": The Bible in the Scottish Reformation' in *The Bible in Scottish Life and Literature*, ed. David Wright, Edinburgh, 1988, 155–78.

Wunderli, Richard, *London Church Courts and Society on the Eve of the Reformation*, Cambridge, Mass., 1981.

Yeoman, Louise, 'Archie's Invisible Worlds Discovered – Spirituality, Madness and Johnston of Wariston's Family', *RSCHS* 27 (1997), 156–86.

———, 'Covenanting Prophetesses' in '*Fantasticall Ymaginations*'*: The Supernatural in Scottish Culture*, East Linton, forthcoming.

Part IV: Unpublished Dissertations and Papers

Byford, M.S., 'The Price of Protestantism: Assessing the Impact of Religious Change in Elizabethan Essex: the Cases of Heydon and Colchester, 1558–1594', Oxford DPhil, 1988.

Dalgleish, George, 'Trinity College Church, Edinburgh: Communion and Baptismal Plate, 1632–1698'.

Dillow, Kevin, 'The Social and Ecclesiastical Significance of Church Seating Arrangements and Pew Disputes, 1500–1740', Oxford DPhil, 1990.

Ewan, Elizabeth, '"Tongue You Lied": The Role of the Tongue in Rituals of Penance in Late Medieval Scotland', paper read at the International Medieval Congress, Kalamazoo, Michigan, May 2001.

Fitch, Audrey-Beth, 'The Search for Salvation: Lay Faith in Scotland, 1480–1560', Glasgow PhD, 1994.

Flett, Iain E.F., 'The Conflict of the Reformation and Democracy in the Geneva of Scotland, 1443–1610: An Introduction to Edited Texts of Documents Relating to the Burgh of Dundee', St Andrews MPhil, 1981.

Kelly, Augustine, 'The Vernacular Devotional Literature of the English Roman Catholic Community 1560–1640', St Andrews PhD, 2001.

Postles, David, 'The Performance of Imposed Penance in England: A Long View (*c.* 1250–1600)'.

Smith, Mark, 'The Presbytery of St Andrews 1586–1605: A Study and Annotated Edition of the Register of the Minutes of the Presbytery of St Andrews, Volume I', St Andrews PhD, 1985.

Verschuur, Mary, 'Perth and the Reformation: Society and Reform 1540–1560', Glasgow PhD, 1985.
White, Alan, 'Religion, Politics, and Society in Aberdeen, 1543–1593', Edinburgh PhD, 1985.
Yeoman, Louise, 'Heart-work: Emotion, Empowerment and Authority in Covenanting Times', St Andrews PhD, 1992.

Index